Dictionary of Contemporary

QUOTATIONS

[2nd Revised Edition]

Edited by John Gordon Burke and Ned Kehde

John Gordon Burke Publisher, Inc.

Bibliographical history: This book, volume 7 of the Dictionary of Contemporary Quotations, supplements both the foundation volume of this series, volume 5, published in 1981 and volume 6, published in 1987. Volume 5 contains all quotations published in volumes 1-4 of the Dictionary of Contemporary Quotations. Both volumes 5 and 6 are available from the publisher. Volume 7 and future volumes of the Dictionary of Contemporary Quotations are supplemented by the Dictionary of Contemporary Quotations Information Service begun in 1988. The Dictionary of Contemporary Quotations Information Service is an electronic service which is available free of charge to all standing order subscribers to the Dictionary of Contemporary Quotations. A subscription license arrangement is available for institutions which desire only to use the Dictionary of Contemporary Quotations Information Service. Note: Prices and conditions of sale of this product are subject to change without notice. ISSN 0360-215X Key Title: Dictionary of Contemporary Quotations ISBN 0-934272-25-5. The Dictionary of Contemporary Quotations is scheduled to be published every three years.

INTRODUCTION

The continuing purpose of the *Dictionary of Contemporary Quotations* is to record contemporary quotations which are historically, sociologically, and politically significant. With the beginning of our electronic data base the *Dictionary of Contemporary Quotations Information Service* in 1988, however, the *Dictionary of Contemporary Quotations* has undertaken the task of building a selection of quotations by contemporary persons based upon quotability as the primary criterion of selection for this book. We no longer record quotations by historic persons found in contemporary media which are not found in standard quotation sources. While quotability is now the primary criterion of selection, the editors' judgment about a quotation's significance can also be important. Our purpose is to record quotations that deserve being recalled in the future because of the content of the quotation or the speaker responsible for it.

This is volume 7 of the *Dictionary of Contemporary Quotations*. It supplements both volumes 5 and 6 of the *Dictionary of Contemporary Quotations* and is itself supplemented by the *Dictionary of Contemporary Quotations Information Service*. Because of this relationship, for example, not all quotations recorded between 1987 and 1990 about the Iran–Contra Affair are included in this volume. Approximately twenty percent of the quotations contained in volume 6 have been replaced and we have deleted a number of quotations based upon our primary criterion of selection. We have also found, in some instances, that quotations deserved being recalled from a previously published volume because their subject or speaker has assumed new national prominence. George Bush is an example of such a case. It is expected future volumes of the *Dictionary of Contemporary Quotations* will reflect this pattern of revision.

The new content of this volume results from a survey of approximately 175 periodicals and newspapers from 1987 to 1990. As in previous editions, when a quotation is cited, it is not necessarily the original source of the published quotation. In instances where a quotation appears in more than one source, the original source of publication is cited if it can be determined. Otherwise, the published source most widely available to users is cited. As a result, weekly news magazines sometimes replace newspapers as the source of quotations.

Quotations are cited by the *Dictionary of Contemporary Quotations* by both Author and Subject. In the Author section, a quotation includes the following information: name of speaker and descriptive annotation if appropriate; quotation and explanatory amplification if necessary, and quotation source. For example:

> **Ashbery,** John. If one is a famous poet, one still isn't famous. (Details 6:99 Mar 88)

This quotation appeared in the March 1988 issue of Details magazine, volume 6, page 99. Additional examples of quotations are:

> **Bellow,** Saul. Writers are readers inspired to emulation. (Harvard Magazine 89:78 Jan/Feb 87)

Black Stalin (Singer). In Calypso, there is no retirement plan. (Spin 3:12 Dec 87)

Davis, Stuart. I was a Cubist until somebody threw me a curve. (Interview 17:124 Dec 87)

Haldeman, Harry Robbins. He'd (George Bush) do anything for the cause. (Time 132:28 Nov 21, 88)

Quotations listed in the subject section now include source of publication. See and see also references have also been added to the subject section of the book to facilitate its use.

The *Dictionary of Contemporary Quotations* is regularly supplemented by the *Dictionary of Contemporary Quotations Information Service*. This electronic data base contains all quotations previously published, as well as the quotations published in this book. As previously noted, it also contains some quotations which have not been published. The current subject authority list for the *Dictionary of Contemporary Quotations Information Service* may be found on page 288. Revised subject authority lists will be published in future volumes of the *Dictionary of Contemporary Quotations* which are scheduled to be published approximately every three years.

We hope that the *Dictionary of Contemporary Quotations* and its electronic data base will continue to be useful to the student of social science and humanities as well as to the student of popular culture. It is our purpose to develop this resource into a reference book which will in time become a standard resource in this subject area.

The Editors

Authors

AALTO, Alvar. True architecture exists only where man stands in the center. (Newsweek 94:97 July 16, 79)

ABBOTT, Berenice. It took two lives to build Atget's reputation: his and mine. (American Photographer 21:11 Oct 88)

ABBOTT, Berenice. You have to have the courage to be poor (about photography as a profession). (Life 5:126 May 82)

ABBOUD, A. Robert. Inflation is a product of—and can only be cured by—the people. (New Republic 180:8 June 30, 79)

ABDULLAH, Ismail Sabry. No nation, no matter how rich, can develop another country. (Time 106:42 Dec 22, 75)

ABE, Kobo. In the love for the weak there is always an intent to kill. (New York Times Magazine 86 April 29, 79)

ABE, Kobo. Once a writer throws away his mask he's finished. (New York Times Magazine 78 April 29, 79)

ABOUREZK, James. Anybody who really changed things for the better in this country could never be elected President anyway. (Playboy 26:105-06 Mar 79)

ABOUREZK, James. Don't worry about your enemies, it's your allies who will do you in (in politics). (Playboy 26:106 Mar 79)

ABOUREZK, James. If you want to curry favor with a politician, give him credit for something someone else did. (Washingtonian 15:140 Nov 79)

ABOUREZK, James. In politics, people will do whatever is necessary to get their way. (Playboy 26:106 Mar 79)

ABOUREZK, James. Politics is like the farmer's dog. If you run too fast you get nipped in the ass. If you stand still too long you get screwed. (Politicks & Other Human Interests 1:17 April 25, 78)

ABOUREZK, James. The bigger the appropriations bill, the shorter the debate. (Playboy 26:106 Mar 79)

ABOUREZK, James. When voting on the confirmation of a Presidential appointment, it's always safer to vote against the son of a bitch, because if he's confirmed, it won't be long before he proves how wise you were. (Playboy 26:106 Mar 79)

ABZUG, Bella. Richard Nixon self-impeached himself. He gave us Gerald Ford as his revenge. (Rolling Stone 227:43 Dec 2, 76)

ACCIARI, Larry. Presidents come and go, but Walter Cronkite—he's an institution. (Newsweek 88:37 July 26, 76)

ACE, Jane. Well, time wounds all heels. (Village Voice 22:20 Dec 26, 77)

ADAMS, Alice. I don't like good-looking men—one always thinks they'll be dumb. (People Weekly 9:53 April 3, 78)

ADAMS, Ansel. They (Ronald Reagan's staff) know the cost of everything but the value of nothing. (California 8:54 Sept 83)

ADAMS, Ansel. You don't take a photograph, you make it. (Time 124:46 Dec 31, 84)

ADAMS, Cecil. The average oilman has the moral development of a newt. (The Reader (Chicago's Free Weekly) 8:2 April 27, 79)

ADAMS, Henry Brooks. A teacher affects eternity; he can never tell where his influence stops. (Kansas City Star 97:15B April 6, 77)

ADAMS, Randall Dale. If there ever was a hell on earth, it's Dallas County (Texas). (Chicago Tribune 162:8 Section 1 June 11, 89)

ADAMS, Sherman. I believe that a president should above all understand his own prejudices. (Time 119:12 April 5, 82)

ADDAMS, Jane. I do not believe that women are better than men. We have not wrecked railroads, nor corrupted legislatures, nor done many unholy things that men have done; but then we must remember that we have not had the chance. (Working Woman 1:8 Nov 76)

ADDERLEY, Julian (Cannonball). God smiles on certain individuals, and they get the privilege to have certain beautiful, artistic vibrations pass through them. (Time 106:56 Aug 18, 75)

ADELMAN, Morris A. (economist). The (energy) gap is like the horizon, always receding as you walk, ride, or fly toward it. (Time 110:61 Oct 10, 77)

ADENAUER, Konrad. History is the sum total of the things that could have been avoided. (Kansas City Times 109:12H Dec 9, 76)

ADJANI, Isabelle. Life is worth being lived but not worth being discussed all the time. (Time 113:67 Feb 12, 79)

ADKINS, Janet. I have no regrets. I have loved life fully and I have lived life fully. (New York Times 139:A13 June 7, 90)

ADLER, Alfred. The chief danger in life is that you may take too many precautions. (Kansas City Times 109:14C Jan 24, 77)

ADLER, Mortimer. Philosophy is everybody's business. (Time 110:57 July 25, 77)

ADLER, Mortimer. Political democracy will not work unless it is accompanied by economic democracy. (Time 110:57 July 25, 77)

ADLER, Mortimer. We are hypocrites if we continue to think that the equality of citizenship belongs to all, but not the equality of educational opportunity. (Time 110:57 July 25, 77)

AGEE, Philip. The CIA claims that secrecy is necessary to hide what it's doing from the enemies of the United States. I claim that the real reason for secrecy is to hide what the CIA is doing from the American people. (Playboy 22:49 Aug 75)

AGEE, Philip. The CIA is nothing more than the secret police of American capitalism, plugging up leaks in the political dam night and day so that shareholders of U.S. companies operating in poor countries can continue enjoying their rip-off. (Time 106:62 Aug 4, 75)

AGNELLI, Giovanni. At twenty, it would be fun to retire. It's silly at sixty. At sixty, what can you do anymore? (Esquire 89:38 June 20, 78)

AGNEW, Spiro Theodore. If you've seen one slum, you've seen them all. (New York Times 127:1 Section 4 April 2, 78)

AIKEN, George. I don't know how you go about containing an idea. I also don't know how you go about containing 700 million people. (Kansas City Times 117:A-24 Nov 22, 84)

AIKEN, George. The way to get out of Vietnam is to declare victory and leave (1966). (Time 124:46 Dec 31, 84)

AIKEN, George David. I have never seen so many incompetent persons in high office. Politics and legislation have become more mixed and smellier than ever (commenting on the U.S. Senate in his book Aiken: Senate Diary). (New York Times 125:23 June 29, 76)

ALAIA, Azzedine. For me, there is no vulgarity and the street is never in bad taste. (Town & Country 216:79 Aug 86)

ALBEE, Edward. If Attila the Hun were alive today, he'd be a dramatic critic. (Stagebill 52 Dec 81)

ALBERT, Claude. You have to love the business (journalism) for what it is, not for what you'd like it to be. (Connecticut 41:32 Feb 78)

ALDA, Alan. If I were a politician, I'd be a decent politician. (Newsweek 94:62 Aug 27, 79)

ALDERSON, M. H. If at first you don't succeed, you are running about average. (Reader's Digest 108:122 Feb 76)

ALEXANDER, Bill. Mr. Gingrich is a congressional Jimmy Swaggart, who condemns sin while committing hypocrisy. (Village Voice 33:18 May 9, 89)

ALEXANDER, Shana. (Journalism) offers the maximum of vicarious living with a minimum of emotional involvement. (New

York Times Book Review 3 May 6, 79)

ALGREN, Nelson. In what other city can you be so sure a judge will keep his word for five hundred dollars (about Chicago)? (New York Times 138:9 Jan 12, 89)

ALGREN, Nelson. Never eat at a place called Mom's. Never play cards with a man named Doc. And never lie down with a woman who's got more troubles than you. (Washingtonian 14:152 Nov 78)

ALI, Muhammad. After I go, boxing will go to the graveyard. (Sporting News 204:63 Oct 12, 87)

ALI, Muhammad. Wars on nations are fought to change maps, but wars on poverty are fought to map change. (Playboy 22:68 Nov 75)

ALLEN, Agnes. Almost anything is easier to get into than to get out of. (Omni 1:131 May 79)

ALLEN, Dick. If horses won't eat it, I don't want to play on it. (Esquire 89:30 Mar 28, 78)

ALLEN, Ethan. If you told him to bunt, he bunted (about George Bush). (Newsweek 111:19 June 27, 88)

ALLEN, Fred. California is a great place to live...if you happen to be an orange. (New West 1:104 Nov 22, 76)

ALLEN, Fred. Hollywood is a place where people from Iowa mistake each other for stars. (Chicago Tribune Magazine 6 Oct 16, 83)

ALLEN, Fred. Imitation is the sincerest form of television. (Emmy 3:46 Fall 81)

ALLEN, Fred. Television is a triumph of equipment over people, and the minds that control it are so small that you could put them in a gnat's navel with room left over for two caraway seeds and an agent's heart. (CoEvolution Quarterly 16:153 Winter 77/78)

ALLEN, Fred. Television is chewing gum for the eyes. (Playboy 23:150 June 76)

ALLEN, George. Only winners are truly alive. Winning is living. Every time you win, you're reborn. When you lose, you die a little. (Chicago Tribune 76:1 Section 2 Mar 17, 78)

ALLEN, Marty. A study of economics usually reveals that the best time to buy anything is last year. (Atlanta 15:26 Jan 75)

ALLEN, Maryon. People in the South love their politics better than their food on the table. (Time 112:32 Oct 9, 78)

ALLEN, Woody. Death is the big obsession behind all the things I've done. (Time 113:64 April 30, 79)

ALLEN, Woody. Drama stays with people more, like meat and potatoes, while comedy is a dessert, like meringue.

(Newsweek 85:87B June 23, 75)

ALLEN, Woody. I can't understand why more people aren't bisexual. It would double your chances for a date on Saturday night. (Rolling Stone 272:14 Aug 24, 78)

ALLEN, Woody. If my film makes one more person feel miserable, I'll feel I've done my job. (Time 113:69 April 30, 79)

ALLEN, Woody. In terms of human attributes, what really counts is courage. (Time 113:69 April 30, 79)

ALLEN, Woody. Sex is dirty only when it's done right. (Cosmopolitan 197:288 Oct 84)

ALLEN, Woody. The lion and the calf shall lie down together, but the calf won't get much sleep. (Time 113:25 Feb 26, 79)

ALLEN, Woody. The meaning of life is that nobody knows the meaning of life. (Rolling Stone 216:88 July 1, 76)

ALLEN, Woody. There have been times when I've thought of suicide, but with my luck it'd probably be a temporary solution. (Time 106:47 Dec 15, 75)

ALLEN, Woody (attributed by Marshall Brickman). Showing up is 80 percent of life. (New York Times 126:11 Section 2 Aug 21, 77)

ALLMAN, T. D. Haiti is to this hemisphere what black holes are to outer space. (Vanity Fair 52:8 Jan 89)

ALSOP, Stewart. A fashionable gentleman who much concerns himself with the fashions of gentlemen is neither fashionable nor a gentleman. (Newsweek 83:108 April 15, 74)

ALTMAN, Robert. Every time you make a film, you live a full lifetime. (Newsweek 85:46 June 30, 75)

ALTMAN, Robert. If I'd gone through school, gotten a good job and not gotten into films, I'd probably be dead today or a drunk. (Newsweek 85:50 June 30, 75)

ALTMAN, Robert. Making movies is like playing baseball—the fun is the playing. (Time 105:68 June 16, 75)

ALVAREZ, A. Divorce transforms habit into drama. (Time 119:76 Feb 8, 82)

ALVES, Reuben. Science is what it is, not what scientists think they do. (New York Times 128:A8 July 13, 79)

ANDERSON, Jack. The founding fathers intended us to be watchdogs, not lapdogs. (Time 106:78 Nov 24, 75)

ANDERSON, Jack. The networks don't recognize a story until it's in the New York Times. They aren't competent; they're incompetent. (TV Guide 23:7 Nov 15, 75)

ANDERSON, John B. George Bush is just a tweedier version of Ronald Reagan. (New York Times Magazine 44 Feb 17, 80)

ANDERSON, John B. We (Republicans) are a staid and proper bunch. (Rolling Stone 315:48 April 17, 80)

ANDERSON, John B. You cannot become weary in well-doing. (Sierra Club Bulletin 65:23 May/June 80)

ANDERSON, Laurie. You don't have to be a surrealist to think the world is strange. (Playboy 32:141 April 85)

ANDERSON, Paul. I have yet to see any problem, however complicated, which, when you looked at it in the right way, did not become still more complicated. (Washingtonian 14:152 Nov 78)

ANDERSON, Thomas J. The only secrets the American government has are the secrets it keeps from its own people. (American Opinion 18:17 June 75)

ANDREOTTI, Giulio. In politics there is a clause that is always valid: rebus sic stantibus (circumstances being what they are). (Time 108:54 Dec 13, 76)

ANDREOTTI, Giulio. There are two German states, and there must remain two German states. (Time 134:34 Sept 11, 89)

ANGER, Kenneth. I have always considered movies evil. (Chicago Tribune 295:15E Section 5 Oct 23, 86)

ANGLETON, James. Our generation believed that you go in naked and you leave naked (about working for the CIA). (Time 113:95 April 30, 79)

ANKA, Paul. I didn't want to find a horse's head in my bed (explaining why he allowed Frank Sinatra to first record My Way). (Rolling Stone 257:15 Jan 26, 78)

ANONYMOUS. A clean desk is the sign of a sick mind. (Chicago Magazine 27:104 Jan 78)

ANONYMOUS. A statesman is a dead politician. (Newsweek 94:35 July 2, 79)

ANONYMOUS. A used car is like a bad woman—no matter how good you treat it, it'll give you more trouble than it's worth. (The Reader (Chicago's Free Weekly) 7:11 Section 1 April 7, 78)

ANONYMOUS. Any country that goes to this much trouble to account for every soldier it loses probably ought not to fight a war. (Time 109:18 Mar 28, 77)

ANONYMOUS. Anybody who believes in astrology was probably born under the wrong sign. (Macleans 90:46 Aug 22, 77)

ANONYMOUS. As long as the bosses pretend they are paying us a decent wage, we will pretend that we are working (Soviet worker's saying). (New York Times 126:25 Section 12 Jan 30, 77)

ANONYMOUS. Get behind a judge on

Monday in case you find yourself in front of him on Tuesday (about Chicago). (Los Angeles Times 97:1 Part 1 Nov 29, 78)

ANONYMOUS. If God had meant for Texans to ski, He would have made bullshit white. (Texas Observer 72:7 Sept 19, 80)

ANONYMOUS. If you're bored in New York, you're boring. (Chicago Tribune 193:1 July 11, 76)

ANONYMOUS. In Cannes, a producer is what any man calls himself if he owns a suit, a tie, and hasn't recently been employed as a pimp. (Village Voice 22:26 June 6, 77)

ANONYMOUS. Northern Ireland has too many Catholics and twice as many Protestants, but very few Christians. (Time 104:30 Dec 30, 74)

ANONYMOUS. Tennis isn't a matter of life and death—it's more important than that (sign at the John Gardiner Tennis Clinic, Warren, Vermont). (New Times 5:48 Aug 8, 75)

ANONYMOUS. The Arabs cannot make war without the Egyptians, but they cannot make peace without the Palestinians. (Time 111:35 Mar 27, 78)

ANONYMOUS. The right governs, the left thinks (about French politics). (Time 114:31 Aug 13, 79)

ANONYMOUS. The socialization of medicine is coming...the time now is here for the medical profession to acknowledge that it is tired of the eternal struggle for advantage over one's neighbor (editorial comment in the Journal of the American Medical Association, 1914). (New York Times Magazine 12 Jan 9, 77)

ANONYMOUS. To err is human; to blame it on the other party is politics. (Washingtonian 15:142 Nov 79)

ANONYMOUS. We do it all for you (McDonald's jingle). (Life 2:86 Dec 79)

ANONYMOUS. When the water rises, the fish eat the ants, but when the water recedes, the ants eat the fish (Khmer Rouge slogan). (Guardian Weekly 143:23 Aug 12, 90)

ANONYMOUS (COROLLARY TO MURPHY'S LAW). Everything will take longer than you think it will. (The Reader (Chicago's Free Weekly) 5:2 May 28, 76)

ANONYMOUS (COROLLARY TO MURPHY'S LAW). If everything appears to be going well, you have obviously overlooked something. (Washingtonian 13:7 Dec 77)

ANONYMOUS (COROLLARY TO MURPHY'S LAW). If there is a possibility of several things going wrong, the one that will go wrong is the one that will do

the most damage. (Washingtonian 13:7 Dec 77)

ANONYMOUS (COROLLARY TO MURPHY'S LAW). Nothing is as easy as it looks. (The Reader (Chicago's Free Weekly) 5:2 May 28, 76)

ANONYMOUS (FRENCH POLITICIAN). It seems that the more Paris resembles New York, the more anti-American we become. (Christian Science Monitor 71:7 Aug 14, 79)

ANONYMOUS (HAIGHT-ASHBURY DIGGERS SLOGAN). Today is the first day of the rest of your life. (New Times 9:68 Aug 19, 77)

ANONYMOUS (MURPHY'S LAW). If anything can go wrong, eventually it will. (The Reader (Chicago's Free Weekly) 5:2 May 28, 76)

ANSELMI, Tina (first Italian woman cabinet member). If people outside Italy have the impression that Italy is always on strike, that is because it is. (New York Times 126:21 Section 1 Oct 10, 76)

ANTHONY, Susan B. Failure is impossible. (Chicago Tribune 176:2 Section 2 June 25, 78)

ANTONIONI, Michelangelo. Hollywood is like being nowhere and talking to nobody about nothing. (Chicago Tribune Magazine 6 Oct 16, 83)

APODACA, Jerry. Let there be no mistake, the West will not become an energy colony for the rest of the nation. (Newsweek 85:65 May 5, 75)

APOLLONIO, Spencer. When four fishermen get together, there's always a fifth. (Down East 22:108 Dec 31, 75)

ARAFAT, Yasir. I have come bearing an olive branch and a freedom fighter's gun. Do not let the olive branch fall from my hand (addressing the United Nations (1974)). (Time 104:43 Nov 25, 74)

ARAFAT, Yasir. I have very few cards, but I have the strongest cards. (Time 114:27 Aug 20, 79)

ARAFAT, Yasir. Palestine is my wife. (Time 104:36 Nov 11, 74)

ARAFAT, Yasir. Palestine is the cement that holds the Arab world together, or it is the explosive that blows it apart. (Time 104:27 Nov 11, 74)

ARAFAT, Yasir. The future of the United States of America, the American interest in this part of the world, is with the Arab people, not with Israel. (Chicago Sun-Times 32:3 Aug 12, 79)

ARAFAT, Yasir. The Russian bear is thirsty and he sees the water. (The Observer 9833:9 Feb 10, 80)

ARAFAT, Yasir. There is nothing greater

than to die for Palestine's return. (Time 111:36 Mar 27, 78)

ARAFAT, Yasir. Until I return to my homeland in Palestine, every Arab country is a temporary home for me and my people. (USA Today 1:10A April 11, 83)

ARANOFF, Ezra. There's no room for a slow poke in a prize fight. (Chicago Sun-Times 31:6 Mar 6, 78)

ARBOLEYA, Carlos. History will write Miami's future in Spanish and English. (Time 112:48 Oct 16, 78)

ARBUS, Diane. I mean it's very subtle and a little embarrassing to me, but I really believe that there are things which nobody would see unless I photographed them. (Town & Country 131:64 Feb 77)

ARDEN, Elizabeth. Nothing that costs only a dollar is worth having. (Chicago Tribune 176:2 Section II June 25, 78)

AREGOOD, Richard. They say only the good die young. Generalissimo Francisco Franco was 82. Seems about right. (More 6:55 July/Aug 76)

ARLEDGE, Roone. The single biggest problem of television is that everyone talks so much. (Time 110:61 Aug 22, 77)

ARLEN, Michael J. Every civilization creates its own cultural garbage and ours is television (commenting in his book The View from Highway 1). (Washington Post 352:E4 Nov 21, 76)

ARLEN, Michael J. TV is a kind of language that people have learned how to read. (Time 110:44 Dec 5, 77)

ARMEY, Dick. Demagoguery beats data every time. (Newsweek 16:22 July 16, 90)

ARMSTRONG, Louis. There are some things which, if there ain't nobody said them, there must be a reason. (Chicago 16:57 July 81)

ARMSTRONG, Neil A. That's one small step for man, one giant leap for mankind (upon stepping on the Moon). (New York Times 128:A12 July 20, 79)

ARNON, Jacob (Former Israeli Finance Ministry director). There comes a point when defense spending becomes so enormous that it presents just as much danger to our survival as do our Arab enemies. (Time 107:49 Jan 5, 76)

ARON, Jean-Paul. Avarice is the predominant French characteristic because of (our) long peasant history. (Newsweek 88:62 Nov 22, 76)

ARON, Raymond. Marxism is the opium of the intellectuals. (Time 114:41 July 9, 79)

ARON, Raymond. There is only one field in which the Soviet Union is successful: the projection of its military power throughout the world. (US News & World Report 85:67 Nov 27, 78)

ARRAU, Claudio. Every concert must be an event, never a routine. (Horizon 20:9 Dec 77)

ASHBERY, John. If one is a famous poet, one still isn't famous. (Details 6:99 Mar 88)

ASHLEY, Elizabeth. Money is the long hair of the Eighties. (Life 5:142 Jan 82)

ASIMOV, Isaac. A lot of people can write. I have to. (Time 113:80 Feb 26, 79)

ASIMOV, Isaac. We are the only creatures ever to inhabit the Earth who have truly seen the stars. (Omni 2:90 April 80)

ASIMOV, Isaac. Women tend to be dirtier but less clever than men. I don't know why, but they can be surprisingly vulgar (about women and limericks). (Time 111:74 April 24, 78)

ASPINALL, Wayne. The conservation extremists demand too much of our public land for their own private use. (American Opinion 18:150 July/Aug 75)

ASSAD, Hafez. Sadat is a traitor to his own people and the Arab nation. (Newsweek 93:25 April 2, 79)

ASSAD, Hafez. Step-by-step might be all right if the steps were giant steps, but they are tortoise steps. (Time 106:29 Dec 8, 75)

ASTAIRE, Fred. I don't dance—ever—and I don't intend to ever again. (Chicago Tribune 1:25 Section 1 Jan 1, 78)

ASTOR, Nancy. I married beneath me. All women do. (The Observer 9822:35 Nov 25, 79)

ATKINS, Christopher. It's nice to be beautiful, but it's beautiful to be nice. (The Atlantic 265:24 Jan 90)

ATWATER, Harvey Lee. I really had two goals in life: one, to manage a presidential campaign, and to be chairman of my party. (New York Times 138:9 Nov 18, 88)

ATWATER, Lee. Democrats get totally preoccupied with things voters don't care about. (Chicago Tribune 190:4 Section 4 July 9, 89)

ATWOOD, Margaret. Anybody who says they like all women just because they are women is an idiot—or lying. (Chicago Tribune 78:6 Section 6 Mar 19, 89)

AUCHINCLOSS, Louis. I am neither a satirist nor a cheerleader. I am strictly an observer. (New York Times Book Review 7 Sept 23, 79)

AUCHINCLOSS, Louis. Prizes are for the birds. They fill the head of one author with vanity and 30 others with misery. (Time 118:61 Sept 21, 81)

AUDEN, Wystan Hugh. Among those whom I like, I can find no common denominator;

but among those whom I love, I can: all of them make me laugh. (Reader's Digest 107:78 Nov 75)

AUDEN, Wystan Hugh. Biographies of writers, whether written by others or themselves, are always superfluous and usually in bad taste. A writer is a maker, not a man of action. (The American Book Review 1:8 April/May 78)

AUDEN, Wystan Hugh. Had one to name the author who comes nearest to bearing the same kind of relation to our age as Dante, Shakespeare and Goethe bore to theirs, Kafka is the first one would think of. (Time 111:80 Jan 30, 78)

AUDEN, Wystan Hugh. I do not know of anyone in the United States who writes better prose (about M. F. K. Fisher). (Bon Appetit 23:127 Nov 78)

AUDEN, Wystan Hugh. Literary confessors are contemptible, like beggars who exhibit their sores for money, but not so contemptible as the public that buys their books. (Time 114:98 Nov 19, 79)

AUDEN, Wystan Hugh. Poetry makes nothing happen. (Washingtonian 13:166 Dec 77)

AUDEN, Wystan Hugh (attributed by Peter Conrad). The economic vice of Europeans is avarice, while that of Americans is waste. (Time 115:40 Mar 31, 80)

AUERBACH, Jerold S. Equal justice under law (often means) unequal justice under lawyers. (Time 111:59 April 10, 78)

AUERBACH, Red. There are only three teams in sports that have achieved true national status. The old Yankees, the Dallas Cowboys and us. That's not ego, that's just fact. (Sports Illustrated 67:73 Nov 9, 87)

AUGUSTINE, Norman. If today were half as good as tomorrow is supposed to be, it would probably be twice as good as yesterday was. (Business Month 129:30 June 87)

AUMONT, Jean-Pierre. Marriages are not eternal, so why should divorce be? (W 6:2 July 8, 77)

AUTRY, Gene. I'm gonna die with my boots on. (Chicago Tribune Magazine 62 Dec 3, 78)

AUTRY, Gene. We had no violence when I did the westerns, just fist fights and comedy. (Newsweek 85:9 Mar 3, 75)

AXELSON, Walter. If a man is reluctant to pay the taxes levied by his democratically elected government, he does not love his country, he loves money. (Chicago Tribune 289:10 Oct 15, 88)

AYCKBOURN, Alan. There are very few

people on top of life, and the rest of us don't like them very much. (Newsweek 128:4 Mar 25, 79)

BAAR, James A. Regardless of what you say or do, some of the people will hate you all of the time. (Wharton Magazine 2:16 Fall 77)

BABBITT, Bruce E. It's time we told every polluter: if you poison our water you will go to jail and your money will be spent to clean up the mess. (Chicago Tribune 70:4 Mar 11, 87)

BABBITT, Bruce E. Far too many corporations think they have a smart system and stupid workers. They've got it backwards. (Lawrence (Kansas) Journal-World 130:1A Jan 5, 88)

BABENCO, Hector. Brazil is a country that can only be understood by metaphors, where the reality of things violently exceeds fiction. (New York Times 127:10 April 30, 78)

BABENCO, Hector. I think a people without a cinema is like a person without a mirror. (American Film 10:72 Oct 84)

BACALL, Lauren. I agree with the Bogart theory that all an actor owes the public is a good performance. (The Observer 9777:11 Jan 14, 79)

BACKUS, Jim. Many a man owes his success to his first wife and his second wife to his success. (Cosmopolitan 197:184 Sept 84)

BACON, Francis. I believe you are born, then you die. You do what you can in between the two. (Elle 4:210 Oct 88)

BAEZ, Joan. Here we are back at square one. The world's blowing up, and I'm singing a concert (1983). (Life 7:113 Jan 84)

BAGNOLD, Enid. I wasn't a born writer, but I was born a writer. (Human Behavior 7:17 May 78)

BAGNOLD, Enid. The state of the world depends on one's newspaper. (Washington Post 351:C1 Nov 21, 75)

BAILEY, F. Lee. I defend crime; I'm not in favor of it. (Boston 70:72 Dec 78)

BAILEY, Pearl. I never ask myself how I do what I do. After all, how does it rain? (W 7:8 June 9, 78)

BAILEY, Pearl. There's a period of life when we swallow a knowledge of ourselves and it becomes either good or sour inside. (Chicago Tribune 176:2 Section 2 June 25, 78)

BAKER, Bobby. It's very important for the American people to know who's buying their politicians. (Chicago Sun-Times 31:8 July 7, 78)

BAKER, Howard Henry. In Washington I'm

thought of as a conservative, but in Tennessee I'm thought of as a Bolshevik. (Time 107:15 Aug 9, 76)

BAKER, Russell. In Washington when you cash in your public service for a big payday, the trick is not to offend anybody important on the way to the bank. (New York Times 135:27 April 30, 86)

BAKER, Russell. Inanimate objects are classified scientifically into three major categories—those that don't work, those that break down, and those that get lost. (Washingtonian 15:140 Nov 79)

BAKER, Russell. Misery no longer loves company. Nowadays it insists upon it. (Washingtonian 14:152 Nov 78)

BAKER, Russell. Televiso ergo sum—I am televised, therefore I am. (Time 116:9 Sept 22, 80)

BAKHTIAR, Shapour. We have replaced an old and corrupt dictatorship with a dictatorship accompanied by anarchy. (The Observer 9787:1 Mar 25, 79)

BAKKER, Jim. Jim and Tammy are a tad flamboyant. (Newsweek 109:62 June 8, 87)

BAKKER, Tammy. Christian television is basically very boring. (Newsweek 109:69 June 8, 87)

BAKKER, Tammy. You don't have to be dowdy to be a Christian. (Newsweek 109:69 June 8, 87)

BAKSHIAN, Aram. Speechwriting is to writing as Muzak is to music. (Washingtonian 17:31 Feb 82)

BALANCHINE, George. Ballet is woman. (Time 111:64 Feb 6, 78)

BALANCHINE, George. I am the mother in this world of dance. (Time 115:87 May 19, 80)

BALANCHINE, George. In England you have to be dignified; if you are awake it is already vulgar. (The Observer 9813:14 Sept 23, 79)

BALANCHINE, George. There are no mothers-in-law in ballet. (Ballet News 5:46 July 83)

BALANCHINE, George. You see a little bit of Astaire in everybody's dancing. (Time 130:58 Dec 28, 87)

BALDWIN, James. Everybody wants an artist on the wall or on the shelf, but nobody wants him in the house. (Time 122:65 Sept 26, 83)

BALDWIN, James. It (language) is the most vivid and crucial key to identity. (Saturday Review 6:14 Oct 13, 79)

BALDWIN, James. Love does not begin and end the way we seem to think it does. Love is a battle, love is a war; love is a growing up. (Cosmopolitan 188:268 Feb

80)

BALDWIN, James. The range (and rein) of accents on that damp little island make England coherent for the English and totally incomprehensible for everyone else. (Saturday Review 6:14 Oct 13, 79)

BALDWIN, Roger. I'm a crusader and crusaders don't stop. (Chicago Tribune 52:1 Section 3 Feb 21, 79)

BALL, George W. (Lyndon Johnson) did not suffer from a poor education, he suffered from the belief that he had a poor education. (Washingtonian 11:102 June 76)

BALL, Lucille. The ham always rises. (US 3:13 Aug 11, 86)

BALTZELL, Edward Digby, Jr. I believe in inherited wealth. Society needs to have some people who are above it all. (Town & Country 132:97 July 78)

BALTZELL, Edward Digby, Jr. The masses who have no roots are far less dangerous to a society than an elite with no roots. (Town & Country 132:97 July 78)

BALTZELL, Edward Digby, Jr. When class authority declines, money talks. (Town & Country 132:97 July 78)

BANI-ASSADI, Hossein. Islam has no kings. (New York Times 128:12 Feb 25, 79)

BANISADR, Abolhassan. In our campaign against the U.S., the hostages are our weakness, not our strength. (Time 115:31 Mar 21, 80)

BANKHEAD, Tallulah. Cocaine isn't habit-forming. I should know—I've been using it for years. (Playboy 26:26 Oct 79)

BANKHEAD, Tallulah. Here's a rule I recommend: Never practice two vices at once. (Cosmopolitan 196:332 Oct 83)

BARBOUR, Hugh R. There is nothing like a good negative review to sell a book. (Newsweek 90:69 Oct 31, 77)

BARDOT, Brigitte. I leave before being left. I decide. (Chicago Tribune 176:2 Section 2 June 25, 78)

BARDOT, Brigitte. It's better to be old than dead. (The Observer 9812:10 Sept 16, 79)

BARDOT, Brigitte. Men are beasts and even beasts don't behave as they do. (Viva 4:26 Feb 77)

BARENBOIM, Daniel. When they want to be difficult, the French can seem impossible. But when they decide to get something done, there's no one better. (Time 125:65 June 17, 85)

BARKLEY, Alben. Three months is a generation in politics. (Time 106:9 July 14, 75)

BARNARD, Christiaan. I believe in destiny,

and there's very little you can do to change it. (Time 126:65 July 22, 85)

BARNARD, Christiaan. There is one message I would give to young doctors and that is that the goal of medicine is not to prolong life. It is to alleviate suffering and improve the quality of life. (Chicago Tribune 64:14 Mar 5, 78)

BARON, Alan. We have divided the presidential election process from the governing process. (Time 115:27 Jan 28, 80)

BARRAGAN, Luis. Art is made by the alone for the alone. (Time 115:50 May 12, 80)

BARROW, Willie. It's easier being black than being a woman. (Sepia 26:12 Sept 75)

BARRY, Lynda. The problem with the left is that they don't realize that people have genitals. (In These Times 14:15 Oct 24, 90)

BARRYMORE, John. There's something about a closet that makes a skeleton terribly restless. (Kansas City Times 109:14B July 8, 77)

BARTH, John. God was a pretty good novelist; the only trouble was that He was a realist. (New York Times Book Review 33 April 1, 79)

BARTH, John. My books are allowed to know one another, as children of the same father, but they must lead their lives independently. (Time 114:96 Oct 8, 78)

BARTHELME, Donald. The principle of collage is the central principle of all art in the 20th Century. (Chicago Tribune 207:12 Section 2 July 26, 89)

BARTHOLOMEW, Summer (Miss U.S.A.— 1975). I believe in equal pay for equal jobs, but not communal toilets or anything like that. (Washingtonian 10:21 July 75)

BARUCH, Bernard Mannes (attributed by William Flanagan). I buy low and sell high (when asked how he had made a fortune in the stock market). (New York 10:56 May 2, 77)

BARYSHNIKOV, Mikhail. With Balanchine I grew up. (Newsweek 94:82 July 2, 79)

BARZINI, Luigi. We (Italians) might be the first developed country to turn itself back into an underdeveloped country. (Time 111:63 April 3, 78)

BATTISTA, O. A. The fellow who says he'll meet you halfway usually thinks he's standing on the dividing line. (Washingtonian 15:140 Nov 79)

BAULER, (Paddy). Chicago ain't ready for reform yet. (Harper's Weekly 3168:8 Aug 23, 76)

BAUMAN, Robert E. Anytime the House is in session the American people are probably in danger. (New York Times 125:31 April 6, 76)

BAXLEY, Bill. (George Bush is) a pin-stripin' pole playin umbrella-totin' Ivy Leaguer, born with a silver spoon so far back in his mouth that you conldn't get it out with a crowbar. (The Atlantic 260:62 July 87)

BAYH, Birch Evans. If there is one symbol of the Establishment ripping off the people, it is the oil companies. (Time 107:56 June 28, 76)

BEARD, Peter. Nixon is what America deserved and Nixon is what America got. (Photograph 5:5 April 78)

BEATON, Sir Cecil. Perhaps the world's second worst crime is boredom; the first is being a bore. (Time 115:89 Jan 28, 80)

BEATTY, Warren. When a reporter enters the room, your privacy ends and his begins. (Life 7:40 Jan 84)

BEAUVOIR, Simone De. I cannot be angry at God, in whom I do not believe. (The Observer 9776:10 Jan 7, 79)

BEAUVOIR, Simone De. One is not born a woman, one becomes one. (Ms 6:16 July 77)

BECKER, Jules. It is much harder to find a job than to keep one. (Washingtonian 14:152 Nov 78)

BECKETT, Samuel. All I want to do is sit on my ass and fart and think of Dante. (Newsweek 91:96 June 5, 78)

BECKETT, Samuel. There's man all over for you, blaming his boots for the faults of his feet. (Philadelphia 69:187 Sept 78)

BEGIN, Menachem. Europe's rivers are still red with Jewish blood. This Europe cannot teach us how to maintain our security. (Christian Science Monitor 70:5 Dec 2, 77)

BEGIN, Menachem. Jerusalem will remain undivided for all generations until the end of the world. (The Observer 9762:15 Oct 1, 78)

BEGIN, Menachem. This region isn't Switzerland. (The Observer 9795:9 May 20, 79)

BEHAN, Brendan. I have never seen a situation so dismal that a policeman couldn't make it worse. (Cleveland 4:118 Aug 75)

BEHAN, Brendan. I think anything is all right provided it is done in private and doesn't frighten the horses. (Cleveland 4:118 Aug 75)

BELL, Griffin. I think we have too many crimes, and I definitely have the view that we have too many laws. (Time 108:16 Dec 27, 76)

BELL, Helen Choate. The French are a low lot. Give them two more legs and a tail, and there you are. (New York 10:88 Jan 31, 77)

BELL, James (Cool Papa). If you don't live to get old, you die young. (St Louis Magazine 16:79 Oct 84)

BELL, Terrence H. We need to liberalize vocational education—and vocationalize liberal education. (Money 5:48 April 76)

BELLA, Ben. It is an illusion to think you can have a revolution without prisons. (New York Times 128:3 Section 4 July 8, 79)

BELLI, Melvin. I'd rather have Adolf Hitler as the executor of my will than the president of an insurance company. (Chicago Sun-Times 35:16 Mar 10, 82)

BELLOW, Saul. By the time the latest ideas reach Chicago, they're worn thin and easy to see through. (Time 119:77 Jan 18, 82)

BELLOW, Saul. I know you think I'm a square, Freifeld, but there's no name for the shape I'm in. (Newsweek 86:39 Sept 1, 75)

BELLOW, Saul. I see politics—ultimately— as a buzzing preoccupation that swallows up art and the life of the spirit. (Newsweek 86:39 Sept 1, 75)

BELLOW, Saul. Writers are readers inspired to emulation. (Harvard Magazine 89:78 Jan/Feb 87)

BENCHLEY, Nathaniel. Contrary to popular opinion there is not a college education in that bottle; you don't get smarter with every drink you take. (Writer's Digest 58:28 Oct 78)

BENCHLEY, Robert. I have tried to know absolutely nothing about a great many things, and I have succeeded fairly well. (Rocky Mountain News 31:64 April 23, 80)

BENCHLEY, Robert. There may be said to be two classes of people in the world: those who constantly divide the people of the world into two classes and those who do not. (Washingtonian 14:152 Oct 31, 78)

BENCHLEY, Robert. Traveling with children corresponds roughly to traveling third class in Bulgaria. (Time 113:76 June 25, 79)

BENES, Bernardo. God gave us our geography and Fidel Castro gave us our biculturalism (about Miami). (Miami Magazine 27:27 Nov 75)

BENNETT, Arnold. The price of justice is eternal publicity. (Time 113:85 April 30, 79)

BENNETT, William J. Why don't you admit what everybody knows, which is there are a lot of teachers...who have no business in being in classrooms? (Lawrence (Kansas) Journal-World 130:1 Mar 30, 88)

BENNETT, William J. Higher education is not underfunded, it is underaccountable and underproductive. (Chicago Tribune 110:10 April 20, 87)

BENNY, Jack. I'm a simple guy. For a comedian I'm surprisingly normal. I have never been to a psychiatrist and I've only been married once. (Newsweek 85:63 Jan 6, 75)

BENTON, Thomas Hart. I feel in my very soul that I was born to be great. (New York Times 138:9 April 13, 89)

BENTSEN, Lloyd. I just wasn't able to convince voters that 'Dukakis' was Greek for 'Bubba'. (Newsweek 112:15 Dec 19, 88)

BENTSEN, Lloyd. Jack Kennedy was a friend of mine. Senator, you're no Jack Kennedy (to Dan Quayle). (Chicago Tribune 280:1 Oct 6, 88)

BENTSEN, Lloyd. When it comes to defending America, you can trust the Democrats. (Chicago Tribune 239:6 Section 1 Aug 26, 88)

BERGE, Pierre. Except for white ruffles, pasta and opera, the Italians can't be credited with anything. (Time 119:60 April 5, 82)

BERGMAN, Ingmar. Each film is my last. (Village Voice 28:44 Jan 4, 83)

BERGMAN, Ingmar. Possessiveness is neurotic, but this is how I am. (New West 2:24 April 25, 77)

BERGMAN, Ingrid. A kiss is a lovely trick designed by nature to stop speech when words become superfluous. (Viva 4:26 May 77)

BERGSON, Henri. Think like a man of action, and act like a man of thought. (Kansas City Star 97:4B Feb 6, 77)

BERHANGER, Elio. Fashion has become like an old prostitute. Nobody even uses the word elegance anymore. (W 7:8 Mar 17, 78)

BERLE, Milton. The best way a new comic can start is to have funny bones. (People Weekly 9:96 April 3, 78)

BERLIN, Irving. There wasn't anyone in show business who will be missed as much as Bing Crosby, not only as a performer, but also as a person. (New York Times 126:42 Oct 16, 77)

BERMER, Richard. The question is no longer whether there will be a recession but how deep it will be and how long it will last (1990). (Time 136:38 Aug 20, 90)

BERNSTEIN, Carl. Let me say no one has successfully challenged the accuracy of this book (The Final Days) or any single assertion in it. (Meet the Press 20:9 April 18, 76)

BERRA, Yogi. A nickel ain't worth a dime anymore. (Duns Business Month 127:50 Jan 31, 86)

BERRA, Yogi. In baseball, you don't know nothing. (New West 4:116 April 9, 79)

BERRIGAN, Daniel. When we get locked up now, there's a sigh of ennui (on the declining state of civil disobedience (1978)). (Time 111:67 Mar 20, 78)

BERRY, Chuck. I never looked for recognition. I was paying for a home and a new car. (Newsweek 108:19 Nov 3, 86)

BERRY, Chuck. The minute you toot your horn, it seems like society will try and disconnect your battery. (US 3:6 Nov 16, 87)

BERRY, Wendell. Learning to farm is learning to farm a farm. (The Nation 249:418 Oct 16, 89)

BERTOLUCCI, Bernardo. To make a film it is not necessary to know anything technical at all. It will all come with time. (Texas Monthly 4:40 Aug 76)

BESTON, Henry. Peace with the earth is the first peace. (Blair & Ketchum's Country Journal 3:88 Aug 76)

BHUTTO, Zulfikar Ali. A politician is like a spring flower: he blossoms, he blooms, and a time comes for him to fade. (Time 107:38 May 2, 77)

BHUTTO, Zulfikar Ali. Democracy demands reciprocity. (Time 106:26 Dec 29, 75)

BIDEN, Joseph. Half the people don't know the difference between SALT and pepper. (Time 113:37 April 16, 79)

BILLINGTON, James. Violence is not only "as American as cherry pie," it is likely to remain a la mode for some time to come. (Newsweek 86:13 Oct 6, 75)

BIRD, Rose. The press has become the modern equivalent of peer group pressure. (Wilson Library Bulletin 62:21 Sept 87)

BISHOP, Elizabeth. Poetry shouldn't be used as a vehicle for any personal philosophy. (Chicago Tribune 155:1 Section 5 June 4, 78)

BLACK ELK. Sometimes I think it might have been better if we had stayed together and made them kill us all. (Quest/78 2:113 Sept/Oct 78)

BLACK STALIN (SINGER). In Calypso, there is no retirement plan. (Spin 3:12 Dec 87)

BLACKMUR, R. P. Literature exists to remind the powers that be, simple and corrupt as they are, of the turbulence they have to control. (New York Times Book Review 32 Sept 23, 79)

BLAKE, Eubie. When she (Alberta Hunter) sang the blues, you felt so sorry for her

you would want to kill the guy she was singing about. (Newsweek 90:101 Oct 31, 77)

BLASS, Bill. Design is like the theatre—the bug bites you early. (Bookviews 1:36 June 78)

BLASS, Bill. I'd rather help raise money for museums than diseases. (US 3:64 Nov 4, 85)

BLASS, Bill. L. A. stinks, and I can say that because I'm not running for anything. (Time 122:49 Sept 12, 83)

BLOCK, Herbert L. (Jimmy Carter) looks a little like both Jack Kennedy and Eleanor Roosevelt. (Time 110:92 Dec 12, 77)

BLOCK, Herbert L. If it's good, they'll stop making it. (Time 113:25 Feb 26, 79)

BLOND, Susan. If you're beautiful, you can get away with anything. (Vanity Fair 48:42 May 85)

BLUMENTHAL, W. Michael. Most bureaucratic regulations look like Chinese to me—and I can read Chinese. (Washingtonian 12:11 Aug 77)

BOCUSE, Paul. Nothing is on the plate and everything is on the bill (about nouvelle cuisine). (Chicago 38:276 Dec 89)

BOCUSE, Paul. The only place for them (women) is in bed. Anyone who doesn't change his woman every week or so lacks imagination. (Newsweek 86:53 Aug 11, 75)

BOEHEIM, Jim. I ain't a bad guy. People see me on the sidelines and they think I'm an idiot or a maniac. That's just coaching. (Topeka Capital-Journal SportsPlus 11 April 7, 87)

BOESKY, Ivan F. I think greed is healthy. You can be greedy and still feel good about yourself. (Newsweek 108:48 Dec 1, 86)

BOESKY, Ivan F. It's OK to make money. It's a good thing. You go to heaven if you do it. (Kansas Cith Star 107:8A Nov 18, 86)

BOGART, Humphrey. Sinatra's idea of paradise is a place where there are plenty of women and no newspapermen. He doesn't know it, but he'd be better off if it were the other way 'round. (US 3:64 Dec 16, 85)

BOHANNAN, Paul. Margaret Mead was, in fact, a centipede; she had that many shoes. (Time 112:57 Nov 27, 78)

BOHR, Niels. But horseshoes have a way of bringing you luck even when you don't believe in them. (Village Voice 21:25 June 28, 76)

BOHR, Niels. When it comes to atoms, language can be used only as in poetry. (Discover 3:70 Dec 82)

BOK, Derek. If you think education is expensive—try ignorance. (Town &

Country 133:140 May 79)

BOMBECK, Erma. A child needs your love most when he deserves it the least. (Family Circle 97:14 Jan 3, 84)

BOND, Edward. Laughter that's not also an idea is cruel. (Washingtonian 21:42 Jan 85)

BONO, Sonny. I've never been qualified for anything I've done. (Newsweek 110:13 July 13, 87)

BOONE, Pat. I think my life is a vindication of what Middle America wants. (TV Guide 26:34 April 1, 78)

BOORSTIN, Daniel J. Our national politics has become a competition for images or between images, rather than between ideals. (Time 113:84 April 9, 79)

BOORSTIN, Daniel J. Reading is a lot like sex. It is a private and often secret activity. It is often undertaken in bed, and people are not inclined to underestimate either the extent or the effectiveness of their activity. (Life 7:39 Jan 84)

BOORSTIN, Daniel J. The contemporary time is always the best time to live. It is a mistake to say the best age is one without problems. (Time 106:53 Sept 1, 75)

BOORSTIN, Daniel J. The courage we inherit from our Jeffersons and Lincolns and others is not the Solzhenitsyn courage of the true believer, but the courage to doubt. (Time 111:21 June 26, 78)

BOORSTIN, Daniel J. We suffer primarily not from our vices or our weaknesses, but from our illusions. (Time 114:133 Nov 12, 79)

BORGES, Jorge Luis. America is still the best hope. But the Americans themselves will have to be the best hope too. (Time 107:51 July 5, 76)

BORGES, Jorge Luis. Had I to choose one literature, my choice would be the English literature. (The (Montreal) Gazette B-6 June 1, 85)

BORGES, Jorge Luis. I think most people are more important than their opinions. (The Times 8067:39 Feb 5, 78)

BORGES, Jorge Luis. If my works are read for pleasure, thats all they have to do. (Chicago Tribune 169:3 Section 5 June 18, 86)

BORK, Robert. I don't care how free enterprise you are, once you deal with a publisher you'll want to nationalize the industry. (Chicago Tribune 82:13 Section 1 Mar 22, 88)

BORK, Robert. Roe v. Wade contains almost no legal reasoning. (Chicago Tribune 259:11 Sept 16, 87)

BORMAN, Frank. Capitalism without bankruptcy is like Christianity without hell. (Chicago Tribune 79:2 Section 5 Mar 21, 90)

BOTHA, Pieter W. I am going to keep order, and nobody is going to stop me. (Time 127:48 Dec 30, 85)

BOTHA, Pieter W. To both friend and foe, the United States is becoming constructively irrelevant (1987). (Chicago Tribune 14:17 Jan 14, 87)

BOTSTEIN, Leon. The English language is dying, because it is not taught. (Time 106:34 Aug 25, 75)

BOULANGER, Nadia. Education is to bring people to be themselves, and at the same time, know how to conform to the limits. (New York Times 126:D25 Sept 11, 77)

BOULDING, Kenneth E. The purpose of education is to transmit information from decrepit old men to decrepit young men. (Omni 2:31 April 80)

BOURKE-WHITE, Margaret. Know your subject thoroughly, saturate yourself with your subject, and your camera will take you by the hand. (Blair & Ketchum's Country Journal 4:78 June 77)

BOW, Clara. He was hung like a horse, and he could go all night (about Gary Cooper). (Cosmopolitan 197:190 Mar 84)

BOWEN, Elizabeth. All your youth you want to have your greatness taken for granted; when you find it taken for granted, you are unnerved. (Kansas City Star 97:15C Sept 22, 76)

BOWLES, Paul. Everything gets worse. (Vanity Fair 48:131 Sept 85)

BOYLE, Charles. If not controlled, work will flow to the competent man until he submerges. (Time 113:25 Feb 26, 79)

BOYLES, Tiny. Getting beat up is like eating hot food. After the first bite you don't feel the rest. (Oui 8:52 May 79)

BRAGA, Sonia. All my life, intuition has put me in the right place at the right time. (Playboy 31:91 Oct 84)

BRAGA, Sonia. I have no idea what acting is. I just try to understand the mind of the women I play. (Chicago Tribune 269:7 Section 5 Sept 26, 85)

BRAGG, W. L. The essence of science lies not in discovering facts but in discovering new ways of thinking about them. (Omni 1:29 April 79)

BRAND, Stewart. I thought the sixties went on too long. (Outside 1:68 Dec 77)

BRAND, Stewart. My expectation is that the sky will fall. My faith is that there's another sky behind it. (Omni 2:50 Dec 79)

BRAND, Stewart. While we were out in the streets marching, the real revolutionaries were in the computer labs. (Inc 7:53 July 85)

BRANDO, Marlon. Acting is an empty profession. I do it for the money because for me there is no pleasure. (Time 107:74 May 24, 76)

BRANDO, Marlon. Carter has done something no other President has done: He has brought into the sharpest contrast the hypocrisy of the U.S. in respect to human rights. (Playboy 26:126 Jan 77)

BRANDO, Marlon. If there are men who have a clean soul, he's (Tennessee Williams) one of them. (Playboy 26:140 Jan 77)

BRANDO, Marlon. If you're rich and famous you don't have any trouble getting laid. (Players 3:32 Feb 77)

BRANDO, Marlon. The only reason I'm in Hollywood is that I don't have the moral courage to refuse the money. (Los Angeles 34:210 Mar 89)

BRANDO, Marlon. The principal benefit acting has offered me is the money to pay my psychiatrists. (Los Angeles 23:181 Nov 78)

BRANDT, Willy. Unity is only a question of time. (Chicago Tribune 361:19 Section 1 Dec 27, 89)

BRAUDEL, Fernand. The preserve of the few, capitalism is unthinkable without society's active complicity. (World Issues 3:30 Oct 78)

BRAUDEL, Fernand (French historian). A historian never judges. He is not God. The power the historian has is to make the dead live. It is a triumph over death. (Time 109:78 May 23, 77)

BREAUX, John. If these do-gooders have their way you'll need a permit to turn on a faucet in the bathroom (commenting on environmentalists' causes). (Outside 1:17 Dec 77)

BRECHT, Bertolt. Because things are the way they are things will not stay the way they are. (Philadelphia Magazine 68:305 Nov 77)

BRECHT, Bertolt. Grub first, art after. (New York Times Magazine 22 Jan 23, 77)

BRECHT, Bertolt. I hope that because of my life, the powerful will sleep less comfortably (on his epitaph). (Guardian Weekly 120:17 April 29, 79)

BREL, Jacques. Dying is man's only natural act. (Atlas World Press Review 25:49 Dec 78)

BRENAN, Gerald. Miracles are like jokes. They relieve our tension suddenly by setting us free from the chain of cause and effect. (Time 113:147 Feb 5, 79)

BRENAN, Gerald. When the coin is tossed, either love or lust will fall uppermost. But if the metal is right, under the one will always lie the other. (Time 113:147-48 Feb 5, 79)

BRENNAN, William. If there is a bedrock principle underlying the First Amendment, it is that the Government may not prohibit the expression of an idea simply because society finds the idea itself offensive or disagreeable. (Time 134:14 July 3, 89)

BRENNAN, William. It is my hope that the Court during my years of service has built a legacy of interpreting the Constitution and Federal laws to make them responsive to the needs of the people whom they were intended to benefit and protect. (Time 136:17 July 30, 90)

BRENNAN, William. We do not consecrate the flag by punishing its descration for in doing so we dilute the freedom that this cherished emblem represents. (Newsweek 114:20 July 3, 89)

BRENNER, David. A vegetarian is a person who won't eat anything that can have children. (Cosmopolitan 197:184 Sept 84)

BRESLIN, Catherine. A freelancer lives at the end of a sawed-off limb. (Time 111:77 April 10, 78)

BRESLIN, Jimmy. Don't trust a brilliant idea unless it survives the hangover. (Washingtonian 23:149 Dec 87)

BRESLIN, Jimmy. If this is what happens when you let them out of the kitchen, I'm all for it (commenting on Gael Greene's first novel Blue Skies, No Candy). (New York Times 126:52 Nov 16, 76)

BRESSLER, Marvin. There is no crisis to which academics will not respond with a seminar. (Washingtonian 15:140 Nov 79)

BRETT, Ken. The worst curse in the world is unlimited potential. (Arkansas Times 12:67 July 86)

BREWSTER, Kingman. A diplomat does not have to be a eunuch. (W 7:37 Aug 31, 15)

BREZHNEV, Leonid I. Building Detente requires no little political courage. (Newsweek 93:41 Jan 22, 79)

BREZHNEV, Leonid I. God will not forgive us if we fail (about Strategic Arms Limitation Talks). (New York Times 128:1 June 17, 79)

BRICKMAN, Marshall. Open marriage is nature's way of telling you you need a divorce. (Cosmopolitan 188:268 Feb 80)

BRIGGS, John. When it comes to politics, anything is fair. (Village Voice 23:62 Oct 16, 78)

BROCK, Bill. Reagan has this remarkable ability to project decency, a sense of knowing where he is and where he is going. (Time 116:13 July 28, 80)

BROCK, Bill. This (Republican) party is a new party—we are on our way up (1980). (Time 116:10 July 28, 80)

BROCK, Lou. If you can perceive a goal and then make it happen, you live a dream. (Newsweek 94:49 Aug 27, 79)

BRODER, David S. Anybody who wants the presidency so much that he'll spend two years organizing and campaigning for it is not to be trusted with the office. (Time 113:25 Feb 26, 79)

BRODER, David S. He (Richard Strout) must get out of bed every day as if it's his first chance to set the world right. (Time 111:83 Mar 27, 78)

BRODEUR, Richard (goalie for Vancouver Canucks). What he does best is make you look bad (commenting on Wayne Gretzky). (The Sporting News 193:8 Jan 30, 82)

BROGAN, D. W. Democracy is like a raft. It never sinks, but damn it, your feet are always in the water. (Time 107:25 May 2, 77)

BRONFMAN, Edgar. To turn $100 into $110 is work. To turn $100 million into $110 million is inevitable. (Newsweek 106:62 Dec 2, 85)

BRONSON, Charles. I'm not one of my favorite characters. (US 3:4 May 4, 87)

BROOKS, Jim. Businessmen commit a fraud when they say they're interested in anything but profit. (New West 1:17 Dec 20, 76)

BROOKS, Mel. Everything we do in life is based on fear, especially love. (Playboy 26:26 Oct 79)

BROOKS, Mel. I don't think in terms of results. I think: what next insanity can I shock the world with. (Maclean's 91:10 April 17, 78)

BROONZY, Bill (Big). It's all folk music, cause horses don't sing (in response to Studs Terkel's question, are the Blues folk music). (Stereo Review 37:62 July 76)

BROUN, Heywood Hale. If anyone corrects your pronunciation of a word in a public place, you have every right to punch him in the nose. (Kansas City Times 109:14B July 8, 77)

BROUN, Heywood Hale. Sport is a preparation for more sport and not a businessmen's ROTC. (New York Times Book Review 8 July 29, 79)

BROWN, Dale. If you don't violate NCAA rules, you're in a coma or in a crematorium. (Lawrence (Kansas) Journal-World 129:5B Mar 25, 87)

BROWN, Edmund Gerald, Jr. California is the place where the rest of the country and the rest of the world look for

leadership and I want to keep it that way. (San Francisco Chronicle This World 1978:29 Feb 26, 78)

BROWN, Edmund Gerald, Jr. Communications erodes provincialism. (Esquire 89:64 Jan 31, 78)

BROWN, Edmund Gerald, Jr. I think it's time for the President, certainly the next President, to say no to nuclear power (1979). (New York Times 128:A18 April 26, 79)

BROWN, Edmund Gerald, Jr. In California, you've got to realize one thing: you don't mess around with a man's cars or his guns. (New West 3:54 Dec 18, 78)

BROWN, Edmund Gerald, Jr. In this business (politics) a little vagueness goes a long way. (New Times 6:18 May 28, 76)

BROWN, Edmund Gerald, Jr. Issues are the last refuges of scoundrels. (Washingtonian 15:140 Nov 79)

BROWN, Edmund Gerald, Jr. People are ready to make sacrifice for the betterment of this country, but only on a basis that we all bear up the burdens and bear under them on an equal basis, and that is not happening today. (Meet The Press 19:2 Oct 5, 75)

BROWN, Edmund Gerald, Jr. The first rule of politics is to be different. (Newsweek 93:24 April 23, 79)

BROWN, Edmund Gerald, Jr. The nation is not governable without new ideas. (Time 114:21 Nov 12, 79)

BROWN, Edmund Gerald, Jr. The power of the executive is like a chess game; there are very few moves that one can make. (Gold Coast Pictorial 13:9 Feb 77)

BROWN, Edmund Gerald, Jr. The reason why everybody likes planning is because nobody has to do anything. (The Coevolution Quarterly 10:23 Summer 76)

BROWN, Edmund Gerald, Jr. There is a limit to the good things we have in this country. We're coming up against those limits. It's really a very salutary exercise to learn to live with them. (Time 106:18 Dec 8, 75)

BROWN, Edmund Gerald, Jr. We must sacrifice for the future, or else we steal from it. (The Tennessean 74:6 April 11, 79)

BROWN, Edmund Gerald, Jr. You don't have to do things. Maybe by avoiding doing things you accomplish a lot. (New York Times 125:17 April 26, 76)

BROWN, Edmund Gerald, Jr. You lean a little to the left and then a little to the right in order to always move straight ahead (on the art of governing). (Time 112:89 Oct 2, 78)

BROWN, Harold. (Russia) has shown no

response to U.S. restraint—when we build, they build; when we cut, they build. (Newsweek 93:104 June 25, 79)

BROWN, Harold. A lesson we learned from Vietnam is that we should be very cautious about intervening in any place where there's a poor political base for our presence. (Time 109:24 May 23, 77)

BROWN, James. I think God made sure there will never by another me. (Newsweek 108:13 Aug 25, 86)

BROWN, John Mason. To many, dramatic criticism must seem like an attempt to tattoo soap bubbles. (Stagebill 52 Dec 81)

BROWN, Michael. We have planted thousands of toxic time bombs; it is only a question of time before they explode (commenting on U. S. chemical dumps). (Life 4:21 Jan 81)

BROWN, Phyllis George. A smart woman will suggest things to a man and let him take the credit. (New Woman 10:12 May 80)

BROWN, Rita Mae. Love is the wild card of existence. (Chicago Sun-Times 34:53 Sept 2, 81)

BROWN, Ron. It is disingenuous for the people who ran the Willie Horton ads to express shock and dismay over David Duke. (Time 133:29 Mar 6, 89)

BROWN, Sam. Never offend people with style when you can offend them with substance. (Washingtonian 14:152 Nov 78)

BROWN, Sam. Never trust anybody over 30. (Chicago Sun-Times 31:26 June 4, 78)

BROWNMILLER, Susan. It (rape) is nothing more or less than a conscious process of intimidation by which all men keep all women in a state of fear. (Time 106:48 Oct 13, 75)

BRUCE, Lenny. I only said it, man. I didn't do it. (Oui 7:51 Feb 78)

BRUSTEIN, Robert. Once we allow lawmakers to become art critics, we take the first step into the world of Ayatollah Khomeini. (The Progressive 53:9 Aug 89)

BRYANT, Anita. God says that someone who practices homosexuality shall not inherit the Kingdom of God. God is very plain on that. (Ms 6:50 July 77)

BRYANT, Paul W. (Bear). No coach ever won a game by what he knows; it's what his players have learned. (Time 118:68 Dec 7, 81)

BRZEZINSKI, Zbigniew. A big country like the U.S. is not like a speedboat on a lake. It can't veer suddenly to the right or left. It's like a large ship. There's continuity to

its course. (Time 111:18 May 29, 78)

BRZEZINSKI, Zbigniew. By the time we're through, the world will have been reordered. (W 7:33 Nov 10, 78)

BRZEZINSKI, Zbigniew. Pessimism is a luxury that policymakers can't afford because pessimism, on the part of people who try to shape events, can become a self-fulfilling prophecy. (Time 112:26 Aug 21, 78)

BUCHAN, Alastair. Respectability depends on whose side you're on. To the Turks, Lawrence of Arabia was a terrorist. (Time 104:44 Nov 25, 74)

BUCHANAN, Patrick J. The day the United States ceases to produce soldiers of the kidney and spleen and heart and soul of Oliver North is the day this country enters on its irreversible decline. (Washington Post National Weekly Edition 4:5 Dec 29, 86)

BUCHWALD, Art. As the economy gets better, everything else gets worse. (Book Digest 6:32 Dec 79)

BUCHWALD, Art. In 80 percent of the countries in the world today, guys like myself would be in jail. (Book Digest 4:27 Sept 77)

BUCHWALD, Art. In this country, when you attack the Establishment, they don't put you in jail or a mental institution. They do something worse. They make you a member of the Establishment. (Time 110:67 Dec 5, 77)

BUCHWALD, Art. The day you leave Russia is the happiest day of your life. (Book Digest 4:30 Sept 77)

BUCK, Pearl. One faces the future with one's past. (Chicago Tribune 176:2 Section 2 June 25, 78)

BUCKLEY, Pat. A New Yorker is anyone possessing a Green Card. (W 13:9 Feb 10, 84)

BUCKLEY, Pat. Women were born to be taken care of by men—I do think that's the law of the universe. (W 6:1 Oct 14, 77)

BUCKLEY, William Frank, Jr. All adventure is now reactionary. (Time 109:87 May 23, 77)

BUCKLEY, William Frank, Jr. If people would just take my advice, everything would go well. (W 7:2 April 14, 78)

BUCKLEY, William Frank, Jr. We should be big enough to grant a little people what we ourselves fought for 200 years ago (commenting on the Panama Canal). (San Francisco Chronicle This World 1978:2 Jan 22, 78)

BUCY, Fred. Nothing is ever accomplished by a reasonable man. (Book Digest 6:30 Dec 79)

BUJOLD, Genevieve. Caesar was Cleopatra's guru and Guinness was mine. (Newsweek 85:32 Jan 6, 76)

BUKOWSKI, Charles. Sexual intercouse is kicking death in the ass while singing. (Playboy 32:16 Feb 85)

BUNDY, McGeorge. One of the things we've always valued about Henry Ford is candor. (Harper's 254:32 Mar 77)

BUNDY, Theodore. I deserve, certainly, the most extreme punishment society has. I think society deserves to be protected from me and from others like me. (Chicago Tribune 33:23 Section 1 Feb 2, 89)

BUNEUL, Luis. A religious education and Surrealism have marked me for life. (In These Times 7:21 Aug 24, 83)

BUNUEL, Luis. Sex without sin is like an egg without salt. (New Times 5:5 Nov 28, 75)

BURGER, Warren Earl. The very discussion of independence reminds us how much each freedom is dependent on other freedoms. (American Legion Magazine 99:36 Nov 75)

BURGER, Warren Earl. We may be well on our way to a society overrun by hordes of lawyers, hungry as locusts, and brigades of judges in numbers never before contemplated. (Time 109:40 June 27, 77)

BURGESS, Anthony. We need beauty queens more than politicians. (The Observer 9809:10 Aug 26, 79)

BURGESS, Anthony. Women cannot help moving, and men cannot help being moved. (Playboy 24:346 Dec 77)

BURNHAM, Daniel. Make no little plans. (Chicago 26:160 Dec 77)

BURNS, Arthur Frank. Anyone who is convinced that he can fine-tune the economy doesn't know what he is talking about. (Time 130:58 Dec 28, 87)

BURNS, Arthur Frank. The ultimate consequence of inflation could well be a significant decline of economic and political freedom for the American people. (Time 111:33 Jan 9, 78)

BURNS, George. Now, they say, you should retire at 70. When I was 70 I still had pimples. (Time 112:69 Aug 7, 78)

BURNS, George. The secret to longevity is three martini's before dinner and always dance close. (W Supplement 131 July 27, 87)

BURNS, George. Too bad that all the people who know how to run the country are busy driving taxicabs and cutting hair. (Life 2:117 Dec 79)

BURNS, George. When I do go, I plan to take my music with me. I don't know what's out there, but I want to be sure it's in my key. (Playboy 22:48 Dec 75)

BURNS, George (attributed by David Steinberg). (Critics are) eunuchs at a gang-bang. (New Times 10:38 Jan 9, 78)

BURNS, John. We expect very little of our (state) legislatures, and they continually live up to our expectations. (Time 111:101 May 29, 78)

BURROUGHS, Edgar Rice. The less I know about a thing the better I can write about it. (Chicago 38:172 Dec 89)

BURROUGHS, John. If you want to see birds, you must have birds in your heart. (Outside 1:11 Dec 77)

BURROUGHS, William S. Life is a cut-up. (University Daily Kansan 93:11 April 25, 83)

BURROUGHS, William S. What you want to do is eventually what you will do anyway. Sooner or later. (Village Voice 22:44 May 16, 77)

BURSTYN, Ellen. What a lovely surprise to finally discover how unlonely being alone can be. (Cosmopolitan 196:332 Oct 83)

BURTON, Richard. Clint (Eastwood) is in the great line of Spencer Tracy and James Stewart and Bob Mitchum. They have a kind of dynamic lethargy. They appear to do nothing and they do everything. (Esquire 89:45 Mar 14, 78)

BURTON, Richard. I only see a movie when I can't avoid it. (W 5:16 July 23, 76)

BURTON, Richard. I was a star from the moment I first walked on the stage. (Chicago Tribune 284:2 Section 2 Oct 11, 77)

BUSH, Barbara. I am a liberal. (Newsweek 104:27 Nov 27, 89)

BUSH, Barbara. I have great faith. Every night before I go to bed I pray out loud; so does George. (W 17:28 Jan 2, 89)

BUSH, Earl (press aide to Richard J. Daley). Don't print what he says; print what he means (about Richard J. Daley). (Chicago Sun-Times 33:2 Oct 17, 80)

BUSH, George. Everyone says they are going to reinvent the wheel, that their Vice President is going to be in on developing North-South strategy and other great projects. But it never happens. Two years later, you wake up and find he's still going to funerals. (Time 116:12 July 28, 80)

BUSH, George. Flag burning is wrong— dead wrong. (Time 134:15 Judy 3, 89)

BUSH, George. Government should be an opportunity for public service, not for public gain. (Chicago Tribune 36:6 Section 4 Feb 5, 89)

BUSH, George. He's (Dan Quayle) going to be one of the greatest vice presidents. You watch him closely, America, because you're going to respect what you see. (Chicago Tribune 315:16 Section 1 Nov 10, 88)

BUSH, George. He's the right man for the job and I'm very pleased that he will lead the Bush team in the White House (about John H Sununu). (New York Times 138:8 Nov 18, 88)

BUSH, George. I am a non-politician, as of now (1976). (Meet the Press 20:9 Feb 22, 76)

BUSH, George. I can feel it in my bones. I'm going to be President (1980). (Time 115:26 Feb 4, 80)

BUSH, George. I will not use food as a foreign policy weapon (1988). (Chicago Tribune 231:1 Section 4 Aug 19, 90)

BUSH, George. I'll be a great conservation and environmental president. I plan to hunt and fish as much as I can. (Outside 14:19 Mar 89)

BUSH, George. I'll prevail over Reagan because it is right that I prevail (1980). (New York 13:44 Jan 21, 80)

BUSH, George. I'm from the federal government, and I'm here to help you [are] the eleven most frightening words in the English language. (Chicago Tribune 21:4 Section 4 Jan 22, 89)

BUSH, George. Iraq will not be permitted to annex Kuwait. That's not a threat, not a boast. That's just the way it's going to be. (Time 136:32 Sept 24, 89)

BUSH, George. Read my lips: No new taxes (1988). (Chicago Tribune 178:1 Section 1 June 27, 90)

BUSH, George. The single most important job of the President is the national security of the United States. (Time 136:20 Aug 20, 90)

BUSH, George. They are, in fact, hostages (August 20, 1990). (Chicago Tribune 233:1 Section 1 Aug 21, 90)

BUSH, George. We love your adherence to democratic principles—and to the democratic process (about Ferdinand Marcos). (Mother Jones 7:28 Feb 82)

BUSH, George. When I said I wanted a kinder and gentler nation, I meant it—And I mean it. (Newsweek 112:9 Nov 21, 88)

BUSH, Neil. I sleep soundly at night knowing I live an honest life. (Chicago Tribune 207:21 July 26, 90)

BUTHELEZI, Gatsha (Zulu Chief). South Africa is one country. It has one destiny. Those who are attempting to divide the land of our birth are attempting to stem the tide of history. (New York Times 125:4 April 23, 76)

BUTLER, Dick. If you took three words out of the English language, most players and

umpires would be mute. (Time 122:55 Oct 10, 83)

BUTLER, Nicholas Murray. An expert is one who knows more and more about less and less. (Kansas City Times 109:14B July 8, 77)

BUTZ, Earl Lauer. It was stupid—like General Motors breaking into Ford to steal Edsel plans (commenting on Watergate, in the long term). (People Weekly 5:84 April 19, 76)

BUTZ, Earl Lauer. Our capitalism is no longer capitalism; it is a weakened mixture of government regulations and limited business opportunities. (American Legion Magazine 99:21 Dec 75)

BYRD, Robert. Do not run a campaign that would embarrass your mother. (Kansas City Times 120:A-9 Oct 13, 87)

BYRD, Robert. The Senate is very much like a violin. The sound will change with the weather, the dampness, the humidity. The Senate is a place of great moods. (Time 110:14 Oct 10, 77)

BYRNE, Jane. Diamonds are a girl's best friend, and Federal grants are second. (Newsweek 96:24 Sept 29, 80)

BYRNE, Jane. Wind chill factor or not, Chicago is America's warmest city. (Chicago 31:127 Dec 31, 81)

BYRNE, Jane. With the Irish, you know, only the strongest survive. (New York Times Magazine 77 Mar 9, 80)

CABELL, James Branch. There is no memory with less satisfaction in it than the memory of some temptation we resisted. (Forbes 120:100 July 15, 77)

CADDELL, Patrick. Clearly, God is a Democrat. (Boston 68:115 Sept 76)

CADDELL, Patrick. I don't know any politicians in America who could run against himself and win. (Time 115:18 April 7, 80)

CADDELL, Patrick. I'm less influential than I'd like to think I am, and a lot more than I deserve. (Time 114:14 Aug 6, 79)

CALDWELL, Zoe. Acting is like being a sibling and directing is like being a parent. (W 15:30 Jan 27, 86)

CALIFANO, Joseph A., Jr. No just society can deny the right of its citizens to the health care they need. We are the only industrial society that does. (New York Times 136:2 Jan 13, 87)

CALIFANO, Joseph A., Jr. Writing things clearly does not necessarily mean writing them short. (Washingtonian 13:11 Nov 77)

CALLAGHAN, James. I believe all good people should be in bed by 11 o'clock at night. (The Observer 9775:9 Dec 31, 78)

CALLAGHAN, James. Spain's self-inflicted isolation is brought about not just by a single act of brutality, but by injustices over a generation or more. (Time 106:37 Oct 13, 75)

CALLAS, Maria. To be an opera singer, you have to be an actress. (Newsweek 90:67 Nov 7, 77)

CALLOWAY, Cab. Women, horses, cars, clothes. I did it all. And do you know what that's called. It's called living. (Sepia 26:10 Jan 77)

CAMERON, James. While other people's deaths are deeply sad, one's own is sure to be a bit of a joke. (The Observer 9933:11 Jan 17, 82)

CAMERON, John. In order to get a loan you must first prove you don't need it. (Washingtonian 14:154 Nov 78)

CAMERON, John. When your opponent is down, kick him. (Town & Country 133:140 May 79)

CAMERON, Simon. An honest politician is one who, when he is bought, will stay bought. (Village Voice 21:16 Nov 8, 76)

CAMPBELL, William J. The grand jury is the total captive of the prosecutor, who, if he is candid, will concede that he can indict anybody, at any time, for almost anything, before any grand jury. (Time 110:61 July 4, 77)

CAMUS, Albert. Alas, after a certain age every man is responsible for his face. (CoEvolution Quarterly 17:30 Spring 78)

CAMUS, Albert. Illness is a convent which has its rule, its austerity, its silences, and its inspirations. (Time 112:74 July 10, 78)

CAMUS, Albert. Not only is there no solution but there aren't even any problems. (Time 112:74 July 10, 78)

CAMUS, Albert. The purpose of the writer is to keep civilization from destroying itself. (Time 120:K8 Sept 13, 82)

CANBY, Vincent. Bland has always been big in television. (New York Times 126:15 Section 2 Nov 13, 77)

CANETTI, Elias. To be the last man to remain alive is the deepest urge of every real seeker after power. (New York Times Book Review 58 April 29, 79)

CANZERI, Joseph. Ask him (Dan Quayle) to turn off a light, and by the time he gets to the switch, he's forgotten what he went for. (Chicago Tribune 200:3 Section 1 July 19, 89)

CAPONE, Alphonse. Let the worthy citizens of Chicago get their liquor the best way they can. I'm sick of the job. It's a thankless job and full of grief. (Chicago 24:186 Dec 75)

CAPONE, Alphonse. When I sell liquor, it's called bootlegging; when my patrons serve it on silver trays on Lake Shore Drive, it's called hospitality. (Aspen 3:43 Spring 77)

CAPONE, Alphonse. You can get much further with a kind word and a gun than you can with a kind word alone. (Playboy 31:22 May 84)

CAPOTE, Truman. All Southerners go home sooner or later, even if in a box. (Southern Magazine 2:29 May 88)

CAPOTE, Truman. Good writing is rewriting. (New York 17:60 Nov 26, 84)

CAPOTE, Truman. He's a sphinx without a secret (commenting on Andy Warhol). (People Weekly 5:15 May 10, 76)

CAPOTE, Truman. I mean I can create any kind of social world I want, anywhere I want. (New York 9:49 Feb 9, 76)

CAPOTE, Truman. It is not writing; it is only typing (about Jack Kerouac). (Village Voice 22:52 Oct 31, 77)

CAPOTE, Truman. The good thing about masturbation is that you don't have to dress up for it. (Playboy 32:16 Feb 85)

CAPOTE, Truman. The only one who can destroy a really strong and talented writer is himself. (Kansas City Star 108:8E June 12, 88)

CAPP, Al. The martyrs at Kent State were the kids in National Guard uniforms. (Newsweek 90:50 Oct 17, 77)

CAPUTO, Philip J. The impetus or the impulse that makes people heroic in wars is the very thing that can make them monsters. (Chicago Tribune Magazine 23 Mar 19, 78)

CARAMANLIS, Constantine. So we Greeks have been from ancient times: we are skillful at making idols, not that we may worship them, but that we may have the pleasure of destroying them. (Time 110:51 Dec 5, 77)

CARDIN, Pierre. Chanel never influenced fashion one bit. (W 8:5 Mar 16, 79)

CARDIN, Pierre. I have to do things differently from anyone else. For that, they say I am crazy. (Chicago Tribune 286:24 Oct 13, 77)

CARDIN, Pierre. If I can put a Maxim's in Peking, I can put a Maxim's on the moon. (Life 7:142 Jan 83)

CAREY, Hugh. A hard worker but he is perceived otherwise (about Ted Kennedy). (New York Times 128:A18 Nov 22, 78)

CAREY, Hugh. My mind doesn't govern my conscience, my conscience governs my mind. (New York Times 127:A1 April 6, 78)

CARLSON, Norman A. Until the behavioral sciences can give us clues as to what motivates the criminal offender, we cannot assure rehabilitation. All we can do is offer offenders the opportunity to rehabilitate themselves. (Behavior Today 7:4 Jan 5, 76)

CARLSON, Phil. Don't ever try to eat where they don't want to feed you. (Washingtonian 15:140 Oct 31, 79)

CARMICHAEL, Stokely. The only position for women in the movement is prone. (New York Times Magazine 91 April 10, 77)

CARPENTER, Elizabeth. Aging has become very stylish, all the best people are doing it. (Time 131:68 Feb 22, 88)

CARPENTER, Elizabeth. If John Connally had been around at the Alamo, he would have organized Texans for Santa Anna. (Texas Monthly 4:10 Sept 76)

CARR, Jesse. Being powerful is like being a lady. If you have to tell people you are, you ain't. (Newsweek 88:77 Sept 27, 76)

CARRERA, Barbara. Straight men make life very difficult. (M 1:87 Mar 84)

CARROLL, Larry. It's like that old saying that your're not a Marine until you've been shot. (Kansas City Times 120:D-3 Oct 22, 87)

CARSWELL, James. Whenever man comes up with a better mousetrap, nature invariably comes up with a better mouse. (Omni 1:132 May 79)

CARTER, Don. One of the advantages bowling has over golf is that you seldom lose a bowling ball. (Sports Illustrated 43:8 Aug 11, 75)

CARTER, Hodding, III. The thing you have to remember about Southerners is that we're always generous and forgiving— with our friends. (New York 9:28 July 26, 76)

CARTER, James Earl. (Republicans are) men of narrow vision who are afraid of the future and whose leaders are inclined to shoot from the hip. (Time 116:13 July 28, 80)

CARTER, James Earl. As is the case in time of war there is potential war profiteering in the impending energy crisis. This could develop with the passing months as the biggest rip-off in history (1977). (New York Times 126:A16 Oct 14, 77)

CARTER, James Earl. Civil service reform will be the centerpiece of government reorganization during my term in office. (Washington Post Magazine 11 Dec 3, 78)

CARTER, James Earl. Doubts are the stuff of great decisions, but so are dreams. (Time 113:24 Mar 26, 79)

CARTER, James Earl. I am against any creation of a separate Palestinian state. (Chicago Sun-Times 32:3 Aug 12, 79)

CARTER, James Earl. I can't resign from the human race because there's discrimination, and I don't intend to resign from my own church because there's discrimination. (Time 108:22 Nov 22, 76)

CARTER, James Earl. I cannot think of a single international or diplomatic achievement that's been realized by Ronald Reagan. (Chicago Tribune 273:2 Sept 30, 86)

CARTER, James Earl. I have never detected or experienced any conflict between God's will and my political duties. (Time 111:13 June 26, 78)

CARTER, James Earl. I have never met an Arab leader that in private professed the desire for an independent Palestinian state. (New York Times 128:21 Sept 1, 79)

CARTER, James Earl. I think the government ought to stay out of the prayer business... (New York Times 128:2 April 8, 79)

CARTER, James Earl. I think the President is the only person who can change the direction or attitude of our nation. (Encore American & Worldwide News 5:4 June 21, 76)

CARTER, James Earl. I'd rather commit political suicide than hurt Israel. (Time 110:30-33 Oct 17, 77)

CARTER, James Earl. In trying to brief him on matters of supreme importance, I was very disturbed at his lack of interest (about Ronald Reagan). (Kansas City Times 115:D1 Jan 1, 83)

CARTER, James Earl. In war, we offer our very lives as a matter of routine. We must be no less daring, no less steadfast, in the pursuit of peace. (Time 113:12 Mar 26, 79)

CARTER, James Earl. Inflation has become embedded in the very tissue of our economy (1978). (Time 111:66 April 24, 78)

CARTER, James Earl. No one knows what he stands for, or even where he comes from (about George Bush). (Chicago Tribune 199:10 Section 1 July 17, 88)

CARTER, James Earl. No one should mistake the energy problem for what it is—a fundamental crisis that threatens Americans and America's way of life. (Time 109:63 May 23, 77)

CARTER, James Earl. No poor, rural, weak, or black person should ever have to bear the additional burden of being deprived of the opportunity of an education, a job, or simple justice. (New York 9:57 July 19, 76)

CARTER, James Earl. The American people and our government will continue our firm commitment to promote respect for human rights not only in our own country but also abroad (to Andrei Sakharov). (Newsweek 89:17 Feb 28, 77)

CARTER, James Earl. The duty of our generation of Americans is to renew our nation's faith—not focused just against foreign threats, but against the threat of selfishness, cynicism and apathy. (Time 113:10 Feb 5, 79)

CARTER, James Earl. The survival of Israel is not a political issue. It is a moral imperative. (Time 107:13 June 21, 76)

CARTER, James Earl. There are many things in life that are not fair. (Village Voice 23:11 Jan 2, 78)

CARTER, James Earl. There is nothing for nothing. (Newsweek 96:55 July 14, 80)

CARTER, James Earl. We are now free of that inordinate fear of Communism which once led us to embrace any dictator who joined us in our fear. (Time 107:9 June 6, 77)

CARTER, James Earl. We must face a time of national austerity (1978). (US News & World Report 85:17 Nov 6, 78)

CARTER, James Earl. When I finish my term, I want black people to say that I did more for them in my presidency than any other President in their lifetime. (Sepia 26:12 April 77)

CARTER, Lillian. Hunger and poverty are things I cannot live with, and I cannot live with myself unless I work to do something about them. (Newsweek 102:84 Nov 14, 83)

CARTER, Lillian. Jimmy's not sexy, he's my son. (People Weekly 13:114 Mar 3, 80)

CARTER, Lillian. Marriage ain't easy but nothing that's worth much ever is. (Chicago Sun-Times 32:33 July 16, 79)

CARTER, Rosalynn. I have always been more political than (Jimmy). (Time 114:13 Aug 6, 79)

CARTER, Rosalynn. I've always worked hard, and that's why they call me 'The Steel Magnolia'. (Maclean's 89:8 Nov 29, 76)

CARTER, Rosalynn. Jimmy (Carter) would have been impeached if he had done some of the things this administration (Ronald Reagan) has gotten away with. (Newsweek 108:29 Nov 24, 86)

CARTER, Rubin (Hurricane). The kindest thing I can say about my childhood is that I survived it. (Chicago Sun-Times 28:86 Dec 16, 75)

CARTIER-BRESSON, Henri. For me the camera is an instrument of intuition and spontaneity, the master of the instant. (The Times 8104:5 Nov 5, 78)

CARTLAND, Barbara. Being 18 is like visiting Russia. You're glad you've had the experience, but you'd never want to repeat it. (The Observer 9764:14 Oct 15, 78)

CARTLAND, Barbara. I'm the only author with 200 virgins in print. (Town & Country 131:144 Dec 77)

CASALS, Pablo. The truly important things in life—love, beauty and one's own uniqueness—are constantly being overlooked. (Forbes 119:312 May 15, 77)

CASH, Johnny. I guess the record shows I'm far from perfect—but I want to keep trying. (US News & World Report 84:60 Feb 27, 78)

CASTANEDA, Jorge. We would like to see the U.S. treat us (Mexico) as an adult country capable of managing our own affairs. (Newsweek 94:26 Oct 1, 79)

CASTRO, Fidel. I do not believe that revolution is an exportable item. (Newsweek 103:38 Jan 9, 84)

CASTRO, Fidel. I reached the conclusion long ago that the one last sacrifice I must make for public health is to stop smoking. (Time 127:83 Jan 6, 86)

CASTRO, Fidel. Men are very fragile. We disappear and go up in smoke for almost any reason. (Time 107:51 Jan 5, 76)

CASTRO, Fidel. My motto for good health is simple: eat little, sleep little and exercise a lot. (Newsweek 103:51 Jan 16, 84)

CATER, Douglass. If power corrupts, being out of power corrupts absolutely. (Book Digest 6:32 Dec 79)

CATLEDGE, Turner. When in doubt, do it. (Newsweek 101:76 May 9, 83)

CAVAZOS, Agapito Gonzales. They come to exploit us, they do not come to help us (about the maquiladora industry). (Chicago Tribune 126:11D Section 7 May 6, 90)

CEZANNE, Paul. I am the primitive of the method I have invented. (Newsweek 78:40 Oct 17, 77)

CHABROL, Claude. I ask audiences to contemplate a character, not identify with him. (Time 106:76 Sept 29, 75)

CHAGALL, Marc. Great art picks up where nature ends. (Time 127:54 Dec 30, 85)

CHAGALL, Marc. Me, I do not understand Chagall. (Time 109:95 May 23, 77)

CHAMBERS, Marilyn. In straight films you have to do it to get a part. In porno films, you do it after you sign the contract. (Connecticut 47:11 Sept 30, 84)

CHAMBERS, Whittaker (attributed by Ralph de Toledano). Joe McCarthy's a rascal, but he's our rascal. (Chicago Tribune 22:11 Section 5 Jan 22, 86)

CHANCELLOR, John. Eric (Sevareid) never told people what he thought, but what he learned. (Time 110:111 Dec 12, 77)

CHANCELLOR, John. Television is good at the transmission of experience. Print is better at the transmission of facts. (Time 115:71 Feb 25, 80)

CHANDLER, A. B. (Happy). We Americans are a peculiar people. We are for the underdog no matter how much of a dog he is. (Reader's Digest 107:78 Nov 75)

CHANDLER, Raymond. All us tough guys are hopeless sentimentalists at heart. (Village Voice 26:42 Nov 25, 81)

CHANDLER, Raymond. If my books had been any worse, I should not have been invited to Hollywood...if they had been any better, I should not have come. (Bookviews 1:21 April 78)

CHANDLER, Raymond. It is always a misfortune to be taken seriously in a field of writing where quality is not expected or desired. (Westways 74:67 Jan 82)

CHANDLER, Raymond. People who make pictures are not all idiots. They just behave as if they were. (Westways 74:67 Jan 82)

CHANEL, Coco. Youth is something very new: twenty years ago no one mentioned it. (Chicago Tribune 176:2 Section 2 June 25, 78)

CHAPLIN, Charles Spencer. I am known in parts of the world by people who have never heard of Jesus Christ. (Chicago Tribune 58:12 Feb 27, 78)

CHAPLIN, Charles Spencer. In the end, everything is a gag. (Newsweek 102:79 July 11, 83)

CHAPLIN, Charles Spencer. Life is a tragedy when seen in close-up, but a comedy in long-shot. (Guardian Weekly 118:5 Jan 1, 78)

CHAPLIN, Charles Spencer. My prodigious sin was and still is, being a nonconformist. Although I am not a Communist, I refused to fall in line by hating them. (Guardian Weekly 118:5 Jan 1, 78)

CHAPMAN, Marshall. As far as I'm concerned, feminists have done to women what the Baptists did to religion. (Stereo Review 41:90 Dec 78)

CHAPMAN, Robert W. A quotation, like a pun, should come unsought, and then be welcomed only for some propriety or felicity justifying the intrusion (from "The Art of Quotation"). (Writer's Digest 57:11 May 77)

CHARLES, Prince of Wales. The thing that appalls me about the newspaper business is the number of trees it consumes. (Kansas City Times 107:B-8 Nov 2, 87)

CHARLES, Ray (attributed by Arthur Ashe). When you leave New York, you ain't goin' nowhere. (Travel & Leisure 13:164 June 83)

CHARLES, PRINCE OF WALES. All the people I have in my office, they can't speak English properly, they can't write English properly. All the letters sent from my office I have to correct myself, and that is because English is taught so bloody badly. (Chicago Tribune 181:2 Section 1 June 30, 89)

CHARLES, PRINCE OF WALES. Much of British management does not seem to understand the human factor. (The Observer 9783:11 Feb 25, 79)

CHARLES, PRINCE OF WALES. Our protection depends, I believe, on the mystical power which from time immemorial has been called God. (The Observer 9937:13 Feb 14, 82)

CHARLES, PRINCE OF WALES. Women's liberationists rather annoy me because they tend to argue all the time and start calling you a male chauvinist pig and, frankly, it becomes rather uncivilized. (Los Angeles Times 94:2 Part 1 Nov 18, 75)

CHAVEZ, Cesar. We will win in the end. We learned many years ago that the rich may have the money, but the poor have the time. (Newsweek 86:67B Sept 22, 75)

CHAYEFSKY, Paddy. Television is democracy at it's ugliest. (New York Times 126:18 Section 2 Nov 14, 76)

CHEEVER, John. Fiction is our most intimate and acute means of communication. (US News & World Report 86:92 May 21, 79)

CHEEVER, John. If you are an artist, self-destruction is quite expected of you. (Time 112:125 Oct 16, 78)

CHEEVER, John. It (plot) is a calculated attempt to hold the reader's interest at the sacrifice of moral conviction. (Esquire 90:35 Nov 21, 78)

CHEEVER, John. Literature is much more a conversation than a discourse. (US News & World Report 86:92 May 21, 79)

CHENEY, Richard B. Basically, I am skeptical about the ability of government to solve problems, and I have a healthy respect for the ability of people to solve problems on their own. (Washington Post 336:A3 Nov 6, 75)

CHENEY, Richard B. SDI is alive and well, but like everything else, it has to fit into a reduced budget. (New York Times 138:19 April 25, 89)

CHER. For me, forever is probably five or

ten years. (US 3:8 Feb 20, 89)

CHEVALIER, Maurice. Old age is a wonderful thing...when you consider the alternative. (Saturday Evening Post 251:40 Feb 28, 79)

CHILD, Julia. I just hate health food. (San Francisco 25:32 Aug 83)

CHILD, Julia. Life itself is the proper binge. (Cosmopolitan 180:178 May 76)

CHILES, Lawton M., Jr. Secrecy in government has become synonymous, in the public mind, with deception by the government. (Christian Science Monitor 67:3 Nov 4, 75)

CHINOY, Mike. China is a place where what was right yesterday is wrong today. (Chicago Tribune 183:24 Section 13 July 2, 89)

CHOMSKY, Noam. Anybody who teaches at age fifty what he was teaching at age twenty-five had better find another profession. (Omni 6:114 Nov 83)

CHRISTIE, Agatha. If I could write like Elizabeth Bowen, Muriel Spark or Graham Greene, I should jump to high heaven with delight, but I know that I can't. (Time 110:127-32 Nov 28, 77)

CHRISTIE, Agatha. The happy people are failures because they are on such good terms with themselves that they don't give a damn. (Lawrence (Kansas) Journal-World 127:3D Oct 28, 84)

CHURCH, Frank. Somehow, some day, this country has got to learn to live with revolution in the Third World. (Time 124:46 Dec 31, 84)

CHURCH, Frank. The Presidency is no place for on-the-job training. I've always advocated the politics of substance, not the politics of style. (Encore American & Worldwide News 5:4 June 21, 76)

CHURCH, Frank. There is no reason to transform a revolution in any of the countries of Central America, regardless from where it draws its initial external support, into a security crisis for us. (The Nation 241:588 Nov 30, 85)

CHURCHILL, Sir Winston. A preposition is a terrible word to end a sentence with. (Lawrence (Kansas) Journal-World 125:5 Sept 30, 83)

CHURCHILL, Sir Winston. Don't argue the difficulties. They argue for themselves. (Christian Science Monitor 69:15 June 27, 77)

CHURCHILL, Sir Winston. Foster Dulles is the only case I know of a bull who carries his china shop with him. (Time 111:83 Feb 27, 78)

CHURCHILL, Sir Winston. It (democracy) is the worst system—except for all those other systems that have been tried and failed. (Time 106:63 July 14, 75)

CHURCHILL, Sir Winston. Russia is a riddle wrapped in an enigma. (Village Voice 22:77 Nov 28, 77)

CHURCHILL, Sir Winston. The inherent vice of capitalism is the unequal sharing of the blessings; the inherent virtue of socialism is the equal sharing of the miseries. (Kansas City Star 108:1F Dec 27, 87)

CHURCHILL, Sir Winston. You don't make the poor richer by making the rich poorer. (To The Point International 3:39 Nov 1, 76)

CHURCHILL, Sir Winston (attributed by Michael Korda). Willie (W. Somerset Maugham) may be an old bugger, but by God, he's never tried to bugger me. (Newsweek 94:105 Nov 5, 79)

CHYLAK, Nestor. An umpire's job is the only one in the world that everybody else can do better. (University Daily Kansan 92:10 Feb 18, 82)

CIARDI, John. Early to bed and early to rise probably indicates unskilled labor. (Kansas City Star 97:2D Feb 20, 77)

CIARDI, John. Love is the word used to label the sexual excitement of the young, the habituation of the middle-aged, and the mutual dependence of the old. (Chicago Tribune 212:1 Section 2 July 31, 78)

CISNEROS, Henry. A party that appeals only to minorities is going to remain a minority party. (Kansas City Times 117:A-19 Nov 8, 84)

CLAIBORNE, Craig. I think that some people, and I suspect a great number of people, are born with the gustatory equivalent of perfect pitch. (New York Times 126:C6 Nov 22, 76)

CLANCY, Tom. A lawyer is just like an attack dog, only without a conscience. (Chicago Tribune 222:15 Section 1 Aug 9, 88)

CLANCY, Tom. Every book you write is a first novel. (Washingtonian 24:73 Jan 89)

CLARK, Alan. Librarians are standing in their graves. (New York Times 128:26 April 8, 79)

CLARK, Alex. It's always darkest just before the lights go out. (Washingtonian 14:152 Nov 78)

CLARK, Joseph. A leader should not get too far in front of his troops or he will be shot in the ass. (Washingtonian 15:140 Nov 79)

CLARK, Kenneth. Integration is a painful job. It is social therapy, and like personal therapy it is not easy. (Time 106:14 Sept 22, 75)

CLARK, Ramsey. The Democratic Party is a party in name only, not in shared belief.

(Time 116:12 Aug 25, 80)

CLARKE, Arthur C. Any sufficiently advanced technology is undistinguishable from magic. (Omni 2:87 April 80)

CLARKE, Arthur C. Experience has shown that the most important results of any technological breakthrough are those that are not obvious. (American Film 2:67 Oct 76)

CLARKE, Arthur C. The facts of the future can hardly be imagined ab initio by those who are unfamiliar with the fantasies of the past. (Omni 2:94 April 80)

CLARKE, Arthur C. The only way to find the limits of the possible is by going beyond them to the impossible. (Omni 2:85 April 80)

CLARKE, Arthur C. The time may come when men control the destinies of the stars. (Time 114:27 July 26, 79)

CLARKE, Arthur C. When a distinguished but elderly scientist says that something is possible he is almost certainly right. When he says it is impossible, he is very probably wrong. (Omni 2:82 April 80)

CLAY, Andrew Dice. I'm just filthy. And the filthier I am, the funnier it is. (Vanity Fair 53:148 June 90)

CLAY, William. Whenever I see certain elements in the press show favoritism to a Black man running for a position of power, I know there's a nigger in the woodpile somewhere. (Sepia 26:10 May 76)

CLEAVER, Eldridge. A black pig, a white pig, a yellow pig, a pink pig—a dead pig is the best pig of all. We encourage people to kill them (in 1970). (Newsweek 85:40 Mar 17, 75)

CLEAVER, Eldridge. If it came down to the choice between a woman and a radio, I'd choose a radio. It brings the outside world in. (Sepia 24:12 June 75)

CLIFFORD, Clark. Jimmy Carter has the best mind of any President I have known. (Time 110:16 Oct 3, 77)

CLINE, Ray S. The First Amendment is not the central purpose of our Constitution. (More 8:21 Feb 78)

CLINE, Ray S. The most urgent task for the U. S. is to stop wars of national liberation. (Mother Jones 10:39 Aug 85)

CLINE, Ray S. The only unrestricted intelligence organization in this country is the American press. (Time 106:10 Aug 4, 75)

CLINTON, Bill. He (George Bush) campaigns like a right-wing Republican and governs like a moderate Democrat. (New York Times 138:12 Aug 2, 89)

CLOSE, Del (Director of Chicago's Second City). Laughter is a response to a gestalt formation where two previously incompatible or dissimilar ideas suddenly form into a new piece of understanding— the energy released during that reaction comes out in laughter. (New Times 10:42 Jan 9, 78)

COCA, Imogene. I've never figured out why we work so well together, except that we both laugh at exactly the same time. (about herself and Sid Caesar). (Time 110:98 Sept 19, 77)

COCKBURN, Alexander. A nation that love Hailsham and re-elects Thatcher deserves everything it gets. (Village Voice 28:15 June 14, 83)

COCKBURN, Alexander. A vice president traditionally has the same relationship to power as that of a circus cleaner to an elephant. (Spin 4:77 Nov 88)

COCKBURN, Alexander. An accident is normalcy raised to the level of drama. (The Nation 250:623 May 7, 90)

COCKBURN, Alexander. Descriptions of sin are what we want at the breakfast table, not admonitions against it. (Village Voice 23:13 Jan 9, 78)

COCKBURN, Alexander. History is the propaganda of the victors. (The Nation 251:190 Sept 3, 90)

COCKBURN, Claud. Never underestimate the effectiveness of a straight cash bribe. (Village Voice 21:39 Oct 4, 76)

CODEVILLA, Angelo. I am aware that active duty agents of the Central Intelligence Agency worked for the George Bush primary election campaign (in 1980). (Village Voice 33:20 Oct 25, 1988)

COFFIN, William Sloane. If you get an Evangelical with a social conscience you've got one of God's true saints. (Time 110:58 Dec 26, 77)

COHEN, Jamie. The biggest industrial health problem in America today is unemployment (1986). (Southern Exposure 14:55 Sept 86)

COHEN, Mark B. Nothing can so alienate a voter from the political system as backing a winning candidate. (Washingtonian 14:152 Nov 78)

COHEN, Mickey. I never killed a man that didn't deserve it. (Playboy 31:22 May 84)

COHEN, Richard. His (Richard Nixon) career is blemished only by his time in public office. (Kansas City Times 121:A-8 May 22, 89)

COHEN, Richard. The best stories never check out. (The Nation 231:663 Dec 20, 80)

COHEN, William. Congress is designed to be slow and inefficient because it represents the total diversity of this country. (Time 105:22 June 9, 75)

COHODAS, Howard L. If it looks too good to be true, it is too good to be true. (Washingtonian 15:151 Nov 79)

COLBERT, Claudette. I'd give my soul for a Tootsie Roll. (Vanity Fair 49:60 Feb 86)

COLBY, William Egan. By the way, did you ever work for the CIA? (to Bob Woodward upon agreeing to issue an official denial that Woodward had ever worked for the CIA). (New York 8:50 July 28, 75)

COLBY, William Egan. I have definitional problems with the word violence. I don't know what the word violence means. (Rolling Stone 196:32 Sept 25, 75)

COLBY, William Egan. I'm convinced it's possible to run a secret agency as part of a constitutional society. (Time 107:17 Jan 19, 76)

COLE, David. If free expression is to exist in this country, people must be as free to burn the flag as they are to wave it. (Time 134:15 July 3, 89)

COLE, Edward N. Kick the hell out of the status quo. (Time 109:87 May 16, 77)

COLETTE, Sidonie Gabrielle Claudine. It is not a bad thing that children should occasionally, and politely, put parents in their place. (Chicago Tribune 176:2 Section 2 June 25, 78)

COLLINS, Judy. Aging does have its rewards. (Newsweek 93:79 Mar 12, 79)

COLSON, Charles Wendell. I would do anything that Richard Nixon asks me to do. (Time 103:13 Mar 11, 74)

COLSON, Charles Wendell. The only good guys to emerge from Watergate are those self-justified, upright fellows writing their own accounts. Since everyone has written a book, the sum of all the books is that no one was guilty, just everyone else.... (National Review 30:474 April 14, 78)

COMFORT, Alex. Nobody is safe being prejudiced against what they themselves are going to become (commenting on aging). (New York Times 126:24 Oct 25, 76)

COMINS, David H. People will accept your idea more readily if you tell them Benjamin Franklin said it first. (Washingtonian 14:152 Nov 78)

COMMAGER, Henry Steele. History is what you make of it. (Geo 6:20 June 84)

COMMONER, Barry. Our system today no more resembles free enterprise than a freeway resembles a dirt road. (Time 114:19 Aug 13, 79)

COMMONER, Barry. When you fully understand the situation it is worse than you think. (Life 2:170 Dec 79)

COMPTON-BURNETT, Ivy. We must use

words as they are used or stand aside from life. (Time 111:36 Jan 2, 78)

CONABLE, Barber. The trouble with Carter is he's listening only to God—and God doesn't pay taxes. (Time 111:11 May 1, 78)

CONDON, Richard. I'm a man of the marketplace as well as an artist. I am a pawnbroker of myth. (New York Times Magazine 45 Sept 2, 79)

CONDON, Richard. If you are writing about politicians, you are writing about marshmallows and smoke. (International Herald Tribune 33367:24 June 7, 79)

CONDON, Richard. When you don't know the whole truth, the worst you can imagine is probably close. (D Magazine 15:38 April 88)

CONLIN, Roxanne. Being rude and killing someone are about on par here (in Iowa). (Time 131:14 Jan 25, 88)

CONNALLY, John Bowden. All hat and no cattle (about George Bush). (Kansas City Times 112:A15 July 23, 80)

CONNALLY, John Bowden. I don't subscribe to the notion that everyone around President Nixon was tarnished. (New York 12:8 July 9, 79)

CONNALLY, John Bowden. The power of this country, in spite of all the misconceptions that exist, is in the Congress of the United States and not in the White House. (US News & World Report 86:30 July 2, 79)

CONNALLY, John Bowden. There's a little larceny in the hearts of all of us. (New York 12:8 July 9, 79)

CONNALLY, John Bowden (attributed by Henry Alfred Kissinger). You will be measured in (Washington D.C.) by the enemies you destroy. The bigger they are, the bigger you are. (Time 114:45 Oct 8, 79)

CONNOLLY, Cyril. Everything is a dangerous drug to me except reality, which is unendurable. (Chicago Tribune Magazine 6 Aug 19, 84)

CONNOLLY, Cyril. Imprisoned in every fat man a thin one is wildly signalling to be let out. (Newsweek 85:74B Jan 20, 75)

CONNOLLY, Cyril. Nothing dates like hate. (Village Voice 22:52 Oct 31, 77)

CONROY, Jack. I've never given a bad review. Some are more favorable than others, but I have never given a bad one. (Kansas City Star 110:A-18 Mar 3, 90)

COOKE, Alistair. I seem to be perceived in America as a benign old English gentleman, and in England as an enlightened American. (Time 122:79 Dec 5, 83)

COOLEY, Denton. A successful surgeon should be a man who, when asked to name the three best surgeons in the world, would have difficulty deciding on the other two. (The Atlantic 244:56 Sept 79)

COOPER, Alexander. Scratch any real estate developer and you'll find an anarchist. (M 4:73 Mar 87)

COOVER, Robert. You make a million or you don't even get printed. (New Times 8:53 Aug 19, 77)

COPLAND, Aaron. The ideal listener, above all else, possesses the ability to lend himself to the power of music. (Washington Post 352:G1 Nov 21, 76)

CORKEY, P. J. The rich used to give us libraries, museums, universities. Now they give us themselves. (Kansas City Times 119:A-1 Oct 3, 86)

COSELL, Howard. I think I've made a difference in my phase of the broadcast industry, but I don't think I've impacted on the world in the manner of Franklin Roosevelt. (Life 8:72 Jan 85)

COSELL, Howard. Indiana should be No. 1. They probably have a bigger payroll than the New York Knicks (1976). (Chicago Tribune 123:3 Section 3 May 2, 76)

COSTA-GAVRAS. Film is the only way now to reach out to people all around the world. The time of the book is over. (Village Voice 20:106 Dec 8, 75)

COUNTRYMAN, Vernon (Harvard professor). The bar is still dominated by shortsightedness and self-interest. Spotting change there is like watching a glacier move. (Time 110:52 Aug 8, 77)

COUSINS, Norman. A hospital is no place for a person who is seriously ill. (Time 115:71 June 30, 80)

COUSINS, Norman. History is an accumulation of error. (Saturday Review 5:13 April 15, 78)

COUSINS, Norman. I am no pessimist. I doubt that any man knows enough to be a pessimist. (Saturday Review 5:12 April 15, 78)

COUSINS, Norman. Infinity converts the possible into the inevitable. (Saturday Review 5:18 April 15, 78)

COUSINS, Norman. Life is an adventure in forgiveness. (Saturday Review 5:12 April 15, 78)

COUSTEAU, Jacques Yves. Today I don't swim at all because I haven't the time to go 10 to 12 miles offshore to find clean water. (Washington Post 226:B2 July 19, 77)

COWLEY, Malcolm. Conrad Aiken remained just a heavy drinker until he died at 84. By that time he had possibly consumed more gin than anyone else in the world. (Writer's Digest 58:26 Oct 78)

COWLEY, Malcolm. No complete son-of-a-bitch ever wrote a good sentence. (Inquiry 1:28 July 24, 78)

COWLEY, Malcolm. One compensation of age is simply sitting still. (Life 1:77 Dec 78)

COZZENS, James Gould. The longer I watch men and life, the surer I get that success whenever more than minor comes of luck alone. By comparison, no principles, ideas, goals, and standards of conduct matter much in an achieving of it. (New York Times 127:39 July 30, 78)

CRAMER, Jerome. Schools are now asked to do what people used to ask God to do. (Time 115:59 June 16, 80)

CRANE, Philip. If you asked central casting in Hollywood for somebody to play the role of President, they'd send you John Connally. (US News & World Report 86:29 July 2, 79)

CRANE, Philip. It's always better to stand on your principles and lose than to lose your principles and win. (Newsweek 93:37 Mar 19, 79)

CRANSON, Maurice. (Government is) a necessary evil that allows for tyranny by the collectivity over the individual. (Time 110:57 July 25, 77)

CRESPI, Consuelo. In Italy now you want to feel rich and look poor. (Time 111:53 May 15, 78)

CRICHTON, Michael. I quit medicine as a service to my patients. (Chicago Tribune 175:1 Section 5 June 24, 87)

CRICHTON, Michael. I think we can all agree that American medicine, the way it is now, is not successful. But there's no evidence that the Government can run anything. If you like the Post Office, you'll like socialized medicine. (Time 111:91 Jan 9, 78)

CRISP, Quentin. For flavor, instant sex will never supercede the stuff you have to peel and cook. (Cosmopolitan 197:288 Oct 84)

CRISP, Quentin. Style is out of fashion. (Connoisseur 215:88 Nov 85)

CRISP, Quenton. The English think incompetence is the same thing as sincerity. (New York Times 126:7 Section 12 Jan 30, 77)

CRISWELL, W. A. I think it is better for the colored to go to their churches and for us to go to ours (1956). (Texas Monthly 12:166 Oct 84)

CRISWELL, W. A. I was brought up to love God and hate the Methodists (1968).

(Texas Monthly 12:166 Oct 84)

CRISWELL, W. A. In order to uphold the idea of communism, the idea of pacifism was conceived (1954). (Texas Monthly 12:166 Oct 84)

CRONKITE, Walter. It is not the reporter's job to be a patriot or to presume to determine where patriotism lies. His job is to relate the facts. (Time 115:60 Feb 11, 80)

CROSBY, Bing. Family life is the basis for a strong community and a great nation. (National Catholic Reporter 12:8 July 2, 76)

CROSBY, Bing. He was an average guy who could carry a tune (on his epitaph). (Newsweek 90:102 Oct 24, 77)

CROSS, George L. We want to build a university the football team can be proud of (about the University of Oklahoma). (Chicago Sun-Times 32:69 Nov 8, 79)

CROW, Trammel. Work is so much more fun than fun, it is improperly called work. (New York Times 133:13 Aug 14, 84)

CROW, Trammell. I have yet to have one disappointment in dealing with the Japanese. (Chicago Tribune 365:1 Section 16 Dec 31, 89)

CUKOR, George. If you live long enough you get rediscovered. (Toronto Star C3 Jan 30, 83)

CUMMINGS, Sam. The arms business is founded on human folly. That is why its depths will never be plumbed, and why it will go on forever. (Esquire 90:64 Mar 1, 78)

CURTIS, Carl Thomas. In the whole history of the world, whenever a meateating race has gone to war against a non-meateating race, the meat eaters won. It produces superior people. (Washingtonian 11:22-23 Dec 75)

CURTIS, John. Between owners and players, a manager today has become a wishbone. (Sports Illustrated 47:18 July 18, 77)

CURTIS, Tony. There's simply no other way for a man to feel his manliness, his kingliness if you will, than to be loved by a beautiful woman. (The Observer 9778:10 Jan 21, 79)

DALEY, Richard J. But then you can never go as low as a newspaper. A newspaper is the lowest thing there is. (Newsweek 85:55 May 5, 75)

DALEY, Richard J. The police are not here to create disorder. They are here to preserve disorder (commenting during the 1968 Democratic Convention in Chicago). (Time 108:46 Jan 3, 77)

DALEY, Steve. In the age of television,

history bores us. That's why everything is a surprise. (Chicago Tribune 84:1 Section 5 Mar 24, 88)

DALI, Salvador. The difference between a madman and me is that I am not mad. (Time 115:76 Mar 3, 80)

DANIELS, Billy. Life is a lot like a good song; take is slow and easy, the music will carry you through. (Chicago Tribune 290:2 Section 13 Oct 16, 88)

DANNEMEYER, William. God's plan for man was Adam and Eve, not Adam and Steve. (Lawrence (Kansas) Journal-World 127:2 Oct 3, 85)

DARBOUZE, Father. Dying of hunger and being executed by the government are the same thing. (Newsweek 96:31 July 7, 80)

DASMANN, Raymond F. We are hooked like junkies, dependent on the drug of wasteful consumption. (New York Times 126:A18 Dec 1, 76)

DAUGHERTY, Duffy. All of those football coaches who hold dressing room prayers before a game should be forced to attend church once a week. (Kansas City Star 106:1C Jan 8, 86)

DAVIS, Angela. I'm not pessimistic about change in this country. I'm convinced that this country will one day be socialist. (New York 11:43 April 17, 78)

DAVIS, Bette. I divide women into two categories. The female and the broad. Me? I'm a broad. (Time 112:98 Oct 23, 78)

DAVIS, Bette. I was always eager to salt a good stew. The trouble is that I was expected to supply the meat and potatoes as well. (Viva 5:29 Oct 77)

DAVIS, Bette. My biggest mistake was that no matter what troubles came my way, I always took the blame. (US 3:64 Feb 24, 86)

DAVIS, Bette. My contention is that producers won't make repulsive films if the public don't go to see them. (The Observer 9813:9 Sept 23, 79)

DAVIS, Bette. You've got to know someone pretty well to hate them. (Village Voice 21:105 July 19, 76)

DAVIS, Edward Michael. America is on the verge of a crime wave like the world has never seen before. (Coronet 13:70 Nov 75)

DAVIS, Evelyn Y. A company is only as good or as bad as its chef executive officer. (M 6:62 Aug 89)

DAVIS, Harry. One can look at business as metaphor and drama (upon announcing the Second City Improvisionational Theater Group will teach Masters' of Business Administration students at the

University of Chicago). (Chicago Tribune 171:1 Section 3 June 20, 89)

DAVIS, Stuart. I was a Cubist until somebody threw me a curve. (Interview 17:124 Dec 87)

DAY, Dorothy. Don't call me a saint, I don't want to be dismissed so easily. (Village Voice 32:40 Nov 3, 87)

DAY, Dorothy. The best thing to do with the best things in life is to give them up. (Life Special Report American Women 39 1976)

DAY, Morris. I'm a man who believes that women have a place, and that they should be kept there. (US 3:64 Jan 27, 86)

DAY, Samuel H., Jr. While prison is the proper place for those who break the law in the interest of peace and justice, it is no place at all for most of the remaining 99.9 per cent who find themselves incarcerated today. (Progressive 54:28 Jan 90)

DAYAN, Moshe. I, Moshe Dayan, as an individual am not a coward. But as a Jew I am a very frightened man. (Time 110:30 Oct 17, 77)

DAYAN, Moshe. You cannot get the Arab opinion by sitting and talking to Jews. (The Observer 9810:10 Sept 2, 79)

DE CHIRICO, Giorgio. I paint what I see with my eyes closed. (New York Times 128:B5 Nov 22, 78)

DE CHIRICO, Giorgio. Modernism is dying in all the countries of the world. Let us hope it will soon be just an unhappy memory. (New York Times 128:B5 Nov 22, 78)

DE GAULLE, Charles. There is no point in taking special precautions when those who want to kill me are as incompetent as those who are supposed to protect me. (Time 106:23 Oct 6, 75)

DE GAULLE, Charles. Treaties fade as quickly as young girls and roses. (New York Times Magazine 42 April 27, 80)

DE GAULLE, Charles. We may as well go to the moon, but that's not very far. The greatest distance we have to cover still lies within us. (Omni 2:36 April 80)

DE GAULLE, Sandra. Everyone in the world loves him except the Americans (about Richard Nixon). (W 9:4 Dec 5, 80)

DE KLERK, F. W. The season of violence is over. The time for reconstruction and reconciliation has arrived. (Chicago Tribune 46:25 Feb 15, 90)

DE LAURENTIIS, Dino. To make a movie is not like to make a book. A movie is much, much more—not just pushing a pencil in a room. (Los Angeles Times Calendar 60 Nov 28, 76)

DE LEMPICKA, Tamara. Do not copy!

(Toronto Life Fashion 43 Spring Preview 88)

DE MILLE, Agnes. Art is the best therapy. (Ballet News 5:14 Sept 83)

DE MILLE, Agnes. Dance today is terrifying (1978). (Los Angeles Times Calendar 70 June 11, 78)

DE MILLE, Agnes. Folk dance is the truest history of the people. (Ballet News 5:14 Sept 83)

DE MILLE, Agnes. I am a theater woman. I am not a saint. (W 6:24 Dec 9, 77)

DE MILLE, Agnes. Isadora Duncan took Western dancing out of the brothel and into the temple. (Ballet News 5:14 Sept 83)

DE MILLE, Agnes. The theater gives us one rule: don't be a bore. (W 6:24 Dec 9, 77)

DE VRIES, Peter. I love being a writer. What I can't stand is the paperwork. (New York Times Book Review 35 July 15, 79)

DE VRIES, Peter. Reality is impossible to take neat, we must dilute it with alcohol. (Writer's Digest 58:29 Oct 78)

DEAN, Dizzy. It ain't bragging if you've done it. (Kansas City Times 107:A-16 April 30, 87)

DEAN, Dizzy. Let the teachers learn the kids English! Ol' Diz will learn the kids baseball. (The Sporting News 195:70 Dec 31, 84)

DEAN, John Wesley, III. He's running for the office of ex-president and he's won (about Richard Nixon). (US 3:64 June 30, 86)

DEAN, John Wesley, III. I don't want to be known as the all-time snitch. (People Weekly 6:122 Dec 13, 76)

DEAN, John Wesley, III. Prisons are emotional zoos filled with paranoids, manic depressives, homosexuals, schizophrenics and assorted fruits and vegetables without labels. (Newsweek 40:9 July 4, 77)

DEAN, John Wesley, III. Washington is a much better place if you are asking questions rather than answering them. (Washingtonian 14:153 Nov 78)

DECROW, Karen Lipshultz. I like the companionship of men. I don't want to cut myself off from half the human race. (New York Times 125:15 Oct 28, 75)

DEEN, Braswell (Georgia judge). This monkey mythology of Darwin is the cause of permissiveness, promiscuity, pills, prophylactics, perversions, pregnancies, abortions, pornotherapy, pollution, poisoning and proliferation of crimes of all types. (Life 5:58 Jan 82)

DELACROIX, Eugene. A taste for simplicity cannot endure for long. (Time 113:57 Jan 8, 79)

DELLA FEMINA, Jerry. If God called my office looking for advertising, I'd check out his references. You can never be too sure in this business. (Oui 3:74 Feb 81)

DEMPSTER, Nigel. If you can't take it (gossip), then don't give it. (Viva 4:105 Oct 76)

DENG XIAOPING. In the 1960's and 1970's there were many student movements and turmoils in the United States. Did they have any other recourse but to mobilize police and troops, arrest people and shed blood. (Newsweek 114:15 July 3, 89)

DENIRO, Robert. I'm spending about $600 a week talking to my analyst. I guess that's the price of success. (The Star 4:2 July 26, 77)

DENIRO, Robert. There is a certain combination of anarchy and discipline in the way I work. (Time 110:60 July 25, 77)

DENIRO, Robert. You have to earn the right to play a character. (New York Times 126:13 Section 2 Mar 6, 77)

DENNIS, Richard. Someone must support unpopular truths and unconventional points of view. (Town & Country 143:164 Dec 89)

DERROW, Martin. Ronald Reagan is the prototype American politician of the '70s: mindless, witless, positionless and worthless. (Time 106:4 Dec 15, 75)

DERSHOWITZ, Alan M. If he (Warren Burger) were one of the Founding Fathers, he would have voted against the Bill of Rights. (Saturday Review 6:20 Nov 30, 79)

DERSHOWITZ, Alan M. Judges are the weakest link in our system of justice, and they are also the most protected. (Newsweek 91:76 Feb 20, 78)

DERSHOWITZ, Alan M. Screw is a despicable magazine, but that's what the First Amendment was designed to protect. (Newsweek 90:53 Nov 7, 77)

DESAE, Morarji. An expert seldom gives an objective view. He gives his own view. (Time 111:47 Feb 27, 78)

DEVORE, Irven. Males are a vast breeding experiment run by females. (Time 110:63 Aug 1, 77)

DEVRIES, Peter. Man is vile, I know, but people are wonderful. (Chicago 31:24 Sept 82)

DEVRIES, Peter. Marriage has driven more than one man to sex. (Penthouse 16:152 Nov 84)

DIANA, Princess of Wales. If men had to have babies, they would have only one each. (Life 8:102 Jan 85)

DICK, A. E. For thirty years, minorities, especially blacks, have been special

wards of the [Supreme] Court. That no longer appears true (1989). (Newsweek 113:16-17 June 26, 89)

DICKEY, James. Flight is the only truly new sensation that men have achieved in modern history. (New York Times Book Review 15 July 15, 79)

DICKSTEIN, Morris. The history of the sixties was written as much in the Berkeley Barb as in the New York Times. (New West 4:52 Jan 1, 79)

DIDION, Joan. California is a place in which a boom mentality and a sense of Chekhovian loss meet in uneasy suspension. (New York Times Magazine 36 June 17, 79)

DIDION, Joan. I think nobody owns land until their dead are in it. (Chicago Tribune 176:2 Section 2 June 25, 78)

DIETRICH, Marlene. Once a woman has forgiven her man, she must not reheat his sins for breakfast. (Cosmopolitan 188:268 Feb 80)

DIGGS, Charles C. As an American, I regret that the United States has allowed the Soviet Union to become identified as the principal supporter of African liberation. (New York Times 125:6 Jan 12, 76)

DILLINGER, John. Never trust an automatic pistol or a D.A.'s deal. (Playboy 31:22 May 84)

DIRKSEN, Everett McKinley. A billion here and a billion there, and pretty soon it adds up to real money. (Kansas City Times 114:A-14 Mar 18, 82)

DIRKSEN, Everett McKinley. The oil can is mightier than the sword. (Washingtonian 14:153 Nov 78)

DISNEY, Walt. I love Mickey Mouse more than any woman I've ever known. (Penthouse 16:152 Nov 84)

DISRAELI, Benjamin. Travel teaches toleration. (Time 110:68 Oct 10, 77)

DOBIE, J. Frank. The average Ph.D. thesis is nothing but a transference of bones from one graveyard to another. (Rocky Mountain News 37:70 May 29, 80)

DOCTOROW, E. L. There is no longer any such thing as fiction or nonfiction; there's only narrative. (New York Times Book Review 3 Jan 27, 80)

DODDS, Deloss. Football is one of the single most important things in people's lives. (Chicago Tribune 187:9 Section 3 July 6, 87)

DOLAN, Terry. The Republican Party is a fraud. It's a social club where rich people go to pick their noses. (Time 114:21 Aug 20, 79)

DOLCI, Danilo. We in Sicily are still parched by the sun, plagued by poverty and milked by the Mafia. (New York Times 127:49 Oct 30, 77)

DOLE, Bob. I've got a feeling a little three day invasion wouldn't make anybody unhappy down there, if you just overthrew Ortega. But that's just my guess. (Newsweek 110:21 Sept 21, 87)

DOLE, Robert J. A Republican has to have a sense of humor because there are so few of us. (Time 108:26 Aug 30, 76)

DOLE, Robert J. George Meany could run for President. But why should he step down? (Wall Street Journal 56:1 Sept 7, 76)

DOLE, Robert J. I regret that I have but one wife to give for my counry's infrastructure. (Chicago Tribune 334:18 Section 1 Nov 29, 84)

DOLE, Robert J. If you liked Richard Nixon, you'll love Bob Dole. (Christian Science Monitor 68:17 Sept 10, 76)

DOLE, Robert J. Jimmy Carter is chicken-fried McGovern. (Washingtonian 20:111 Sept 30, 84)

DOLE, Robert J. Rural America never had a better friend (about Edward Zorinsky). (Chicago Tribune 67:7 Section 2 Mar 8, 87)

DOLE, Robert J. Thank goodness whenever I was in the Oval Office I only nodded (commenting on the Watergate tapes). (Christian Science Monitor 68:17 Sept 10, 76)

DOLE, Robert J. When I ran for vice-president in 1976, they told me to go for the jugular. I did. My own. (US 3:59 Dec 15, 86)

DOLE, Robert J. With all respect, Connally, Goldwater and Rockefeller are great men but they don't indicate any forward thrust in our party. We've got to start building from the bottom up instead of the top down. (Time 108:30 Aug 30, 76)

DONALDSON, Sam. George Bush picked Dan Quayle because he wanted a nonentity that would not threaten him in any way, shape or form. (M 6:127 Sept 89)

DONLEAVY, J. P. Authors don't have any respect at all in terms of a profession in America—and this is quite a good and stimulating thing. (Newsweek 94:95 Oct 22, 79)

DONLEAVY, J. P. Nearly everybody who pans my books doesn't get anywhere in the literary trade. (Newsweek 94:95 Oct 22, 79)

DONLEAVY, J. P. Writing is turning one's worst moments into money. (Playboy 26:135 May 79)

DORFMAN, Dan. To lie to the press on a

public matter is, in effect, to lie to the people. (New York 10:9 May 9, 77)

DORNFELD, Arnold (attributed by Mike Royko). If your mother says she loves you, check it out (on the journalist's responsibility). (Town & Country 132:173 Sept 78)

DOTY, William R. Connally will always be remembered for his bright Nixon button and his weakness for milk shakes. (Texas Monthly 3:8 Aug 75)

DOUGLAS, Norman. You can tell the ideals of a nation by its advertisements. (Omni 4:37 July 82)

DOUGLAS, William Orville. A lifetime diet of the law alone turns judges into dull, dry husks. (Newsweek 86:46 Nov 24, 75)

DOUGLAS, William Orville. I forgot to tell you that this gang in power (the Nixon administration) is not just in search of the truth. They are 'search and destroy' people. (Kansas City Star 108:1A Nov 27, 87)

DOUGLAS, William Orville. The great and invigorating influences in American life have been the unorthodox; the people who challenge an existing institution or way of life, or say and do things that make people think. (Kansas City Times 109:14C Jan 22, 77)

DOUGLAS, William Orville. The press has a preferred position in our constitutional scheme not to enable it to make money, not to set newsmen apart as a favored class, but to bring fulfillment to the public's right to know. (New York Times 127:2 Section 4 Aug 6, 78)

DOWNEY, Thomas. George Bush has decided he would rather see the government of the United States shut down than tax the wealthy. (Chicago Tribune 294:3 Section 4 Oct 21, 90)

DRABBLE, Margaret. I think when you are young, you are obliged to be excessively interested in yourself. (Toronto Life Fashion Magazine 34 Fall 87)

DRINAN, Robert. Politics is the formation of public morality. (Chicago Tribune 261:20 Sept 17, 80)

DRUCKER, Peter F. Capital formation is shifting from the entrepreneur who invests in the future to the pension trustee who invests in the past. (New York Times 125:15 Section 3 May 16, 76)

DRUCKER, Peter F. In all recorded history there has not been one economist who had to worry about where the next meal would come from. (New York Times 125:15 Section 3 May 16, 76)

DRUCKER, Peter F. Look at governmental programs for the past fifty years. Every single one—except for warfare—achieved the exact opposite of its announced goal. (New York Times 125:15 Section 3 May 16, 76)

DRUCKER, Peter F. So much of what we call management consists in making it difficult for people to work. (New York Times 125:15 Section 3 May 16, 76)

DRUCKER, Peter F. The main impact of the computer has been the provision of unlimited jobs for clerks. (New York Times 125:15 Section 3 May 16, 76)

DRUCKER, Peter F. The only things that evolve by themselves in an organization are disorder, friction and malperformance. (The Wharton Magazine 1:14 Fall 76)

DRUCKER, Peter F. The wonder of modern institutions is not that they work so badly, but that anything works at all. (The Wharton Magazine 1:14 Fall 76)

DRUCKER, Peter F. What managers decide to stop doing is often more important then what they decide to do. (Kansas City Star 109:2F Dec 25, 88)

DRYANSKY, G. Y. Paris is becoming more vulgar, New York more refined. (W 8:8 Jan 19, 79)

DUBOS, Rene. Each civilization has its own kind of pestilence and controls it only by reforming itself. (Skeptic 19:29 May 77)

DUBUFFET, Jean. Many artists begin with the pig and make sausages. I begin with the sausages from which I reconstitute a pig. (Time 125:93 May 27, 85)

DUBUS, Andre. Romance dies hard, because its very nature is to want to live. (Boston 69:236 Dec 77)

DUCHAMP, Marcel. I was interested in ideas—not in merely visual products. I wanted to put painting once again at the service of the mind. (New York Times 128:1 Section 7 Feb 11, 79)

DUDNEY, Bob. The country would have recovered from the death of John Kennedy, but it hasn't recovered yet from the death of Lee Harvey Oswald and probably never will. (Esquire 85:62 Feb 76)

DUFFY, Sean. The chance of a meaningful relationship with a member of the opposite sex is inversely proportional to their amount of beauty. (Omni 1:132 May 79)

DUGGAN, B. To every Ph.D. there is an equal and opposite Ph.D. (Washingtonian 14:153 Nov 78)

DUGGER, Ronnie. To be from Texas will always have a kind of gusto to it. (New York Times 129:B12 Oct 15, 79)

DUKAKIS, Michael. I told the truth (about taxes) and I paid the price. Mr. Bush did not and we're all now going to have to pay the price for that. (Chicago Tribune V 178:14 Section 1 June 27, 90)

DUKAKIS, Michael. We're going to win because we are the party that believes in the American Dream. (Chicago Sun-Times 41:14 Section Com July 24, 88)

DUKAKIS, Michael. What George Bush is doing to the truth in this campaign is a crime (1988). (Newsweek 112:25 Oct 3, 88)

DUKE, David. Black people have organizations that fight for black power, and Jews look out for each other. But there isn't anyone except the Klan who will fight for the rights of white people. (Newsweek 90:45 Nov 14, 77)

DUKE, David. I feel more comfortable in the Republican Party. (Time 133:29 Mar 6, 89)

DUNAWAY, Faye. I've always thought that acting is an art of creating accidents. (W 5:15 Nov 26, 76)

DUNCAN, Isadora. With what a price we pay for the glory of motherhood. (Chicago Tribune 176:2 Section 2 June 25, 78)

DUNDEE, Chris. Middle age is when you start for home about the same time you used to start for somewhere else. (Sports Illustrated 44:10 Mar 29, 76)

DUNDES, Alan. Football is a healthy outlet for male-to-male affections just as spin the bottle and post office are healthy outlets for adolescent heterosexual needs. (Time 112:112 Nov 13, 78)

DUNNE, John Gregory. Hollywood is the only place where you fail upwards. (US 1:12 Feb 21, 78)

DURANT, Will. One of the lessons of history is that nothing is often a good thing to do and always a clever thing to say. (Washingtonian 14:153 Nov 78)

DURANT, Will. We are living in a time when woman thinks she has been emancipated, but I'm afraid that's a complimentary way of saying she's been industrialized. (Chicago Sun-Times 28:30 Nov 6, 75)

DURANTE, Jimmy. There's a million good-lookin' guys, but I'm a novelty. (New York Times 129:1 Jan 30, 80)

DURENBERGER, David. I wouldn't trust Elliott Abrams any further than I could throw Oliver North. (Village Voice 32:20 Mar 3, 87)

DURKIN, John. In New Hampshire today, the Ayatullah Khomeini could beat Carter (1979). (Time 113:52 April 9, 79)

DUROCHER, Leo. If you lose you're going to be fired, and if you win you only put off the day you're going to be fired. (The

Sporting News 197:10 June 11, 84)

DURY, Ian. Sex is about as important as a cheese sandwich. (Chicago Sun-Times 31:6 June 20, 78)

DUTTON, Fred. Lawyers have become secular priests. (Time 111:58 April 10, 78)

DUTTON, Fred. Washington is like a woman who is always waiting to be seduced. (Time 109:26 Feb 7, 77)

DYLAN, Bob. Money doesn't exist because I don't recognize it. (New Times 10:45 Feb 6, 78)

DYLAN, Bob. Rock and roll ended with Little Anthony and the Imperials. (Rolling Stone 257:42 Jan 26, 78)

DYLAN, Bob. Somebody called me the Ed Sullivan of rock and roll. I don't know what that means, but it sounds right. (TV Guide 24:4 Sept 11, 78)

DYSON, Freeman. The only certainty in (the) remote future is that radically new things will be happening. (Omni 2:40 June 80)

EARHART, Amelia. There are two kinds of stones, as everyone knows, one of which rolls. (Chicago Tribune 176:2 Section 2 June 25, 78)

EASTWOOD, Clint. Everybody talks about love, but the thing that keeps marriage together for me is friendship. (Chicago Tribune Magazine 174:25 Aug 1, 76)

EATON, Cyrus S. We must either learn to live with the Communists or resign ourselves to perish with them. (Time 113:93 May 21, 79)

EATON, Richard. Life is subject to change without notice. (More 8:9 June 78)

EBAN, Abba Solomon. Better to be disliked than pitied. (New York 9:38 July 26, 76)

EBAN, Abba Solomon. You cannot have peace without risks. (Time 111:37 Mar 6, 78)

ECKHARDT, Nadine. Most politicians are just little men who couldn't get it up in high school. (Newsweek 86:38 Oct 13, 75)

EDDINGTON, Arthur. The stuff of the universe is mind stuff. (Human Behavior 7:32 May 78)

EDER, Richard. A critic may write for an institution, but he shouldn't be one. (Village Voice 22:97 Mar 28, 77)

EDISON, Thomas Alva. Anything that won't sell, I don't want to invent. (New York Times Book Review 7 Feb 25, 79)

EDISON, Thomas Alva. Deafness has been of great advantage to me as my business is thinking. (Newsweek 93:104 Mar 26, 79)

EDWARDS, Don. The CIA is a real basket of snakes compared to the FBI. (Chicago Tribune 79:19 Mar 20, 87)

EDWARDS, James B. I don't believe the South will buy Jimmy Carter. He is nothing more than a Southern-talking George McGovern. (New York Times 125:51 June 29, 76)

EDWARDS, Shelton. The way to get somewhere in politics is to find a crowd that's going some place and get in front of it. (Time 112:16 Aug 28, 78)

EHRLICH, Paul. The petrochemical industry is at about the intellectual and moral level of the people who sell heroin to high school kids. (Outside 1:10 July 78)

EHRLICHMAN, John D. I have done my time. I don't think he (Richard Nixon) is ever going to stop doing his time. (Time 111:67 May 15, 78)

EHRLICHMAN, John D. Narcotics suppression is a very sexy political issue. (Playboy 23:174 Nov 76)

EHRLICHMAN, John D. We operate in this country, and in the media and the courts, on a situational ethics base. (Time 106:21 Dec 1, 75)

EINSTEIN, Albert. An empty stomach is not a good political adviser. (Kansas City Times 109:14B May 11, 77)

EINSTEIN, Albert. Everything should be made as simple as possible, but not simpler. (Newsweek 93:100 April 16, 79)

EINSTEIN, Albert. God may be subtle, but He isn't mean. (The Observer 9785:9 Mar 11, 79)

EINSTEIN, Albert. Let every man be respected as an individual and no man idolized. (Parade 4 July 1, 79)

EINSTEIN, Albert. Nationalism is an infantile disease. It is the measles of mankind. (Chicago Tribune 281:2 Section 2 Oct 8, 78)

EINSTEIN, Albert. Princeton is a wonderful little spot. A quaint and ceremonious village of puny demigods on stilts. (Philadelphia Magazine 66:116 Aug 75)

EINSTEIN, Albert. Sit with a pretty girl for an hour, and it seems like a minute; sit on a hot stove for a minute, and it seems like an hour—that's relativity. (Rocky Mountain News 235:104 Dec 13, 79)

EINSTEIN, Albert. The world needs heroes and it's better they be harmless men like me than villains like Hitler. (Newsweek 92:43 Nov 27, 78)

EINSTEIN, Albert. To punish me for my contempt for authority, Fate made me an authority myself. (Chicago Tribune 281:1 Section 2 Oct 8, 78)

EINSTEIN, Albert. To the village square we must carry the facts of atomic energy. From there must come America's voice (commenting in 1946). (Newsweek 85:23

Feb 24, 75)

EINSTEIN, Albert. When a man after long years of searching chances upon a thought which discloses something of the beauty of this mysterious universe, he should not therefore be personally celebrated. He is already sufficiently paid by his experience of seeking and finding. (New York Times 128:18 Section 4 Nov 10, 78)

EINSTEIN, Albert (attributed by Yousuf Karsh). Curiosity has its own reason for existence. (Parade 7 Dec 3, 78)

EISELEY, Loren. There is but one way into the future: the technological way. (Time 110:61 July 25, 77)

EISENHOWER, David. Journalists aren't nearly as interesting as they think they are. (Esquire 87:35 June 30, 77)

EISENHOWER, Dwight David. It has been the tough-minded optimist whom history has proved right in America. (Newsweek 85:18 Feb 24, 75)

EISENHOWER, Dwight David. The path to America's future lies down the middle of the road. (Time 116:32 July 28, 80)

EISENHOWER, Dwight David. These are not bad people... All they are concerned about is to see that their sweet little girls are not required to sit in schools alongside some big overgrown Negroes. (Time 109:66 Mar 28, 77)

EISENHOWER, Mamie Geneva (Doud). I let Ike run the country and I ran the home. (New York Times 126:26 Section 1 Nov 14, 76)

ELDRIDGE, Paul. Man is always ready to die for an idea, provided that idea is not quite clear to him. (Washingtonian 15:141 Nov 79)

ELGIN, Duane S (futurologist). Once you discover that space doesn't matter, or that time can be traveled through at will so that time doesn't matter, and that matter can be moved by consciousness so that matter doesn't matter—well, you can't go home again. (New York 10:55 Dec 27, 76)

ELIOT, Thomas Stearns. Humankind cannot bear very much reality. (Chicago Tribune Magazine 6 Aug 19, 84)

ELIOT, Thomas Stearns. Those who say they give the public what it wants begin by underestimating public taste and end by debauching it. (American Film 5:83 Nov 79)

ELLISON, Ralph. People who want to write sociology should not write a novel. (Newsweek 91:21 Feb 20, 78)

ELY, Bert. Banker's don't know squat about insurance. (Chicago Tribune 50:4 Section 4 Feb 19, 89)

EMERSON, Eric. The second is never as good as the first. (Omni 1:131 May 79)

EMERSON, William A., Jr. A foolish consistency is the hobgoblin of small committees. (Wilson Library Bulletin 52:534 Mar 78)

EMERSON, William A., Jr. New Yorkers are an endangered species. (Newsweek 86:9 Dec 29, 75)

EMERY, Fred J. Regulation is the substitution of error for chance. (Washingtonian 15:141 Nov 79)

EPHRON, Nora. For a lot of women, the women's movement has just given them a political rationalization for their fear of success. (Christian Science Monitor 69:2 Dec 10, 76)

EPHRON, Nora. The plain fact is that a celebrity is anyone People (magazine) writes about. (USA Today 1:10A May 16, 83)

EPSTEIN, Edward Jay. Corporate America is the perpetrator, not the victim, of greenmail. (Manhattan, Inc. 4:26 Feb 87)

EPSTEIN, Joseph. A few things ought to be said on behalf of the 1970's—not the least among them that they weren't the 1960's. (Time 115:39 Jan 7, 80)

EPSTEIN, Thomas A. With extremely few exceptions, nothing is worth the trouble. (Omni 1:131 May 79)

ERHARD, Werner. You are perfect exactly the way you are. (Life 2:86 Dec 79)

ERISH, Andrew. America is 90 percent corn. (New York Times 128:23 Nov 25, 78)

ERVIN, Samuel James. Nobody I know wanted to see Nixon go to jail, (but) there's an old saying that mercy but murders, pardoning those that kill. (Newsweek 85:24 Jan 13, 75)

ESPOSITO, Meade H. If I wrote a book, no one would come to my wake. (New York Times 133:2 Jan 27, 84)

ESQUERRA, Maria Antonia (Chicana nun). The theology of liberation in North America will-be written by the oppressed. (Time 106:34 Sept 1, 75)

ESTES, Billie Sol. You win by losing, hold on by letting go, increase by diminishing, and multiply by dividing. These are the principles that have brought me success. (New York Times 128:23 Feb 25, 79)

EVANS, Harold. Publishing is: Talk softly and carry a big stick, but don't let them see the big stick. (Chicago Tribune 316:5 Section 5 Nov 12, 90)

EVANS, Medford. It usually takes disciplined organization to dislodge entrenched power. (American Opinion 18:29 Nov 75)

EVANS, Robert. Success means never have

to admit you're unhappy. (Chicago Tribune Magazine 4 July 22, 84)

EVANS, Walker. Photography isn't a matter of taking pictures. It's a matter of having an eye. (Chicago Tribune 226:2 Section 6 Aug 14, 77)

EVTUSHENKO, Evgenii Aleksandrovich. Distrust is the mother of war and political racism. (Atlas World Press Review 23:10 Nov 76)

EYSENCK, H. J. Scientists, especially when they leave the particular field in which they have specialized, are just as ordinary, pig-headed and unreasonable as anybody else. (Omni 2:49 Dec 79)

FABER, Harold. If there isn't a law, there will be. (Book Digest 6:32 Dec 79)

FADIMAN, Clifton. No woman of our time has gone further with less mental equipment (Clare Boothe Luce). (New York 15:70 Mar 1, 82)

FAHD, KING OF SAUDI ARABIA. If Iran goes, God help us. (The Observer 9777:11 Jan 14, 79)

FAHRENKOPF, Frank. Every time a Democrat gets into trouble, it's sex, every time a Republican does, it's money. (Washingtonian 22:99 July 87)

FAIRCHILD, Morgan. Hair and cleavage— that's all they need me for. (US 3:4 May 4, 87)

FAIRCHILD, Morgan. They told me a good bitch was hard to find, and so I became a good bitch (on her career). (US 3:64 May 5, 86)

FAIRLIE, Henry. Celebrity has become the main threat to journalism, especially in Washington. (Washingtonian 24:119 April 89)

FAIRLIE, Henry. Religion in America leaves me, especially a European, with the impression that in place of churches there are only Do-It-Yourself God Kits. (Chicago Tribune 123:3 May 3, 87)

FAIRLIE, Henry. The once rambunctious American spirit of innovation and adventurousness is today being paralyzed by the desire to build a risk-free society. (Time 114:71 Oct 22, 79)

FAIRLIE, Henry. Where there is no theology, there is no religion. (Chicago Tribune 123:3 May 3, 87)

FALLOWS, James. I came to think that Carter believes fifty things, but no one thing. (New York Times 128:23 April 26, 79)

FALLOWS, James. I'm inclined to doubt this government can be changed, by Carter or any other President. (Time 112:91 Dec 4, 78)

FALWELL, Jerry. Christians, like slaves and

soldiers, ask no questions. (Penthouse 13:65 Dec 81)

FALWELL, Jerry. Not only should we register them (Communists), but we should stamp it on their foreheads and send them back to Russia. This is a free country. (Washington Post 275:B3 Sept 6, 77)

FALWELL, Jerry. Textbooks are Soviet propaganda. (Kansas City Star 112:1E Dec 7, 80)

FALWELL, Jerry. You can't be a good Christian and a liberal at the same time. (Oklahoma Observer 21:12 Jan 25, 89)

FANG LIZHI. China's hope at present lies in the fact that more and more people have broken free from blind faith in the leadership (1989). (Newsweek 113:27 June 26, 89)

FANG LIZHI. It (Marxism) is a thing of the past...and like a worn-out dress it should be discarded. (Fame 1:50 Mar 90)

FARMER, Robert. The main reason people give to political campaigns is because they don't want to say no to the person who asked them. (New England Monthly 5:38 July 88)

FARRELL, James T. There's one good kind of a writer—a dead writer. (Chicago Sun-Times 32:53 Aug 24, 79)

FASSBINDER, Rainer Werner. I long for a little naivete but there's none around. (Film Comment 12:2 Jan 75)

FAULKNER, William. I believe that man will not merely endure: he will prevail (commenting in his 1950 Nobel Prize acceptance speech). (New York Times Magazine 42 Dec 5, 76)

FAULKNER, William. I gave the world what it wanted—guts and genitals. (True 57:14 Dec 75)

FAULKNER, William. If a writer has to rob his mother, he will not hesitate; the Ode on a Grecian Urn is worth any number of old ladies. (New York Times Book Review 3 Aug 16, 81)

FAULKNER, William. Living is a process of getting ready to be dead for a long time. (Parade 18 Sept 13, 81)

FAULKNER, William. The past is never dead; it is not even past. (Newsweek 89:87 Feb 21, 77)

FAULKNER, William. You can cure human beings of almost anything except marrying. (Playboy 32:130 Jan 85)

FEATHER, William. No plan is worth a damn unless somebody makes it work. (Forbes 120:186 Oct 15, 77)

FEENEY, Leonard. The first American girl who 'made good' according to God's exact standards (about Elizabeth Seton).

(Time 106:53 Sept 22, 75)

FEIN, Leonard. Israel is squandering recklessly its most critical and natural resource—the good will that many people around the world, and in this country in particular, feel for this gutsy country. (Time 114:43 July 23, 79)

FEISAL, KING OF SAUDI ARABIA. If anyone feels wrongly treated, he has only himself to blame for not telling me. What higher democracy can there be. (Time 105:22 April 7, 75)

FELA, 1938-. Music is the weapon of the future. (Newsweek 106:67 July 15, 85)

FELA, 1938-. Nigerians like to fight, that's why they like me. (New York Times 138:15 Nov 18, 88)

FELD, Eliot. Each time I make a dance, it's like being a virgin. (People Weekly 11:45 May 14, 79)

FELDMAN, Marty. Humor is like sex. Those who do it don't talk about it. (People Weekly 6:103 Dec 27/Jan 3, 77)

FELDMAN, Marty. Well, any melodrama inverted is good material for a comedy. (Chicago Tribune 207:7 July 26, 77)

FELIX, Virginia. Decision makers are those who have the greatest vested interest in the decision. (Omni 1:132 May 79)

FELLINI, Federico. I don't have problems with actors—they have problems with me. (Time 107:76 May 17, 76)

FERNANDES, Millor (Brazilian playwright). In a democracy we are all equal before the law. In a dictatorship we are all equal before the police. (New York Times 126:8 May 24, 77)

FERRIS, Earle. There's nothing neither good nor bad that can't be made more so. (Washingtonian 15:143 Nov 79)

FIEDLER, Leslie. There can be no terror without the hope for love and love's defeat. (New York Arts Journal 9:15 April 78)

FIELD, Marshall, V. They all started out with nothing in those days, and the biggest crooks won. I was just lucky to come from a line of successful crooks. (Esquire 89:96 Mar 28, 78)

FIELDS, W. C. There comes a time in the affairs of men when you must take the bull by the tail and face the situation. (San Francisco Chronicle This World 1978:40 Jan 29, 78)

FIELDS, W. C. Women are like elephants. They're nice to look at but I wouldn't want to own one. (Viva 5:26 Dec 77)

FIERSTEIN, Harvey. I assume everyone is gay unless I'm told otherwise. (Life 7:40 Jan 84)

FINK, Stanley. There are times when

reasonable people come to no solution. (New York 10:9 July 25, 77)

FINLEY, Charles Oscar. I've never seen so many damned idiots as the owners in sport. (Time 106:42 Aug 18, 75)

FISHER, Carrie. Show me a child with a simple, happy, uncomplicated childhood, and I'll show you Dan Quayle. (Chicago Tribune 288:11 Section 1 Oct 15, 90)

FITZGERALD, F. Scott. Having once found the intensity of art, nothing else that can happen in life can ever again seem as important as the creative process. (Forbes 120:186 Oct 15, 77)

FITZGERALD, F. Scott. I talk with the authority of failure—Ernest (Hemingway) with the authority of success. (Time 111:89 April 3, 78)

FITZGERALD, F. Scott. The test of a first-rate intelligence is the ability to hold two opposed ideas in the mind at the same time, and still retain the ability to function. (New York Times Book Review 23 Mar 4, 79)

FITZGERALD, F. Scott. There never was a good biography of a good novelist. There couldn't be. He is too many people, if he's any good. (Writer's Digest 56:6 Dec 76)

FITZGERALD, Robert. Translating is writing poetry to the full extent of the product. (Connoisseur 215:83 Sept 85)

FITZGERALD, Zelda. A vacuum can only exist, I imagine, by the things which enclose it. (Chicago Tribune 176:2 Section 2 June 25, 78)

FITZHUGH, Gilbert W. The Republicans fight like cats and go home and sulk. The Democrats fight like cats, and suddenly there are more cats. (Time 107:11 Aug 23, 76)

FITZSIMMONS, Frank E. The Teamsters are without peer as an organization dedicated to the service of mankind. (New York Times Magazine 31 Nov 7, 76)

FLANAGAN, Fionnula. The one thing you must not commit with the Irish is to succeed. (TV Guide 26:22 April 29, 78)

FLANNER, Janet. I'm not one of those journalists with a staff. I don't even have a secretary. I act as a sponge. I soak it up and squeeze it out in ink every two weeks. (New York Times 28:B10 Nov 8, 78)

FLANNER, Janet. She (Elsa Maxwell) was built for crowds. She has never come any closer to life than the dinner table. (New York Times 128:B10 Nov 8, 78)

FLEENER, Terre. What the Jewish people endured does not give them the right to visit violence on other people. (Chicago Sun-Times 32:100 July 1, 79)

FLEISHMAN, Stanley. There are more

citizens in jail in the United States today for publishing books, magazines, newspapers, and films than there are in all the countries of the world put together. (American Film 2:4 June 77)

FLEMING, John. Show me your books, and I'll tell you who you are. (Esquire 89:71 Jan 31, 78)

FLOOD, Curt. Being black is always having people being cautious about what they call you. (Esquire 89:46 Mar 1, 78)

FLOREZ, Elisa (Missy). When you start getting paid big money to take your clothes off, and people tell you look good, it does wonders for you. (Washingtonian 22:24 April 87)

FLYNT, Larry. If you ask me, yes, I am a born-again Christian. But I am going to continue publishing pornography, and anybody who doesn't like it can go kiss a rope. (New York Times 127:A16 Feb 2, 78)

FLYNT, Larry. There's only one commandment: do unto others as you would have them do unto you—but do it first. (Vanity Fair 47:47 Jan 31, 84)

FOLEY, Thomas S. There is a mood in this country that government action is not necessarily always the perfect solution to social problems. (US News & World Report 84:24 Jan 23, 78)

FONDA, Jane. (Robert Redford) is, and remains, a bourgeois in the worst sense of the word. (Chicago Tribune 314:28 Nov 10, 77)

FONDA, Jane. Conservation is the religion of the future. (Life 2:170 Dec 79)

FONDA, Jane. I think that every movie is political. (New Times 10:58 Mar 20, 78)

FONDA, Jane. It is time to look at crime in the suites, not just in the streets. (Time 114:31 Oct 8, 79)

FONDA, Peter. I'm heir to nothing but a legend, which is full of ...air. (Chicago Tribune Magazine 70 Nov 6, 77)

FONTAINE, Joan. The physical side of being a woman is detestable. (The Observer 9767:13 Nov 5, 78)

FORBES, Malcolm S. A bore is someone who persists in holding his own views after we have enlightened him with ours. (Reader's Digest 108:261 May 76)

FORBES, Malcolm S. I'd say capitalism's worst excess is in the large number of crooks and tinhorns who get too much of the action. (Playboy 26:108 April 79)

FORBES, Malcolm S. People who never get carried away should be. (Town & Country 130:166 Nov 76)

FORD, Edsel, II. I've got engines in my blood. (W 12A:8 July 29, 83)

FORD, Gerald Rudolph. A President should never promise more than he can deliver and a President should always deliver everything that he's promised. (Time 108:15 Oct 4, 76)

FORD, Gerald Rudolph. Detente means moderate and restrained behavior between two superpowers—not a license to fish in troubled waters. (American Legion Magazine 99:36 Nov 75)

FORD, Gerald Rudolph. Eurocommunism is not, as their propagandists say, Communism with a human face. It is Stalinism in a mask and tyranny in disguise. (New York Times 127:2 Oct 30, 77)

FORD, Gerald Rudolph. Having become Vice President and President without expecting or seeking either, I have a special feeling toward these high offices. To me, the presidency and vice presidency were not prizes to be won, but a duty to be done. (Time 108:22 Aug 30, 76)

FORD, Gerald Rudolph. I don't think the United States should ever involve itself in the internal situation in any country. (New York 9:33 Feb 23, 76)

FORD, Gerald Rudolph. I learned a long time ago in politics, never say never. (New York Times 128:17 April 22, 79)

FORD, Gerald Rudolph. I'm a better President than a campaigner. (Time 107:16 June 28, 76)

FORD, Gerald Rudolph. Most of the important things that happen in the world happen in the middle of the night. (San Francisco Chronicle This World 1978:2 Feb 26, 78)

FORD, Gerald Rudolph. My motto towards the Congress is communication, conciliation, compromise and cooperation. (Time 104:27 Dec 2, 74)

FORD, Gerald Rudolph. There is no Soviet domination of Eastern Europe and there never will be under a Ford Administration. (Chicago Sun-Times 29:2 Oct 8, 76)

FORD, Gerald Rudolph. Things are more like they are now than they've ever been. (The Nation 237:385 Oct 29, 83)

FORD, Gerald Rudolph. We cannot improve this agency by destroying it (commenting on the CIA at the installation ceremony for George Bush as director). (New York Times 125:1 Jan 31, 76)

FORD, Gerald Rudolph. We skiers know that falling down isn't important; it's getting up again. (New York 10:104 Nov 14, 77)

FORD, Henry. History is more or less bunk. (Time 111:74 Jan 9, 78)

FORD, Henry. Thinking is the hardest work there is—which is probably the reason why so few engage in it. (Forbes 121:96 Feb 6, 78)

FORD, Henry, II. Never complain, never explain. (New York Times 128:19 Mar 26, 79)

FORD, Henry, II. This country developed in a particular way because of the automobile, and you can't just push a button and change it. (Time 105:71 Feb 10, 75)

FOREMAN, George. Boxing is like jazz. The better it is, the less people appreciate it. (Sepia 25:12 Sept 76)

FOREMAN, Percy. Man's inhumanity to man is only exceeded by woman's inhumanity to woman. (Newsweek 88:93 Nov 8, 76)

FOREMAN, Percy. You don't approach a case with the philosophy of applying abstract justice—you go in to win. (USA Today 1:10A May 5, 83)

FORSTER, E. M. If I had to choose between betraying my country and betraying my friend, I hope I should have the guts to betray my country. (Time 115:78 June 2, 80)

FORTAS, Abe. The law of revenge has its roots in the deep recesses of the human spirit, but that is not a permissible reason for retaining capital punishment. (New York Times Magazine 9 Jan 23, 77)

FOWLES, John. Cherish the poet; there seemed many great auks till the last one died. (The American Book Review 1:21 Dec 77)

FRAIN, Andy. Never trust a man with a mustache or a man who carries an umbrella. (The Reader (Chicago's Free Weekly) 7:14 Jan 27, 78)

FRANK, Barney. The anti-abortionists believe that the right to life begins at conception—and ends at birth. (Boston 73:13 Dec 81)

FRANKEL, Charles. Scholarship must be free to follow crooked paths to unexpected conclusions. (Time 113:8 May 14, 79)

FRANKEL, Charles. Whatever happens in government could have happened differently, and it usually would have been better if it had. (The Reader (Chicago's Free Weekly) 5:2 May 28, 76)

FRASER, Douglas. The President (Jimmy Carter) is a nice man, an intelligent man and he likes his job. But he doesn't have any fire in his belly. (Chicago Sun-Times 32:2 April 27, 79)

FREIFELD, Sam. Saul Bellow is a great writer who is smaller than life. (Chicago 28:176 Dec 79)

FREMONT-SMITH, Eliot. Booksellers are good at drinking; librarians are better. (Village Voice 20:49 June 9, 75)

FREUD, Sigmund. My cigar is not a symbol. It is only a cigar. (Washingtonian 12:112 April 77)

FREUD, Sigmund. One is very crazy when in love. (Playboy 26:26 Oct 79)

FREUD, Sigmund. The first human who hurled a curse instead of a weapon against his adversary was the founder of civilization. (Rocky Mountain News 244:58 Dec 22, 79)

FREUD, Sigmund. The less a man knows about the past and the present, the more insecure must be his judgment of the future. (Kansas City Star 106:5A Dec 30, 85)

FRIEDBERG, A. Alan. Boston is a city with champagne tastes and beer pocketbooks. (Time 114:82 July 16, 79)

FRIEDMAN, Milton. Governments never learn. Only people learn. (The Observer 9840:11 Mar 30, 80)

FRIEDMAN, Milton. In the United States the Federal Reserve has never practiced monetarism. (Washington Post 106:C4 May 29, 83)

FRIEDMAN, Milton. In this day and age, we need to revise the old saying to read, Hell hath no fury like a bureaucrat scorned. (Newsweek 86:47 Dec 29, 75)

FRIEDMAN, Milton. Inflation is the one form of taxation that can be imposed without legislation. (American Opinion 18:37 April 75)

FRIEDMAN, Milton. Let me propose that we take as our major motto what I would like to see as an 11th commandment: that everyone shall be free to do good at his own expense. (American Legion Magazine 103:12 Aug 77)

FRIEDMAN, Milton. There is no such thing as a free lunch. That is the sum of my economic theory. The rest is elaboration. (Reader's Digest 112:190 Feb 78)

FRIENDLY, Fred. Television makes so much money doing its worst that it can'd afford to do its best. (US 3:11 Aug 25, 86)

FRIENDLY, Fred. The news is the one thing networks can point to with pride. Everything else they do is crap, and they know it. (Time 115:74 Jan 14, 80)

FRIENDLY, Fred. TV still basically indexes rather than reports the news. (Time 115:70 Feb 25, 80)

FROHNMAYER, John E. Holocaust victims might be inappropriate for display in the entrance of a museum where all would have to confront it, whether they chose to or not. (New York Times 139:B3 Aug 2, 90)

FROM, Al. The Republicans win when they draw the line between the poor and the rest of us. The Democrats win when we draw the line between the rich and the rest of us. (New York Times 138:15 Feb 19, 89)

FROMME, Lynette (Squeaky). Anybody can kill anybody. (Time 106:19 Sept 15, 75)

FROST, Robert. A liberal is a man who can't take his own side in an argument. (Harvard Magazine 87:68 Sept 84)

FROST, Robert. Half the world is composed of people who have something to say and can't, and the other half who have nothing to say and keep on saying it. (Kansas City Star 97:38 July 14, 77)

FROST, Robert. Home is the place where when you have to go there, they have to take you in. (Rocky Mountain News 134:44 Sept 3, 79)

FUENTES, Carlos. (The U. S.) is a country in love with itself and it cares about the world only in the measure that the world cares about the United States. (Fame 3:24 Feb 90)

FUENTES, Carlos. Mexicans have always asked themselves why a people so close to God should be so near the United States. (W 5:9 Oct 29, 76)

FUENTES, Carlos. There are two things one never should do after fifty: change wives and give interviews. (Nuestro 2:36 Nov 78)

FUENTES, Carlos. What the United States does best is to understand itself. What it does worst is understand others. (Time 127:52 June 16, 86)

FULBRIGHT, James William. If once the press was excessively orthodox and unquestioning of Government policy, it has now become almost sweepingly iconoclastic. (Time 106:78 Nov 24, 75)

FULBRIGHT, James William. It is one of the perversities of human nature that people have a far greater capacity for enduring disasters than for preventing them, even when the danger is plain and imminent. (American Legion Magazine 98:20 Jan 75)

FULLER, R. Buckminster. Sometimes I think we're alone. Sometimes I think we're not. In either case, the thought is quite staggering. (Omni 2:39 April 80)

FULLER, R. Buckminster. The future is a choice between Utopia and oblivion. (Analog Science Fiction/Science Fact 99:97 Oct 79)

GABOR, Zsa Zsa. A man in love is incomplete until he has married. Then he's finished. (Village Voice 22:20 Dec 26, 77)

GABOR, Zsa Zsa. I have never hated a man enough to give his diamonds back. (Cosmopolitan 188:268 Feb 80)

GABOR, Zsa Zsa. Macho does not prove mucho. (Washingtonian 15:143 Nov 79)

GABOR, Zsa Zsa. You're never too young to be younger. (Oui 8:82 Jan 78)

GALBRAITH, John Kenneth. Anyone who says he isn't going to resign, four times, definitely will. (Town & Country 133:140 May 79)

GALBRAITH, John Kenneth. Capitalism will survive. (New York Times Book Review 31 Sept 30, 79)

GALBRAITH, John Kenneth. I reserve judgment on whether God is a conservative or not. (Life 5:58 Jan 82)

GALBRAITH, John Kenneth. Modesty is a vastly overrated virtue. (Washingtonian 18:127 Sept 83)

GALBRAITH, John Kenneth. No ethic is as ethical as the work ethic. (Cosmopolitan 188:264 June 80)

GALBRAITH, John Kenneth. The (tax) revolt of the affluent, which now has politicans so frightened, is not a violent thing. The response in the ghettoes if life there is allowed further to deteriorate might be different. (New York Times 128:A23 Jan 12, 79)

GALBRAITH, John Kenneth. There's just a growing feeling that Wall Street is a sort of irresponsible beehive of young people who don't know what they're doing. (Kansas City Star 108:6A Oct 27, 87)

GALLUP, George. I could prove God statistically. (Omni 2:42 Nov 79)

GANDHI, Indira (Nehru). The freedom of the people cannot be allowed to come in the way of the freedom of the masses. (People Weekly 4:33 Dec 29/Jan 5, 76)

GANDHI, Indira (Nehru). We should be vigilant to see that our march to progress is not hampered in the name of the Constitution. (New York Times 125:5 Section 1 Dec 28, 75)

GANDHI, Indira (Nehru). Well, I've lived with danger all my life, and I think I've had a pretty full life, and it makes no difference whether you die in bed or you die standing up. (The New Yorker 60:39 Nov 12, 84)

GANNETT, Lewis. The great days in New York were just before you got there. (Country Journal 5:10 Dec 78)

GARAGIOLA, Joe. You could plant two thousand rows of corn with the fertilizer he spreads around (commenting on Tom Lasorda, manager of the L. A. Dodgers). (The Sporting News 193:10 May 3, 82)

GARDNER, Brian. Polluters must be made

to pay so much that the fines—continuously leveled until the pollution stops—are so high that not to pollute is a cheaper alternative. (New Scientist 76:516 Nov 24, 77)

GARDNER, Richard. Italy is a poor country full of right people. (The Observer 9931:13 Jan 3, 82)

GARLAND, Judy. I have gone through hell, I tell you, a hell no one, no person, no man, no beast, not even a fire hydrant could endure. (Newsweek 85:52 May 26, 75)

GARMENT, Leonard. He is the antithesis of a stuffed judicial robe (about Robert Bork). (Time 130:13 July 13, 87)

GARN, Jake. I frankly don't give a damn if a 14-legged bug or the woundfin minnow live or die. (Outside 1:10 July 78)

GARROWAY, Dave. Television started off mediocre and went steadily downhill. (Channels 3:53 Sept 83)

GARVEY, Ed. When you talk about civil liberties in professional sports, it's like talking about virtue in a whorehouse. (Village Voice 20:37 Dec 8, 75)

GASICH, Welko (Vice President of Northrop Aircraft Corporation). Until we have a bona fide world police force, it's still Dodge City and everyone wants a rifle over his door. (Time 105:44 Mar 3, 75)

GAULD, Joseph. The rod (physical discipline) is only wrong in the wrong hands. (Time 107:51 Aug 9, 76)

GEISEL, Theodor. Adults are obsolete children and the hell with them. (Time 113:93 May 7, 79)

GENTRY, Charles B. Unrestrained individualism is incompatible with civilization. (The Atlantic 266:6 Sept 90)

GENTRY, Dave Tyson. True friendship comes when silence between two people is comfortable. (Reader's Digest 107:56B Sept 75)

GEORGE, Phyllis. The most popular labor-saving device is still money. (Cosmopolitan 196:332 Oct 83)

GEORGE F, Will. American children do better than Japanese children in English. For now. (Kansas City Times 121:A-11 Feb 13, 89)

GETTY, Gordon Peter. I think I will be remembered not for my music, but for my economic theories. (Chicago Tribune 50:14B Section 7 Feb 19, 89)

GETTY, Jean Paul. I suffer no guilt complexes or conscience pangs about my wealth. The Lord may have been disproportionate, but that is how He—or nature, if you like—operates. (Time 107:41 May 24, 76)

GETTY, Jean Paul. If you can count your money, you don't have a billion dollars. (Newsweek 87:55 June 14, 76)

GETTY, Jean Paul. Remember, a billion dollars isn't worth what it used to be. (Newsweek 94:166 Nov 19, 79)

GETTY, Jean Paul. The meek shall inherit the earth, but not its mineral rights. (Time 113:25 Feb 26, 79)

GHORBAL, Ashraf. Terrorism has become the lens through which the Americans look at the Middle East. (Time 127:19 June 16, 86)

GIAMATTI, A. Bartlett. The university must be a tributary to a larger society, not a sanctuary from it. (Time 112:89 Oct 2, 78)

GIBBS, Lawrence. A taxpaying public that doesn't understand the law is a taxpaying public that can't comply with the law. (Chicago Tribune 79:19 Mar 20, 87)

GIBBS, Philip. It's better to give than to lend, and it costs about the same. (Kansas City Star 97:38 July 14, 77)

GIELGUD, John (attributed by Leslie Caron). Never show your good side—show your faults (instruction to actors). (New York Times 126:31 Section 2 Aug 28, 77)

GILDER, George. This is what sexual liberation chiefly accomplishes—it liberates young women to pursue married men. (Newsweek 108:31 Dec 8, 86)

GILL, Brendan. God is thought to be housed better than the rest of us, and He usually is. (Chicago 36:26 July 87)

GILL, Brendan. The rich have no need to pronounce words correctly. They can leave all that to their lawyers and accountants. (Andy Warhol's Interview 8:60 Dec 78)

GILLESPIE, Dizzy. It took me all my life to learn the biggest music lesson of them all—what not to play. (Sepia 25:10 Dec 76)

GILLESPIE, Marcia Ann. I did not stand up for my rights as a black person in America to be told that I have to sit down because I'm a woman. (Time 114:99 Oct 29, 79)

GILMORE, Gary Mark. Death is the only inescapable, unavoidable, sure thing. We are sentenced to die the day we're born. (Chicago Sun-Times 29:2 Nov 17, 76)

GILMORE, Gary Mark. Let's do it. (Chicago Daily News 13 Dec 30, 77)

GINGRICH, Arnold. To stand out, for a man or a magazine, it is necessary to stand for something. Otherwise you stand still. (Newsweek 88:78 July 19, 76)

GINGRICH, Newt. I am now a famous person (1985). (Washingtonian 20:5 July 85)

GINSBERG, Allen. I like a varied

audience—little old ladies, homosexuals, weirdos. (Time 113:81 Mar 5, 79)

GINZBURG, Alexander. The Russian (people) do not believe in Communism. (US News & World Report 86:17 June 18, 79)

GIONO, Jean. Reality pushed to its extreme ends in unreality. (Village Voice 21:93 Sept 27, 76)

GIROUX, Robert. Editors used to be known by their authors; now some of them are known by their restaurants. (Time 119:73 Jan 18, 82)

GISCARD D'ESTAING, Valery. Nuclear energy is at the crossroads of the two independences of France: the independence of her defense and the independence of her energy supply. (Time 110:31 Aug 15, 77)

GISCARD D'ESTAING, Valery. You do not fear freedom for yourself, do not then fear it for your friends and allies. (New York Times 125:2 May 19, 76)

GISH, Lillian. Films are the greatest force ever to move the hearts and minds of the world. (The Observer 9772:10 Oct 31, 78)

GISH, Lillian. I don't think actresses have the right to marry and ruin a man's life. (Chicago Sun-Times 32:33 Nov 30, 98)

GISH, Lillian. I've had the best life of anyone I know, or knew, Dear. And I knew some amazing people. (Guardian Weekly 120:19 May 6, 79)

GISH, Lillian. Movies have to answer a great deal for what the world is today. (Time 105:44 Feb 3, 75)

GIULIANI, Rudolph W. Ed Koch has always taken the low road. (New York Times 138:14 May 25, 89)

GIULINI, Carlo Maria. I always think I am a very small man. When I shave myself, I look in the mirror and see behind me Beethoven and Brahms. (Time 111:63 April 3, 78)

GIVENCHY, Hubert De. After I open a collection and see people trying on my clothes and treating them roughly, I suffer. My dresses are like my family. (Time 110:67 Sept 26, 77)

GLEASON, Jackie. How sweet it is! (Time 13:58 Dec 28, 87)

GLEASON, Jackie. I drank because it removed the warts and blemishes. Not from me but from the people I associated with. It sort of dimmed the lights. (Chicago Tribune Magazine 17 Mar 26, 78)

GLEASON, Jackie. Thin people are beautiful, but fat people are adorable. (People Weekly 5:29 May 3, 76)

GLEASON, Jackie. Vanity is an actor's courage. (Emmy 5:48 Jan 83)

GLENN, John. Our objective is to prevent the people of this country from getting economically raped (arguing against the decontrol of petroleum prices). (Time 106:61 Oct 13, 75)

GLENVILLE, Peter. Compared to ordinary men with ordinary ambitions, Larry (Olivier) was a sea monster. (New York Times Magazine 62 Mar 25, 79)

GODART, Suzanne. Keep a girl in jeans from 4 to 14, and you'll wind up with a Butch on your hands. (W 9:8 Jan 18, 80)

GOLD, Herbert. Never trust a newspaper over 10. (New West 4:52 Jan 1, 79)

GOLD, Herbert. The rubber-stamp expression is a rubber stamp even the first time it is pressed into our brains. (Newsweek 93:11 Feb 5, 79)

GOLDBERG, Alan. Public TV is for the humor-impaired. (Washington Journalism Review 5:40 Nov 83)

GOLDBERG, Arthur Joseph. We need a world in which it is safe to be human. (Kansas City Times 109:28 Jan 4, 77)

GOLDBERGER, Paul. Other cities consume culture, New York creates it. (Town & Country 131:14 Sept 77)

GOLDSMITH, James. Four necessary attributes for success: appetite, luck, the right people and fear. (Kansas City Star 106:5A Dec 30, 85)

GOLDSMITH, James. We (British) have reached the state where the private sector is that part of the economy the Government controls and the public sector is the part that nobody controls. (The Observer 9787:11 Mar 25, 79)

GOLDSTEIN, Al. A hard-on is its own redeeming value. (Penthouse 8:106 Jan 76)

GOLDSTEIN, Al. Most porn films I've seen are a wonderful argument in favor of blindness. (TV Guide 32:38 June 30, 84)

GOLDSTEIN, Al. When it comes to pornography, I know two kinds of people: those who don't know what they're talking about, and those who don't know what they're missing. (Washington Post 353:D3 Nov 22, 76)

GOLDWATER, Barry Morris. A book should not be charged the same rate for mailing as a brick. (New York Times 126:16 Section 4 Jan 30, 77)

GOLDWATER, Barry Morris. Eternal vigilance is the price of liberty. (Texas Observer 70:2 Aug 11, 78)

GOLDWATER, Barry Morris. Every good Christian ought to kick Falwell right in the ass. (Newsweek 99:44 Jan 4, 82)

GOLDWATER, Barry Morris. Extremism in

the defense of liberty is no vice.
Moderation in the pursuit of justice is no
virtue. (Family Weekly 4 Dec 30, 84)

GOLDWATER, Barry Morris. I don't care if
I'm called a Democrat or a Republican as
long as I'm in bed with people of the same
thinking. (Rolling Stone 227:43 Dec 2, 76)

GOLDWATER, Barry Morris. I don't object
to a woman doing anything in combat as
long as she gets home in time to cook
dinner. (Viva 5:29 Oct 77)

GOLDWATER, Barry Morris. I have no use
for Nixon. I call him the world's biggest
liar, and he's never done anything to
disprove that. (New York Times 138:12
Oct 4, 88)

GOLDWATER, Barry Morris. I think the
Senate is beginning to look like a bunch
of jackasses. (Life 8:102 Jan 84)

GOLDWATER, Barry Morris. If he (Richard
Nixon) wants to do this country a favor, he
might stay in China. (Family Weekly 4 Dec
30, 84)

GOLDWATER, Barry Morris. Sex and
politics are a lot alike. You don't have to
be good at them to enjoy them.
(University Daily Kansan 94:9 Jan 25, 84)

GOLDWATER, Barry Morris. There are only
so many lies you can take, and now there
has been one too many. Nixon should get
his ass out of the White House—today
(after leaving a conference with Nixon
before his resignation as president).
(Time 104:21 Aug 19, 74)

GOLDWATER, Barry Morris. This is a great
country where anybody can grow up to
be President—except me. (Chicago
Tribune 245:20 Sept 2, 77)

GOLDWATER, Barry Morris. You can't be
raised in the South, and not be a
segregationist. (New York Times 138:12
Oct 4, 88)

GOLDWATER, Barry Morris, Jr. Without a
sense of privacy, the Bill of Rights'
guarantees cease to function. (Time
110:17 July 18, 77)

GOLDWYN, Samuel. A verbal contract isn't
worth the paper it's written on.
(Washingtonian 14:154 Nov 78)

GOLDWYN, Samuel. If ya wanna send a
message, call Western Union. (Mother
Jones 2:61 Sept 77)

GOLEMBO, Eri. People will buy any
product that has been made smaller if it
retains the functionality of the larger
product and has a handle. (PC Magazine
5:148 Mar 25, 86)

GOMEZ, Eden Pastora. Anyone who
recommends invading Nicaragua is
insane. (Life 7:113 Jan 83)

GOMEZ, Lefty. If you don't throw it, they

can't hit it. (Washingtonian 15:141 Nov
79)

GONCALVES, Vasco dos Santos. Emotion
is not incompatible with lucidity. (Time
105:40 May 5, 75)

GONICK, Jean. For women, life is a series
of leaking tampons. (GQ 57:99 May 87)

GOODFELLOW, Geoff. The floppy disk is
the punch card of the Eighties. (Popular
Computing 4:28 Feb 28, 85)

GOODHART, Charles. Any measure of the
money supply that is officially controlled
promptly loses its meaning. (Chicago
Sun-Times 34:50 Feb 1, 82)

GOODMAN, Benny. Everything I own,
whatever I have accomplished, all that I
am, really, I owe to music. (People Weekly
9:80 Jan 23, 78)

GOODMAN, Ellen. It has begun to occur to
me that life is a stage I'm going through.
(Time 114:125 Dec 10, 79)

GOODWIN, Richard N. He's not even an
accidental president. He's a
double-misfortune president—president
by grace of the criminal code and modern
electronics (about Gerald R. Ford). (New
York 8:43 Aug 18, 75)

GORBACHEV, Mikhail S. History punishes
those who come late. (Vanity Fair 53:189
Feb 90)

GORBACHEV, Mikhail S. It is now clear that
he deserved the Nobel Prize (about
Andrei Sakharov). (Chicago Tribune
341:14 Section 1 Dec 19, 89)

GORBACHEV, Mikhail S. It is only now that
the real Perestroika begins (1990). (Time
135:29-30 Feb 19, 90)

GORBACHEV, Mikhail S. The guilt of Stalin
and his immediate entourage before the
party and the people for the wholesale
repressive measures and the acts of
lawlessness is enormous and
unforgivable. This is a message for all
generations. (Kansas City Star 5C Nov 2,
87) (108)

GORDIMER, Nadine. The facts are always
less than what really happened. (Time
110:93 Sept 19, 77)

GORMAN, Paul (Former commander of U.
S. Southern Command). You're not going
to knock off the Sandinistas with a
conventional force, and that's what the
Contras are. (Chicago Tribune 67:30
Section 1 Mar 8, 87)

GORTAZAR, Jesus. The bullfight is the only
thing that really begins on time in Mexico.
(Western Houseman 52:24 April 87)

GOSSAGE, Howard. The only fit work for an
adult is to save the world. (California
13:13 May 88)

GOTLIEB, Allan E. It's never over till it's

over, and in the U.S. system of government it's never over. (New York Times 138:10 Jan 12, 89)

GOTTLIEB, Robert. The editor of the New Yorker is treated as a living god. (Manhattan, Inc. 7:57 June 90)

GRABLE, Betty. There are only two reasons for my success, and I'm standing on them. (New Orleans 10:108 July 31, 76)

GRACE, J. Peter. Congressmen have two goals, to be elected and to be re-elected. (Texas Observer 77:23 Sept 27, 85)

GRAHAM, Benjamin. (The stock market is) a Falstaffian joke that frequently degenerates into a madhouse. (Money 5:36 July 76)

GRAHAM, Benjamin. Never having to balance your checkbook (a definition of financial success). (Money 5:37 July 76)

GRAHAM, Bill. San Francisco is not a part of America. (Chicago Daily News Panorama 4 Dec 31, 21)

GRAHAM, Billy. I believe I have demonic forces opposed to me wherever I preach. (The Observer 9832:9 Feb 3, 80)

GRAHAM, Billy. In her own way she (Ethel Waters) did as much for race relations as any American in the 20th Century. (Chicago Tribune 245:5 Sept 2, 77)

GRAHAM, Billy. Most Houstonians will spend eternity in Hell. (Texas Monthly 6:154 Feb 78)

GRAHAM, Billy. Nixon in my judgement was a true intellectual. (Chicago Tribune Magazine 46 Nov 6, 77)

GRAHAM, Billy. The pressures of being a well-known clergyman are unbelievable, and I'd like to escape to heaven if I could. (Chicago Tribune Magazine 32 Nov 6, 77)

GRAHAM, Billy. Transcendental Meditation is evil because...it opens space within you for the devil. (Ms 6:50 July 77)

GRAHAM, Billy. When you say that you pray and stop a hurricane, a few things like that, it gives the press something to distort (on Pat Robertson). (Newsweek 108:23 Oct 13, 86)

GRAHAM, Katharine. This company (The Washington Post) is not now and never has been antiunion. (Newsweek 86:44 Dec 22, 75)

GRAMM, Phil. Balancing the budget is like going to heaven—everybody wants to balance the budget but nobody wants to do what you have to do to balance the budget. (Kansas City Star 107:6B June 29, 87)

GRANT, Cary. My formula for living is quite simple. I get up in the morning and go to bed at night. In between times, I occupy myself as best I can. (Los Angeles Times Calendar 39 June 11, 78)

GRASS, Gunter. If you don't face it, it means two things: you lost the war and you've also lost the ability to make clear why it happened (about Vietnam). (Time 112:77 Nov 13, 78)

GRAY, Francine du Plessix. Women are the only exploited group in history who have been idealized into powerlessness. (Time 111:76 Jan 30, 78)

GREELEY, Andrew. Only a charlatan or a lunatic would be hopeful about the present state of Catholicism. (Psychology Today 10:51 June 76)

GREEN, Mark. While piously proclaiming an interest in the public good, the bar's Canons of Ethics have operated as Canons of Profits. (Time 110:52 Aug 8, 77)

GREENBERG, David. An oldtimer is someone who can remember when a naughty child was taken to the woodshed instead of to a psychiatrist. (American Opinion 18:29 Nov 75)

GREENBERG, Mike. Half of San Antonio's population is of Mexican descent; the other half just eats that way. (Chicago 24:112 Sept 75)

GREENBERG, Stanley. Writing isn't an exact science. It is more like chasing a butterfly you're not sure you want to catch. (Writer's Digest 56:5 May 76)

GREENE, Graham. God forbid people should read our books to find the juicy passages. (The Observer 9816:11 Oct 14, 79)

GREENE, Graham. There is far more religious faith in Russia than in England. (The Observer 9850:13 June 8, 80)

GREENFELD, Josh. Cinema is a form of Danish. (Time 111:97 April 10, 78)

GREENFELD, Josh. New Jersey looks like the back of an old radio. (Time 111:97 April 10, 78)

GREENFIELD, Jeff. You will get what you want if you vote for the candidate who says exactly the opposite of what you most deeply believe. (Penthouse 10:123 Nov 78)

GREENSPAN, Alan. The current level of inflation, let alone an increase, is not acceptable (1989). (Time 133:51 Mar 6, 89)

GREENSPAN, Alan. When I met Ayn Rand, I was a free enterpriser in the Adam Smith sense, impressed with the theoretical structure and efficiency of markets. What she did was to make me see that capitalism is not only efficient and practical, but also moral. (Newsweek 85:61 Feb 24, 75)

GREER, Germaine. Everyone I know is either married or dotty. (The Observer 9790:10 April 15, 79)

GREER, Germaine. I love men like some people like good food or wine. (The Observer 9782:10 Feb 18, 79)

GREER, Germaine. It's sheer myth that feminists are anti-child—we're the only people who're going to give children a better deal. (People Weekly 5:72 Jan 26, 76)

GREER, Germaine. Security is when everything is settled, when nothing can happen to you; security is a denial of life. (Redbook 148:57 Mar 77)

GREIDER, William. When the Federal Reserve was created, the realm of acceptable political discourse shrank. (Harvard Business Review 66:23 May/June 88)

GRIFFITH, Calvin. He's the P.T. Barnum of baseball. (about Charles Oscar Finley). (Time 106:42 Aug 18, 75)

GROENING, Matt. The people who are my fans now frighten me (about The Simpsons). (Newsweek 115:June 18, 90

GROMYKO, Andrei. Age is a stubborn thing and there is no getting away from it. (Manchester Guardian Weekly 141:1 July 9, 89)

GRUBER, Jack. Integration is not something you win at, it's something you work at. (Time 110:21 Oct 31, 77)

GUARE, John. Innocence is ignorance where you're not getting caught. (Village Voice 22:35 Aug 15, 77)

GUBER, Peter. In Hollywood, it's all just the size of your dick. (Vanity Fair 53:194 Feb 90)

GUCCI, Aldo. We are not businessmen, we are poets. (Town & Country 131:193 Dec 77)

GUEST, Lucy Cochrane (C.Z.). I think manners are the most important thing in life. (Mother Jones 2:10 Aug 77)

GUEVARA, Nacha. In life the things you want always arrive after you've stopped waiting. (Chicago Sun-Times 32:8 Section 4 July 1, 79)

GUGGENHEIM, Peggy. I don't like art today, I think it has gone to hell. (W 8:24 Oct 12, 79)

GUMBEL, Bryant. I love to gamble, it's a real weakness. (US 3:64 Sept 9, 85)

GUND, Gordon. The greatest satisfactions in life come from endeavors which directly or indirectly have a positive impact on others at the same time they impact on you. (Town & Country 143:161 Dec 89)

GUNTHER, John. All happiness depends on a leisurely breakfast. (Washingtonian 14:154 Nov 78)

GURFEIN, Murray. A cantankerous press must be suffered by those in authority in order to preserve freedom of expression and the right of the people to know. (Time 114:59 Dec 31, 79)

GURLEY, George H., Jr. Crime is one of the country's few growth industries. (Kansas City Star 111:1C Oct 4, 90)

GURLEY, George H., Jr. Our problem is that we live in a culture dominated by shameless bad taste. (Kansas City Times 120:1B Nov 3, 87)

GURLEY, George H., Jr. The omnipresence of vulgar sexual imagery reflects our taste in love in the same way that Chicken McNuggets represent our taste in food. (Kansas City Times 120:1B Nov 3, 87)

GUTHRIE, Arlo. If we want to hold hands around the world, we have to learn to use both hands. (Village Voice 26:28 Feb 18, 81)

GUTHRIE, Arlo. The world has shown me what it has to offer...It's a nice plce to visit, but I wouldn't want to live there. (Rolling Stone 268:36 June 29, 78)

GUTHRIE, Janet. I am a racing driver who happens to be a woman. (New York Times 125:6 Section 5 April 18, 76)

GUTHRIE, Woody. You can't write a good song about a whorehouse unless you been in one. (Los Angeles Times Calendar 82 Mar 26, 78)

GYSI, Gregor. I have never been in America in my life, but I think it is a country that should not give up its responsibilities for Europe. (New York Times 139:1 Dec 15, 89)

HAGEDORN, Tom. As far as I'm concerned, environmentalists and food stamp cheaters are the same thing. (Potomac: Magazine of the Washington Post 4 Mar 7, 76)

HAGGARD, Merle. I was born the running kind, with leaving always on my mind. (Village Voice 25:8 July 2, 80)

HAHN, Jessica. I spoke with God and asked for a miracle. The next day, Playboy called. (Chicago Tribune 54:22 Section 1 Feb 23, 89)

HAIG, Alexander M. If you knew the true story, it would make your hair stand on end (on President Reagan's illness following the 1981 assassination attempt on his life). (Chicago Tribune 282:27 Oct 9, 87)

HAIG, Alexander M. Military service and public service are not unakin. (The Observer 9776:10 Jan 7, 79)

HAIG, Alexander M. The arms race is the only game in town. (Esquire 90:31 Sept

26, 78)

HAIG, Alexander M. The next war could be a come-as-you-are party. (Esquire 90:31 Sept 26, 78)

HAILE SELASSIE I, Emperor of Ethiopia. Death changes everything, sweeps everything away. Even mistakes. (Newsweek 86:32 Sept 8, 75)

HALDEMAN, Harry Robbins. He'd (George Bush) do anything for the cause. (Time 132:28 Nov 21, 88)

HALDEMAN, Harry Robbins. I'll approve of whatever will work and am concerned with results—not methods. (Time 103:12 Mar 11, 74)

HALES, E. E. Y. Hell is where you are free to be yourself, and nothing but yourself (commenting in his novel Chariot of Fire). (Time 109:92 Mar 7, 77)

HALEY, Jack. I don't believe there's no business like show business. (Newsweek 93:90 June 18, 79)

HALL, Daryl. It's socially immoral for a white person to act like a black person. (Creem 9:34 Aug 77)

HALL, Donald. Less is more, in prose as in architecture. (Writer's Digest 58:8 Nov 78)

HALL, Jerry. Often I think the main point of life is having something to talk about at dinner. (US 3:64 July 1, 85)

HALL, Joyce. Good taste is good business. (Village Voice 27:15 Feb 10, 82)

HALL, Keith W. The word 'necessary' seldom is. (Washingtonian 15:141-42 Nov 79)

HALL, Monty. You can learn more about America by watching one half-hour of Let's Make a Deal than you can by watching Walter Cronkite for an entire month. (Time 115:85 Feb 18, 80)

HAMILTON, Lee. Those involved, whether public official or private citizen, had no doubt they were acting on the authority of the President of the United States. (Kansas City Star 107:6B June 10, 87)

HAMMER, Armand. Having spent my lifetime fighting injustice, this vindication reinforces my abiding faith in the American system of justice (upon being pardoned for illegal campaign contributions to Richard Nixon's 1972 presidential campaign). (Chicago Tribune 243:27 Aug 31, 89)

HAMMER, Armand. Luck seems to come to the guy who works 14 hours a day, seven days a week. (Kansas City Star 108:1F Dec 27, 87)

HANSEN, George. Firearms are not the problem. People are. (American Opinion 18:29 Sept 75)

HARDEN, Frank. Every time you come up with a terrific idea, you find that someone else thought of it first. (Washingtonian 14:154 Nov 78)

HARDING, Warren Gamaliel. Our most dangerous tendency is to expect too much of government, and at the same time to do for it too little (inaugural address—1921). (Christian Science Monitor 69:14 Jan 20, 77)

HARE, David. Critics believe in the right to judge, to which the artist cannot possibly accede. (Connoisseur 216:124 Feb 86)

HARLOW, Bryce N. Our only protection against the presidency is the character of the president. (Washingtonian 11:103 June 76)

HARRELL, John R. The black man's angry, the yellow man's angry. Everybody's angry but the white man, and he's asleep. (Time 114:8 Nov 5, 79)

HARRELSON, Ken. Baseball is the only sport I know that when you're on offense, the other team controls the ball. (Sports Illustrated 44:14 Sept 6, 76)

HARRIMAN, Averell. The Russians are not nuts, they are not crazy people, they're not Hitler. But they are trying to dominate the world by their ideology and we are killing the one instrument which we have to fight that ideology, the CIA. (W 4:16 Nov 16, 75)

HARRIS, Fred. Our current economic problems are not a failure of the system, they are a failure of economic leadership. (Village Voice 20:28 July 7, 75)

HARRIS, Fred. Sometimes it seems we are willing to prop up any two-bit dictator who can afford the price of a pair of sunglasses. (Time 106:25 Dec 22, 75)

HARRIS, Fred. The basic issue in 1976 is privilege. It's time to take the rich off welfare. (Newsweek 86:24 Dec 22, 75)

HARRIS, Fred. We've got to dismantle the monster (about the CIA). (Time 106:24 Sept 29, 75)

HARRIS, Marvin. Women's liberation did not create the working woman; rather the working woman—especially the working housewife—created women's liberation. (Time 119:89 Jan 11. 82)

HARRIS, Patricia Roberts. Poverty is not so much the absence of money as the absence of aspiration, of the knowledge that it is possible to go anywhere else. (Skeptic 19:10 May 77)

HARRIS, Sidney J. The paradox in games is that most games are no fun unless you take them seriously; but when you take them seriously, they cease being games. (Chicago Daily News 8 May 5, 77)

HARRIS, Sydney J. Any philosophy that can be 'put in a nutshell' belongs there. (Washingtonian 14:154 Nov 78)

HARRIS, Sydney J. It is not criminals, but laws that are the worst enemy of Law. (Chicago Daily News 8 May 5, 77)

HARRIS, Sydney J. The art of living consists in knowing which impulses to obey and which must be made to obey. (Kansas City Times 109:28 Jan 4, 77)

HARRISON, Elizabeth (former wife of Rex Harrison). Rex is the only man in the world who would disdainfully send back the wine in his own home. (Time 106:41 Dec 29, 75)

HARRISS, Joseph. Parisians have always recognized the human need for the superfluous. (Time 110:38 July 18, 77)

HART, Gary. Follow me around. I don't care. I'm serious. If anybody wants to put a tail on me, go ahead. They'd be very bored. (Kansas City Star 107:1B May 10, 87)

HART, Gary. I think it's time we as Americans kind of grow up...and instead of expecting our leaders to be perfect, we are going to have to expect them to be human. (Lawrence (Kansas) Journal-World 130:1A Jan 8, 87)

HART, Gary. It was a bad mistake. It was a damn fool mistake. But I don't think it disqualifies me from governing this country (about Donna Rice). (Chicago Tribune 6:15 Jan 6, 88)

HART, Gary. To get the government off your back, get your hands out of the government's pockets. (Newsweek 90:36 Nov 7, 77)

HART, Gary. We can't be defensive on defense. (New York 19:26 May 5, 86)

HASKINS, Caryl. It's funny that we often value what is rare and specialized. What is truly precious is what is common and unspecialized. (Washington Post 70:H7 Feb 13, 77)

HATCH, Orrin. Capital punishment is our society's recognition of the sanctity of human life. (Newsweek 111:15 June 6, 88)

HATFIELD, Mark. If one argues that a prisoner deserves whatever he or she gets in prison, then one must also be prepared to argue that society deserves what it gets when the prisoner is eventually released. (USA Today 1:10A Jan 12, 83)

HAUPTMANN, Bruno Richard. I have said it all, I am innocent. There is nothing else I could tell. (New York 9:76 Nov 22, 76)

HAUSER, Philip M. (Chicago) has lace pants in the front, and soiled drawers behind. (Chicago Tribune 71:1 Mar 12, 78)

HAVEL, Vaclav. You can help us most of all

if you help the Soviet Union on its irreversible but immensely complicated road to democracy. (Newsweek 115:28 Mar 5, 90)

HAWATMEH, Nayef. The Palestine Liberation Organization is returning to the golden age of unity, and the phase of divisiveness is gone forever (1987). (Chicago Tribune 110:9 April 20, 87)

HAWKINS, Erick. Dance is the most beautiful metaphor of existence in the world. (New York Times 128:12 Section 2 July 1, 79)

HAWKINS, Paula. Nicaragua is involved in an insidious plot to cripple our youth in America (1985). (Mother Jones 10:11 Aug 85)

HAYAKAWA, Samuel Ichiye. If you see in any given situation only what everyone else can see, you can be said to be so much a representative of your culture that you are a victim of it. (Phoenix 18:94 April 83)

HAYAKAWA, Samuel Ichiye. There is only one thing age can give you, and that is wisdom. (New West 1:17 July 5, 76)

HAYDEN, Thomas. During the 1960s, we fought the pigs. Now we fight the high price of bacon. (Newsweek 90:36 Nov 7, 77)

HAYDEN, Thomas. I don't believe that any defense contract ought to be cut in the face of mass unemployment. (US News & World Report 18:12 Nov 3, 75)

HAYDEN, Thomas. If it weren't for the Bill of Rights people like me would be in jail instead of running for office (commenting on his bid for the Senate). (Los Angeles Times 95:3 Part 1 Jan 5, 76)

HAYDEN, Thomas. Jerry Brown's mortal sin is that he is ahead of his time. (New West 6:184 Oct 31, 81)

HAYES, Helen. There is no racial or religious prejudice among people in the theater. The only prejudice is against bad actors, especially successful ones. (Time 114:85 Dec 17, 79)

HAYES, Woody. Football is about the only unifying force left in America today. (Life 2:87 Dec 79)

HAZZARD, Shirley. Nothing supplies the truth except the will for it. (Fame 1:38 Mar 90)

HEAL, Sylvia. The dark age of Thatcherism is drawing to a close (1990). (Newsweek 115:31 April 2, 90)

HEALEY, Denis. Mrs. Thatcher is doing for monetarism what the Boston Strangler did for door-to-door salesmen. (The Observer 9825:10 Dec 16, 79)

HEARST, Austine. After 40, a woman needs

a lover and a good facelift. And after 50, cash. (W 7:2 Oct 27, 78)

HEASTER, Jerry. Everybody says they want to go to heaven, but nobody wants to die to get there. (Kansas City Star 1E Nov 8, 87) (108)

HEATH, Edward. I started out studying music but very quickly went downhill and into politics. (Time 116:93 Sept 15, 80)

HEFFERAN, Colien. The woman who once saw marriage as a form of security now finds that she can provide her own security. (US News & World Report 85:83 Nov 27, 78)

HEFNER, Hugh Marston. I am an incurable romantic. (US 3:6 May 2, 88)

HEFNER, Hugh Marston. I'm not primarily an entrepreneurial businessman. I'm primarily a playboy philosopher. (Chicago Tribune 124:1 Section 1 May 3, 76)

HEFNER, Hugh Marston. I've had a bachelor party for 30 years, why do I need one now (upon his marriage in 1989). (Chicago Tribune 183:8 Section 1 July 2, 89)

HEFNER, Hugh Marston. If I told you, for example that Playboy, in its 22 years, was one of the major things that contributed to the women's movement, you might find it a mindboggler, but it happens to be true. (Chicago Tribune 124:1 Section 1 May 3, 76)

HEIDE, Wilma Scott. I do not refer to myself as a housewife for the reason that I did not marry a house. (Viva 4:26 Aug 77)

HEIDEGGER, Martin. He who does not know what homesickness is, cannot philosophize. (Time 107:59 June 7, 76)

HELLER, Joseph. If I could be clever on demand, I'd still be in advertising. (Life 2:16 June 79)

HELLER, Joseph. No one governs. Everyone performs. Politics has become a social world. (New York Times 128:15 Section 6 Mar 4, 79)

HELLER, Walter. By mid-year double digit inflation should be behind us (Jan 23, 1980). (Kansas City Star 102:9A Oct 12, 81)

HELLER, Walter. Only an ostrich could have missed the contradictions in Reaganomics. (Life 5:33 Jan 82)

HELLER, Walter. Waiting for supply-side economics to work is like leaving the landing lights on for Amelia Earhart. (Dun's Business Month 127:51 Feb 86)

HELLMAN, Lillian. I don't understand personal salvation. It seems to me a vain idea. (Rolling Stone 233:55 Feb 24, 77)

HELLMAN, Lillian. I think (Watergate and the McCarthy Era) are deeply connected, with Mr. Nixon being the connection, the rope that carries it all through. (New York Times 125:28 Nov 7, 75)

HELLMAN, Lillian. I would like to have had the courage to do what I wrote about. (American Theatre 1:13 May 84)

HELLMAN, Lillian. If I had to give young writers advice, I would say, Don't listen to writers talking about writing or about themselves. (Time 110:40 Sept 5, 77)

HELLMAN, Lillian. Nobody can argue any longer about the rights of women. It's like arguing about earthquakes. (Rolling Stone 233:56 Feb 24, 77)

HELLMAN, Lillian. We have no national memory. (Time 113:28 April 23, 79)

HELM, Levon. Music is medicine, and if the doctor is going to make house calls, he better know how to play. (Newsweek 90:102 Oct 31, 77)

HELMS, Jesse. If Environmental Action had its way, the American people would starve and freeze to death in the dark. (Chicago Sun-Times 31:2 June 5, 78)

HELMS, Richard McGarrah. I think he was yielding to that human impulse of the greater good (explaining why the CIA scientist in charge of the Chemical Weapons Division did not destroy shellfish toxin as ordered by President Nixon). (Rolling Stone 199:34 Nov 6, 75)

HELMS, Richard McGarrah. If I ever do decide to talk, there are going to be some very embarrassed people in this town, you can bet on that (commenting after testifying to the Watergate Committee on CIA involvement in domestic intelligence operations). (Newsweek 85:21 Feb 24, 75)

HELMS, Richard McGarrah. We're not in the Boy Scouts (about the Central Intelligence Agency). (The Atlantic 244:36 Aug 79)

HEMENWAY, Russell. He's (Jimmy Carter) the first president in recent history that would occupy the most important office in the world without any commitment to anybody. (New York 9:8 July 12, 76)

HEMINGWAY, Ernest. A writer must write what he has to say, not speak it. (Time 119:71 April 5, 82)

HEMINGWAY, Ernest. I know it means I will never have any dough but I know I shouldn't work in pictures when I go well enough in books. (American Film 6:12 May 81)

HEMINGWAY, Ernest. I wish him (James Jones) no luck at all and hope he goes out and hangs himself as soon as plausible. (Kansas City Star 106:1K Dec 29, 85)

HEMINGWAY, Ernest. If she (Marlene Dietrich) had nothing but her voice, she could break your heart with it. (Book Digest 5:99 April 78)

HEMINGWAY, Ernest. Make a thing as true as possible, and it will live. (New York Times Book Review 30 July 23, 78)

HEMINGWAY, Ernest. The first and final thing you have to do in this world is to last in it and not be smashed by it. (Kansas City Times 109:1A Feb 3, 77)

HEMINGWAY, Ernest. There are only three true sports: fencing, bullfighting and auto racing. Everything else is just a game. (D Magazine 11:143 June 84)

HEMINGWAY, Ernest. Writing is something that you never do as well as it can be done. (D Magazine 12:168 Mar 85)

HEMINGWAY, Mary. Books are helpful in bed. But they are not responsive (commenting on widowhood). (People Weekly 6:49 Dec 13, 76)

HEMINGWAY, Mary. I'm too old to waste my time being sentimental. (Time 110:41 July 25, 77)

HEMMINGS, David. Acting is a wonderful profession for immature people. (US 3:64 Mar 7, 88)

HENDERSON, Vivian Wilson. We have programs for combatting racial discrimination, but not for combatting economic class distinctions. (Time 107:71 Feb 9, 76)

HENDRIX, Jimi. It's funny the way most people love the dead. Once you are dead, you are made for life. (Rolling Stone 227:81 Dec 2, 76)

HENSHAW, Paul C. Gold is how you survive when everything else is down the drain. (New West 1:11 July 5, 76)

HEPBURN, Katharine. Acting really isn't a very high-class way to make a living, is it? (The Observer 9779:10 Jan 21, 79)

HEPBURN, Katharine. First God made England, Ireland and Scotland. That's when He corrected His mistakes and made Wales. (Time 112:69 Aug 7, 78)

HEPBURN, Katharine. I think that one terrifying thing that has happened now is that the truth has gone out of style. (Toronto Globe and Mail 138:1 Nov 28, 81)

HEPBURN, Katharine. Sometimes I wonder if men and women really suit each other. Perhaps they should live next door and just visit now and then. (Cosmopolitan 188:268 Feb 80)

HERNETT, Lance (Lucky). You can steal a cowboy's girlfriend, but never touch his hat or screw with his horse. (Phoenix 22:50 Mar 87)

HEROLD, Don. Many people have character who have nothing else.

(Chicago Sun-Times 32:25 July 14, 79)

HERZBERG, Donald. Never leave hold of what you've got until you've got hold of something else. (Washingtonian 14:155 Nov 78)

HERZOG, Werner. You should look straight at a film; that's the only way to see one. Film is not the art of scholars but of illiterates. (New York Times 126:D19 Sept 11, 77)

HESBURGH, Theodore. The Catholic University is where the church does its learning. (Newsweek 109:75 May 11, 87)

HESTON, Charlton. Acting is the oldest profession, no matter what claims are made by the other trade. (People Weekly 10:102 Sept 4, 78)

HESTON, Charlton. Truly, I would rather play a senator than be one. (US 3:64 Aug 26, 85)

HEWITT, Don. People are finding that truth is more fascinating than fiction. (US News & World Report 85:52 Nov 20, 78)

HIGGINSON, John. We now know there are a hundred causes of cancer, and eighty of them are cigarettes. (Texas Monthly 6:174 June 76)

HIGHTOWER, Jim. Bush was born on third base and he thinks he got there by hitting a triple. (Chicago Sun-Times 41:4 July 24, 88)

HILL, Clinton J. If I had reacted just a little bit quicker, I could have (saved Kennedy), I guess, and I'll live with that to my grave. (Chicago Tribune 341:16 Section 1 Dec 7, 75)

HILLMAN, Sidney. Politics is the science of how who gets what, when and why. (Rocky Mountain News 62:36 June 23, 80)

HINCKLEY, John W., Jr. I helped his presidency. After I shot him his polls went up 20 percent (about Ronald Reagan). (Kansas City Times 115:D1 Jan 1, 84)

HINTON, Deane R. Bobby proved himself to be a fine, young Democrat (about Roberto D'Aubuisson). (Newsweek 104:23 July 2, 84)

HITCHCOCK, Alfred Joseph. All actors should be treated like cattle. (Chicago Sun-Times 32:1 Section 3 Mar 4, 79)

HITCHCOCK, Alfred Joseph. Always make an audience suffer as much as possible. (Family Circle 44 Jan 12, 82)

HITCHCOCK, Alfred Joseph. Conversation is the enemy of good wine and food. (Time 112:99 Oct 9, 78)

HITCHCOCK, Alfred Joseph. I wouldn't be able to sleep nights if I thought I had to spend even $10 million on a picture...When you work with a smaller budget, you're forced to use ingenuity and imagination and you almost always come up with a better picture. (Chicago Tribune 339:16 Dec 5, 77)

HITCHCOCK, Alfred Joseph. Most people make mystery films. I don't. I make films of suspense. A surprise in a film takes 10 seconds, suspense takes up an hour. (Chicago Daily News 92:29 April 9, 76)

HITCHCOCK, Alfred Joseph. There is no terror in a bang, only in the anticipation of it. (Village Voice 23:1 Jan 23, 78)

HITCHENS, Ivon. My pictures are painted to be listened to. (The Observer 9787:14 Mar 25, 79)

HITLER, Adolf. You know, everybody has a price—and you'd be surprised how low it is. (New York Times Book Review 23 July 24, 77)

HO CHI MINH. It is better to sniff French dung for a while than to eat China's all our lives. (New York Times 128:1 Section 4 Feb 25, 79)

HOCHMANN, John L. After all, publishing is a business, literature is a happy accident. (New York Times Book Review 35 July 30, 78)

HOCKNEY, David. I'm a Puritan at heart. I also think I'm the world's most overrated, overpaid artist. (Newsweek 90:73 Nov 14, 77)

HOCKNEY, David. Three hundred homosexuals rule the world and I know every one of them. (Manchester Guardian Weekly 140:29 May 21, 89)

HODEL, Donald. (Environmentalism is) a crusade to stop all development in this country. (Wall Street Journal 56:1 Dec 17, 75)

HOFFA, James Riddle. I don't cheat nobody. I don't lie about nobody. I don't frame nobody. I don't talk bad about people. If I do, I tell 'em. So what the hell's people gonna try to kill me for? (Playboy 22:73 Dec 75)

HOFFA, James Riddle. The only guy who needs a bodyguard is a liar, a cheat, a guy who betrays friendship. (Time 106:63 Nov 24, 75)

HOFFER, Eric. I hang onto my prejudices. They are the testicles of my mind. (New York Times 128:9 Section 7 Jan 28, 79)

HOFFMAN, Abbie. The movie isn't over yet (1989). (Chicago Tribune 104:10 Section 2 April 14, 89)

HOFFMAN, Jack. He didn't die with a Rolex. He died with a full heart (about Abbie Hoffman). (Chicago Tribune 109:3 Section 1 April 19, 89)

HOFMANN, Hans. They are so good you would not know they were done by a woman (about Lee Krasner's art). (Newsweek 104:23 July 2, 84)

HOFSTADTER, Richard. The United States was the only country in the world that began with perfection and aspired to progress. (Wisconsin Trails 17:5 Winter 76)

HOLLAND, Jack. The tragedy of Northern Ireland is that it is now a society in which the dead console the living. (New York Times Magazine 39 July 15, 79)

HOLLOW, Norman. In the olden days the Indian peoples defended themselves with bows and arrows. Now, politics is the only way our rights can be developed. (New York Times 125:1 Section 1 Dec 21, 75)

HOLMES, Oliver Wendell. Taxes are the price that society pays for civilization. (Time 112:60 Sept 25, 78)

HOLTZMAN, Elizabeth. Government follows Newton's law of physics. Objects stay at rest until they're pushed. (Newsweek 96:27 Sept 8, 80)

HOOKS, Benjamin Lawson. If we don't solve this race problem, this country isn't going to ever rest in peace. (Newsweek 88:46 Nov 22, 76)

HOOVER, John Edgar. I regret to say that we of the FBI are powerless to act in cases of oral-genital intimacy, unless it has in some way obstructed interstate commerce. (New York 13:14 Oct 6, 80)

HOOVER, John Edgar. Justice is incidental to law and order. (USA Today 1:8A Mar 15, 83)

HOOVER, John Edgar. The cure for crime is not the electric chair but the high chair. (Chicago Sun-Times 29:76 July 9, 76)

HOPE, Bob. I don't think I'd do anything if it were a sacrifice. (Rolling Stone 311:47 Mar 20, 80)

HOPE, Bob. I think we're running out of perversions to put in film, and I'm looking forward to it (on pornographic movies). (Los Angeles Times 96:2 Part 1 Dec 30, 76)

HORN, Trevor. Kids want to buy records by people they want to mate with. (New York 17:22 Aug 20, 84)

HOROWITZ, Rachel. If you're a public employee and your job depends on public officials, you have to be in politics. (Newsweek 96:27 July 14, 80)

HOROWITZ, Vladimir. I had to go back to Russia before I died. (Time 127:56 May 5, 86)

HOROWITZ, Vladimir. You can't be serious 24 hours a day. You have to take half an hour or an hour a day to be childish. (Time 112:88 Oct 16, 78)

HOUDE, Camillien. A mob is like a river—it

never runs uphill. (Macleans 90:63 July 11, 77)

HOUSEMAN, John. There is no question but that Marlon Brando would have been America's Olivier if he had continued in the classical theater. (W 4:11 Dec 12, 75)

HOVING, Walter. It is in poor taste for a man to wear a diamond ring. (W Supplement 131 July 27, 87)

HOWARD, Robert T. The family hour seems to have become just another cop-out used by creative people to explain their failure. (Los Angeles Times 94:13 Part 4 Nov 4, 75)

HOWE, Sir Geoffrey. Finance must determine expenditure; expenditure must not determine finance. (The Observer 9799:9 June 17, 79)

HOWE, Tina. I'm not identified as a feminist writer, yet I'm convinced I am one—and one of the fiercer ones, to boot. (American Theatre 2:12 Sept 85)

HOWE, Tina. The love story is the acid test for any writer. (Elle 2:42 Nov 86)

HOYLE, Fred. There is a coherent plan in the universe, though I don't know what it's a plan for. (Omni 2:40 April 80)

HUA, Kuo-Feng. Peace cannot be got by begging. War cannot be averted by yielding. (The Observer 9819:9 Nov 4, 79)

HUBBARD, Elbert. Never explain. Your friends do not need it and your enemies will not believe you anyway. (Kansas City Star 97:4B Oct 10, 76)

HUBBARD, Elbert. This will never be a civilized country until we spend more money for books than we do for chewing gum. (Human Behavior 6:12 May 77)

HUBBARD, Harry. Making Texans stand in line for gas is like making Kansans stand in line for wheat (1979). (Newsweek 94:22 July 2, 79)

HUBBARD, L. Ron. If a man really wants to make a million dollars, the best way would be to start his own religion. (Time 127:86 Feb 10, 86)

HUFSTEDLER, Shirley. A man cannot be very kind unless he is also very strong. (New York Times Magazine 104 June 8, 80)

HUFSTEDLER, Shirley. There is a little nonsense and sloth in the seams and marrow of all human industry. (New York Times Magazine 94 June 8, 80)

HUGHES, Robert. Not even Pablo Picasso was Pablo Picasso. (Art & Antiques 87 Oct 84)

HUGO, Richard. In the world of imagination, all things belong. (New York Times Book Review 11 Mar 25, 79)

HUMPHREY, Hubert Horatio. A man with no tears is a man with no heart. (Chicago Tribune 263:2 Sept 20, 77)

HUMPHREY, Hubert Horatio. Compassion is not weakness and concern for the unfortunate is not socialism. (Time 111:25 Jan 23, 78)

HUMPHREY, Hubert Horatio. I would rather be honestly wrong than to be a deliberate hypocrite. (New Times 10:72 Feb 6, 78)

HUMPHREY, Hubert Horatio. Life was not meant to be endured, but enjoyed. (New Times 10:51 Feb 6, 78)

HUMPHREY, Hubert Horatio. Oh, my friend, it isn't what they take away from you that counts—it's what you do with what you have left. (Newsweek 89:43 July 25, 77)

HUMPHREY, Hubert Horatio. Politics isn't a matter of making love. It's making choices. (Newsweek 91:22 Jan 23, 78)

HUMPHREY, Hubert Horatio. The biggest corruption in politics, friends, is not money. It's publicity. (New York 9:100 May 10, 76)

HUMPHREY, Hubert Horatio. The greatest gift of life is friendship and I have received it. (Time 110:23 Nov 7, 77)

HUMPHREY, Hubert Horatio. The hardest job for a politician today is to have the courage to be moderate. (Time 111:22-24 Jan 23, 78)

HUMPHREY, Hubert Horatio. The Senate is a place filled with goodwill and good intentions, and if the road to hell is paved with them, then it's a pretty good detour. (Newsweek 91:23 Jan 23, 78)

HUMPHREY, Hubert Horatio. The time has arrived for the Democratic Party to get out of the shadow of states' rights and walk forthrightly into the bright sunshine of human rights (at the 1948 Democratic National Convention). (Time 111:22 Jan 23, 78)

HUMPHREY, Hubert Horatio. We made judgements about that part of the world (Southeast Asia) based on our experience in Europe. We were a world power with a half-world knowledge. (Time 105:20 May 12, 75)

HUNDLEY, William G. The worst defense lawyers I know are those who become convinced their clients are innocent. (Time 111:89 Mar 6, 78)

HUNG, Tran Van (Vietnamese refugee). We are shrubs, planted in a new place, needing care and water to grow again. (Newsweek 94:52 July 2, 79)

HUNGATE, William. The electorate knows more and believes less and expresses it louder than at any time in history. (Wall Street Journal 56:1 April 28, 76)

HUNT, Everette Howard. No one is entitled to the truth. (Rolling Stone 239:40 May 19, 77)

HUNT, Haroldson Lafayette. Money is just something to make bookkeeping convenient. (Time 104:44 Dec 9, 74)

HUNT, Nelson Bunker. A billion dolalrs isn't what it used to be. (Life 7:39 Jan 83)

HUNT, Nelson Bunker. Money never meant anything to us. It was just sort of how we kept score. (Dun's Business Month 127:50 Feb 86)

HUNT, Nelson Bunker. People who know how much they're worth aren't usually worth that much. (Time 115:56 May 12, 80)

HUNTER, Ross. Every one of us in Hollywood is overpaid. (W 8:2 Mar 16, 79)

HURT, Mary Beth. Acting is like a sexual disease. You get it and you can't get rid of it. (US 3:6 Oct 5, 87)

HUSSEIN, Saddam. Kuwait belongs to Iraq, and we will never give it up even if we have to fight over it for one thousand years. (Time 136:26 Oct 8, 90)

HUSSEIN, Saddam. We would rather die than be humiliated, and we will pluck out the eyes of those who attack the Arab nation. (Chicago Tribune 227:17 Section 1 Aug 15, 90)

HUSSEIN, KING OF JORDAN. It's amusing. The Americans have changed Presidents six times since I've been King. And they talk to the Arabs about stability? (People Weekly 6:122 Dec 13, 76)

HUSTON, John. (Charles Bronson is) a hand grenade with the pin pulled. (Time 111:52 Jan 9, 78)

HUTTON, Barbara. All the unhappiness in my life has been caused by men. (New York Times 128:1 May 13, 79)

HUXLEY, Thomas. It is the customary fate of new truths to begin as heresies and to end as superstitions. (Omni 2:36 June 80)

HYLAND, William G. Protectionism is the ally of isolationism, and isolationism is the Dracula of American foreign policy. (New York Times 136:2 May 17, 87)

IACOCCA, Lee A. A little righteous anger really brings out the best in the American personality. (Cleveland Magazine 12:149 Nov 83)

IACOCCA, Lee A. Don Regan shouldn't be president of the U.S.—and he is. Make no mistake about it. (US 3:17 Sept 22, 86)

IACOCCA, Lee A. I never invent anything any more. Everything I do is to meet a law. (Time 114:71 Oct 22, 79)

IACOCCA, Lee A. The free-enterprise system has gone to hell. (Time 114:74 Oct 8, 79)

IANNI, Francis (American sociologist). As in business, politics and education, there will be equal opportunities in crime. You can't have Bella Abzugs without Bonnie Parkers. (Time 106:8 Dec 1, 75)

IBARRURI, Dolores (Spanish Civil War activist). It is better to die on your feet than live on your knees. (Time 109:50 May 23, 77)

IGUINIZ, Javier (Peruvian economist). The growth of capitalism is the same as the growth of world poverty. (Time 106:34 Sept 1, 75)

INGERSOLL, Ralph. The owners of newspapers don't give a damn who's president. (Progressive 49:50 June 30, 85)

INOUYE, Daniel. I see it as a chilling story, a story of deceit and duplicity and the arrogant disregard of the rule of law. (Kansas City Star 107:5A Aug 4, 86)

IONESCO, Eugene. Basically I think it is stupid not to believe in God. (Harvard Magazine 89:24 Nov 86)

IRANI, C. R. The only protection for a free press is the courage to demand it. (Chicago Tribune 233:4 Section 2 Aug 21, 77)

IRVING, John. I think those of us who into our adult lives maintain good relations with our parents probably do it at the expense of total honesty. (New York Times Book Review 3 Aug 16, 81)

IRVING, John. Let no one forget that when I say I'm only a storyteller, I'm not being humble. (New York Times 138:16 April 25, 89)

IZAWA, Osamu. The irony is that no matter how much the American companies claim their products are better than the Japanese, the American public may not believe so. (Newsweek 99:69 April 12, 82)

JACKSON, Glenda. The important thing about acting is to be able to laugh and cry on cue. (Kansas City Star 110:D-1 May 7, 90)

JACKSON, Jack. No rule is ever so good, or so well written, or covers so many contingencies, that it can't be replaced by another, much better, more appropriate rule (with the exception of this rule). (Washingtonian 14:26 Dec 78)

JACKSON, Jesse. A school system without parents at its foundation is just like a bucket with a hole in it. (Time 112:46 July 10, 78)

JACKSON, Jesse. Affirmative action is a moot point if you don't learn to read and write. (Time 114:42 Aug 6, 79)

JACKSON, Jesse. Apartheid is violence by definition. (Newsweek 94:36 Aug 13, 79)

JACKSON, Jesse. If we can have a Miss America, we can have a Mr. President. (Philadelphia 74:176 Nov 83)

JACKSON, Jesse. In a hot war we (Blacks) die first; in a cold war, we starve first. (Newsweek 94:27 Sept 3, 79)

JACKSON, Jesse. People in South Africa only have the Bible as a constitution. (Chicago Sun-Times 32:32 July 20, 79)

JACKSON, Jesse. We too often condemn blacks who succeed and excel, calling them Uncle Toms. The ideal ought to be for all of us to succeed and excel. (Sepia 25:12 Sept 76)

JACKSON, Jesse. What does it matter if we have a new book or an old book, if we open neither? (Time 112:46 July 10, 78)

JACKSON, Jesse. Whether I win or lose, American politics will never be the same. (Time 124:26 Dec 31, 84)

JACKSON, Maynard. If Richard Nixon were black, he would be catching so much hell, he would rather be in jail. (Sepia 24:10 Jan 75)

JACKSON, Reggie. Hitting is better than sex. (Esquire 89:98 Mar 1, 78)

JACKSON, Reggie. I don't mind getting beaten, but I hate to lose. (Sepia 26:10 Mar 77)

JACOB, John. Reaganomics is giving voodoo a bad name. (Lawrence (Kansas) Journal-World 124:5A Nov 7, 82)

JACOBS, Andrew, Jr. (Ralph) Nader has become a legend in his own mind. (Time 112:21 Aug 7, 78)

JAGGER, Bianca. What do I really want as a woman? I want it all. (Playboy 26:186 Jan 79)

JAGGER, Mick. I'd rather be dead than sing Satisfaction when I'm 45. (People Weekly 7:58 May 2, 77)

JAGGER, Mick. Keith and I are two of the nicest people we know. (Creem 10:55 Jan 78)

JAGGER, Mick. Politics, like the legal system, is dominated by old men. (Life 2:117 Dec 79)

JAGGER, Mick. We will probably be making albums until we enter some sort of future senior-citizens facility. (Time 118:61 Sept 7, 81)

JAMES, Clive. Eloquence might get you started with a woman but it is often taciturnity that seals the bargain. (Chicago Tribune 19:3 Section 5 Jan 19, 87)

JAMES, Clive. For the lost soul, the university is the modern monastery. (The New Yorker 62:95 Dec 29, 86)

JAMES, Clive. She (Marilyn Monroe) was good at playing abstract confusion in the same way a midget is good at being short. (Details 8:25 Oct 89)

JAMES, Henry (attributed by William L. Shirer). It's a complex fate, being an American. (New York Times Book Review 25 July 24, 77)

JAMES, P. D. I've never met a stupid person who liked detective stories. (Chiago Tribune 35:1 Section 14 Feb 4, 90)

JAMISON, Judith. Every dancer lives on the threshold of chucking it. (New York Times Magazine 148 Dec 5, 76)

JANEWAY, Eliot. The thrill of making a fast buck follows only the thrill of love at first sight. Everyone needs to take an occasional fling with money...and with love. (Chicago Tribune 95:14 April 5, 77)

JANKLOW, William. The only way we want to give them arms is dropping them from the bay of a B-1 bomber. (Newsweek 109:17 Mar 16, 87)

JANOV, Arthur. The world is having a nervous breakdown. Valium is the only glue that holds it together. (Rolling Stone 219:19 Aug 12, 76)

JARUZELSKI, Wojceich. Thank goodness we don't live in medieval times when people fight wars over ideas. (Time 119:43 Jan 4, 82)

JARUZELSKI, Wojciech. Our country is on the edge of the abyss (declaring martial law). (Newsweek 99:49 Jan 4, 82)

JARVIS, Felton (Elvis Presly's producer). It's like someone just came up and told me there aren't going to be any more cheeseburgers in the world (commenting on Elvis Presley's death). (Country Music 7:36 Dec 77)

JARVIS, Howard. I didn't promise anybody that Prop 13 would reduce rent. (Newsweek 93:71 June 4, 79)

JARVIS, Howard. The only way to cut Government spending is not to give them the money to spend in the first place. (New West 3:32 July 3, 78)

JENKINS, Robin. It is not the goodness of saints that makes us feel there is hope for humanity: it is the goodness of obscure men. (New York Times Book Review 14 Feb 3, 80)

JENNINGS, Waylon. Honesty is something you can't wear out. (Country Music 7:55 Jan 79)

JEROME, Jerome K. It is always the best policy to speak the truth, unless of course you are an exceptionally good liar. (Kansas City Star 97:26 May 2, 77)

JEROME, Jerome K. It is impossible to enjoy idling thoroughly unless one has plenty of work to do. (Rocky Mountain

News 79:86 July 10, 80)

JOHN, Elton. People in England are so
bloody nosey. (The Observer 9820:10
Nov 11, 79)

JOHN PAUL I, POPE. If I hadn't been a
bishop, I would have wanted to be a
journalist. (Time 112:80 Sept 11, 78)

JOHN PAUL I, POPE. If someone had told
me I would be Pope one day, I would have
studied harder. (The Observer 9761:14
Sept 24, 78)

JOHN PAUL I, POPE. If St. Paul returned to
the world now as a journalist he would not
only direct Reuters but seek time on
television. (The Observer 9758:9 Sept 3,
78)

JOHN PAUL I, POPE. Those who treat
theology as a human science rather than
a sacred science, or exaggerate their
freedom, lack faith. (Time 112:66 Sept 4,
78)

JOHN PAUL II, Pope. Social injustice and
unjust social structures exist only because
individuals and groups of individuals
deliberately maintain or tolerate them.
(Kansas City Star 107:10A Sept 14, 87)

JOHN PAUL II, POPE. It is the right of the
faithful not to be troubled by theories and
hypotheses that they are not expert in
judging or that are easily simplified or
manipulated by public opinion. (Time
114:68 Oct 22, 79)

JOHN PAUL II, POPE. Our times demand
not to enclose ourselves in inflexible
borders, especially when human good is
concerned. (New York Times 128:1 June
11, 79)

JOHN PAUL II, POPE. Priesthood is
forever—we do not return the gift once
given. (Time 114:21 Oct 15, 79)

JOHN PAUL II, POPE. There is but one
thing more dangerous than sin: the
murder of man's sense of sin. (New York
Times 128:7 April 2, 79)

JOHN PAUL II, POPE. Violence always
delays the day of justice (to the IRA). (The
Observer 9814:1 Sept 30, 79)

JOHNS, Glynnis. For me, most relationships
with men have been like pregnancies—
they last about nine months. (Chicago
Tribune 226:2 Section 5 Aug 14, 77)

JOHNSON, Claudia Alta (Taylor). A
politician ought to be born a foundling
and remain a bachelor. (Time 106:56 Dec
1, 75)

JOHNSON, Claudia Alta (Taylor). The First
Lady is an unpaid public servant elected
by one person: her husband.
(Washington Post 266:K7 Aug 28, 77)

JOHNSON, Flora. There is nothing like
death. Everything that approaches it is

metaphor. (Chicago 25:115 June 30, 76)

JOHNSON, Haynes. As work and space
expand and collide they breed their own
reaction. (Washington Post 252:A3 Aug
14, 77)

JOHNSON, Haynes. Jimmy Carter met the
press and they were his (commenting
after Carter's first press conference as
President). (Time 109:11 Feb 11, 77)

JOHNSON, Lyndon Baines. Boys, it is just
like the Alamo. Somebody should have
by God helped those Texans. I'm going to
Viet Nam. (Time 105:28 May 12, 75)

JOHNSON, Lyndon Baines. Cast your
bread upon the waters and the sharks'll
eat it. (D Magazine 10:7 Jan 83)

JOHNSON, Lyndon Baines. I never
believed that Oswald acted alone,
although I can accept that he pulled the
trigger. (Skeptic 9:55 Sept 75)

JOHNSON, Lyndon Baines. I never trust a
man unless I've got his pecker in my
pocket. (Village Voice 21:16 Nov 8, 76)

JOHNSON, Lyndon Baines. I'd druther
have him (J. Edgar Hoover) inside the tent
pissin' out than outside pissin' in.
(Washingtonian 13:221 Mar 78)

JOHNSON, Lyndon Baines. I'm not going
to be the first President to lose a war.
(Time 105:28 May 12, 75)

JOHNSON, Lyndon Baines. If Walter
Cronkite would say on television what he
says on radio, he would be the most
powerful man in America. (Newsweek
93:91 April 30, 79)

JOHNSON, Lyndon Baines. If you don't
blow your horn, somebody will steal it.
(TV Guide 25:A4 Dec 24, 78)

JOHNSON, Lyndon Baines. Killing, rioting,
and looting are contrary to the best
traditions of this country. (Texas Monthly
3:93 Dec 75)

JOHNSON, Lyndon Baines. The most
important thing a man has to tell you is
what he is not telling you. (Time 114:13
Aug 20, 79)

JOHNSON, Philip. All cultures that can be
called cultures have built monuments.
(Time 113:59 Jan 8, 79)

JOHNSON, Philip. Houston is only more
interesting than Dallas because I've built
more there. (Texas Homes 9:85 May 85)

JOHNSON, Sterling. In the heroin business,
the Mexicans are the short-order cooks.
The French are the chefs. (Rolling Stone
204:30 Jan 15, 76)

JOHNSTON, Jill. All women are lesbians
except those who don't know it yet. (Ms
4:80 Nov 75)

JOHNSTON, Jill. Feminism at heart is a
massive complaint. Lesbianism is the

solution. (Time 106:39 Sept 8, 75)

JONES, Bertram Hays. Football plays are like accounting problems. They baffle you at first, but once you've learned the system they're easy. (People Weekly 6:36 Dec 27/Jan 3, 77)

JONES, Bob. We're in a bad fix in America when eight evil old men and one vain and foolish woman can speak a verdict on American liberties. (The American Lawyer 5:93 Sept 83)

JONES, David. Man is the only maker, neither beast nor angel share this dignity with him. (New York Times 128:9 Section 7 Feb 18, 79)

JONES, Franklin P. One thing in which the sexes are equal is in thinking that they're not. (Reader's Digest 108:261 May 76)

JONES, James Thurman. I am God; there is no other God and religion is the opium of the people. (New York Times 128:A17 Nov 21, 78)

JONES, Thomas. Friends may come and go, but enemies accumulate. (Washingtonian 14:155 Nov 78)

JONG, Erica. Everyone has talent. What is rare is the courage to follow the talent to the dark place where it leads. (Los Angeles Times 97:6 Part 4 Feb 3, 78)

JONG, Erica. I cannibalized real life. (Newsweek 85:71 May 5, 75)

JONG, Erica. I want to set an example of a woman poet who doesn't kill herself. (Kansas City Star 117:6B Dec 3, 84)

JONG, Erica. If Jackie Kennedy did not exist, the press would have to invent her. (In The Know 1:9 Nov 75)

JONG, Erica. It seems to me that sooner or later all intelligent women become feminists. (New York Times 125:32 Nov 8, 75)

JONG, Erica. The trouble is, if you don't risk anything, you risk even more. (Cosmopolitan 196:332 Oct 83)

JONG, Erica. You don't have to beat a woman if you can make her feel guilty. (Viva 4:28 April 77)

JORDAN, Barbara. My faith in the Constitution is whole—complete—total. (Newsweek 88:70 July 4, 76)

JORDAN, Hamilton. Historically, I think there probably is an inferiority complex associated with being Southern. (Esquire 89:79 Mar 28, 78)

JORDAN, Hamilton. If after the inauguration you find a Cy Vance as Secretary of State and Zbigniew Brzezinski (of Columbia University) as head of national security, then I would say we failed. And I'd quit. But that's not going to happen. (Christian Science Monitor 69:3 Dec 6, 76)

JORDAN, Hamilton. Perhaps the strongest feeling in this country today (1972) is the general distrust and disillusionment of government and politicians at all levels. (New York Times 128:A17 July 19, 79)

JOUBERT, Joseph. Space is to place as eternity is to time. (Omni 2:39 April 80)

JUNG, Carl Gustav. Nothing has a stronger influence on their children than the unlived lives of the parents. (Boston 70:97 June 78)

JUNOT, Philippe. Society's ills come from people having lost the taste for enjoyment. (Rolling Stone 271:16 Aug 10, 78)

KADISHAI, Yechiel. We want to settle so many Jews that the West Bank and Gaza can't be given back to the Arabs. (USA Today 1:10A April 11, 83)

KAEL, Pauline. Hollywood is the only place where you can die of encouragement. (After Dark 13:20 Sept 80)

KAHN, Alfred. All life is a concatenation of ephemeralities. (Barron's 59:5 Feb 19, 79)

KAHN, Alfred. Anybody who isn't schizophrenic these days isn't thinking clearly. (Life 4:21 Jan 80)

KAHN, Alfred. If you can't explain what you're doing in simple English, you are probably doing something wrong. (Time 111:63 May 8, 78)

KAHN, Herman. Think the unthinkable. (National Catholic Reporter 21:26 Dec 21, 84)

KAHN, J. Kesner. Free market competition, freely advertised, is consumerism at its best. (American Opinion 18:18 June 75)

KAHN, J. Kesner. When politicians come up with a solution for your problem, you have two problems. (American Opinion 18:21 May 75)

KAHN, Roger. His (Jackie Robinson) race was humanity, and he did a great deal for us. (TV Guide 25:14 Aug 6, 77)

KAISER, Henry J. When your work speaks for itself, don't interrupt. (Washingtonian 23:149 Dec 87)

KANE, Walter. It is tragic that Howard Hughes had to die to prove that he was alive. (Newsweek 87:25 April 19, 76)

KAPILOFF, Larry. I believe that politics is 90 percent the profession of cowards. (San Diego Magazine 31:88 May 79)

KAROL, Pamala (La Loca). My work is sort of a psychic vomit that comes from within. (Los Angeles 35:20 April 90)

KASELIONIS, Simas. Writers aren't like mushrooms—you can't grow them. (Chicago 24:23 July 31, 75)

KAUFMAN, George. Satire is what closes Saturday night. (Time 107:72 Feb 2, 76)

KAUFMAN, Irving. It is not enough for justice to be declared. The judge must assure that justice is done. (Time 113:92 Jan 22, 79)

KAUNDA, Kenneth. A new Zimbabwe (Rhodesia) can only be born out of the barrel of a gun. (Time 110:30 July 18, 77)

KAUNDA, Kenneth. An African in Zimbabwe does not need a communist to tell him that he is not free (1977). (To The Point International 4:10 June 20, 77)

KAUNDA, Kenneth. Not every white man is bad. (The Observer 9769:13 Nov 19, 78)

KAVANAGH, Patrick. Whatever will live must touch the heart of the mob in some way. (Washington Post 102:A17 Mar 17, 77)

KAY, Alan. Artificial intelligence is the designer jeans of computer science. (Infoworld 7:13 July 8, 85)

KEILLOR, Garrison. Interviewing celebrities is just a step above calling the morgue. (Mpls/St. Paul 13:26 Sept 30, 85)

KEKER, John W. The evidence will show that when the time came for Oliver North to tell the truth, he lied. When the time came for Oliver North to come clean he shredded, he erased, he altered. When the time came for Oliver North to let the light shine in, he covered up. (New York Times 138:2 Feb 22, 89)

KELLEY, Ken. But history is nothing but a chronology of oppressors oppressing the oppressed. (Rolling Stone 216:38 July 1, 76)

KELLEY, Stanley. Last guys don't finish nice. (Town & Country 133:140 May 79)

KEMP, Jack. I want it known that you cannot balance the budget off the backs of the poor. (Lawrence (Kansas) Journal-World 130:1A Dec 20, 88)

KEMP, Jack. Whether it's politics or football, winning is like shaving: you do it every day or you wind up looking like a bum. (The Sporting News 202:12 Aug 4, 86)

KENDALL, Donald M. If we can get the Soviet people to enjoy good consumer goods, they'll never be able to do without them again. (Chicago Tribune 99:3 Section 1 April 9, 90)

KENNEDY, Edward Moore. I think Mr. Carter has created Ronald Reagan. (The Observer 9856:12 July 20, 80)

KENNEDY, Edward Moore. If and when needed, anti-trust laws are ready and able to promote a diverse and competitive press. (Esquire 91:6 Feb 27, 79)

KENNEDY, Edward Moore. My father always said: 'If it's on the table, eat it'. (The Observer 9813:9 Sept 23, 79)

KENNEDY, Edward Moore. Rethinking our ideas should never be an excuse for retreating from our ideals. The last thing this nation needs in the 1980s is two Republican parties. (Time 120:14 July 12, 82)

KENNEDY, Edward Moore. We cannot afford a foreign policy based on the pangs of unrequited love. (The Tennessean 74:7 Jan 30, 80)

KENNEDY, Edward Moore. Whatever contributions the Kennedys have made are very much tied into the incredible importance and power of that force in our lives, the family. (New York Times Magazine 15 June 17, 79)

KENNEDY, Florynce Rae. If men could get pregnant, abortion would be a sacrament. (Viva 5:28 Nov 77)

KENNEDY, Florynce Rae. If the ass is protecting the system, ass-kicking should be undertaken regardless of the sex, ethnicity, or charm of the ass involved. (Ms 1:89 Mar 73)

KENNEDY, Florynce Rae. Most lawyers are like whores. They serve the client who puts the highest fee on the table. (Ms 1:89 Mar 73)

KENNEDY, Florynce Rae. There are a few jobs that actually require a penis or vagina. All other jobs should be open to everybody. (Ms 1:55 Mar 73)

KENNEDY, Florynce Rae. There's no sex to a brain. (Human Behavior 7:17 May 78)

KENNEDY, John Fitzgerald. And so, my fellow Americans, ask not what your country can do for you; ask what you can do for your country (inaugural address— 1961). (Christian Science Monitor 69:14 Jan 20, 77)

KENNEDY, John Fitzgerald. Domestic policy can only defeat us; foreign policy can kill us. (New York Times Magazine 50 Sept 9, 79)

KENNEDY, John Fitzgerald. He's got no class (about Richard Nixon). (Time 111:20 Mar 6, 78)

KENNEDY, John Fitzgerald. I know that when things don't go well, they like to blame the President, and that is one of the things presidents are paid for. (Rocky Mountain News 185:60 Oct 24, 79)

KENNEDY, John Fitzgerald. If somebody is going to kill me, they are going to kill me. (New Leader 61:15 Nov 6, 78)

KENNEDY, John Fitzgerald. If we are strong, our strength will speak for itself. If we are weak, words will be no help. (Kansas City Times 109:28 Jan 4, 77)

KENNEDY, John Fitzgerald. My father always told me that steel men were sons-of-bitches, but I never realized till now how right he was (in the 1962 steel-price confrontation). (Chicago Tribune 147:2 Section 2 May 29, 77)

KENNEDY, John Fitzgerald. No future American president should be driven into a corner where his only choice is world devastation or submission (1960). (Washingtonian 19:128 Mar 84)

KENNEDY, John Fitzgerald. The worse I do, the more popular I get. (Time 115:31 May 5, 80)

KENNEDY, John Fitzgerald (attributed by David Reckford). Those who make peaceful revolution impossible make violent revolution inevitable. (The Observer 9785:13 Mar 11, 79)

KENNEDY, Joseph P., III. There's no question being a Kennedy can open a lot of doors, but it's also opened a few I didn't want to walk through. (Newsweek 88:24 July 12, 76)

KENNEDY, Robert F. Richard Nixon represents the dark side of the American spirit. (Village Voice Literary Supplement 58:14 Sept 87)

KENNEDY, Robert Francis (attributed by Bill Moyers). I have myself wondered if we did not pay a very great price for being more energetic than wise about a lot of things, especially Cuba. (Washington Post 228:A5 July 21, 77)

KENNEY, Charles. The best cure I know for writer's block is deadline. (Boston 78:27 Oct 86)

KERBY, Phil. Censorship is the strongest drive in human nature. Sex is only a weak second. (Kansas City Times 117:A-6 April 22, 85)

KEROUAC, Jack. Walking on water wasn't built in a day. (The American Book Review 1:8 April 78)

KERR, Clark. Have plenty of football for the alumni, sex for the students, and parking for the faculty. (Washingtonian 15:142 Oct 31, 79)

KERR, Clark. Naderism has taken over education. (Time 110:75 Nov 14, 77)

KERR, Jean. Marrying a man is like buying something you've been admiring for a long time in a shop window. You may love it when you get it home, but it doesn't always go with everything else in the house. (Chicago Tribune 65:1 Section 5 Mar 5, 78)

KESEY, Ken. Always stay in your own movie. (New Times 9:68 Aug 19, 77)

KESEY, Ken. Take what you can use and let the rest go by. (Kansas City Times 119:A-1 Sept 19, 86)

KETTERING, Charles. If you want to kill any idea in the world today, get a committee

working on it. (Omni 4:41 April 82)

KEYNES, John Maynard. My only regret in life is that I did not drink more champagne. (Money 5:53 April 76)

KEYSERLING, Hermann A. The greatest American superstition is belief in facts. (Kansas City Times 109:26 Jan 25, 77)

KHAN, Naved N. Bloomingdale's is more than a store. It is a way of life. (Time 106:4 Dec 22, 75)

KHOMEINI, Ayatollah Ali. Anyone who fights America's aggression has engaged in a holy war in the cause of Allah, and anyone who is killed on that path is a martyr. (Time 136:32 Sept 24, 89)

KHOMEINI, Ayatollah Ruhollah. All western governments are just thieves. Nothing but evil comes from them. (Time 115:22 Jan 7, 80)

KHOMEINI, Ayatollah Ruhollah. As long as I am alive, I will not let the State (Iran) fall into the hands of liberals. (Chicago Tribune 54:2 Section 1 Feb 23, 89)

KHOMEINI, Ayatollah Ruhollah. Dictatorship is the greatest sin in the religion of Islam. Fascism and Islamism are absolutely incompatible. (Time 114:57 Oct 22, 79)

KHOMEINI, Ayatollah Ruhollah. Even if Salman Rushdie repents and becomes the most pious man of all time, it is incumbent on every Moslem to employ everything he's got, his life and wealth, to send him to hell. (Chicago Tribune 57:3 Section 4 Feb 26, 89)

KHOMEINI, Ayatollah Ruhollah. From its very inception, Islam has been afflicted by the Jews. (Newsweek 93:42 Jan 29, 79)

KHOMEINI, Ayatollah Ruhollah. The people of Iran want to be martyrs. (The Observer 9826:9 Dec 23, 79)

KHOMEINI, Ayatollah Ruhollah. We (Iran) did not need these armaments in the past; we will not be in need of them in the future (about U.S. arms). (US News & World Report 85:46 Nov 20, 78)

KHOMEINI, Ayatollah Ruhollah. We have the ideology to distinguish right from wrong, and we should not hesitate to tell misguided people, here and abroad, what is wrong with them. (Time 114:25 Dec 10, 79)

KHRUSHCHEV, Nikita Sergeevich. Call it what you will, incentives are the only way to make people work harder (responding to a charge that the Soviet Union was becoming capitalist). (Time 106:63 July 14, 75)

KHRUSHCHEV, Nikita Sergeevich. Life is short. Live it up. (Viva 4:25 July 77)

KHRUSHCHEV, Nikita Sergeevich.

Politicians are the same the world over: they promise to build a bridge even where there is no river. (Village Voice 22:23 Aug 29, 77)

KHRUSHCHEV, Nikita Sergeevich. The survivors (of a nuclear attack) would envy the dead. (Harper's 259:36 Aug 79)

KIDD, Bruce. We should stop preaching about sport's moral values. Sport, after all, isn't Lent. It's a pleasure of the flesh. (Chicago Tribune 76:1 Section 2 Mar 17, 78)

KILLENS, John O. Let's stop titillating white people. No matter what we black folks do, we always wind up as entertainers. (Sepia 26:10 May 76)

KILPATRICK, James J. Big Bill Bennett, as I may have said before, is the best thing to hit American education since the McGuffey readers. (Kansas City Star 107:11A Feb 5, 87)

KILPATRICK, James J. Find out where the people want to go, then hustle yourself around in front of them. (Washingtonian 15:143 Nov 79)

KING, Billie Jean. Amateur athletes have become the pawn of manipulators and big business. (The Nation 221:654 Dec 20, 75)

KING, Billie Jean. Don't go to college if you want to make your living in sports. (New York Times 127:5 Section 5 Mar 26, 78)

KING, Billie Jean. You put a pink blanket on a little girl and a blue blanket on a little boy, and right there the difference starts. (The Sporting News 205:50 May 2, 88)

KING, Coretta Scott. I don't have the facts, but at this stage I say it appears there was a conspiracy in the death of my husband. (Los Angeles Times 94:12 Part 1 Nov 28, 75)

KING, Coretta Scott. There is a spirit and a need and a man at the beginning of every great human advance. Each of these must be right for that particular moment of history, or nothing happens. (Chicago Tribune 176:2 Section 2 June 25, 78)

KING, Donald. I have risen to the top in the promotion business just as I climbed to the top in the numbers game: by wits and grits and bullshit. (Cleveland 4:90 Nov 75)

KING, Florence. Sharing is not what America is all about; in our hearts, each of us is an only child. (Vanity Fair 47:20 Oct 84)

KING, Larry L. One receives an inverse ratio of romantic opportunities to that which one needs. (Viva 4:72 Dec 76)

KING, Martin Luther, Jr. I'm not fearing any man. Mine eyes have seen the glory of the coming of the Lord. (Playboy 23:127 June 76)

KING, Martin Luther, Sr. Nothing that a man does takes him lower than when he allows himself to fall so far as to hate anyone. (Newsweek 96:92 Sept 15, 80)

KING, Martin Luther, Sr. Surely the Lord sent Jimmy Carter to come on out and bring America back where she belongs. (Washington Post 224:A1 July 16, 76)

KINGMAN, David Arthur. There's no way to be a nice guy and play professional athletics. You have to just go out and be mean. (Chicago Tribune Magazine 21 April 19, 78)

KIRBO, Charles. He's (Jimmy Carter) got faults, like all of us. He's ambitious. But he's not greedy, and he's considerate. (Time 107:17 July 12, 76)

KIRBO, Charles. Once he (John Connally) gets across that Texas line—he's not much. (Newsweek 88:25 Aug 2, 76)

KIRKLAND, Gelsey. My brain was the last of my muscles to develop. (US 3:17 Feb 9, 87)

KIRKLAND, Lane. All sinners belong in the church; all citizens owe fealty to their country; and all true unions belong in the American Federation of Labor and Congress of Industrial Organizations. (New York Times 129:B1 Nov 20, 79)

KIRKLAND, Lane. Any jackass can draw up a balanced budget on paper. (US News & World Report 88:90 May 19, 80)

KIRKLAND, Lane. Carter is your typical, smiling, brilliant, backstabbing, bullshitting, southern nut-cutter. (New Times 7:13 Sept 3, 76)

KIRKLAND, Lane. If hard work were such a wonderful thing, surely the rich would have kept it all to themselves. (Life 7:39 Jan 84)

KIRKPATRICK, Jeane. I have absolutely no intention of running for office—ever. (Chicago Tribune 6:5 Section 1 Mar 27, 85)

KIRKUP, Jon. The sun goes down just when you need it the most. (Washingtonian 14:154 Nov 78)

KIRSTEIN, Lincoln. Transplanting ballet to this country is like trying to raise a palm tree in Dakota. (Newsweek 102:58 Dec 26, 83)

KISSINGER, Henry Alfred. All the Russians can offer is war, but we can bring the peace (commenting on the Mideast situation). (Time 109:16 Jan 24, 77)

KISSINGER, Henry Alfred. Among the many claims on American resources, I would put those of Vietnam in alphabetical order. (Newsweek 89:47 May 16, 77)

KISSINGER, Henry Alfred. Cambodia's agony unfolded with the inevitability of a Greek tragedy. (Newsweek 94:59 Oct 22, 79)

KISSINGER, Henry Alfred. Competing pressures tempt one to believe that an issue deferred is a problem avoided; more often it is a crisis invited. (Time 114:82 Oct 15, 79)

KISSINGER, Henry Alfred. Covert action should not be confused with missionary work. (In These Times 14:5 Oct 3, 90)

KISSINGER, Henry Alfred. Each success only buys an admission ticket to a more difficult problem. (Wilson Library Bulletin 53:513 Mar 79)

KISSINGER, Henry Alfred. High office teaches decision making, not substance. It consumes intellectual capital; it does not create it. (Time 114:81 Oct 15, 79)

KISSINGER, Henry Alfred. I have always thought of foreign policy as bipartisan. (Chicago Tribune 233:6 Section 2 Aug 21, 77)

KISSINGER, Henry Alfred. I think Metternich was an extremely skilled diplomat, but not very creative. (Time 107:33 Jan 12, 76)

KISSINGER, Henry Alfred. If we do not meet the Russian challenge now at modest cost we will find it necessary to do so further down the road when it will be more costly and more dangerous (commenting on why U.S. aid is needed in Angola). (Christian Science Monitor 21:9 Dec 24, 75)

KISSINGER, Henry Alfred. Intellectuals condemn society for materialism when it is prosperous and for injustice when it fails to ensure prosperity. (Time 107:49 June 20, 77)

KISSINGER, Henry Alfred. It is necessary for the Western democracies to recapture the sense that they can control their own destiny. (Time 106:36 Oct 27, 75)

KISSINGER, Henry Alfred. It was hard to avoid the impression that Nixon, who thrived on crisis, also craved disasters. (Time 114:59 Oct 1, 79)

KISSINGER, Henry Alfred. Moderation is a virtue only in those who are thought to have an alternative. (The Observer 9934:13 Jan 24, 82)

KISSINGER, Henry Alfred. Most administrations come to office believing that they are saving the world. This one believes it created the world (commenting on the Carter administration). (Chicago Sun-Times 30:3 May 4, 77)

KISSINGER, Henry Alfred. Nelson Rockefeller was the greatest American I have ever known. (Newsweek 93:27 Feb 5, 79)

KISSINGER, Henry Alfred. No communist country has solved the problem of succession. (Time 113:59 Mar 12, 79)

KISSINGER, Henry Alfred. One had the sense that if (Charles de Gaulle) moved to a window, the center of gravity might shift, and the whole room might tilt everybody into the garden. (Time 114:82 Oct 15, 79)

KISSINGER, Henry Alfred. One thing I don't want around me is a military intellectual. I don't have to worry about you on that score (to Alexander Haig). (Look 1:58 June 11, 79)

KISSINGER, Henry Alfred. Power is the greatest aphrodisiac of all. (Maclean's 91:72 Mar 6, 78)

KISSINGER, Henry Alfred. Sadat is the greatest (statesman) since Bismarck. (Esquire 91:30 Jan 30, 79)

KISSINGER, Henry Alfred. The absence of alternatives (in the Middle East) clears the mind marvelously. (Time 111:35 Jan 2, 78)

KISSINGER, Henry Alfred. The American body politic is basically healthy. Our people want to believe in their government. (Time 106:35 Oct 27, 75)

KISSINGER, Henry Alfred. The cold war was not so terrible and detente was not so exalting. (The Observer 9833:9 Feb 10, 80)

KISSINGER, Henry Alfred. The likelihood of war is extremely low due to the nature of modern weapons. (M 1:48 July 84)

KISSINGER, Henry Alfred. The longer I am out of office, the more infallible I appear to myself. (San Francisco Chronicle This World 1977:2 Oct 16, 77)

KISSINGER, Henry Alfred. The main point...in the mechanics of my success comes from the fact that I have acted alone. (Esquire 89:41-42 Mar 14, 78)

KISSINGER, Henry Alfred. The nice thing about being a celebrity is that when you bore people, they think it's their fault. (Washingtonian 23:150 Dec 87)

KISSINGER, Henry Alfred. The Shah (of Iran) was—despite the travesties of retroactive myth—a dedicated reformer. (Time 114:77 Oct 15, 79)

KISSINGER, Henry Alfred. The tragedy of this war (the Iranian-Iraqi war) is that it has to end someday. (Manhattan, Inc. 5:46 Sept 88)

KISSINGER, Henry Alfred. Two years from now nobody will give a damn if I am up, down or sideways. (Time 106:29 Nov 17, 75)

KISSINGER, Henry Alfred. We are all the president's men, and have got to behave that way. (Meet the Press 20:6 April 18, 76)

KISSINGER, Henry Alfred. We are not going around looking for opportunities to prove our manhood. (Ms 4:63 Oct 75)

KISSINGER, Henry Alfred. We must resist the myth that government is a gigantic conspiracy. We cannot allow the intelligence services of the country to be dismantled. (Washington Post 355:1 Nov 25, 75)

KISSINGER, Henry Alfred. We now face the challenge of the early '80s with forces designed in the '60s. (Chicago Sun-Times 32:2 Aug 1, 79)

KISSINGER, Henry Alfred. We should have bombed the hell out of them the minute we got into office (a week after the 1973 Vietnam peace agreement). (Rolling Stone 188:35 June 5, 75)

KISSLING, Frances. God put me on earth to give the Pope a hard time. (Village Voice 32:24 Jan 27, 87)

KLEIN, Calvin. We live in an age of obsession: obsession with work, obsession with romance. (Interview 14:135 June 85)

KLUGE, Alexander. German (movie) directors are like airplanes always circling the airport but never landing. (Time 111:53 Mar 20, 78)

KNEPPER, Bob. You can be a woman umpire if you want, but that doesn't mean it's right. (The Sporting News 205:36 Mar 28, 88)

KNIGHT, Andrew (Editor of The Economist, London). We are a government of opposition, no matter who is in power. (W 4:2 Sept 19, 75)

KNIGHT, Bob. I'm an imperfect man trying to attain perfection in a game that probably has no chance of being played perfectly. (Topeka Capital-Journal SportsPlus 10 Dec 1, 87)

KNIGHT, Damon. If there is a universal mind, must it be sane? (Village Voice 23:37 Aug 21, 78)

KNOPF, Alfred A. It's peculiar. The older I become the more radical I become. (W 4:2 Oct 31, 75)

KNOWLES, John H. A sense of humor is the prelude to faith and laughter is the beginning of prayer. (New York Times 128:A22 Mar 7, 79)

KNOWLES, John H. Over 99 percent of us are born healthy and made sick as a result of personal misbehavior and environmental conditions. (Time 111:65 June 12, 78)

KOCH, Edward I. Gentrification isn't a dirty word. (Village Voice 31:32 Dec 9, 86)

KOCH, Edward I. I always run for office with the humility of an adopted child. (US 3:64 Feb 10, 86)

KOCH, Edward I. If the United Nations would leave New York, nobody would ever hear of it again. (The Observer 9938:13 Feb 21, 82)

KOCH, Edward I. It happens that intellectual honesty is not the coin of the realm in politics. (New York Times 129:B1 Oct 23, 79)

KOCH, Edward I. My experience with blacks is that they are basically anti-Semitic. (Village Voice 27:12 Mar 9, 82)

KOCH, Edward I. The Constitution is dumb (March 1981). (Village Voice 27:12 Mar 12, 82)

KOCH, Edward I. You're not a nice guy if you have a gun, even if you are a nice guy. (Time 115:63 Mar 3, 80)

KOESTLER, Arthur. Those who deny the influence of environment on the development of the human being should spend a year in prison and observe themselves daily in a mirror. (USA Today 1:8A June 15, 83)

KOHL, Helmut. We have less reason than ever to be resigned to the long-term division of Germany into two states. (New York Times 139:2 Nov 9, 89)

KOHLER, Jerry. I'd just as soon die in Vietnam as in the library. (Salina (Kansas) Journal 10 May 27, 76)

KOJAK, Theo. Hindsight is the only exact science. (Philadelphia 68:113 July 77)

KOMPLEKTOV, Viktor G. At no time, not before, not during the beginning of the crisis, or in the most acute moments of the crisis, neither from the Soviet command there in Cuba nor in Moscow was there, or could there have been, an order to mount (Russian) nuclear warheads on the missles. (Chicago Tribune 38:21 Section 1 Feb 7, 89)

KOON, Larry. Women are best suited for secretarial work, decorating cakes and counter sales, like selling lingerie. (New Woman 10:12 May 80)

KOPPEL, Ted. On television, ambiguity is a virtue. (Newsweek 109:56 June 15, 87)

KORDA, Michael. Accuracy has never been my strongest point. (Chicago Tribune 332:1 Section 3 Nov 28, 79)

KORDA, Michael. An ounce of hypocrisy is worth a pound of ambition. (Playboy 28:97 Sept 81)

KORDA, Michael. Gossip, unlike river water, flows both ways. (Reader's Digest 106:114 June 76)

KORDA, Michael. New York style is that what you do is more important than who you are. (New York 21 Dec 24, 84)

KORDA, Michael. New York—it's a fun place, but by and large, people are here because this is where success matters the most and this where it pays off the most. (New York 19:54 Dec 22, 86)

KOSLOW, Ron. What marijuana was to the Sixties, real estate is to the Seventies. (Esquire 93:17 Feb 80)

KOVAR, Jay. Journalists today are more into jogging than drinking. (Chicago 34:16 July 85)

KOVIC, Ron. The government took the best years of my life away from me and millions of other young men. I just think they're lucky I wrote a book instead of buying a gun. (People Weekly 6:58 Dec 27/Jan 3, 77)

KOWAL, Charles (American astronomer). I enjoy learning things, but a university is the last place in the world to learn anything. (Time 106:75 Oct 27, 75)

KRAUS, Karl. The devil is an optimist if he thinks he can make people worse than they are. (Inquiry 1:25 Jan 23, 78)

KRAUSE, Charles. In the jungle, a press card is just another piece of paper. (Washingtonian 15:142 Nov 79)

KRIENDLER, Peter. If you make it in New York, you got it made. If you make it anywhere else, you've still got something to prove. (New York 108 Dec 24, 84)

KRISTOL, Irving. A neoconservative is a liberal mugged by reality. (Washington Post National Weekly Edition 2:12 Oct 21, 85)

KRISTOL, Irving. Being frustrated is disagreeable, but the real disasters of life begin when you get what you want. (Book Digest 6:28 Dec 79)

KROC, Ray. If you think small, you'll stay small. (Chicago 28:12 Mar 79)

KUBRICK, Stanley. The essence of dramatic form is to let an idea come over people without its being plainly stated. (Time 106:72 Dec 15, 75)

KUGEL, Yerachmiel. Ethics is not a branch of economics. (St. Louis Post-Dispatch 99:2G July 24, 77)

KUPFERBERG, Tuli. What is a beatnik? Why, it's exactly everything that Herbert Hoover hates. (New York 12:82 May 7, 79)

KUROKAWA, Masaaki. The United States will have to follow a set of austerity measures similar, in some sense, to those imposed by the I.M.F. on debt-ridden countries. (New York Times 138:3 Section 3 Feb 19, 89)

KUTLER, Stanley. Richard Nixon is struggling for the soul of history and for the souls of historians. Historians ought to worry about theirs. (Chicago Tribune 342:17 Dec 8, 87)

KY, Nguyen Cao. Never believe what any Vietnamese tells you, including me (commenting in 1966). (Newsweek 85:17 May 19, 75)

LADD, Cheryl. Jaclyn (Smith) is the only girl I know that has the body of a go-go dancer and the mind of an angel. (Chicago Tribune 76:18 Mar 17, 78)

LAFFER, Arthur. The U.S. is the fastest 'undeveloping' country in the world. (Time 114:36 Aug 27, 79)

LAIRD, Melvin. Conservation alone is a slow walk down a dead-end street. (Time 110:62 Oct 10, 77)

LAKER, Freddie. The man that doesn't change his mind doesn't think. (The Observer 9804:9 July 22, 79)

LAMARR, Hedy. Any girl can be glamorous. All you have to do is stand still and look stupid. (Chicago Sun-Times 30:21 Jan 28, 78)

LANCE, Thomas Bertram. Folks are serious about three things—their religion, their family, and most of all, their money. (Time 108:20 Dec 6, 76)

LANCE, Thomas Bertram. He (Jimmy Carter) campaigns liberal, but he governs conservative. (Washington Post 61:A3 Jan 31, 77)

LAND, Edwin. Anything worth doing is worth doing to excess. (Time 107:66 May 9, 77)

LAND, Edwin. I am addicted to at least one good experiment a day. (Time 115:68 Mar 17, 80)

LANDERS, Ann. If nobody minds, it doesn't matter. (Washingtonian 23:150 Dec 87)

LANDERS, Ann. Love is the most precious thing in all the world. Whatever figures in second place doesn't even come close. (New York 9:68 Feb 16, 76)

LANDON, Melville. Levity is the soul of wit. (San Francisco Chronicle This World 1978:40 Jan 29, 78)

LANDOR, Walter Savage. Men cannot bear to be deprived of anything they are used to; not even of their fears. (Kansas City Star 97:4B Oct 10, 76)

LANDRY, Tom. God doesn't make any losers. (Chicago Sun-Times 32:32 April 21, 79)

LANDRY, Tom. Nothing funny ever happens on the football field. (Time 111:75 Jan 16, 78)

LANGLOIS, Henri. Most people advance through life walking backward. Those artists who face forward are likely to be put in jail—or the madhouse. (New York Times 126:D13 Jan 23, 77)

LANGLOIS, Henri. There is no Garbo, no Dietrich. There is only Louise Brooks. (Newsweek 106:71 Aug 19, 85)

LANSKY, Meyer. We're bigger than U. S. Steel. (Playboy 31:22 May 84)

LAPHAM, Lewis H. Democracy means that you and I must fight. Democracy means a kind of Darwinism for ideas. (Time 111:84 Jan 23, 78)

LAPHAM, Lewis H. I take for granted Jefferson's dictum that money, not morality, constitutes the principle of commercial nations. (Harper's 254:32 Feb 77)

LARKIN, Philip. Generally speaking, the further one gets from home, the greater the misery. (New York 17:22 June 11, 84)

LARKIN, Philip. I see life more as an affair of solitude diversified by company than as an affair of company diversified by solitude. (The Observer 9825:35 Dec 16, 79)

LAROUCHE, Lyndon. I am the leading economist of the century. (Inquiry 6:21 Feb 28, 83)

LARTIGUE, Jacques-Henri. When you fall in love with a woman, it's because she's ready, she has chosen you. (Vanity Fair 47:82 April 84)

LASCH, Christopher. Radicalism in the United States has no great triumphs to record. (Time 110:67 Aug 15, 77)

LASCH, Christopher. The mother's power originates in the imposition of her own madness on everybody else. (New York Times Magazine 14 May 13, 79)

LASORDA, Tom. Managing is like holding a dove in your hand. Squeeze too hard and you kill it; not hard enough and it flies away. (Toronto Life 84 May 84)

LASSER, Louise. When you are a celebrity, you are totally a victim. (Time 111:56 June 19, 78)

LASZLO, Ervin. The materialistic growth ethic is not an immutable expression of human nature. (Time 107:56 April 26, 76)

LAUGHLIN, Tom. Never trust a man with ideas. (New York 8:51 Aug 4, 75)

LAUREN, Ralph. I can do anything I want. (W 7:8 Dec 8, 79)

LAWRENCE, David Herbert. The essential American soul is hard, stoic, isolate and a killer. (Time 111:53 Jan 9, 78)

LAWTON, George E. If it is important to give the human animal a good start in life, it is just as important to see that he makes a good finish. (Saturday Evening Post 251:98 Feb 28, 79)

LAXALT, Paul D. If there's an elder statesman in our party right now, it's Richard Nixon. (Newsweek 107:27 May 19, 86)

LAYNE, Bobby. Living in a small town (Lubbock) in Texas ain't half bad—if you own it. (Kansas City Times 111:10 Nov 17, 78)

LAZAR, Irving L (Swifty). Dostoevsky couldn't get a publisher today. (Chicago Tribune 40:18 Section 1 Feb 9, 82)

LE CARRE, John. He (Andrei Sakharov) really has contributed to a change in history. (New York Times 138:15 May 22, 89)

LE CARRE, John. People are very secretive creatures—secret even from themselves. (The Observer 9833:9 Feb 10, 80)

LE GUIN, Ursula. If science fiction becomes respectable, it may die. (Newsweek 86:74 Dec 22, 75)

LEACHMAN, Cloris. Fat people pollute the esthetic environment. (People Weekly 5:29 May 3, 76)

LEAR, Amanda. I hate to spread rumors, but what else can you do with them. (Interview 8:32 Mar 78)

LEAR, Norman. TV executives don't make decisions based on their own sense of showmanship. They make decisions based on fear. (Emmy 1:12 Winter 79)

LEAR, Norman. When I give advice to rising starlets I say, just remember, Hollywood is the land of the definite maybe. (US 1:81 June 14, 77)

LEARY, Timothy. You have to remember, the truth is funny. (Cleveland 8:17 Nov 79)

LEBOWITZ, Fran. A dog who thinks he is a man's best friend is a dog who obviously has never met a tax lawyer. (Book World 11:5 Sept 81)

LEBOWITZ, Fran. Having been unpopular in high school is not just cause for book publication. (New York Times Book Review 39 June 17, 79)

LEBOWITZ, Fran. I can't write if there's another person in the building. (W 17:52 Sept 19, 88)

LEBOWITZ, Fran. If God had meant for everything to happen at once, he would not have invented desk calendars. (Time 111:K3 May 29, 78)

LEBOWITZ, Fran. Rome is a very loony city in every respect. One needs but spend an hour or two there to realize that Fellini makes documentaries. (Andy Warhol's Interview 7:46 July 75)

LEBOWITZ, Fran. Sleep is death without the responsibility. (Time 111:K3 May 29, 78)

LEBRON, Lolita. Until my last breath I will fight for the liberation and freedom of Puerto Rico. (New York Times 128:1 Sept 12, 79)

LEFEBVRE, Marcel. Rome, and not I, is in

error. (Guardian Weekly 120:6 Jan 28, 79)

LEFEBVRE, Marcel. The church is full of thieves, mercenaries and wolves. During the past 20 years, the Vatican has become the friend of our enemies. (Time 110:64 July 11, 77)

LEFEVRE, William M. Fears expressed by the majority of investors are very often like bad dreams—they rarely come true in real life. (Kansas City Star 106:5A Dec 30, 85)

LEFEVRE, William M. There are only two emotions in Wall Street: fear and greed. (Time 111:42 May 1, 78)

LEGMAN, Gershon. Make love, not war. (Village Voice 29:43 May 1, 84)

LEHMAN, Ernest. If writer's block is soluble in alcohol, so is the liver. (Writer's Digest 58:26 Oct 78)

LEHMAN, Ernest. Very few people realize, when they go to a movie theatre and want to be entertained, what sort of blood has flowed in order that they might have a good time. (Chicago Tribune 282:18 Section 6 Oct 9, 77)

LEHRER, Tom. When Henry Kissinger can get the Nobel Peace Prize, what is there left for satire? (Chicago Sun-Times 33:76 July 9, 80)

LELAND, Mickey. It's a white mark on America's history for us to have hungry children in our society. (The New Yorker 65:31 Sept 11, 89)

LEMONS, Abe. Basketball is a game, not a religion. (Arkansas Times 11:87 Mar 31, 85)

LENNON, John. A working class hero is something to be. (Sports Illustrated 65:77 Oct 27, 86)

LEONE, Mama. No one ever filed for divorce on a full stomach. (Viva 4:26 May 77)

LEOPOLD, Aldo. The first prerequisite of intelligent tinkering is to save all the pieces. (Washingtonian 13:149 Sept 78)

LESCHAK, Peter M. Whenever an individual is ostracized from society, suspect society first. (Mpls/St. Paul 15:228 Mar 87)

LEVANT, Oscar. Happiness is not a thing you experience, but something you remember. (Chicago 31:22 July 31, 82)

LEVANT, Oscar. I never read bad reviews about myself because my best friends invariably tell me about them. (Chicago 31:22 July 31, 82)

LEVENSON, Sam. The reason grandparents and grandchildren get along so well is that they have a common enemy. (Cosmopolitan 197:184 Sept 84)

LEVESQUE, Rene. The quality of a civilized society is the treatment it affords minorities. (New York Times 128:23 April 5, 79)

LEVI-STRAUSS, Claude. Age removes the confusion, only possible in youth, between physical and moral characteristics. (Time 111:99 April 24, 78)

LEVIN, S. Jay. Stocks do not move unless they are pushed. (Book Digest 6:32 Dec 79)

LEVY, Bernard-Henri. Between the barbarity of capitalism, which censures itself much of the time, and the barbarity of socialism, which does not, I guess I might choose capitalism. (Time 111:30 Mar 13, 78)

LEVY, Bernard-Henri. Solzhenitsyn is the Shakespeare of our time, the only one who knows how to point out the monsters. (Time 110:29 Sept 12, 77)

LEVY, Bernard-Henri. The only successful revolution of this century is totalitarianism. (Time 110:29 Sept 12, 77)

LEWI, Morris. I never wasted time resisting temptation. (Kansas City Star 108:5C Oct 7, 87)

LEWIS, Anthony. In making a prison for others, the Afrikaners have imprisoned themselves. (Chicago Daily News 14 Nov 30, 93)

LEWIS, C. S. A young man who wishes to remain a sound atheist cannot be too careful of his reading. God is, if I may say it, very unscrupulous. (New York Times 126:B1 Dec 20, 76)

LEWIS, C. S. All that is not eternal is eternally out of date. (Time 110:92 Dec 5, 77)

LEWIS, Jerry. Only the man who does nothing makes no mistakes. (Boston 69:74 Sept 77)

LEWIS, Jerry Lee. That dead son of a gun is still riding on my coattails (about Elvis Presley). (New York Times Magazine 45 Mar 25, 79)

LEWIS, Joe E. You're not really drunk if you can lie on the floor without hanging on. (Playboy 26:26 Oct 79)

LEWIS, Jonathan. Most politicians get elected by being all things to all people. Jerry (Brown) survives by being nothing to everyone. (Harper's 259:14 July 79)

LEWIS, Robert A. (co-pilot of the B-29 Enola Gay). If I live to be a hundred, I'll never quite get these few minutes out of my mind. (Time 122:48 July 4, 83)

LIBERMAN, Alexander. All serious art is against convention. (New York Times Magazine 61 May 13, 79)

LIDBERG, A. A. Distribute dissatisfaction uniformly. (Washingtonian 15:140 Nov 79)

LIDDY, G. Gordon. Before going to prison I believed that criticism of the criminal justice system for its treatment of the poor was so much liberal bleating and bunk. I was wrong. (Connecticut 40:48 Feb 77)

LIDDY, G. Gordon. I think in all fairness to the man, you'd have to put him right up there with Judas Iscariot (about John Dean). (More 5:11 July 75)

LIDDY, G. Gordon. Obviously crime pays, or there'd be no crime. (Newsweek 108:19 Nov 10, 86)

LIEBERMANN, Rolf. Running an opera is like running a restaurant. If the boss is not there, the food gets bad and the service even worse. (Time 108:58 Sept 20, 76)

LIEBLING, A. J. Freedom of the press belongs to those who own one. (American Film 3:67 July/Aug 78)

LIEBLING, A. J. The only way to write is well and how you do it is your own damn business. (Gentlemen's Quarterly 56:76 June 86)

LIEBLING, A. J. The people who have something to say don't talk; the others insist on talking. (Washingtonian 15:142 Nov 79)

LIEBOW, Elliot. Most people would be ashamed for their children to see them at work. (Washingtonian 16:82 Mar 81)

LILLY, Doris. Gossip and manure are only good for one thing—and that's spreading. Gossip doesn't mean a damn thing unless you spread it around. (W 4:2 Aug 22, 75)

LINDBERGH, Anne Morrow (attributed by Julie Nixon Eisenhower). Life is a gift, given in trust—like a child. (Christian Science Monitor 69:21 June 23, 77)

LINDBERGH, Charles Augustus. I've had enough fame for a dozen lives; it's not what it's cracked up to be. (New York Times Magazine 12 May 8, 77)

LINDBERGH, Charles Augustus. Life is like a landscape. You live in the midst of it, but can describe it only from the vantage point of distance. (Washington Post 161:G2 May 15, 77)

LINDSAY, John Vliet. Flattery isn't harmful unless inhaled. (Chicago Tribune 22:1 Section 2 Jan 22, 78)

LINDSAY, John Vliet. If you want gratitude, get yourself a dog. (Chicago Tribune 22:2 Section 2 Jan 22, 78)

LIPPMANN, Walter. America has always been not only a country but a dream. (American West 20:8 Nov 83)

LIPPMANN, Walter. The final test of a leader is that he leaves behind him in other men the conviction and the will to carry on. (Sports Illustrated 65:66 Oct 6, 86)

LIPPMANN, Walter. The theory of a free press is that the truth will emerge from free reporting and free discussions, not that it is presented perfectly and instantly

in any one account. (Chicago Tribune 57:2 Section 5 Feb 26, 89)

LIPPMANN, Walter. When all think alike, no one is thinking. (Book Digest 6:28 Dec 79)

LIPSEN, Chuck. Folklore has it that the oldest profession is prostitution. I always thought it was lobbying. (W 6:2 Sept 16, 77)

LISAGOR, Peter. Washington is a place where the truth is not necessarily the best defense. It surely runs a poor second to the statute of limitations. (Time 108:71 Dec 20, 76)

LITTLE RICHARD. If there was anything I loved better than a big penis it was a bigger penis. (Spin 2:12 Mar 87)

LITTLE RICHARD. Prince is me in this generation. (US 3:4 April 6, 87)

LITTLE RICHARD. Real women don't want to climb telephone poles. (New Woman 10:12 May 80)

LODGE, John Davis. Man is born into the world as a pig and is civilized by women. (W 6:2 Feb 18, 77)

LOGAN, Ben. TV is hydraulic. You push down violence and up pops exploitative sex. (Newsweek 91:54 Feb 20, 78)

LOLLOBRIGIDA, Gina. Whatever we learn, we learn too late. (Chicago Tribune Magazine 2 July 5, 87)

LOMBARD, Carole. You know how much I love Pappy, but to tell you the honest truth, he isn't such a hell of a good lay (about Clark Gable). (Cosmopolitan 197:190 Mar 84)

LOMBARDI, Vince. Winning isn't everything. It is the only thing. (Newsweek 94:166 Nov 19, 79)

LOMBARDO, Guy. When I go, I'll take New Year's Eve with me. (Newsweek 90:126 Nov 14, 77)

LONG, Russell. Those who defame us, curse us, abuse us and lie about us, would be in one hell of a fix without us (about energy producers). (Time 114:84 Nov 26, 79)

LONGWORTH, Alice Roosevelt. Fill what's empty. Empty what's full. And scratch where it itches. (Washingtonian 15:142 Nov 79)

LONGWORTH, Alice Roosevelt. He was the best company there ever was (about John L. Lewis). (New York Times 124:15 Section 4 Aug 17, 75)

LONGWORTH, Alice Roosevelt. The secret of eternal youth is arrested development. (Washington Post 103:1 Section C Feb 24, 80)

LOOS, Anita. Gentlemen don't prefer blondes. If I were writing that book today,

I'd call it 'Gentlemen Prefer Gentlemen'. (Newsweek 85:72 May 12, 75)

LOPES, Davey. If he ain't struck you out, you ain't nobody (about Nolan Ryan). (Time 134:70 Sept 4, 89)

LOPEZ PORTILLO, Jose. Mexico is neither on the list of United States priorities nor on that of United States respect. (New York Times 128:A8 Nov 20, 78)

LORD, Winston. The Trilateral Commission doesn't secretly run the world. The Council on Foreign Relations does that. (W 7:9 Aug 4, 78)

LOREN, Sophia. I will be a very wise and serene old lady. As I get older, I get quieter, because now I know myself better. (Chicago Tribune 15:33 Jan 15, 78)

LOREN, Sophia. Spaghetti can be eaten most successfully if you inhale it like a vacuum cleaner. (Time 119:76 April 26, 82)

LOREN, Sophia. The mob that adores you is the most wonderful tribute there can be. (Newsweek 96:63 Oct 6, 80)

LOREN, Sophia. We actors are the damned of the earth. (The Observer 9862:12 Aug 31, 80)

LOUGHRIGE, Alan Craig. The middle of the road is the best place to get run over. (Washingtonian 15:142 Nov 79)

LOUIS, Joe. You can run, but you can't hide. (Mother Jones 3:65 Dec 77)

LOVELL, James, Jr. We will fly women into space and use them the same way we use them on Earth—and for the same purpose. (Ms 6:49 July 77)

LOWE, Nick. (Grace Slick) is like somebody's mom who's had a few too many drinks at a cocktail party. (Time 111:46 June 26, 78)

LOWELL, Robert. Almost all good women poets are either divorced or lesbian. (San Francisco Chronicle 111:19 May 25, 77)

LOWERY, Joseph. Twenty years later, everything has changed and nothing has changed (on the 20th anniversary of the assassination of Martin Luther King Jr.). (Chicago Tribune 103:17 Section 1 April 12, 1988)

LOWREY, Bette. Inflation is just a high priced depression. (Cleveland 4:15 May 75)

LOY, Myrna. Nobody seems to like each other anymore. (Viva 5:108 Oct 77)

LUCAS, George. I'm not out to be thought of as a great artist. It's a big world and everybody doesn't have to be significant. (Time 115:73 May 19, 80)

LUCE, Clare Boothe. A man's home may seem to be his castle on the outside; inside it is more often his nursery.

(Cosmopolitan 196:332 Oct 83)

LUCE, Clare Boothe. Censorship, like charity, should begin at home, but unlike charity, it should end there. (USA Today 1:8A Aug 9, 83)

LUCE, Clare Boothe. It is ridiculous to think you can spend your entire life with just one person. Three is about the right number. Yes, I imagine three husbands would do it. (The Observer 9931:13 Jan 3, 82)

LUCE, Clare Boothe. There aren't many women now I'd like to see as President—but there are fewer men. (Newsweek 94:95 Oct 22, 79)

LUCE, Clare Boothe. Widowhood is a fringe benefit of marriage. (Washingtonian 21:121 Jan 85)

LUCE, Clare Boothe (attributed by Paul Dickson). No good deed goes unpunished. (Playboy 25:22 May 78)

LUCE, Henry. Make money, be proud of it; make more money, be prouder of it. (Washington Journalism Review 1:22 April 78)

LUCIANO, Ron. Old managers never die. They just end up working for George Steinbrenner. (Time 120:93 Sept 13, 82)

LUDLAM, Charles. My work is eclectic not ethnocentric. It is a Rosetta Stone of theatrical conventions. (Village Voice 20:120 Nov 17, 75)

LUEDERS, Edward. Solitude leads to amplitude. (Country Journal 5:105 Aug 78)

LUMBARD, J. Edward. In areas of doubt and conflicting considerations, it is thought better to err on the side of free speech. (American Legion Magazine 102:22 June 77)

LYNCH, James. If we do not live together, we will die—prematurely—alone. (Guardian Weekly 117:17 Sept 18, 77)

MABLEY, Moms. A woman is a woman until the day she dies, but a man's a man only as long as he can. (Sepia 24:10 Jan 75)

MACARTHUR, Douglas. Duty, honor, country: Those three hallowed words reverently dictate what you want to be, what you can be, and what you will be...The long gray line has never failed us (at the U.S. Military Academy at West Point, May 12, 1962). (Washington Post 208:B1 July 1, 77)

MACARTHUR, Douglas. It's the orders you disobey that make you famous. (Time 112:89 Sept 11, 78)

MACARTHUR, John D. Anybody who knows what he's worth, isn't worth very much (upon being asked how much he was worth). (Chicago Tribune 340:2

Section 1 Dec 5, 76)

MACCARTHY, Desmond. A biographer is an ártist who is on oath. (Time 114:86 July 2, 79)

MACHEL, Samora. We cannot tolerate a bourgeoisie in Mozambique, even a black one. (Time 107:26 May 3, 76)

MACLAINE, Shirley. He (Ronald Reagan) is a true velvet fascist, really smooth. (Chicago Sun-Times 29:12 Feb 17, 76)

MACLAINE, Shirley. I want women to be liberated and still be able to have a nice ass and shake it. (People Weekly 5:27 May 10, 76)

MACLAINE, Shirley. We're bisexual up to the age of 3, but what society won't admit is that we're bisexual most of our lives. (W 6:2 Sept 2, 77)

MACLAINE, Shirley. When you know who you are and you realize what you can do, you can do things better at 40 than when you're 20. (Time 107:39 Feb 16, 76)

MACLEAN, Norman. In our family, there was no clear line between religion and fly fishing. (Lawrence (Kansas) Journal-World 130:2C June 12, 88)

MACLEISH, Archibald. Freedom is still the last great revolutionary cause. (Chicago Tribune 163:2 Section 2 June 11, 78)

MACLEISH, Archibald. What we know to be man is in these stacks (about the Library of Congress). (New York Times 129:B14 Oct 4, 79)

MACMILLAN, Harold. A foreign secretary is forever poised between a cliche and an indiscretion. (Kansas City Star 97:4B Jan 30, 77)

MACNEIL, Robert. TV has created a nation of news junkies who tune in every night to get their fix on the world. (Time 115:65 Feb 25, 80)

MADDOX, Lester Garfield. The reason he (Jimmy Carter) says he never lies is because he thinks the truth originates with him. (Newsweek 88:25 July 19, 76)

MADONNA, (rock musician). I'm just a midwestern girl in a bustier. (US 3:6 July 11, 88)

MAGRUDER, Jeb Stuart. I lost my moral compass. (Newsweek 85:49 May 5, 75)

MAHE, Edward, Jr. Everything Quayle does—or doesn't do—will reflect on George Bush's judgement. (Newsweek 112:13 Nov 21, 88)

MAHER, Leo, Bishop. A pro-choice Catholic is an oxymoron. (Chicago Tribune 341:20 Dec 7, 89)

MAHFOUZ, Naguib. If the rage to write should ever leave me, I want that day to be my last. (Chicago Tribune 300:23 Section 1 Oct 26, 88)

MAILER, Norman. (Thomas Wolfe was) the greatest five-year-old who ever lived. (New York Times Book Review 3 Dec 2, 79)

MAILER, Norman. A writer of the largest dimension can alter the nerves and marrow of a nation. (New York Times Magazine 54 Sept 9, 79)

MAILER, Norman. As many people die from an excess of timidity as from brávery. (New York 16:32 Mar 28, 83)

MAILER, Norman. Ego is the word of the century. (New York Times Magazine 110 Dec 2, 79)

MAILER, Norman. Giving a camera to Diane Arbus is like putting a live grenade in the hands of a child. (Newsweek 104:90 Oct 22, 84)

MAILER, Norman. I can think of very few women who, like Susan Sontag, are first intellectuals and then literary artists. (Village Voice 31:21 Jan 28, 86)

MAILER, Norman. I don't pretend I'm typical, but I've always found promiscuous women interesting. I suspect I would have been promiscuous if I'd been a woman. I certainly have been as a man. (Kansas City Star 110:D-1 May 7, 90)

MAILER, Norman. I've made an ass of myself so many times I often wonder if I am one. (New York Times Magazine 53 Sept 9, 79)

MAILER, Norman. It's hard to get to the top in America, but it's even harder to stay there. (Time 113:74 April 2, 79)

MAILER, Norman. My talent is making money, not managing it. (Kansas City Times 111:2A Jan 25, 79)

MAILER, Norman. Sex is the reward for good work. (M 7:79 Feb 90)

MAILER, Norman. You don't know anything about a woman until you meet her in court. (Penthouse 16:152 Nov 84)

MAKAROVA, Natalia. Even the ears must dance. (Newsweek 85:65 May 19, 75)

MALAMUD, Bernard. I write to know the next room of my fate. (Time 114:86 July 2, 79)

MALCOLM X. This thing with me will be resolved by death and violence. (Playboy 23:127 June 76)

MALINOWSKI, Bronislaw. Every historical change creates its mythology. (Time 109:86 May 23, 77)

MALKOVICH, John. Art is not more important than life. (Newsweek 104:86 Sept 24, 84)

MALKOVICH, John. He's (Dustin Hoffman) the quintessential terminal juvenile. (American Film 11:28 Oct 85)

MALLE, Louis. Being a director is like being

a thief. You steal bits and pieces of the lives around you, and you put them into a movie. (New York Times 126:C6 Nov 19, 76)

MALRAUX, Andre. A minor living art is far more vital than a major dead one. (New York Times Magazine 17 Jan 23, 77)

MALRAUX, Andre. There cannot be another Michelangelo in today's society because our faith in man is too weak. (Time 105:40 May 12, 75)

MAMET, David. Frank Rich and John Simon are the syphilis and gonorrhea of the theater. (Newsweek 107:13 Feb 17, 86)

MAMET, David. I want to change the future of American theatre. (Village Voice 21:101 July 5, 76)

MAMET, David. Intellectually, I'd like to think of them (critics) as running-dog conspirators against the institution of art. But they're just jack-offs like the rest of us. (More 7:31 July 77)

MANDEL, Morris. Always put off until tomorrow what you shouldn't do at all. (Reader's Digest 106:145 April 75)

MANDELA, Nelson. Equality, liberty and the pursuit of happiness are fundamental human rights which are not only inalienable but must, if necessary, be defended with the weapons of war. (Chicago Tribune 178:3 Section 1 June 27, 90)

MANDELA, Nelson. White South Africa has to accept that there will never be peace until the principle of majority rule is fully applied. (Time 135:27 Feb 5, 90)

MANKIEWICZ, Frank Fabian. Since we are not yet serious about guns, let us at least withhold the most costly target (the President). (Newsweek 86:34 Oct 6, 75)

MANKIEWICZ, Frank Fabian. The higher the tuition, the fewer days they spend in school. (Washingtonian 14:154 Oct 31, 78)

MANKIEWICZ, Herman. There but for the grace of God goes God (about Orson Welles). (American Film 4:70 Feb 79)

MANKIEWICZ, Tom. Whatever Jimmy Carter is asking us to be, Superman is already. (Time 110:64 Aug 1, 77)

MANSFIELD, Mike. The crisis you have to worry about most is the one you don't see coming. (US News & World Report 88:42 Oct 31, 77)

MAO, Tse-Tung. (I am) only a lone monk walking the world with a leaky umbrella. (Time 108:37 Sept 20, 76)

MAO, Tse-Tung. All reactionaries are paper tigers. (Newsweek 88:45 Sept 20, 76)

MAO, Tse-Tung. Every Communist must grasp the truth: political power grown out of the barrel of a gun. Our principle is that the party commands the gun and the gun must never be allowed to command the party. (Newsweek 88:40 Sept 20, 76)

MAO, Tse-Tung. I am alone with the masses. (Time 108:38 Sept 20, 76)

MAO, Tse-Tung. If the Americans do not recognize us in 1,000 years, they will recognize us in 1,001 years. (New York Times 126:3 Section 4 Aug 21, 77)

MAO, Tse-Tung. Let a hundred schools of thought contend. Let a hundred flowers blossom (in 1956-57). (New York Times 128:1 Section 4 Dec 3, 78)

MAO, Tse-Tung. Once all struggle is grasped, miracles are possible. (New York Times 128:1 Section 4 Dec 3, 78)

MAO, Tse-Tung. Revolution is a drama of passion. We did not win the People over by appealing to reason but by developing hope, trust, fraternity. (Time 108:41 Sept 20, 76)

MAO, Tse-Tung. Sometimes we have only to fart to stir Americans into moving a battleship or two or even a whole fleet. (Time 108:44 Sept 20, 76)

MAO, Tse-Tung. The most important thing is to be strong. With strength, one can conquer others, and to conquer others gives one virtue. (Time 108:41 Sept 20, 76)

MARCEAU, Marcel. I am a silent witness of my time. (Christian Science Monitor 69:22 Feb 2, 77)

MARCHETTI, Victor. Ours is not yet a totalitarian government, but it is an elitist democracy—and becoming more so every year. (Inquiry 1:24 Feb 6, 78)

MARCINKUS, Paul Casimir. You can't run the church on Hail Marys. (National Catholic Reporter 23:10 Mar 13, 87)

MARCOS, Ferdinand E. I would like to return the Filipino to what he was before he was altered and modified by the softness of Western and other ways. (Time 107:21 Jan 5, 76)

MARCOS, Ferdinand E. It is easier to run a revolution than a government. (Time 107:35 June 6, 77)

MARCOS, Imelda. The Americans need us more than we need them. (USA Today 1:8A Aug 23, 83)

MARCUS, Stanley. A businessman can make no worse mistake than to try to use the muscle of the advertising dollar to try to influence the news. (The Atlantic 241:38 April 78)

MARGOLIS, Susan. Today the gifted as well as the deranged among us are struggling to be famous the way earlier Americans struggled to be saved. (Time 111:56 June

19, 78)

MARK, Sir Robert (chief of London's police force). The real art of policing a free society or a democracy is to win by appearing to lose or at least to win by not appearing to win. (The Observer 9701:13 July 17, 77)

MARLEY, Bob. It takes a revolution to make a solution. (To the Point International 4:17 Sept 12, 77)

MARQUIS, Don. If you make people think they're thinking, they'll love you; but if you really make them think, they'll hate you. (Rocky Mountain News 250:50 Dec 28, 79)

MARSH, Jean. I think poetry is like a diary: people don't tend to write anything in it until something awful happens. (Newsweek 91:32 Feb 13, 78)

MARSH, Jean. We're not sent into this life to be alone, but two-by-two, like in the ark. (W 7:41 Oct 13, 78)

MARSHALL, Throgood. I don't think (he) (Franklin D. Roosevelt) did much for the Negro. (Newsweek 110:21 Sept 21, 87)

MARSHALL, Throgood. I have come to the definite conclusion that if the United States is indeed the great melting pot, the Negro either didn't get in the pot or he didn't get melted down. (Newsweek 110:21 Sept 21, 87)

MARSHALL, Thurgood. The Ku Klux Klan never dies. They just stop wearing sheets because sheets cost too much. (Time 112:91 Dec 4, 78)

MARTIN, Abe. Beauty is only skin deep, but it's a valuable asset if you're poor or haven't any sense. (Human Behavior 7:70 Sept 78)

MARTIN, Abe. Being an optimist after you've got everything you want doesn't count. (Human Behavior 7:70 Sept 78)

MARTIN, Abe. What this country needs is a good five-cent cigar. (Human Behavior 7:70 Sept 78)

MARTIN, Judith. Life is full of situations that cry out not to be commented upon. (Kansas City Times 117:A-23 Oct 25, 84)

MARTIN, Mary. He's (Richard Rodgers) the one person I will never, never wash out of my hair. (New York Times 128:C15 Dec 4, 78)

MARTY, Martin E. A saint has to be a misfit. A person who embodies what his culture considers typical or normal cannot be exemplary. (Time 106:48 Dec 29, 75)

MARVIN, Lee. There's too much damned violence on the screen. I don't go for it. Some of those producers and directors need some sense bashed into their heads. (The Star 4:2 Aug 30, 77)

MARX, Groucho. I never forget a face, but in your case I'll make an exception. (Viva 5:80 Sept 77)

MARX, Groucho. I wouldn't belong to any club that would have me for a member. (New York Times 126:40 Aug 21, 77)

MARX, Groucho. Military intelligence is a contradiction in terms. (San Francisco Chronicle This World 1978:40 Jan 29, 78)

MARX, Leo. The establishment has taken over the art of anti-disestablishmentarianism. (M 6:84 Feb 89)

MARX, Minnie. Where else can people who don't know anything make a living (commenting on show business). (Newsweek 91:76 May 22, 78)

MASON, Tony. The thing is that 90% of the colleges are abiding by the rules, doing things right. The other 10%, they're going to the bowl games. (Sports Illustrated 43:14 Oct 27, 75)

MASTERS, William Howell. Males have made asses of themselves writing about female sexual experience. (Newsweek 85:74 May 5, 75)

MASTROIANNI, Marcello. She is much woman (about Sonia Braga). (Newsweek 112:60 July 18, 88)

MATA-HARI. The dance is a poem and each movement a word. (Andy Warhol's Interview 7:15 May 76)

MATHIAS, Charles McCurdy. People tend to want to follow the beaten path. The difficulty is that the beaten path doesn't seem to be leading anywhere. (Time 106:12 Dec 8, 75)

MATHIS, Andrew W. It's bad luck to be superstitious. (Omni 1:131 May 79)

MATLOVICH, Leonard P. They gave me a medal for killing two men and discharged me for loving one. (Chicago Sun-Times 28:36 Aug 18, 75)

MATTHAU, Carol. You don't stop being a girl because they give you a different number. (W 19:19 July 9, 90)

MATURE, Victor. Apparently, the way to a girl's heart is to saw her in half. (Playboy 26:26 Oct 79)

MAUGHAM, William Somerset. Only a mediocre person is always at his best. (Forbes 120:80 Aug 1, 77)

MAUGHAM, William Somerset. People ask you for criticism, but they only want praise. (Rocky Mountain News 141:44 Sept 10, 79)

MAUGHAM, William Somerset. The unfortunate thing about this world is that good habits are so much easier to get out of than bad ones. (Kansas City Times 109:14C Jan 22, 77)

MAULDIN, Bill. We have more provincialism and bigotry and superstition and prejudice per square mile than almost any other nation. (Rolling Stone 225:56 Nov 4, 76)

MAVERICK, Maury, Jr. When you've got a famous name, you ought to use it to speak up for the people who can't speak up for themselves. (Texas Monthly 16:109 Mar 88)

MAXWELL, Elsa. A good hostess must always proceed upon the assumption that her guests are children, no matter what their age. (Details 7:24 Nov 88)

MAYER, Jean. The ability to arrive at complex decisions is the hallmark of the educated person. (People Weekly 6:44 Nov 15, 76)

MAYS, Benjamin. If this (country) is a melting pot, I don't want the Negro to melt away. (Time 111:49 Feb 13, 78)

MAYS, Willie. I think I was the best baseball player I ever saw. (Newsweek 93:68 Feb 5, 79)

MCARTHUR, Robert. Never imply that they care whether your socks match; and never forget that they do. (Washingtonian 14:46 Jan 78)

MCCARTHY, Eugene Joseph. He (Fritz Mondale) has the soul of a vice-president. (Village Voice 21:14 Oct 11, 76)

MCCARTHY, Eugene Joseph. If you're in the peanut business you learn to think small (about Jimmy Carter). (New York 9:9 Aug 2, 76)

MCCARTHY, Eugene Joseph. Kissinger won a Nobel Peace Prize for watching a war end that he was for. (New York Times Magazine 100 Oct 24, 76)

MCCARTHY, Eugene Joseph. The only thing that saves us from the bureaucracy is inefficiency. An efficient bureaucracy is the greatest threat to liberty. (Time 113:67 Feb 12, 79)

MCCARTHY, Eugene Joseph. The Republican Party is a lower form of plant life, like moss on a rock. It has very low vitality—green in the summer, slightly gray in the winter—but it never dies. If the Republicans had any decency, they'd just go away. (New York Times Magazine 13 Oct 24, 76)

MCCARTHY, Eugene Joseph. The selling of arms is now one of the principal occupations of the Defense Department. (Center Report 8:11 Dec 75)

MCCARTHY, Eugene Joseph. Work is the only kind of property many people have in America. (Center Report 8:12 Dec 75)

MCCARTHY, Eugene Joseph (attributed by Daniel Patrick Moynihan). No one ever was associated with (Lyndon Johnson) who was not in the end somehow diminished. (The Observer 9796:34 May 27, 79)

MCCARTHY, Mary. It really takes a hero to live any kind of spiritual life without religious belief. (The Observer 9816:35 Oct 14, 79)

MCCARTHY, Mary. One has to believe that love is eternal, even if one knows it is not. (The Observer 9816:35 Oct 14, 79)

MCCARTHY, Mary. You mustn't force sex to do the work of love or love to do the work of sex. (Cosmopolitan 197:274 Mar 84)

MCCARTNEY, Linda. Our kids keep asking, what is Daddy going to do when he grows up? (People Weekly 5:35 June 7, 76)

MCCLINTICK, David. There is only one law of the Hollywood jungle, and it is box office. (Time 120:47 July 26, 82)

MCCORMACK, Mike. One man's conservation is all too frequently another man's unemployment. (Time 110:27 Dec 12, 77)

MCCREE, Wade. Washington is the only town in the world where sound travels faster than light. (Chicago Sun-Times 31:6 June 20, 78)

MCCULLERS, Carson. I have more to say than Hemingway, and, God knows, I say it better than Faulkner. (Time 106:E3 July 21, 75)

MCGOVERN, George Stanley. He who tugs Uncle Sam's beard too hard risks reprisal from the mightiest nation on the face of this earth. (The Observer 9822:9 Nov 25, 79)

MCGOVERN, George Stanley. Marching in mindless lockstep is the lowest form of party loyalty. (Village Voice 22:34 May 16, 77)

MCGOVERN, George Stanley. The longer the title, the less important the job . (Town & Country 133:141 May 79)

MCGOVERN, George Stanley. Thoughtful Americans understand that the highest patriotism is not a blind acceptance of official policy, but a love of one's country deep enough to call her to a higher standard. (Life 2:117 Dec 79)

MCGUIRE, Al. The only thing in this country that blacks really dominate, except poverty, is basketball. (Chicago Tribune 63:1 Section 5 Mar 3, 78)

MCKAY, Robert. If war is too important to be left to the generals, surely justice is too important to be left to lawyers. (Time 111:66 April 10, 78)

MCKUEN, Rod. Having been born a bastard, I feel it has given me a head start on all those people who have spent their lives becoming one. (Time 106:30 Dec

29, 75)

MCKUEN, Rod. The best remedy for a cold is to go to bed with a good book, or a friend who's read one. (Viva 4:26 Feb 77)

MCLUHAN, Marshall. Football is itself the biggest dramatization of American business ever invented. (Inside Sports 3:70 Jan 31, 81)

MCLUHAN, Marshall. Most clear writing is a sign that there is no exploration going on. Clear prose indicates an absence of thought. (Time 106:36 Aug 25, 75)

MCLUHAN, Marshall. North America looks, as usual, grim. (Mother Jones 1:9 Nov 76)

MCLUHAN, Marshall. Only the vanquished remember history. (Forbes 120:120 Aug 15, 77)

MCLUHAN, Marshall. Television is not a visual medium. (CoEvolution Quarterly 16:86 Winter 77/78)

MCLUHAN, Marshall. TV is addictive. It's a drug. (Washington Post 161:H1 May 15, 77)

MCNULTY, Franklin L. With adequate integrity, guts can be located. (Parade 4 May 27, 79)

MEAD, Margaret. At least 50 percent of the human race doesn't want their mother-in-law within walking distance. (Newsweek 92:75 Nov 27, 78)

MEAD, Margaret. For the first time the young are seeing history being made before it is censored by their elders (in defense of TV). (Time 112:57 Nov 27, 78)

MEAD, Margaret. I expect to die someday but I'll never retire. (Change 9:12 Sept 77)

MEAD, Margaret. Women, it is true, make human beings, but only men can make men. (Chicago Tribune 176:2 Section 2 June 25, 78)

MEANY, George. Everything in this world that affects life, liberty and happiness is the business of the American trade union movement. (American Legion Magazine 100:9 Feb 76)

MEANY, George. Foreign policy is too damned important to be left to the Secretary of State. (Time 106:7 Sept 8, 75)

MEANY, George. The fight against inflation must be on the basis of the equality of sacrifice, not the sacrifice of equality. (Time 113:9 Feb 5, 79)

MEANY, George. They say Carter is the first businessman ever to sit in the White House. But why did they have to send us a small businessman? (Time 112:62 Nov 27, 78)

MEDLIN, James. The most healthy thing in

L.A. is to do nothing. (New West 3:Oct 9, 78

MEESE, Edwin. The progressive income tax is immoral. (USA Today 1:8A July 22, 83)

MEESE, Edwin. We are literally going to have to put criminals in jail and throw away the key. (USA Today 1:8A June 15, 83)

MEESE, Edwin. You don't name many suspects who are innocent of a crime. (Texas Observer 79:10 Sept 11, 87)

MEHTA, Asoka. Socialism is an attractive goal, but concentration of power is as dangerous as concentration of capital. (Time 111:30 Mar 13, 78)

MEIER, Hans. What you suffer does not defile you; what you do does. (Chicago Tribune 81:2 Section 5 Mar 22, 89)

MEIGHEN, Arthur. We are not in the same boat, but we are pretty much in the same waters. (New York Times 129:E5 Section 4 Nov 4, 79)

MEIR, Golda. Don't be humble, you're not that great. (New York Times Book Review 39 June 17, 79)

MEIR, Golda. I may not have been a great prime minister, but I would have been a great farmer. (Chicago Tribune 306:18 Nov 2, 77)

MEIR, Golda. I wouldn't accept the West Bank and Gaza as part of Israel if they were offered on a silver platter. (Village Voice 25:8 Oct 8, 80)

MEKAS, Jonas. Avant-garde film doesn't want to and can't be part of any business. (Village Voice 20:72 July 7, 75)

MEKAS, Jonas. I am minister of interior for independent filmmakers. (Elle 2:46 Nov 86)

MELLON, Paul. One of the main things money provides is privacy. (Time 111:79 May 8, 78)

MENCKEN, Henry Louis. For every human problem, there is a neat, plain solution— and it is always wrong. (Washingtonian 14:155 Nov 78)

MENCKEN, Henry Louis. Immorality is the morality of those who are having a better time. (New York Times 139:31 Dec 13, 89)

MENCKEN, Henry Louis. One horse laugh is worth ten thousand syllogisms. (New York Times Book Review 27 Sept 7, 80)

MENKE-GLUCKERT, Peter. Environment has become the Viet Nam of the middle class. (Time 107:48 April 25, 77)

MENNINGER, Karl. 'Insane' is an expression we psychiatrists don't use until we get to court. Insanity is a question of public opinion. (Time 106:57 Oct 20, 75)

MENNINGER, Karl. Sex and sexuality never

made anyone ill and never made anyone feel guilty. It is the hate and destructiveness concealed in them which produce strange aberrations and bitter regret. (Playboy 24:203 Dec 77)

MENNINGER, Karl. The jail is a horrible institution manned by amateurs and politicians. (Los Angeles Times 96:2 Part 1 Oct 2, 77)

MENNINGER, Karl. The worst disease in the world is the plague of vengeance. (New York Times 133:24 Oct 30, 83)

MERCOURI, Melina. I have been playing a woman with a past since I was five years old. (Time 107:93 June 6, 77)

MEREDITH, Don. The higher you climb the flagpole, the more people see your rear end. (Life 7:141 Jan 84)

MERKIN, Richard. Paintings in galleries sell for twice the price they command at auction. (CoEvolution Quarterly 35:5 Fall 82)

MERMAN, Ethel. (Cole Porter) sang like a hinge. (Time 114:97 Oct 1, 79)

MERMAN, Ethel. Broadway has been very good to me—but then, I've been very good to Broadway. (Time 124:47 Dec 31, 84)

METZENBAUM, Howard. The President can't stand up to the military-industrial complex, and neither can Congress. (Penthouse 14:175 Oct 82)

MEYER, Russ. My films are like a reptile you beat with a club. You think you've killed it, but then you turn around and it gets you in the ankle. (Washington Post 340:B1 Nov 9, 76)

MEYNER, Helen. Let the best man win, whomever she may be. (Life 2:140 Dec 79)

MIDLER, Bette. (Fans) make me think that maybe there's more to me than I know. (Newsweek 94:37 July 2, 79)

MIDLER, Bette. I want to be a legend. (TV Guide 25:22 Dec 3, 77)

MIDLER, Bette. The worst part of having success is to try finding someone who is happy for you. (Chicago Sun-Times 29:32 Mar 3, 76)

MIKULSKI, Barbara A. Some people like to raise flowers; I like to raise hell, I want to be the Amelia Earhart of Congress. I want to fly into the areas of the unknown, like she did, for the fun of it. (Time 108:48 Nov 15, 76)

MIKVA, Abner J. My definition of a liberal is someone who can look at an idea and see that it doesn't work, even if it was a liberal idea. (Chicago Tribune 222:4 Section 3 Aug 10, 78)

MIKVA, Abner J. Someone once said that

politics is like poker—it's only fun when you play for a trifle more than you can afford to lose. (Chicago Sun-Times 31:5 Nov 9, 78)

MILLAY, Edna St. Vincent. It is not true that life is one damn thing after another; it's one damn thing over and over. (Viva 4:25 July 77)

MILLER, Ann. All my life I've tried to be an eight-by-ten glossy. (Newsweek 85:52 May 26, 75)

MILLER, Ann. No matter what you've achieved, if you're not loved (by a man), Honey, you ain't nothin' but a hound dog. (New Woman 10:12 May 80)

MILLER, Arthur. I always doubted that writers ever really understand more than anyone else. All you can hope is that maybe you feel a little more. (The Observer 9812:35 Sept 16, 79)

MILLER, Arthur. I think a play ought to cast a shadow; it ought to be something you can walk around. (New York Times 128:6 Section 2 June 17, 79)

MILLER, Arthur. I think that you don't take seriously any art that's not dealing finally with whether we are doomed or not. (Christian Science Monitor 69:30 Aug 8, 77)

MILLER, Arthur. I welcome him as the world's first avant-garge president. (Newsweek 115:28 Mar 5, 90)

MILLER, Arthur. I've always written in the back of my head for the great unwashed. (New York Times 128:6 Section 2 June 17, 79)

MILLER, Arthur. Part of being a playwright is being an actor. One way or another, whether surreptitiously or not, a good playwright is an actor. (Connecticut 41:115 Jan 78)

MILLER, Arthur. The paranoia of stupidity is always the worst, since its fear of destruction by intelligence is reasonable. (Forbes 121:28 April 3, 78)

MILLER, Arthur. Violence is the last refuge of scoundrels (commenting on TV violence). (Christian Science Monitor 69:30 Aug 8, 77)

MILLER, George William. Don't rationalize mediocrity. (Time 112:62 July 17, 78)

MILLER, George William. Inflation (is) a clear and present danger. (New York Times 128:10 Section 4 Aug 12, 79)

MILLER, George William. There is no penalty for overachievement. (Time 112:62 July 17, 78)

MILLER, Henry. I'm going to beat those bastards (when asked how he would write his epitaph). (People Weekly 10:62 Aug 21, 78)

MILLER, Henry. To the person who thinks with his head, life is a comedy. To those who think with their feelings, or work through their feelings, life is a tragedy. (Soho News 5:3 Jan 26, 78)

MILLIGAN, Spike. Money can't buy friends, but you can get a better class of enemy. (Washingtonian 21:120 Jan 85)

MILLS, Chuck. When it comes to football, God is prejudiced—toward big, fast kids (commenting on religion and football). (New York Times 125:3 Feb 1, 76)

MILNES, Richard Monckton. My exit is the result of too many entrees. (Writer's Digest 58:11 Oct 78)

MINGUS, Charles. Don't call me a jazz musician. The word jazz means nigger, discrimination, second-class citizenship, the back-of-the-bus bit. (Time 113:77 Jan 22, 79)

MINOW, Newton. The most important educational institution in the country is not Harvard or Yale or Caltech—it's television. (Time 113:50 May 28, 79)

MINOW, Newton. There is no contract you can't get out of for money. (Wilson Library Bulletin 53:507 Mar 79)

MIRO, Joan. Fools do not make art. (New York Arts Journal 7:8 Nov 77)

MITCHELL, Clarence M., Jr. Lyndon B. Johnson was the greatest American President on civil rights. (New York Times 128:28 April 15, 79)

MITCHUM, Robert. I do films for the greatest return, for the least effort. (The Times 8042:3 Aug 7, 77)

MITFORD, Nancy. Sisters stand between one and life's cruel circumstances. (Ms 6:65 Sept 77)

MITTERAND, Francois. The day when racial segragation ceases to be identified with social segregation hasn't come yet. And so long as racial protest is joined to social protest, watch out. Even if there are periods of calm, the awakening will be rude (about the United States). (Village Voice 31:32 June 3, 86)

MIX, Tom (attributed by Heywood Hale Broun). Straight shooters always win. (Travel & Leisure 11:138 Feb 80)

MIZNER, Wilson. A dramatic critic is a person who surprises the playwright by informing him what he meant. (Stagebill 52 Dec 81)

MOHAMMED REZA PAHLEVI, SHAH OF IRAN. I'm not just another dictator. I'm a hereditary monarch. (Village Voice 23:19 Aug 21, 78)

MOHAMMED REZA PAHLEVI, SHAH OF IRAN. In a man's life, women count only if they're beautiful and graceful and know how to stay feminine. (Washingtonian 10:21 July 75)

MOHAMMED REZA PAHLEVI, SHAH OF IRAN. Nobody can overthrow me—I have the power. (US News & World Report 84:37 June 26, 78)

MONACO, James. Film has come of age as an art, probably because television now receives the brunt of contempt from the remaining proponents of an elite culture. (New York Times Book Review 11 April 1, 79)

MONAGHAN, Jim. I guess every day in New Orleans is like a B-movie. (New Orleans 10:30 Jan 75)

MONDALE, Walter Frederick. If you are sure you understand everything that is going on, you are hopelessly confused. (Book Digest 6:28 Dec 79)

MONDALE, Walter Frederick. It shows above all that Americans are no good at all at killing, lying and covering up and I'm glad that's the case (on CIA assassination attempts on foreign leaders). (Washington Post 351:1 Nov 21, 75)

MONDALE, Walter Frederick. There is no way on earth people can take the Vice-president of the United States seriously (originally quoted by columnist Jim Klobuchar in the Minneapolis Tribune in 1974). (Rolling Stone 221:16 Sept 9, 76)

MONDALE, Walter Frederick. There must be some fundamental changes in America's intelligence activities or they will fundamentally change America. (Foreign Policy 23:58 Summer 76)

MONDALE, Walter Frederick. What we have today is government of the rich, by the rich and for the rich. (Newsweek 104:33 Aug 27, 83)

MONNET, Jean. The world is divided into those who want to become someone and those who want to accomplish something. (Time 113:47 Mar 26, 79)

MONROE, Marilyn. After one night with Frankie, I don't have to see my analyst for weeks (about Frank Sinatra). (Cosmopolitan 197:190 Mar 84)

MONROE, Marilyn. I think I made his back feel better (about John F. Kennedy). (Time 106:11 Dec 29, 75)

MONTAGU, Ashley. Most psychiatrists need to have their heads examined. Analysis, it has been said, is the study of the id by the odd. (Chicago Tribune 142:3 Section 5 May 22, 77)

MONTAGU, Ashley. Science has proof without any certainty. Creationists have certainty without any proof. (Time 118:61 Sept 21, 81)

MONTAGU, Ashley. The idea is to die young as late as possible. (Town & Country 133:141 May 79)

MONTANER, Carlos Alberto. The U.S. is a neurotic Midas who homogenizes everything he touches. (Atlas World Press Review 23:39 Nov 76)

MONTRESOR, Beni. Compared to what you see around the world, New York is mummified. (W 18:22 Jan 25, 88)

MOON, Keith. Some of the things I've done, I couldn't have anything but the reputation of being a lunatic. (Newsweek 92:93 Sept 18, 78)

MOON, Sun Myung. God has been very good to me. (Newsweek 92:81 Dec 4, 78)

MOON, Sun Myung. God sent me to America in the role of a doctor. (People Weekly 6:35 Dec 27, 76)

MOON, Sun Myung. The time will come when my words will serve as law. (New York 10:97 Mar 7, 77)

MOON, Sun Myung. Without me, on earth everything will be nullified. (New West 4:62 Jan 29, 79)

MOORE, George C. No, we never gave it a thought (in response to whether the FBI had ever discussed the constitutional or legal authority for its Cointelpro Program). (New York Times 125:1 Section 4 May 2, 76)

MOORE, Henry. Looking at sculpture teaches people to use their inborn sense of form, to improve their own surroundings, to make life marvelous. (Chicago Tribune 237:1 Section 3 Aug 25, 78)

MOORE, Henry. Sculpture should always at first sight have some obscurities and further meanings. People should want to go on looking and thinking. (Mankind 6:43 May 78)

MOORE, Henry. Some people ask me why I live and work in the country. Space, light and distance are three good reasons. (Mankind 6:10 May 78)

MOORE, Henry. Stonehenge is not a building, it is a carving. (Quest 2:26 Nov 78)

MOORE, Jonathan. We're not getting as conservative as much as we are becoming less liberal (1978). (US News & World Report 84:24 Jan 23, 78)

MOORE, Marianne. A writer is unfair when he is unable to be hard on himself. (Writer's Digest 58:6 Feb 78)

MOORE, Mary Tyler. Behind each beautiful wild fur there is an ugly story. It is a brutal, bloody and barbaric story. The animal is not killed—it is tortured. I don't think a fur coat is worth it. (Chicago Sun-Times 28:3 Nov 18, 75)

MOORE, Mary Tyler. Worrying is a necessary part of life. (Chicago Tribune 32:16 Feb 1, 78)

MOORE, Roger. My real attitude toward women is this, and it hasn't changed because of any movement or anything: basically, women like to be treated as sex objects. (Playboy 25:102 May 78)

MOREAU, Jeanne. Age does not protect you from love. But love, to some extent, protects you from age. (People Weekly 3:66 Feb 3, 75)

MORGAN, Charles, Jr. If Moses had gone to Harvard Law School and spent three years working on the Hill, he would have written the Ten Commandments with three exceptions and a savings clause. (Rolling Stone 205:30 Jan 15, 76)

MORGAN, Marabel. It is only when a woman surrenders her life to her husband, reveres and worships him, and is willing to serve him, that she becomes really beautiful to him. (Ms 7:64 June 79)

MORGAN, Ted. One has come to America to get a sense of life's possibilities. (Philadelphia 69:179 Nov 78)

MORGAN, Thomas B. Koch had the opportunity to be the national urban leader, but he fled from it. (Manhattan, Inc. 6:9 Jan 89)

MORLEY, Robert. Commercials are the last things in life you can count on for a happy ending. (Time 111:53 Feb 6, 78)

MORRIS, Richard B. The United States is still the last best hope of man. (US News & World Report 81:73 July 5, 76)

MORRISON, Toni. What is curious to me is that bestial treatment of human beings never produces a race of beasts. (New York Times Magazine 40 May 20, 79)

MORROW, Dwight. One of the troubles is that we judge ourselves by our motives and others by their actions. (Christian Science Monitor 70:47 Dec 7, 77)

MORROW, Lance. Celebrities are intellectual fast food. (Time 111:57 June 12, 78)

MORROW, Lance. It bewilders Americans to be hated. (The Observer 9829:9 Jan 13, 80)

MORROW, Lance. When fame ceases to bear any relation to worth or accomplishment, then the whole currency of public recognition is debased. (Time 111:56 June 19, 78)

MORTON, Arnie (attributed by Victor Lownes). He's (Hugh Hefner) the nicest, kindest, most selfish man I've ever met. (USA Today 1:50 June 30, 83)

MOSES, Robert. As long as you're on the

side of parks, you're on the side of the angels. (New York Times 130:11 July 30, 81)

MOSES, Robert. If the end doesn't justify the means, what does? (New York Times 130:11 July 30, 81)

MOSES, Robert. If you elect a matinee idol as mayor, you get a musical-comedy administration. (New York 10:58 Sept 5, 77)

MOSES, Robert. Nothing I have ever done has been tinged with legality. (New York Times 130:11 July 30, 81)

MOSES, Robert. The important thing is to get things done. (New York Times 130:11 July 30, 81)

MOSES, Robert. Those who can, build. Those who can't, criticize. (New York Times 130:1 July 30, 81)

MOTHER TERESA. I am unworthy (upon winning the Nobel Peace Prize). (New York Times 129:1 Oct 18, 79)

MOTHER TERESA. Jesus said love one another. He didn't say love the whole world. (The Observer 9836:9 Mar 2, 80)

MOTHER TERESA. Loneliness and the feeling of being unwanted is the most terrible poverty. (Time 106:49 Dec 29, 75)

MOTHER TERESA. Those countries with legalized abortions are the poorest countries in the world. (The Observer 9825:10 Dec 16, 79)

MOTHERWELL, Robert. Every intelligent painter carries the whole culture of modern painting in his head. It is his real subject, of which anything he paints is both an homage and a critique. (Los Angeles Times Calendar 96:86 July 31, 77)

MOUNTBATTEN, Louis. If the Third World War is fought with nuclear weapons, the fourth will be fought with bows and arrows. (Maclean's 88:73 Nov 17, 75)

MOWAT, Farley. Everything outrages me that outrages nature—and most of what modern man does outrages nature. (People Weekly 13:65 Mar 31, 80)

MOYERS, Bill D. Dick Goodwin was no saint, not close, but if there's a hereafter, I'd rather spend it with Goodwin than with Gabriel. (New York 8:38 Aug 18, 75)

MOYERS, Bill D. It isn't wisdom or intelligence that influences a President, it's opportunity. (Newsweek 91:22 April 17, 78)

MOYERS, Bill D. Nixon systematically robbed the country of its ability and willingness to trust the President. (Newsweek 83:80 April 15, 74)

MOYERS, Bill D. Of all the myths of journalism, objectivity is the greatest.

(National Review 31:1021 Aug 12, 79)

MOYERS, Bill D. TV personalities are like celluloid. They're very perishable. (Newsweek 83:80 April 15, 74)

MOYNIHAN, Daniel Patrick. (The multinational corporation) is arguably the most creative international institution of the 20th century. (Time 106:62 July 14, 75)

MOYNIHAN, Daniel Patrick. As the lights go out in the rest of the world, they shine all the brighter here. (Time 107:28 Jan 26, 76)

MOYNIHAN, Daniel Patrick. I don't think there's any point in being Irish if you don't know that the world is going to break your heart eventually. (New York Times Book Review 15 April 30, 78)

MOYNIHAN, Daniel Patrick. If the U.N. didn't exist, it would be impossible to invent it. (Time 107:27 Jan 26, 76)

MOYNIHAN, Daniel Patrick. Most politicians have a right to feel morally superior to their constituencies. (Rolling Stone 219:43 Aug 12, 76)

MOYNIHAN, Daniel Patrick. Nixon understood more about liberals than liberals ever understood about him. (The Observer 9796:33 May 27, 79)

MOYNIHAN, Daniel Patrick. The great corporations of this country were not founded by ordinary people. They were founded by people with extraordinary energy, intelligence, ambition, aggressiveness. All those factors go into the primordial capitalist urge. (Time 111:27 June 19, 78)

MOYNIHAN, Daniel Patrick. The time may have come when the issue of race could benefit from a period of 'benign neglect' (to Richard Nixon in 1970). (Newsweek 94:90 Nov 19, 79)

MOYNIHAN, Daniel Patrick. There is no nation so poor that it cannot afford free speech, but there are few elites which will put up with the bother of it. (Time 107:28 Jan 26, 76)

MOYNIHAN, Daniel Patrick. When a person goes to a country and finds their newspapers filled with nothing but good news, he can bet there are good men in jail. (University Daily Kansan 87:4 Feb 16, 77)

MUCHOW, David. Budgeting is a black art practiced by bureaucratic magicians. (Chicago Sun-Times 29:2 Nov 19, 76)

MUGGERIDGE, Malcolm. (Journalism) is the ideal profession for those who find power fascinating and its exercise abhorrent. (Time 114:73 Aug 13, 79)

MUGGERIDGE, Malcolm. It is only

believers in the Fall of Man who can really appreciate how funny men are. (The Observer 9762:15 Oct 1, 78)

MUGGERIDGE, Malcolm. Western society suffers from a largely unconscious collective death wish. (Time 114:86 Sept 10, 79)

MUHAMMAD, Wallace D. I doubt if the Pope knows as much about Scripture as I do. I may not be the best orator, I may not have gone very far in school, but I am the boldest nigger you ever saw. (Newsweek 85:71 June 30, 75)

MULRONEY, Brian. Today we must guard against two dangers. First, to despair that anything can be done and, second, to delude ourselves that nothing has happened (after the failure of the Meech Lake Accord). (Chicago Tribune 179:27 Section 1 June 28, 90)

MUNRO, Alice. Love is not kind or honest and does not contribute to happiness in any reliable way. (California 10:71 Sept 85)

MUNRO, Ross H. Communist countries never expel correspondents for telling lies. (New York Times 127:11 Nov 27, 77)

MURDOCH, Iris. A bad review is even less important than whether it is raining in Patagonia. (The Observer 9770:12 Nov 26, 78)

MURDOCH, Rupert. I cannot avoid the temptation of wondering whether there is any other industry (than newspaper publishing) in this country which seeks to presume so completely to give the customer what he does not want. (Time 107:46 May 30, 77)

MURDOCH, Rupert. We will never be boring (about his newspapers). (M 7:95 Feb 90)

MURROW, Edward R (attributed by Charles Kuralt). Just because you speak in a voice loud enough to be heard over television by 16 million people, that doesn't make you any smarter than you were when you spoke loudly enough to be heard only at the other end of the bar. (Mpls/St. Paul 42 Jan 77)

MURTAUGH, Danny. A bad call (in baseball) is one that goes against you. (TV Guide 26:14 May 6, 78)

MUSE, Clarence. The public believed in the Negro's voice, but not in his intelligence. (Time 114:123 Oct 29, 79)

MUSGRAVE, John. There is nothing more ruthless on the face of this earth than an 18-year-old rifleman who wants to be 19. (University Daily Kansan 97:1 Feb 26, 87)

MYERSON, Bess. You can't be beautiful and hate. (Forbes 122:200 Oct 30, 78)

MYRDAL, Gunnar. It is natural for the ordinary American when he sees something wrong to feel not only that there should be a law against it but also that an organization should be formed to combat it. (Time 112:34 Aug 7, 78)

NABOKOV, Vladimir. Anonymous praise hurts nobody. (New York Times Book Review 27 July 31, 77)

NABOKOV, Vladimir. Great novels are above all great fairy tales. Literature does not tell the truth but makes it up. (Newsweek 90:42 July 18, 77)

NABOKOV, Vladimir. I am an American writer, born in Russia and educated in England, where I studied French literature before spending 15 years in Germany. (Washington Post 212:C4 July 5, 77)

NADER, Ralph. I start with the premise that the function of leadership is to produce more leaders, not more followers. (Time 108:41 Nov 8, 76)

NADER, Ralph. If nuclear power is so safe, why won't the insurance industry insure it? (Newsweek 85:24 Feb 24, 75)

NADER, Ralph. Information is the currency of democracy. (Chicago Tribune 258:3 Sept 15, 89)

NADER, Ralph. No lawyer in any other city is treated with such awe and fear as Don Reuben is treated in the city of Chicago. (Chicago 31:107 Feb 82)

NADER, Ralph. The speed of exit of a civil servant is directly proportional to the quality of his service. (Town & Country 133:141 May 79)

NADER, Ralph. There is not an energy crisis. There is an energy monopoly crisis, too many of the energy decisions are being made by a few large corporations instead of by a broader aggregate of consumer determinants. (Meet the Press 21:3 April 17, 77)

NADER, Ralph. This (the Three Mile Island accident) is the beginning of the end of nuclear power in this country. (Time 113:8 April 9, 79)

NAIPAUL, V. S. Africa has no future. (New York Times Book Review 36 May 13, 79)

NAIPAUL, V. S. Ignorant people in preppy clothes are more dangerous to America than oil embargoes. (Life 7:39 Jan 83)

NAKAGAMA, Sam. I would say that you can discount almost anything you read in the Wall Street Journal. (Manhattan, Inc. 5:56 Nov 88)

NAKASONE, Yasuhiro. To master the mysteries of taxation, one must learn how to shear a sheep without its bleating. (Chicago Tribune 72:21 Mar 13, 87)

NAM DUCK WOO, (Deputy Prime Minister of South Korea). There is not one developing country in the world where Western democracy really works. (Time 107:32 June 6, 77)

NASH, Graham. Serious musicians who read music don't understand what goes on with hippies. (People Weekly 8:57 Dec 12, 77)

NASH, Ogden. Marriage is the alliance of two people, one of whom never remembers birthdays and the other never forgets them. (Cosmopolitan 188:268 Feb 80)

NASH, Ogden. Progress might have been all right once, but it's gone on too long. (Reader's Digest 106:98 Feb 75)

NATHAN, George Jean. An artist never strikes; he leaves such things to plumbers and streetsweepers. (Village Voice 25:47 Dec 24, 80)

NAVRATILOVA, Martina. When I win, it is routine. When I lose, life comes to an end. (Life 7:141 Jan 83)

NEARING, Scott. Do the thing you believe in. Do it with all your might. (Down East 30:171 Aug 83)

NEAS, Ralph. There was more damage done to civil rights statutes in the last 2 1/2 weeks than in the last 2 1/2 decades (1989). (Chicago Tribune 181:3 Section 3 July 1, 89)

NEEDHAM, Richard J. Men are foolish, they think money should be taken from the rich and given to the poor. Women are sensible, they think money should be taken from the rich and given to them. (Toronto Globe and Mail 134:6 July 13, 77)

NEEDHAM, Richard J. You should treat your children as strangers whom you happen to like. If, that is, you happen to like them. (Toronto Globe and Mail 134:6 July 13, 77)

NEIZVESTNY, Ernst. A man should stand on his own two feet, even if he has only one leg. (New York Times 128:C19 Dec 1, 78)

NEL, Louis. We do not have censorship. What we have is a limitation on what newspapers can report (in South Africa). (New York Times 135:A3 June 26, 86)

NELSON, Jack. I think there is a real contempt for the press within the Reagan Administration, and I think it starts at the top. (Time 128:88 Nov 17, 86)

NELSON, Willie. To write songs, I usually need a reason. Like not having any money. (Newsweek 92:53 Aug 14, 78)

NESSEN, Ron. Press conferences force more policy decisions than anything else. (Time 106:32 May 5, 75)

NEUMAN, Alfred E. Today, it takes more

brains and effort to make out the Income Tax Form than it does to make the income. (Mad Magazine 175:1 June 75)

NEWELL, Guy. The cancer problem has not been solved, but it has never been more solvable. (American Legion Magazine 102:7 May 77)

NEWFIELD, Jack. Justice is a meat grinder. (Chicago Tribune 46:1 Section 7 Feb 15, 76)

NEWMAN, Edwin. I believe some silence is helpful to thought. And I believe to some extent radio and television discourage thought and reflection. (Chicago Tribune 1:23 Jan 1, 78)

NEWMAN, Paul. He makes the Sphinx look like a blabber-mouth (about Robert Redford). (Newsweek 103:75 May 28, 84)

NEWMAN, Paul. I figure that on my tombstone, it's going to say, 'He was a terrific actor until one day his eyes turned brown'. (Chicago Tribune 319:31 Section 1 Nov 14, 76)

NEWMAN, Paul. If you don't have enemies, you don't have character. (First Run 2 June 10, 79)

NEWMAN, Paul. There's no way that what people see on celluloid has anything to do with me. (Chicago 25:86 July 76)

NEWMAN, Susan. Making movies has nothing to do with acting. (Time 111:52 Feb 6, 78)

NGUYEN VAN THIEU, (former President of South Vietnam). A coalition (government) is like a sugar-coated poison pill. When the sugar melts, the poison kills you. (Time 105:12 April 14, 75)

NICHOLAS, N. J. The journalism business has very much become as much entertainment as it is journalism. (Manhattan, Inc. 6:76 May 89)

NICHOLS, Mike. Directing is one of the few professions you can practice without knowing what it is. (American Theatre 1:32 Sept 84)

NICHOLSON, Jack. She's like a delicate fawn crossed with a Buick (about Jessia Lange). (Vanity Fair 47:72 Oct 84)

NIEBUHR, Reinhold. Man's capacity for justice makes democracy possible, but man's inclination to injustice makes democracy necessary. (Rocky Mountain News 122:54 Dec 17, 80)

NIES, John. The effort expended by the bureaucracy in defending any error is in direct proportion to the size of the error. (Washingtonian 14:155 Nov 78)

NIN, Anais. Writers make love to whatever they need. (Vanity Fair 49:127 Sept 86)

NISBET, Robert. The doctrine of a benevolent state grows stronger. Very big government is not going to disappear. (Newsweek 90:34 Nov 7, 77)

NIVEN, David. Actors don't retire, they just get offered fewer parts. (W 6:18 July 8, 77)

NIXON, Patricia Ryan. I gave up everything I've ever loved (commenting in 1960 on the price of political life). (Good Housekeeping 187:158 Aug 78)

NIXON, Patricia Ryan. If they had been my tapes, I would have burned or destroyed them because they were like a private diary, not public property. (Village Voice 23:62 Aug 7, 78)

NIXON, Richard Malhous. When he is in top form, he can make the eagles scream. (Newsweek 110:21 Sept 21, 87)

NIXON, Richard Milhous. (Watergate) was worse than a crime, it was a blunder. (The Observer 9771:14 Dec 3, 78)

NIXON, Richard Milhous. A man is not finished when he is defeated, he is defeated when he quits. (Fame 1:94 Mar 90)

NIXON, Richard Milhous. All I want is a prosecution, not a persecution (upon firing Archibald Cox). (Washington Post National Weekly Edition 4:24 Mar 16, 87)

NIXON, Richard Milhous. As Brazil goes, so will the rest of the Latin American continent (commenting in 1971). (Time 108:30 Nov 29, 76)

NIXON, Richard Milhous. From a personal standpoint, what I would prefer to be remembered for is the example I set for surviving and coming back from adversity. (Fame 1:97 Mar 90)

NIXON, Richard Milhous. Henry (Kissinger) likes to say outrageous things....he was fascinated by the celebrity set and he liked being one himself. (Time 109:41 May 23, 77)

NIXON, Richard Milhous. History will justifiably record that my handling of the Watergate crisis was an unmitigated disaster. (Chicago Sun-Times 32:35 Sept 17, 79)

NIXON, Richard Milhous. I brought myself down. I have impeached myself. (New York Times 127:38 April 30, 78)

NIXON, Richard Milhous. I have often thought that if there had been a good rap group around in those days I might have chosen a career in music instead of politics. (Newsweek 116:13 July 30, 90)

NIXON, Richard Milhous. I would have made a good Pope. (US 3:64 Mar 10, 86)

NIXON, Richard Milhous. I'd like to see people, instead of spending so much time on the ethical problem, get after the problems that really affect the people of this country. (Newsweek 114:15 July 10, 89)

NIXON, Richard Milhous. If it hadn't been for Martha (Mitchell), there'd have been no Watergate. (Washingtonian 13:11 Nov 77)

NIXON, Richard Milhous. If the United States doesn't stand up for our friends when they are in trouble, we're going to wind up without any friends. (New York Times 128:B6 July 12, 79)

NIXON, Richard Milhous. In our own lives, let each of us ask—not just what will government do for me, but what can I do for myself (inaugural address—1973). (Christian Science Monitor 69:14 Jan 20, 77)

NIXON, Richard Milhous. Just destroy all the tapes (on the greatest lesson of Watergate). (Newsweek 107:17 May 5, 86)

NIXON, Richard Milhous. Knowing a little about everything won't work. Knowing a great deal about important things is essential (for Presidents). (Time 112:16 Aug 28, 78)

NIXON, Richard Milhous. My political life is over (1978). (New York Times 128:A5 Dec 1, 78)

NIXON, Richard Milhous. One thing I really hate is exercise for exercise's sake. (Philadelphia 69:131 April 78)

NIXON, Richard Milhous. Presidents come and go, but the Supreme Court, through its decisions, goes on forever. (Playboy 26:111 April 79)

NIXON, Richard Milhous. The ideological battle is won. You can't sell the idea that Marxism works. It doesn't. (Kansas City Star 108:21A Dec 10, 87)

NIXON, Richard Milhous. The next President's qualifications should be tested against foreign policy. If he fails there, we all fail. (Time 114:27 Sept 10, 79)

NIXON, Richard Milhous. The trouble with most conservatives is that those who have brains lack guts and those who have guts lack brains. (Village Voice 29:19 April 17, 84)

NIXON, Richard Milhous. The worst thing a politician can be is dull. (Newsweek 107:32 May 19, 86)

NIXON, Richard Milhous. There is one thing solid and fundamental in politics—the law of change. What's up today is down tomorrow. (Time 104:40 Aug 19, 74)

NIXON, Richard Milhous. We are a compromised country at the moment (1975). (Ladies' Home Journal 92:40 Nov 30, 75)

NIXON, Richard Milhous. We are now in a

war called peace. (Time 114:27 Sept 10, 79)

NIXON, Richard Milhous. When news is concerned, nobody in the press is a friend—they are all enemies. (Time 111:104 April 17, 78)

NIXON, Richard Milhous. Won some, lost some, all interesting (commenting on his political career). (Chicago Tribune 206:13 Section 1 July 25, 90)

NIXON, Richard Milhous. Writing is the toughest thing I've ever done. (Rolling Stone 227:43 Dec 2, 76)

NIXON, Richard Milhous. You have to dissemble, you have to recognize that you can't say what you think about an individual because you may have to use him or need him sometime in the future (on the nature of international diplomacy). (Kansas City Times 115:D1 Jan 1, 83)

NKOMO, Joshua. I do not think the British know what genuine majority rule is. (The Observer 9806:10 Aug 5, 79)

NKOMO, Joshua. There's no such thing to me as whites. (The Observer 9760:13 Sept 17, 78)

NOFZIGER, Lyn. Elections in this country are won in the center. (Newsweek 102:26 Oct 31, 83)

NOGUCHI, Isamu. Stones are like people, some more alive than others. (Chicago Tribune 366:1 Dec 31, 88)

NOLAN, John T. If you outsmart your own lawyer, you've got the wrong lawyer. (Washingtonian 15:142 Nov 79)

NOONAN, Peggy. It's disorienting because it's hard to know who to assign the evil role to. (Chicago Tribune 47:19 Feb 16, 90)

NORDERN, Michael. Making a movie is rather like warfare—99 percent boredom and 1 percent terror. (New York Times 132:22 Section 2 Jan 9, 82)

NORMAN, Edward. Truth does not cease because people give up believing it. (The Observer 9767:13 Nov 5, 78)

NORMAN, Marsha. Playwrights, I believe, lead lives of enormous drama. (Chicago Tribune 154:3 Section 5 June 4, 89)

NORODOM SIHANOUK, KING OF CAMBODIA (ABDICATED 1955). When they no longer need me, they will spit me out like a cherry pit (about the Khmer Rouge). (Time 106:38 Sept 22, 75)

NORRIS, Clarence (the sole surviving Scottsboro Boy). The lesson to Black people, to my children, to everybody, is that you should always fight for your rights even if it costs you your life. Stand up for your rights, even if it kills you (commenting on his struggle to clear his

name upon being pardoned by the state of Alabama). (New York Times 126:1 Oct 26, 76)

NORRIS, Kathleen. If ambition doesn't hurt you, you haven't got it. (Kansas City Star 97:4B Feb 6, 77)

NORRIS, William. We talk a lot about human rights, but I don't know of any human right that is more important than a job. (Time 111:61 April 3, 78)

NORTH, Oliver L., Jr. I assumed that the President was aware of what I was doing and had, through my superiors, approved. (Time 130:40 Dec 28, 87)

NORTH, Oliver L., Jr. I never carried out a single act, not one, in which I did not have authority from my superiors. (Kansas City Star 107:6A July 8, 86)

NORTH, Oliver L., Jr. Those accusations (Iran-Contra indictments) are not a brand. They are a badge of honor. (Chicago Tribune 130:15 Section 1 May 9, 88)

NORTH, Oliver L., Jr. What we are facing in Central America and in Nicaragua is much more than just a regional crisis. We are fighting for our ability to survive and to prevent another world war. (Kansas City Star 107:2A July 14, 87)

NOSAKA, Akiyuke. There is no doubt in my mind that Japan wants to rule Asia again, but this time it wants to do it as an American subcontractor. (Chicago Tribune 14:21 Jan 14, 87)

NOSSITER, Bernard D. There are no conflicts of interest when bankers' pockets are to be lined. (The Nation 251:441 Oct 22, 90)

NOVA, Leo. The other person's attitude depends on which direction the money moves between you. (Omni 1:131-32 May 79)

NOVAK, Michael. Reagan has done more to help the poor than Carter. (USA Today 2:10A Nov 7, 83)

NOVICK, Julius. It is a well-known and infuriating fact of life that in any relationship, if one party really and truly does not give a damn, that party will inevitably have the upper hand. Indifference is power (ask any cat). (Village Voice 21:81 Feb 14, 77)

NOYES, Eliot F. (industrial designer). Familiarity breeds acceptance. (Time 110:71 Aug 1, 77)

NUKAZAWA, Kazuo. The United States is over the hill, and blaming the discomfort on an easy target (Japan). (Newsweek 115:22 April 2, 90)

NUNN, Sam. I've never gotten up in the morning, looked in the mirror, and seen a president staring me in the face.

(Newsweek 108:30 Oct 27, 86)

NUREEV, Rudolf. I do not try to dance better than anyone else. I only try to dance better than myself. (Newsweek 85:32 Jan 6, 76)

NUREEV, Rudolf. Men are better at everything. (Chicago Tribune 349:11 Section 5 Dec 15, 83)

NYERERE, Julius Kamberage. South Africa is no different from Rhodesia. The struggle by blacks in both countries is exactly the same—for majority rule. So what happens in Rhodesia will happen in South Africa. (People Weekly 6:40 Dec 27/Jan 3, 77)

NYIREGYHAZI, Ervin. Music is a wonderful way of life but a terrible career. (Stereo Review 41:61 July 78)

O'BRIAN, Hugh. There is quite enough grief when one is alone. Why compound it by getting married? (upon his founding Marriage Anonymous). (People Weekly 5:72 Jan 26, 76)

O'BRIAN, Jack. (Truman Capote is) Jackie Susann with an education. (Time 107:68 June 28, 76)

O'CONNELL, David (IRA tactician). Put your faith in the Provos and Ireland will be free. We will abolish British rule, we will smash it. (New York Times 125:7 April 26, 76)

O'CONNOR, Flannery. (Fame) is a comic distinction shared with Roy Rogers's horse and Miss Watermelon of 1955. (Time 113:86 Mar 5, 79)

O'CONNOR, Flannery. Anybody that admires Thomas Wolfe can be expected to like good fiction only by accident. (New York Times Book Review 3 Dec 2, 79)

O'CONNOR, Flannery. For a fiction writer, to believe nothing is to see nothing. (Ms 8:39 July 79)

O'CONNOR, Flannery. What (Graham Greene) does, I think, is try to make religion respectable to the modern unbeliever by making it seedy. (Time 113:86 Mar 5, 79)

O'CONNOR, John J. Exposure to television is not necessarily fatal. (New York Times 127:33 Section 2 Nov 27, 77)

O'HARA, John. An artist is his own fault. (Mirabella 1:33 Feb 90)

O'KEEFFE, Georgia. I am not a woman artist. (New York Times 138:19 Nov 18, 88)

O'KEEFFE, Georgia. I'll paint what I see but I'll paint it big to say what is to me the wideness and wonder of the world as I live it. (Newsweek 88:76 Nov 22, 76)

O'LEARY, John. There isn't a gasoline shortage. There's a driving surplus (1979). (Time 113:66 June 25, 79)

O'MALLEY, Frank Ward. Life is just one damned thing after another. (Viva 4:25 July 77)

O'NEILL, Eugene. Born in a hotel room—and God damn it—died in a hotel room. (New York Times 128:5 Section D Nov 26, 78)

O'NEILL, Eugene. Life is a tragedy, hurrah. (New York Times 128:15 Section 6 Mar 4, 79)

O'NEILL, Thomas P. (Tip). If this were France, the Democratic Party would be five parties. (Time 112:42 Nov 20, 78)

O'NEILL, Thomas P. (Tip). When it comes to giving tax breaks to the wealthy of this country, the President has a heart of gold. (Life 5:33 Jan 81)

O'NEILL, Thomas P.(Tip). I hate to say it about such an agreeable man, but it was sinful that Ronald Reagan ever became president. (University Daily Kansan 98:7B Aug 26, 87)

O'ROURKE, Joseph. The antiabortionists are antifree, antiwomen and anti-Christian. (Time 114:27 July 9, 79)

O'ROURKE, P. J. All I really do is say in print what all the other reporters say at 10 at night in the bar. (Washington Journalism Review 10:22 Sept 88)

OATES, Joyce Carol. Sometimes my work is very savage, very harsh. But so is life. My material is not sordid, it's just a realistic reflection of a society that is in turmoil. (People Weekly 6:66 Nov 15, 76)

OBEY, David R. Joe McCarthy made me an independent, Stevenson made me a Liberal, and Eisenhower made me a Democrat. (New York Times 128:B20 Mar 1, 79)

OCCHIOGROSSO, Peter. Sonny Rollins is the Vladimir Nabokov of the tenor saxophone. (Soho Weekly News 6:27 Nov 2, 78)

OCHS, Adolph Simon. When a tabloid prints it, that's smut. When the Times prints it, that's sociology. (Time 110:75 Aug 15, 77)

OGILVEY, David. The consumer is not a moron. She is your wife. (Viva 4:26 Aug 77)

OGILVY, David. Ninety-nine percent of advertising doesn't sell much of anything. (Chicago Tribune 3:6 Section 3 Jan 4, 84)

OKUN, Arthur M. Society can transport money from rich to poor only in a leaky bucket. (Time 115:83 April 7, 80)

OKUN, Arthur M. The world is not safe for incumbents. (New York Times 128:15 Section 3 June 24, 79)

OLDENBURG, Claes. To give birth to form is the only act of man that has any consequence. (Chicago 25:18 Nov 76)

OLIANSKY, Joel. TV writing is the country of the blind where the one-eyed man is king. (Writer's Yearbook 61 1977)

OLIVIER, Laurence. Acting great parts devours you. (The Observer 9788:9 April 1, 79)

OLIVIER, Laurence. Acting is a masochistic form of exhibitionism. (Los Angeles Times Calendar 33 Feb 26, 78)

OLIVIER, Laurence. I am an actor because that is all I am qualified to do. (Los Angeles Times Calendar 33 Feb 26, 78)

OLIVIER, Laurence. I love comedy every bit as much as tragedy, perhaps more, because the whole scene of humanity is under its roof. (New York Times Magazine 60 Mar 25, 79)

OLIVIER, Laurence. I'm not sure what I'm like and I'm not sure I want to know. (New York Times Magazine 56 Mar 25, 79)

OLIVIER, Laurence. Living is strife and torment, disappointment and love and sacrifice, golden sunsets and black storms. (Los Angeles Times Calendar 35 Feb 26, 78)

OLIVIER, Laurence. Probably every great actor in history was the son of a clergyman. (Chicago Tribune 201:20 July 20, 79)

OLIVIER, Laurence. You can't just run. You have to look as if you're running (about acting). (New York Times Magazine 20 Mar 25, 79)

ONASSIS, Jacqueline Lee (Bouvier) Kennedy. I always wanted to be some kind of writer or newspaper reporter. But after college—I did other things. (New York Times 126:A10 Jan 14, 77)

ONO, Yoko. Keep your intentions in a clear bottle and leave it on the shelf when you rap. (Chicago Tribune 176:2 Section 2 June 25, 78)

OPPENHEIMER, J. Robert. The optimist thinks this is the best of all possible worlds, and the pessimist knows it. (Town & Country 133:141 May 79)

ORBEN, Robert. I feel that if God had really wanted us to have enough oil, He never would have given us the Department of Energy. (Time 113:71 Feb 26, 79)

ORESKES, Michael. He (Jim Wright) is a man abundantly endowed with a quality in dangerously short supply in politics today: guts. (New York Times 138:12 May 22, 89)

ORLANS, Harold. Logic is a game men play as cats play with balls of string, whereas reality is a game the gods play with us. (Change 9:34 April 77)

ORMANDY, Eugene. The Philadelphia

sound—its me. (Time 127:57 Dec 30, 85)

ORTEGA SAAVEDRA, Daniel. We do not consider it an acceptable cease-fire when we cease and the Contras fire. (Time 134:49 Nov 13, 89)

ORTON, Joe. All classes are criminal today. We live in an age of equality. (After Dark 11:51 Dec 78)

ORWELL, George. Any life when viewed from the inside is simply a series of defeats. (Toronto Globe and Mail 136:5 Section 5 Nov 17, 79)

ORWELL, George. If you want a picture of the future, imagine a boot stamping on the human face—forever...and remember that it is forever. (Omni 2:94 April 80)

OSBORN, Kenneth Barton. There are icebergs, and we are the Titanic (about the Central Intelligence Agency). (Playboy 22:58 Aug 75)

OSBORNE, John. Asking a working writer what he thinks about critics is like asking a lamppost what it feels about dogs. (Time 110:77 Oct 31, 77)

OUTHIER, Louis. You don't get fat from a good kitchen—only from a bad one. (W 4:11 Nov 28, 75)

OZAWA, Seiji. Slava (Mstislav Rostropovich) doesn't interpret, he feels. His music is really his character. He is conducting his life. (Time 110:84 Oct 24, 77)

PAGE, Clarence. Any concept can be sold to the media as long as it can be described in two words. (Chicago Tribune 5:17 Section 4 Jan 5, 85)

PAGE, Geraldine. The sadness I feel is that half my life or more is over, the list of films so short, and the people won't see all of what I could have shown them (1978). (Los Angeles Times Calendar 27 Sept 3, 78)

PAGNOL, Marcel. The most difficult secret for a man to keep is the opinion he has of himself. (Reader's Digest 107:166 Oct 75)

PAIGE, Satchel. How old would you be if you didn't know how old you was? (Chicago Tribune 37:2 Section 2 Feb 6, 78)

PALEY, William S. Jack (Benny) wasn't witty or even funny in real life. (M 2:66 July 85)

PANIGATI, Angelo. Afghanistan will always impose itself on the foreigner, no matter how hard he may try to make it otherwise. (New York Times 138:7 April 13, 89)

PANNENBERG, Wolfhart. The greatest deception (of our era is the idea that) political change can satisfy a religious need. (Time 107:65 Mar 8, 76)

PANZA DI BIUMO, Giuseppe. For me, art is the visualization of philosophy.

(Newsweek 86:69 Aug 11, 75)

PAPP, Joseph. The true dramatist of our time is a poet; the true poet, a dramatist. (New York Times 128:C24 Dec 1, 78)

PARKER, Charlie. Romance without finance ain't got no chance. (The Animator 4:1 Fall 76)

PARKER, Dorothy. An author really hasn't made it until he no longer shows his books to his friends. (Writer's Digest 56:11 Dec 78)

PARKER, Gail Thain. We must not be misled by snobbery into thinking that there is only one way to become educated. (Time 111:90 April 10, 78)

PARKINSON, C. Northcote. Expenditure rises to meet income. (Washingtonian 14:155 Nov 78)

PARKINSON, C. Northcote. Nonsense expands so as to fill the space available (Corollary to Parkinson's Law). (Wilson Library Bulletin 52:219 Nov 77)

PARKINSON, C. Northcote. Work expands to fill the time allotted to it, or, conversely, the amount of work completed is in inverse proportion to the number of people employed. (The Reader (Chicago's Free Weekly) 5:2 May 28, 76)

PARKS, Gordon. Huddie (Ledbetter) was meant for music and born for trouble. (New York 9:66 May 10, 76)

PARTON, Dolly. A real important thing is that, though I rely on my husband for love, I rely on myself for strength. (Chicago Sun-Times 32:33 July 16, 79)

PARTON, Dolly. If people think I'm a dumb blonde because of the way I look, then they're dumber than they think I am. (Ms 7:16 June 79)

PARTON, Dolly. When I sit back in my rocker, I want to have done it all. (Time 109:73 April 18, 77)

PARTRIDGE, Eric. I always wanted to become a writer, and I consider myself to be one. (Time 110:76 Oct 17, 77)

PASCHKE, Ed. Painting is like rock 'n' roll. It should never get safe. (Chicago Tribune 259:23 Section 10 Sept 16, 90)

PASQUA, Charles (French interior minister). Democracy ends where the interest of the State begins. (The Progressive 51:10 July 87)

PATERNO, Joe. If I ever need a brain transplant, I want one from a sportswriter because I know its never been used. (Chicago Tribune 273:3 Section 4 Sept 39, 90)

PATMAN, Wright (attributed by James T. Molloy). Next to the church, credit unions do more good for the people than any other institution. (Chicago Sun-Times

29:22 Mar 10, 76)

PATON, Alan. Sometimes, you think of apartheid as a fort. Often it is seen as a prison. But it is really a grave the Afrikaner has dug for himself. (New York Times 127:32 Oct 30, 77)

PATTERSON, L. Ray. The concern of the public (about crime) is not so much for vindictive retribution, but for some retribution. (Time 112:54 Sept 18, 78)

PATTON, George S. In war, just as in loving, you've got to keep on shoving. (Playboy 26:26 Oct 79)

PATTON, George S. Now I want you to remember that no bastard ever won a war by dying for his country. You won it by making the other poor dumb bastard die for his country. (American West 22:22 Nov 85)

PAUL VI, POPE. If you want peace, work for justice. (National Catholic Reporter 22:1 April 25, 86)

PAULUCCI, Jeno F. It pays to be ignorant, for when you're smart you already know it can't be done. (New York Times 126:5 Section 3 Nov 7, 76)

PAULUCCI, Jeno F. The meek have to inherit the earth—they sure don't know how to market it. (New York Times 126:5 Section 3 Nov 7, 76)

PAYTON, Walter. I don't watch much football. It's boring. (US 3:17 Nov 3, 86)

PAZ, Octavio. The prize is not a passport to immortality, but it does give a poet the possibility of a wider audience, and every writer needs a wider audience. (Chicago Tribune 288:11 Section 1 Oct 15, 90)

PAZ, Octavio. The soul has become a department of sex, and sex has become a department of politics. (Newsweek 94:137 Nov 19, 79)

PEALE, Norman Vincent. If Jesus were alive today he would be at the Super Bowl. (Time 119:82 Feb 8, 82)

PECK, Bernice. Money isn't everything, but you can buy the rest. (Village Voice 31:43 Jan 7, 86)

PEKAR, Harvey. A person who can't relate to comic books is like somebody who can't relate to opera. They're both culturally deprived. (Cleveland 5:153 July 76)

PENDEN, Bill. Atomic energy is a future idea whose time is past. Renewable energy is a future idea whose time has come. (Atlas World Press Review 24:38 April 77)

PENDLETON, Clarence. The best way to help poor folks is not to be one. (Mother Jones 7:25 Feb 82)

PERCY, Walker. Every novelist I know is miserable. (New York Times Book Review

31 June 29, 80)

PEREIRE, Anita. Gardening is a combination of being an architect and an interior designer. (W 15:29 June 16, 86)

PERES, Shimon. Stroking a tiger (the P.L.O.) will not make it a pussycat. (Time 109:24 April 18, 77)

PERETZ, Martin. You know, the thing I really disliked most about Chavez was the way he established himself as a tool of the Kennedy elite. (Boston Magazine 67:66 July 75)

PEREZ, Manuel Benitez. Bullfighting is an animal inside me, and it is one that I cannot dominate—it dominates me. (Newsweek 96:12 Sept 8, 80)

PERKINS, Maxwell. You have to throw yourself away when you write (to Elizabeth Lemmon). (Esquire 89:65 July 18, 78)

PERLS, Fritz. Learning is discovering that something is possible. (Omni 2:36 Nov 79)

PERLS, Klaus. Never talk to an artist about his work. If you do, what you get are total lies. (M 6:228 Oct 88)

PEROT, H. Ross. T There's only two places a 28-year-old can make a half million dollars—Wall Street and dealing dope. (Newsweek 112:143 July 11, 88)

PEROT, H. Ross. This country has enough problems without inflicting me on it. (Chicago Tribune 72:21 Mar 13, 87)

PEROT, H. Ross. We've got to nuke the GM system. (Kansas City Times 120:A-2 Jan 30, 88)

PERRY, Joe. The only aging rock star is a dead one. (Creem 10:30 Dec 78)

PETER, Laurence J. Bureaucracy defends the status quo long past the time when the quo has lost its status. (San Francisco Chronicle This World 1978:40 Jan 29, 78)

PETER, Laurence J. If two wrongs don't make a right, try three (Nixon's principle). (Washingtonian 14:155 Nov 78)

PETER, Laurence J. If you don't know where you are going, you will probably end up somewhere else. (San Francisco Chronicle This World 1978:40 Jan 29, 78)

PETER, Laurence J. In a hierarchy, every employee tends to rise to the level of his own incompetence. (The Reader (Chicago's Free Weekly) 5:2 May 28, 76)

PETER, Laurence J. In the country of the blind, the one-eyed King can still goof up. (San Francisco Chronicle This World 1978:40 Jan 29, 78)

PETER, Laurence J. Most hierarchies were established by men who now occupy the upper levels, thus depriving women of an equal opportunity to achieve their levels of incompetence. (San Francisco Chronicle

This World 1978:40 Jan 29, 78)

PETER, Laurence J. The cream rises until it sours. (San Francisco Chronicle This World 1978:40 Jan 29, 78)

PETERS, Charles. In Washington, bureaucrats confer, the President proclaims and the Congress legislates, but the impact on reality is negligible, if evident at all. (Time 115:14 June 30, 80)

PETERSON, Esther. If a man fights his adversaries, he's called determined. If a woman does it, she's frustrated. (National Observer 16:18 June 13, 77)

PHILBY, Kim. John Foster Dulles was a strong personality with views as narrow as a small-gauge railway. (Esquire 89:53 Mar 28, 78)

PHILBY, Kim. Now I can abandon my earlier reserve and call him an idle, ignorant, ungenerous old fraud (about Dwight Eisenhower). (Esquire 89:55 Mar 28, 78)

PHILLIPS, Michelle. Deep down, I may be a very shallow person. (US 3:59 Dec 15, 86)

PICASSO, Jacqueline. Living with Picasso was like living with a blowtorch; he was a consuming flame. (Time 108:70 Nov 8, 76)

PICASSO, Pablo. After Matisse, Chagall is the only artist who really knows color. (ARTnews 76:48 Summer 77)

PICASSO, Pablo. Art is lies that tell the truth. (More 8:34 June 78)

PICASSO, Pablo. Every child is an artist. The problem is how to remain an artist once he grows up. (Time 108:68 Oct 4, 76)

PICASSO, Pablo. For me there are only two kinds of women—goddesses and doormats. (People Weekly 13:37 May 26, 80)

PICASSO, Pablo. I paint forms as I think them, not as I see them. (Art & Antiques 1:53 Sept 84)

PICASSO, Pablo. It takes a long time to grow young. (Town & Country 135:179 May 81)

PIERCE, Webb. One drink is too many and a million is not enough. (Country Music 5:63 April 77)

PIERSON, L. R. If you're coasting, you're going downhill. (Washingtonian 14:155 Nov 78)

PINERO, Miguel. I'd like to die with my back against the wall and two guns smokin'. (Andy Warhol's Interview 7:27 Nov 77)

PINOCHET, Augusto. When people don't listen to words, they'll listen to deeds. (The Times 8126:10 Mar 23, 80)

PIPPIN, Horace (folk artist). Pictures just come to my mind and then I tell my heart to go ahead. (Newsweek 90:60 Aug 22, 77)

PIRANDELLO, Luigi. Life is little more than a loan shark: it exacts a very high rate of interest for the few pleasures it concedes. (The Reader (Chicago's Free Weekly) 7:2 Dec 23, 77)

PISIER, Marie-France. People wear resort clothes but actually Hollywood is an enormous factory. People work ten times harder than anywhere else. (Newsweek 89:47 May 16, 77)

PITMAN, Keith A. All generalizations are untrue. (Washingtonian 14:26 Dec 78)

PLANT, Robert. The lifestyle of rock 'n' roll is to live well and take a good woman. (Creem 9:49 July 77)

PLOTKIN, Stanley. It is shameful that a country as rich as this does so poor a job immunizing its infants. (New York Times 139:A14 May 22, 90)

PODHORETZ, Norman. The role of Jews who write in both the Jewish and general press is to defend Israel, and not join in the attacks on Israel. (Mother Jones 12:21 Mar/April 87)

POGO, (Cartoon Character). We have met the enemy and they is us. (Philadelphia 69:188 Sept 78)

POIROT, Paul L. Multiplying wealth is by far the fastest way to help the poor. Dividing the wealth and subsidizing poverty is the fastest way to starve everyone. (American Opinion 18:29 Nov 75)

POLYKOFF, Shirley. If I've only one life, let me live it as a blonde! (advertising slogan). (New York 9:37 Aug 23, 76)

PORTER, Sir George. If sunbeams were weapons of war, we would have had solar energy centuries ago. (Omni 2:37 June 80)

POST, Emily. An overdose of praise is like 10 lumps of sugar in coffee; only a very few people can swallow it. (Kansas City Times 109:14C Jan 22, 77)

POUND, Ezra. At seventy, I realized that instead of being a lunatic, I was a moron. (Horizon 21:96 Mar 78)

POVICH, Maury. We love being married, but we're not to sure about living together (about Connie Chung). (US 3:17 Sept 22, 86)

POWELL, Paul. I can smell the meat a-cookin'. If you can't get a meal, take a sandwich (advice to lawmakers). (Chicago 27:11 June 78)

PRENDERGAST, George Washington. I never took a dime from the public till; it's all been honest graft. (Change 8:60 Aug 76)

PRESLEY, Elvis. I don't know anything about music. In my line I don't have to. (Creem 11:30 Feb 80)

PRICE, Reynolds. The classical world decided wisely that any human accorded the honors of a hero must be, above all, dead. (Saturday Review 5:17 Dec 78)

PRICE, Roger. If everybody doesn't want it, nobody gets it. (Texas Observer 76:22 Nov 23, 84)

PRINZE, Freddie. Hollywood is one big whore. It breeds decadence. (Playboy 24:110 June 77)

PRIOLO, Paul. What that guy (Jerry Brown) does is enough to make a grown Republican cry. (The Times 8102:9 Oct 22, 78)

PRITCHETT, V. S. It is the role of the poet to look at what is happening in the world and to know that quite other things are happening. (New York Times Book Review 50 June 3, 79)

PRITCHETT, V. S. There are rules for old men who are in love with young girls, all the stricter when the young girls are in love with them. It has to be played as a game. (Time 114:127 Nov 12, 79)

PRIZEMAN, John. Collecting books is like collecting other people's minds, like having people on the shelves—only, you can just put them away when you want to. (Esquire 89:76 Jan 31, 78)

PRUDHOMME, Paul. When the taste changes with every bite and the last bite is as good as the first, that's Cajun. (Cook's Magazine 20:57 June 30, 85)

PRUSZYNSKA, Elzbieta. In Poland, it seems it's a rule that whoever is in power is ruining us. (Chicago Tribune 161:1 Section 4 June 10, 90)

PRYOR, David. While this (the Senate) is said to be the most exclusive club in the world, no one ever said it's the most productive. (Newsweek 111:17 Jan 4, 88)

PUZO, Mario. (Film writing) is the most crooked business that I've ever had any experience with. You can get a better shake in Vegas than you can in Hollywood. (Time 112:72 Aug 28, 78)

PUZO, Mario. A novelist should never take the movie business seriously. (New York Times 128:40 Section 7 Feb 18, 79)

PUZO, Mario. I find that the only thing that really stands up, better than gambling, better than booze, better than women, is reading. (Time 111:72 June 26, 78)

PUZO, Mario. I never knew anybody so determined to be unhappy (about Joseph Heller). (New York Times 128:16 Section 6 Mar 4, 79)

QADDAFI, Muammar. From time to time, I weep, but only when I am alone. (Time

127:29 April 21, 86)

QADDAFI, Muammar. My people have the right to liquidate opponents inside and outside the country even under broad daylight. (Time 127:29 April 21, 86)

QADDAFI, Muammar. People are getting killed everywhere by their leaders. (The Observer 9799:9 June 17, 79)

QUAMMEN, David. A man wrote a book, and lives were changed. That doesn't happen often (about Edward Abbey). (Outside 14:25 June 89)

QUANT, Mary. Good taste is death, vulgarity life. (Life 2:83 Nov 79)

QUAYLE, Dan. I'm going to be a vice-president very much like George Bush was. (New York 22:49 Mar 13, 89)

QUAYLE, Dan. The problem in Central America is not El Salvador. The problem in Central America is Nicaragua, and let us not forget that. (New York 22:46 Mar 13, 89)

QUAYLE, Dan. You won't see me being the so-called spear carrier for all the so-called conservative issues. (Chicago Tribune 142:10 Section 1 Dec 1, 88)

QUAYLE, Marilyn. I believe in creationism. I think the Bible is correct in that. (Chicago Tribune 15:8 Section 5 Jan 15, 89)

QUAYLE, Marilyn. Regular people are not equipped to deal with the viciousness of the media. (W 17:18 Nov 14, 88)

QUIN, Percy Edwards. A man must sometimes rise above principle. (Washingtonian 15:143 Nov 79)

QUINN, Sally. Washington society is ruled with unwavering severity by a handful of aging widows, dowagers and old maids who subsist on fortunes inherited from robber-baron husbands or corrupt political daddies. (Atlanta 16:124 Jan 76)

RABIN, Yitzhak. For me, peace means reconciliation of the Arab countries with the existence of Israel as a Jewish state. (Newsweek 88:47 Dec 20, 76)

RAFKO, Kaye Lani Rae (Miss America). I'm a professional individual. (US 3:6 Nov 2, 87)

RAHIM, Abdur. The war (in Afghanistan) is like a good love affair. All the action happens at night. (Time 113:44 May 14, 79)

RAHV, Philip. Nothing can last in America more than ten years. (Time 110:67 Aug 15, 77)

RAM DASS. If I'm saving the whale, why am I eating tuna fish? (New Times 11:39 Sept 4, 78)

RAND, Ayn. The state of today's culture is so low that I do not care to spend my time watching and discussing it. (Time 107:32

Jan 12, 76)

RANDALL, Tony. People don't call you mad or eccentric if you are well-heeled. It's only when you're poor that they call you a nut.... (Chicago Tribune 170:14 June 19, 79)

RAPPOLT, Richard T. It's easier to get people off of heroin than coffee. (Rolling Stone 234:39 Mar 10, 77)

RATHER, Dan. I'm at my relaxed and effective best when I'm reporting stories. (Newsweek 111:17 Feb 1, 88)

RATHER, Dan. In television news, no good deed goes unpunished. (Newsweek 112:6 Aug 22, 88)

RATTIGAN, Terrence. I could never see why craftsmanship should be equated with insincerity. (The Times 8059:35 Dec 4, 77)

RATTIGAN, Terrence. What a lovely world we're in, if only we'd let ourselves see it. (Guardian Weekly 117:4 Dec 11, 77)

RAUSCHENBERG, Robert. Painting relates to both art and life. I try to act in the gap between the two. (Chicago 26:112 Dec 77)

RAVEL, Jean-Francois. Stalinism is the essence of Communism. (Time 107:32 Feb 2, 76)

RAVITZ, Justin Charles. I understand the function of American media. Essentially, they exist to please their advertisers. (Mother Jones 2:51 Sept 77)

RAY, Dixie Lee. Anything that the private sector can do, government can do it worse. (Mother Jones 2:31 May 77)

RAY, Man. I have always preferred inspiration to information (commenting on photography). (ARTnews 76:52 Jan 76)

RAY, Man. I would like to go to only one funeral, mine. (Andy Warhol's Interview 7:23 Feb 76)

RAY, Man. The pursuit of liberty and the pursuit of pleasure—that takes care of my whole art. (Newsweek 88:53 Nov 29, 76)

RAY, Man. The streets are full of admirable craftsmen, but so few practical dreamers. (ARTnews 76:52 Jan 76)

RAY, Man. There is no progress in art any more than there is progress in making love. There are simply different ways of doing it. (New York Times Book Review 1 Feb 26, 78)

RAYBURN, Sam. A whore's vote is just as good as a debutante's. (D Magazine 6:86 June 79)

RAYBURN, Sam. If you want to get along, go along. (Washingtonian 14:155 Nov 78)

RAYBURN, Sam. No one has a finer command of language than the person who keeps his mouth shut. (Lawrence

(Kansas) Daily Journal-World 120:24 Aug 29, 78)

RAYBURN, Sam. Son, always tell the truth. Then you'll never have to remember what you said the last time. (Chicago Sun-Times 32:32 June 28, 79)

RAYBURN, Sam. The three most important words in the English language are 'wait a minute'. (Time 107:15 Aug 9, 76)

READ, David H. C. The worst sin is dullness. (Time 114:65 Dec 31, 79)

REAGAN, Maureen. A member of the United States military who lies to the commander-in-chief is guilty of treason and should be court-martialed (about Oliver North and John Poindexter). (Chicago Tribune 79:19 Mar 20, 87)

REAGAN, Nancy. A woman is like a teabag—only in hot water do you realize how strong she is. (The Observer 9931:13 Jan 3, 82)

REAGAN, Nancy. I think people would be alive today if there were a death penalty. (Life 5:142 Jan 82)

REAGAN, Nancy. My life began with Ronnie. (Newsweek 86:38 Oct 13, 75)

REAGAN, Ronald. A president should never say never. (Life 7:113 Jan 83)

REAGAN, Ronald. All the wastes in a year from a nuclear power plant could be stored under a desk. (USA Today 1:8A Mar 22, 83)

REAGAN, Ronald. America is back, standing tall. (Time 124:25 Dec 31, 84)

REAGAN, Ronald. America's best days are yet to come. You ain't seen nothin' yet (1984). (Time 124:50 Nov 19, 84)

REAGAN, Ronald. As a matter of fact, Nancy never had any interest in politics or anything else when we got married (denying charges that his wife is the real political power in the family). (Rolling Stone 219:19 Aug 12, 76)

REAGAN, Ronald. Eighty percent of air pollution comes from plants and trees. (Time 116:18 Aug 25, 80)

REAGAN, Ronald. He (Oliver North) is a national hero. (Chicago Tribune 67:7 Section 5 Mar 8, 87)

REAGAN, Ronald. I always grew up believing that if you build a better mousetrap, the world will beat a path to your door. Now if you build a better mousetrap the government comes along with a better mouse. (Chicago Tribune 323:1 Section 1 Nov 19, 75)

REAGAN, Ronald. I believe that government is the problem, not the answer. (Washington Post 137:A5 April 20, 76)

REAGAN, Ronald. I did not come here to balance the budget—not at the expense of my tax cutting and defense programs. If we can't do it in 1984, we'll have to do it later (November 1981). (Life 5:33 Jan 82)

REAGAN, Ronald. I do not think it (the Iran arms sale) was a mistake. (Time 128:18 Dec 8, 86)

REAGAN, Ronald. I don't know of anyone today that has less influence in this country than business. (Washington Post 353:A14 Nov 23, 75)

REAGAN, Ronald. I don't resent his (Mikhail Gorbachev) popularity or anything else. Good Lord, I costarred with Errol Flynn once. (Chicago Tribune 342:17 Dec 8, 87)

REAGAN, Ronald. I finally figured out this politics. It's like show business. You start with a big opening act, coast, and close with a great crescendo. (Time 106:16 Nov 24, 75)

REAGAN, Ronald. I happen to be one who believes that it it wasn't for women, us men would still be walking around in skin suits carrying clubs. (Life 7:172 Jan 84)

REAGAN, Ronald. I never found that Wall Street is a source of good economic advice. (Life 5:33 Jan 81)

REAGAN, Ronald. I think we took the only action we could have in Iran (1986). (Time 128:18 Dec 8, 86)

REAGAN, Ronald. I was not fully informed (about Iran arms sales). (Time 128:16 Dec 8, 86)

REAGAN, Ronald. I wasn't a Great Communicator, but I communicated great things. (New York Times 138:8 Jan 12, 89)

REAGAN, Ronald. I worry about Kissinger. He needed someone like Nixon to keep him on that tough track. He has to have someone around who can keep him from giving away the store. (Time 106:22 Nov 17, 75)

REAGAN, Ronald. I'd like to go back to those days when the press never quoted the President without permission. (SA Today 1:4A Jan 12, 83)

REAGAN, Ronald. I'm beginning to wonder if the symbol of the United States pretty soon isn't going to be an ambassador with a flag under his arm climbing into the escape helicopter. (Time 113:11 Mar 5, 79)

REAGAN, Ronald. I've noticed that everybody who's for abortion has already been born. (Life 4:68 Jan 81)

REAGAN, Ronald. If I have to appoint another one, I'll try to find one they'll object to just as much as this one (about Robert Bork). (Chicago Tribune 287:1 Oct 14, 87)

REAGAN, Ronald. If I were really lucky, I wouldn't have this job. (US 3:64 May 5, 86)

REAGAN, Ronald. If we get the federal government out of the classroom, maybe we'll get God back in. (The Washingtonian 11:97 July 76)

REAGAN, Ronald. It is my desire to have the full story about Iran come out now—the alleged transfer of funds, the Swiss bank accounts, who was involved—everything. (New York Times 136:2 Dec 17, 86)

REAGAN, Ronald. Middle age is when you're faced with two temptations and you choose the one that will get you home by 9:30 (commenting on the 27th anniversary of his 39th birthday). (Washington Post 65:C6 Feb 8, 77)

REAGAN, Ronald. My fellow Americans, I'm pleased to tell you today that I've signed legislation that will outlaw Russia forever. We begin bombing in five minutes. (Life 9:72 Jan 84)

REAGAN, Ronald. No policy or decision in my mind has ever been influenced by astrology. (Kansas City Star 108:8c May 4, 88)

REAGAN, Ronald. Of the four wars in my lifetime, none came about because the U.S. was too strong. (The Observer 9853:12 June 29, 80)

REAGAN, Ronald. Once you've seen one redwood, you've seen them all. (New York Times Magazine 71 July 4, 76)

REAGAN, Ronald. Take away the arms of the citizenry and where is its defense. (Time 106:24 Nov 24, 75)

REAGAN, Ronald. The (Carter) administration doesn't know the difference between being a diplomat and a doormat. (US News & World Report 86:54 May 7, 79)

REAGAN, Ronald. The deficit is big enough to take care of itself. (Newsweek 112:29 Nov 21, 88)

REAGAN, Ronald. The entire graduated-income-tax structure was created by Karl Marx. (New York 13:28 April 28, 80)

REAGAN, Ronald. The Latin American countries have a respect for macho. I think if the United States reacts with firmness and fairness, we might not earn their love, but we would earn their respect. (Time 107:12 May 17, 76)

REAGAN, Ronald. The minimum wage has caused more misery and unemployment than anything since the Great Depression. (Time 116:11 Sept 1, 80)

REAGAN, Ronald. The national Democratic leadership is going so far left they've left America. (Washington Post National Weekly Edition 1:12 Aug 6, 84)

REAGAN, Ronald. The problem isn't a shortage of fuel, it's a surplus of government. (Newsweek 94:21 Oct 1, 79)

REAGAN, Ronald. The trouble with (the Carter) administration is that for everybody they got in, it was a step up. They never had it so good. (Time 115:16 June 30, 80)

REAGAN, Ronald. The West won't contain communism; it will transcend communism. (Time 119:39 Jan 4, 82)

REAGAN, Ronald. There ain't no smoking gun (about the Iran Arms-Contra Aid Case). (Newsweek 109:19 June 29, 87)

REAGAN, Ronald. There is nothing better for the inside of a man than the outside of a horse. (Time 130:52 Dec 28, 87)

REAGAN, Ronald. They still won't believe us, but we are going to balance this budget by 1984 (September 1981). (Life 5:33 Jan 82)

REAGAN, Ronald. This is not a campaign; it's a crusade. (Tennessean 75:7 July 16, 80)

REAGAN, Ronald. Thou shalt not criticize other Republicans. (Time 116:13 July 28, 80)

REAGAN, Ronald. Treaties invite nationalization (about the Panama Canal). (Time 107:19 May 17, 76)

REAGAN, Ronald. Unemployment insurance is a prepaid vacation plan for freeloaders. (Time 116:16 Aug 25, 80)

REAGAN, Ronald. Using taxes to cure deficits in like using leeches to cure anemia. (Chicago Tribune 174:15 June 23, 87)

REAGAN, Ronald. Walter Mondale accuses us of ad-libbing our foreign policy. Not true. We read it right off the three-by-five cards. (Washingtonian 20:113 Oct 84)

REAGAN, Ronald. We are not doing anything to try and overthrow the Nicaraguan government. (USA Today 1:10A April 18, 83)

REAGAN, Ronald. We could pave the whole country and put parking stripes on it and still be home by Christmas (about winning the Vietnamese War). (New York 13:28 April 28, 80)

REAGAN, Ronald. We don't have a budget deficit because our people aren't taxed enough, we have a budget deficit because Congress spends too much (1989). (Chicago Tribune 38:11 Section 1 Feb 7, 89)

REAGAN, Ronald. We have got to get to where we can run a foreign policy without a committee of 535 telling us what we can do. (New York 18:32 June 10, 84)

REAGAN, Ronald. We made the Republican Party into the party of the working people, the family, the neighborhood, the defense of freedom, and, yes, the American flag and the Pledge of Allegiance. (Chicago Tribune 290:3 Section 4 Oct 16, 88)

REAGAN, Ronald. You know, politics has been called the second oldest profession. Sometimes there is a similarity to the first. (Chicago Tribune 323:1 Section 1 Nov 19, 75)

REDFORD, Robert. Health food may be good for the conscience, but Oreos taste a hell of a lot better. (Chicago Tribune 27:12 Jan 27, 78)

REDFORD, Robert. I spent most of my life feeling like an academic failure—largely because I was. (US 3:4 Mar 23, 87)

REDFORD, Robert. I've always had a very low regard for cynicism; I think it is the beginning of dying. (Time 107:55 Mar 29, 76)

REDFORD, Robert. If you stay in Beverly Hills too long you become a Mercedes. (Time 107:58 Mar 29, 76)

REDGRAVE, Vanessa. California is a place with lots of warm weather and lots of cold people. (US 1:80 June 28, 77)

REED, Lou. I'm like an Elvis Presley with brains, or Bob Dylan with looks. (Time 111:79 April 24, 78)

REED, Rex. In Hollywood, if you don't have happiness, you send out for it. (Chicago Tribune Magazine 6 Oct 16, 83)

REESE, Charley. The Soviet Union has a powerful lobby in the United States which consists of Communists, socialists, greedy bankers and businessmen, pacifists, and cowards. (The Progressive 47:13 Nov 83)

REEVE, Christopher. Women keep asking me if I really am Superman. My reply to them is, 'only if you're Lois Lane'. (W 7:33 Nov 10, 78)

REEVES, Richard. Politics is sex in a hula-hoop. (New York 9:99 June 14, 76)

REEVES, Richard. Television, of course, is dangerous. But that does not mean it is necessarily bad. (Esquire 89:57 April 25, 78)

REEVES, Richard. The people of New York have no political leader. (New York 8:33 Aug 4, 75)

REICH, Steve. You must love music or be a duck. (Ear 4:8 Feb 78)

REINHARDT, Ad. Art is art. Everything else is everything else. (Village Voice 25:78 Dec 24, 80)

REINHARDT, Ad. The eyes are in the head for a reason. (Art in America 65:72 Mar 77)

REMARQUE, Erich Maria. Not to laugh at the 20th century is to shoot yourself. (Time 111:94 April 3, 78)

RESTON, James. Old men running for the Presidency of the United States are like old men who take young brides. It's an exciting idea for a while but it seldom works. (New York Times 128:25 Jan 26, 79)

RESTON, James. Washington has no memory. (The Observer 9811:9 Sept 9, 79)

REUBEN, Don. Lawyers are impossible to manage, they are contemptious and egotistical. (American Lawyer 10:15 July/Aug 88)

REVSON, Charles. I don't meet competition. I crush it. (Duns Business Month 127:51 Feb 86)

REYNOLDS, Burt. I'm trying very subtly and subliminally to ease myself away from Billy Clyde Puckett and toward Cary Grant. I may be the most unsophisticated Cary Grant in 20 years, but I'm going to get there. (Time 111:54 Jan 9, 78)

RHODES, Frank H. T. The great universities are those in which people grow by contact with others in ever-widening circles. (Time 110:51 Nov 14, 77)

RHYS, Jean. If you want to write the truth, you must write about yourself. (Newsweek 93:103 May 28, 79)

RICE, Donna. I am not a party girl. (Washington Post National Weekly 5:9 Jan 4, 88)

RICE, Kathleen Brown. Contrary to his reputation, he is not a flake, and he does have a sense of humor (about Jerry Brown). (New York Times 128:C5 Mar 6, 79)

RICH, Lee. People enjoy watching wealthy people with more problems than they have (about television programs). (American Film 6:28 May 81)

RICH, Lee. Public broadcasting has become a joke. They spend more time fighting with each other than they do putting shows on the air. (Emmy 1:13 Winter 79)

RICHARD, Cliff. Just because someone isn't married doesn't mean he's homosexual. (People Weekly 13:55 Feb 18, 80)

RICHARD, Ivor. The U.N. will not abolish sin, but it can make it more difficult for the sinner. (US News & World Report 87:62 Sept 17, 79)

RICKEY, Branch. Luck is the residue of design. (Toronto Life 22 May 84)

RICKOVER, Hyman G. I never start to like a

man until I tell him off three or four times a day. (People Weekly 7:36 June 20, 77)

RICKOVER, Hyman G. Learning isn't fun. (Texas Observer 76:22 Sept 28, 84)

RICKOVER, Hyman G. Politics is to government like sex is to conception. (University Daily Kansan 94:1 Sept 30, 83)

RIDGEWAY, Matthew B. Candidates are no better or worse than those who choose and elect them, and therein lies the answer to what we are to become. (American Legion Magazine 101:21 Aug 76)

RIDING, Alan. Never commit yourself fully to anyone; always leave numerous options open; be all things to all men, and, keep your true sentiments well hidden (rule number 1 of long-term survival in Mexican politics). (New York Times Magazine 130 Sept 16, 79)

RIESMAN, David. The question is not whether leadership is obsolete but whether democracy is governable. (Time 114:26 Aug 6, 79)

RIESMAN, David. The road to the board room leads through the locker room. (Time 111:59 June 26, 78)

RIFKIND, Simon. (Judicial) impartiality is an acquired taste, like olives. You have to be habituated to it. (Time 114:49 Aug 20, 79)

RIMBAUD, Arthur. My greatest fear is that people will see me as I see them. (Newsweek 83:103 Mar 25, 74)

RINFRET, Pierre A. Consensus is the security blanket of the insecure. (Challenge 19:42 May 76)

RINGER, Barbara A. The basic human rights of individual authors throughout the world are being sacrificed more and more on the altar of the technological revolution. (American Legion Magazine 99:21 Dec 75)

RINGER, Robert J. Everything worthwhile has a price. (Playboy 28:97 Sept 81)

RINGER, Robert J. The women behind the (women's liberation) movement want the same thing all group leaders want and have wanted through history: ego assuagement. (Playboy 25:110 May 78)

RIVERA, Diego. I have never believed in God, but I believe in Picasso. (Connoisseur 214:28 Mar 84)

RIVERS, Larry. Is photography art? Art is everything. (Andy Warhol's Interview 7:12 Nov 75)

RIZZO, Frank Lazzaro. I get confused about figures over 100. (Chicago Tribune 306:5 Nov 2, 86)

RIZZO, Frank Lazzaro. If you want fiction, read the news pages; if you want facts,

read the comic pages. (Philadelphia Magazine 69:253 Nov 78)

RIZZO, Frank Lazzaro. We need excellence in public education and if the teachers can't do it, we'll send in a couple of policemen. (Time 110:40 Oct 24, 77)

RIZZO, Frank Lazzaro. When I see the American flag, my blood still runs cold. (New York Times 128:29 Section 2 Jan 21, 79)

ROBBINS, Harold. I'm the best novelist in the world. (Book Digest 7:22 Aug 80)

ROBBINS, Jerome. He's (George Balanchine) the Mozart of dance. (Newsweek 101:89 Mar 9, 83)

ROBERTS, Dale. He is a man of letters—all of them lower case. (Writer's Digest 58:11 Oct 78)

ROBERTSON, Pat. When I pray, I get answers. (Newsweek 108:13 Aug 25, 86)

ROBESON, Paul. American democracy is Hitler fascism. (Newsweek 86:58 Oct 6, 75)

ROBINSON, Frank. It's nice to come into town and be referred to as the manager of the Cleveland Indians instead of as the first black manager. (Sepia 26:10 Jan 75)

ROBINSON, Joan. I am an optimist by temperament, but a pessimist by intellect. (Time 122:74 Aug 22, 83)

ROCHBERG, George. The business of art is to praise God. (Newsweek 93:73 Feb 19, 79)

ROCHE, Kevin. Architecture is an intuitive activity, and the discussion, the polemic, the rationalizations all come afterwards, after the act, never before. (Connoisseur 218:86 Feb 88)

ROCKEFELLER, David. Although I work downtown, my family does have something of a stake in a small parcel of land which abuts Fifth Avenue (commenting on Rockefeller Center and his ties to the Fifth Avenue area in New York City). (New York Times 126:A13 Oct 22, 76)

ROCKEFELLER, David. Basically I operate on the principle that you should never do something for yourself that you can get someone else to do for you. (Penthouse 12:64 Oct 80)

ROCKEFELLER, John Davison III (attributed by an aide). I am too rich to steal. (Time 110:81 Oct 24, 77)

ROCKEFELLER, John Davison, III. I don't have a whole lot of faith in what the oil companies say. (Time 114:61 July 16, 79)

ROCKEFELLER, Nelson Aldrich. Being a Rockefeller is like living in a goldfish bowl. The goldfish get used to it and so do we. (New York Times 128:26 Jan 28, 79)

ROCKEFELLER, Nelson Aldrich. Congressional actions in the past few years, however well intentioned, have hamstrung the presidency and usurped the presidential prerogative in the conduct of foreign affairs. (Christian Science Monitor 68:2 May 11, 76)

ROCKEFELLER, Nelson Aldrich. One thing I can't stand is a goddamned bleeding heart. (American Spectator 15:22 Oct 82)

ROCKNE, Knute. You show me a good and gracious loser, and I'll show you a failure! (Argosy 384:15 Nov 76)

ROCKWELL, Geo. Making something perfectly clear only confuses everybody. (Down East 22:108 Jan 76)

RODGERS, Richard. When the lyrics are right, it's easier for me to write a tune than to bend over and tie my shoelaces. (Time 115:83 Jan 14, 80)

RODIA, Simon. I had in mind to do something big and I did (about the Watts Towers). (Travel & Leisure 8:67 Oct 78)

ROGERS, Ginger. If you don't stand for something, you will stand for anything. (Parade 9 June 18, 78)

ROGERS, Jimmy. Nobody in government understands Wall Street. And very few people on Wall Street understands Wall Street. (Kansas City Star 108:6A Oct 27, 87)

ROGERS, Roy. They'll have to shoot me first to take my gun. (Time 120:61 Aug 2, 82)

ROGERS, Will. Any man who thinks civilization has advanced is an egoist. (Time 104:92 Oct 7, 74)

ROGERS, Will. Everything is funny as long as it is happening to somebody else. (Kansas City Star 97:2A April 10, 77)

ROGERS, William D. Making foreign policy is a little bit like making pornographic movies. It's more fun doing it than watching it. (Chicago Sun-Times 29:9 June 29, 76)

ROGOW, Bruce. One person's vulgarity is another person's art. (Chicago Tribune 278:27 Section 1 Oct 5, 90)

ROHATYN, Felix. I have been in business for almost 40 years, and I cannot recall a period in which greed and corruption appeared as prevalent as they are today (1986). (Washington Post National Weekly Edition 4:5 Dec 29, 86)

ROHATYN, Felix. We ought to change the sign on the Statue of Liberty to read, 'this time around, send us your rich'. (Newsweek 92:88 Nov 27, 78)

ROLLINS, Sonny. Music is an open sky. (Soho Weekly News 6:27 Nov 2, 78)

ROMERO, Oscar Arnulfo. They can kill me, but the voice of justice will never be stilled. (Newsweek 95:47 April 7, 80)

RONSTADT, Linda. I'm so disorganized, what I really need is a good wife. (People Weekly 4:54 Nov 17, 75)

ROOSEVELT, Eleanor. Do what you feel in your heart to be right, for you will be criticized anyway. (Kansas City Times 115:A-1 Jan 13, 83)

ROOSEVELT, Eleanor. No one can make you feel inferior without your consent. (San Francisco Chronicle This World 1978:40 Jan 29, 78)

ROOSEVELT, Franklin Delano. Government has the definite duty to use all its power and resources to meet new social problems with new social controls. (Newsweek 92:27 Nov 27, 78)

ROOSEVELT, Franklin Delano. If you treat people right they will treat you right—90 percent of the time. (Kansas City Times 109:14C Jan 14, 77)

ROOSEVELT, Franklin Delano. Nothing just happens in politics. If something happens you can be sure it was planned that way. (Oui 7:107 May 78)

ROOSEVELT, Franklin Delano. Obedience to the law is demanded as a right, not asked as a favor. (The Oklahoma Observer 16:13 Jan 25, 84)

ROOSEVELT, Franklin Delano. Our true destiny is not to be ministered unto but to minister to ourselves and to our fellow men (inaugural address—1933). (Christian Science Monitor 69:14 Jan 20, 77)

ROOSEVELT, Franklin Delano. The only way to do anything in the American government is to bypass the Senate (returning from Yalta). (Chicago Tribune 147:2 Section 2 May 29, 77)

ROOSEVELT, Franklin Delano. When you get to the end of your rope, tie a knot and hang on. (Kansas City Star 97:2F June 5, 77)

ROOSEVELT, James. My uncle Teddy stole it, my father Franklin kept it going, and as far as I'm concerned they can now give it back (commenting on the Panama Canal). (Rolling Stone 262:36 April 6, 78)

ROREM, Ned. I do my very best to say mean things about Beethoven. (Philadelphia 79:89 May 88)

ROREM, Ned. I have suffered far less from being a homosexual than I have from being a composer. (People Weekly 10:40 Aug 21, 78)

ROSE, Billy. Never invest your money in anything that eats or needs repairing. (Duns Business Month 127:50 Feb 86)

ROSE, Billy. Sun is for apricots and exercise is for horses. (Food & Wine 10:64 Feb 87)

ROSE, Pete. I'd be willing to bet you, if I was a betting man, that I have never bet on baseball. (Time 133:85 April 3, 89)

ROSE, Pete. I'm not the greatest hitter ever. I just have the most hits. (The Sporting News 200:16 Sept 23, 85)

ROSE, Pete. Singles hitters drive Fords. Home-run hitters drive Cadillacs. (New West 4:116 April 9, 79)

ROSE, Richard. Even an atheist must be a Protestant atheist or Catholic atheist in order to have status in the society (commenting on life in Northern Ireland). (Time 104:30 Dec 30, 74)

ROSENBERG, Harold. In linking art to the modern consciousness, no artist is more relevant than Steinberg. (Time 111:92 April 17, 78)

ROSENBLATT, Roger. Liberals are radicals with assets. (US 3:14 Dec 2, 85)

ROSENTHAL, A. M. I don't care if you screw an elephant, just don't cover the circus. (New West 4:17 Mar 26, 79)

ROSSELLINI, Roberto. I believe that the cinema has failed in its mission of being the art of our century. (Newsweek 89:75 July 13, 77)

ROSSITER, Clinton. The essence of (Franklin) Roosevelt's Presidency was his airy eagerness to meet the age head on. (Time 114:11 July 16, 79)

ROSSNER, Judith. What is going on in my typewriter is going on in my life. (Life 6:30 Oct 83)

ROSSY, Paul (former vice chairman, Swiss Banking Commission). God, after all, created Switzerland for one purpose—to be the clearinghouse of the world. (Time 110:74 July 18, 77)

ROSTEN, Leo. Any man who hates dogs and babies can't be all bad (about W. C. Fields). (TV Guide 26:29 Dec 30, 78)

ROSTENKOWSKI, Dan. The art of politics is finding the center. (Washington Post National Weekly Edition 3:5 Dec 9, 85)

ROSTROPOVICH, Mstislav. When I play for an audience, I feel that I am making my confession to those people. (New York Times Magazine 66 April 18, 78)

ROTH, Philip. The road to hell is paved with works-in-progress. (New York Times Book Review 1 July 15, 79)

ROTH, Philip. When you publish a book, it's the world's book. The world edits it. (New York Times Book Review 13 Sept 2, 79)

ROTH, William V., Jr. Public confidence and trust in the federal government are low not only because of Watergate or our experience in Vietnam, but also because too many politicians have promised more than the government can deliver.

(Chicago Tribune 311:1 Section 1 Nov 7, 75)

ROTHKO, Mark. There is no such thing as a good painting about nothing. (Texas Monthly 7:166 April 79)

ROTHSCHILD, Emma. For the last 20 years, America's influence on Europe has had more to do with food and animal feed than with high politics or low diplomacy. (New York Times 127:19 Section E April 16, 78)

ROTHSCHILD, Marie-Helene De. I'm not a bit ashamed of being rich. I think it's very healthy to have big parties now and again, like they did in history. (Time 105:48 June 9, 75)

ROWAN, Carl. Carter turned out to be not a populist but a small-town businessman. (Time 115:73 June 9, 80)

ROWEN, Phyllis. When you grow as a designer, you realize that nothing is forever. (Architectural Digest 32:122 Nov 75)

ROWSE, A. L. I've always thought of myself as a parallel to D.H. Lawrence. (The Times 8062:35 Jan 1, 78)

ROWSE, A. L. Most people's opinions are of no value at all. (The Observer 9809:10 Aug 26, 79)

ROWSE, A. L. This filthy 20th century. I hate its guts. (Time 112:K9 Nov 13, 78)

ROYKO, Mike. He seldom exited the same sentence he entered (about Richard J. Daley). (Chicago Tribune 40:3 Section 1 Feb 9, 89)

ROYKO, Mike. If you can't find a good bar in Chicago, you ought to give up drinking. (Chicago 31:127 Dec 31, 81)

ROYKO, Mike. The motto of the (Chicago) City Council is: never do today what somebody else can do today or tomorrow. (Chicago Sun-Times 32:2 Nov 26, 78)

ROYSTER, Vermont. When things go wrong somewhere, they are apt to go wrong everywhere. (Washingtonian 14:155 Nov 78)

ROZELLE, Pete. Sporting events give people time off from the problems of the world. (US News & World Report 85:62 Oct 16, 78)

ROZELLE, Pete. The world knows no less rational person than a losing bettor (commenting in opposition to efforts to legalize betting on professional football). (Time 108:69 Sept 20, 76)

RUBIN, Jerry. I'm famous. That's my job. (Christian Science Monitor 68:30 April 26, 76)

RUBIN, Jerry. Most men act so tough and strong on the outside because on the inside, we are scared, weak, and fragile.

Men, not women, are the weaker sex. (Chicago Tribune 75:24 Mar 16, 78)

RUBINSTEIN, Artur. I'm not a drug fiend, I'm not a drunkard, but I am the laziest man I ever met. (Time 105:39 Feb 10, 75)

RUBINSTEIN, Artur. It's more important to play the wrong note right than the right note wrong. (High Fidelity (Musical America Edition) 35:17 May 85)

RUBINSTEIN, Artur. Most people ask for happiness on condition. Happiness can only be felt if you don't set any condition. (Kansas City Star 97:15C Sept 22, 76)

RUBINSTEIN, Artur. To get as old as I am (91) one must drink a glass of whiskey every morning, smoke a long cigar and chase beautiful girls. (People Weekly 10:144 Nov 20, 78)

RUBINSTEIN, Michael. The ultimate blasphemy must be censorship. (The Observer 9701:13 July 17, 77)

RUCKELSHAUS, Jill. It occurred to me when I was 13 and wearing white gloves and Mary Janes and going to dancing school, that no one should have to dance backwards all their lives. (Chicago Sun-Times 30:21 Jan 28, 78)

RUDKIN, David. The play should liberate itself from the personal origins of the author. (Village Voice 22:89 June 27, 77)

RUMSFELD, Donald. If you try to please everybody, somebody is not going to like it. (Washingtonian 12:107 Feb 77)

RUNYON, Damon. All life is six-to-five against. (New York 9:36 Nov 1, 76)

RUNYON, Damon. Man's only weapon against a woman is his hat. He should grab it and run. (Viva 4:28 April 77)

RUSHDIE, Salman. The Satanic Verses is not, in my view, an antireligious novel. (Chicago Tribune 57:3 Section 4 Feb 26, 89)

RUSSELL, Bertrand. I believe myself that romantic love is the source of the most intense delights that life has to offer. (Chicago Tribune 212:1 Section 2 July 31, 78)

RUSSELL, Bertrand. It matters little what you believe, so long as you don't altogether believe it. (Kansas City Star 106:5A Dec 30, 85)

RUSSELL, Ken. All good art, all good entertainment, shocks people. (Village Voice 26:46 Jan 21, 81)

RUSSELL, Ken. It's possible to think three things at once. (Village Voice 26:46 Jan 21, 81)

RUSSELL, Rosalind. Flops are a part of life's menu, and I'm never a girl to miss out on any of the courses. (Time 108:102 Dec 13, 76)

RUTLER, George William. Anti-Catholicism has become the Anti-Semitism of the liberals. (Chicago Tribune 68:16 Mar 9, 86)

RYAN, Cornelius. The mathematics of self-pity can be raised to infinity. (Time 114:83 Aug 6, 79)

RYAN, John. Bribes are just bad business. (Mother Jones 2:50 July 77)

RYKIEL, Sonia. Every woman must create her own ambience; it is not I or Yves St. Laurent but the woman who has to create herself and be a unique person. (Time 110:54 Nov 7, 77)

SADAT, Anwar. I have dealt with three presidents, Nixon, Ford and this Carter. I can say that everything is improving. (Time 111:32 Jan 2, 78)

SADAT, Anwar. No one ever knows what I am thinking, not even my own family. I go alone. (Time 111:22 Jan 2, 78)

SAFFIOTTI, Umberto. Cancer in the last quarter of the 20th century can be considered a social disease, a disease whose causation and control are rooted in the technology and economy of our society. (Time 106:67 Oct 20, 75)

SAFIRE, William. (Jimmy Carter is) the best U.S. President the Soviet Union ever had. (Time 114:116 Nov 19, 79)

SAFIRE, William. Gerald Ford's Presidency was unique in this century for not producing a single memorable phrase. (New York Times Magazine 90 Nov 19, 78)

SAFIRE, William. I think that one of Nixon's great contributions to civil liberties was getting caught doing what the two presidents before him got away with. (Book Digest 4:28 July 77)

SAFIRE, William. My business (is) writing informed polemics—with a satisfying zap. (Newsweek 93:94 April 23, 79)

SAHL, Mort. The more you stay the same, the more they say you've changed. (Newsweek 92:16 Dec 11, 78)

SAINT JAMES, Margo. (We've already) got legalized prostitution: marriage. (Washington Post 138:B7 April 21, 76)

SAINT LAURENT, Yves. Fashions fade, style is eternal. (Andy Warhol's Interview 5:13 April 75)

SAKATA, Michita. Security is like sun, water or air. When they are plentiful you don't appreciate their value. (Newsweek 86:53 Oct 6, 75)

SAKHAROV, Andrei Dmitrievich. I hope this prize is not only an acknowledgement of my personal merits, but of the merits of all those who fight for human rights (commenting on his Nobel Peace Prize).

(People Weekly 4:26 Oct 27, 75)

SAKHAROV, Andrei Dmitrievich. There is, of course, no alternative to Mikhail Gorbachev as leader of the Soviet Union at this decisive moment in its history. (Chicago Tribune 365:5 Section 1 Dec 31, 89)

SAKHAROV, Andrei Dmitrievich. Thermonuclear warfare has already become a dark reality of modern times, like Auschwitz, the Gulag and famine. (Time 106:44 Oct 20, 75)

SALEM, Elie. Whatever the target, Lebanon is always the victim. (Life 7:114 Jan 84)

SALINGER, J. D. Some of my best friends are children. In fact, all of my best friends are children. (Washington Star 323:1 Section D Nov 19, 78)

SALK, Jonas. It is becoming clear that a diagnosis of HIV positivity need not be regarded as a death sentence (1989). (Chicago Tribune 160:3 Section 1 June 9, 89)

SALK, Jonas. The best thing to do (for people worried about cancer-causing substances) is quit reading the newspaper. (Chicago Sun-Times 29:54 Mar 17, 76)

SALMORE, Stephen. In the 1960s, the burden of proof against change rested with those accepting the status quo. In the 1970s, the burden of proof rests with those who want change. (US News & World Report 84:25 Jan 23, 78)

SAMPLES, Alvin (Junior). I'd rather be wise and act dumb than be dumb and act wise. (Lawrence (Kansas) Journal-World 125:15 Nov 14, 83)

SAMUELS, John S., III. Texas is sort of an opera. (New York Times 128:17 Section 2 Jan 21, 79)

SANCHEZ, Robert. In looking backward, we must renew our faith in God. In looking forward, we must renew our faith in men. (National Catholic Reporter 12:8 July 2, 76)

SANDBURG, Carl. A baby is God's opinion that the world should go on. (Kansas City Star 97:2D Feb 20, 77)

SANDBURG, Carl. Life is like an onion: you peel it off one layer at a time and sometimes you weep. (San Francisco Chronicle This World 1978:40 Jan 29, 78)

SANDBURG, Carl. Slang is language that takes off its coat, spits on its hands, and goes to work. (Kansas City Times 109:17C July 15, 77)

SANDERS, Ed. Just because you're paranoid doesn't mean they're not trying to get you. (The Reader (Chicago's Free Weekly) 7:4 Section 1 April 7, 78)

SANDERSEN, Ann. When I'm in New York I'm homesick for Aspen, and when I'm in Aspen I'm homesick for Aspen. (Outside 1:25 Sept 78)

SANTAYANA, George. Fanatics are those people who know what they are doing is what God would be doing if He only had all the facts. (Time 112:94 Oct 9, 78)

SANTAYANA, George. Our dignity is not in what we do, but in what we understand. (Kansas City Star 97:4B Oct 10, 76)

SANTAYANA, George. Sometimes we have to change the truth in order to remember it. (Time 106:57 July 28, 75)

SARBANES, Paul. A working man voting for Reagan is like a chicken voting for Colonel Sanders. (Washingtonian 20:328 Nov 84)

SARNOFF, David. Competition brings out the best in products and the worst in people. (Dun's Business Month 127:51 Feb 86)

SAROYAN, William. I would rather write, even pompously, than celebrate meaninglessness. (New York Times Book Review 20 July 15, 79)

SARRIS, Andrew. We New Yorkers are the most naive and provincial people in the world to put so much faith not in princes and priests, but in a mere publication (about the New York Times). (Village Voice 20:63 Aug 11, 75)

SARTRE, Jean-Paul. We can only see the somber recesses in our selves if we try to become transparent to others. (Chicago Tribune 282:4 Section 7 Oct 9, 77)

SASSER, Jim. He's (Ronald Reagan) become a kindly old relative that you don't have to pay much attention to. He's just run his course (1987). (Newsweek 109:19 June 29, 87)

SASSOON, Vidal. I call myself a lucky barber. (The Observer 9786:10 Mar 18, 79)

SAUL, Peter. Becoming an artist is kind of like stocks and bonds: complicated. You have to go against the advice of very intelligent people who surround you. (Chicago Tribune 246:9 Section 9 Sept 3, 89)

SAVALAS, Telly. I am a loud, extraverted friendly person, but never rude. (Time 107:38 June 28, 76)

SAVITCH, Jessica. The thing you need most in this business (TV journalism) is stamina. (Ms 8:86 Aug 79)

SAWYER, Charles. The United States, like Atlas, is holding up the world. But who holds up Atlas? American business. (Time 113:85 April 23, 79)

SCAMMON, Richard. There's nothing wrong with the Republican Party that double-digit inflation won't cure. (Guardian Weekly 119:17 Nov 12, 78)

SCHEER, Robert. The journalist's job is to get the story by breaking into their offices, by bribing, by seducing people, by lying, by anything else to break through that palace guard. (Time 107:56 April 4, 77)

SCHEUCH, Erwin. (Helmut) Schmidt is an above-average average German. (Time 113:32 June 11, 79)

SCHLAFLY, Phyllis. Ask yourself: When you are rescued from the third floor of a burning building, do you want to be carried down the ladder by a man or a woman? (National NOW Times 11:6 Aug 78)

SCHLAFLY, Phyllis. The atomic bomb is a marvelous gift given to America by a wise God. (The Times 8142:8 July 13, 80)

SCHLESINGER, Arthur, Jr. 'Gay' used to be one of the most agreeable words in the language. Its appropriation by a notably morose group is an act of piracy. (Time 111:36 Jan 2, 78)

SCHLESINGER, Arthur, Jr. History can be a high-risk occupation. (The Observer 9769:13 Nov 19, 78)

SCHLESINGER, Arthur, Jr. It is evident that what pretends to be a Democratic administration has deliberately and methodically chosen Republican policies. (Washington Post 102:3 June 24, 79)

SCHLESINGER, Arthur, Jr. John Kennedy was a realist brilliantly disguised as a romantic; Robert Kennedy, a romantic stubbornly disguised as a realist. (Newsweek 92:78 Sept 4, 78)

SCHLESINGER, Arthur, Jr. The higher loyalty, it has always seemed to me, is to truth, public enlightenment, and history. (The Atlantic 244:28 Aug 79)

SCHLESINGER, James Rodney. The American role in maintaining a worldwide military balance is better understood in Moscow than it is in this country. (American Legion Magazine 98:20 Jan 74)

SCHMIDT, Helmut. He (Jimmy Carter) is making (foreign) policy from the pulpit. (Time 107:14 May 9, 77)

SCHMIDT, Helmut. We Germans are in the heart of Europe. In any new war, we have everything to lose and nothing to gain. (Newsweek 96:37 July 14, 80)

SCHMITT, Harrison. Space represents the kind of resource for the human spirit that North America was three hundred years ago: a new stimulus for the spirit of freedom. (Omni 2:82 June 80)

SCHNABEL, Artur. Great music is music that is written better than it can be played.

(Chicago Sun-Times 39:17 Dec 30, 85)

SCHNEIDER, William. Liberalism is a problem that could be overcome by finding the right theme (about the Democratic Party). (Chicago Tribune 267:4 Section 4 Sept 24, 89)

SCHNEIDERMAN, David. I belong to the (Rupert) Murdoch school of journalism, er, business: When you have an idea and think you are on to something, go for it. (Washington Journalism Review 9:14 Jan/Feb 87)

SCHNEIDERS, Greg. He (Jimmy Carter) is the opposite of macho. He's soft on the outside and hard on the inside. (Washington Post 352:B3 Nov 19, 76)

SCHORR, Daniel. All news is an exaggeration of life. (Village Voice 20:134 May 26, 75)

SCHORR, Daniel. The joys of martyrdom are considerably overrated. (Time 107:62 Mar 8, 76)

SCHORR, Daniel. To betray a source would be to betray myself, my career and my life. I cannot do it (commenting in his testimony before the Pike committee). (Time 108:76 Oct 11, 76)

SCHOTT, Phil. Paranoia among politicians is simply a state of heightened awareness. (San Diego Magazine 35:168 Sept 83)

SCHRADER, Paul. I like to fire a movie like a bullet. Then I stay with it until it hits its target. (Chicago Sun-Times 31:1 Section 3 Mar 12, 78)

SCHREINER, Olive. We are men or women in the second place, human beings in the first. (Ms 6:94 Aug 77)

SCHROEDER, Patricia. America is man enough to elect a woman President. (Time 130:20 Aug 3, 87)

SCHROEDER, Patricia. I am a fiscally conservative liberal. (Newsweek 110:76 Aug 17, 87)

SCHROEDER, Patricia. When men talk about defense, they always claim to be protecting women and children, but they never ask the women and children what they think. (New York Times Book Review 35 Feb 17, 80)

SCHULLER, Robert. The church is in the business of retailing religion. (Time 105:38 Feb 24, 75)

SCHULTZ, George. Central America is West. The East must get out. (New York 18:32 June 10, 84)

SCHULTZE, Charles. If you can't measure output, then you measure input. (Washingtonian 14:155 Nov 78)

SCHUMACHER, Ernst F. As a good friend says, most of the modern economics as taught is a form of brain damage. (The

Reader (Chicago's Free Weekly) 6:27 Mar 25, 77)

SCHUMACHER, Ernst F. It's impossible to discuss economic problems without concepts like temptation and seduction. In economics this is translated into free consumer choice. (The Reader (Chicago's Free Weekly) 6:27 Mar 25, 77)

SCHUMACHER, Ernst F. People always called me a crank, but I didn't carry any resentment about that because it is an excellent thing, a crank. It is not expensive, it is relatively nonviolent, and it causes revolutions. (Christian Science Monitor 69:1 June 27, 77)

SCHUMACHER, Ernst F. Production by the masses, rather than mass production. (Newsweek 90:72 Sept 19, 77)

SCHUMACHER, Ernst F. They're spending their time rearranging the deck chairs on the Titanic (commenting on his fellow economists). (The Reader (Chicago's Free Weekly) 6:27 Mar 25, 77)

SCHUMAN, William. In my own music, I'm alone, absolutely alone. (New York Times 129:19 Section D Aug 3, 80)

SCHUMAN, William. The simple is not easy (about Virgil Thomson). (Village Voice 31:112 Dec 16, 86)

SCHWAB, Charles M. Personality is to a man what perfume is to a flower. (Kansas City Times 109:1 April 15, 77)

SCHWARTZ, Delmore. No reputation is more than a snowfall. (Times Literary Supplement 3969:2 April 28, 78)

SCHWEITZER, Albert (attributed by Norman Cousins). We are at our best when we give the doctor who resides within each patient a chance to go to work. (Newsweek 94:99 Sept 24, 79)

SCOTT, George C. The actor is never rewarded in film. Film stardom is a peripheral and distorted kind of fulfillment. (New York Times Magazine 12 Jan 23, 77)

SCOTT, Ulric. An Independent-Republican is an elephant that is trying to forget. (Time 106:8 Dec 1, 75)

SCRANTON, William W. The only universality that one can honestly associate with the Universal Declaration of Human Rights is universal lip service. (New York Times 126:10 Nov 25, 76)

SEALE, Bobby. Those who know don't talk; and those who talk don't know. (New York Times Magazine 53 Nov 20, 77)

SEAMAN, Barbara. (A feminist is) a woman who is for women, which does not mean being against men. (New York Times 125:32 Nov 8, 75)

SEARS, John. Politics is motion and excitement. (Time 114:22 Nov 12, 79)

SEARS, John. You never really win anything in politics. All you get is a chance to play for higher stakes and perform at a higher level. (Time 115:32 Jan 21, 80)

SEEGER, Pete. TV must become our council fire, our town hall. (CoEvolution Quarterly 16:153 Winter 77/78)

SEGOVIA, Andres. Artists who say they practice eight hours a day are liars or asses. (The Observer 9839:10 Mar 23, 80)

SEIDENBAUM, Art. A city worrying about image enhancement is like a man considering a wig; each faces the world with a shining inferiority complex. (Wall Street Journal 56:14 June 25, 76)

SELLARS, Peter (theatrical director). Great art is created on the run. (Boston 75:108 Oct 83)

SELLARS, Peter (theatrical director). We need to understand the music in Shakespeare and the Shakespeare in music. (USA Today 2:5D Oct 20, 83)

SELLECK, Tom. In the scheme of things, I'm not as important as Dr. Jonas Salk. (Life 7:141 Jan 83)

SELLERS, Peter. The older I get, the less I like the film industry and the people in it. In fact, I'm at a stage where I almost loathe them. (Time 115:73 Mar 3, 80)

SELYE, Hans. Stress is the nonspecific response of the body to any demand. (Human Nature 1:58 Feb 78)

SENGHOR, Leopold Sedar. Africa will teach rhythm to a world dead with machinery and cannon. (Time 116:5 July 7, 80)

SEVAREID, Eric. On balance, TV is better for us than bad for us. (USA Today 1:10A Jan 10, 83)

SEVAREID, Eric. The chief cause of problems is solutions. (Town & Country 133:141 May 79)

SEVAREID, Eric. The problem is not so much finding out what the news is, it's making sense of it. (TV Guide 25:A55 Dec 13, 77)

SEVAREID, Eric. There is an immense amount of biased listening and inaccurate listening (commenting on TV news audiences). (TV Guide 25:A55 Dec 13, 77)

SEVAREID, Eric. We are a turbulent society but a stable republic. The mind goes blank at the thought of a world without one such power. (Time 110:111 Dec 12, 77)

SEXTON, Anne. Creative people must not avoid the pain that they get dealt. (Time 110:124 Nov 28, 77)

SEXTON, Anne. I wonder if the artist ever lives his life—he is so busy recreating it.

(The American Book Review 1:4 Dec 77)

SEYMOUR, Steven. Translations are like women. When they are pretty, chances are they won't be very faithful. (Rolling Stone 260:16 Mar 9, 78)

SHAFFER, Floyd. I believe it would be healthier if the church could laugh because I believe that God laughs. (Newsweek 86:64 Sept 29, 75)

SHALES, Tom. People, I have found, are a poor substitute for television. (Interview 14:180 Sept 84)

SHANKER, Albert. Power is a good thing. It is better than powerlessness. (Time 106:17 Sept 22, 75)

SHANKER, Albert. Teaching is no longer seen as a woman's job. Teaching is seen as a tough, exciting place where things are happening. (Ms 6:85 July 77)

SHANLEY, John Patrick. I see no difference between writing a play and living my life. (Los Angeles 33:53 Mar 88)

SHANNON, William V. What is actually happening is often less important than what appears to be happening. (Book Digest 6:30 Dec 79)

SHAPIRO, Joseph H. Aesthetics is to art what ornithology is to birds. (Chicago 26:178 Sept 77)

SHAPIRO, Joseph H. Great art is so complex and has so many levels of meaning it carries its own equivocation. (Chicago 26:178 Sept 77)

SHAPIRO, Joseph H. Nowhere is a man's imagination so fertile as in the discovery of new ways to say no to a man who asks for money. (Chicago 26:178 Sept 77)

SHARON, Ariel. In order to overcome our problems, the first thing to do is to eliminate the heads of the terrorist organizations, and the first one is Yasir Arafat. (Chicago Tribune 208:27 Section 1 July 27, 89)

SHARON, Ariel. Jordan is the Palestinian state. (USA Today 1:8A Dec 22, 82)

SHARPE, Cornelia. I think sex is the greatest thing since Coca-Cola. (Viva 2:21 Sept 75)

SHAW, Artie. If she didn't breathe by reflex, she'd probably forget to (about Lana Turner). (US 3:60 Oct 21, 85)

SHAW, George Bernard. An Englishman thinks he is moral when he is only uncomfortable. (Time 120:15 Oct 4, 82)

SHAW, George Bernard. Gambling promises the poor what property performs for the rich—something for nothing. (Rocky Mountain News 333:70 Mar 20, 80)

SHAWN, William (attributed by Brendan Gill). Liebling wants to live like a stockbroker, but he doesn't want to be a stockbroker. (Andy Warhol's Interview 8:60 Dec 78)

SHCHARANSKY, Anatoly. I am happy that I have lived honestly and in peace with my conscience, and never lied even when I was threatened with death. (Guardian Weekly 119:7 July 23, 78)

SHEED, Wilfrid. Criticism is what every reviewer would like to write if he had the time. (New York Times 128:9 Section 7 Jan 21, 79)

SHEED, Wilfrid. One reason the human race has such a low opinion of itself is that it gets so much of its wisdom from writers. (New York Times 128:9 Section 7 Jan 21, 79)

SHEED, Wilfrid. Suicide is the sincerest form of criticism life gets. (The Tennessean 74:11 June 27, 79)

SHEEHAN, George A. To know running is to know life. (New York Times Book Review 30 Dec 3, 78)

SHEEN, Charlie. Alcohol is the devil's urine. (US 3:8 Oct 17, 88)

SHEEN, Fulton J. Freedom is the right to do what you ought to do. (Time 114:84 Dec 24, 79)

SHEEN, Martin. I don't believe in God, but I do believe that Mary was His mother. (Rolling Stone 303:48 Nov 1, 79)

SHEPARD, Sam. I don't want to be a playwright. I want to be a rock 'n' roll star. (Santa Fe Reporter 8:24 Feb 24, 82)

SHEPARD, Sam. If you can stay right in the middle of a contradiction, that's where life is. (Interview 18:76 Sept 88)

SHEPHERD, Cybill. It's divorce that's the problem with marriage. (US 3:4 May 4, 87)

SHERRILL, Henry Knox. Far too many people in the church have very great convictions about very small things. (Newsweek 95:93 May 26, 80)

SHERRILL, Robert. No politician ever deserved our hatred more than (Lyndon) Johnson because, simply, no politician ever did more than he to destroy the country. (Texas Observer 82:14 April 6, 90)

SHERROD, William Forrest (Blackie). Sportswriting is just like driving a taxi. It ain't the work you enjoy. It's the people you run into. (Texas Monthly 3:93 Dec 75)

SHIELDS, Brooke. Smoking can kill you, and if you've been killed, you've lost a very important part of your life. (The Atlantic 265:24 Jan 90)

SHIELDS, Gerald R. It is obvious that the photocopying issue is to be decided soon and that the odds favor turning libraries into some sort of reprint warehouse for publisher's products. (Library Journal 100:2307 Dec 15, 75)

SHIELDS, Mark. I don't think Carter and self-doubt have ever met. (Washingtonian 11:103 June 76)

SHOR, Toots. A good saloonkeeper is the most important man in the community. (Time 106:44 Sept 22, 75)

SHOR, Toots. I don't want to be a millionaire, I just want to live like one. (New York Times 126:36 Jan 25, 77)

SHRIVER, Eunice. Mistakes were obviously made in terms of the investigation, but I'm satisfied with their conclusions (on the Warren Commission). (Christian Science Monitor 68:8 Dec 3, 75)

SHUTTLEWORTH, John. We are still much too preoccupied with taking our machines out into the woods, instead of making a place for the forest in our hearts. (The Mother Earth News 35:7 Sept 75)

SIDEY, Hugh. Bureaucrats are the only people in the world who can say absolutely nothing and mean it. (Time 108:13 Nov 29, 76)

SIDEY, Hugh. One must always remember that freedom from action and freedom from purpose constitute the philosophical bases of creative bureaucracy. (Time 108:13 Nov 29, 76)

SIDEY, Hugh. The measurement of the gestation period of an original thought in a bureaucracy is still pending. (Time 108:13 Nov 29, 76)

SIDEY, Hugh. When a bureaucrat makes a mistake and continues to make it, it usually becomes the new policy. (Time 108:13 Nov 29, 76)

SIKINGER, Maximilian. It's better to be a hungry coyote than to be a satisfied dog. (Village Voice 22:32 May 9, 77)

SILBER, John R. I don't speak plastic like other politicians. (New York Times 139:A10 April 6, 90)

SILBER, John R. I know as a (political) candidate I should kiss your ass, but I haven't learned to do that with equanimity yet (to the press). (Newsweek 115:17 Feb 5, 90)

SILBERMAN, Laurence. The legal process, because of its unbridled growth, has become a cancer which threatens the vitality of our forms of capitalism and democracy. (Time 111:56 April 10, 78)

SIMELS, Steve. John Denver (is) Johnny Mathis disguised as a hillbilly. He has never written a decent song, his voice is an Irish tenor only a whit less offensive than Dennis Day's, and, as far as I can tell, his only function is to provide adolescent girls with records to cry over in the privacy of their bedrooms. (Stereo Review 35:72 Dec 75)

SIMMEL, Marianne L. Methodology is the last refuge of a sterile mind. (Kansas City Star 109:2 F Dec 25, 88)

SIMON, George T. Only God can make a tree and only men can play good jazz. (National NOW Times 11:12 Aug 78)

SIMON, John. Every era gets the leader it deserves; John Wayne is ours. (Newsweek 93:77 June 25, 79)

SIMON, John. I always thought Miss (Liza) Minelli's face deserving—of first prize in the beagle category. (Time 110:34 Dec 26, 77)

SIMON, John. I love plays, but I love them in a different way. I'm not blind. I don't gush. I love the theater as it might be. (Time 110:34 Dec 26, 77)

SIMON, John. The culture of the nation's capital would seem to be a capital joke. (New York 8:76 May 12, 75)

SIMON, Paul. I am not a neo-anything. I'm a Democrat. (Newsweek 109:17 April 20, 87)

SIMON, Paul. If money alone could do the trick, John Connally would be president. (Newsweek 111:15 Mar 14, 88)

SIMON, William E. Bad politicians are sent to Washington by good people who don't vote. (Atlanta 16:130 Aug 76)

SIMON, William E. In the United States today, we already have more government than we need, more government than most people want, and certainly more government than we are willing to pay for. (Vital Speeches 42:72 Nov 15, 75)

SIMON, William E. Show me a good loser and I'll show you a loser. (Washingtonian 11:24 April 76)

SIMON, William E. Washington is the only city where sound travels faster than light. (Atlanta 16:130 Aug 76)

SIMON, William E. We're going to have a taxpayers' revolt if we don't begin to make the tax system more simple, more understandable, so that everyone knows that everybody is paying his fair share. (Chicago Tribune 11:1 Section 1 Jan 11, 76)

SIMONE, Nina. Jazz lets black people know, everytime they hear it, that they have their hands on the pulse of life. (Sepia 26:10 June 77)

SINATRA, Frank. I am a symmetrical man, almost to a fault. (New York 13:32 April 28, 80)

SINCLAIR, Clive. High tech is high fashion. (Village Voice 27:71 Mar 30, 82)

SINCLAIR, John. You can't make a

revolution if you have to make a living. (Newsweek 90:26 Sept 5, 77)

SINCLAIR, Upton. I tried to touch America's conscience and all I did was hit it in the stomach (commenting on the effect of his novel The Jungle). (Philadelphia 67:65 Nov 76)

SINGER, Isaac Bashevis. A Marxist has never written a good novel. (New York Times Magazine 42 Nov 26, 78)

SINGER, Isaac Bashevis. A writer, like a woman, never knows why people like him, or why people dislike him. We never know. (Time 112:69 Aug 7, 78)

SINGER, Isaac Bashevis. Fiction can entertain and stir the mind; it does not direct it. (Time 112:82 July 3, 78)

SINGER, Isaac Bashevis. I did not become a vegetarian for my health. I did it for the health of the chickens. (Time 123:79 Jan 2, 84)

SINGER, Isaac Bashevis. I never forget that I am only a storyteller. (Time 112:129 Oct 16, 78)

SINGER, Isaac Bashevis. I'm a pessimist with cheerfulness. It's a riddle even to me, but this is how I am. (Chicago Tribune 291:20 Oct 18, 78)

SINGER, Isaac Bashevis. I'm afraid the whole world is going to become a second Lebanon. (New York 19:56 Nov 22, 86)

SINGER, Isaac Bashevis. Literature is the memory of humanity. (US News & World Report 85:60 Nov 6, 78)

SINGER, Isaac Bashevis. The supernatural is like the ocean, while the so-called natural is only a little island on it. And even this little island is a great riddle. (New York Times 128:18 Section 4 Dec 3, 78)

SINGER, Isaac Bashevis. The whole human history is a holocaust. (Chicago Tribune 174:3 Section 5 June 23, 87)

SINGER, Isaac Bashevis. When I was a little boy, they called me a liar, but now that I am grown up, they call me a writer. (Time 122:53 July 18, 83)

SINGER, Isaac Bashevis. Writers were not born to change the world. (Time 112:82 July 3, 78)

SINGH, Vishwanath Pratap. This is a government of the poor, for the poor (about India). (Chicago Tribune 344:22 Section 1 Sept 10, 89)

SIRICA, John J. I hope no political party will ever stoop so low as to embrace the likes of Richard Nixon again. (The Tennessean 74:10 Section F May 13, 79)

SIRICA, John J. Nixon should have been indicted. (Chicago Tribune 119:2 Section 2 April 29, 79)

SITWELL, Edith. The public will believe anything, so long as it is not founded on truth. (Kansas City Star 97:2D Feb 20, 77)

SKINNER, B. F. The more reason we have to pay attention to life, the less we have to pay attention to death. (Kansas City Star 104:1A Oct 11, 83)

SKINNER, B. F. The real problem is not whether machines think but whether men do. (Omni 4:36 July 82)

SKINNER, B. F. You must find or create a world in which you can act in a sensible way. (Kansas City Star 104:11A Oct 11, 83)

SKINNER, Cornelia Otis. A woman's virtue is man's greatest invention. (Time 114:76 July 23, 79)

SKODACK, Debra. A person is not an investor until he has delt with a bad stock market. (Kansas City Times 120:D-3 Oct 22, 87)

SLATER, Jim. As you get better at a thing it gets less interesting. (The Observer 9761:14 Sept 24, 78)

SLOANE, Harvey. He's maturing like good Kentucky bourbon (about Jimmy Carter). (Time 107:10 May 24, 76)

SMATHERS, George. They say life is a game, but you keep score in money. (Washingtonian 17:66 Aug 82)

SMEAL, Eleanor. I feel it is important to march to your own drummer. (Washington Post National Weekly Edition 3:7 Dec 9, 85)

SMELSER, Neil. Californians believe the best is behind them. (Time 110:23 July 18, 77)

SMITH, Adam. If you don't know who you are, the stock market is an expensive place to find out. (Kansas City Star 109:2F Dec 25, 88)

SMITH, Alexis. Women who are only involved with how they look are always dull. (Chicago Tribune 123:16 Section 1 May 3, 77)

SMITH, Charles Merrill. In a democracy you can be respected though poor, but don't count on it. (Time 113:25 Feb 26, 79)

SMITH, Howard K. The trouble with Ronald Reagan is that he thinks the whole world began in Dixon, Illinois. (USA Today 1:2D Jan 3, 83)

SMITH, Ian Douglas. I do not believe in black majority rule in Rhodesia—not in a thousand years. (People Weekly 5:45 June 7, 76)

SMITH, Ian Douglas. I have got to admit that things haven't gone quite the way I wanted (1979). (The Observer 9797:10 June 3, 79)

SMITH, Maggie. I'm always very relieved to be somebody else, because I'm not sure at all who I am. (New York Times 128:C26 Sept 12, 79)

SMITH, Patti. As far as I'm concerned, being any gender is a drag. (Playboy 26:26 Oct 79)

SMITH, Patti. I want every faggot, grandmother, five-year-old and Chinaman to be able to hear my music and say YEAH. (Time 107:76 Jan 5, 76)

SMITH, Patti. Jesus died for somebody's sins but not mine. (Philadelphia 69:185 Sept 78)

SMITH, Patti. Not even boot camp is as tough as being in rock and roll. (Chicago Tribune 340:3 Section 6 Dec 13, 76)

SMITH, Red. Writing is very easy. All you do is sit in front of a typewriter keyboard until little drops of blood appear on your forehead. (Writers' Digest 55:4 Nov 75)

SMITH, Roger. I'd rather be remembered as the guy that lost market share and increased profits than the guy who increased market share and lost profits. (Chicago Tribune 215:21 Section 1 Aug 3, 90)

SMITH, Sam. He stood on his own (about Elvis Presley). (New York Times Magazine 45 Mar 25, 79)

SMITH, W. Eugene. I carry a torch with my camera. (Life 1:56 Dec 78)

SMITH, Walter (Red). He might have been a great athlete, except that he is small, puny, slow, inept, uncoordinated, myopic and yellow (speaking of himself). (Time 119:85 Jan 25, 82)

SMITH, William French. We must recognize that bigness in business does not necessarily mean badness. (Newsweek 98:57 July 6, 81)

SNOW, C. P. Literary intellectuals at one pole—at the other, scientists...Between the two a gulf of mutual incomprehension. (Omni 1:39 Mar 79)

SNOW, C. P. Money is not so important as a pat on the head. (The Observer 9723:11 Dec 18, 77)

SOFFER, Gerald. All the signs suggest that life exists on Mars, but we can't find any bodies. (Omni 2:40 April 80)

SOKOLSKY, Leon. Those who have never made a mistake work for those who have dared to. (Kansas City Star 106:5A Dec 30, 85)

SOLTI, Sir Georg. Chicago should erect a statue to me for what I have done. (Chicago 26:152 Dec 77)

SOLZHENITSYN, Aleksandr Isaevich. For us in Russia Communism is a dead dog, while for many people in the West it is still a living lion. (The Observer 9782:10 Mar 18, 79)

SOLZHENITSYN, Aleksandr Isaevich. Hastiness and superficiality are the psychic disease of the 20th century. (Time 111:33 June 19, 78)

SOLZHENITSYN, Aleksandr Isaevich. The entire period from 1945 to 1975 can be viewed as another world war that was lost by the West without a battle. (Time 115:48 Feb 18, 80)

SOLZHENITSYN, Aleksandr Isaevich. The Soviet Union's economy is on such a war footing that even if it were the unanimous opinion of all members of the Politburo not to start a war, this would no longer be in their power. (New York Times 125:26 Mar 3, 76)

SOLZHENITSYN, Aleksandr Isaevich. To defend oneself, one must also be ready to die; there is little such readiness in a society raised in the cult of material well-being. (Time 111:18 June 26, 78)

SOLZHENITSYN, Aleksandr Isaevich. When changes occur in the Soviet regime, the whole orbit of life on earth will change. (The Observer 9783:11 Feb 25, 79)

SOMERS, Suzanne. If you've got it, bump it with a trumpet. (Playboy 26:26 Oct 79)

SONDHEIM, Stephen. Books are what the musical theater is about. (Los Angeles 30:46 Nov 85)

SONTAG, Susan. Nobody ever discovered ugliness through photographs. But many, through photographs, have discovered beauty. (Vogue 168:185 June 78)

SONTAG, Susan. There are some elements in life—above all, sexual pleasure—about which it isn't necessary to have a position. (Village Voice 21:77 Mar 22, 76)

SOREL, Edward. At what I do, I am the best there is. (Guardian Weekly 119:17 Nov 12, 78)

SOUTER, David. I have not got any agenda on what should be done with Roe v. Wade if that case was brought before me. I have not made up my mind. (Chicago Tribune 261:19 Section 1 Sept 18, 90)

SPARK, Muriel. People who have hope are sad because they are so often disappointed. (New York Times Book Review 47 May 20, 79)

SPAULDING, Jim. When newspapers write about themselves, they lie. (New West 3:65 Jan 16, 78)

SPEAKES, Larry. If you tell the same story five times, it's true. (Spy 32:June 89

SPEAKES, Larry. Remember, you don't have to explain what you say (advice to new White House spokesman). (Newsweek 109:15 Feb 16, 87)

SPENCE, Gary. There is no justice in seeking justice anymore. (W 4:86 April

87)

SPENDER, Stephen. He (Robert Graves) was one of those rare people whom, whatever their foibles, one knows to be ultimately true and good. (Manchester Guardian Weekly 133:5 Dec 15, 85)

SPIELBERG, Steven. I wanted a creature only a mother could love (about E.T.). (Kansas City Times 115:D1 Jan 1, 83)

SPIELBERG, Steven. My advice to anyone who wants to be a movie director is to make home movies. I started out by shooting 8 millimeter home movies with neighbors and friends. (Texas Monthly 4:38 Aug 76)

SPIELBERG, Steven. The most expensive habit in the world is celluloid, not heroin, and I need a fix every few years. (Time 113:97 April 26, 79)

SPIKOL, Art. The fact is that most people don't drive cars that reflect what they are: they drive the closest thing they can find to what they'd like to be. (Philadelphia Magazine 66:198 Nov 75)

SPILLANE, Mickey. Freud's stupid. I didn't like Jung or Adler, either. I go along with Samuel Goldwyn: he said anybody who has to see a psychiatrist ought to have to have his head examined. (Gentlemen's Quarterly 55:327 Oct 85)

SPILLANE, Mickey. Hey, if Shakespeare was selling big today, I'd write like Shakespeare. (Village Voice 29:102 Feb 21, 84)

SPILLANE, Mickey. Mike Hammer drinks beer, not cognac, because I can't spell cognac. (American Bookseller 11:23 Dec 87)

SPILLER, Roger. Military history is the laboratory of the professional officer in time of peace. (Chicago Tribune 104:19 Section 1 April 14, 89)

SPINKS, Leon. You can take a man out of the ghetto, but you can't take the ghetto out of a man. (The Observer 9760:13 Sept 17, 78)

SPOCK, Benjamin. You know more than you think you do. (Yankee 48:75 Dec 84)

SPROLES, Judy. If there is an opinion, facts will be found to support it. (Omni 1:132 May 79)

STAFFORD, Jean. I write for myself and God and a few close friends. (Time 113:78 April 9, 79)

STALLONE, Frank. He's a frustrated musician, been that way all his life. (US 3:6 Nov 2, 87)

STALLONE, Sylvester. Actors are a walking, throbbing mass of unhealed scar tissue by the time they get anywhere. (Chicago Sun-Times 32:3 Section 3 Nov 5, 78)

STALLONE, Sylvester. I make my living with my mind. My muscles I consider merely machinery to carry my mind around. (Chicago Tribune 210:16 July 29, 77)

STALLONE, Sylvester. My temperature was higher than my combined SAT scores. (US 3:64 July 1, 85)

STALLONE, Sylvester. Playing polo is a lot like trying to hit a golf ball during an earthquake. (Metro 5:68 1990)

STALLONE, Sylvester. Some people have skeletons in their closets, but I have a graveyard. (US 3:64 Oct 7, 85)

STANDISH, David. The blues hasn't died out; it's turned white. (Chicago 27:236 Jan 78)

STARR, Kevin O. Perhaps if we find a way to save our Presidents, we can find a way to save ourselves. (Newsweek 86:34 Oct 6, 75)

STARR, Kevin O. There is no stable intellectual tradition in California except utopianism. (Esquire 89:134 Jan 31, 78)

STEICHEN, Edward. The mission of photography is to explain man to man and each man to himself. (Camera 35 20:37 July 76)

STEIN, Gertrude. Considering how dangerous everything is, nothing is really frightening. (Human Behavior 7:17 May 78)

STEIN, Gertrude. Everybody gets so much information all day long that they lose their common sense. (Chicago Tribune 176:2 Section 2 June 25, 78)

STEIN, Gertrude. I do want to get rich, but I never want to do what there is to do to get rich. (Cosmopolitan 196:332 Oct 83)

STEIN, Gertrude. Money is always there but the pockets change; it is not in the same pockets after a change, and that is all there is to say about money. (Time 106:E8 Oct 13, 75)

STEIN, Gertrude. Nothing can, or will, happen in Africa. (New York Times Book Review 10 July 1, 79)

STEIN, Gertrude. One of the great things about not going to movies is that you get lots of surprises. (Film Comment 12:2 Jan 76)

STEIN, Gertrude. We are always the same age inside. (Omni 2:38 April 80)

STEINBECK, John. Competing with Hemingway isn't my idea of good business. (Time 106:48 Dec 1, 75)

STEINBECK, John. The profession of book writing makes horse racing seem like a solid, stable business. (Time 112:68 Aug 28, 78)

STEINBECK, John (attributed by John Kenneth Galbraith). Unless the bastards have the courage to give you unqualified praise, I say ignore them. (Esquire 99:88 April 30, 83)

STEINBERG, Saul. The doodle is the brooding of the hand. (Time 112:88 Oct 16, 78)

STEINBERG, Saul. The life of the creative man is led, directed and controlled by boredom. (Time 111:92 April 17, 78)

STEINBERG, Saul. Unlike writing, drawing makes up its own syntax as it goes along. The line can't be reasoned in the mind. It can only be reasoned on paper. (Time 111:92 April 17, 78)

STEINBERG, William. Great conductors do not dance. (Newsweek 91:93 May 29, 78)

STEINEM, Gloria. A pedestal is as much a prison as any small space. (Playboy 26:26 Oct 79)

STEINEM, Gloria. Feminism means that each woman has power over her own life and can decide what to do for herself. (Chicago Tribune 338:1 Dec 4, 78)

STEINEM, Gloria. I can't mate in captivity. (Life 7:40 Jan 83)

STEINEM, Gloria. If the secretaries and wives told each other what we know, we could take over the world. (Chicago Sun-Times 34:41 April 27, 81)

STEINEM, Gloria. Some of us are becoming the men we wanted to marry. (Chicago Sun-Times 34:41 April 27, 81)

STEINEM, Gloria. The average secretary in the U.S. is better educated than the average boss. (Time 112:61 Sept 11, 78)

STEINEM, Gloria. The first problem for all of us, men and women, is not to learn, but to unlearn. (Human Behavior 7:17 May 78)

STEINEM, Gloria. Today a woman without a man is like a fish without a bicycle. (New York 9:26 Aug 9, 76)

STEINEM, Gloria. Women now face the threat of having their bodies nationalized. (Life 5:58 Jan 82)

STEINER, George. The world of Auschwitz lies outside speech as it lies outside reason. (Time 111:53 May 1, 78)

STEINFELS, Peter. Rather than getting the government they want, the people should want the government they get; they should be retutored to fit its current capacities. (Newsweek 94:74 July 2, 79)

STENGEL, Charles Dillon (Casey). If you walk backward you'll find out that you can go forward and people won't know if you're coming or going. (Newsweek 86:47 Aug 11, 75)

STENGEL, Charles Dillon (Casey). Never make predictions, especially about the future. (New York 18:20 June 3, 85)

STERLING, Donald T. Buy it. Improve it.

Keep it...forever. (California 14:60 July 89)

STERN, Isaac. You don't realize how close it is to you, how much it is a part of your body, until it is gone (about the violin).. (New York Times Magazine 15 Aug 12, 79)

STEVENS, Cat. Nobody put a sword to my neck to make me a Moslem. (Toronto Globe and Mail 141:1 Aug 25, 84)

STEVENS, John Paul. It's always been my philosophy to decide cases on the narrowest grounds possible and not to reach out. (New York Times 125:1 Dec 9, 75)

STEVENS, John Paul. Judges should impose on themselves the discipline of deciding no more than is before them. (American Legion Magazine 100:9 Feb 76)

STEVENS, John Paul. One of the strongest arguments against regulating obscenity through criminal law is the inherent vagueness of the obscenity concept. (Chicago Tribune 161:12 Section 1 June 10, 77)

STEVENSON, Adlai, II. A free society is one where it is safe to be unpopular. (Human Behavior 7:68 May 78)

STEVENSON, Adlai, II. An editor is someone who separates the wheat from the chaff and then prints the chaff. (Texas Observer 68:7 Dec 24, 76)

STEVENSON, Adlai, II. By the time a man is nominated for the Presidency of the United States, he is no longer worthy to hold the office. (Washingtonian 15:143 Nov 79)

STEVENSON, Adlai, II. Good government cannot exist side by side with bad politics: the best government is the best politics. (Kansas City Star 97:4B Jan 30, 77)

STEVENSON, Adlai, II. He's (Hubert Humphrey) a politician with more solutions than there are problems. (Washingtonian 16:22 June 81)

STEVENSON, Adlai, II. I have been tempted to make a proposal to our Republican friends: that if they stop telling lies about us, we would stop telling the truth about them. (Human Behavior 7:68 May 78)

STEVENSON, Adlai, II. I have often thought that if I had any epitaph that I would rather have more than another, it would be to say that I had disturbed the sleep of my generation. (Newsweek 90:120 Oct 24, 77)

STEVENSON, Adlai, II. It is better to light one candle than to curse the darkness. (New York Times Magazine 45 July 4, 76)

STEVENSON, Adlai, II. Man does not live by

words alone, despite the fact that sometimes he has to eat them. (Human Behavior 7:69 May 78)

STEVENSON, Adlai, II. Nixon is the kind of politician who would cut down a redwood tree, then mount the stump for a speech on conservation. (Human Behavior 7:68 May 78)

STEVENSON, Adlai, II. The government must be the trustee for the little man, because no one else will be. The powerful can usually help themselves—and frequently do. (Human Behavior 7:68 May 78)

STEVENSON, Adlai, II. The journey of a thousand leagues begins with a single step. So we must never neglect any work of peace within our reach, however small. (Human Behavior 7:69 May 78)

STEVENSON, Adlai, II. There was a time when a fool and his money were soon parted, but now it happens to everybody. (New York Times 128:A19 June 11, 79)

STEVENSON, Adlai, II. You can tell the size of a man by the size of the thing that makes him mad. (Texas Observer 78:7 June 18, 76)

STEVENSON, Adlai, III. I don't think ideas are incompatible with political reality. (Time 113:18 Feb 26, 79)

STEWART, James. The most important thing about acting is to approach it as a craft, not as an art and not as some mysterious type of religion. (Chicago Tribune 105:25 Section 1 April 17, 77)

STEWART, Potter. It's better to go too soon than to stay too long. (Time 127:57 Dec 30, 85)

STEWART, Rod. I'm a rock star because I couldn't be a soccer star. (Elle 2:37 Dec 86)

STIEGLITZ, Alfred. Let all the art in the world be destroyed. It will rise again, for the art spirit is inherent in man. (Los Angeles Times Book Review 96:10 July 31, 77)

STIEGLITZ, Alfred. Photography is photography, neither more nor less. (American Photographer 22:7 Mar 89)

STIMSON, Henry. Gentlemen do not read each other's mail. (Maclean's 89:72 April 5, 76)

STING, (Musician). When you're a rock star, you're allowed to be a petulant child and many other things you'r supposed to grow out of. (Life 7:40 Jan 83)

STOCKMAN, David. None of us really understands what's going on with all these numbers (commenting on budget figures). (Life 5:33 Jan 82)

STOCKMAN, David. We've had a referendum on what we want in the budget, and what we don't. What's left, most of the people want. And we're going to have to raise taxes to pay for it. (Washington Post National Weekly Edition 2:4 Oct 21, 85)

STOESSINGER, John G. The President holds our future in his hands. His personality may be our destiny. (Time 114:20 Dec 31, 79)

STOKOWSKI, Leopold. Music appeals to me for what can be done with it. (Time 110:54 Sept 26, 77)

STOKOWSKI, Leopold. The history of popular music shows that it is the true art form of the people. (Newsweek 90:94 Sept 26, 77)

STOLLEY, Richard. Young sells better than old, pretty sells better than ugly, music sells better than television, television better than movies, and politics doesn't sell at all. (New York 10:15 Sept 12, 77)

STONE, Isidor Feinstein. Every government is run by liars. Nothing they say should be believed. (The Progressive 53:4 Aug 89)

STONE, Isidor Feinstein. I'd like to say that I never though of myself as an investigative journalist, because from my boyhood I felt that every reporter investigates what he's writing about. If he doesn't he's an idiot who just rewrites press releases. (The Nation 249:40 July 10, 89)

STONE, Isidor Feinstein. If you live long enough, you get accused of things you never did and praised for virtues you never had. (American Spectator 17:17 July 84)

STONE, Isidor Feinstein. The biggest menace to American freedom is the intelligence community. (Wilson Library Bulletin 51:25 Sept 76)

STONE, John S. Trammell Crow is the kind of person Donald Trump ought to want to be when Donald Trump grows up. (Chicago Tribune 365:1 Section 16 Dec 31, 89)

STONE, Richard. One privilege of home ownership is the right to have lousy taste and display it. (Time 111:24 April 17, 78)

STOPPARD, Tom. Ambushing the audience is what theater is all about. (Newsweek 103:82 Jan 16, 84)

STOPPARD, Tom. I suppose my purpose as a playwright, if such a thing can be stated at all, has been to marry the play of ideas with comedy or farce. (Los Angeles Times Calendar 46 Jan 9, 77)

STOPPARD, Tom. I think that plays should disturb certainties as well as affirm them. (Newsweek 103:83 Jan 16, 84)

STOPPARD, Tom. My feeling is that in the

theater the emotions should be gratified as well as the intellect. (Newsweek 103:82 Jan 16, 84)

STOPPARD, Tom. Skill without imagination is craftsmanship and gives us many useful objects as wickerwork picnic baskets. Imagination without skill gives us modern art. (Kansas City Times 119:A-19 July 11, 87)

STOTESBURY, E. T. A good servant should never be in the way and never out of the way. (Town & Country 131:95 Mar 77)

STRAUSS, Robert S. Everybody in government is like a bunch of ants on a log floating down a river. Each one thinks he is guiding the log, but it's really just going with the flow. (Time 111:47 April 17, 78)

STRAUSS, Robert S. I didn't come to town yesterday on a load of watermelons. (Newsweek 94:5 July 16, 79)

STRAUSS, Robert S. If you're in politics, you're a whore anyhow. It doesn't make any difference who you sleep with. (Texas Monthly 6:132 Feb 78)

STRAUSS, Robert S. There ain't but one good job in this government, and you got it (to Jimmy Carter). (Time 116:12 Sept 22, 80)

STRAUSS, Robert S. You know, it's awfully easy to tell people to go to hell. But it's another thing to get them there. (Newsweek 94:47 July 16, 79)

STRAVINSKY, Igor Fedorovich. A good composer does not imitate; he steals. (Whole Earth Review 57:108 Winter 87)

STRAVINSKY, Igor Fedorovich. If everything would be permitted to me, I would feel lost in this abyss of freedom. (New York Times 126:D25 Sept 11, 77)

STROESSNER, Alfredo. Human rights is a Trojan horse of international Communism. (Mother Jones 3:8 June 78)

STROUT, Richard. (American Democracy is) the only governmental vehicle on earth that has two steering wheels: one for the President, one for the Congress. You never can tell who's driving. (Time 111:83 Mar 27, 78)

STURGEON, Theodore. Ninety percent of science fiction is crud. But then, 90 percent of everything is crud. (Kansas City Star 114:1A Dec 30, 81)

STYRON, William. I think a great novel could even come out of Beverly Hills. (New York Times Book Review 18 May 27, 79)

SULLIVAN, Frank. Jane Byrne was the supreme misjudgement of Richard J. Daley's life. (Chicago Tribune 76:3 Section 5 Mar 17, 89)

SUMMERS, Andy. One night stands don't have to be tacky. (Playboy 31:90 April 84)

SUSANN, Jacqueline. I don't have any peers, as far as writers go. (After Dark 8:35 Aug 75)

SUSKIND, Sigmund. Cheating (in colleges) is not endemic, it's epidemic. (Time 107:29 June 7, 76)

SUTTON, Willie. I always figured that being a good robber was like being a good lawyer. (Village Voice 21:118 Sept 13, 76)

SWAGGART, Jimmy Lee. All I want to do is jack off awhile. (Village Voice 33:25 June 21, 88)

SWANSON, Gloria. It's hereditary, all in the genes. But no one can have skin like a baby's bottom if they're going to stuff that hole in their face with chocolate and banana splits. (Chicago Tribune 320:11 Section 5 Nov 16, 75)

SWAYDUCK, Edward. When we examine Ford's political and legislative record, we must ask the crucial question: Is Ford really an Edsel. (Washingtonian 11:294 Dec 75)

SWITZER, Barry. Some people are born on third base and go through life thinking they hit a triple. (Kansas City Times 107:1F Nov 22, 86)

SYMINGTON, Stuart. (Charles Finley) is one of the most disreputable characters to enter the American sports scene. (New York Times 125:2 Section 5 Sept 19, 76)

SZASZ, Thomas. Just as (mental) illness is not a crime, so crime is not an illness. (TV Guide 28:32 May 17, 80)

SZENT-GYOERGYI VON NAGYRAPOLT, Albert. Discovery consists of seeing what everybody has seen and thinking what nobody has thought. (Omni 2:45 Dec 79)

TALBERT, Bob. Resisting temptation is easier when you think you'll probably get another chance later on. (Reader's Digest 107:166 Oct 75)

TALBERT, Diron. There ain't but one time to go fishin' and that's whenever you can. (Washingtonian 11:116 Sept 76)

TALBOTT, Basil, Jr. Chicago may have nominated its first mayor who goes to a beauty shop, but she is in the city's oldest tradition. (Chicago Sun-Times 32:5 Section 2 Mar 4, 79)

TALESE, Gay. Lawyers have become the third force in publishing. I see them as the new enemy. (Time 115:51 Mar 17, 80)

TALMADGE, Betty. If you love the law and you love good sausage, don't watch either of them being made. (The Reader (Chicago's Free Weekly) 7:23 Nov 25, 77)

TALMADGE, Betty. There's not much difference between selling a ham and selling a political idea. (Time 112:23 July 31, 78)

TALMADGE, Herman. Virtually everything is under federal control nowadays except the federal budget. (American Legion Magazine 99:17 Aug 75)

TANEN, Ned (former Hollywood agent). There's no orphan like the movie that doesn't work; a hit movie has 90 fathers. (New York Times Magazine 18 Aug 7, 77)

TANIGUCHI, Yoshiko. Affluence made many Americans content with their lives. This has begun to show in their products. (Newsweek 115:19 April 2, 90)

TANNER, Chuck. Having Willie Stargell on your ball club is like having a diamond ring on your finger. (Time 114:108 Oct 29, 79)

TANNER, Jack. A person without character always does what is right. (Challenge 19:5 Mar/April 76)

TANNER, Jack. An editor has no friends. (Challenge 19:5 Mar/April 76)

TANNER, Jack. Fame is empty. But it is better to find that out afterwards. (Challenge 19:5 Mar/April 76)

TANNER, Jack. Nothing could discredit capitalism more than a decision by the Russians to try it. (Challenge 19:4 Mar/April 76)

TANNER, Jack. What is counted as truth in one age is counted as myth in the next. (Challenge 19:4 Mar/April 76)

TANNER, Jack. When God created the world, He said it was good. That was His second mistake. (Challenge 19:5 Mar/April 76)

TARTIKOFF, Brandon. Hollywood is like Harvard. Once you're accepted, you can't flunk out. (New Times 10:31 Jan 9, 78)

TATI, Jacques. Comedians speak with their legs. (Times Literary Supplement 3969:460 April 28, 78)

TAUPIN, Bernie. We've all made assholes of ourselves. (Playboy 31:90 April 84)

TAWIL, Raymonde. We (Palestinians) are like grass. The more you cut it, the more it will grow. (Time 111:36 Mar 27, 78)

TAYAC, Turkey (Chief of the Piscataway Indians). They don't know about Indians any more than a buzzard knows about ice cream (about the Bureau of Indian Affairs). (Washingtonian 10:103 May 75)

TAYLOR, Elizabeth. I didn't know I was destroying a famous actor (about Richard Burton). (Vanity Fair 52:84 Feb 89)

TAYLOR, Elizabeth. I'm confident that he's (Jimmy Carter) a short-term President. (Chicago Tribune 212:44 July 31, 79)

TAYLOR, Elizabeth. When people say: she's got everything, I've only one answer: I haven't had tomorrow. (Chicago Tribune 176:2 Section 2 June 25, 78)

TAYLOR, Francis H. The trick is to buy the right thing at the wrong time (about collecting). (Philadelphia 75:153 Sept 84)

TEAGUE, Freeman, Jr. Nothing is so simple it cannot be misunderstood. (Omni 1:132 May 79)

TEKANAWA, Kiri. Nothing is worse than a musical snob. (W 12A:13 July 29, 83)

TELLER, Edward. I am forever described as the father of the H-bomb. I would much prefer to be known as the father of two wonderful children. (Outside 1:13 Oct 77)

TELLER, Edward. Nuclear power is not an option—it is a part of the fight for the survival of freedom. (New York Times 129:A30 Dec 12, 79)

TENG, Hsiao-Ping. If the masses feel some anger, we must let them express it. (The Observer 9771:14 Dec 3, 78)

TENG, Hsiao-Ping. It doesn't matter whether you climb Mount Everest by its North slope or its South slope as long as you get to the top. (Newsweek 93:36 Feb 5, 79)

TENG, Hsiao-Ping. You can sign all the treaties you want, but you cannot trust the Russians. (Chicago Tribune 38:3 Section 3 Feb 7, 79)

TERKEL, Studs. Dissent is not merely the right to dissent—it is the duty. (National Catholic Reporter 12:7 July 2, 76)

TERKEL, Studs. He was a North Star to me (about I. F. Stone). (Chicago Tribune 170:1 June 19, 89)

TERKEL, Studs. I would like to see the end of institutional brutalities and stupidities. I would like to see the abolition of the CIA, which symbolizes those things, and I would like people to look at the FBI as the secret police system it is, rather than something sacred. (Chicago Tribune 343:4 Section 1 Dec 8, 75)

THALBERG, Irving. Nothing is unfair in politics. (The Nation 239:77 Aug 4, 84)

THARP, Twyla. Art is the only way to run away from home without leaving home. (Ms 5:66 Oct 76)

THARP, Twyla. Dancing is like bank robbery, it takes split-second timing. (Ms 5:68 Oct 76)

THARP, Twyla. I sometimes find structure a riot. (Chicago Tribune 198:3 Section 6 July 17, 77)

THATCHER, Margaret Hilda. Britain's progress toward socialism has been an alternation of two steps forward with half a step back. (Time 105:30 Feb 10, 75)

THATCHER, Margaret Hilda. Foreign policy is simply a matter of national self-interest.

(New York Times Magazine 56 April 29, 79)

THATCHER, Margaret Hilda. I am controversial. That means I stand for something. (Time 115:34 Jan 7, 80)

THATCHER, Margaret Hilda. I am extraordinary patient, provided I get my own way in the end. (The Observer 9944:8 April 4, 82)

THATCHER, Margaret Hilda. I never read books. (The Observer 9774:7 Dec 24, 79)

THATCHER, Margaret Hilda. I'm not a consensus politician, or a pragmatic politician, but a conviction politician. (Newsweek 93:52 April 9, 79)

THATCHER, Margaret Hilda. If a Tory does not believe that private property is one of the main bulwarks of individual freedom, then he had better become a socialist and have done with it. (Time 105:30-31 Feb 24, 75)

THATCHER, Margaret Hilda. If you want anything said, ask a man; if you want anything done, ask a woman. (New York Times Magazine 52 April 29, 79)

THATCHER, Margaret Hilda. It is important not to be so obsessed with yesterday's danger that we fail to detect today's. (The Observer 9822:9 Nov 25, 79)

THATCHER, Margaret Hilda. Opportunity means nothing unless it includes the right to be unequal. (The Illustrated London News 263:26 Oct 31, 75)

THATCHER, Margaret Hilda. There can be no liberty unless there is economic liberty. (Village Voice 24:35 May 14, 79)

THATCHER, Margaret Hilda. We (Conservatives) believe that you get a responsible society when you get responsible individuals. (New York Times Magazine 36 April 29, 79)

THATCHER, Margaret Hilda. We are not short of summits. The only thing we are short of is the results from summits. (The Observer 9723:11 Dec 18, 77)

THATCHER, Margaret Hilda. What Britain needs is an iron lady. (Newsweek 93:50 May 14, 79)

THATCHER, Margaret Hilda. You cannot have national welfare before someone has created national wealth. (Time 112:61 Sept 11, 78)

THEROUX, Paul. Travel is glamorous only in retrospect. (The Observer 9815:10 Oct 7, 79)

THEROUX, Paul. You are not what you eat; but where you eat is who you are. (Travel & Leisure 7:76 July 31, 77)

THICKE, Alan. I can count my Canadian media friends on the fingers of one hand, and I express my feelings for the rest of them with one finger. (US 3:6 Mar 9, 89)

THIEBAUD, Wayne. Living in California allows one to escape preciousness and the predictable. (Connoisseur 217:66 Feb 87)

THOMAS, Caitlin (wife of Dylan Thomas). Dylan wanted us to be young and unwise forever—to be permanently naughty children. He managed this by killing himself with booze, but I was left to grow old. (Time 106:46 Dec 15, 75)

THOMAS, Lewis. We do not, in any real way, run the (world). It runs itself, and we are part of the running. (Time 111:85 May 29, 78)

THOMAS, Lowell. After the age of 80, everything reminds you of something else. (Time 112:62 Nov 27, 78)

THOMAS, Marlo. A man has to be Joe McCarthy to be called ruthless. All a woman has to do is put you on hold. (New York Times Book Review 35 Feb 17, 80)

THOMAS, Marlo. Nothing is either all masculine or all feminine except sex. (People Weekly 8:50 Dec 19, 77)

THOMPSON, Hunter S. Crack is ruining the drug culture. (Newsweek 116:17 Oct 8, 90)

THOMPSON, Hunter S. Huge brains, small necks, weak muscles, and fat wallets— these are the dominant characteristics of the 80s—the generation of swine. (Spin 2:50 April 30, 86)

THOMPSON, Hunter S. I don't plan to give up any of my guns until the cops give up theirs. (The California Aggie 96:6 Mar 2, 78)

THOMPSON, Hunter S. I don't think incompetence is any excuse for being a dumb President. (The California Aggie 96:6 Mar 2, 78)

THOMPSON, Hunter S. I'm basically a lazy person. And proud of it. (The California Aggie 96:6 Mar 2, 78)

THOMPSON, Hunter S. There's no such thing as a 'nice' reporter. That's like saying somebody's a nice liberal. (W 5:11 Sept 3, 76)

THOMPSON, Hunter S. Today's pig is tomorrow's bacon. (Kansas City Star 110:A-6 May 23, 90)

THOMPSON, James. If I could be president, I'd like to be president. I'm immodest enough to think that I could be a good one. (Chicago Tribune 72:21 Mar 13, 87)

THOMPSON, James. It is better to make fun of yourself than let your opponent do it for you. (San Francisco Chronicle This World 1977:2 Oct 16, 77)

THOMPSON, Lord Roy Herbert. I am in business to make money, and I buy more newspapers to make more money to buy more newspapers. (New York Times 125:28 Aug 5, 76)

THOMPSON, Mike. Franklin Roosevelt couldn't be nominated today. A Bruce Jenner could beat him. (Time 115:26 Jan 28, 80)

THOMSON, Campbell. If it ever was true that a hospital was a charity organization, it no longer is true. (San Francisco Examiner 1977:1 May 1, 77)

THOMSON, Meldrim. Henry Kissinger is the cunning architect of America's planned destruction. (American Opinion 18:27 Oct 75)

THOMSON, Virgil. It's (musical criticism) a minor art best practiced by composers. (Newsweek 98:84 Dec 7, 81)

THOMSON, Virgil. Music in any generation is not what the public thinks of it but what the musicians make of it. (New York Times 127:13 Section 2 July 2, 78)

THURBER, James. One martini is all right, two is too many, three is not enough. (Rocky Mountain News 327:86 Mar 14, 80)

THURBER, James. There is no safety in numbers, or in anything else. (Washingtonian 14:155 Nov 78)

THURMOND, Strom. I admire people who have a lot of money. (W 12:9 Feb 12, 82)

THURMOND, Strom. There are not enough laws on the books of the nation, nor can there be enough laws, to break down segregation in the South (commenting in 1948 as he accepted the presidential nomination of the Dixiecrat Party). (Washington Post 264:A3 Aug 27, 77)

TINKERBELLE. You don't need much money when the best things in life are handouts. (Vanity Fair 50:85 Jan 87)

TISELIUS, Arne. The world is full of people who should get the Nobel Prize but haven't got it and won't get it. (Time 112:81 Sept 25, 78)

TOKLAS, Alice B. The young men of today seem mostly to be interested in the manner rather than the matter. (Chicago Tribune 176:2 Section 2 June 25, 78)

TOMLIN, Lily. I worry about kids today. Because of the sexual revolution they're going to grow up and never know what dirty means. (Time 109:71 Mar 28, 77)

TOMLIN, Lily. If love is the answer, could you rephrase the question? (Cosmopolitan 188:268 Feb 80)

TOMLIN, Lily. Sometimes I worry about being a success in a mediocre world. (New Times 9:47 Jan 9, 78)

TOMLIN, Lily. Why is it we are always hearing about the tragic cases of too

much, too soon? What about the rest of us? Too little, too late. (Time 109:71 Mar 28, 77)

TONSOR, Stephen. New Deal liberals are as dead as a dodo. The only problem is they don't know it. (Newsweek 90:34 Nov 7, 77)

TOON, Malcolm (United States Ambassador to Russia). I am not in a position to explain why the Soviets have or have not done certain things. I have never been able to explain what makes them tick. (People Weekly 6:34 Dec 13, 76)

TORRICELLI, Robert. Foreign assistance should be goods provided by Americans, arriving on American ships flying American flags, so we can be seen giving assistance to grateful people. (In These Times 14:4 Nov 8, 89)

TORRIJOS, Omar. In truth, the (Panama Canal Zone) treaty is like a little pebble which we shall be able to carry in our shoe for 23 years, and that is better than the stake we have had to carry in our hearts. (Time 110:10 Aug 22, 77)

TOSCANINI, Arturo. I kissed my first girl and smoked my first cigarette on the same day. I haven't had time for tobacco since. (Playboy 32:16 Feb 85)

TOSCANINI, Arturo. I kissed my first woman and smoked my first cigarette on the same day; I've never had time for tobacco since. (Kansas City Star 97:26 May 2, 77)

TOUREL, Jennie. You see, it isn't just boiled potatoes, what I do. (Stereo Review 35:80 Nov 75)

TOWER, John. I am not a mindless hawk. I am a realist. (Chicago Tribune 33:23 Section 1 Feb 2, 89)

TOWER, John. I used to be a pretty good scotch drinker. (New York 22:16 Mar 13, 89)

TOWNE, Robert. Directing a script you wrote is somewhere between shooting yourself in the foot, shooting yourself in the head, and shooting yourself in the nuts. (Vanity Fair 52:40 Jan 89)

TOWNSHEND, Peter. It isn't enough any more to write books: publishers expect you to sell them. (W 7:39 Nov 10, 78)

TOWNSHEND, Peter. The way all societies are is that some people get, and some people don't. (Rolling Stone 325:35 June 26, 80)

TOYNBEE, Arnold. The Englishman's truly distinctive disease is his cherished habit of waiting until the 13th hour. (Time 106:30 Aug 4, 75)

TOYNBEE, Arnold. To be able to fill leisure intelligently is the last product of civilization. (Chicago Tribune 67:1 Section

5 Mar 8, 78)

TRACHTENBERG, Stephen. The truth is that 80 percent of research is done by 20 percent of professors who are at 10 percent of our universities. (Chicago Tribune 110:10 April 20, 87)

TREVINO, Lee. Pressure is playing for ten dollars when you don't have a dime in your pocket. (Esquire 93:44 Jan 31, 80)

TRUDEAU, Garry. America is one of the few places where the failure to promote oneself is widely regarded as arrogance. (Time 126:57 Oct 7, 85)

TRUDEAU, Garry. I can't write a joke to save my ass. (Newsweek 116:61 Oct 15, 89)

TRUDEAU, Garry. I've been trying for some time now to develop a life-style that doesn't require my presence. (Time 118:47 July 20, 81)

TRUDEAU, Garry. Satire has nothing to do with equal time. (Chicago Tribune 328:5 Section 13 Nov 24, 85)

TRUDEAU, Margaret. I was not so much a hippy as a failed hippy; a hippy without a cause. (Guardian Weekly 120:18 June 17, 79)

TRUDEAU, Margaret. It takes two to destroy a marriage. (Cosmopolitan 188:268 Feb 80)

TRUDEAU, Pierre Elliott. The atmosphere of Watergate has polluted the atmosphere of other democratic countries. Nobody trusts anybody anymore. (American Legion Magazine 98:32 May 75)

TRUDEAU, Pierre Elliott. The Tory future is worse than the Liberal past. (New York Times 128:3 May 20, 79)

TRUFFAUT, Francois. In love, women are professionals, men are amateurs. (Rolling Stone 293:43 June 14, 79)

TRUFFAUT, Francois. The words British cinema are a contradiction in terms. (The Reader (Chicago's Free Weekly) 12:14 April 22, 83)

TRUFFAUT, Francois. They (tomorrow's films) will resemble the men who make them, and the number of spectators will be about equal to the number of the director's friends. They will be an act of love. (Print 30:85 May/June 77)

TRUMAN, Harry S. (John Kennedy) had his ear so close to the ground it was full of grasshoppers. (Time 111:89 Mar 20, 78)

TRUMAN, Harry S. I never did give anybody hell. I just told the truth, and they thought it was hell. (Time 105:45 June 9, 75)

TRUMAN, Harry S. That Richard Nixon, boys, is a no-good lying son of a bitch (commenting during one of his Presidential press conferences). (Newsweek 85:89 May 12, 75)

TRUMAN, Harry S. The C students run the world. (Time 108:32 Nov 8, 76)

TRUMAN, Harry S. The only things worth learning are the things you learn after you know it all. (Reader's Digest 106:145 April 75)

TRUMAN, Harry S. You want a friend in this life, get a dog. (New West 3:33 Dec 4, 78)

TRUMP, Donald. I can be very happy living in a one-bedroom apartment, believe me. (Newsweek 115:15 Mar 5, 90)

TRUMP, Donald. I love quality, but I don't believe in paying top price for quality. (Time 133:50 Jan 16, 89)

TRUMP, Donald. I'm not running for president, but if I did...I'd win. (US 3:6 Nov 2, 87)

TRUMP, Donald. The 1990s sure aren't like the 1980s'. (Newsweek 115:June 18, 90)

TUCHMAN, Barbara. I never became a journalist because I wasn't pushy enough. (W Supplement 16:47 July 27, 87)

TUCKER, Sophie. From birth to age 18, a girl needs good parents. From 18 to 35, she needs good looks. From 35 to 55, she needs a good personality. From 55 on, she needs good cash. (Chicago Sun-Times 30:21 Jan 28, 78)

TUCKER, Sophie. I've been rich and I've been poor, and rich is better. (Philadelphia 78:59 Aug 87)

TURBEVILLE, Deborah. I'm as far as you can get from a romantic. I'm tough, not sweet. (Mirabella 2:20 July 89)

TURNER, Lana. I never did dig sex very much. (Life 7:39 Jan 83)

TURNER, R. E. (Ted). "If I fail" doesn't exist in my vocabulary. (TV Guide 33:7 Dec 28, 85)

TURNER, R. E. (Ted). I want to be the first trillionaire. (Southpoint 2:29 April 89)

TURNER, R. E. (Ted). If being against stuffiness and pompousness and bigotry is bad behavior, then I plead guilty. (Time 110:84 Sept 19, 77)

TURNER, R. E. (Ted). Lots of sex for everybody, that's a solution to the world's problems. (Playboy 25:67 Aug 78)

TURNER, R. E. (Ted). My desire to excel borders on the unhealthy. (Time 120:50 Aug 9, 82)

TUTU, Desmond. As long as some of God's children are not free, none of God's children will be free. (Time 127:48 Dec 30, 85)

TUTU, Desmond. Mandela has become the symbol of our people. (Chicago Tribune 182:13 Section 1 July 1, 90)

TYNAN, Kenneth. A critic is a man who knows the way but can't drive the car. (Stagebill 52 Dec 81)

TYRRELL, R. Emmett, Jr. In America there has always been a market for a certain kind of cheap thought. (Arkansas Times 11:37 June 85) (1)

UDALL, Morris King. A boss is a political leader who is on somebody else's side. (ABC News Issues and Answers 1 April 25, 76)

ULLMANN, Liv. A good director is the same all over the world. A good director is one who provides the inspiration and courage for you to use what is inside you. (Washington Post 77:K9 Feb 20, 77)

ULLMANN, Liv. You must put more in your life than a man. (Time 113:65 Jan 29, 79)

ULTRA VIOLET. He (Andy Warhol) was a shy, near-blind, bald, gay albino from an ethnic Pittsburgh ghetto. (Manchester Guardian Weekly 140:29 May 21, 89)

UNITED STATES. CONGRESS. SENATE. SELECT COMMITTEE ON INTELLIGENCE OPERATIONS. There is no inherent Constitutional authority for the President or any intelligence agency to violate the law. (New York Times 125:14 Section 4 May 2, 76)

UNRUH, Jesse. As a Governor, Reagan was better than most Democrats would concede, though not nearly as good as most Republicans like to think. (Time 106:19 Nov 24, 75)

UNRUH, Jesse. If I had slain all my political enemies, I wouldn't have any friends today. (New West 1:8 Sept 13, 76)

UNRUH, Jesse. Money is the mother's milk of politics. (US News & World Report 85:50 Sept 18, 78)

UPDIKE, John. Every man is a failed boy. (Village Voice Literary Supplement 29:8 Sept 30, 84)

UPDIKE, John. I've never been able to take sins of the flesh awfully seriously, nor do I believe that God takes them terribly seriously. (Kansas City Star 119:4C Oct 14, 86)

USTINOV, Peter. An optimist is someone who knows exactly how sad and bad the world can be. (The Observer 9826:9 Dec 23, 79)

VALLEE, Jacques. The theory of space and time is a cultural artifact made possible by the invention of graph paper. (CoEvolution Quarterly 16:82 Winter 77/78)

VALLEE, Rudy. I thought my freshman English instructor at Yale was crazy when he said life was cold, cruel, rotten, hard and it stinks. But I found out he was right. (Washington Post 333:B7 Nov 3, 75)

VALLI, Frankie. There's nothing wrong with the world, only the people in it. And the same goes for music. (New York 8:62 Aug 4, 75)

VALVANO, Jim. Monday through Friday they want you to be like Harvard. On Saturday, they want you to play like Oklahoma. (Kansas City Times 120:E-3 Jan 20, 88)

VAN DE WETERING, Janwillem. I've meditated for thousands of hours now, and I still don't know nothing. It's disgusting. (Chicago Tribune 291:1 Section 2 Oct 18, 79)

VAN DER ROHE, Mies. Buildings are the will of an epoch translated into space. (Chicago Tribune Magazine 10 June 10, 90)

VAN DERBUR, Marilyn (former Miss America). The vital, successful people I have met all had one common characteristic. They had a plan. (People Weekly 6:23 Dec 13, 76)

VAN DOREN, Mark (attributed by Robert Giroux). A classic is a book that is never out of print. (New York Times Book Review 23 Jan 6, 80)

VANCE, Cyrus R. In pursuing a human rights policy, we must always keep in mind the limits of our power and of our wisdom. (New York Times 126:2 Section 1 May 1, 76)

VANDERBILT, Amy. One face to the world, another at home makes for misery. (Chicago Tribune 176:2 Section 2 June 25, 78)

VANDERBILT, Gloria. A woman can never be too thin or too rich. (Chicago Sun-Times 32:3 Dec 18, 80)

VANDERBILT, William K. Inherited wealth is a real handicap to happiness. It is as certain a death to ambition as cocaine is to morality. (Times Literary Supplement 3960:198 Feb 17, 78)

VARESE, Edgar. Scientists are the poets of today. (Artspace 9:30 Fall 85)

VEECK, Bill. Baseball is the only orderly thing in a very unorderly world. If you get three strikes, even Edward Bennett Williams can't get you off. (Sports Illustrated 43:14 June 2, 75)

VEECK, Bill. I'd like to be devious, but I can't find it in myself. (Chicago 27:99 July 78)

VEECK, Bill. It's not the high price of stars that's expensive. It's the high price of mediocrity. (Kansas City Star 106:1 Sports Jan 5, 86)

VIDAL, Gore. Any man who can win a contemporary presidential campaign ought not to be President. (Rolling Stone 319:42 May 15, 80)

VIDAL, Gore. As now set up, the best one can hope for in a President is that he not be entirely insane. (Rolling Stone 319:42

May 15, 80)

VIDAL, Gore. Better the zero of Carter than the minus of Kennedy. (Rolling Stone 319:42 May 15, 80)

VIDAL, Gore. Early on I wanted to be Franklin Roosevelt. (Vanity Fair 50:87 June 87)

VIDAL, Gore. I write to make art and change society. (San Diego Magazine 34:156 Feb 82)

VIDAL, Gore. In writing and politicking, it's best not to think about it, just do it. (Bookviews 1:24 June 78)

VIDAL, Gore. It is not enough to succeed, a friend must also fail. (In The Know 1:47 June 75)

VIDAL, Gore. Most American writers I find phony, but it's a phony country. (Bookviews 1:24 June 78)

VIDAL, Gore. Power is far more exciting than sex. (Chicago Tribune 173:3 Section 5 June 22, 87)

VIDAL, Gore. Sex is politics. (Playboy 26:177 Jan 77)

VIDAL, Gore. The genius of the American ruling class, and this goes back to the beginning of the Republic, has been its ability to get people to vote against their own interests. (San Diego Magazine 34:156 Feb 82)

VIDAL, Gore. There are two invitations one never turns down: sex and television. (Chicago Tribune 22:1 Section 5 Jan 22, 87)

VIDAL, Gore. Truman (Capote) has made lying an art. A minor art. (Viva 5:105 Oct 77)

VIDOR, King. Good films, like good wine, improve with age. (New York Times 126:C6 Jan 14, 77)

VIDOR, King. I don't think one can sum up Russia in one word, but 'grim' might do. (W 8:12 Oct 12, 79)

VIGUERIE, Richard. Defunding the Left should be a principal priority of the Reagan administration. (Mother Jones 8:7 Jan 82)

VIGUERIE, Richard. We've already taken control of the conservative movement. And conservatives have taken control of the Republican Party. The remaining thing is to see if we can take control of the country. (Oklahoma Observer 21:12 Jan 25, 89)

VINCENT, Jan-Michael. My father said if I was too nervous to steal and too dumb to lie, than I'd better be an actor. (Kansas City Times 117:B-5 Aug 20, 85)

VIORST, Judith. Brevity may be the soul of wit, but not when someone's saying 'I love you'. (Chicago Tribune 176:2 Section 2 June 25, 78)

VIVA. Your kids always seem to obtain, somehow, what you could never afford to buy for yourself. (Village Voice 29:33 July 24, 84)

VIZINCZEY, Stephen. No girl, however intelligent and warmhearted, can possibly know or feel half as much at 20 as she will at 35. (Time 111:99 April 24, 78)

VOIGT, Jon. The real dream (of America) is that with independence there is more strength and more beauty. (Rolling Stone 292:50 May 31, 79)

VOIGT, Jon. Things don't have to be about politics to be political. (Rolling Stone 292:50 May 31, 79)

VOLCKER, Paul A. The standard of living of the average American has to decline. (New York Times 129:1 Oct 18, 79)

VOLLBRACHT, Michaele. If you have to talk about fashion, then you are not in it. (Village Voice 22:63 Mar 14, 77)

VON BRAUN, Werner. I look forward to the day when mankind will join hands to apply the combined technological ingenuity of all nations to the exploration and utilization of outer space for peaceful uses. (Time 109:72 June 27, 77)

VON HAYEK, Friedrich. The pursuit of gain is the only way in which people can serve the needs of others whom they do not know. (Kansas City Star 108:1F Dec 27, 87)

VON HAYEK, Friedrich. You can have economic freedom without political freedom, but you cannot have political freedom without economic freedom. (Village Voice 24:35 May 14, 79)

VON HOFFMAN, Nicholas. If he (William Paley) is remembered at all, it will be as the man who gave America 'Hee Haw'. (New York 12:109 April 30, 79)

VON HOFFMAN, Nicholas. It's getting so this society has no left, except in baseball. (Chicago Tribune 86:19 Section 1 Mar 27, 85)

VON HOFFMAN, Nicholas. Professionalism is a cheap and easy way of disciplining labor. (More 8:25 Feb 78)

VONNEGUT, Kurt. Life in our country has become one big TV serial. (Lawrence (Kansas) Journal-World 128:1 Oct 23, 86)

VONNEGUT, Kurt. We are what we pretend to be so we must be careful what we pretend to be. (Miami/South Florida Magazine 38:68 Aug 84)

VORONEL, Nina. Soviet life is so absurd that when I write realistically, it becomes the theatre of the absurd. (New York Times 125:28 Nov 7, 75)

VORONTSOV, Yuli. For the government of

Najb, every new day of not losing is winning. And for the Mjuahedeen, every new day without winning is losing. (Chicago Tribune 183:4 Section 4 July 2, 89)

VOZNESENSKY, Andrei. When Man put on clothes for the first time, he challenged the Lord and became His equal. (Vogue 168:193 Feb 78)

VREELAND, Diana. Air conditioning is like power and love. In the wrong hands, it'll kill you. (W 7:13 July 7, 78)

VREELAND, Diana. Either one's life is attractive or it isn't. (Town & Country 129:79 June 75)

VREELAND, Diana. Elegance is innate...it has nothing to do with being well dressed. (Time 134:70 Sept 4, 89)

VREELAND, Diana. New York City is the leading light of the Twentieth Century. (New York 17:27 Dec 24, 84)

VREELAND, Diana. Show me a fashionable woman, and I will show you a woman who accomplished something. (Newsweek 91:3 Jan 2, 78)

WAGNER, Richard. A poet is nothing if not someone who knows without having made a study. (New York Times Book Review 9 April 1, 79)

WAGNER, Robert. A person's state of happiness is almost directly related to the amount of gas in his tank (1979). (New York Times 128:A10 July 13, 79)

WAGNER, Winifred. If Hitler walked through the door today, I would be just as glad and happy to see and have him here as ever. (Time 106:33 Aug 18, 75)

WAITS, Tom. Reality is for those who can't face drugs. (Playboy 26:26 Oct 79)

WALD, Jeffrey. I don't think I made her a star. I know I did (about Helen Reddy). (People Weekly 3:64 May 12, 75)

WALD, Richard. California understands the real purpose of television is to collect a crowd of advertisers. (Esquire 89:62 Jan 31, 78)

WALDHEIM, Kurt. A head of state must not retreat in the face of slanders, hateful demonstrations and wholesale condemnations. (Chicago Tribune 55:17 Section 1 Feb 24, 88)

WALDHEIM, Kurt. The whole war generation would have to be incriminated if knowledge of atrocities was a crime. (Chicago Tribune 45:3 Section 4 Feb 15, 88)

WALESA, Lech. I was always the leader of the class. (Time 119:16 Jan 4, 82)

WALESA, Lech. We should leave the political situation as it is now (1989). (Newsweek 104:35 Nov 27, 89)

WALKER, Doak. He was the greatest two-minute quarterback ever. Bobby Layne simply never lost a game. Sometimes, time just ran out on him. (The Sporting News 202:61 Dec 15, 86)

WALKER, Jimmy. A reformer is a guy who rides through a sewer in a glass-bottomed boat. (New York Times 129:A15 July 7, 80)

WALLACE, Clinton. Money is the means by which you can purchase everything but happiness and health, and will pay your ticket to all places but Heaven. (National Review 30:282 Mar 3, 78)

WALLACE, George Corley. I draw the line in the dust and toss the gauntlet before the feet of tyranny. And I say, segregation now. Segregation tomorrow. Segregation forever. (New York 8:36 July 28, 75)

WALLACE, George Corley. Let 'em call me a racist in the press. It don't make any difference. Hell, I want 'em to. 'Cause if you want to know the truth, race is what's gonna win this thing for us. (Sepia 26:10 Feb 76)

WALLACE, George Corley. Segregation is a moot question, and integration is the law of the land. It is a moot question, and therefore we don't want to go back, nor make any attempt to change what is now a fact accomplished. (Meet the Press 20:5 Mar 28, 76)

WALLACE, George Corley. The Supreme Court has to write a hundred pages on what pornography is. The average man who works in a steel mill can tell you right off whether that's filth or not. (Newsweek 85:44 April 21, 75)

WALLACE, Mike. There are no indiscreet questions, there are only indiscreet answers. (Washington Post 190:L2 June 10, 79)

WALTER, Bruno. Talent is the one real power. (Chicago 32:24 Sept 83)

WALTERS, Vernon A. I describe myself as a pragmatist tinged with idealism. (New York Times 134:6 May 31, 85)

WARHOL, Andy. Art is what you can get away with. (Mother Jones 6:10 July 81)

WARHOL, Andy. Bad taste makes the day go faster. (Houston Home/Garden 5:42 Nov 78)

WARHOL, Andy. Good business is the best art. (Time 106:32 July 28, 75)

WARHOL, Andy. I don't believe in it (death), because you're not around to know that it's happened. (Time 106:32 July 28, 75)

WARHOL, Andy. I never fall apart because I never fall together. (Newsweek 86:69 Sept 15, 75)

WARHOL, Andy. I wish I were as rich as

Jackson Pollock. (Art & Antiques 87 Oct 84)

WARHOL, Andy. If I go into a hospital, I won't come out. (New York 20:40 Mar 9, 87)

WARHOL, Andy. In the future everybody will be world famous for at least 15 minutes. (Time 107:8 May 31, 76)

WARHOL, Andy. Movies are the new novels. No one is going to read anymore. Everyone is going to do movies, because movies are easier to do. (Texas Monthly 4:42 Aug 76)

WARHOL, Andy. The best dates are when you take the office with you. (Manchester Guardian Weekly 140:29 May 21, 89)

WARREN, Earl. A jurist's mind cannot operate in a vacuum. (Christian Science Monitor 69:27 Aug 3, 77)

WARREN, Earl. Tricky (Richard Nixon) is perhaps the most despicable President this nation has ever had. He was a cheat, a liar and a crook, and he brought my country, which I love, into disrepute. Even worse than abusing his office, he abused the American people. (Esquire 83:83 Mar 31, 75)

WARREN, Robert Penn. What is man but his passion? (Saturday Review 5:19 Dec 78)

WASHINGTON, Booker T., III. Being the sensitive man he was about his race, I think the present day Harlem scene would bring tears to my grandfather's eyes. (Sepia 26:10 Feb 77)

WASHINGTON, Pamela. He's (George Bush) not a pork rinds, county music person. He's an easy-listening, lobster-eating politician if I ever saw one. (New York Times 138:19 Nov 10, 88)

WASHTON, Arnold M. Taking cocaine is dropping an atomic bomb on your brain. (Topeka Capital-Journal Sportsplus 2 July 8, 86)

WATERS, Craig. About 15 years ago, Jack Rosenberg changed his name to Werner Hans Erhard. His motive for doing so is unknown, but, with the switch, the son of a Jewish restaurant proprietor became an apparent Aryan: a son of history's perpetual victim became an heir apparent to one of history's greatest victimizers. (Boston Magazine 30:48 Sept 75)

WATERS, John. I always wanted to sell out, but nobody would buy me. (University Daily Kansan 98:3 Nov 17, 87)

WATT, James. If you want an example of the failure of socialism, don't go to Russia. Come to America and go to the American Indian reservations. (Life 7:176 Jan 83)

WATT, James. We don't have to worry about endangered species—why, we

can't even get rid of the cockroach. (Life 5:33 Jan 81)

WATTENBERG, Ben. How can a nation that believes it hasn't done anything right in the recent past even consider that it can do anything right, or bold, or creative in the immediate future. (Washington Post 72:B1 Feb 15, 77)

WATTENBERG, Ben. Poland is one of those great events that happen once in a generation to unmask the truth. (Time 119:20 Jan 11, 83)

WATTENBERG, Ben. There is nothing so powerful as an old idea whose time has come again. (Washingtonian 15:143 Nov 79)

WATTS, Andre. Here lies a man who never played Petrouchka (on his epitaph). (Horizon 20:13 Dec 77)

WATTS, Glenn. Unions must be prepared to change with the times, or they run the risk of being run over by them. (USA Today 1:10A Sept 6, 83)

WAUGH, Evelyn. An artist must be a reactionary. He has to stand out against the tenor of the age and not go flopping along. (Time 113:96 Feb 12, 79)

WAUGH, Evelyn. I regard writing not as investigation of character, but as an exercise in the use of language. (Time 113:96 Feb 12, 79)

WAUGH, Evelyn. It is impudent and exorbitant to demand truth from the lower classes. (Time 110:102 Oct 17, 77)

WAUGH, Evelyn. My children weary me. I can only see them as defective adults; feckless, destructive, frivolous, sensual, humourless. (Time 110:102 Oct 17, 77)

WAUGH, Evelyn. Punctuality is the virtue of the bored. (Time 110:102 Oct 17, 77)

WAUGH, Evelyn. You have no idea how much nastier I would be if I was not a Catholic. Without supernatural aid I would hardly be a human being. (Newsweek 86:119 Nov 24, 75)

WAVY GRAVY. The nineties will be the sixties standing on your head. (California 14:83 Dec 89)

WAYNE, John. I stay away from nuances. (Time 113:50 June 25, 79)

WAYNE, John. In my opinion Senator Joseph McCarthy was one of the greatest Americans that ever lived. (Guardian Weekly 120:6 June 17, 79)

WAYNE, John. Nobody likes my acting but the public. (The Tennessean 74:2 June 12, 79)

WEAVER, Earl. Bad ballplayers make good managers. (Toronto Life 22 April 30, 84)

WEILER, A. H. Nothing is impossible for the man who doesn't have to do it himself.

(Washingtonian 14:155 Nov 78)

WEINBERGER, Caspar. If the movement from Cold War to detente is progress, then let me say we cannot afford much more progress. (Life 5:33 Jan 81)

WEIZENBAUM, Joseph. A computer will do what you tell it to do, but that may be much different from what you had in mind. (Time 111:45 Feb 20, 78)

WEIZENBAUM, Joseph. We are rapidly losing, have perhaps already lost, physical and mental control of our society. (Omni 2:50 Dec 79)

WEIZMAN, Ezer. Anyone who says he is not emotional is not getting what he should out of life. (Time 112:115 Oct 30, 78)

WELCH, Robert (founder of the John Birch Society). Every President since Theodore Roosevelt has committed a treasonable act except—maybe—Warren G. Harding, Calvin Coolidge, and Herbert Hoover. (Chicago Tribune 194:14 July 13, 77)

WELLES, Orson. Nobody gets justice— people get good luck or bad luck. (US 3:64 Sept 23, 85)

WELLES, Orson. Patty Hearst is the central victim of our time...the best human story in the last thirty years—better than Kane. (Esquire 91:38 Feb 27, 79)

WELLES, Orson. The director is the most overrated artist in the world. (Time 119:69 Mar 8, 82)

WERTMUELLER, Lina. I'm the last ballbuster left. (Time 107:59 Feb 16, 76)

WEST, Mae. He who hesitates is last. (Chicago Tribune 176:2 Section 2 June 25, 78)

WEST, Mae. I never needed Panavision and stereophonic sound to woo the world. I did it in black and white on a screen the size of a postage stamp. Honey, that's talent. (Rolling Stone 245:27 Aug 11, 77)

WEST, Mae. I'm for peace. I have yet to wake up in the morning and hear a man say, I've just had a good war. (Viva 4:26 Aug 77)

WEST, Mae. I've said it before and I'll say it again—I like a man that takes his time. (Coronet 13:37 Sept 75)

WEST, Mae. It's better to be looked over than overlooked. (Lawrence (Kansas) Journal-World 127:3D Feb 3, 85)

WEST, Mae. Marriage is a great institution, but I'm not ready for an institution yet. (American Spectator 15:34 Feb 82)

WEST, Mae. My motto is keem a diary, and one day it will keep you. (Interview 16:70 July 86)

WEST, Mae. To err is human—but it feels divine. (Viva 4:24 Jan 77)

WEST, Mae. To me a star is somebody who

has a little bit more than somebody else. (In The Know 1:35 Sept 75)

WEST, Mae. Too much of a good thing can be wonderful. (Human Behavior 7:17 May 78)

WEST, Mae. When I'm good, I'm very good; but when I'm bad, I'm better. (Oui 8:82 Jan 78)

WEST, Mae. You should marry for sex or money and you're really lucky if you can get both. (Chicago Tribune 64:1 Section 5 Mar 5, 78)

WEST, Morris. In discourse the Italians are the most eloquent people in the world. In action they are either apathetic or impulsive to the point of insanity. (Esquire 89:81 April 25, 78)

WEST, Rebecca. The main difference between men and women is that men are lunatics and women are idiots. (Chicago Tribune 303:1 Section 5 Oct 30, 87)

WEST, Rebecca. There are jungles of people, and jungles of facts—which make it harder to recognize the great things when they do happen. (New York Times Book Review 14 Oct 2, 77)

WEST, Tom. Every patient that every doctor has is going to die. (Lawrence (Kansas) Journal-World 130:5A Dec 20, 88)

WESTMORELAND, William Childs. Despite the final failure of the South Vietnamese, the record of the American military services of never having lost a war is still intact. (Los Angeles Times 94:25 Part 1 Oct 30, 75)

WESTMORELAND, William Childs. Television is an instrument which can paralyze this country. (Time 119:57 April 5, 82)

WESTMORELAND, William Childs. We met the enemy, and he was us. (Rolling Stone 263:41 April 20, 78)

WETZSTEON, Ross. Sex, to paraphrase Clausewitz, is the continuation of war by other means. (Village Voice 20:89 April 28, 77)

WHARTON, William. After I muddle in other people's puddles, I find out it's all one, big lonesome ocean. (National Catholic Reporter 21:13 May 17, 85)

WHEATON, James R. Given what's happening today in Eastern Europe, in South America, even what the students have been trying to do in China, the state of democracy in America is shameful. (Los Angeles Times 109:A24 Mar 31, 90)

WHITE, Donald (President of Hughes Aircraft Company). If you did a survey on whether the American public can trust military-defense contractors, I'm afraid the score would not be too high. (Los

Angeles 34:131 Mar 89)

WHITE, E. B. Before I start to write, I always treat myself to a nice dry martini. (Writer's Digest 58:25 Oct 78)

WHITE, E. B. Humor can be dissected, as a frog can, but the thing dies in the process and the innards are discouraging to any but the pure scientific mind. (New York Times Magazine 70 Dec 2, 79)

WHITE, E. B. New Yorkers temperamentally do not crave comfort and convenience. If they did, they would live elsewhere. (Time 112:20 Aug 21, 78)

WHITE, E. B. No one can write decently who is distrustful of the reader's intelligence. (New York Times 126:C19 Nov 17, 76)

WHITE, E. B. Non-commercial television should address itself to the ideal of excellence, not the ideal of acceptability. (Harper's 259:78 Aug 79)

WHITE, E. B. The way to approach a manuscript is on all fours, in utter amazement. (Washington Post 352:E2 Nov 21, 76)

WHITE, Kevin Hagen. Charismatic leadership is hungered for, but at the same time we fear it. (Time 107:10 Feb 9, 76)

WHITE, Kevin Hagen. Everybody knows that Washington, D.C. has no culture—they have to buy it. (Time 113:71 April 23, 79)

WHITE, Theodore. Class is a matter of style in leadership. It is the magic that translates the language of the street into the language of history. (Time 111:20 Mar 6, 78)

WHITE, Theodore. If you go back through 2000 years, I guess luck, Marx, and God have made history, the three of them together. (Firing Line 15 July 26, 75)

WHITE, Theodore. It's about time women had their say in the laws governing them—laws that for 5,000 years have been made by old men, mostly with shriveled-up groins, who have long since forgotten what it was like to be young and never knew what it was like to be a woman. (W 7:41 Sept 15, 78)

WHITE, Theodore. Politics in America is the binding secular religion. (Firing Line 5 July 26, 75)

WHITE, Theodore. The true crime of Richard Nixon was simple: he destroyed the myth that binds America together, and for this he was driven from power. (Esquire 91:34 Feb 27, 79)

WHITE, William Allen. In education we are striving not to teach youth to make a living, but to make a life. (Kansas City Times 109:11B Feb 4, 77)

WHITEHEAD, Alfred North. Even perfection will not bear the tedium of indefinite repetition. (The Atlantic 244:29 Sept 79)

WHITEHEAD, Alfred North. Nobody has a right to speak more clearly than he thinks. (Washingtonian 15:143 Nov 79)

WHITEHEAD, Alfred North. The aims of scientific thought are to see the general in the particular and the eternal in the transitory. (Omni 2:41 Nov 79)

WHITLOCK, Ralph. Good beomes ill when pushed to excess. (Manchester Guardian Weekly 138:29 May 1, 88)

WHITMAN, Alden. Carter's sermons (on human rights) might be more credible if he had a priority program to end poverty. (Rolling Stone 242:59 June 30, 77)

WHITTLE, Christopher. People call me a great salesman when they want to damn me with faint praise. (Vanity Fair 53:229 Mar 90)

WICKER, Tom. A reporter should write and his newspaper should print what they know. (Texas Observer 70:9 April 28, 78)

WICKER, Tom. Government expands to absorb revenue—and then some. (Washingtonian 14:155 Nov 78)

WICKER, Tom. To know things as they are is better than to believe things as they seem. (Reader's Digest 107:121 July 75)

WIDEMAN, John Edgar. Being a writer these days includes self-promotion. (Chicago Tribune 162:10 Section 5 June 11, 89)

WILDER, Billy. As soon as you have chosen a subject for a film, you have already made a success or a failure. (New York 8:43 Nov 24, 75)

WILDER, Billy. France is a country where the money falls apart in your hands and you can't tear the toilet paper. (New York 8:43 Nov 24, 75)

WILDER, Billy. If there's one thing I hate more than not being taken seriously, it's being taken too seriously. (New York 8:43 Nov 24, 75)

WILDER, Gene. Everything I write is a love story and emotionally autobiographical. (Time 107:70 May 30, 77)

WILDER, Gene. It has been my experience that a producer gets more money than anyone else for what is essentially a $6.50-an-hour job. (The Star 4:2 July 26, 77)

WILDER, Roy. Tennis adds years to your life and life to your years. (New York Times 125:5 Section 5 Sept 12, 76)

WILDER, Thornton. The highest tribute to the dead is not grief but gratitude. (Parade 20 Sept 13, 81)

WILEY, Ralph. A National Football League

center once said that potential is a French word meaning you aren't worth a damn yet. (Sports Illustrated 65:27 Oct 6, 86)

WILKINS, Roy. Black power can only mean black death. (Newsweek 99:51 Jan 4, 82)

WILL, George F. Education should be primarily an inoculation against the disease of our time, which is disdain for times past. (Washington Post 172:A15 May 26, 77)

WILL, George F. Eighty years ago, Henry James defined journalism as the science of beating the sense out of words. (Lawrence (Kansas) Journal-World 126:5A Sept 23, 84)

WILL, George F. Inflation is a great conservatizing issue. (Newsweek 90:36 Nov 7, 77)

WILL, George F. Nationalism is another supposed anachronism whose time has come 'round again. (Kansas City Times 115:A-15 Feb 15, 83)

WILL, George F. People do not want to be equal to their neighbors. They want to be richer than their neighbors. (Kansas City Times 119:A-7 Mar 17, 87)

WILL, George F. People who use word processors should not be surprised if what they write is to prose as process cheese is to real cheese. (Lawrence (Kansas) Journal-World 125:4 Dec 18, 83)

WILL, George F. Politics is more difficult than you think. (Gentlemen's Quarterly 56:68 May 86)

WILL, George F. Reagan's policy is detente without intellect. (Time 119:51 April 19, 82)

WILL, George F. The universe is not only stranger than we suppose, it is stranger than we suppose. (Kansas City Times 115:A-19 Nov 11, 82)

WILL, George F. When affirmative action came to Ann Arbor and Morningside Heights, dawn came up like thunder. (Newsweek 90:44 Nov 7, 77)

WILL, George F. World War II was the last government program that really worked (to the Association of American Publishers). (Washingtonian 10:22 July 75)

WILLIAMS, Tennessee. I was brought up puritanically. I try to outrage that puritanism. (Time 122:88 Mar 7, 83)

WILLIAMS, Tennessee. Men are rather inscrutable to me. (W 8:14 April 13, 79)

WILLIAMS, Tennessee. They teach it (The Glass Menagerie) in college now, and everybody approaches it as though it were a place of worship. Frankly, I fall asleep at times. (Time 106:31 Dec 29, 75)

WILLIAMS, Tennessee. Time is the longest

distance between two places. (Omni 2:38 July 80)

WILLIAMS, William Appleman. The act of imposing one people's morality upon another people is an imperial denial of self-determination. (Chicago Tribune 71:6 Section 2 Mar 12, 90)

WILLS, Garry. (John Paul II's) theological conservatism undercuts his political liberalism. (Time 114:35 Oct 15, 79)

WILLS, Garry. Politicians fascinate because they constitute such a paradox: they are an elite that accomplishes mediocrity for the public good. (Time 113:86 April 23, 79)

WILLS, Garry. The CIA is an unconstitutional body. (Washington Post Magazine 32 June 28, 87)

WILSON, David B. Sam Wilson used to say that any damn fool can stand adversity; but it takes real quality to stand prosperity. (Kansas City Times 119:A-7 Oct 14, 86)

WILSON, Earl. Middle age is when your clothes no longer fit, and it's you who need the alterations. (Reader's Digest 108:146 Feb 76)

WILSON, Edwin. If I wasn't in jail, I'd have headed up this (Iran-contra aid) operation. (Newsweek 109:22 May 11, 87)

WILSON, Helen S. One cannot buy wisdom in the marketplace. (Chicago Tribune 362:1 Section 7 Dec 2, 86)

WILSON, James Q. There aren't any liberals left in New York. They've all been mugged by now. (American Spectator 18:18 April 85)

WILSON, Robert Anton. If a man's ideas aren't frightening enough to get him imprisoned, you can be sure he's not really thinking something new and important. (Fate 30:7 Oct 77)

WILSON, Sloan. A man who wants time to read and write must let the grass grow long. (New York 9:46 May 24, 76)

WILSON, Sloan. A writer's job is sticking his neck out. (Writer's Digest 58:9 Feb 78)

WILSON, Sloan. It is impossible to treat a woman too well. (New York 9:46 May 24, 76)

WINFIELD, Dave. Everything you read about George Steinbrenner is true. That's the problem. (Kansas City Star 106:1C Jan 8, 86)

WINNER, Michael. Film audiences are people who are seeking light relief in a dark room for an hour and a half. (Chicago Tribune 324:22 Section 6 Nov 20, 77)

WINPISINGER, William (union leader). I don't mind being called a lefty. We're being centered to death. (Time 110:52

July 11, 77)

WIRIN, Abraham Lincoln. The rights of all persons are wrapped in the same constitutional bundle as those of the most hated member of the community. (Time 111:94 Feb 20, 78)

WISEMAN, Frederick. The final film is a theory about the event, about the subject in the film. (Film Quarterly 31:15 Spring 78)

WOLFE, Tom. Fashion, to put it most simply, is the code language of status. (Mother Jones 8:18 Jan 83)

WOLFE, Tom. Rental property should sell for 100 times the monthly rental income. (CoEvolution Quarterly 35:5 Fall 82)

WOLFE, Tom. There's not too much reason to come to Manhattan unless you're ambitious. (Kansas City Times 116:A-2 June 29, 84)

WOLFE, Tom. You can be denounced from the heavens, and it only makes people interested. (Time 114:82 Sept 24, 79)

WOLFERT, Paula. There's a culinary renaissance in America today. The trouble is, we have no Michelangelos. (Metropolitan Home 18:92 June 86)

WONDER, Stevie. How can you even think of being conceited—with the universe as large as it is? (Penthouse 7:131 Feb 76)

WOOD, Gordon. People in Texas believe in slow-talking football coaches more than they believe in fast-talking politicians. (Chicago Tribune 67:6 Mar 8, 87)

WOOD, Lowell. The things most discussed in public are the ones the government is least interested in (about space weapons). (Newsweek 105:38 June 17, 85)

WOOD, Natalie. Anyone who says it doesn't hurt when (critics) zap you is not to be believed. (Time 114:101 Dec 10, 79)

WOODS, Mike. If Jesse Helms ran against Jesus Christ, I think Jesus Christ would win by a very slim margin. (Southpoint 2:8 May 90)

WOODS, Rose Mary. There's more to life than money. (W 12:4 April 23, 82)

WOODSON, Robert. A kinder, gentler nation doesn't have to be a more expensive one. (Chicago Tribune 4:15 Section 1 Jan 4, 89)

WOODWARD, Joanne. You cannot be an actor without being willing to make a fool of yourself. (Chicago Tribune Magazine 38 Aug 7, 77)

WOOLF, Virginia. The best letters of our times are those that can never be published. (Village Voice 27:25 July 6, 82)

WOOLF, Virginia. The history of men's opposition to women's emancipation is

more interesting perhaps than the story of that emancipation itself. (Los Angeles Times 97:6 Part 4 Feb 3, 78)

WRIGHT, Frank Lloyd. A doctor can bury his mistakes, but an architect can only advise his client to plant vines. (Chicago Tribune Magazine 6 July 18, 82)

WRIGHT, Frank Lloyd. I have been black and blue in some spot, somewhere, almost all my life from too intimate contact with my own early furniture. (Chicago Tribune 24:1 Section 2 Jan 24, 78)

WRIGHT, Jim. Members (of Congress) are now more concerned about image and less about substance. (Time 119:13 April 26, 82)

WRIGHT, Jim. The Sandinistas have had a history of snatching defeat from the jaws of victory. (Kansas City Star 108:6A Dec 15, 87)

WRIGHT, Jim. The Wright broad rule is that broads ought to be able to type (commenting when asked to state a broad rule for avoiding Congressional sex scandals). (Wall Street Journal 57:1 Dec 31, 76)

WRIGHT, Jim. When people are drowning, there is no time to build a better ship. (Chicago Sun-Times 30:2 Feb 2, 77)

WRIGHT, Stephen. Anywhere's in walking distance is you've got the time. (Outside 10:13 Dec 85)

WRISTON, Walter. I believe there are no institutional values, only personal values. (Guardian Weekly 124:16 Jan 25, 81)

WURF, Jerry. If Jimmy Carter emerges as a strong President and keeps the promises he made in 1976, then there is still time for him to be born again politically. (New York Times 128:A10 July 13, 79)

WYETH, Andrew. True reality goes beyond reality itself. (Christian Science Monitor 70:24 Sept 28, 78)

WYNETTE, Tammy. My life has been a soap opera. (US 3:64 June 30, 86)

YAMASHITA, Sachio (Painter). Art, color are the vitamins of the soul. (Time 105:8 Mar 3, 75)

YARMOLINSKY, Adam. It is plain foolishness to have fewer and fewer well trained soldiers operating more and more complicated equipment. (USA Today 1:10A Jan 14, 83)

YEW, Lee Kuan. The Russians say that there are many different roads to socialism, and that sounds good to new nations. But the United States seems to be saying that there is only one road to democracy. (American Legion Magazine 103:12 Aug 77)

YOUNG, Andrew. (Jimmy) Carter does not

hand out nickels after a campaign (about political rewards for supporting him). (Time 107:18 June 28, 76)

YOUNG, Andrew. Black folks didn't need much selling on Carter. They have a special kind of radar about whether white folks are for real. (New York 9:91 July 12, 76)

YOUNG, Andrew. Eleven o'clock Sunday morning is still the most segregated hour of the week, and I don't know that anybody can be self-righteous about church integration. (Issues and Answers 2 Nov 14, 76)

YOUNG, Andrew. Georgia is more liberal than New York. (Atlanta 19:60 Nov 79)

YOUNG, Andrew. I don't think affirmative action for blacks requires discrimination against whites. (Sepia 24:10 July 75)

YOUNG, Andrew. I was taught to fight when people called me nigger. That's when I learned that negotiation is better than fighting. (Time 108:13 Dec 27, 76)

YOUNG, Andrew. Influence is like a savings account. The less you use it, the more you've got. (People Weekly 6:30 Dec 27/Jan 3, 1977)

YOUNG, Andrew. Nothing is illegal if 100 businessmen decide to do it, and that's true anywhere in the world. (Rolling Stone 235:35 Mar 24, 77)

YOUNG, Andrew. The Russians are the worst racists in the world. (Life 2:117 Dec 79)

YOUNG, Loretta. A beautiful face gets you the first five minutes. After that you're on your own. (New Hampshire Profiles 27:18 May 78)

YOUNGQUIST, Wayne. People want leaders with vision rather than programs. Even if conservatism is overtaking liberalism and individualism is prized over collective action, vision is always in demand and often rewarded at the polls. (Time 112:23 Oct 23, 78)

ZADORA, Pia. I can buy and sell any of these people who are always criticizing me. (US 3:64 July 15, 85)

ZALEZNICK, Abraham. I think if we want to understand the entrepreneur, we should look at the juvenile delinquent. (Inc 7:17 Aug 85)

ZAPPA, Frank. A wise man once said that the only difference between a cult and a religion is the amount of real estate they own. (National Catholic Reporter 23:10 Aug 14, 87)

ZAPPA, Frank. High school isn't a time and a place. It's a state of mind. (Human Behavior 5:65 Aug 76)

ZAPPA, Frank. Most rock journalism is people who can't write, interviewing people who can't talk, for people who can't read. (Chicago Tribune 18:12 Jan 18, 78)

ZAPPA, Frank. The biggest dangers we face today don't even need to sneak past our billion-dollar defense system. They issue the contracts for them. (Rolling Stone 205:22 Jan 29, 76)

ZAPPA, Frank. There will be no nuclear war. There's too much real estate involved. (Life 8:90 Jan 84)

ZEFFIRELLI, Franco. You must be as tough as rubber and as soft as steel. (Times Literary Supplement 3969:460 April 28, 78)

ZELZER, Harry. Good music is not as bad as it sounds. (Chicago 27:12 Oct 78)

ZIA UL-HAQ, Mohammad. The army is the only stable institution in Pakistan. (The Observer 9701:13 July 17, 77)

ZIEGLER, Ronald Louis. I never knowingly lied, but certainly history shows that many things I said were incorrect. (Newsweek 91:22 April 17, 78)

ZISK, Richie (baseball player). Chicago is the kind of place where, if you fall flat on your face, there's someone to pick you up instead of stomping on your face. (Chicago Tribune 248:20 Sept 5, 77)

ZUKOR, Adolph. Look ahead a little and gamble a lot (a formula for success). (Time 107:55 June 21, 76)

Subjects

ABBEY, EDWARD

Quammen, David. A man wrote a book, and lives were changed. That doesn't happen often (about Edward Abbey). (Outside 14:25 June 89)

ABILITY

Brett, Ken. The worst curse in the world is unlimited potential. (Arkansas Times 12:67 July 86)

ABORTION

Carter, James Earl. There are many things in life that are not fair. (Village Voice 23:11 Jan 2, 78)

Kennedy, Florynce Rae. If men could get pregnant, abortion would be a sacrament. (Viva 5:28 Nov 77)

Maher, Leo, Bishop. A pro-choice Catholic is an oxymoron. (Chicago Tribune 341:20 Dec 7, 89)

Mother Teresa. Those countries with legalized abortions are the poorest countries in the world. (The Observer 9825:10 Dec 16, 79)

O'Rourke, Joseph. The antiabortionists are antifree, antiwomen and anti-Christian. (Time 114:27 July 9, 79)

Reagan, Ronald. I've noticed that everybody who's for abortion has already been born. (Life 4:68 Jan 81)

Steinem, Gloria. Women now face the threat of having their bodies nationalized. (Life 5:58 Jan 82)

ABORTION—LAWS AND LEGISLATION

Bork, Robert. Roe v. Wade contains almost no legal reasoning. (Chicago Tribune 259:11 Sept 16, 87)

Souter, David. I have not got any agenda on what should be done with Roe v. Wade if that case was brought before me. I have not made up my mind. (Chicago Tribune 261:19 Section 1 Sept 18, 90)

ABRAMS, ELLIOTT

Durenberger, David. I wouldn't trust Elliott Abrams any further than I could throw Oliver North. (Village Voice 32:20 Mar 3, 87)

ACCIDENTS

Cockburn, Alexander. An accident is normalcy raised to the level of drama. (The Nation 250:623 May 7, 90)

ACHIEVEMENT

Miller, George William. There is no penalty for overachievement. (Time 112:62 July 17, 78)

ACTING

Caldwell, Zoe. Acting is like being a sibling and directing is like being a parent. (W 15:30 Jan 27, 86)

DeNiro, Robert. You have to earn the right to play a character. (New York Times 126:13 Section 2 Mar 6, 77)

Dunaway, Faye. I've always thought that acting is an art of creating accidents. (W 5:15 Nov 26, 76)

Gielgud, John (attributed by Leslie Caron). Never show your good side—show your faults (instruction to actors). (New York Times 126:31 Section 2 Aug 28, 77)

Hemmings, David. Acting is a wonderful profession for immature people. (US 3:64 Mar 7, 88)

Hepburn, Katharine. Acting really isn't a very high-class way to make a living, is it? (The Observer 9779:10 Jan 21, 79)

Heston, Charlton. Acting is the oldest profession, no matter what claims are made by the other trade. (People Weekly 10:102 Sept 4, 78)

Hurt, Mary Beth. Acting is like a sexual disease. You get it and you can't get rid of it. (US 3:6 Oct 5, 87)

Jackson, Glenda. The important thing about acting is to be able to laugh and cry on cue. (Kansas City Star 110:D-1 May 7, 90)

Newman, Susan. Making movies has nothing to do with acting. (Time 111:52 Feb 6, 78)

Olivier, Laurence. Acting great parts devours you. (The Observer 9788:9 April 1, 79)

Olivier, Laurence. Acting is a masochistic form of exhibitionism. (Los Angeles Times Calendar 33 Feb 26, 78)

Olivier, Laurence. You can't just run. You have to look as if you're running (about acting). (New York Times Magazine 20 Mar 25, 79)

Scott, George C. The actor is never rewarded in film. Film stardom is a peripheral and distorted kind of fulfillment. (New York Times Magazine 12 Jan 23, 77)

Stewart, James. The most important thing about acting is to approach it as a craft, not as an art and not as some mysterious type of religion. (Chicago Tribune 105:25 Section 1 April 17, 77)

Ullmann, Liv. A good director is the same all over the world. A good director is one who provides the inspiration and courage for you to see what is inside you. (Washington Post 77:K9 Feb 20, 77)

Woodward, Joanne. You cannot be an actor without being willing to make a fool of yourself. (Chicago Tribune Magazine 38 Aug 7, 77)

Young, Loretta. A beautiful face gets you the first five minutes. After that you're on your own. (New Hampshire Profiles 27:18 May 78)

ACTORS AND ACTRESSES

Atkins, Christopher. It's nice to be beautiful, but it's beautiful to be nice. (The Atlantic 265:24 Jan 90)

Bacall, Lauren. I agree with the Bogart theory that all an actor owes the public is a good performance. (The Observer 9777:11 Jan 14, 79)

Ball, Lucille. The ham always rises. (US 3:13 Aug 11, 86)

DeNiro, Robert. You have to earn the right to play a character. (New York Times 126:13 Section 2 Mar 6, 77)

Gish, Lillian. I don't think actresses have the right to marry and ruin a man's life. (Chicago Sun-Times 32:33 Nov 30, 98)

Gleason, Jackie. Vanity is an actor's courage. (Emmy 5:48 Jan 83)

Hitchcock, Alfred Joseph. All actors should be treated like cattle. (Chicago Sun-Times 32:1 Section 3 Mar 4, 79)

Loren, Sophia. We actors are the damned of the earth. (The Observer 9862:12 Aug 31, 80)

Niven, David. Actors don't retire, they just get offered fewer parts. (W 6:18 July 8, 77)

Olivier, Laurence. Probably every great actor in history was the son of a clergyman. (Chicago Tribune 201:20 July 20, 79)

Stallone, Sylvester. Actors are a walking, throbbing mass of unhealed scar tissue by the time they get anywhere. (Chicago Sun-Times 32:3 Section 3 Nov 5, 78)

West, Mae. To me a star is somebody who has a little bit more than somebody else. (In The Know 1:35 Sept 75)

ACTORS AND ACTRESSES see also ALDA, ALAN; AUTRY, GENE; BANKHEAD, TALLULAH; BARDOT, BRIGITTE; BRANDO, MARLON; BUJOLD, GENEVIEVE; BURNS, GEORGE; BURTON, RICHARD; DAVIS, BETTE; DENIRO, ROBERT; DUNAWAY, FAYE; EASTWOOD, CLINT; FIELDS, W. C.; GABOR, ZSA ZSA; GARLAND, JUDY; GISH, LILLIAN .; GRABLE, BETTY; GRANT, CARY; GUINNESS, SIR ALEC; HALEY, JACK; HARRISON, REX; HUTTON, BARBARA; JOHNS, GLYNNIS; LASSER, LOUISE; MACLAINE, SHIRLEY; MERCOURI, MELINA; MILLER, ANN; MITCHUM, ROBERT; MONROE, MARILYN; NEWMAN, PAUL; PAGE, GERALDINE; REDFORD, ROBERT; REEVE, CHRISTOPHER; RUSSELL, ROSALIND; SAVALAS, TELLY; SHEEN, MARTIN; SMITH, MAGGIE; STALLONE, SYLVESTER; WILDER, GENE

ADKINS, JANET

Adkins, Janet. I have no regrets. I have loved life fully and I have lived life fully. (New York Times 139:A13 June 7, 90)

ADVANCEMENT see PROGRESS

ADVENTURE

Buckley, William Frank, Jr. All adventure is now reactionary. (Time 109:87 May 23, 77)

ADVERTISING

Douglas, Norman. You can tell the ideals of

a nation by its advertisements. (Omni 4:37 July 82)

Morley, Robert. Commercials are the last things in life you can count on for a happy ending. (Time 111:53 Feb 6, 78)

Ogilvey, David. The consumer is not a moron. She is your wife. (Viva 4:26 Aug 77)

Ogilvy, David. Ninety-nine percent of advertising doesn't sell much of anything. (Chicago Tribune 3:6 Section 3 Jan 4, 84)

ADVERTISING INDUSTRY

Della Femina, Jerry. If God called my office looking for advertising, I'd check out his references. You can never be too sure in this business. (Oui 3:74 Feb 81)

AESTHETICS

Shapiro, Joseph H. Aesthetics is to art what ornithology is to birds. (Chicago 26:178 Sept 77)

AFGHANISTAN see also REVOLUTIONS—AFGHANISTAN

AFGHANISTAN—POLITICS AND GOVERNMENT

Panigati, Angelo. Afghanistan will always impose itself on the foreigner, no matter how hard he may try to make it otherwise. (New York Times 138:7 April 13, 89)

Vorontsov, Yuli. For the government of Najb, every new day of not losing is winning. And for the Mjuahedeen, every new day without winning is losing. (Chicago Tribune 183:4 Section 4 July 2, 89)

AFRICA

Naipaul, V. S. Africa has no future. (New York Times Book Review 36 May 13, 79)

Stein, Gertrude. Nothing can, or will, happen in Africa. (New York Times Book Review 10 July 1, 79)

AFRICA see also ANGOLA

AFRICA—RACE QUESTION

Kaunda, Kenneth. Not every white man is bad. (The Observer 9769:13 Nov 19, 78)

AGE

Gromyko, Andrei. Age is a stubborn thing and there is no getting away from it. (Manchester Guardian Weekly 141:1 July 9, 89)

Hayakawa, Samuel Ichiye. There is only one thing age can give you, and that is wisdom. (New West 1:17 July 5, 76)

Levi-Strauss, Claude. Age removes the confusion, only possible in youth, between physical and moral characteristics. (Time 111:99 April 24, 78)

Stein, Gertrude. We are always the same age inside. (Omni 2:38 April 80)

AGED

Chevalier, Maurice. Old age is a wonderful thing...when you consider the alternative.

(Saturday Evening Post 251:40 Feb 28, 79)

Comfort, Alex. Nobody is safe being prejudiced against what they themselves are going to become (commenting on aging). (New York Times 126:24 Oct 25, 76)

Cowley, Malcolm. One compensation of age is simply sitting still. (Life 1:77 Dec 78)

Lawton, George E. If it is important to give the human animal a good start in life, it is just as important to see that he makes a good finish. (Saturday Evening Post 251:98 Feb 28, 79)

Skinner, B. F. The more reason we have to pay attention to life, the less we have to pay attention to death. (Kansas City Star 104:1A Oct 11, 83)

AGED—PSYCHOLOGY

Paige, Satchel. How old would you be if you didn't know how old you was? (Chicago Tribune 37:2 Section 2 Feb 6, 78)

AGING

Bardot, Brigitte. It's better to be old than dead. (The Observer 9812:10 Sept 16, 79)

Bell, James (Cool Papa). If you don't live to get old, you die young. (St Louis Magazine 16:79 Oct 84)

Camus, Albert. Alas, after a certain age every man is responsible for his face. (CoEvolution Quarterly 17:30 Spring 78)

Carpenter, Elizabeth. Aging has become very stylish, all the best people are doing it. (Time 131:68 Feb 22, 88)

Collins, Judy. Aging does have its rewards. (Newsweek 93:79 Mar 12, 79)

Comfort, Alex. Nobody is safe being prejudiced against what they themselves are going to become (commenting on aging). (New York Times 126:24 Oct 25, 76)

Longworth, Alice Roosevelt. The secret of eternal youth is arrested development. (Washington Post 103:1 Section C Feb 24, 80)

Matthau, Carol. You don't stop being a girl because they give you a different number. (W 19:19 July 9, 90)

Moreau, Jeanne. Age does not protect you from love. But love, to some extent, protects you from age. (People Weekly 3:66 Feb 3, 75)

Paige, Satchel. How old would you be if you didn't know how old you was? (Chicago Tribune 37:2 Section 2 Feb 6, 78)

Picasso, Pablo. It takes a long time to grow young. (Town & Country 135:179 May 81)

Pierson, L. R. If you're coasting, you're going downhill. (Washingtonian 14:155 Nov 78)

Skinner, B. F. The more reason we have to pay attention to life, the less we have to pay attention to death. (Kansas City Star 104:1A Oct 11, 83)

Thomas, Lowell. After the age of 80, everything reminds you of something else. (Time 112:62 Nov 27, 78)

AIDS

Salk, Jonas. It is becoming clear that a diagnosis of HIV positivity need not be regarded as a death sentence (1989). (Chicago Tribune 160:3 Section 1 June 9, 89)

AIKEN, CONRAD

Cowley, Malcolm. Conrad Aiken remained just a heavy drinker until he died at 84. By that time he had possibly consumed more gin than anyone else in the world. (Writer's Digest 58:26 Oct 78)

AIKEN, GEORGE DAVID

Aiken, George David. I have never seen so many incompetent persons in high office. Politics and legislation have become more mixed and smellier than ever (commenting on the U.S. Senate in his book Aiken: Senate Diary). (New York Times 125:23 June 29, 76)

AIR CONDITIONING

Vreeland, Diana. Air conditioning is like power and love. In the wrong hands, it'll kill you. (W 7:13 July 7, 78)

AIR POLLUTION

Reagan, Ronald. Eighty percent of air pollution comes from plants and trees. (Time 116:18 Aug 25, 80)

ALAIA, AZZEDINE

Alaia, Azzedine. For me, there is no vulgarity and the street is never in bad taste. (Town & Country 216:79 Aug 86)

ALCOHOLIC BEVERAGES

Apollonio, Spencer. When four fishermen get together, there's always a fifth. (Down East 22:108 Dec 31, 75)

Benchley, Nathaniel. Contrary to popular opinion there is not a college education in that bottle; you don't get smarter with every drink you take. (Writer's Digest 58:28 Oct 78)

De Vries, Peter. Reality is impossible to take neat, we must dilute it with alcohol. (Writer's Digest 58:29 Oct 78)

Sheen, Charlie. Alcohol is the devil's urine. (US 3:8 Oct 17, 88)

Thurber, James. One martini is all right, two is too many, three is not enough. (Rocky Mountain News 327:86 Mar 14, 80)

ALCOHOLIC BEVERAGES see also BEER; CHAMPAGNE

ALCOHOLISM

Pierce, Webb. One drink is too many and a million is not enough. (Country Music

5:63 April 77)

ALCOHOLISM AND AUTHORSHIP

Lehman, Ernest. If writer's block is soluble in alcohol, so is the liver. (Writer's Digest 58:26 Oct 78)

ALDA, ALAN

Alda, Alan. If I were a politician, I'd be a decent politician. (Newsweek 94:62 Aug 27, 79)

ALLEN, GEORGE

Allen, George. Only winners are truly alive. Winning is living. Every time you win, you're reborn. When you lose, you die a little. (Chicago Tribune 76:1 Section 2 Mar 17, 78)

ALLEN, WOODY

Allen, Woody. If my film makes one more person feel miserable, I'll feel I've done my job. (Time 113:69 April 30, 79)

Allen, Woody. There have been times when I've thought of suicide, but with my luck it'd probably be a temporary solution. (Time 106:47 Dec 15, 75)

ALPERT, RICHARD see RAM DASS

ALTMAN, ROBERT

Altman, Robert. If I'd gone through school, gotten a good job and not gotten into films, I'd probably be dead today or a drunk. (Newsweek 85:50 June 30, 75)

AMBITION

Norris, Kathleen. If ambition doesn't hurt you, you haven't got it. (Kansas City Star 97:4B Feb 6, 77)

Wolfe, Tom. There's not too much reason to come to Manhattan unless you're ambitious. (Kansas City Times 116:A-2 June 29, 84)

AMERICA

Boorstin, Daniel J. We suffer primarily not from our vices or our weaknesses, but from our illusions. (Time 114:133 Nov 12, 79)

Borges, Jorge Luis. America is still the best hope. But the Americans themselves will have to be the best hope too. (Time 107:51 July 5, 76)

Douglas, William Orville. The great and invigorating influences in American life have been the unorthodox; the people who challenge an existing institution or way of life, or say and do things that make people think. (Kansas City Times 109:14C Jan 22, 77)

Graham, Bill. San Francisco is not a part of America. (Chicago Daily News Panorama 4 Dec 31, 21)

Rahv, Philip. Nothing can last in America more than ten years. (Time 110:67 Aug 15, 77)

AMERICA see also UNITED STATES

AMERICAN CIVIL LIBERTIES UNION see also BALDWIN, ROGER

AMERICANS

Auden, Wystan Hugh (attributed by Peter Conrad). The economic vice of Europeans is avarice, while that of Americans is waste. (Time 115:40 Mar 31, 80)

Carter, James Earl. The duty of our generation of Americans is to renew our nation's faith—not focused just against foreign threats, but against the threat of selfishness, cynicism and apathy. (Time 113:10 Feb 5, 79)

Chandler, A. B. (Happy). We Americans are a peculiar people. We are for the underdog no matter how much of a dog he is. (Reader's Digest 107:78 Nov 75)

Iacocca, Lee A. A little righteous anger really brings out the best in the American personality. (Cleveland Magazine 12:149 Nov 83)

James, Henry (attributed by William L. Shirer). It's a complex fate, being an American. (New York Times Book Review 25 July 24, 77)

Lawrence, David Herbert. The essential American soul is hard, stoic, isolate and a killer. (Time 111:53 Jan 9, 78)

Morrow, Lance. It bewilders Americans to be hated. (The Observer 9829:9 Jan 13, 80)

AMERICANS see also UNITED STATES

ANGER

Stevenson, Adlai, II. You can tell the size of a man by the size of the thing that makes him mad. (Texas Observer 78:7 June 18, 76)

ANTHROPOLOGISTS see also MEAD, MARGARET

ANTI-CATHOLICISM

Rutler, George William. Anti-Catholicism has become the Anti-Semitism of the liberals. (Chicago Tribune 68:16 Mar 9, 86)

APARTHEID

Jackson, Jesse. Apartheid is violence by definition. (Newsweek 94:36 Aug 13, 79)

Paton, Alan. Sometimes, you think of apartheid as a fort. Often it is seen as a prison. But it is really a grave the Afrikaner has dug for himself. (New York Times 127:32 Oct 30, 77)

ARAB STATES—POLITICS AND GOVERNMENT

Hussein, King of Jordan. It's amusing. The Americans have changed Presidents six times since I've been King. And they talk to the Arabs about stability? (People Weekly 6:122 Dec 13, 76)

ARAFAT, YASIR

Arafat, Yasir. I have come bearing an olive branch and a freedom fighter's gun. Do not let the olive branch fall from my hand (addressing the United Nations (1974)). (Time 104:43 Nov 25, 74)

Arafat, Yasir. Palestine is my wife. (Time 104:36 Nov 11, 74)

Sharon, Ariel. In order to overcome our problems, the first thing to do is to eliminate the heads of the terrorist organizations, and the first one is Yasir Arafat. (Chicago Tribune 208:27 Section 1 July 27, 89)

ARBUS, DIANE

Arbus, Diane. I mean it's very subtle and a little embarrassing to me, but I really believe that there are things which nobody would see unless I photographed them. (Town & Country 131:64 Feb 77)

Mailer, Norman. Giving a camera to Diane Arbus is like putting a live grenade in the hands of a child. (Newsweek 104:90 Oct 22, 84)

ARCHITECTS

Wright, Frank Lloyd. A doctor can bury his mistakes, but an architect can only advise his client to plant vines. (Chicago Tribune Magazine 6 July 18, 82)

ARCHITECTURE

Aalto, Alvar. True architecture exists only where man stands in the center. (Newsweek 94:97 July 16, 79)

Burnham, Daniel. Make no little plans. (Chicago 26:160 Dec 77)

Hall, Donald. Less is more, in prose as in architecture. (Writer's Digest 58:8 Nov 78)

Johnson, Philip. All cultures that can be called cultures have built monuments. (Time 113:59 Jan 8, 79)

Roche, Kevin. Architecture is an intuitive activity, and the discussion, the polemic, the rationalizations all come afterwards, after the act, never before. (Connoisseur 218:86 Feb 88)

Van der Rohe, Mies. Buildings are the will of an epoch translated into space. (Chicago Tribune Magazine 10 June 10, 90)

ARGUMENTS

Sproles, Judy. If there is an opinion, facts will be found to support it. (Omni 1:132 May 79)

ARRAU, CLAUDIO

Arrau, Claudio. Every concert must be an event, never a routine. (Horizon 20:9 Dec 77)

ART

Barragan, Luis. Art is made by the alone for the alone. (Time 115:50 May 12, 80)

Barthelme, Donald. The principle of collage is the central principle of all art in the 20th Century. (Chicago Tribune 207:12 Section 2 July 26, 89)

Brecht, Bertolt. Grub first, art after. (New York Times Magazine 22 Jan 23, 77)

Chagall, Marc. Great art picks up where nature ends. (Time 127:54 Dec 30, 85)

De Lempicka, Tamara. Do not copy! (Toronto Life Fashion 43 Spring Preview 88)

Guggenheim, Peggy. I don't like art today, I think it has gone to hell. (W 8:24 Oct 12, 79)

Liberman, Alexander. All serious art is against convention. (New York Times Magazine 61 May 13, 79)

Malkovich, John. Art is not more important than life. (Newsweek 104:86 Sept 24, 84)

Malraux, Andre. A minor living art is far more vital than a major dead one. (New York Times Magazine 17 Jan 23, 77)

Miro, Joan. Fools do not make art. (New York Arts Journal 7:8 Nov 77)

O'Hara, John. An artist is his own fault. (Mirabella 1:33 Feb 90)

Oldenburg, Claes. To give birth to form is the only act of man that has any consequence. (Chicago 25:18 Nov 76)

Panza di Biumo, Giuseppe. For me, art is the visualization of philosophy. (Newsweek 86:69 Aug 11, 75)

Picasso, Pablo. Art is lies that tell the truth. (More 8:34 June 78)

Ray, Man. There is no progress in art any more than there is progress in making love. There are simply different ways of doing it. (New York Times Book Review 1 Feb 26, 78)

Reinhardt, Ad. Art is art. Everything else is everything else. (Village Voice 25:78 Dec 24, 80)

Rivers, Larry. Is photography art? Art is everything. (Andy Warhol's Interview 7:12 Nov 75)

Rochberg, George. The business of art is to praise God. (Newsweek 93:73 Feb 19, 79)

Rogow, Bruce. One person's vulgarity is another person's art. (Chicago Tribune 278:27 Section 1 Oct 5, 90)

Russell, Ken. All good art, all good entertainment, shocks people. (Village Voice 26:46 Jan 21, 81)

Saul, Peter. Becoming an artist is kind of like stocks and bonds: complicated. You have to go against the advice of very intelligent people who surround you. (Chicago Tribune 246:9 Section 9 Sept 3, 89)

Shapiro, Joseph H. Aesthetics is to art what ornithology is to birds. (Chicago 26:178 Sept 77)

Shapiro, Joseph H. Great art is so complex and has so many levels of meaning it carries its own equivocation. (Chicago

26:178 Sept 77)

Stieglitz, Alfred. Let all the art in the world be destroyed. It will rise again, for the art spirit is inherent in man. (Los Angeles Times Book Review 96:10 July 31, 77)

Tharp, Twyla. Art is the only way to run away from home without leaving home. (Ms 5:66 Oct 76)

Varese, Edgar. Scientists are the poets of today. (Artspace 9:30 Fall 85)

Warhol, Andy. Art is what you can get away with. (Mother Jones 6:10 July 81)

Warhol, Andy. Good business is the best art. (Time 106:32 July 28, 75)

Yamashita, Sachio (Painter). Art, color are the vitamins of the soul. (Time 105:8 Mar 3, 75)

ART see also PAINTING

ART AND POLITICS

Brustein, Robert. Once we allow lawmakers to become art critics, we take the first step into the world of Ayatollah Khomeini. (The Progressive 53:9 Aug 89)

ART CRITICISM

Hughes, Robert. Not even Pablo Picasso was Pablo Picasso. (Art & Antiques 87 Oct 84)

ART SALES

Merkin, Richard. Paintings in galleries sell for twice the price they command at auction. (CoEvolution Quarterly 35:5 Fall 82)

ART, MODERN

Stoppard, Tom. Skill without imagination is craftsmanship and gives us many useful objects as wickerwork picnic baskets. Imagination without skill gives us modern art. (Kansas City Times 119:A-19 July 11, 87)

ART—MODERNISM

De Chirico, Giorgio. Modernism is dying in all the countries of the world. Let us hope it will soon be just an unhappy memory. (New York Times 128:B5 Nov 22, 78)

ARTIFICIAL INTELLIGENCE

Kay, Alan. Artificial intelligence is the designer jeans of computer science. (Infoworld 7:13 July 8, 85)

ARTISTS

Cheever, John. If you are an artist, self-destruction is quite expected of you. (Time 112:125 Oct 16, 78)

Langlois, Henri. Most people advance through life walking backward. Those artists who face forward are likely to be put in jail—or the madhouse. (New York Times 126:D13 Jan 23, 77)

Motherwell, Robert. Every intelligent painter carries the whole culture of modern painting in his head. It is his real subject, of which anything he paints is both an

homage and a critique. (Los Angeles Times Calendar 96:86 July 31, 77)

O'Hara, John. An artist is his own fault. (Mirabella 1:33 Feb 90)

Perls, Klaus. Never talk to an artist about his work. If you do, what you get are total lies. (M 6:228 Oct 88)

Picasso, Pablo. Every child is an artist. The problem is how to remain an artist once he grows up. (Time 108:68 Oct 4, 76)

Ray, Man. The streets are full of admirable craftsmen, but so few practical dreamers. (ARTnews 76:52 Jan 76)

Reinhardt, Ad. The eyes are in the head for a reason. (Art in America 65:72 Mar 77)

Waugh, Evelyn. An artist must be a reactionary. He has to stand out against the tenor of the age and not go flopping along. (Time 113:96 Feb 12, 79)

ARTISTS see also CEZANNE, PAUL; CHAGALL, MARC; DUCHAMP, MARCEL; HITCHENS, IVON; O'KEEFFE, GEORGIA; PICASSO, PABLO; RAY, MAN; SENGHOR, LEOPOLD SEDAR

ARTISTS—SELF PERCEPTION

Steinberg, William. Great conductors do not dance. (Newsweek 91:93 May 29, 78)

ARTS

Baldwin, James. Everybody wants an artist on the wall or on the shelf, but nobody wants him in the house. (Time 122:65 Sept 26, 83)

Malraux, Andre. A minor living art is far more vital than a major dead one. (New York Times Magazine 17 Jan 23, 77)

Miller, Arthur. I think that you don't take seriously any art that's not dealing finally with whether we are doomed or not. (Christian Science Monitor 69:30 Aug 8, 77)

Sellars, Peter (theatrical director). Great art is created on the run. (Boston 75:108 Oct 83)

ARTS AND SOCIETY

Brecht, Bertolt. Grub first, art after. (New York Times Magazine 22 Jan 23, 77)

Malraux, Andre. There cannot be another Michelangelo in today's society because our faith in man is too weak. (Time 105:40 May 12, 75)

ARTS—AFRICA

Senghor, Leopold Sedar. Africa will teach rhythm to a world dead with machinery and cannon. (Time 116:5 July 7, 80)

ARTS—CENSORSHIP

Frohnmayer, John E. Holocaust victims might be inappropriate for display in the entrance of a museum where all would have to confront it, whether they chose to or not. (New York Times 139:B3 Aug 2, 90)

Rogow, Bruce. One person's vulgarity is another person's art. (Chicago Tribune 278:27 Section 1 Oct 5, 90)

ARTS—CHICAGO

Solti, Sir Georg. Chicago should erect a statue to me for what I have done. (Chicago 26:152 Dec 77)

ARTS—CRITICISM

Burns, George (attributed by David Steinberg). (Critics are) eunuchs at a gang-bang. (New Times 10:38 Jan 9, 78)

Osborne, John. Asking a working writer what he thinks about critics is like asking a lamppost what it feels about dogs. (Time 110:77 Oct 31, 77)

ARTS—NEW YORK (CITY)

Montresor, Beni. Compared to what you see around the world, New York is mummified. (W 18:22 Jan 25, 88)

ASIMOV, ISAAC

Asimov, Isaac. A lot of people can write. I have to. (Time 113:80 Feb 26, 79)

ASPEN, COLORADO

Sandersen, Ann. When I'm in New York I'm homesick for Aspen, and when I'm in Aspen I'm homesick for Aspen. (Outside 1:25 Sept 78)

ASSASSINATION

Gandhi, Indira (Nehru). Well, I've lived with danger all my life, and I think I've had a pretty full life, and it makes no difference whether you die in bed or you die standing up. (The New Yorker 60:39 Nov 12, 84)

ASSASSINATION—UNITED STATES

Fromme, Lynette (Squeaky). Anybody can kill anybody. (Time 106:19 Sept 15, 75)

ASSAULT AND BATTERY

Boyles, Tiny. Getting beat up is like eating hot food. After the first bite you don't feel the rest. (Oui 8:52 May 79)

ASTAIRE, FRED

Astaire, Fred. I don't dance—ever—and I don't intend to ever again. (Chicago Tribune 1:25 Section 1 Jan 1, 78)

Balanchine, George. You see a little bit of Astaire in everybody's dancing. (Time 130:58 Dec 28, 87)

ASTOR, NANCY

Astor, Nancy. I married beneath me. All women do. (The Observer 9822:35 Nov 25, 79)

ASTROLOGY

Anonymous. Anybody who believes in astrology was probably born under the wrong sign. (Macleans 90:46 Aug 22, 77)

Reagan, Ronald. No policy or decision in my mind has ever been influenced by astrology. (Kansas City Star 108:8c May 4, 88)

ASTRONAUTS see also WOMEN ASTRONAUTS

ASTROTURF

Allen, Dick. If horses won't eat it, I don't want to play on it. (Esquire 89:30 Mar 28, 78)

ATGET, EUGENE

Abbott, Berenice. It took two lives to build Atget's reputation: his and mine. (American Photographer 21:11 Oct 88)

ATHEISM

Lewis, C. S. A young man who wishes to remain a sound atheist cannot be too careful of his reading. God is, if I may say it, very unscrupulous. (New York Times 126:B1 Dec 20, 76)

ATHLETES

Garvey, Ed. When you talk about civil liberties in professional sports, it's like talking about virtue in a whorehouse. (Village Voice 20:37 Dec 8, 75)

King, Billie Jean. Amateur athletes have become the pawn of manipulators and big business. (The Nation 221:654 Dec 20, 75)

ATOMIC BOMB

Lewis, Robert A. (co-pilot of the B-29 Enola Gay). If I live to be a hundred, I'll never quite get these few minutes out of my mind. (Time 122:48 July 4, 83)

Schlafly, Phyllis. The atomic bomb is a marvelous gift given to America by a wise God. (The Times 8142:8 July 13, 80)

ATOMIC POWER

Brown, Edmund Gerald, Jr. I think it's time for the President, certainly the next President, to say no to nuclear power (1979). (New York Times 128:A18 April 26, 79)

Einstein, Albert. To the village square we must carry the facts of atomic energy. From there must come America's voice (commenting in 1946). (Newsweek 85:23 Feb 24, 75)

Nader, Ralph. This (the Three Mile Island accident) is the beginning of the end of nuclear power in this country. (Time 113:8 April 9, 79)

Penden, Bill. Atomic energy is a future idea whose time is past. Renewable energy is a future idea whose time has come. (Atlas World Press Review 24:38 April 77)

Teller, Edward. Nuclear power is not an option—it is a part of the fight for the survival of freedom. (New York Times 129:A30 Dec 12, 79)

ATOMIC POWER INDUSTRY

Nader, Ralph. If nuclear power is so safe, why won't the insurance industry insure it? (Newsweek 85:24 Feb 24, 75)

ATOMIC POWER PLANTS

Reagan, Ronald. All the wastes in a year from a nuclear power plant could be stored under a desk. (USA Today 1:8A Mar 22, 83)

ATOMIC POWER—FRANCE

Giscard d'Estaing, Valery. Nuclear energy is at the crossroads of the two independences of France: the independence of her defense and the independence of her energy supply. (Time 110:31 Aug 15, 77)

ATOMIC WARFARE

Khrushchev, Nikita Sergeevich. The survivors (of a nuclear attack) would envy the dead. (Harper's 259:36 Aug 79)

Mountbatten, Louis. If the Third World War is fought with nuclear weapons, the fourth will be fought with bows and arrows. (Maclean's 88:73 Nov 17, 75)

Sakharov, Andrei Dmitrievich. Thermonuclear warfare has already become a dark reality of modern times, like Auschwitz, the Gulag and famine. (Time 106:44 Oct 20, 75)

Zappa, Frank. There will be no nuclear war. There's too much real estate involved. (Life 8:90 Jan 84)

ATOMIC WEAPONS see also TELLER, EDWARD

AUCHINCLOSS, LOUIS

Auchincloss, Louis. I am neither a satirist nor a cheerleader. I am strictly an observer. (New York Times Book Review 7 Sept 23, 79)

AUDEN, WYSTAN HUGH

Auden, Wystan Hugh. Among those whom I like, I can find no common denominator; but among those whom I love, I can: all of them make me laugh. (Reader's Digest 107:78 Nov 75)

AUSCHWITZ CONCENTRATION CAMP

Steiner, George. The world of Auschwitz lies outside speech as it lies outside reason. (Time 111:53 May 1, 78)

AUTHORITY, DELEGATION OF see DELEGATION OF AUTHORITY

AUTHORS

Abe, Kobo. Once a writer throws away his mask he's finished. (New York Times Magazine 78 April 29, 79)

Auden, Wystan Hugh. Biographies of writers, whether written by others or themselves, are always superfluous and usually in bad taste. A writer is a maker, not a man of action. (The American Book Review 1:8 April/May 78)

Bellow, Saul. Writers are readers inspired to emulation. (Harvard Magazine 89:78 Jan/Feb 87)

Breslin, Catherine. A freelancer lives at the end of a sawed-off limb. (Time 111:77 April 10, 78)

Camus, Albert. The purpose of the writer is to keep civilization from destroying itself. (Time 120:K8 Sept 13, 82)

Capote, Truman. The only one who can destroy a really strong and talented writer is himself. (Kansas City Star 108:8E June 12, 88)

Chandler, Raymond. It is always a misfortune to be taken seriously in a field of writing where quality is not expected or desired. (Westways 74:67 Jan 82)

Cheever, John. If you are an artist, self-destruction is quite expected of you. (Time 112:125 Oct 16, 78)

Farrell, James T. There's one good kind of a writer—a dead writer. (Chicago Sun-Times 32:53 Aug 24, 79)

Faulkner, William. If a writer has to rob his mother, he will not hesitate; the Ode on a Grecian Urn is worth any number of old ladies. (New York Times Book Review 3 Aug 16, 81)

Fitzgerald, F. Scott. There never was a good biography of a good novelist. There couldn't be. He is too many people, if he's any good. (Writer's Digest 56:6 Dec 76)

Hemingway, Ernest. A writer must write what he has to say, not speak it. (Time 119:71 April 5, 82)

Miller, Arthur. I always doubted that writers ever really understand more than anyone else. All you can hope is that maybe you feel a little more. (The Observer 9812:35 Sept 16, 79)

Moore, Marianne. A writer is unfair when he is unable to be hard on himself. (Writer's Digest 58:6 Feb 78)

Nin, Anais. Writers make love to whatever they need. (Vanity Fair 49:127 Sept 86)

Parker, Dorothy. An author really hasn't made it until he no longer shows his books to his friends. (Writer's Digest 56:11 Dec 78)

Percy, Walker. Every novelist I know is miserable. (New York Times Book Review 31 June 29, 80)

Roberts, Dale. He is a man of letters—all of them lower case. (Writer's Digest 58:11 Oct 78)

Sexton, Anne. I wonder if the artist ever lives his life—he is so busy recreating it. (The American Book Review 1:4 Dec 77)

Sheed, Wilfrid. One reason the human race has such a low opinion of itself is that it gets so much of its wisdom from writers. (New York Times 128:9 Section 7 Jan 21, 79)

Steinbeck, John. Competing with Hemingway isn't my idea of good business. (Time 106:48 Dec 1, 75)

Townshend, Peter. It isn't enough any more

to write books: publishers expect you to sell them. (W 7:39 Nov 10, 78)

Waugh, Evelyn. An artist must be a reactionary. He has to stand out against the tenor of the age and not go flopping along. (Time 113:96 Feb 12, 79)

Wilson, Sloan. A writer's job is sticking his neck out. (Writer's Digest 58:9 Feb 78)

AUTHORS RIGHTS

Ringer, Barbara A. The basic human rights of individual authors throughout the world are being sacrificed more and more on the altar of the technological revolution. (American Legion Magazine 99:21 Dec 75)

AUTHORS, AMERICAN

Donleavy, J. P. Authors don't have any respect at all in terms of a profession in America—and this is quite a good and stimulating thing. (Newsweek 94:95 Oct 22, 79)

Mailer, Norman. It's hard to get to the top in America, but it's even harder to stay there. (Time 113:74 April 2, 79)

Susann, Jacqueline. I don't have any peers, as far as writers go. (After Dark 8:35 Aug 75)

AUTHORS, AMERICAN see also AIKEN, CONRAD; ASIMOV, ISAAC; AUCHINCLOSS, LOUIS; BARTH, JOHN; BELLOW, SAUL; BUCHWALD, ART; CAPOTE, TRUMAN; CONDON, RICHARD; DEVRIES, PETER; DONLEAVY, J. P.; FAULKNER, WILLIAM; FISHER, M. F. K.; GREENE, GAEL; HELLER, JOSEPH; HOFFER, ERIC; KOVIC, RON; MALAMUD, BERNARD; MCCULLERS, CARSON; NABOKOV, VLADIMIR; OATES, JOYCE CAROL; RAND, AYN; ROBBINS, HAROLD; SALINGER, J. D.; SAROYAN, WILLIAM; SINCLAIR, UPTON; SUSANN, JACQUELINE; WHITE, E. B.; WOLFE, THOMAS

AUTHORS, AMERICAN—WOMEN

Mailer, Norman. I can think of very few women who, like Susan Sontag, are first intellectuals and then literary artists. (Village Voice 31:21 Jan 28, 86)

AUTHORS, ENGLISH see also BOWEN, ELIZABETH; GREENE, GRAHAM; MURDOCH, IRIS; RHYS, JEAN; WAUGH, EVELYN

AUTHORS, FRENCH see also GIONO, JEAN

AUTHORS, IRISH see also BECKETT, SAMUEL

AUTHORS—FAME

Schwartz, Delmore. No reputation is more than a snowfall. (Times Literary Supplement 3969:2 April 28, 78)

AUTHORS—RELATIONS—MOVING PICTURE INDUSTRY

Puzo, Mario. A novelist should never take the movie business seriously. (New York Times 128:40 Section 7 Feb 18, 79)

AUTHORSHIP

Abe, Kobo. Once a writer throws away his mask he's finished. (New York Times Magazine 78 April 29, 79)

Auden, Wystan Hugh. Literary confessors are contemptible, like beggars who exhibit their sores for money, but not so contemptible as the public that buys their books. (Time 114:98 Nov 19, 79)

Bakshian, Aram. Speechwriting is to writing as Muzak is to music. (Washingtonian 17:31 Feb 82)

Capote, Truman. Good writing is rewriting. (New York 17:60 Nov 26, 84)

Cheever, John. It (plot) is a calculated attempt to hold the reader's interest at the sacrifice of moral conviction. (Esquire 90:35 Nov 21, 78)

Clancy, Tom. Every book you write is a first novel. (Washingtonian 24:73 Jan 89)

Cowley, Malcolm. No complete son-of-a-bitch ever wrote a good sentence. (Inquiry 1:28 July 24, 78)

De Laurentiis, Dino. To make a movie is not like to make a book. A movie is much, much more—not just pushing a pencil in a room. (Los Angeles Times Calendar 60 Nov 28, 76)

Donleavy, J. P. Writing is turning one's worst moments into money. (Playboy 26:135 May 79)

Ellison, Ralph. People who want to write sociology should not write a novel. (Newsweek 91:21 Feb 20, 78)

Gordimer, Nadine. The facts are always less than what really happened. (Time 110:93 Sept 19, 77)

Greenberg, Stanley. Writing isn't an exact science. It is more like chasing a butterfly you're not sure you want to catch. (Writer's Digest 56:5 May 76)

Hall, Donald. Less is more, in prose as in architecture. (Writer's Digest 58:8 Nov 78)

Hellman, Lillian. If I had to give young writers advice, I would say, Don't listen to writers talking about writing or about themselves. (Time 110:40 Sept 5, 77)

Hemingway, Ernest. Writing is something that you never do as well as it can be done. (D Magazine 12:168 Mar 85)

Howe, Tina. The love story is the acid test for any writer. (Elle 2:42 Nov 86)

Jong, Erica. I cannibalized real life. (Newsweek 85:71 May 5, 75)

Kaselionis, Simas. Writers aren't like mushrooms—you can't grow them. (Chicago 24:23 July 31, 75)

Kenney, Charles. The best cure I know for writer's block is deadline. (Boston 78:27 Oct 86)

Lebowitz, Fran. Having been unpopular in high school is not just cause for book publication. (New York Times Book

Review 39 June 17, 79)

Liebling, A. J. The only way to write is well and how you do it is your own damn business. (Gentlemen's Quarterly 56:76 June 86)

MacCarthy, Desmond. A biographer is an artist who is on oath. (Time 114:86 July 2, 79)

Mailer, Norman. A writer of the largest dimension can alter the nerves and marrow of a nation. (New York Times Magazine 54 Sept 9, 79)

McLuhan, Marshall. Most clear writing is a sign that there is no exploration going on. Clear prose indicates an absence of thought. (Time 106:36 Aug 25, 75)

O'Connor, Flannery. For a fiction writer, to believe nothing is to see nothing. (Ms 8:39 July 79)

Rhys, Jean. If you want to write the truth, you must write about yourself. (Newsweek 93:103 May 28, 79)

Roth, Philip. The road to hell is paved with works-in-progress. (New York Times Book Review 1 July 15, 79)

Roth, Philip. When you publish a book, it's the world's book. The world edits it. (New York Times Book Review 13 Sept 2, 79)

Singer, Isaac Bashevis. A Marxist has never written a good novel. (New York Times Magazine 42 Nov 26, 78)

Singer, Isaac Bashevis. A writer, like a woman, never knows why people like him, or why people dislike him. We never know. (Time 112:69 Aug 7, 78)

Singer, Isaac Bashevis. When I was a little boy, they called me a liar, but now that I am grown up, they call me a writer. (Time 122:53 July 18, 83)

Singer, Isaac Bashevis. Writers were not born to change the world. (Time 112:82 July 3, 78)

Smith, Red. Writing is very easy. All you do is sit in front of a typewriter keyboard until little drops of blood appear on your forehead. (Writers' Digest 55:4 Nov 75)

Steinbeck, John. The profession of book writing makes horse racing seem like a solid, stable business. (Time 112:68 Aug 28, 78)

Vidal, Gore. In writing and politicking, it's best not to think about it, just do it. (Bookviews 1:24 June 78)

Waugh, Evelyn. I regard writing not as investigation of character, but as an exercise in the use of language. (Time 113:96 Feb 12, 79)

White, E. B. No one can write decently who is distrustful of the reader's intelligence. (New York Times 126:C19 Nov 17, 76)

White, E. B. The way to approach a manuscript is on all fours, in utter amazement. (Washington Post 352:E2 Nov 21, 76)

Wideman, John Edgar. Being a writer these days includes self-promotion. (Chicago Tribune 162:10 Section 5 June 11, 89)

Will, George F. People who use word processors should not be surprised if what they write is to prose as process cheese is to real cheese. (Lawrence (Kansas) Journal-World 125:4 Dec 18, 83)

AUTHORSHIP see also ALCOHOLISM AND AUTHORSHIP; TELEVISION AUTHORSHIP

AUTOBIOGRAPHY

Auden, Wystan Hugh. Literary confessors are contemptible, like beggars who exhibit their sores for money, but not so contemptible as the public that buys their books. (Time 114:98 Nov 19, 79)

AUTOMOBILES

Ford, Henry, II. This country developed in a particular way because of the automobile, and you can't just push a button and change it. (Time 105:71 Feb 10, 75)

Spikol, Art. The fact is that most people don't drive cars that reflect what they are: they drive the closest thing they can find to what they'd like to be. (Philadelphia Magazine 66:198 Nov 75)

AUTOMOBILES—USED

Anonymous. A used car is like a bad woman—no matter how good you treat it, it'll give you more trouble than it's worth. (The Reader (Chicago's Free Weekly) 7:11 Section 1 April 7, 78)

AUTRY, GENE

Autry, Gene. I'm gonna die with my boots on. (Chicago Tribune Magazine 62 Dec 3, 78)

AVARICE

Aron, Jean-Paul. Avarice is the predominant French characteristic because of (our) long peasant history. (Newsweek 88:62 Nov 22, 76)

Boesky, Ivan F. I think greed is healthy. You can be greedy and still feel good about yourself. (Newsweek 108:48 Dec 1, 86)

Rohatyn, Felix. I have been in business for almost 40 years, and I cannot recall a period in which greed and corruption appeared as prevalent as they are today (1986). (Washington Post National Weekly Edition 4:5 Dec 29, 86)

BABIES see INFANTS

BACON, FRANCIS

Bacon, Francis. I believe you are born, then you die. You do what you can in between the two. (Elle 4:210 Oct 88)

BAEZ, JOAN

Baez, Joan. Here we are back at square one. The world's blowing up, and I'm singing a concert (1983). (Life 7:113 Jan 84)

BAGNOLD, ENID
Bagnold, Enid. I wasn't a born writer, but I was born a writer. (Human Behavior 7:17 May 78)

BAILEY, F. LEE
Bailey, F. Lee. I defend crime; I'm not in favor of it. (Boston 70:72 Dec 78)

BAILEY, PEARL
Bailey, Pearl. I never ask myself how I do what I do. After all, how does it rain? (W 7:8 June 9, 78)

BAKER, HOWARD HENRY
Baker, Howard Henry. In Washington I'm thought of as a conservative, but in Tennessee I'm thought of as a Bolshevik. (Time 107:15 Aug 9, 76)

BAKKER, JIM
Bakker, Jim. Jim and Tammy are a tad flamboyant. (Newsweek 109:62 June 8, 87)

BAKKER, TAMMY
Bakker, Jim. Jim and Tammy are a tad flamboyant. (Newsweek 109:62 June 8, 87)

BALANCHINE, GEORGE
Balanchine, George. I am the mother in this world of dance. (Time 115:87 May 19, 80)
Baryshnikov, Mikhail. With Balanchine I grew up. (Newsweek 94:82 July 2, 79)
Robbins, Jerome. He's (George Balanchine) the Mozart of dance. (Newsweek 101:89 Mar 9, 83)

BALDWIN, ROGER
Baldwin, Roger. I'm a crusader and crusaders don't stop. (Chicago Tribune 52:1 Section 3 Feb 21, 79)

BANKHEAD, TALLULAH
Bankhead, Tallulah. Cocaine isn't habit-forming. I should know—I've been using it for years. (Playboy 26:26 Oct 79)

BANKRUPTCY
Borman, Frank. Capitalism without bankruptcy is like Christianity without hell. (Chicago Tribune 79:2 Section 5 Mar 21, 90)

BANKS AND BANKING
Ely, Bert. Banker's don't know squat about insurance. (Chicago Tribune 50:4 Section 4 Feb 19, 89)
Nossiter, Bernard D. There are no conflicts of interest when bankers' pockets are to be lined. (The Nation 251:441 Oct 22, 90)
Wriston, Walter. I believe there are no institutional values, only personal values. (Guardian Weekly 124:16 Jan 25, 81)

BARDOT, BRIGITTE
Bardot, Brigitte. I leave before being left. I decide. (Chicago Tribune 176:2 Section 2 June 25, 78)

BARS AND BARROOMS
Shor, Toots. A good saloonkeeper is the most important man in the community. (Time 106:44 Sept 22, 75)

BARS AND BARROOMS—CHICAGO
Royko, Mike. If you can't find a good bar in Chicago, you ought to give up drinking. (Chicago 31:127 Dec 31, 81)

BARTH, JOHN
Barth, John. My books are allowed to know one another, as children of the same father, but they must lead their lives independently. (Time 114:96 Oct 8, 78)

BARUCH, BERNARD MANNES
Baruch, Bernard Mannes (attributed by William Flanagan). I buy low and sell high (when asked how he had made a fortune in the stock market). (New York 10:56 May 2, 77)

BARYSHNIKOV, MIKHAIL
Baryshnikov, Mikhail. With Balanchine I grew up. (Newsweek 94:82 July 2, 79)

BASEBALL
Allen, Dick. If horses won't eat it, I don't want to play on it. (Esquire 89:30 Mar 28, 78)
Berra, Yogi. In baseball, you don't know nothing. (New West 4:116 April 9, 79)
Butler, Dick. If you took three words out of the English language, most players and umpires would be mute. (Time 122:55 Oct 10, 83)
Harrelson, Ken. Baseball is the only sport I know that when you're on offense, the other team controls the ball. (Sports Illustrated 44:14 Sept 6, 76)
Jackson, Reggie. Hitting is better than sex. (Esquire 89:98 Mar 1, 78)
Veeck, Bill. Baseball is the only orderly thing in a very unorderly world. If you get three strikes, even Edward Bennett Williams can't get you off. (Sports Illustrated 43:14 June 2, 75)

BASEBALL see also BROCK, LOU; FINLEY, CHARLES OSCAR; JACKSON, REGGIE; MAYS, WILLIE; PITCHING (BASEBALL); ROBINSON, FRANK; ROBINSON, JACKIE; STARGELL, WILLIE; VEECK, BILL

BASEBALL—HITTING
Rose, Pete. Singles hitters drive Fords. Home-run hitters drive Cadillacs. (New West 4:116 April 9, 79)

BASEBALL—HITTING—RECORDS
Rose, Pete. I'm not the greatest hitter ever. I just have the most hits. (The Sporting News 200:16 Sept 23, 85)

BASEBALL—MANAGERS
Curtis, John. Between owners and players, a manager today has become a wishbone. (Sports Illustrated 47:18 July 18, 77)

Durocher, Leo. If you lose you're going to be fired, and if you win you only put off the day you're going to be fired. (The Sporting News 197:10 June 11, 84)

Lasorda, Tom. Managing is like holding a dove in your hand. Squeeze too hard and you kill it; not hard enough and it flies away. (Toronto Life 84 May 84)

Luciano, Ron. Old managers never die. They just end up working for George Steinbrenner. (Time 120:93 Sept 13, 82)

Weaver, Earl. Bad ballplayers make good managers. (Toronto Life 22 April 30, 84)

BASEBALL—SALARIES, PENSIONS, ETC.

Veeck, Bill. It's not the high price of stars that's expensive. It's the high price of mediocrity. (Kansas City Star 106:1 Sports Jan 5, 86)

BASEBALL—STUDY AND TEACHING

Dean, Dizzy. Let the teachers learn the kids English. Ol' Diz will learn the kids baseball. (The Sporting News 195:70 Dec 31, 84)

BASEBALL—UMPIRING

Chylak, Nestor. An umpire's job is the only one in the world that everybody else can do better. (University Daily Kansan 92:10 Feb 18, 82)

Murtaugh, Danny. A bad call (in baseball) is one that goes against you. (TV Guide 26:14 May 6, 78)

BASKETBALL

Lemons, Abe. Basketball is a game, not a religion. (Arkansas Times 11:87 Mar 31, 85)

BASKETBALL, COLLEGE

Brown, Dale. If you don't violate NCAA rules, you're in a coma or in a crematorium. (Lawrence (Kansas) Journal-World 129:5B Mar 25, 87)

Valvano, Jim. Monday through Friday they want you to be like Harvard. On Saturday, they want you to play like Oklahoma. (Kansas City Times 120:E-3 Jan 20, 88)

BASKETBALL, COLLEGE see also INDIANA. UNIVERSITY

BASKETBALL, COLLEGE—COACHES

Boeheim, Jim. I ain't a bad guy. People see me on the sidelines and they think I'm an idiot or a maniac. That's just coaching. (Topeka Capital-Journal SportsPlus 11 April 7, 87)

Knight, Bob. I'm an imperfect man trying to attain perfection in a game that probably has no chance of being played perfectly. (Topeka Capital-Journal SportsPlus 10 Dec 1, 87)

BASKETBALL, PROFESSIONAL— BLACKS

McGuire, Al. The only thing in this country that blacks really dominate, except poverty, is basketball. (Chicago Tribune 63:1 Section 5 Mar 3, 78)

BEATNIKS

Kupferberg, Tuli. What is a beatnik? Why, it's exactly everything that Herbert Hoover hates. (New York 12:82 May 7, 79)

BEATON, SIR CECIL

Beaton, Sir Cecil. Perhaps the world's second worst crime is boredom; the first is being a bore. (Time 115:89 Jan 28, 80)

BEAUTY, PERSONAL

Chanel, Coco. Youth is something very new: twenty years ago no one mentioned it. (Chicago Tribune 176:2 Section 2 June 25, 78)

Duffy, Sean. The chance of a meaningful relationship with a member of the opposite sex is inversely proportional to their amount of beauty. (Omni 1:132 May 79)

Lamarr, Hedy. Any girl can be glamorous. All you have to do is stand still and look stupid. (Chicago Sun-Times 30:21 Jan 28, 78)

Martin, Abe. Beauty is only skin deep, but it's a valuable asset if you're poor or haven't any sense. (Human Behavior 7:70 Sept 78)

Myerson, Bess. You can't be beautiful and hate. (Forbes 122:200 Oct 30, 78)

Somers, Suzanne. If you've got it, bump it with a trumpet. (Playboy 26:26 Oct 79)

West, Mae. It's better to be looked over than overlooked. (Lawrence (Kansas) Journal-World 127:3D Feb 3, 85)

BEAUTY, PERSONAL—MEN

Adams, Alice. I don't like good-looking men—one always thinks they'll be dumb. (People Weekly 9:53 April 3, 78)

BEAUVOIR, SIMONE DE

Beauvoir, Simone De. I cannot be angry at God, in whom I do not believe. (The Observer 9776:10 Jan 7, 79)

BECKETT, SAMUEL

Beckett, Samuel. All I want to do is sit on my ass and fart and think of Dante. (Newsweek 91:96 June 5, 78)

BEHAVIOR (PSYCHOLOGY)

Ace, Jane. Well, time wounds all heels. (Village Voice 22:20 Dec 26, 77)

Durant, Will. One of the lessons of history is that nothing is often a good thing to do and always a clever thing to say. (Washingtonian 14:153 Nov 78)

Wharton, William. After I muddle in other people's puddles, I find out it's all one, big lonesome ocean. (National Catholic Reporter 21:13 May 17, 85)

BEHAVIOR (PSYCHOLOGY) see also MEN—BEHAVIOR (PSYCHOLOGY)

BELIEF

Russell, Bertrand. It matters little what you believe, so long as you don't altogether believe it. (Kansas City Star 106:5A Dec 30, 85)

BELIEF AND DOUBT

Shields, Mark. I don't think Carter and self-doubt have ever met. (Washingtonian 11:103 June 76)

Sitwell, Edith. The public will believe anything, so long as it is not founded on truth. (Kansas City Star 97:2D Feb 20, 77)

BELLOW, SAUL

Bellow, Saul. I know you think I'm a square, Freifeld, but there's no name for the shape I'm in. (Newsweek 86:39 Sept 1, 75)

Freifeld, Sam. Saul Bellow is a great writer who is smaller than life. (Chicago 28:176 Dec 79)

BENCHLEY, ROBERT

Benchley, Robert. I have tried to know absolutely nothing about a great many things, and I have succeeded fairly well. (Rocky Mountain News 31:64 April 23, 80)

BENNETT, WILLIAM J.

Kilpatrick, James J. Big Bill Bennett, as I may have said before, is the best thing to hit American education since the McGuffey readers. (Kansas City Star 107:11A Feb 5, 87)

BENNY, JACK

Benny, Jack. I'm a simple guy. For a comedian I'm surprisingly normal. I have never been to a psychiatrist and I've only been married once. (Newsweek 85:63 Jan 6, 75)

Paley, William S. Jack (Benny) wasn't witty or even funny in real life. (M 2:66 July 85)

BENTON, THOMAS HART

Benton, Thomas Hart. I feel in my very soul that I was born to be great. (New York Times 138:9 April 13, 89)

BERGMAN, INGMAR

Bergman, Ingmar. Each film is my last. (Village Voice 28:44 Jan 4, 83)

Bergman, Ingmar. Possessiveness is neurotic, but this is how I am. (New West 2:24 April 25, 77)

BERRY, CHUCK

Berry, Chuck. I never looked for recognition. I was paying for a home and a new car. (Newsweek 108:19 Nov 3, 86)

BEVERLY HILLS, CALIFORNIA

Redford, Robert. If you stay in Beverly Hills too long you become a Mercedes. (Time 107:58 Mar 29, 76)

Styron, William. I think a great novel could even come out of Beverly Hills. (New York Times Book Review 18 May 27, 79)

BIOGRAPHY

Auden, Wystan Hugh. Biographies of writers, whether written by others or themselves, are always superfluous and usually in bad taste. A writer is a maker, not a man of action. (The American Book Review 1:8 April/May 78)

Fitzgerald, F. Scott. There never was a good biography of a good novelist. There couldn't be. He is too many people, if he's any good. (Writer's Digest 56:6 Dec 76)

MacCarthy, Desmond. A biographer is an artist who is on oath. (Time 114:86 July 2, 79)

BIOGRAPHY see also AUTOBIOGRAPHY

BIRD STUDY

Burroughs, John. If you want to see birds, you must have birds in your heart. (Outside 1:11 Dec 77)

BISEXUALITY

Allen, Woody. I can't understand why more people aren't bisexual. It would double your chances for a date on Saturday night. (Rolling Stone 272:14 Aug 24, 78)

MacLaine, Shirley. We're bisexual up to the age of 3, but what society won't admit is that we're bisexual most of our lives. (W 6:2 Sept 2, 77)

BLACK BASEBALL MANAGERS see also ROBINSON, FRANK

BLACK MUSLIMS

Malcolm X. This thing with me will be resolved by death and violence. (Playboy 23:127 June 76)

BLACK POLITICIANS

Clay, William. Whenever I see certain elements in the press show favoritism to a Black man running for a position of power, I know there's a nigger in the woodpile somewhere. (Sepia 26:10 May 76)

BLACKS

Barrow, Willie. It's easier being black than being a woman. (Sepia 26:12 Sept 75)

Carter, James Earl. When I finish my term, I want black people to say that I did more for them in my presidency than any other President in their lifetime. (Sepia 26:12 April 77)

Hall, Daryl. It's socially immoral for a white person to act like a black person. (Creem 9:34 Aug 77)

Jackson, Maynard. If Richard Nixon were black, he would be catching so much hell, he would rather be in jail. (Sepia 24:10 Jan 75)

Killens, John O. Let's stop titillating white people. No matter what we black folks do, we always wind up as entertainers. (Sepia 26:10 May 76)

Marshall, Throgood. I have come to the definite conclusion that if the United

States is indeed the great melting pot, the Negro either didn't get in the pot or he didn't get melted down. (Newsweek 110:21 Sept 21, 87)

McGuire, Al. The only thing in this country that blacks really dominate, except poverty, is basketball. (Chicago Tribune 63:1 Section 5 Mar 3, 78)

Muse, Clarence. The public believed in the Negro's voice, but not in his intelligence. (Time 114:123 Oct 29, 79)

Norris, Clarence (the sole surviving Scottsboro Boy). The lesson to Black people, to my children, to everybody, is that you should always fight for your rights even if it costs you your life. Stand up for your rights, even if it kills you (commenting on his struggle to clear his name upon being pardoned by the state of Alabama). (New York Times 126:1 Oct 26, 76)

Simone, Nina. Jazz lets black people know, everytime they hear it, that they have their hands on the pulse of life. (Sepia 26:10 June 77)

Wilkins, Roy. Black power can only mean black death. (Newsweek 99:51 Jan 4, 82)

BLACKS AND POLITICS

Jackson, Jesse. If we can have a Miss America, we can have a Mr. President. (Philadelphia 74:176 Nov 83)

BLACKS—CHICAGO

Hauser, Philip M. (Chicago) has lace pants in the front, and soiled drawers behind. (Chicago Tribune 71:1 Mar 12, 78)

BLACKS—CIVIL RIGHTS—HISTORY

Eisenhower, Dwight David. These are not bad people... All they are concerned about is to see that their sweet little girls are not required to sit in schools alongside some big overgrown Negroes. (Time 109:66 Mar 28, 77)

BLACKS—ECONOMIC CONDITIONS

Jackson, Jesse. In a hot war we (Blacks) die first; in a cold war, we starve first. (Newsweek 94:27 Sept 3, 79)

Jackson, Jesse. We too often condemn blacks who succeed and excel, calling them Uncle Toms. The ideal ought to be for all of us to succeed and excel. (Sepia 25:12 Sept 76)

BLACKS—EDUCATION

Jackson, Jesse. A school system without parents at its foundation is just like a bucket with a hole in it. (Time 112:46 July 10, 78)

Jackson, Jesse. Affirmative action is a moot point if you don't learn to read and write. (Time 114:Aug 6, 79) (148)

Jackson, Jesse. What does it matter if we have a new book or an old book, if we open neither? (Time 112:46 July 10, 78)

BLACKS—PSYCHOLOGY

Flood, Curt. Being black is always having people being cautious about what they call you. (Esquire 89:46 Mar 1, 78)

BLACKS—SOCIAL CONDITIONS

Washington, Booker T., III. Being the sensitive man he was about his race, I think the present day Harlem scene would bring tears to my grandfather's eyes. (Sepia 26:10 Feb 77)

BLACKS—UNITED STATES

Mays, Benjamin. If this (country) is a melting pot, I don't want the Negro to melt away. (Time 111:49 Feb 13, 78)

BLASS, BILL

Blass, Bill. I'd rather help raise money for museums than diseases. (US 3:64 Nov 4, 85)

BLOOMINGDALE'S (DEPARTMENT STORE)

Khan, Naved N. Bloomingdale's is more than a store. It is a way of life. (Time 106:4 Dec 22, 75)

BOESKY, IVAN F.

Boesky, Ivan F. It's OK to make money. It's a good thing. You go to heaven if you do it. (Kansas Cith Star 107:8A Nov 18, 86)

BOHR, NIELS

Bohr, Niels. But horseshoes have a way of bringing you luck even when you don't believe in them. (Village Voice 21:25 June 28, 76)

BONO, SONNY

Bono, Sonny. I've never been qualified for anything I've done. (Newsweek 110:13 July 13, 87)

BOOK REVIEWERS AND REVIEWING

Barbour, Hugh R. There is nothing like a good negative review to sell a book. (Newsweek 90:69 Oct 31, 77)

Conroy, Jack. I've never given a bad review. Some are more favorable than others, but I have never given a bad one. (Kansas City Star 110:A-18 Mar 3, 90)

Murdoch, Iris. A bad review is even less important than whether it is raining in Patagonia. (The Observer 9770:12 Nov 26, 78)

Sheed, Wilfrid. Criticism is what every reviewer would like to write if he had the time. (New York Times 128:9 Section 7 Jan 21, 79)

BOOKS

Hemingway, Mary. Books are helpful in bed. But they are not responsive (commenting on widowhood). (People Weekly 6:49 Dec 13, 76)

Roth, Philip. When you publish a book, it's the world's book. The world edits it. (New York Times Book Review 13 Sept 2, 79)

Van Doren, Mark (attributed by Robert Giroux). A classic is a book that is never out of print. (New York Times Book Review 23 Jan 6, 80)

BOOKS AND READING

Boorstin, Daniel J. Reading is a lot like sex. It is a private and often secret activity. It is often undertaken in bed, and people are not inclined to underestimate either the extent or the effectiveness of their activity. (Life 7:39 Jan 84)

Greene, Graham. God forbid people should read our books to find the juicy passages. (The Observer 9816:11 Oct 14, 79)

BOOKS—COLLECTORS AND COLLECTING

Prizeman, John. Collecting books is like collecting other people's minds, like having people on the shelves—only, you can just put them away when you want to. (Esquire 89:76 Jan 31, 78)

BOOKSELLERS AND BOOKSELLING

Barbour, Hugh R. There is nothing like a good negative review to sell a book. (Newsweek 90:69 Oct 31, 77)

BOONE, PAT

Boone, Pat. I think my life is a vindication of what Middle America wants. (TV Guide 26:34 April 1, 78)

BOREDOM

Anonymous. If you're bored in New York, you're boring. (Chicago Tribune 193:1 July 11, 76)

Beaton, Sir Cecil. Perhaps the world's second worst crime is boredom; the first is being a bore. (Time 115:89 Jan 28, 80)

BORGES, JORGE LUIS

Borges, Jorge Luis. Had I to choose one literature, my choice would be the English literature. (The (Montreal) Gazette B-6 June 1, 85)

Borges, Jorge Luis. If my works are read for pleasure, thats all they have to do. (Chicago Tribune 169:3 Section 5 June 18, 86)

BORK, ROBERT

Bork, Robert. Roe v. Wade contains almost no legal reasoning. (Chicago Tribune 259:11 Sept 16, 87)

Garment, Leonard. He is the antithesis of a stuffed judicial robe (about Robert Bork). (Time 130:13 July 13, 87)

Reagan, Ronald. If I have to appoint another one, I'll try to find one they'll object to just as much as this one (about Robert Bork). (Chicago Tribune 287:1 Oct 14, 87)

BOSS RULE

Udall, Morris King. A boss is a political leader who is on somebody else's side. (ABC News Issues and Answers 1 April 25, 76)

BOSTON—DESCRIPTION

Friedberg, A. Alan. Boston is a city with champagne tastes and beer pocketbooks. (Time 114:82 July 16, 79)

BOSTON. BASKETBALL CLUB (NATIONAL ASSOCIATION)

Auerbach, Red. There are only three teams in sports that have achieved true national status. The old Yankees, the Dallas Cowboys and us. That's not ego, that's just fact. (Sports Illustrated 67:73 Nov 9, 87)

BOWEN, ELIZABETH

Bowen, Elizabeth. All your youth you want to have your greatness taken for granted; when you find it taken for granted, you are unnerved. (Kansas City Star 97:15C Sept 22, 76)

BOWLING

Carter, Don. One of the advantages bowling has over golf is that you seldom lose a bowling ball. (Sports Illustrated 43:8 Aug 11, 75)

BOXING

Ali, Muhammad. After I go, boxing will go to the graveyard. (Sporting News 204:63 Oct 12, 87)

Aranoff, Ezra. There's no room for a slow poke in a prize fight. (Chicago Sun-Times 31:6 Mar 6, 78)

Foreman, George. Boxing is like jazz. The better it is, the less people appreciate it. (Sepia 25:12 Sept 76)

King, Donald. I have risen to the top in the promotion business just as I climbed to the top in the numbers game: by wits and grits and bullshit. (Cleveland 4:90 Nov 75)

Louis, Joe. You can run, but you can't hide. (Mother Jones 3:65 Dec 77)

BOXING see also CARTER, RUBIN (HURRICANE); FOREMAN, GEORGE; KING, DONALD

BRAGA, SONIA

Braga, Sonia. All my life, intuition has put me in the right place at the right time. (Playboy 31:91 Oct 84)

Braga, Sonia. I have no idea what acting is. I just try to understand the mind of the women I play. (Chicago Tribune 269:7 Section 5 Sept 26, 85)

Mastroianni, Marcello. She is much woman (about Sonia Braga). (Newsweek 112:60 July 18, 88)

BRAND, STEWART

Brand, Stewart. My expectation is that the sky will fall. My faith is that there's another sky behind it. (Omni 2:50 Dec 79)

BRANDO, MARLON

Brando, Marlon. Acting is an empty profession. I do it for the money because for me there is no pleasure. (Time 107:74 May 24, 76)

Brando, Marlon. The only reason I'm in Hollywood is that I don't have the moral courage to refuse the money. (Los Angeles 34:210 Mar 89)

Brando, Marlon. The principal benefit acting has offered me is the money to pay my psychiatrists. (Los Angeles 23:181 Nov 78)

Houseman, John. There is no question but that Marlon Brando would have been America's Olivier if he had continued in the classical theater. (W 4:11 Dec 12, 75)

BRAZIL

Babenco, Hector. Brazil is a country that can only be understood by metaphors, where the reality of things violently exceeds fiction. (New York Times 127:10 April 30, 78)

Nixon, Richard Milhous. As Brazil goes, so will the rest of the Latin American continent (commenting in 1971). (Time 108:30 Nov 29, 76)

BREAKFASTS

Gunther, John. All happiness depends on a leisurely breakfast. (Washingtonian 14:154 Nov 78)

BRECHT, BERTOLT

Brecht, Bertolt. I hope that because of my life, the powerful will sleep less comfortably (on his epitaph). (Guardian Weekly 120:17 April 29, 79)

BRENNAN, WILLIAM

Brennan, William. It is my hope that the Court during my years of service has built a legacy of interpreting the Constitution and Federal laws to make them responsive to the needs of the people whom they were intended to benefit and protect. (Time 136:17 July 30, 90)

BRIBERY

Cockburn, Claud. Never underestimate the effectiveness of a straight cash bribe. (Village Voice 21:39 Oct 4, 76)

Ryan, John. Bribes are just bad business. (Mother Jones 2:50 July 77)

BRITISH

Crisp, Quenton. The English think incompetence is the same thing as sincerity. (New York Times 126:7 Section 12 Jan 30, 77)

John, Elton. People in England are so bloody nosey. (The Observer 9820:10 Nov 11, 79)

Shaw, George Bernard. An Englishman thinks he is moral when he is only uncomfortable. (Time 120:15 Oct 4, 82)

Toynbee, Arnold. The Englishman's truly distinctive disease is his cherished habit of waiting until the 13th hour. (Time 106:30 Aug 4, 75)

BROCK, LOU

Brock, Lou. If you can perceive a goal and then make it happen, you live a dream. (Newsweek 94:49 Aug 27, 79)

BRONSON, CHARLES

Bronson, Charles. I'm not one of my favorite characters. (US 3:4 May 4, 87)

Huston, John. (Charles Bronson is) a hand grenade with the pin pulled. (Time 111:52 Jan 9, 78)

BROOKS, LOUISE

Langlois, Henri. There is no Garbo, no Dietrich. There is only Louise Brooks. (Newsweek 106:71 Aug 19, 85)

BROOKS, MEL

Brooks, Mel. I don't think in terms of results. I think: what next insanity can I shock the world with. (Maclean's 91:10 April 17, 78)

BROWN, EDMUND GERALD, JR.

Brown, Edmund Gerald, Jr. California is the place where the rest of the country and the rest of the world look for leadership and I want to keep it that way. (San Francisco Chronicle This World 1978:29 Feb 26, 78)

Brown, Edmund Gerald, Jr. You don't have to do things. Maybe by avoiding doing things you accomplish a lot. (New York Times 125:17 April 26, 76)

Brown, Edmund Gerald, Jr. You lean a little to the left and then a little to the right in order to always move straight ahead (on the art of governing). (Time 112:89 Oct 2, 78)

Hayden, Thomas. Jerry Brown's mortal sin is that he is ahead of his time. (New West 6:184 Oct 31, 81)

Lewis, Jonathan. Most politicians get elected by being all things to all people. Jerry (Brown) survives by being nothing to everyone. (Harper's 259:14 July 79)

Priolo, Paul. What that guy (Jerry Brown) does is enough to make a grown Republican cry. (The Times 8102:9 Oct 22, 78)

Rice, Kathleen Brown. Contrary to his reputation, he is not a flake, and he does have a sense of humor (about Jerry Brown). (New York Times 128:C5 Mar 6, 79)

BROWN, JAMES

Brown, James. I think God made sure there will never by another me. (Newsweek 108:13 Aug 25, 86)

BRUCE, LENNY

Bruce, Lenny. I only said it, man. I didn't do it. (Oui 7:51 Feb 78)

BRYANT, ANITA

Bryant, Anita. God says that someone who practices homosexuality shall not inherit the Kingdom of God. God is very plain on that. (Ms 6:50 July 77)

BUCHWALD, ART

Buchwald, Art. In 80 percent of the countries in the world today, guys like myself would be in jail. (Book Digest 4:27 Sept 77)

BUCKLEY, WILLIAM FRANK, JR.

Buckley, William Frank, Jr. If people would just take my advice, everything would go well. (W 7:2 April 14, 78)

BUDGET

Muchow, David. Budgeting is a black art practiced by bureaucratic magicians. (Chicago Sun-Times 29:2 Nov 19, 76)

BUDGET, PERSONAL

Parkinson, C. Northcote. Expenditure rises to meet income. (Washingtonian 14:155 Nov 78)

BUDGET—UNITED STATES

Dirksen, Everett McKinley. A billion here and a billion there, and pretty soon it adds up to real money. (Kansas City Times 114:A-14 Mar 18, 82)

Gramm, Phil. Balancing the budget is like going to heaven—everybody wants to balance the budget but nobody wants to do what you have to do to balance the budget. (Kansas City Star 107:6B June 29, 87)

Kirkland, Lane. Any jackass can draw up a balanced budget on paper. (US News & World Report 88:90 May 19, 80)

Reagan, Ronald. I did not come here to balance the budget—not at the expense of my tax cutting and defense programs. If we can't do it in 1984, we'll have to do it later (November 1981). (Life 5:33 Jan 82)

Reagan, Ronald. They still won't believe us, but we are going to balance this budget by 1984 (September 1981). (Life 5:33 Jan 82)

Reagan, Ronald. We don't have a budget deficit because our people aren't taxed enough, we have a budget deficit because Congress spends too much (1989). (Chicago Tribune 38:11 Section 1 Feb 7, 89)

Stockman, David. None of us really understands what's going on with all these numbers (commenting on budget figures). (Life 5:33 Jan 82)

Stockman, David. We've had a referendum on what we want in the budget, and what we don't. What's left, most of the people want. And we're going to have to raise taxes to pay for it. (Washington Post National Weekly Edition 2:4 Oct 21, 85)

Talmadge, Herman. Virtually everything is under federal control nowadays except the federal budget. (American Legion Magazine 99:17 Aug 75)

Wicker, Tom. Government expands to absorb revenue—and then some. (Washingtonian 14:155 Nov 78)

BUDGETING

Muchow, David. Budgeting is a black art practiced by bureaucratic magicians. (Chicago Sun-Times 29:2 Nov 19, 76)

BUJOLD, GENEVIEVE

Bujold, Genevieve. Caesar was Cleopatra's guru and Guinness was mine. (Newsweek 85:32 Jan 6, 76)

BUNDY, THEODORE

Bundy, Theodore. I deserve, certainly, the most extreme punishment society has. I think society deserves to be protected from me and from others like me. (Chicago Tribune 33:23 Section 1 Feb 2, 89)

BUNEUL, LUIS

Buneul, Luis. A religious education and Surrealism have marked me for life. (In These Times 7:21 Aug 24, 83)

BUREAUCRACY

Blumenthal, W. Michael. Most bureaucratic regulations look like Chinese to me—and I can read Chinese. (Washingtonian 12:11 Aug 77)

Friedman, Milton. In this day and age, we need to revise the old saying to read, Hell hath no fury like a bureaucrat scorned. (Newsweek 86:47 Dec 29, 75)

Hufstedler, Shirley. There is a little nonsense and sloth in the seams and marrow of all human industry. (New York Times Magazine 94 June 8, 80)

McCarthy, Eugene Joseph. The only thing that saves us from the bureaucracy is inefficiency. An efficient bureaucracy is the greatest threat to liberty. (Time 113:67 Feb 12, 79)

Nies, John. The effort expended by the bureaucracy in defending any error is in direct proportion to the size of the error. (Washingtonian 14:155 Nov 78)

Peter, Laurence J. Bureaucracy defends the status quo long past the time when the quo has lost its status. (San Francisco Chronicle This World 1978:40 Jan 29, 78)

Sidey, Hugh. Bureaucrats are the only people in the world who can say absolutely nothing and mean it. (Time 108:13 Nov 29, 76)

Sidey, Hugh. One must always remember that freedom from action and freedom from purpose constitute the philosophical bases of creative bureaucracy. (Time 108:13 Nov 29, 76)

Sidey, Hugh. The measurement of the gestation period of an original thought in a bureaucracy is still pending. (Time 108:13 Nov 29, 76)

Sidey, Hugh. When a bureaucrat makes a mistake and continues to make it, it usually becomes the new policy. (Time 108:13 Nov 29, 76)

BURGER, WARREN EARL

Dershowitz, Alan M. If he (Warren Burger) were one of the Founding Fathers, he would have voted against the Bill of Rights. (Saturday Review 6:20 Nov 30, 79)

BURNS, GEORGE

Burns, George. Now, they say, you should retire at 70. When I was 70 I still had pimples. (Time 112:69 Aug 7, 78)

Burns, George. When I do go, I plan to take my music with me. I don't know what's out there, but I want to be sure it's in my key. (Playboy 22:48 Dec 75)

BURROUGHS, EDGAR RICE

Burroughs, Edgar Rice. The less I know about a thing the better I can write about it. (Chicago 38:172 Dec 89)

BURTON, RICHARD

Burton, Richard. I only see a movie when I can't avoid it. (W 5:16 July 23, 76)

Burton, Richard. I was a star from the moment I first walked on the stage. (Chicago Tribune 284:2 Section 2 Oct 11, 77)

Taylor, Elizabeth. I didn't know I was destroying a famous actor (about Richard Burton). (Vanity Fair 52:84 Feb 89)

BUSH, BARBARA

Bush, Barbara. I am a liberal. (Newsweek 104:27 Nov 27, 89)

Bush, Barbara. I have great faith. Every night before I go to bed I pray out loud; so does George. (W 17:28 Jan 2, 89)

BUSH, GEORGE

Allen, Ethan. If you told him to bunt, he bunted (about George Bush). (Newsweek 111:19 June 27, 88)

Anderson, John B. George Bush is just a tweedier version of Ronald Reagan. (New York Times Magazine 44 Feb 17, 80)

Baxley, Bill. (George Bush is) a pin-stripin' pole playin umbrella-totin' Ivy Leaguer, born with a silver spoon so far back in his mouth that you conldn't get it out with a crowbar. (The Atlantic 260:62 July 87)

Bush, Barbara. I have great faith. Every night before I go to bed I pray out loud; so does George. (W 17:28 Jan 2, 89)

Bush, George. I am a non-politician, as of now (1976). (Meet the Press 20:9 Feb 22, 76)

Bush, George. I can feel it in my bones. I'm going to be President (1980). (Time 115:26 Feb 4, 80)

Bush, George. I'll be a great conservation and environmental president. I plan to

hunt and fish as much as I can. (Outside 14:19 Mar 89)

Bush, George. I'll prevail over Reagan because it is right that I prevail (1980). (New York 13:44 Jan 21, 80)

Bush, George. When I said I wanted a kinder and gentler nation, I meant it—And I mean it. (Newsweek 112:9 Nov 21, 88)

Carter, James Earl. No one knows what he stands for, or even where he comes from (about George Bush). (Chicago Tribune 199:10 Section 1 July 17, 88)

Clinton, Bill. He (George Bush) campaigns like a right-wing Republican and governs like a moderate Democrat. (New York Times 138:12 Aug 2, 89)

Codevilla, Angelo. I am aware that active duty agents of the Central Intelligence Agency worked for the George Bush primary election campaign (in 1980). (Village Voice 33:20 Oct 25, 1988)

Connally, John Bowden. All hat and no cattle (about George Bush). (Kansas City Times 112:A15 July 23, 80)

Dukakis, Michael. What George Bush is doing to the truth in this campaign is a crime (1988). (Newsweek 112:25 Oct 3, 88)

Haldeman, Harry Robbins. He'd (George Bush) do anything for the cause. (Time 132:28 Nov 21, 88)

Hightower, Jim. Bush was born on third base and he thinks he got there by hitting a triple. (Chicago Sun-Times 41:4 July 24, 88)

Mahe, Edward, Jr. Everything Quayle does—or doesn't do—will reflect on George Bush's judgement. (Newsweek 112:13 Nov 21, 88)

Washington, Pamela. He's (George Bush) not a pork rinds, county music person. He's an easy-listening, lobster-eating politician if I ever saw one. (New York Times 138:19 Nov 10, 88)

BUSH, GEORGE—ECONOMIC POLICY

Downey, Thomas. George Bush has decided he would rather see the government of the United States shut down than tax the wealthy. (Chicago Tribune 294:3 Section 4 Oct 21, 90)

BUSH, GEORGE—PRESIDENTIAL CAMPAIGN—1988

Atwater, Harvey Lee. I really had two goals in life: one, to manage a presidential campaign, and to be chairman of my party. (New York Times 138:9 Nov 18, 88)

Dukakis, Michael. What George Bush is doing to the truth in this campaign is a crime (1988). (Newsweek 112:25 Oct 3, 88)

BUSH, NEIL

Bush, Neil. I sleep soundly at night knowing I live an honest life. (Chicago Tribune 207:21 July 26, 90)

BUSINESS

LeFevre, William M. There are only two emotions in Wall Street: fear and greed. (Time 111:42 May 1, 78)

Reagan, Ronald. I don't know of anyone today that has less influence in this country than business. (Washington Post 353:A14 Nov 23, 75)

Riesman, David. The road to the board room leads through the locker room. (Time 111:59 June 26, 78)

Ryan, John. Bribes are just bad business. (Mother Jones 2:50 July 77)

Smith, William French. We must recognize that bigness in business does not necessarily mean badness. (Newsweek 98:57 July 6, 81)

Warhol, Andy. Good business is the best art. (Time 106:32 July 28, 75)

BUSINESS ETHICS

Rohatyn, Felix. I have been in business for almost 40 years, and I cannot recall a period in which greed and corruption appeared as prevalent as they are today (1986). (Washington Post National Weekly Edition 4:5 Dec 29, 86)

Young, Andrew. Nothing is illegal if 100 businessmen decide to do it, and that's true anywhere in the world. (Rolling Stone 235:35 Mar 24, 77)

BUSINESS MANAGEMENT AND ORGANIZATION

Babbitt, Bruce E. Far too many corporations think they have a smart system and stupid workers. They've got it backwards. (Lawrence (Kansas) Journal-World 130:1A Jan 5, 88)

Drucker, Peter F. So much of what we call management consists in making it difficult for people to work. (New York Times 125:15 Section 3 May 16, 76)

Drucker, Peter F. What managers decide to stop doing is often more important then what they decide to do. (Kansas City Star 109:2F Dec 25, 88)

Iacocca, Lee A. I never invent anything any more. Everything I do is to meet a law. (Time 114:71 Oct 22, 79)

Peter, Laurence J. In a hierarchy, every employee tends to rise to the level of his own incompetence. (The Reader (Chicago's Free Weekly) 5:2 May 28, 76)

BUSINESS—INTERNATIONAL ASPECTS

Kugel, Yerachmiel. Ethics is not a branch of economics. (St. Louis Post-Dispatch 99:2G July 24, 77)

BUSINESS—PUBLIC RELATIONS

Marcus, Stanley. A businessman can make no worse mistake than to try to use the muscle of the advertising dollar to try to influence the news. (The Atlantic 241:38 April 78)

BUSINESS—RELATIONS—FOOTBALL

McLuhan, Marshall. Football is itself the biggest dramatization of American business ever invented. (Inside Sports 3:70 Jan 31, 81)

BUSINESS—STUDY AND TEACHING

Davis, Harry. One can look at business as metaphor and drama (upon announcing the Second City Improvisionational Theater Group will teach Masters' of Business Administration students at the University of Chicago). (Chicago Tribune 171:1 Section 3 June 20, 89)

BUSINESS—UNITED STATES

Iacocca, Lee A. A little righteous anger really brings out the best in the American personality. (Cleveland Magazine 12:149 Nov 83)

Sawyer, Charles. The United States, like Atlas, is holding up the world. But who holds up Atlas? American business. (Time 113:85 April 23, 79)

BUSINESSMEN

Brooks, Jim. Businessmen commit a fraud when they say they're interested in anything but profit. (New West 1:17 Dec 20, 76)

Hefner, Hugh Marston. I'm not primarily an entrepreneurial businessman. I'm primarily a playboy philosopher. (Chicago Tribune 124:1 Section 1 May 3, 76)

Peter, Laurence J. In a hierarchy, every employee tends to rise to the level of his own incompetence. (The Reader (Chicago's Free Weekly) 5:2 May 28, 76)

Riesman, David. The road to the board room leads through the locker room. (Time 111:59 June 26, 78)

Young, Andrew. Nothing is illegal if 100 businessmen decide to do it, and that's true anywhere in the world. (Rolling Stone 235:35 Mar 24, 77)

BUSINESSMEN—GREAT BRITAIN

Charles, Prince of Wales. Much of British management does not seem to understand the human factor. (The Observer 9783:11 Feb 25, 79)

BUSINESSMEN—PUBLIC RELATIONS

Marcus, Stanley. A businessman can make no worse mistake than to try to use the muscle of the advertising dollar to try to influence the news. (The Atlantic 241:38 April 78)

BYRNE, JANE

Byrne, Jane. Diamonds are a girl's best friend, and Federal grants are second. (Newsweek 96:24 Sept 29, 80)

Sullivan, Frank. Jane Byrne was the supreme misjudgement of Richard J. Daley's life. (Chicago Tribune 76:3 Section 5 Mar 17, 89)

Talbott, Basil, Jr. Chicago may have nominated its first mayor who goes to a beauty shop, but she is in the city's oldest tradition. (Chicago Sun-Times 32:5 Section 2 Mar 4, 79)

CABLE TELEVISION INDUSTRY see also TURNER, R. E. (TED)

CADDELL, PATRICK

Caddell, Patrick. I'm less influential than I'd like to think I am, and a lot more than I deserve. (Time 114:14 Aug 6, 79)

CAESAR, SID

Coca, Imogene. I've never figured out why we work so well together, except that we both laugh at exactly the same time. (about herself and Sid Caesar). (Time 110:98 Sept 19, 77)

CALIFORNIA

Didion, Joan. California is a place in which a boom mentality and a sense of Chekhovian loss meet in uneasy suspension. (New York Times Magazine 36 June 17, 79)

Starr, Kevin O. There is no stable intellectual tradition in California except utopianism. (Esquire 89:134 Jan 31, 78)

Thiebaud, Wayne. Living in California allows one to escape preciousness and the predictable. (Connoisseur 217:66 Feb 87)

CALIFORNIA see also BEVERLY HILLS, CALIFORNIA; HOMOSEXUALS—CIVIL RIGHTS—CALIFORNIA

CALIFORNIA—DESCRIPTION

Allen, Fred. California is a great place to live...if you happen to be an orange. (New West 1:104 Nov 22, 76)

Brown, Edmund Gerald, Jr. In California, you've got to realize one thing: you don't mess around with a man's cars or his guns. (New West 3:54 Dec 18, 78)

Redgrave, Vanessa. California is a place with lots of warm weather and lots of cold people. (US 1:80 June 28, 77)

Smelser, Neil. Californians believe the best is behind them. (Time 110:23 July 18, 77)

CALIFORNIA—POLITICS AND GOVERNMENT

Brown, Edmund Gerald, Jr. California is the place where the rest of the country and the rest of the world look for leadership and I want to keep it that way. (San Francisco Chronicle This World 1978:29 Feb 26, 78)

CALIFORNIA—POLITICS AND GOVERNMENT see also UNRUH, JESSE

CALLOWAY, CAB

Calloway, Cab. Women, horses, cars, clothes. I did it all. And do you know what that's called. It's called living. (Sepia 26:10 Jan 77)

CAMBODIA

Kissinger, Henry Alfred. Cambodia's agony unfolded with the inevitability of a Greek tragedy. (Newsweek 94:59 Oct 22, 79)

CAMBODIA—POLITICS AND GOVERNMENT

Anonymous. When the water rises, the fish eat the ants, but when the water recedes, the ants eat the fish (Khmer Rouge slogan). (Guardian Weekly 143:23 Aug 12, 90)

Norodom Sihanouk, King Of Cambodia (Abdicated 1955). When they no longer need me, they will spit me out like a cherry pit (about the Khmer Rouge). (Time 106:38 Sept 22, 75)

CANADA—POLITICS AND GOVERNMENT

Levesque, Rene. The quality of a civilized society is the treatment it affords minorities. (New York Times 128:23 April 5, 79)

Mulroney, Brian. Today we must guard against two dangers. First, to despair that anything can be done and, second, to delude ourselves that nothing has happened (after the failure of the Meech Lake Accord). (Chicago Tribune 179:27 Section 1 June 28, 90)

Trudeau, Pierre Elliott. The Tory future is worse than the Liberal past. (New York Times 128:3 May 20, 79)

CANADA—RELATIONS—UNITED STATES

Meighen, Arthur. We are not in the same boat, but we are pretty much in the same waters. (New York Times 129:E5 Section 4 Nov 4, 79)

CANCER

Saffiotti, Umberto. Cancer in the last quarter of the 20th century can be considered a social disease, a disease whose causation and control are rooted in the technology and economy of our society. (Time 106:67 Oct 20, 75)

Salk, Jonas. The best thing to do (for people worried about cancer-causing substances) is quit reading the newspaper. (Chicago Sun-Times 29:54 Mar 17, 76)

CANCER—CAUSES

Higginson, John. We now know there are a hundred causes of cancer, and eighty of them are cigarettes. (Texas Monthly 6:174 June 76)

Newell, Guy. The cancer problem has not been solved, but it has never been more solvable. (American Legion Magazine 102:7 May 77)

CANNES INTERNATIONAL FILM FESTIVAL

Anonymous. In Cannes, a producer is what any man calls himself if he owns a suit, a tie, and hasn't recently been employed as a pimp. (Village Voice 22:26 June 6, 77)

CAPITAL

Drucker, Peter F. Capital formation is shifting from the entrepreneur who invests in the future to the pension trustee who invests in the past. (New York Times 125:15 Section 3 May 16, 76)

CAPITAL INVESTMENTS

Drucker, Peter F. Capital formation is shifting from the entrepreneur who invests in the future to the pension trustee who invests in the past. (New York Times 125:15 Section 3 May 16, 76)

CAPITAL PUNISHMENT

Fortas, Abe. The law of revenge has its roots in the deep recesses of the human spirit, but that is not a permissible reason for retaining capital punishment. (New York Times Magazine 9 Jan 23, 77)

Gilmore, Gary Mark. Let's do it. (Chicago Daily News 13 Dec 30, 77)

Hatch, Orrin. Capital punishment is our society's recognition of the sanctity of human life. (Newsweek 111:15 June 6, 88)

Hoover, John Edgar. The cure for crime is not the electric chair but the high chair. (Chicago Sun-Times 29:76 July 9, 76)

Reagan, Nancy. I think people would be alive today if there were a death penalty. (Life 5:142 Jan 82)

CAPITAL PUNISHMENT see also GILMORE, GARY MARK

CAPITALISM

Borman, Frank. Capitalism without bankruptcy is like Christianity without hell. (Chicago Tribune 79:2 Section 5 Mar 21, 90)

Braudel, Fernand. The preserve of the few, capitalism is unthinkable without society's active complicity. (World Issues 3:30 Oct 78)

Butz, Earl Lauer. Our capitalism is no longer capitalism; it is a weakened mixture of government regulations and limited business opportunities. (American Legion Magazine 99:21 Dec 75)

Churchill, Sir Winston. The inherent vice of capitalism is the unequal sharing of the blessings; the inherent virtue of socialism is the equal sharing of the miseries. (Kansas City Star 108:1F Dec 27, 87)

Forbes, Malcolm S. I'd say capitalism's worst excess is in the large number of crooks and tinhorns who get too much of the action. (Playboy 26:108 April 79)

Galbraith, John Kenneth. Capitalism will survive. (New York Times Book Review 31 Sept 30, 79)

Greenspan, Alan. When I met Ayn Rand, I was a free enterpriser in the Adam Smith sense, impressed with the theoretical structure and efficiency of markets. What she did was to make me see that capitalism is not only efficient and practical, but also moral. (Newsweek 85:61 Feb 24, 75)

Iguiniz, Javier (Peruvian economist). The growth of capitalism is the same as the growth of world poverty. (Time 106:34 Sept 1, 75)

Janeway, Eliot. The thrill of making a fast buck follows only the thrill of love at first sight. Everyone needs to take an occasional fling with money...and with love. (Chicago Tribune 95:14 April 5, 77)

Levy, Bernard-Henri. Between the barbarity of capitalism, which censures itself much of the time, and the barbarity of socialism, which does not, I guess I might choose capitalism. (Time 111:30 Mar 13, 78)

Moynihan, Daniel Patrick. The great corporations of this country were not founded by ordinary people. They were founded by people with extraordinary energy, intelligence, ambition, aggressiveness. All those factors go into the primordial capitalist urge. (Time 111:27 June 19, 78)

Tanner, Jack. Nothing could discredit capitalism more than a decision by the Russians to try it. (Challenge 19:4 Mar/April 76)

Teng, Hsiao-Ping. It doesn't matter whether you climb Mount Everest by its North slope or its South slope as long as you get to the top. (Newsweek 93:36 Feb 5, 79)

Von Hayek, Friedrich. The pursuit of gain is the only way in which people can serve the needs of others whom they do not know. (Kansas City Star 108:1F Dec 27, 87)

CAPITALISM see also FREE ENTERPRISE

CAPONE, ALPHONSE

Capone, Alphonse. Let the worthy citizens of Chicago get their liquor the best way they can. I'm sick of the job. It's a thankless job and full of grief. (Chicago 24:186 Dec 75)

Capone, Alphonse. When I sell liquor, it's called bootlegging; when my patrons serve it on silver trays on Lake Shore Drive, it's called hospitality. (Aspen 3:43

Spring 77)

CAPOTE, TRUMAN

Capote, Truman. I mean I can create any kind of social world I want, anywhere I want. (New York 9:49 Feb 9, 76)

O'Brian, Jack. (Truman Capote is) Jackie Susann with an education. (Time 107:68 June 28, 76)

Vidal, Gore. Truman (Capote) has made lying an art. A minor art. (Viva 5:105 Oct 77)

CARAMANLIS, CONSTANTINE

Caramanlis, Constantine. So we Greeks have been from ancient times: we are skillful at making idols, not that we may worship them, but that we may have the pleasure of destroying them. (Time 110:51 Dec 5, 77)

CARDIN, PIERRE

Cardin, Pierre. I have to do things differently from anyone else. For that, they say I am crazy. (Chicago Tribune 286:24 Oct 13, 77)

CARDS

Algren, Nelson. Never eat at a place called Mom's. Never play cards with a man named Doc. And never lie down with a woman who's got more troubles than you. (Washingtonian 14:152 Nov 78)

CAREY, HUGH

Carey, Hugh. My mind doesn't govern my conscience, my conscience governs my mind. (New York Times 127:A1 April 6, 78)

CARTER, JAMES EARL

Block, Herbert L. (Jimmy Carter) looks a little like both Jack Kennedy and Eleanor Roosevelt. (Time 110:92 Dec 12, 77)

Brando, Marlon. Carter has done something no other President has done: He has brought into the sharpest contrast the hypocrisy of the U.S. in respect to human rights. (Playboy 26:126 Jan 77)

Carter, James Earl. Civil service reform will be the centerpiece of government reorganization during my term in office. (Washington Post Magazine 11 Dec 3, 78)

Carter, James Earl. I can't resign from the human race because there's discrimination, and I don't intend to resign from my own church because there's discrimination. (Time 108:22 Nov 22, 76)

Carter, James Earl. The American people and our government will continue our firm commitment to promote respect for human rights not only in our own country but also abroad (to Andrei Sakharov). (Newsweek 89:17 Feb 28, 77)

Carter, James Earl. When I finish my term, I want black people to say that I did more for them in my presidency than any other

President in their lifetime. (Sepia 26:12 April 77)

Carter, Lillian. Jimmy's not sexy, he's my son. (People Weekly 13:114 Mar 3, 80)

Carter, Rosalynn. Jimmy (Carter) would have been impeached if he had done some of the things this administration (Ronald Reagan) has gotten away with. (Newsweek 108:29 Nov 24, 86)

Clifford, Clark. Jimmy Carter has the best mind of any President I have known. (Time 110:16 Oct 3, 77)

Conable, Barber. The trouble with Carter is he's listening only to God—and God doesn't pay taxes. (Time 111:11 May 1, 78)

Dole, Robert J. Jimmy Carter is chicken-fried McGovern. (Washingtonian 20:111 Sept 30, 84)

Durkin, John. In New Hampshire today, the Ayatullah Khomeini could beat Carter (1979). (Time 113:52 April 9, 79)

Edwards, James B. I don't believe the South will buy Jimmy Carter. He is nothing more than a Southern-talking George McGovern. (New York Times 125:51 June 29, 76)

Fallows, James. I came to think that Carter believes fifty things, but no one thing. (New York Times 128:23 April 26, 79)

Fraser, Douglas. The President (Jimmy Carter) is a nice man, an intelligent man and he likes his job. But he doesn't have any fire in his belly. (Chicago Sun-Times 32:2 April 27, 79)

Hemenway, Russell. He's (Jimmy Carter) the first president in recent history that would occupy the most important office in the world without any commitment to anybody. (New York 9:8 July 12, 76)

Kennedy, Edward Moore. I think Mr. Carter has created Ronald Reagan. (The Observer 9856:12 July 20, 80)

King, Martin Luther, Sr. Surely the Lord sent Jimmy Carter to come on out and bring America back where she belongs. (Washington Post 224:A1 July 16, 76)

Kirbo, Charles. He's (Jimmy Carter) got faults, like all of us. He's ambitious. But he's not greedy, and he's considerate. (Time 107:17 July 12, 76)

Kirkland, Lane. Carter is your typical, smiling, brilliant, backstabbing, bullshitting, southern nut-cutter. (New Times 7:13 Sept 3, 76)

Kissinger, Henry Alfred. Most administrations come to office believing that they are saving the world. This one believes it created the world (commenting on the Carter administration). (Chicago Sun-Times 30:3 May 4, 77)

Lance, Thomas Bertram. He (Jimmy Carter) campaigns liberal, but he governs conservative. (Washington Post 61:A3 Jan 31, 77)

Maddox, Lester Garfield. The reason he (Jimmy Carter) says he never lies is because he thinks the truth originates with him. (Newsweek 88:25 July 19, 76)

Mankiewicz, Tom. Whatever Jimmy Carter is asking us to be, Superman is already. (Time 110:64 Aug 1, 77)

McCarthy, Eugene Joseph. If you're in the peanut business you learn to think small (about Jimmy Carter). (New York 9:9 Aug 2, 76)

Meany, George. They say Carter is the first businessman ever to sit in the White House. But why did they have to send us a small businessman? (Time 112:62 Nov 27, 78)

Novak, Michael. Reagan has done more to help the poor than Carter. (USA Today 2:10A Nov 7, 83)

Rowan, Carl. Carter turned out to be not a populist but a small-town businessman. (Time 115:73 June 9, 80)

Sadat, Anwar. I have dealt with three presidents, Nixon, Ford and this Carter. I can say that everything is improving. (Time 111:32 Jan 2, 78)

Safire, William. (Jimmy Carter is) the best U.S. President the Soviet Union ever had. (Time 114:116 Nov 19, 79)

Schlesinger, Arthur, Jr. It is evident that what pretends to be a Democratic administration has deliberately and methodically chosen Republican policies. (Washington Post 102:3 June 24, 79)

Schmidt, Helmut. He (Jimmy Carter) is making (foreign) policy from the pulpit. (Time 107:14 May 9, 77)

Schneiders, Greg. He (Jimmy Carter) is the opposite of macho. He's soft on the outside and hard on the inside. (Washington Post 352:B3 Nov 19, 76)

Shields, Mark. I don't think Carter and self-doubt have ever met. (Washingtonian 11:103 June 76)

Sloane, Harvey. He's maturing like good Kentucky bourbon (about Jimmy Carter). (Time 107:10 May 24, 76)

Strauss, Robert S. There ain't but one good job in this government, and you got it (to Jimmy Carter). (Time 116:12 Sept 22, 80)

Taylor, Elizabeth. I'm confident that he's (Jimmy Carter) a short-term President. (Chicago Tribune 212:44 July 31, 79)

Vidal, Gore. Better the zero of Carter than the minus of Kennedy. (Rolling Stone 319:42 May 15, 80)

Whitman, Alden. Carter's sermons (on human rights) might be more credible if he had a priority program to end poverty. (Rolling Stone 242:59 June 30, 77)

Wurf, Jerry. If Jimmy Carter emerges as a strong President and keeps the promises he made in 1976, then there is still time for him to be born again politically. (New York Times 128:A10 July 13, 79)

Young, Andrew. (Jimmy) Carter does not hand out nickels after a campaign (about political rewards for supporting him). (Time 107:18 June 28, 76)

Young, Andrew. Black folks didn't need much selling on Carter. They have a special kind of radar about whether white folks are for real. (New York 9:91 July 12, 76)

CARTER, JAMES EARL—RELATIONS WITH THE PRESS

Johnson, Haynes. Jimmy Carter met the press and they were his (commenting after Carter's first press conference as President). (Time 109:11 Feb 11, 77)

CARTER, JAMES EARL—RELATIONS— RELIGION

Carter, James Earl. I have never detected or experienced any conflict between God's will and my political duties. (Time 111:13 June 26, 78)

CARTER, JAMES EARL—STAFF

Jordan, Hamilton. If after the inauguration you find a Cy Vance as Secretary of State and Zbigniew Brzezinski (of Columbia University) as head of national security, then I would say we failed. And I'd quit. But that's not going to happen. (Christian Science Monitor 69:3 Dec 6, 76)

Reagan, Ronald. The trouble with (the Carter) administration is that for everybody they got in, it was a step up. They never had it so good. (Time 115:16 June 30, 80)

CARTER, JAMES EARL—STAFF see also CADDELL, PAT

CARTER, LILLIAN

Carter, Lillian. Hunger and poverty are things I cannot live with, and I cannot live with myself unless I work to do something about them. (Newsweek 102:84 Nov 14, 83)

CARTER, ROSALYNN

Carter, Rosalynn. I have always been more political than (Jimmy). (Time 114:13 Aug 6, 79)

Carter, Rosalynn. I've always worked hard, and that's why they call me 'The Steel Magnolia'. (Maclean's 89:8 Nov 29, 76)

CARTER, RUBIN (HURRICANE)

Carter, Rubin (Hurricane). The kindest thing I can say about my childhood is that I survived it. (Chicago Sun-Times 28:86

Dec 16, 75)

CARTIER-BRESSON, HENRI

Cartier-Bresson, Henri. For me the camera is an instrument of intuition and spontaneity, the master of the instant. (The Times 8104:5 Nov 5, 78)

CARTLAND, BARBARA

Cartland, Barbara. I'm the only author with 200 virgins in print. (Town & Country 131:144 Dec 77)

CARTOONISTS see also TRUDEAU, GARRY

CASH, JOHNNY

Cash, Johnny. I guess the record shows I'm far from perfect—but I want to keep trying. (US News & World Report 84:60 Feb 27, 78)

CASTRO, FIDEL

Castro, Fidel. I reached the conclusion long ago that the one last sacrifice I must make for public health is to stop smoking. (Time 127:83 Jan 6, 86)

CATHOLIC CHURCH

Hesburgh, Theodore. The Catholic University is where the church does its learning. (Newsweek 109:75 May 11, 87)

John Paul II, Pope. It is the right of the faithful not to be troubled by theories and hypotheses that they are not expert in judging or that are easily simplified or manipulated by public opinion. (Time 114:68 Oct 22, 79)

Lefebvre, Marcel. The church is full of thieves, mercenaries and wolves. During the past 20 years, the Vatican has become the friend of our enemies. (Time 110:64 July 11, 77)

Maher, Leo, Bishop. A pro-choice Catholic is an oxymoron. (Chicago Tribune 341:20 Dec 7, 89)

CATHOLIC CHURCH IN THE UNITED STATES

Greeley, Andrew. Only a charlatan or a lunatic would be hopeful about the present state of Catholicism. (Psychology Today 10:51 June 76)

CATHOLIC CHURCH—FINANCE

Marcinkus, Paul Casimir. You can't run the church on Hail Marys. (National Catholic Reporter 23:10 Mar 13, 87)

CATHOLIC COLLEGES AND UNIVERSITIES

Hesburgh, Theodore. The Catholic University is where the church does its learning. (Newsweek 109:75 May 11, 87)

CATHOLICISM

Waugh, Evelyn. You have no idea how much nastier I would be if I was not a Catholic. Without supernatural aid I would hardly be a human being. (Newsweek 86:119 Nov 24, 75)

CAUCASIAN RACE

Harrell, John R. The black man's angry, the yellow man's angry. Everybody's angry but the white man, and he's asleep. (Time 114:8 Nov 5, 79)

CAUSATION

Shannon, William V. What is actually happening is often less important than what appears to be happening. (Book Digest 6:30 Dec 79)

CELEBRITIES

Blond, Susan. If you're beautiful, you can get away with anything. (Vanity Fair 48:42 May 85)

Ephron, Nora. The plain fact is that a celebrity is anyone People (magazine) writes about. (USA Today 1:10A May 16, 83)

Keillor, Garrison. Interviewing celebrities is just a step above calling the morgue. (Mpls/St. Paul 13:26 Sept 30, 85)

Kissinger, Henry Alfred. The nice thing about being a celebrity is that when you bore people, they think it's their fault. (Washingtonian 23:150 Dec 87)

CELEBRITIES—CONDUCT OF LIFE

Maverick, Maury, Jr. When you've got a famous name, you ought to use it to speak up for the people who can't speak up for themselves. (Texas Monthly 16:109 Mar 88)

CELEBRITIES—SEXUAL BEHAVIOR

Brando, Marlon. If you're rich and famous you don't have any trouble getting laid. (Players 3:32 Feb 77)

CELLISTS see also ROSTROPOVICH, MSTISLAV

CENSORSHIP

Irani, C. R. The only protection for a free press is the courage to demand it. (Chicago Tribune 233:4 Section 2 Aug 21, 77)

Kerby, Phil. Censorship is the strongest drive in human nature. Sex is only a weak second. (Kansas City Times 117:A-6 April 22, 85)

Luce, Clare Boothe. Censorship, like charity, should begin at home, but unlike charity, it should end there. (USA Today 1:8A Aug 9, 83)

Rubinstein, Michael. The ultimate blasphemy must be censorship. (The Observer 9701:13 July 17, 77)

CENSORSHIP see also ARTS—CENSORSHIP

CENSORSHIP—SOUTH AFRICA

Nel, Louis. We do not have censorship. What we have is a limitation on what newspapers can report (in South Africa). (New York Times 135:A3 June 26, 86)

CENTRAL AMERICA—POLITICS AND

GOVERNMENT

Quayle, Dan. The problem in Central America is not El Salvador. The problem in Central America is Nicaragua, and let us not forget that. (New York 22:46 Mar 13, 89)

CEZANNE, PAUL

Cezanne, Paul. I am the primitive of the method I have invented. (Newsweek 78:40 Oct 17, 77)

CHABROL, CLAUDE

Chabrol, Claude. I ask audiences to contemplate a character, not identify with him. (Time 106:76 Sept 29, 75)

CHAGALL, MARC

Chagall, Marc. Me, I do not understand Chagall. (Time 109:95 May 23, 77)

Picasso, Pablo. After Matisse, Chagall is the only artist who really knows color. (ARTnews 76:48 Summer 77)

CHAMPAGNE

Keynes, John Maynard. My only regret in life is that I did not drink more champagne. (Money 5:53 April 76)

CHANCE

Runyon, Damon. All life is six-to-five against. (New York 9:36 Nov 1, 76)

CHANDLER, RAYMOND

Chandler, Raymond. All us tough guys are hopeless sentimentalists at heart. (Village Voice 26:42 Nov 25, 81)

Chandler, Raymond. If my books had been any worse, I should not have been invited to Hollywood...if they had been any better, I should not have come. (Bookviews 1:21 April 78)

CHANGE

Brecht, Bertolt. Because things are the way they are things will not stay the way they are. (Philadelphia Magazine 68:305 Nov 77)

Pannenberg, Wolfhart. The greatest deception (of our era is the idea that) political change can satisfy a religious need. (Time 107:65 Mar 8, 76)

CHANGE see also SOCIAL CHANGE

CHAPLIN, CHARLES SPENCER

Chaplin, Charles Spencer. I am known in parts of the world by people who have never heard of Jesus Christ. (Chicago Tribune 58:12 Feb 27, 78)

Chaplin, Charles Spencer. My prodigious sin was and still is, being a nonconformist. Although I am not a Communist, I refused to fall in line by hating them. (Guardian Weekly 118:5 Jan 1, 78)

CHARACTER

Herold, Don. Many people have character who have nothing else. (Chicago Sun-Times 32:25 July 14, 79)

CHARACTERS AND CHARACTERISTICS

Anonymous. A clean desk is the sign of a sick mind. (Chicago Magazine 27:104 Jan 78)

Benchley, Robert. There may be said to be two classes of people in the world: those who constantly divide the people of the world into two classes and those who do not. (Washingtonian 14:152 Oct 31, 78)

Forbes, Malcolm S. A bore is someone who persists in holding his own views after we have enlightened him with ours. (Reader's Digest 108:261 May 76)

Frost, Robert. Half the world is composed of people who have something to say and can't, and the other half who have nothing to say and keep on saying it. (Kansas City Star 97:38 July 14, 77)

Hitler, Adolf. You know, everybody has a price—and you'd be surprised how low it is. (New York Times Book Review 23 July 24, 77)

Kerouac, Jack. Walking on water wasn't built in a day. (The American Book Review 1:8 April 78)

Maugham, William Somerset. Only a mediocre person is always at his best. (Forbes 120:80 Aug 1, 77)

Meir, Golda. Don't be humble, you're not that great. (New York Times Book Review 39 June 17, 79)

Newman, Paul. If you don't have enemies, you don't have character. (First Run 2 June 10, 79)

Randall, Tony. People don't call you mad or eccentric if you are well-heeled. It's only when you're poor that they call you a nut.... (Chicago Tribune 170:14 June 19, 79)

Spinks, Leon. You can take a man out of the ghetto, but you can't take the ghetto out of a man. (The Observer 9760:13 Sept 17, 78)

Stevenson, Adlai, II. You can tell the size of a man by the size of the thing that makes him mad. (Texas Observer 78:7 June 18, 76)

Tanner, Jack. A person without character always does what is right. (Challenge 19:5 Mar/April 76)

CHARACTERS AND CHARACTERISTICS—FRANCE

Aron, Jean-Paul. Avarice is the predominant French characteristic because of (our) long peasant history. (Newsweek 88:62 Nov 22, 76)

Barenboim, Daniel. When they want to be difficult, the French can seem impossible. But when they decide to get something done, there's no one better. (Time 125:65 June 17, 85)

Bell, Helen Choate. The French are a low lot. Give them two more legs and a tail, and there you are. (New York 10:88 Jan 31, 77)

CHARACTERS AND CHARACTERISTICS—GREAT BRITAIN

Crisp, Quenton. The English think incompetence is the same thing as sincerity. (New York Times 126:7 Section 12 Jan 30, 77)

John, Elton. People in England are so bloody nosey. (The Observer 9820:10 Nov 11, 79)

Shaw, George Bernard. An Englishman thinks he is moral when he is only uncomfortable. (Time 120:15 Oct 4, 82)

Toynbee, Arnold. The Englishman's truly distinctive disease is his cherished habit of waiting until the 13th hour. (Time 106:30 Aug 4, 75)

CHARACTERS AND CHARACTERISTICS—IRELAND

Flanagan, Fionnula. The one thing you must not commit with the Irish is to succeed. (TV Guide 26:22 April 29, 78)

Moynihan, Daniel Patrick. I don't think there's any point in being Irish if you don't know that the world is going to break your heart eventually. (New York Times Book Review 15 April 30, 78)

CHARACTERS AND CHARACTERISTICS—ITALY

Berge, Pierre. Except for white ruffles, pasta and opera, the Italians can't be credited with anything. (Time 119:60 April 5, 82)

West, Morris. In discourse the Italians are the most eloquent people in the world. In action they are either apathetic or impulsive to the point of insanity. (Esquire 89:81 April 25, 78)

CHARACTERS AND CHARACTERISTICS—MEN

Hufstedler, Shirley. A man cannot be very kind unless he is also very strong. (New York Times Magazine 104 June 8, 80)

Rubin, Jerry. Most men act so tough and strong on the outside because on the inside, we are scared, weak, and fragile. Men, not women, are the weaker sex. (Chicago Tribune 75:24 Mar 16, 78)

Toklas, Alice B. The young men of today seem mostly to be interested in the manner rather than the matter. (Chicago Tribune 176:2 Section 2 June 25, 78)

CHARACTERS AND CHARACTERISTICS—NEW YORK (CITY)

Korda, Michael. New York style is that what you do is more important than who you are. (New York 21 Dec 24, 84)

CHARACTERS AND CHARACTERISTICS—SOUTH

Allen, Maryon. People in the South love their politics better than their food on the table. (Time 112:32 Oct 9, 78)

Goldwater, Barry Morris. You can't be raised in the South, and not be a segregationist. (New York Times 138:12 Oct 4, 88)

Jordan, Hamilton. Historically, I think there probably is an inferiority complex associated with being Southern. (Esquire 89:79 Mar 28, 78)

CHARACTERS AND CHARACTERISTICS—UNITED STATES

Lawrence, David Herbert. The essential American soul is hard, stoic, isolate and a killer. (Time 111:53 Jan 9, 78)

CHAVEZ, CESAR

Peretz, Martin. You know, the thing I really disliked most about Chavez was the way he established himself as a tool of the Kennedy elite. (Boston Magazine 67:66 July 75)

CHEATING (EDUCATION) see also COLLEGES AND UNIVERSITIES—CHEATING

CHEEVER, JOHN

Cheever, John. It (plot) is a calculated attempt to hold the reader's interest at the sacrifice of moral conviction. (Esquire 90:35 Nov 21, 78)

CHER

Cher. For me, forever is probably five or ten years. (US 3:8 Feb 20, 89)

CHICAGO

Byrne, Jane. Wind chill factor or not, Chicago is America's warmest city. (Chicago 31:127 Dec 31, 81)

Royko, Mike. If you can't find a good bar in Chicago, you ought to give up drinking. (Chicago 31:127 Dec 31, 81)

Zisk, Richie (baseball player). Chicago is the kind of place where, if you fall flat on your face, there's someone to pick you up instead of stomping on your face. (Chicago Tribune 248:20 Sept 5, 77)

CHICAGO see also BLACKS—CHICAGO; CHICAGO—POLITICS AND GOVERNMENT; SEGREGATION—CHICAGO

CHICAGO SYMPHONY ORCHESTRA

Solti, Sir Georg. Chicago should erect a statue to me for what I have done. (Chicago 26:152 Dec 77)

CHICAGO—DESCRIPTION

Bellow, Saul. By the time the latest ideas reach Chicago, they're worn thin and easy to see through. (Time 119:77 Jan 18, 82)

CHICAGO—POLICE

Daley, Richard J. The police are not here to create disorder. They are here to preserve disorder (commenting during the 1968

Democratic Convention in Chicago). (Time 108:46 Jan 3, 77)

CHICAGO—POLITICS AND GOVERNMENT

Algren, Nelson. In what other city can you be so sure a judge will keep his word for five hundred dollars (about Chicago)? (New York Times 138:9 Jan 12, 89)

Anonymous. Get behind a judge on Monday in case you find yourself in front of him on Tuesday (about Chicago). (Los Angeles Times 97:1 Part 1 Nov 29, 78)

Bauler, (Paddy). Chicago ain't ready for reform yet. (Harper's Weekly 3168:8 Aug 23, 76)

Royko, Mike. The motto of the (Chicago) City Council is: never do today what somebody else can do today or tomorrow. (Chicago Sun-Times 32:2 Nov 26, 78)

CHICAGO—SOCIAL LIFE AND CUSTOMS—PROHIBITION

Capone, Alphonse. When I sell liquor, it's called bootlegging; when my patrons serve it on silver trays on Lake Shore Drive, it's called hospitality. (Aspen 3:43 Spring 77)

CHILDBIRTH

Diana, Princess of Wales. If men had to have babies, they would have only one each. (Life 8:102 Jan 85)

CHILDREN

Geisel, Theodor. Adults are obsolete children and the hell with them. (Time 113:93 May 7, 79)

Greenberg, David. An oldtimer is someone who can remember when a naughty child was taken to the woodshed instead of to a psychiatrist. (American Opinion 18:29 Nov 75)

Greer, Germaine. It's sheer myth that feminists are anti-child—we're the only people who're going to give children a better deal. (People Weekly 5:72 Jan 26, 76)

Viva. Your kids always seem to obtain, somehow, what you could never afford to buy for yourself. (Village Voice 29:33 July 24, 84)

CHILDREN—CLOTHING AND DRESS

Godart, Suzanne. Keep a girl in jeans from 4 to 14, and you'll wind up with a Butch on your hands. (W 9:8 Jan 18, 80)

CHILDREN—GROWTH AND DEVELOPMENT

Jung, Carl Gustav. Nothing has a stronger influence on their children than the unlived lives of the parents. (Boston 70:97 June 78)

CHILDREN—SEXUAL BEHAVIOR

Tomlin, Lily. I worry about kids today. Because of the sexual revolution they're going to grow up and never know what dirty means. (Time 109:71 Mar 28, 77)

CHILE—POLITICS AND GOVERNMENT

Pinochet, Augusto. When people don't listen to words, they'll listen to deeds. (The Times 8126:10 Mar 23, 80)

CHINA (PEOPLE'S REPUBLIC)

Aiken, George. I don't know how you go about containing an idea. I also don't know how you go about containing 700 million people. (Kansas City Times 117:A-24 Nov 22, 84)

Mao, Tse-Tung. Revolution is a drama of passion. We did not win the People over by appealing to reason but by developing hope, trust, fraternity. (Time 108:41 Sept 20, 76)

CHINA (PEOPLE'S REPUBLIC)— DESCRIPTION

Mao, Tse-Tung. Let a hundred schools of thought contend. Let a hundred flowers blossom (in 1956-57). (New York Times 128:1 Section 4 Dec 3, 78)

CHINA (PEOPLE'S REPUBLIC)— HISTORY see also **MAO, TSE-TUNG**

CHINA (PEOPLE'S REPUBLIC)— MILITARY POLICY

Mao, Tse-Tung. The most important thing is to be strong. With strength, one can conquer others, and to conquer others gives one virtue. (Time 108:41 Sept 20, 76)

CHINA (PEOPLE'S REPUBLIC)— POLITICS AND GOVERNMENT

Chinoy, Mike. China is a place where what was right yesterday is wrong today. (Chicago Tribune 183:24 Section 13 July 2, 89)

Deng Xiaoping. In the 1960's and 1970's there were many student movements and turmoils in the United States. Did they have any other recourse but to mobilize police and troops, arrest people and shed blood. (Newsweek 114:15 July 3, 89)

Fang Lizhi. China's hope at present lies in the fact that more and more people have broken free from blind faith in the leadership (1989). (Newsweek 113:27 June 26, 89)

Fang Lizhi. It (Marxism) is a thing of the past...and like a worn-out dress it should be discarded. (Fame 1:50 Mar 90)

Mao, Tse-Tung. Once all struggle is grasped, miracles are possible. (New York Times 128:1 Section 4 Dec 3, 78)

Teng, Hsiao-Ping. If the masses feel some anger, we must let them express it. (The Observer 9771:14 Dec 3, 78)

CHINA (PEOPLE'S REPUBLIC)— POLITICS AND GOVERNMENT see also **MAO, TSE-TUNG**

CHOREOGRAPHY
Feld, Eliot. Each time I make a dance, it's like being a virgin. (People Weekly 11:45 May 14, 79)

CHOREOGRAPHY see also BALANCHINE, GEORGE

CHRISTIANITY
Bakker, Tammy. You don't have to be dowdy to be a Christian. (Newsweek 109:69 June 8, 87)

Falwell, Jerry. Christians, like slaves and soldiers, ask no questions. (Penthouse 13:65 Dec 81)

CHRISTIANS
Falwell, Jerry. You can't be a good Christian and a liberal at the same time. (Oklahoma Observer 21:12 Jan 25, 89)

CHRISTIE, AGATHA
Christie, Agatha. If I could write like Elizabeth Bowen, Muriel Spark or Graham Greene, I should jump to high heaven with delight, but I know that I can't. (Time 110:127-32 Nov 28, 77)

CHUNG, CONNIE
Povich, Maury. We love being married, but we're not to sure about living together (about Connie Chung). (US 3:17 Sept 22, 86)

CHURCH AND BELIEF
Sherrill, Henry Knox. Far too many people in the church have very great convictions about very small things. (Newsweek 95:93 May 26, 80)

CHURCH AND RACE PROBLEMS
Carter, James Earl. I can't resign from the human race because there's discrimination, and I don't intend to resign from my own church because there's discrimination. (Time 108:22 Nov 22, 76)

CHURCH AND STATE
Carter, James Earl. I think the government ought to stay out of the prayer business... (New York Times 128:2 April 8, 79)

CHURCH ATTENDANCE—SEGREGATION
Young, Andrew. Eleven o'clock Sunday morning is still the most segregated hour of the week, and I don't know that anybody can be self-righteous about church integration. (Issues and Answers 2 Nov 14, 76)

CHURCHES
Gill, Brendan. God is thought to be housed better than the rest of us, and He usually is. (Chicago 36:26 July 87)

CHURCHES—DESEGREGATION
Criswell, W. A. I think it is better for the colored to go to their churches and for us to go to ours (1956). (Texas Monthly 12:166 Oct 84)

CIGARS
Freud, Sigmund. My cigar is not a symbol. It is only a cigar. (Washingtonian 12:112 April 77)

CITIES AND TOWNS
Seidenbaum, Art. A city worrying about image enhancement is like a man considering a wig; each faces the world with a shining inferiority complex. (Wall Street Journal 56:14 June 25, 76)

CIVIL DISOBEDIENCE
Berrigan, Daniel. When we get locked up now, there's a sigh of ennui (on the declining state of civil disobedience (1978)). (Time 111:67 Mar 20, 78)

CIVIL LIBERTY see LIBERTY

CIVIL RIGHTS
Carter, James Earl. No poor, rural, weak, or black person should ever have to bear the additional burden of being deprived of the opportunity of an education, a job, or simple justice. (New York 9:57 July 19, 76)

Carter, James Earl. The American people and our government will continue our firm commitment to promote respect for human rights not only in our own country but also abroad (to Andrei Sakharov). (Newsweek 89:17 Feb 28, 77)

Garvey, Ed. When you talk about civil liberties in professional sports, it's like talking about virtue in a whorehouse. (Village Voice 20:37 Dec 8, 75)

Moynihan, Daniel Patrick. When a person goes to a country and finds their newspapers filled with nothing but good news, he can bet there are good men in jail. (University Daily Kansan 87:4 Feb 16, 77)

Neas, Ralph. There was more damage done to civil rights statutes in the last 2 1/2 weeks than in the last 2 1/2 decades (1989). (Chicago Tribune 181:3 Section 3 July 1, 89)

Norris, Clarence (the sole surviving Scottsboro Boy). The lesson to Black people, to my children, to everybody, is that you should always fight for your rights even if it costs you your life. Stand up for your rights, even if it kills you (commenting on his struggle to clear his name upon being pardoned by the state of Alabama). (New York Times 126:1 Oct 26, 76)

Sakharov, Andrei Dmitrievich. I hope this prize is not only an acknowledgement of my personal merits, but of the merits of all those who fight for human rights (commenting on his Nobel Peace Prize). (People Weekly 4:26 Oct 27, 75)

Scranton, William W. The only universality

that one can honestly associate with the Universal Declaration of Human Rights is universal lip service. (New York Times 126:10 Nov 25, 76)

CIVIL RIGHTS see also UNITED STATES—FOREIGN POLICY—CIVIL RIGHTS; UNIVERSAL DECLARATION OF HUMAN RIGHTS

CIVIL RIGHTS—PARAGUAY

Stroessner, Alfredo. Human rights is a Trojan horse of international Communism. (Mother Jones 3:8 June 78)

CIVIL RIGHTS—ZIMBABWE

Kaunda, Kenneth. An African in Zimbabwe does not need a communist to tell him that he is not free (1977). (To The Point International 4:10 June 20, 77)

Nkomo, Joshua. There's no such thing to me as whites. (The Observer 9760:13 Sept 17, 78)

CIVILIZATION

Dubos, Rene. Each civilization has its own kind of pestilence and controls it only by reforming itself. (Skeptic 19:29 May 77)

Freud, Sigmund. The first human who hurled a curse instead of a weapon against his adversary was the founder of civilization. (Rocky Mountain News 244:58 Dec 22, 79)

Rogers, Will. Any man who thinks civilization has advanced is an egoist. (Time 104:92 Oct 7, 74)

CIVILIZATION AND LEISURE

Toynbee, Arnold. To be able to fill leisure intelligently is the last product of civilization. (Chicago Tribune 67:1 Section 5 Mar 8, 78)

CLAY, ANDREW DICE

Clay, Andrew Dice. I'm just filthy. And the filthier I am, the funnier it is. (Vanity Fair 53:148 June 90)

CLERGY

Graham, Billy. The pressures of being a well-known clergyman are unbelievable, and I'd like to escape to heaven if I could. (Chicago Tribune Magazine 32 Nov 6, 77)

Olivier, Laurence. Probably every great actor in history was the son of a clergyman. (Chicago Tribune 201:20 July 20, 79)

CLERGY see also GRAHAM, BILLY

CLOTHING AND DRESS

Voznesensky, Andrei. When Man put on clothes for the first time, he challenged the Lord and became His equal. (Vogue 168:193 Feb 78)

CLOTHING AND DRESS—WOMEN

Rykiel, Sonia. Every woman must create her own ambience; it is not I or Yves St. Laurent but the woman who has to create herself and be a unique person. (Time 110:54 Nov 7, 77)

Vreeland, Diana. Elegance is innate...it has nothing to do with being well dressed. (Time 134:70 Sept 4, 89)

CLOTHING INDUSTRY

Vollbracht, Michaele. If you have to talk about fashion, then you are not in it. (Village Voice 22:63 Mar 14, 77)

CLUBS

Marx, Groucho. I wouldn't belong to any club that would have me for a member. (New York Times 126:40 Aug 21, 77)

COACHES (ATHLETICS) see also ROCKNE, KNUTE

COCA, IMOGENE

Coca, Imogene. I've never figured out why we work so well together, except that we both laugh at exactly the same time. (about herself and Sid Caesar). (Time 110:98 Sept 19, 77)

COCA-COLA COMPANY

Sharpe, Cornelia. I think sex is the greatest thing since Coca-Cola. (Viva 2:21 Sept 75)

COCAINE

Bankhead, Tallulah. Cocaine isn't habit-forming. I should know—I've been using it for years. (Playboy 26:26 Oct 79)

Washton, Arnold M. Taking cocaine is dropping an atomic bomb on your brain. (Topeka Capital-Journal Sportsplus 2 July 8, 86)

COCAINE see also CRACK (COCAINE)

COFFEE

Rappolt, Richard T. It's easier to get people off of heroin than coffee. (Rolling Stone 234:39 Mar 10, 77)

COHEN, MICKEY

Cohen, Mickey. I never killed a man that didn't deserve it. (Playboy 31:22 May 84)

COLBERT, CLAUDETTE

Colbert, Claudette. I'd give my soul for a Tootsie Roll. (Vanity Fair 49:60 Feb 86)

COLBY, WILLIAM EGAN

Colby, William Egan. I have definitional problems with the word violence. I don't know what the word violence means. (Rolling Stone 196:32 Sept 25, 75)

COLD (DISEASE)

McKuen, Rod. The best remedy for a cold is to go to bed with a good book, or a friend who's read one. (Viva 4:26 Feb 77)

COLLECTORS AND COLLECTING

Taylor, Francis H. The trick is to buy the right thing at the wrong time (about collecting). (Philadelphia 75:153 Sept 84)

COLLEGE EDUCATION

Mankiewicz, Frank Fabian. The higher the tuition, the fewer days they spend in school. (Washingtonian 14:154 Oct 31, 78)

COLLEGE EDUCATION, VALUE OF

Duggan, B. To every Ph.D. there is an equal and opposite Ph.D. (Washingtonian 14:153 Nov 78)

King, Billie Jean. Don't go to college if you want to make your living in sports. (New York Times 127:5 Section 5 Mar 26, 78)

Kohler, Jerry. I'd just as soon die in Vietnam as in the library. (Salina (Kansas) Journal 10 May 27, 76)

COLLEGE PROFESSORS AND INSTRUCTORS

Bressler, Marvin. There is no crisis to which academics will not respond with a seminar. (Washingtonian 15:140 Nov 79)

COLLEGES AND UNIVERSITIES

Dobie, J. Frank. The average Ph.D. thesis is nothing but a transference of bones from one graveyard to another. (Rocky Mountain News 37:70 May 29, 80)

Giamatti, A. Bartlett. The university must be a tributary to a larger society, not a sanctuary from it. (Time 112:89 Oct 2, 78)

James, Clive. For the lost soul, the university is the modern monastery. (The New Yorker 62:95 Dec 29, 86)

Kerr, Clark. Have plenty of football for the alumni, sex for the students, and parking for the faculty. (Washingtonian 15:142 Oct 31, 79)

Kowal, Charles (American astronomer). I enjoy learning things, but a university is the last place in the world to learn anything. (Time 106:75 Oct 27, 75)

Rhodes, Frank H. T. The great universities are those in which people grow by contact with others in ever-widening circles. (Time 110:51 Nov 14, 77)

Trachtenberg, Stephen. The truth is that 80 percent of research is done by 20 percent of professors who are at 10 percent of our universities. (Chicago Tribune 110:10 April 20, 87)

COLLEGES AND UNIVERSITIES— CHEATING (EDUCATION)

Suskind, Sigmund. Cheating (in colleges) is not endemic, it's epidemic. (Time 107:29 June 7, 76)

COLSON, CHARLES WENDELL

Colson, Charles Wendell. I would do anything that Richard Nixon asks me to do. (Time 103:13 Mar 11, 74)

COMEDIANS

Berle, Milton. The best way a new comic can start is to have funny bones. (People Weekly 9:96 April 3, 78)

Tati, Jacques. Comedians speak with their legs. (Times Literary Supplement 3969:460 April 28, 78)

COMEDIANS see also ALLEN, WOODY; BENNY, JACK; BURNS, GEORGE; CAESAR, SID; CLAY,

ANDREW DICE; COCA, IMOGENE; DURANTE, JIMMY; HOPE, BOB; MARX, GROUCHO; SAHL, MORT

COMEDY

Allen, Woody. Drama stays with people more, like meat and potatoes, while comedy is a dessert, like meringue. (Newsweek 85:87B June 23, 75)

Feldman, Marty. Well, any melodrama inverted is good material for a comedy. (Chicago Tribune 207:7 July 26, 77)

COMICS (BOOKS, STRIPS, ETC.)

Pekar, Harvey. A person who can't relate to comic books is like somebody who can't relate to opera. They're both culturally deprived. (Cleveland 5:153 July 76)

COMMERCIAL PRODUCTS

Block, Herbert L. If it's good, they'll stop making it. (Time 113:25 Feb 26, 79)

COMMITTEES

Emerson, William A., Jr. A foolish consistency is the hobgoblin of small committees. (Wilson Library Bulletin 52:534 Mar 78)

Kettering, Charles. If you want to kill any idea in the world today, get a committee working on it. (Omni 4:41 April 82)

COMMON SENSE

Stein, Gertrude. Everybody gets so much information all day long that they lose their common sense. (Chicago Tribune 176:2 Section 2 June 25, 78)

COMMUNICATION

Brown, Edmund Gerald, Jr. Communications erodes provincialism. (Esquire 89:64 Jan 31, 78)

Johnson, Lyndon Baines. The most important thing a man has to tell you is what he is not telling you. (Time 114:13 Aug 20, 79)

Rockwell, Geo. Making something perfectly clear only confuses everybody. (Down East 22:108 Jan 76)

COMMUNISM

Aiken, George. I don't know how you go about containing an idea. I also don't know how you go about containing 700 million people. (Kansas City Times 117:A-24 Nov 22, 84)

Aron, Raymond. Marxism is the opium of the intellectuals. (Time 114:41 July 9, 79)

Carter, James Earl. We are now free of that inordinate fear of Communism which once led us to embrace any dictator who joined us in our fear. (Time 107:9 June 6, 77)

Chaplin, Charles Spencer. My prodigious sin was and still is, being a nonconformist. Although I am not a Communist, I refused to fall in line by hating them. (Guardian Weekly 118:5 Jan 1, 78)

Falwell, Jerry. Not only should we register them (Communists), but we should stamp it on their foreheads and send them back to Russia. This is a free country. (Washington Post 275:B3 Sept 6, 77)

Kissinger, Henry Alfred. No communist country has solved the problem of succession. (Time 113:59 Mar 12, 79)

Nixon, Richard Milhous. The ideological battle is won. You can't sell the idea that Marxism works. It doesn't. (Kansas City Star 108:21A Dec 10, 87)

Ravel, Jean-Francois. Stalinism is the essence of Communism. (Time 107:32 Feb 2, 76)

Reagan, Ronald. The West won't contain communism; it will transcend communism. (Time 119:39 Jan 4, 82)

Teng, Hsiao-Ping. It doesn't matter whether you climb Mount Everest by its North slope or its South slope as long as you get to the top. (Newsweek 93:36 Feb 5, 79)

COMMUNISM—AFRICA

Kaunda, Kenneth. An African in Zimbabwe does not need a communist to tell him that he is not free (1977). (To The Point International 4:10 June 20, 77)

COMMUNISM—CHINA (PEOPLE'S REPUBLIC)

Mao, Tse-Tung. Every Communist must grasp the truth: political power grown out of the barrel of a gun. Our principle is that the party commands the gun and the gun must never be allowed to command the party. (Newsweek 88:40 Sept 20, 76)

COMMUNISM—EUROPE

Ford, Gerald Rudolph. Eurocommunism is not, as their propagandists say, Communism with a human face. It is Stalinism in a mask and tyranny in disguise. (New York Times 127:2 Oct 30, 77)

COMMUNISM—RELATIONS— JOURNALISTS

Munro, Ross H. Communist countries never expel correspondents for telling lies. (New York Times 127:11 Nov 27, 77)

COMMUNISM—RUSSIA

Solzhenitsyn, Aleksandr Isaevich. For us in Russia Communism is a dead dog, while for many people in the West it is still a living lion. (The Observer 9782:10 Mar 18, 79)

COMPASSION

Humphrey, Hubert Horatio. Life was not meant to be endured, but enjoyed. (New Times 10:51 Feb 6, 78)

Rockefeller, Nelson Aldrich. One thing I can't stand is a goddamned bleeding heart. (American Spectator 15:22 Oct 82)

COMPETENCE

Boyle, Charles. If not controlled, work will flow to the competent man until he submerges. (Time 113:25 Feb 26, 79)

COMPETITION

Sarnoff, David. Competition brings out the best in products and the worst in people. (Dun's Business Month 127:51 Feb 86)

COMPOSERS

Stravinsky, Igor Fedorovich. A good composer does not imitate; he steals. (Whole Earth Review 57:108 Winter 87)

COMPOSERS, AMERICAN see also
PORTER, COLE; RODGERS, RICHARD; ROREM, NED; SCHUMAN, WILLIAM

COMPROMISE

Battista, O. A. The fellow who says he'll meet you halfway usually thinks he's standing on the dividing line. (Washingtonian 15:140 Nov 79)

COMPUTER INDUSTRY

Brand, Stewart. While we were out in the streets marching, the real revolutionaries were in the computer labs. (Inc 7:53 July 85)

COMPUTERS

Drucker, Peter F. The main impact of the computer has been the provision of unlimited jobs for clerks. (New York Times 125:15 Section 3 May 16, 76)

Weizenbaum, Joseph. A computer will do what you tell it to do, but that may be much different from what you had in mind. (Time 111:45 Feb 20, 78)

COMPUTERS—SOCIAL ASPECTS

Goodfellow, Geoff. The floppy disk is the punch card of the Eighties. (Popular Computing 4:28 Feb 28, 85)

CONCEIT

Wonder, Stevie. How can you even think of being conceited—with the universe as large as it is? (Penthouse 7:131 Feb 76)

CONCENTRATION CAMPS—POLAND see
also AUSCHWITZ CONCENTRATION CAMP

CONDON, RICHARD

Condon, Richard. I'm a man of the marketplace as well as an artist. I am a pawnbroker of myth. (New York Times Magazine 45 Sept 2, 79)

CONDUCT OF LIFE

Adler, Alfred. The chief danger in life is that you may take too many precautions. (Kansas City Times 109:14C Jan 24, 77)

Anderson, John B. You cannot become weary in well-doing. (Sierra Club Bulletin 65:23 May/June 80)

Anderson, Laurie. You don't have to be a surrealist to think the world is strange. (Playboy 32:141 April 85)

Baar, James A. Regardless of what you say or do, some of the people will hate you all of the time. (Wharton Magazine 2:16 Fall 77)

Bacon, Francis. I believe you are born, then you die. You do what you can in between the two. (Elle 4:210 Oct 88)

Bankhead, Tallulah. Here's a rule I recommend: Never practice two vices at once. (Cosmopolitan 196:332 Oct 83)

Burroughs, William S. What you want to do is eventually what you will do anyway. Sooner or later. (Village Voice 22:44 May 16, 77)

Burstyn, Ellen. What a lovely surprise to finally discover how unlonely being alone can be. (Cosmopolitan 196:332 Oct 83)

Callaghan, James. I believe all good people should be in bed by 11 o'clock at night. (The Observer 9775:9 Dec 31, 78)

Cameron, John. When your opponent is down, kick him. (Town & Country 133:140 May 79)

Capone, Alphonse. You can get much further with a kind word and a gun than you can with a kind word alone. (Playboy 31:22 May 84)

Carlson, Phil. Don't ever try to eat where they don't want to feed you. (Washingtonian 15:140 Oct 31, 79)

Castro, Fidel. My motto for good health is simple: eat little, sleep little and exercise a lot. (Newsweek 103:51 Jan 16, 84)

Churchill, Sir Winston. Don't argue the difficulties. They argue for themselves. (Christian Science Monitor 69:15 June 27, 77)

Ciardi, John. Early to bed and early to rise probably indicates unskilled labor. (Kansas City Star 97:2D Feb 20, 77)

Cole, Edward N. Kick the hell out of the status quo. (Time 109:87 May 16, 77)

Day, Dorothy. The best thing to do with the best things in life is to give them up. (Life Special Report American Women 39 1976)

Dillinger, John. Never trust an automatic pistol or a D.A.'s deal. (Playboy 31:22 May 84)

Faulkner, William. Living is a process of getting ready to be dead for a long time. (Parade 18 Sept 13, 81)

Fields, W. C. There comes a time in the affairs of men when you must take the bull by the tail and face the situation. (San Francisco Chronicle This World 1978:40 Jan 29, 78)

Flynt, Larry. There's only one commandment: do unto others as you would have them do unto you—but do it first. (Vanity Fair 47:47 Jan 31, 84)

Ford, Henry, II. Never complain, never explain. (New York Times 128:19 Mar 26, 79)

Fuentes, Carlos. There are two things one never should do after fifty: change wives and give interviews. (Nuestro 2:36 Nov 78)

Gomez, Lefty. If you don't throw it, they can't hit it. (Washingtonian 15:141 Nov 79)

Gossage, Howard. The only fit work for an adult is to save the world. (California 13:13 May 88)

Harris, Sydney J. The art of living consists in knowing which impulses to obey and which must be made to obey. (Kansas City Times 109:28 Jan 4, 77)

Hemingway, Ernest. The first and final thing you have to do in this world is to last in it and not be smashed by it. (Kansas City Times 109:1A Feb 3, 77)

Humphrey, Hubert Horatio. Oh, my friend, it isn't what they take away from you that counts—it's what you do with what you have left. (Newsweek 89:43 July 25, 77)

Johnson, Lyndon Baines. Cast your bread upon the waters and the sharks'll eat it. (D Magazine 10:7 Jan 83)

Johnson, Lyndon Baines. If you don't blow your horn, somebody will steal it. (TV Guide 25:A4 Dec 24, 78)

Jong, Erica. The trouble is, if you don't risk anything, you risk even more. (Cosmopolitan 196:332 Oct 83)

Kaiser, Henry J. When your work speaks for itself, don't interrupt. (Washingtonian 23:149 Dec 87)

Kesey, Ken. Always stay in your own movie. (New Times 9:68 Aug 19, 77)

Khrushchev, Nikita Sergeevich. Life is short. Live it up. (Viva 4:25 July 77)

King, Martin Luther, Sr. Nothing that a man does takes him lower than when he allows himself to fall so far as to hate anyone. (Newsweek 96:92 Sept 15, 80)

Knowles, John H. A sense of humor is the prelude to faith and laughter is the beginning of prayer. (New York Times 128:A22 Mar 7, 79)

Korda, Michael. An ounce of hypocrisy is worth a pound of ambition. (Playboy 28:97 Sept 81)

Land, Edwin. Anything worth doing is worth doing to excess. (Time 107:66 May 9, 77)

Landers, Ann. If nobody minds, it doesn't matter. (Washingtonian 23:150 Dec 87)

Legman, Gershon. Make love, not war. (Village Voice 29:43 May 1, 84)

Lewi, Morris. I never wasted time resisting temptation. (Kansas City Star 108:5C Oct 7, 87)

Lewis, Jerry. Only the man who does

nothing makes no mistakes. (Boston 69:74 Sept 77)

Liebling, A. J. The people who have something to say don't talk; the others insist on talking. (Washingtonian 15:142 Nov 79)

Lollobrigida, Gina. Whatever we learn, we learn too late. (Chicago Tribune Magazine 2 July 5, 87)

Longworth, Alice Roosevelt. Fill what's empty. Empty what's full. And scratch where it itches. (Washingtonian 15:142 Nov 79)

Loughrige, Alan Craig. The middle of the road is the best place to get run over. (Washingtonian 15:142 Nov 79)

Louis, Joe. You can run, but you can't hide. (Mother Jones 3:65 Dec 77)

Luce, Clare Boothe (attributed by Paul Dickson). No good deed goes unpunished. (Playboy 25:22 May 78)

Mailer, Norman. As many people die from an excess of timidity as from bravery. (New York 16:32 Mar 28, 83)

Mandel, Morris. Always put off until tomorrow what you shouldn't do at all. (Reader's Digest 106:145 April 75)

Mansfield, Mike. The crisis you have to worry about most is the one you don't see coming. (US News & World Report 88:42 Oct 31, 77)

Meier, Hans. What you suffer does not defile you; what you do does. (Chicago Tribune 81:2 Section 5 Mar 22, 89)

Mix, Tom (attributed by Heywood Hale Broun). Straight shooters always win. (Travel & Leisure 11:138 Feb 80)

Montagu, Ashley. The idea is to die young as late as possible. (Town & Country 133:141 May 79)

Morrow, Dwight. One of the troubles is that we judge ourselves by our motives and others by their actions. (Christian Science Monitor 70:47 Dec 7, 77)

Moses, Robert. If the end doesn't justify the means, what does? (New York Times 130:11 July 30, 81)

Moses, Robert. The important thing is to get things done. (New York Times 130:11 July 30, 81)

Nearing, Scott. Do the thing you believe in. Do it with all your might. (Down East 30:171 Aug 83)

Neizvestny, Ernst. A man should stand on his own two feet, even if he has only one leg. (New York Times 128:C19 Dec 1, 78)

Peter, Laurence J. If you don't know where you are going, you will probably end up somewhere else. (San Francisco Chronicle This World 1978:40 Jan 29, 78)

Quin, Percy Edwards. A man must

sometimes rise above principle. (Washingtonian 15:143 Nov 79)

Ram Dass. If I'm saving the whale, why am I eating tuna fish? (New Times 11:39 Sept 4, 78)

Rockefeller, David. Basically I operate on the principle that you should never do something for yourself that you can get someone else to do for you. (Penthouse 12:64 Oct 80)

Roosevelt, Eleanor. Do what you feel in your heart to be right, for you will be criticized anyway. (Kansas City Times 115:A-1 Jan 13, 83)

Roosevelt, Franklin Delano. If you treat people right they will treat you right—90 percent of the time. (Kansas City Times 109:14C Jan 14, 77)

Roosevelt, Franklin Delano. When you get to the end of your rope, tie a knot and hang on. (Kansas City Star 97:2F June 5, 77)

Rumsfeld, Donald. If you try to please everybody, somebody is not going to like it. (Washingtonian 12:107 Feb 77)

Samples, Alvin (Junior). I'd rather be wise and act dumb than be dumb and act wise. (Lawrence (Kansas) Journal-World 125:15 Nov 14, 83)

Sikinger, Maximilian. It's better to be a hungry coyote than to be a satisfied dog. (Village Voice 22:32 May 9, 77)

Skinner, B. F. You must find or create a world in which you can act in a sensible way. (Kansas City Star 104:11A Oct 11, 83)

Smeal, Eleanor. I feel it is important to march to your own drummer. (Washington Post National Weekly Edition 3:7 Dec 9, 85)

Sokolsky, Leon. Those who have never made a mistake work for those who have dared to. (Kansas City Star 106:5A Dec 30, 85)

Stein, Gertrude. Considering how dangerous everything is, nothing is really frightening. (Human Behavior 7:17 May 78)

Stein, Gertrude. I do want to get rich, but I never want to do what there is to do to get rich. (Cosmopolitan 196:332 Oct 83)

Stewart, Potter. It's better to go too soon than to stay too long. (Time 127:57 Dec 30, 85)

Strauss, Robert S. You know, it's awfully easy to tell people to go to hell. But it's another thing to get them there. (Newsweek 94:47 July 16, 79)

Tanner, Jack. A person without character always does what is right. (Challenge 19:5 Mar/April 76)

Tinkerbelle. You don't need much money when the best things in life are handouts. (Vanity Fair 50:85 Jan 87)

Vonnegut, Kurt. We are what we pretend to be so we must be careful what we pretend to be. (Miami/South Florida Magazine 38:68 Aug 84)

Weizman, Ezer. Anyone who says he is not emotional is not getting what he should out of life. (Time 112:115 Oct 30, 78)

Welles, Orson. Nobody gets justice—people get good luck or bad luck. (US 3:64 Sept 23, 85)

West, Mae. He who hesitates is last. (Chicago Tribune 176:2 Section 2 June 25, 78)

West, Mae. To err is human—but it feels divine. (Viva 4:24 Jan 77)

West, Mae. Too much of a good thing can be wonderful. (Human Behavior 7:17 May 78)

Whitlock, Ralph. Good beomes ill when pushed to excess. (Manchester Guardian Weekly 138:29 May 1, 88)

Wright, Stephen. Anywhere's in walking distance is you've got the time. (Outside 10:13 Dec 85)

CONDUCT OF LIFE see also MUSICIANS— CONDUCT OF LIFE; NIXON, RICHARD MILHOUS— CONDUCT OF LIFE

CONDUCTORS (MUSIC) see also ROSTROPOVICH, MSTISLAV; STOKOWSKI, LEOPOLD; TOSCANINI, ARTURO

CONFLICT OF GENERATIONS

Brown, Sam. Never trust anybody over 30. (Chicago Sun-Times 31:26 June 4, 78)

CONFLICT OF INTEREST

Nossiter, Bernard D. There are no conflicts of interest when bankers' pockets are to be lined. (The Nation 251:441 Oct 22, 90)

CONFORMITY

Rayburn, Sam. If you want to get along, go along. (Washingtonian 14:155 Nov 78)

CONGRESSMEN

Abourezk, James. When voting on the confirmation of a Presidential appointment, it's always safer to vote against the son of a bitch, because if he's confirmed, it won't be long before he proves how wise you were. (Playboy 26:106 Mar 79)

Grace, J. Peter. Congressmen have two goals, to be elected and to be re-elected. (Texas Observer 77:23 Sept 27, 85)

CONNALLY, JOHN BOWDEN

Carpenter, Elizabeth. If John Connally had been around at the Alamo, he would have organized Texans for Santa Anna. (Texas Monthly 4:10 Sept 76)

Connally, John Bowden. There's a little larceny in the hearts of all of us. (New York 12:8 July 9, 79)

Crane, Philip. If you asked central casting in Hollywood for somebody to play the role

of President, they'd send you John Connally. (US News & World Report 86:29 July 2, 79)

Doty, William R. Connally will always be remembered for his bright Nixon button and his weakness for milk shakes. (Texas Monthly 3:8 Aug 75)

Kirbo, Charles. Once he (John Connally) gets across that Texas line—he's not much. (Newsweek 88:25 Aug 2, 76)

Simon, Paul. If money alone could do the trick, John Connally would be president. (Newsweek 111:15 Mar 14, 88)

CONNOLLY, CYRIL

Connolly, Cyril. Everything is a dangerous drug to me except reality, which is unendurable. (Chicago Tribune Magazine 6 Aug 19, 84)

CONROY, JACK

Conroy, Jack. I've never given a bad review. Some are more favorable than others, but I have never given a bad one. (Kansas City Star 110:A-18 Mar 3, 90)

CONSERVATION

Fonda, Jane. Conservation is the religion of the future. (Life 2:170 Dec 79)

CONSERVATION ASSOCIATIONS

Hodel, Donald. (Environmentalism is) a crusade to stop all development in this country. (Wall Street Journal 56:1 Dec 17, 75)

CONSERVATION OF RESOURCES

Aspinall, Wayne. The conservation extremists demand too much of our public land for their own private use. (American Opinion 18:150 July/Aug 75)

Laird, Melvin. Conservation alone is a slow walk down a dead-end street. (Time 110:62 Oct 10, 77)

McCormack, Mike. One man's conservation is all too frequently another man's unemployment. (Time 110:27 Dec 12, 77)

Reagan, Ronald. Once you've seen one redwood, you've seen them all. (New York Times Magazine 71 July 4, 76)

CONSERVATISM

Chambers, Whittaker (attributed by Ralph de Toledano). Joe McCarthy's a rascal, but he's our rascal. (Chicago Tribune 22:11 Section 5 Jan 22, 86)

Kristol, Irving. A neoconservative is a liberal mugged by reality. (Washington Post National Weekly Edition 2:12 Oct 21, 85)

Moore, Jonathan. We're not getting as conservative as much as we are becoming less liberal (1978). (US News & World Report 84:24 Jan 23, 78)

Nixon, Richard Milhous. The trouble with most conservatives is that those who have brains lack guts and those who have guts lack brains. (Village Voice 29:19

April 17, 84)
Thatcher, Margaret Hilda. We (Conservatives) believe that you get a responsible society when you get responsible individuals. (New York Times Magazine 36 April 29, 79)
Viguerie, Richard. We've already taken control of the conservative movement. And conservatives have taken control of the Republican Party. The remaining thing is to see if we can take control of the country. (Oklahoma Observer 21:12 Jan 25, 89)

CONSUMERS
Kahn, J. Kesner. Free market competition, freely advertised, is consumerism at its best. (American Opinion 18:18 June 75)
Ogilvey, David. The consumer is not a moron. She is your wife. (Viva 4:26 Aug 77)

CONSUMPTION (ECONOMICS)
Dasmann, Raymond F. We are hooked like junkies, dependent on the drug of wasteful consumption. (New York Times 126:A18 Dec 1, 76)
Kesey, Ken. Take what you can use and let the rest go by. (Kansas City Times 119:A-1 Sept 19, 86)

CONTRACTS
Goldwyn, Samuel. A verbal contract isn't worth the paper it's written on. (Washingtonian 14:154 Nov 78)
Minow, Newton. There is no contract you can't get out of for money. (Wilson Library Bulletin 53:507 Mar 79)

CONVERSATION
Frost, Robert. Half the world is composed of people who have something to say and can't, and the other half who have nothing to say and keep on saying it. (Kansas City Star 97:38 July 14, 77)
Hitchcock, Alfred Joseph. Conversation is the enemy of good wine and food. (Time 112:99 Oct 9, 78)

COOKE, ALISTAIR
Cooke, Alistair. I seem to be perceived in America as a benign old English gentleman, and in England as an enlightened American. (Time 122:79 Dec 5, 83)

COOKERY
Child, Julia. I just hate health food. (San Francisco 25:32 Aug 83)
Outhier, Louis. You don't get fat from a good kitchen—only from a bad one. (W 4:11 Nov 28, 75)

COOKERY see also NOUVELLE CUISINE
COOKERY, CAJUN
Prudhomme, Paul. When the taste changes with every bite and the last bite is as good as the first, that's Cajun. (Cook's Magazine 20:57 June 30, 85)

COOKERY—UNITED STATES
Wolfert, Paula. There's a culinary renaissance in America today. The trouble is, we have no Michelangelos. (Metropolitan Home 18:92 June 86)

COOPER, GARY
Bow, Clara. He was hung like a horse, and he could go all night (about Gary Cooper). (Cosmopolitan 197:190 Mar 84)

COPYRIGHT—UNITED STATES
Ringer, Barbara A. The basic human rights of individual authors throughout the world are being sacrificed more and more on the altar of the technological revolution. (American Legion Magazine 99:21 Dec 75)
Shields, Gerald R. It is obvious that the photocopying issue is to be decided soon and that the odds favor turning libraries into some sort of reprint warehouse for publisher's products. (Library Journal 100:2307 Dec 15, 75)

CORPORAL PUNISHMENT
Gauld, Joseph. The rod (physical discipline) is only wrong in the wrong hands. (Time 107:51 Aug 9, 76)

CORPORATIONS, INTERNATIONAL
Moynihan, Daniel Patrick. (The multinational corporation) is arguably the most creative international institution of the 20th century. (Time 106:62 July 14, 75)

CORPULENCE see OBESITY
COSELL, HOWARD
Cosell, Howard. I think I've made a difference in my phase of the broadcast industry, but I don't think I've impacted on the world in the manner of Franklin Roosevelt. (Life 8:72 Jan 85)

COSMOLOGY
Clarke, Arthur C. The time may come when men control the destinies of the stars. (Time 114:27 July 26, 79)

COST OF LIVING
Glenn, John. Our objective is to prevent the people of this country from getting economically raped (arguing against the decontrol of petroleum prices). (Time 106:61 Oct 13, 75)

COUNCIL ON FOREIGN RELATIONS
Lord, Winston. The Trilateral Commission doesn't secretly run the world. The Council on Foreign Relations does that. (W 7:9 Aug 4, 78)

COURAGE
Allen, Woody. In terms of human attributes, what really counts is courage. (Time 113:69 April 30, 79)

Boorstin, Daniel J. The courage we inherit from our Jeffersons and Lincolns and others is not the Solzhenitsyn courage of the true believer, but the courage to doubt. (Time 111:21 June 26, 78)
Gleason, Jackie. Vanity is an actor's courage. (Emmy 5:48 Jan 83)
McNulty, Franklin L. With adequate integrity, guts can be located. (Parade 4 May 27, 79)

COUSINS, NORMAN

Cousins, Norman. I am no pessimist. I doubt that any man knows enough to be a pessimist. (Saturday Review 5:12 April 15, 78)

COVERT AMERICAN MILITARY ASSISTANCE

Kissinger, Henry Alfred. Covert action should not be confused with missionary work. (In These Times 14:5 Oct 3, 90)

CRACK (COCAINE)

Thompson, Hunter S. Crack is ruining the drug culture. (Newsweek 116:17 Oct 8, 90)

CREATION

Quayle, Marilyn. I believe in creationism. I think the Bible is correct in that. (Chicago Tribune 15:8 Section 5 Jan 15, 89)
Tanner, Jack. When God created the world, He said it was good. That was His second mistake. (Challenge 19:5 Mar/April 76)

CREATION (LITERARY, ARTISTIC, ETC.)

Adderley, Julian (Cannonball). God smiles on certain individuals, and they get the privilege to have certain beautiful, artistic vibrations pass through them. (Time 106:56 Aug 18, 75)
Breslin, Jimmy. Don't trust a brilliant idea unless it survives the hangover. (Washingtonian 23:149 Dec 87)
Fitzgerald, F. Scott. Having once found the intensity of art, nothing else that can happen in life can ever again seem as important as the creative process. (Forbes 120:186 Oct 15, 77)

Hemingway, Ernest. Make a thing as true as possible, and it will live. (New York Times Book Review 30 July 23, 78)
Sexton, Anne. Creative people must not avoid the pain that they get dealt. (Time 110:124 Nov 28, 77)
Steinberg, Saul. The life of the creative man is led, directed and controlled by boredom. (Time 111:92 April 17, 78)

CREATION—STUDY AND TEACHING

Montagu, Ashley. Science has proof without any certainty. Creationists have certainty without any proof. (Time 118:61 Sept 21, 81)

CREDIT UNIONS

Patman, Wright (attributed by James T. Molloy). Next to the church, credit unions do more good for the people than any other institution. (Chicago Sun-Times 29:22 Mar 10, 76)

CRICHTON, MICHAEL

Crichton, Michael. I quit medicine as a service to my patients. (Chicago Tribune 175:1 Section 5 June 24, 87)

CRIME AND CRIMINALS

Bell, Griffin. I think we have too many crimes, and I definitely have the view that we have too many laws. (Time 108:16 Dec 27, 76)
Fonda, Jane. It is time to look at crime in the suites, not just in the streets. (Time 114:31 Oct 8, 79)
Gurley, George H., Jr. Crime is one of the country's few growth industries. (Kansas City Star 111:1C Oct 4, 90)
Harris, Sydney J. It is not criminals, but laws that are the worst enemy of Law. (Chicago Daily News 8 May 5, 77)
Hoover, John Edgar. The cure for crime is not the electric chair but the high chair. (Chicago Sun-Times 29:76 July 9, 76)
Johnson, Lyndon Baines. Killing, rioting, and looting are contrary to the best traditions of this country. (Texas Monthly 3:93 Dec 75)
Liddy, G. Gordon. Obviously crime pays, or there'd be no crime. (Newsweek 108:19 Nov 10, 86)
Meese, Edwin. You don't name many suspects who are innocent of a crime. (Texas Observer 79:10 Sept 11, 87)
Patterson, L. Ray. The concern of the public (about crime) is not so much for vindictive retribution, but for some retribution. (Time 112:54 Sept 18, 78)

CRIME AND CRIMINALS see also SUTTON, WILLIE; WOMEN CRIMINALS

CRIME AND CRIMINALS—RELATIONS— MENTAL HYGIENE

Szasz, Thomas. Just as (mental) illness is not a crime, so crime is not an illness. (TV Guide 28:32 May 17, 80)

CRIME AND CRIMINALS—UNITED STATES

Carlson, Norman A. Until the behavioral sciences can give us clues as to what motivates the criminal offender, we cannot assure rehabilitation. All we can do is offer offenders the opportunity to rehabilitate themselves. (Behavior Today 7:4 Jan 5, 76)
Davis, Edward Michael. America is on the verge of a crime wave like the world has never seen before. (Coronet 13:70 Nov 75)

CRIMINAL JUSTICE, ADMINISTRATION OF

Hatfield, Mark. If one argues that a prisoner deserves whatever he or she gets in prison, then one must also be prepared to argue that society deserves what it gets when the prisoner is eventually released. (USA Today 1:10A Jan 12, 83)

Meese, Edwin. We are literally going to have to put criminals in jail and throw away the key. (USA Today 1:8A June 15, 83)

Patterson, L. Ray. The concern of the public (about crime) is not so much for vindictive retribution, but for some retribution. (Time 112:54 Sept 18, 78)

CRIMINAL JUSTICE, ADMINISTRATION OF—ASPEN, COLORADO

Thompson, Hunter S. Today's pig is tomorrow's bacon. (Kansas City Star 110:A-6 May 23, 90)

CRISWELL, W. A.

Criswell, W. A. I was brought up to love God and hate the Methodists (1968). (Texas Monthly 12:166 Oct 84)

CRITICISM

Maugham, William Somerset. People ask you for criticism, but they only want praise. (Rocky Mountain News 141:44 Sept 10, 79)

Steinbeck, John (attributed by John Kenneth Galbraith). Unless the bastards have the courage to give you unqualified praise, I say ignore them. (Esquire 99:88 April 30, 83)

Tynan, Kenneth. A critic is a man who knows the way but can't drive the car. (Stagebill 52 Dec 81)

Wood, Natalie. Anyone who says it doesn't hurt when (critics) zap you is not to be believed. (Time 114:101 Dec 10, 79)

CRITICS

Hare, David. Critics believe in the right to judge, to which the artist cannot possibly accede. (Connoisseur 216:124 Feb 86)

CRONKITE, WALTER

Acciari, Larry. Presidents come and go, but Walter Cronkite—he's an institution. (Newsweek 88:37 July 26, 76)

Johnson, Lyndon Baines. If Walter Cronkite would say on television what he says on radio, he would be the most powerful man in America. (Newsweek 93:91 April 30, 79)

CROSBY, BING

Berlin, Irving. There wasn't anyone in show business who will be missed as much as Bing Crosby, not only as a performer, but also as a person. (New York Times 126:42 Oct 16, 77)

Crosby, Bing. He was an average guy who could carry a tune (on his epitaph).

(Newsweek 90:102 Oct 24, 77)

CROW, TRAMMELL

Stone, John S. Trammell Crow is the kind of person Donald Trump ought to want to be when Donald Trump grows up. (Chicago Tribune 365:1 Section 16 Dec 31, 89)

CUBAN MISSILE CRISIS, 1962

Komplektov, Viktor G. At no time, not before, not during the beginning of the crisis, or in the most acute moments of the crisis, neither from the Soviet command there in Cuba nor in Moscow was there, or could there have been, an order to mount (Russian) nuclear warheads on the missiles. (Chicago Tribune 38:21 Section 1 Feb 7, 89)

CULTS

Zappa, Frank. A wise man once said that the only difference between a cult and a religion is the amount of real estate they own. (National Catholic Reporter 23:10 Aug 14, 87)

CULTURE

Hayakawa, Samuel Ichiye. If you see in any given situation only what everyone else can see, you can be said to be so much a representative of your culture that you are a victim of it. (Phoenix 18:94 April 83)

Rand, Ayn. The state of today's culture is so low that I do not care to spend my time watching and discussing it. (Time 107:32 Jan 12, 76)

CURIOSITY

Einstein, Albert (attributed by Yousuf Karsh). Curiosity has its own reason for existence. (Parade 7 Dec 3, 78)

CYNICISM

Redford, Robert. I've always had a very low regard for cynicism; I think it is the beginning of dying. (Time 107:55 Mar 29, 76)

D'AUBUISSON, ROBERTO

Hinton, Deane R. Bobby proved himself to be a fine, young Democrat (about Roberto D'Aubuisson). (Newsweek 104:23 July 2, 84)

DALEY, RICHARD J.

Bush, Earl (press aide to Richard J. Daley). Don't print what he says; print what he means (about Richard J. Daley). (Chicago Sun-Times 33:2 Oct 17, 80)

Daley, Richard J. The police are not here to create disorder. They are here to preserve disorder (commenting during the 1968 Democratic Convention in Chicago). (Time 108:46 Jan 3, 77)

Royko, Mike. He seldom exited the same sentence he entered (about Richard J. Daley). (Chicago Tribune 40:3 Section 1 Feb 9, 89)

Sullivan, Frank. Jane Byrne was the supreme misjudgement of Richard J. Daley's life. (Chicago Tribune 76:3 Section 5 Mar 17, 89)

DALI, SALVADOR

Dali, Salvador. The difference between a madman and me is that I am not mad. (Time 115:76 Mar 3, 80)

DALLAS COUNTY, TEXAS

Adams, Randall Dale. If there ever was a hell on earth, it's Dallas County (Texas). (Chicago Tribune 162:8 Section 1 June 11, 89)

DALLAS. FOOTBALL CLUB (NATIONAL LEAGUE)

Auerbach, Red. There are only three teams in sports that have achieved true national status. The old Yankees, the Dallas Cowboys and us. That's not ego, that's just fact. (Sports Illustrated 67:73 Nov 9, 87)

DANCE

Balanchine, George. Ballet is woman. (Time 111:64 Feb 6, 78)

Balanchine, George. There are no mothers-in-law in ballet. (Ballet News 5:46 July 83)

De Mille, Agnes. Dance today is terrifying (1978). (Los Angeles Times Calendar 70 June 11, 78)

Hawkins, Erick. Dance is the most beautiful metaphor of existence in the world. (New York Times 128:12 Section 2 July 1, 79)

Kirstein, Lincoln. Transplanting ballet to this country is like trying to raise a palm tree in Dakota. (Newsweek 102:58 Dec 26, 83)

Makarova, Natalia. Even the ears must dance. (Newsweek 85:65 May 19, 75)

Mata-Hari. The dance is a poem and each movement a word. (Andy Warhol's Interview 7:15 May 76)

Tharp, Twyla. Dancing is like bank robbery, it takes split-second timing. (Ms 5:68 Oct 76)

DANCERS see also JAMISON, JUDITH; NUREEV, RUDOLF

DANCING

Balanchine, George. You see a little bit of Astaire in everybody's dancing. (Time 130:58 Dec 28, 87)

De Mille, Agnes. Art is the best therapy. (Ballet News 5:14 Sept 83)

Jamison, Judith. Every dancer lives on the threshold of chucking it. (New York Times Magazine 148 Dec 5, 76)

DANCING, FOLK

De Mille, Agnes. Folk dance is the truest history of the people. (Ballet News 5:14 Sept 83)

DAVIS, BETTE

Davis, Bette. I divide women into two categories. The female and the broad. Me? I'm a broad. (Time 112:98 Oct 23, 78)

Davis, Bette. I was always eager to salt a good stew. The trouble is that I was expected to supply the meat and potatoes as well. (Viva 5:29 Oct 77)

Davis, Bette. My biggest mistake was that no matter what troubles came my way, I always took the blame. (US 3:64 Feb 24, 86)

DAVIS, STUART

Davis, Stuart. I was a Cubist until somebody threw me a curve. (Interview 17:124 Dec 87)

DAY, DOROTHY

Day, Dorothy. Don't call me a saint, I don't want to be dismissed so easily. (Village Voice 32:40 Nov 3, 87)

DAY, MORRIS—RELATIONS—WOMEN

Day, Morris. I'm a man who believes that women have a place, and that they should be kept there. (US 3:64 Jan 27, 86)

DAYAN, MOSHE

Dayan, Moshe. I, Moshe Dayan, as an individual am not a coward. But as a Jew I am a very frightened man. (Time 110:30 Oct 17, 77)

DE CHIRICO, GIORGIO

De Chirico, Giorgio. I paint what I see with my eyes closed. (New York Times 128:B5 Nov 22, 78)

DE GAULLE, CHARLES

De Gaulle, Charles. There is no point in taking special precautions when those who want to kill me are as incompetent as those who are supposed to protect me. (Time 106:23 Oct 6, 75)

Kissinger, Henry Alfred. One had the sense that if (Charles de Gaulle) moved to a window, the center of gravity might shift, and the whole room might tilt everybody into the garden. (Time 114:82 Oct 15, 79)

DE MILLE, AGNES

De Mille, Agnes. I am a theater woman. I am not a saint. (W 6:24 Dec 9, 77)

DEAN, JOHN WESLEY, III

Dean, John Wesley, III. I don't want to be known as the all-time snitch. (People Weekly 6:122 Dec 13, 76)

Liddy, G. Gordon. I think in all fairness to the man, you'd have to put him right up there with Judas Iscariot (about John Dean). (More 5:11 July 75)

DEATH

Allen, Woody. Death is the big obsession behind all the things I've done. (Time 113:64 April 30, 79)

Brel, Jacques. Dying is man's only natural act. (Atlas World Press Review 25:49 Dec 78)

Burns, George. When I do go, I plan to take my music with me. I don't know what's out there, but I want to be sure it's in my key. (Playboy 22:48 Dec 75)

Cameron, James. While other people's deaths are deeply sad, one's own is sure to be a bit of a joke. (The Observer 9933:11 Jan 17, 82)

Gandhi, Indira (Nehru). Well, I've lived with danger all my life, and I think I've had a pretty full life, and it makes no difference whether you die in bed or you die standing up. (The New Yorker 60:39 Nov 12, 84)

Gilmore, Gary Mark. Death is the only inescapable, unavoidable, sure thing. We are sentenced to die the day we're born. (Chicago Sun-Times 29:2 Nov 17, 76)

Haile Selassie I, Emperor of Ethiopia. Death changes everything, sweeps everything away. Even mistakes. (Newsweek 86:32 Sept 8, 75)

Heaster, Jerry. Everybody says they want to go to heaven, but nobody wants to die to get there. (Kansas City Star 1E Nov 8, 87) (108)

Hendrix, Jimi. It's funny the way most people love the dead. Once you are dead, you are made for life. (Rolling Stone 227:81 Dec 2, 76)

Johnson, Flora. There is nothing like death. Everything that approaches it is metaphor. (Chicago 25:115 June 30, 76)

Lynch, James. If we do not live together, we will die—prematurely—alone. (Guardian Weekly 117:17 Sept 18, 77)

Redford, Robert. I've always had a very low regard for cynicism; I think it is the beginning of dying. (Time 107:55 Mar 29, 76)

Skinner, B. F. The more reason we have to pay attention to life, the less we have to pay attention to death. (Kansas City Star 104:1A Oct 11, 83)

Warhol, Andy. I don't believe in it (death), because you're not around to know that it's happened. (Time 106:32 July 28, 75)

West, Tom. Every patient that every doctor has is going to die. (Lawrence (Kansas) Journal-World 130:5A Dec 20, 88)

Wilder, Thornton. The highest tribute to the dead is not grief but gratitude. (Parade 20 Sept 13, 81)

DEBT, PUBLIC—UNITED STATES

Reagan, Ronald. The deficit is big enough to take care of itself. (Newsweek 112:29 Nov 21, 88)

DECISION MAKING (POLITICAL SCIENCE)

Brown, Edmund Gerald, Jr. The power of the executive is like a chess game; there are very few moves that one can make. (Gold Coast Pictorial 13:9 Feb 77)

Carter, James Earl. Doubts are the stuff of great decisions, but so are dreams. (Time 113:24 Mar 26, 79)

Cheney, Richard B. Basically, I am skeptical about the ability of government to solve problems, and I have a healthy respect for the ability of people to solve problems on their own. (Washington Post 336:A3 Nov 6, 75)

Felix, Virginia. Decision makers are those who have the greatest vested interest in the decision. (Omni 1:132 May 79)

Friedman, Milton. Governments never learn. Only people learn. (The Observer 9840:11 Mar 30, 80)

Kahn, J. Kesner. When politicians come up with a solution for your problem, you have two problems. (American Opinion 18:21 May 75)

Marcos, Ferdinand E. It is easier to run a revolution than a government. (Time 107:35 June 6, 77)

Mayer, Jean. The ability to arrive at complex decisions is the hallmark of the educated person. (People Weekly 6:44 Nov 15, 76)

Ray, Dixie Lee. Anything that the private sector can do, government can do it worse. (Mother Jones 2:31 May 77)

Rinfret, Pierre A. Consensus is the security blanket of the insecure. (Challenge 19:42 May 76)

DELEGATION OF AUTHORITY

Weiler, A. H. Nothing is impossible for the man who doesn't have to do it himself. (Washingtonian 14:155 Nov 78)

DELLA FEMINA, JERRY

Della Femina, Jerry. If God called my office looking for advertising, I'd check out his references. You can never be too sure in this business. (Oui 3:74 Feb 81)

DEMOCRACY

Adler, Mortimer. Political democracy will not work unless it is accompanied by economic democracy. (Time 110:57 July 25, 77)

Bhutto, Zulfikar Ali. Democracy demands reciprocity. (Time 106:26 Dec 29, 75)

Brogan, D. W. Democracy is like a raft. It never sinks, but damn it, your feet are always in the water. (Time 107:25 May 2, 77)

Churchill, Sir Winston. It (democracy) is the worst system—except for all those other systems that have been tried and failed. (Time 106:63 July 14, 75)

Einstein, Albert. Let every man be respected

as an individual and no man idolized. (Parade 4 July 1, 79)

Fernandes, Millor (Brazilian playwright). In a democracy we are all equal before the law. In a dictatorship we are all equal before the police. (New York Times 126:8 May 24, 77)

Kissinger, Henry Alfred. It is necessary for the Western democracies to recapture the sense that they can control their own destiny. (Time 106:36 Oct 27, 75)

Lapham, Lewis H. Democracy means that you and I must fight. Democracy means a kind of Darwinism for ideas. (Time 111:84 Jan 23, 78)

Mark, Sir Robert (chief of London's police force). The real art of policing a free society or a democracy is to win by appearing to lose or at least to win by not appearing to win. (The Observer 9701:13 July 17, 77)

Moynihan, Daniel Patrick. As the lights go out in the rest of the world, they shine all the brighter here. (Time 107:28 Jan 26, 76)

Nader, Ralph. Information is the currency of democracy. (Chicago Tribune 258:3 Sept 15, 89)

Nam Duck Woo, (Deputy Prime Minister of South Korea). There is not one developing country in the world where Western democracy really works. (Time 107:32 June 6, 77)

Niebuhr, Reinhold. Man's capacity for justice makes democracy possible, but man's inclination to injustice makes democracy necessary. (Rocky Mountain News 122:54 Dec 17, 80)

Pasqua, Charles (French interior minister). Democracy ends where the interest of the State begins. (The Progressive 51:10 July 87)

Riesman, David. The question is not whether leadership is obsolete but whether democracy is governable. (Time 114:26 Aug 6, 79)

Smith, Charles Merrill. In a democracy you can be respected though poor, but don't count on it. (Time 113:25 Feb 26, 79)

Stevenson, Adlai, II. A free society is one where it is safe to be unpopular. (Human Behavior 7:68 May 78)

Stevenson, Adlai, II. The government must be the trustee for the little man, because no one else will be. The powerful can usually help themselves—and frequently do. (Human Behavior 7:68 May 78)

DEMOCRATIC PARTY

Atwater, Lee. Democrats get totally preoccupied with things voters don't care about. (Chicago Tribune 190:4 Section 4

July 9, 89)

Bentsen, Lloyd. When it comes to defending America, you can trust the Democrats. (Chicago Tribune 239:6 Section 1 Aug 26, 88)

Caddell, Patrick. Clearly, God is a Democrat. (Boston 68:115 Sept 76)

Cisneros, Henry. A party that appeals only to minorities is going to remain a minority party. (Kansas City Times 117:A-19 Nov 8, 84)

Clark, Ramsey. The Democratic Party is a party in name only, not in shared belief. (Time 116:12 Aug 25, 80)

Dukakis, Michael. We're going to win because we are the party that believes in the American Dream. (Chicago Sun-Times 41:14 Section Com July 24, 88)

Fitzhugh, Gilbert W. The Republicans fight like cats and go home and sulk. The Democrats fight like cats, and suddenly there are more cats. (Time 107:11 Aug 23, 76)

From, Al. The Republicans win when they draw the line between the poor and the rest of us. The Democrats win when we draw the line between the rich and the rest of us. (New York Times 138:15 Feb 19, 89)

Goldwater, Barry Morris. I don't care if I'm called a Democrat or a Republican as long as I'm in bed with people of the same thinking. (Rolling Stone 227:43 Dec 2, 76)

Humphrey, Hubert Horatio. The time has arrived for the Democratic Party to get out of the shadow of states' rights and walk forthrightly into the bright sunshine of human rights (at the 1948 Democratic National Convention). (Time 111:22 Jan 23, 78)

Kennedy, Edward Moore. Rethinking our ideas should never be an excuse for retreating from our ideals. The last thing this nation needs in the 1980s is two Republican parties. (Time 120:14 July 12, 82)

McGovern, George Stanley. Marching in mindless lockstep is the lowest form of party loyalty. (Village Voice 22:34 May 16, 77)

O'Neill, Thomas P. (Tip). If this were France, the Democratic Party would be five parties. (Time 112:42 Nov 20, 78)

Reagan, Ronald. The national Democratic leadership is going so far left they've left America. (Washington Post National Weekly Edition 1:12 Aug 6, 84)

Schneider, William. Liberalism is a problem that could be overcome by finding the right theme (about the Democratic Party).

(Chicago Tribune 267:4 Section 4 Sept 24, 89)

DEMOCRATIC PARTY. NATIONAL CONVENTION, CHICAGO, 1968

Daley, Richard J. The police are not here to create disorder. They are here to preserve disorder (commenting during the 1968 Democratic Convention in Chicago). (Time 108:46 Jan 3, 77)

DENIRO, ROBERT

DeNiro, Robert. I'm spending about $600 a week talking to my analyst. I guess that's the price of success. (The Star 4:2 July 26, 77)

DeNiro, Robert. There is a certain combination of anarchy and discipline in the way I work. (Time 110:60 July 25, 77)

DENNIS, RICHARD

Dennis, Richard. Someone must support unpopular truths and unconventional points of view. (Town & Country 143:164 Dec 89)

DENVER, JOHN

Simels, Steve. John Denver (is) Johnny Mathis disguised as a hillbilly. He has never written a decent song, his voice is an Irish tenor only a whit less offensive than Dennis Day's, and, as far as I can tell, his only function is to provide adolescent girls with records to cry over in the privacy of their bedrooms. (Stereo Review 35:72 Dec 75)

DEPARTMENT STORES—NEW YORK see also **BLOOMINGDALE'S**

DEPRESSION, MENTAL

Baker, Russell. Misery no longer loves company. Nowadays it insists upon it. (Washingtonian 14:152 Nov 78)

DEPRESSIONS

Bermer, Richard. The question is no longer whether there will be a recession but how deep it will be and how long it will last (1990). (Time 136:38 Aug 20, 90)

DESIGN

Noyes, Eliot F. (industrial designer). Familiarity breeds acceptance. (Time 110:71 Aug 1, 77)

Oldenburg, Claes. To give birth to form is the only act of man that has any consequence. (Chicago 25:18 Nov 76)

DETECTIVE AND MYSTERY STORIES

Chandler, Raymond. It is always a misfortune to be taken seriously in a field of writing where quality is not expected or desired. (Westways 74:67 Jan 82)

James, P. D. I've never met a stupid person who liked detective stories. (Chiago Tribune 35:1 Section 14 Feb 4, 90)

DETENTE (POLITICAL SCIENCE)

Kissinger, Henry Alfred. The cold war was not so terrible and detente was not so exalting. (The Observer 9833:9 Feb 10, 80)

DEVIL

Graham, Billy. Transcendental Meditation is evil because...it opens space within you for the devil. (Ms 6:50 July 77)

Kraus, Karl. The devil is an optimist if he thinks he can make people worse than they are. (Inquiry 1:25 Jan 23, 78)

DEVRIES, PETER

De Vries, Peter. I love being a writer. What I can't stand is the paperwork. (New York Times Book Review 35 July 15, 79)

DIARIES

West, Mae. My motto is keem a diary, and one day it will keep you. (Interview 16:70 July 86)

DICTATORSHIP

Fernandes, Millor (Brazilian playwright). In a democracy we are all equal before the law. In a dictatorship we are all equal before the police. (New York Times 126:8 May 24, 77)

Khomeini, Ayatollah Ruhollah. Dictatorship is the greatest sin in the religion of Islam. Fascism and Islamism are absolutely incompatible. (Time 114:57 Oct 22, 79)

DIETRICH, MARLENE

Hemingway, Ernest. If she (Marlene Dietrich) had nothing but her voice, she could break your heart with it. (Book Digest 5:99 April 78)

DIPLOMACY

Kissinger, Henry Alfred. I think Metternich was an extremely skilled diplomat, but not very creative. (Time 107:33 Jan 12, 76)

Nixon, Richard Milhous. You have to dissemble, you have to recognize that you can't say what you think about an individual because you may have to use him or need him sometime in the future (on the nature of international diplomacy). (Kansas City Times 115:D1 Jan 1, 83)

DIPLOMATS

Brewster, Kingman. A diplomat does not have to be a eunuch. (W 7:37 Aug 31, 15)

DISCOVERY

Szent-Gyoergyi von Nagyrapolt, Albert. Discovery consists of seeing what everybody has seen and thinking what nobody has thought. (Omni 2:45 Dec 79)

DISCRIMINATION see also **RACE DISCRIMINATION**

DISCRIMINATION IN EMPLOYMENT

Kennedy, Florynce Rae. There are a few jobs that actually require a penis or vagina. All other jobs should be open to everybody. (Ms 1:55 Mar 73)

Young, Andrew. I don't think affirmative action for blacks requires discrimination against whites. (Sepia 24:10 July 75)

DISEASES see also COLD (DISEASE)

DISNEY, WALT

Disney, Walt. I love Mickey Mouse more than any woman I've ever known. (Penthouse 16:152 Nov 84)

DISSENTERS

Moynihan, Daniel Patrick. When a person goes to a country and finds their newspapers filled with nothing but good news, he can bet there are good men in jail. (University Daily Kansan 87:4 Feb 16, 77)

Terkel, Studs. Dissent is not merely the right to dissent—it is the duty. (National Catholic Reporter 12:7 July 2, 76)

DISSENTERS—RUSSIA see also SHCHARANSKY, ANATOLY

DISSENTERS—UNITED STATES

Douglas, William Orville. The great and invigorating influences in American life have been the unorthodox; the people who challenge an existing institution or way of life, or say and do things that make people think. (Kansas City Times 109:14C Jan 22, 77)

DISTRUST

Evtushenko, Evgenii Aleksandrovich. Distrust is the mother of war and political racism. (Atlas World Press Review 23:10 Nov 76)

DIVORCE

Alvarez, A. Divorce transforms habit into drama. (Time 119:76 Feb 8, 82)

Aumont, Jean-Pierre. Marriages are not eternal, so why should divorce be? (W 6:2 July 8, 77)

Leone, Mama. No one ever filed for divorce on a full stomach. (Viva 4:26 May 77)

Lowell, Robert. Almost all good women poets are either divorced or lesbian. (San Francisco Chronicle 111:19 May 25, 77)

Shepherd, Cybill. It's divorce that's the problem with marriage. (US 3:4 May 4, 87)

DOGS

Lindsay, John Vliet. If you want gratitude, get yourself a dog. (Chicago Tribune 22:2 Section 2 Jan 22, 78)

DOLE, ELIZABETH

Dole, Robert J. I regret that I have but one wife to give for my counry's infrastructure. (Chicago Tribune 334:18 Section 1 Nov 29, 84)

DOLE, ROBERT J.

Dole, Robert J. If you liked Richard Nixon, you'll love Bob Dole. (Christian Science Monitor 68:17 Sept 10, 76)

Dole, Robert J. Thank goodness whenever I was in the Oval Office I only nodded (commenting on the Watergate tapes). (Christian Science Monitor 68:17 Sept 10, 76)

Dole, Robert J. When I ran for vice-president in 1976, they told me to go for the jugular. I did. My own. (US 3:59 Dec 15, 86)

DONLEAVY, J. P.

Donleavy, J. P. Nearly everybody who pans my books doesn't get anywhere in the literary trade. (Newsweek 94:95 Oct 22, 79)

DOUBT see BELIEF AND DOUBT

DRAMA

Allen, Woody. Drama stays with people more, like meat and potatoes, while comedy is a dessert, like meringue. (Newsweek 85:87B June 23, 75)

Howe, Tina. The love story is the acid test for any writer. (Elle 2:42 Nov 86)

Miller, Arthur. I think a play ought to cast a shadow; it ought to be something you can walk around. (New York Times 128:6 Section 2 June 17, 79)

Olivier, Laurence. I love comedy every bit as much as tragedy, perhaps more, because the whole scene of humanity is under its roof. (New York Times Magazine 60 Mar 25, 79)

Rudkin, David. The play should liberate itself from the personal origins of the author. (Village Voice 22:89 June 27, 77)

Stoppard, Tom. I think that plays should disturb certainties as well as affirm them. (Newsweek 103:83 Jan 16, 84)

DRAMATIC CRITICISM

Albee, Edward. If Attila the Hun were alive today, he'd be a dramatic critic. (Stagebill 52 Dec 81)

Brown, John Mason. To many, dramatic criticism must seem like an attempt to tattoo soap bubbles. (Stagebill 52 Dec 81)

Eder, Richard. A critic may write for an institution, but he shouldn't be one. (Village Voice 22:97 Mar 28, 77)

Mamet, David. Frank Rich and John Simon are the syphilis and gonorrhea of the theater. (Newsweek 107:13 Feb 17, 86)

Mamet, David. Intellectually, I'd like to think of them (critics) as running-dog conspirators against the institution of art. But they're just jack-offs like the rest of us. (More 7:31 July 77)

Mizner, Wilson. A dramatic critic is a person who surprises the playwright by informing him what he meant. (Stagebill 52 Dec 81)

DRAMATISTS

Miller, Arthur. Part of being a playwright is being an actor. One way or another, whether surreptitiously or not, a good playwright is an actor. (Connecticut 41:115 Jan 78)

Norman, Marsha. Playwrights, I believe, lead lives of enormous drama. (Chicago Tribune 154:3 Section 5 June 4, 89)

Papp, Joseph. The true dramatist of our time is a poet; the true poet, a dramatist. (New York Times 128:C24 Dec 1, 78)

Rudkin, David. The play should liberate itself from the personal origins of the author. (Village Voice 22:89 June 27, 77)

DRAMATISTS, AMERICAN see also HOWE, TINA; LUDLAM, CHARLES; MAMET, DAVID; MILLER, ARTHUR; O'NEILL, EUGENE; WILLIAMS, TENNESSEE

DRAMATISTS, ENGLISH see also STOPPARD, TOM

DRAMATISTS, RUSSIAN see also VORONEL, NINA

DRAWING

Steinberg, Saul. The doodle is the brooding of the hand. (Time 112:88 Oct 16, 78)

Steinberg, Saul. Unlike writing, drawing makes up its own syntax as it goes along. The line can't be reasoned in the mind. It can only be reasoned on paper. (Time 111:92 April 17, 78)

DRUGS

Waits, Tom. Reality is for those who can't face drugs. (Playboy 26:26 Oct 79)

DRUGS see also LYSERGIC ACID DIETHYLAMIDE; VALIUM

DRUNKENNESS

Lewis, Joe E. You're not really drunk if you can lie on the floor without hanging on. (Playboy 26:26 Oct 79)

DUBUFFET, JEAN

Dubuffet, Jean. Many artists begin with the pig and make sausages. I begin with the sausages from which I reconstitute a pig. (Time 125:93 May 27, 85)

DUCHAMP, MARCEL

Duchamp, Marcel. I was interested in ideas—not in merely visual products. I wanted to put painting once again at the service of the mind. (New York Times 128:1 Section 7 Feb 11, 79)

DUKE, DAVID

Brown, Ron. It is disingenuous for the people who ran the Willie Horton ads to express shock and dismay over David Duke. (Time 133:29 Mar 6, 89)

DULLES, JOHN FOSTER

Churchill, Sir Winston. Foster Dulles is the only case I know of a bull who carries his china shop with him. (Time 111:83 Feb 27, 78)

Philby, Kim. John Foster Dulles was a strong personality with views as narrow as a small-gauge railway. (Esquire 89:53 Mar 28, 78)

DULLNESS

Read, David H. C. The worst sin is dullness. (Time 114:65 Dec 31, 79)

DUNAWAY, FAYE

Dunaway, Faye. I've always thought that acting is an art of creating accidents. (W 5:15 Nov 26, 76)

DUNCAN, ISADORA

De Mille, Agnes. Isadora Duncan took Western dancing out of the brothel and into the temple. (Ballet News 5:14 Sept 83)

DURANTE, JIMMY

Durante, Jimmy. There's a million good-lookin' guys, but I'm a novelty. (New York Times 129:1 Jan 30, 80)

DYLAN, BOB

Dylan, Bob. Money doesn't exist because I don't recognize it. (New Times 10:45 Feb 6, 78)

Dylan, Bob. Somebody called me the Ed Sullivan of rock and roll. I don't know what that means, but it sounds right. (TV Guide 24:4 Sept 11, 76)

E.T. (MOVING PICTURE CHARACTER)

Spielberg, Steven. I wanted a creature only a mother could love (about E.T.). (Kansas City Times 115:D1 Jan 1, 83)

EASTWOOD, CLINT

Burton, Richard. Clint (Eastwood) is in the great line of Spencer Tracy and James Stewart and Bob Mitchum. They have a kind of dynamic lethargy. They appear to do nothing and they do everything. (Esquire 89:45 Mar 14, 78)

Eastwood, Clint. Everybody talks about love, but the thing that keeps marriage together for me is friendship. (Chicago Tribune Magazine 174:25 Aug 1, 76)

EATING

Leone, Mama. No one ever filed for divorce on a full stomach. (Viva 4:26 May 77)

Loren, Sophia. Spaghetti can be eaten most successfully if you inhale it like a vacuum cleaner. (Time 119:76 April 26, 82)

Theroux, Paul. You are not what you eat; but where you eat is who you are. (Travel & Leisure 7:76 July 31, 77)

ECOLOGY

Hodel, Donald. (Environmentalism is) a crusade to stop all development in this country. (Wall Street Journal 56:1 Dec 17, 75)

Shuttleworth, John. We are still much too preoccupied with taking our machines out into the woods, instead of making a place for the forest in our hearts. (The Mother Earth News 35:7 Sept 75)

ECOLOGY see also GARN, JAKE

ECONOMIC ASSISTANCE, AMERICAN

Torricelli, Robert. Foreign assistance should be goods provided by Americans, arriving on American ships flying American flags, so we can be seen giving assistance to grateful people. (In These Times 14:4 Nov 8, 89)

ECONOMIC FORECASTING

Rinfret, Pierre A. Consensus is the security blanket of the insecure. (Challenge 19:42 May 76)

ECONOMIC POLICY

Okun, Arthur M. Society can transport money from rich to poor only in a leaky bucket. (Time 115:83 April 7, 80)

Schumacher, Ernst F. Production by the masses, rather than mass production. (Newsweek 90:72 Sept 19, 77)

ECONOMIC STATISTICS

Goodhart, Charles. Any measure of the money supply that is officially controlled promptly loses its meaning. (Chicago Sun-Times 34:50 Feb 1, 82)

ECONOMICS

Allen, Marty. A study of economics usually reveals that the best time to buy anything is last year. (Atlanta 15:26 Jan 75)

Burns, Arthur Frank. Anyone who is convinced that he can fine-tune the economy doesn't know what he is talking about. (Time 130:58 Dec 28, 87)

Kugel, Yerachmiel. Ethics is not a branch of economics. (St. Louis Post-Dispatch 99:2G July 24, 77)

Lapham, Lewis H. I take for granted Jefferson's dictum that money, not morality, constitutes the principle of commercial nations. (Harper's 254:32 Feb 77)

Thatcher, Margaret Hilda. There can be no liberty unless there is economic liberty. (Village Voice 24:35 May 14, 79)

Von Hayek, Friedrich. You can have economic freedom without political freedom, but you cannot have political freedom without economic freedom. (Village Voice 24:35 May 14, 79)

ECONOMICS—STUDY AND TEACHING

Schumacher, Ernst F. As a good friend says, most of the modern economics as taught is a form of brain damage. (The Reader (Chicago's Free Weekly) 6:27 Mar 25, 77)

Schumacher, Ernst F. It's impossible to discuss economic problems without concepts like temptation and seduction. In economics this is translated into free consumer choice. (The Reader (Chicago's Free Weekly) 6:27 Mar 25, 77)

ECONOMISTS

Drucker, Peter F. In all recorded history there has not been one economist who had to

worry about where the next meal would come from. (New York Times 125:15 Section 3 May 16, 76)

Schumacher, Ernst F. They're spending their time rearranging the deck chairs on the Titanic (commenting on his fellow economists). (The Reader (Chicago's Free Weekly) 6:27 Mar 25, 77)

ECONOMISTS see also GREENSPAN, ALAN; KEYNES, JOHN MAYNARD; SCHUMACHER, ERNST F.

EDISON, THOMAS ALVA

Edison, Thomas Alva. Anything that won't sell, I don't want to invent. (New York Times Book Review 7 Feb 25, 79)

Edison, Thomas Alva. Deafness has been of great advantage to me as my business is thinking. (Newsweek 93:104 Mar 26, 79)

EDITORS AND EDITING

Giroux, Robert. Editors used to be known by their authors; now some of them are known by their restaurants. (Time 119:73 Jan 18, 82)

Stevenson, Adlai, II. An editor is someone who separates the wheat from the chaff and then prints the chaff. (Texas Observer 68:7 Dec 24, 76)

Tanner, Jack. An editor has no friends. (Challenge 19:5 Mar/April 76)

EDITORS AND EDITING see also KORDA, MICHAEL

EDUCATION

Adler, Mortimer. We are hypocrites if we continue to think that the equality of citizenship belongs to all, but not the equality of educational opportunity. (Time 110:57 July 25, 77)

Ball, George W. (Lyndon Johnson) did not suffer from a poor education, he suffered from the belief that he had a poor education. (Washingtonian 11:102 June 76)

Bell, Terrence H. We need to liberalize vocational education—and vocationalize liberal education. (Money 5:48 April 76)

Bok, Derek. If you think education is expensive—try ignorance. (Town & Country 133:140 May 79)

Boulding, Kenneth E. The purpose of education is to transmit information from decrepit old men to decrepit young men. (Omni 2:31 April 80)

Dobie, J. Frank. The average Ph.D. thesis is nothing but a transference of bones from one graveyard to another. (Rocky Mountain News 37:70 May 29, 80)

Kerr, Clark. Naderism has taken over education. (Time 110:75 Nov 14, 77)

Parker, Gail Thain. We must not be misled by snobbery into thinking that there is only one way to become educated. (Time

111:90 April 10, 78)

Rickover, Hyman G. Learning isn't fun. (Texas Observer 76:22 Sept 28, 84)

White, William Allen. In education we are striving not to teach youth to make a living, but to make a life. (Kansas City Times 109:11B Feb 4, 77)

Will, George F. Education should be primarily an inoculation against the disease of our time, which is disdain for times past. (Washington Post 172:A15 May 26, 77)

EDUCATION see also BLACKS—EDUCATION; COLLEGES AND UNIVERSITIES; HIGH SCHOOLS

EDUCATION, HIGHER

Bennett, William J. Higher education is not underfunded, it is underaccountable and underproductive. (Chicago Tribune 110:10 April 20, 87)

EDUCATION—AIMS AND OBJECTIVES

Boulanger, Nadia. Education is to bring people to be themselves, and at the same time, know how to conform to the limits. (New York Times 126:D25 Sept 11, 77)

Cramer, Jerome. Schools are now asked to do what people used to ask God to do. (Time 115:59 June 16, 80)

Kilpatrick, James J. Big Bill Bennett, as I may have said before, is the best thing to hit American education since the McGuffey readers. (Kansas City Star 107:11A Feb 5, 87)

EDUCATION—JAPAN

George F, Will. American children do better than Japanese children in English. For now. (Kansas City Times 121:A-11 Feb 13, 89)

EDUCATION—PHILADELPHIA

Rizzo, Frank Lazzaro. We need excellence in public education and if the teachers can't do it, we'll send in a couple of policemen. (Time 110:40 Oct 24, 77)

EDUCATION—UNITED STATES

George F, Will. American children do better than Japanese children in English. For now. (Kansas City Times 121:A-11 Feb 13, 89)

EFFICIENCY, ADMINISTRATIVE

Drucker, Peter F. Look at governmental programs for the past fifty years. Every single one—except for warfare—achieved the exact opposite of its announced goal. (New York Times 125:15 Section 3 May 16, 76)

Frankel, Charles. Whatever happens in government could have happened differently, and it usually would have been better if it had. (The Reader (Chicago's Free Weekly) 5:2 May 28, 76)

Parkinson, C. Northcote. Work expands to fill the time allotted to it, or, conversely, the amount of work completed is in inverse proportion to the number of people employed. (The Reader (Chicago's Free Weekly) 5:2 May 28, 76)

Ray, Dixie Lee. Anything that the private sector can do, government can do it worse. (Mother Jones 2:31 May 77)

Sidey, Hugh. Bureaucrats are the only people in the world who can say absolutely nothing and mean it. (Time 108:13 Nov 29, 76)

Sidey, Hugh. When a bureaucrat makes a mistake and continues to make it, it usually becomes the new policy. (Time 108:13 Nov 29, 76)

Will, George F. World War II was the last government program that really worked (to the Association of American Publishers). (Washingtonian 10:22 July 75)

EGYPT—FOREIGN RELATIONS—UNITED STATES

Sadat, Anwar. I have dealt with three presidents, Nixon, Ford and this Carter. I can say that everything is improving. (Time 111:32 Jan 2, 78)

EHRLICHMAN, JOHN D.

Ehrlichman, John D. I have done my time. I don't think he (Richard Nixon) is ever going to stop doing his time. (Time 111:67 May 15, 78)

EINSTEIN, ALBERT

Einstein, Albert. Let every man be respected as an individual and no man idolized. (Parade 4 July 1, 79)

Einstein, Albert. To punish me for my contempt for authority, Fate made me an authority myself. (Chicago Tribune 281:1 Section 2 Oct 8, 78)

EISENHOWER, DWIGHT DAVID

Eisenhower, Dwight David. The path to America's future lies down the middle of the road. (Time 116:32 July 28, 80)

Eisenhower, Mamie Geneva (Doud). I let Ike run the country and I ran the home. (New York Times 126:26 Section 1 Nov 14, 76)

Philby, Kim. Now I can abandon my earlier reserve and call him an idle, ignorant, ungenerous old fraud (about Dwight Eisenhower). (Esquire 89:55 Mar 28, 78)

EISENHOWER, MAMIE GENEVA (DOUD)

Eisenhower, Mamie Geneva (Doud). I let Ike run the country and I ran the home. (New York Times 126:26 Section 1 Nov 14, 76)

EL CORDOBES see PEREZ, MANUEL BENITEZ

EL SALVADOR—POLITICS AND GOVERNMENT

Romero, Oscar Arnulfo. They can kill me, but the voice of justice will never be stilled. (Newsweek 95:47 April 7, 80)

EMIGRATION AND IMMIGRATION LAW
Rohatyn, Felix. We ought to change the sign on the Statue of Liberty to read, 'this time around, send us your rich'. (Newsweek 92:88 Nov 27, 78)

EMOTIONS
Forbes, Malcolm S. People who never get carried away should be. (Town & Country 130:166 Nov 76)

Miller, Henry. To the person who thinks with his head, life is a comedy. To those who think with their feelings, or work through their feelings, life is a tragedy. (Soho News 5:3 Jan 26, 78)

EMOTIONS see also FEAR; HAPPINESS; HATE; LOVE; PITY

EMPLOYEES
Peter, Laurence J. In a hierarchy, every employee tends to rise to the level of his own incompetence. (The Reader (Chicago's Free Weekly) 5:2 May 28, 76)

EMPLOYEES, DISMISSAL OF
Galbraith, John Kenneth. Anyone who says he isn't going to resign, four times, definitely will. (Town & Country 133:140 May 79)

EMPLOYEES, PUBLIC
Horowitz, Rachel. If you're a public employee and your job depends on public officials, you have to be in politics. (Newsweek 96:27 July 14, 80)

EMPLOYMENT
Norris, William. We talk a lot about human rights, but I don't know of any human right that is more important than a job. (Time 111:61 April 3, 78)

EMPLOYMENT see also UNEMPLOYMENT

ENEMIES
Jones, Thomas. Friends may come and go, but enemies accumulate. (Washingtonian 14:155 Nov 78)

ENERGY CONSERVATION
Laird, Melvin. Conservation alone is a slow walk down a dead-end street. (Time 110:62 Oct 10, 77)

ENERGY CRISIS see POWER RESOURCES

ENERGY INDUSTRY see FUEL INDUSTRY

ENGLISH see BRITISH

ENGLISH LANGUAGE
Rayburn, Sam. The three most important words in the English language are 'wait a minute'. (Time 107:15 Aug 9, 76)

ENGLISH LANGUAGE—COMPOSITION
Califano, Joseph A., Jr. Writing things clearly does not necessarily mean writing them short. (Washingtonian 13:11 Nov 77)

ENGLISH LANGUAGE—GRAMMAR
Churchill, Sir Winston. A preposition is a terrible word to end a sentence with. (Lawrence (Kansas) Journal-World 125:5 Sept 30, 83)

ENGLISH LANGUAGE—STUDY AND TEACHING
Botstein, Leon. The English language is dying, because it is not taught. (Time 106:34 Aug 25, 75)

Charles, Prince of Wales. All the people I have in my office, they can't speak English properly, they can't write English properly. All the letters sent from my office I have to correct myself, and that is because English is taught so bloody badly. (Chicago Tribune 181:2 Section 1 June 30, 89)

ENGLISH LANGUAGE—USAGE
Dean, Dizzy. Let the teachers learn the kids English. Ol' Diz will learn the kids baseball. (The Sporting News 195:70 Dec 31, 84)

Gold, Herbert. The rubber-stamp expression is a rubber stamp even the first time it is pressed into our brains. (Newsweek 93:11 Feb 5, 79)

ENTERTAINERS
Marx, Minnie. Where else can people who don't know anything make a living (commenting on show business). (Newsweek 91:76 May 22, 78)

ENTERTAINING
Maxwell, Elsa. A good hostess must always proceed upon the assumption that her guests are children, no matter what their age. (Details 7:24 Nov 88)

ENTERTAINMENT INDUSTRY
Marx, Minnie. Where else can people who don't know anything make a living (commenting on show business). (Newsweek 91:76 May 22, 78)

ENTREPRENEURS
Hefner, Hugh Marston. I'm not primarily an entrepreneurial businessman. I'm primarily a playboy philosopher. (Chicago Tribune 124:1 Section 1 May 3, 76)

Zaleznick, Abraham. I think if we want to understand the entrepreneur, we should look at the juvenile delinquent. (Inc 7:17 Aug 85)

ENVIRONMENT
Burroughs, John. If you want to see birds, you must have birds in your heart. (Outside 1:11 Dec 77)

Commoner, Barry. When you fully understand the situation it is worse than you think. (Life 2:170 Dec 79)

Koestler, Arthur. Those who deny the influence of environment on the development of the human being should spend a year in prison and observe themselves daily in a mirror. (USA Today 1:8A June 15, 83)

ENVIRONMENTAL ACTION

(ORGANIZATION)

Helms, Jesse. If Environmental Action had its way, the American people would starve and freeze to death in the dark. (Chicago Sun-Times 31:2 June 5, 78)

ENVIRONMENTAL MOVEMENT

Aspinall, Wayne. The conservation extremists demand too much of our public land for their own private use. (American Opinion 18:150 July/Aug 75)

Breaux, John. If these do-gooders have their way you'll need a permit to turn on a faucet in the bathroom (commenting on environmentalists' causes). (Outside 1:17 Dec 77)

Hagedorn, Tom. As far as I'm concerned, environmentalists and food stamp cheaters are the same thing. (Potomac: Magazine of the Washington Post 4 Mar 7, 76)

Helms, Jesse. If Environmental Action had its way, the American people would starve and freeze to death in the dark. (Chicago Sun-Times 31:2 June 5, 78)

Menke-Gluckert, Peter. Environment has become the Viet Nam of the middle class. (Time 107:48 April 25, 77)

ENVIRONMENTAL MOVEMENT see also ENVIRONMENTAL ACTION (ORGANIZATION)

ENVIRONMENTAL POLICY

Dasmann, Raymond F. We are hooked like junkies, dependent on the drug of wasteful consumption. (New York Times 126:A18 Dec 1, 76)

Hodel, Donald. (Environmentalism is) a crusade to stop all development in this country. (Wall Street Journal 56:1 Dec 17, 75)

EQUALITY

Adler, Mortimer. We are hypocrites if we continue to think that the equality of citizenship belongs to all, but not the equality of educational opportunity. (Time 110:57 July 25, 77)

Carter, James Earl. No poor, rural, weak, or black person should ever have to bear the additional burden of being deprived of the opportunity of an education, a job, or simple justice. (New York 9:57 July 19,76)

Jones, Franklin P. One thing in which the sexes are equal is in thinking that they're not. (Reader's Digest 108:261 May 76)

Kennedy, Florynce Rae. There's no sex to a brain. (Human Behavior 7:17 May 78)

Thatcher, Margaret Hilda. Opportunity means nothing unless it includes the right to be unequal. (The Illustrated London News 263:26 Oct 31, 75)

Will, George F. People do not want to be equal to their neighbors. They want to be richer than their neighbors. (Kansas City

Times 119:A-7 Mar 17, 87)

ERHARD, WERNER

Waters, Craig. About 15 years ago, Jack Rosenberg changed his name to Werner Hans Erhard. His motive for doing so is unknown, but, with the switch, the son of a Jewish restaurant proprietor became an apparent Aryan: a son of history's perpetual victim became an heir apparent to one of history's greatest victimizers. (Boston Magazine 30:48 Sept 75)

ERRORS

Nies, John. The effort expended by the bureaucracy in defending any error is in direct proportion to the size of the error. (Washingtonian 14:155 Nov 78)

ESPOSITO, MEADE H.

Esposito, Meade H. If I wrote a book, no one would come to my wake. (New York Times 133:2 Jan 27, 84)

ESTES, BILLIE SOL

Estes, Billie Sol. You win by losing, hold on by letting go, increase by diminishing, and multiply by dividing. These are the principles that have brought me success. (New York Times 128:23 Feb 25, 79)

ETHICS

Kugel, Yerachmiel. Ethics is not a branch of economics. (St. Louis Post-Dispatch 99:2G July 24, 77)

Mencken, Henry Louis. Immorality is the morality of those who are having a better time. (New York Times 139:31 Dec 13, 89)

ETIQUETTE

Broun, Heywood Hale. If anyone corrects your pronunciation of a word in a public place, you have every right to punch him in the nose. (Kansas City Times 109:14B July 8, 77)

ETIQUETTE see also OFFICES—ETIQUETTE

ETIQUETTE—IOWA

Conlin, Roxanne. Being rude and killing someone are about on par here (in Iowa). (Time 131:14 Jan 25, 88)

EUROPE see also COMMUNISM—EUROPE

EUROPE—POLITICS AND GOVERNMENT

Monnet, Jean. The world is divided into those who want to become someone and those who want to accomplish something. (Time 113:47 Mar 26, 79)

EUROPEANS

Auden, Wystan Hugh (attributed by Peter Conrad). The economic vice of Europeans is avarice, while that of Americans is waste. (Time 115:40 Mar 31, 80)

EUTHANASIA see also ADKINS, JANET

EVANGELICALISM

Cockburn, Alexander. Descriptions of sin are what we want at the breakfast table, not admonitions against it. (Village Voice 23:13 Jan 9, 78)

Coffin, William Sloane. If you get an Evangelical with a social conscience you've got one of God's true saints. (Time 110:58 Dec 26, 77)

EVOLUTION—STUDY AND TEACHING

Deen, Braswell (Georgia judge). This monkey mythology of Darwin is the cause of permissiveness, promiscuity, pills, prophylactics, perversions, pregnancies, abortions, pornotherapy, pollution, poisoning and proliferation of crimes of all types. (Life 5:58 Jan 82)

EXECUTIVES

Davis, Evelyn Y. A company is only as good or as bad as its chef executive officer. (M 6:62 Aug 89)

EXECUTIVES see also SMITH, ROGER

EXERCISE

Nixon, Richard Milhous. One thing I really hate is exercise for exercise's sake. (Philadelphia 69:131 April 78)

EXPENDITURES, PUBLIC

Parkinson, C. Northcote. Expenditure rises to meet income. (Washingtonian 14:155 Nov 78)

EXPERTS

Butler, Nicholas Murray. An expert is one who knows more and more about less and less. (Kansas City Times 109:14B July 8, 77)

Desae, Morarji. An expert seldom gives an objective view. He gives his own view. (Time 111:47 Feb 27, 78)

EXPLANATION

Einstein, Albert. Everything should be made as simple as possible, but not simpler. (Newsweek 93:100 April 16, 79)

Hubbard, Elbert. Never explain. Your friends do not need it and your enemies will not believe you anyway. (Kansas City Star 97:4B Oct 10, 76)

FACTS

Gordimer, Nadine. The facts are always less than what really happened. (Time 110:93 Sept 19, 77)

Keyserling, Hermann A. The greatest American superstition is belief in facts. (Kansas City Times 109:26 Jan 25, 77)

FAILURE

Anonymous (Murphy's Law). If anything can go wrong, eventually it will. (The Reader (Chicago's Free Weekly) 5:2 May 28, 76)

Brett, Ken. The worst curse in the world is unlimited potential. (Arkansas Times 12:67 July 86)

Christie, Agatha. The happy people are failures because they are on such good terms with themselves that they don't give

a damn. (Lawrence (Kansas) Journal-World 127:3D Oct 28, 84)

Simon, William E. Show me a good loser and I'll show you a loser. (Washingtonian 11:24 April 76)

Tomlin, Lily. Why is it we are always hearing about the tragic cases of too much, too soon? What about the rest of us? Too little, too late. (Time 109:71 Mar 28, 77)

Wilson, David B. Sam Wilson used to say that any damn fool can stand adversity; but it takes real quality to stand prosperity. (Kansas City Times 119:A-7 Oct 14, 86)

FAIRCHILD, MORGAN

Fairchild, Morgan. Hair and cleavage— that's all they need me for. (US 3:4 May 4, 87)

Fairchild, Morgan. They told me a good bitch was hard to find, and so I became a good bitch (on her career). (US 3:64 May 5, 86)

FALWELL, JERRY

Goldwater, Barry Morris. Every good Christian ought to kick Falwell right in the ass. (Newsweek 99:44 Jan 4, 82)

FAME

Ashbery, John. If one is a famous poet, one still isn't famous. (Details 6:99 Mar 88)

Bowen, Elizabeth. All your youth you want to have your greatness taken for granted; when you find it taken for granted, you are unnerved. (Kansas City Star 97:15C Sept 22, 76)

Hendrix, Jimi. It's funny the way most people love the dead. Once you are dead, you are made for life. (Rolling Stone 227:81 Dec 2, 76)

Lasser, Louise. When you are a celebrity, you are totally a victim. (Time 111:56 June 19, 78)

Lindbergh, Charles Augustus. I've had enough fame for a dozen lives; it's not what it's cracked up to be. (New York Times Magazine 12 May 8, 77)

Margolis, Susan. Today the gifted as well as the deranged among us are struggling to be famous the way earlier Americans struggled to be saved. (Time 111:56 June 19, 78)

Meredith, Don. The higher you climb the flagpole, the more people see your rear end. (Life 7:141 Jan 84)

Morrow, Lance. Celebrities are intellectual fast food. (Time 111:57 June 12, 78)

Morrow, Lance. When fame ceases to bear any relation to worth or accomplishment, then the whole currency of public recognition is debased. (Time 111:56 June 19, 78)

Nabokov, Vladimir. Anonymous praise hurts nobody. (New York Times Book Review

27 July 31, 77)
O'Connor, Flannery. (Fame) is a comic distinction shared with Roy Rogers's horse and Miss Watermelon of 1955. (Time 113:86 Mar 5, 79)
Rubin, Jerry. I'm famous. That's my job. (Christian Science Monitor 68:30 April 26, 76)
Tanner, Jack. Fame is empty. But it is better to find that out afterwards. (Challenge 19:5 Mar/April 76)
Wolfe, Tom. You can be denounced from the heavens, and it only makes people interested. (Time 114:82 Sept 24, 79)

FAME see also AUTHORS—FAME

FAMILY

Lance, Thomas Bertram. Folks are serious about three things—their religion, their family, and most of all, their money. (Time 108:20 Dec 6, 76)

FAMILY LIFE

Crosby, Bing. Family life is the basis for a strong community and a great nation. (National Catholic Reporter 12:8 July 2, 76)
Mead, Margaret. At least 50 percent of the human race doesn't want their mother-in-law within walking distance. (Newsweek 92:75 Nov 27, 78)

FARMING

Berry, Wendell. Learning to farm is learning to farm a farm. (The Nation 249:418 Oct 16, 89)

FASCISM

Khomeini, Ayatollah Ruhollah. Dictatorship is the greatest sin in the religion of Islam. Fascism and Islamism are absolutely incompatible. (Time 114:57 Oct 22, 79)

FASHION

Alsop, Stewart. A fashionable gentleman who much concerns himself with the fashions of gentlemen is neither fashionable nor a gentleman. (Newsweek 83:108 April 15, 74)
Berhanger, Elio. Fashion has become like an old prostitute. Nobody even uses the word elegance anymore. (W 7:8 Mar 17, 78)
Cardin, Pierre. Chanel never influenced fashion one bit. (W 8:5 Mar 16, 79)
Rykiel, Sonia. Every woman must create her own ambience; it is not I or Yves St. Laurent but the woman who has to create herself and be a unique person. (Time 110:54 Nov 7, 77)
Saint Laurent, Yves. Fashions fade, style is eternal. (Andy Warhol's Interview 5:13 April 75)
Sinclair, Clive. High tech is high fashion. (Village Voice 27:71 Mar 30, 82)

Vollbracht, Michaele. If you have to talk about fashion, then you are not in it. (Village Voice 22:63 Mar 14, 77)
Vreeland, Diana. Show me a fashionable woman, and I will show you a woman who accomplished something. (Newsweek 91:3 Jan 2, 78)
Wolfe, Tom. Fashion, to put it most simply, is the code language of status. (Mother Jones 8:18 Jan 83)

FASHION DESIGN

Blass, Bill. Design is like the theatre—the bug bites you early. (Bookviews 1:36 June 78)

FASHION DESIGNERS

Vollbracht, Michaele. If you have to talk about fashion, then you are not in it. (Village Voice 22:63 Mar 14, 77)

FASHION DESIGNERS see also CARDIN, PIERRE; GIVENCHY, HUBERT DE; LAUREN, RALPH

FAT see also OBESITY

FATE

Barnard, Christiaan. I believe in destiny, and there's very little you can do to change it. (Time 126:65 July 22, 85)

FAULKNER, WILLIAM

Faulkner, William. I gave the world what it wanted—guts and genitals. (True 57:14 Dec 75)

FEAR

Brooks, Mel. Everything we do in life is based on fear, especially love. (Playboy 26:26 Oct 79)
King, Martin Luther, Jr. I'm not fearing any man. Mine eyes have seen the glory of the coming of the Lord. (Playboy 23:127 June 76)
Landor, Walter Savage. Men cannot bear to be deprived of anything they are used to; not even of their fears. (Kansas City Star 97:4B Oct 10, 76)

FEDERAL GOVERNMENT

Bush, George. I'm from the federal government, and I'm here to help you [are] the eleven most frightening words in the English language. (Chicago Tribune 21:4 Section 4 Jan 22, 89)
Cranson, Maurice. (Government is) a necessary evil that allows for tyranny by the collectivity over the individual. (Time 110:57 July 25, 77)
Nisbet, Robert. The doctrine of a benevolent state grows stronger. Very big government is not going to disappear. (Newsweek 90:34 Nov 7, 77)

FEDERAL-STATE CONTROVERSIES

Hart, Gary. To get the government off your back, get your hands out of the government's pockets. (Newsweek 90:36 Nov 7, 77)

FELA

Fela, 1938-. Nigerians like to fight, that's why they like me. (New York Times 138:15 Nov 18, 88)

FELLINI, FEDERICO

Fellini, Federico. I don't have problems with actors—they have problems with me. (Time 107:76 May 17, 76)

FEMINISM

Johnston, Jill. Feminism at heart is a massive complaint. Lesbianism is the solution. (Time 106:39 Sept 8, 75)

Jong, Erica. It seems to me that sooner or later all intelligent women become feminists. (New York Times 125:32 Nov 8, 75)

Steinem, Gloria. Feminism means that each woman has power over her own life and can decide what to do for herself. (Chicago Tribune 338:1 Dec 4, 78)

FEMINISM see also WOMEN—EQUAL RIGHTS

FEMINISTS see also WOMEN'S LIBERATION MOVEMENT

FICTION

Cheever, John. Fiction is our most intimate and acute means of communication. (US News & World Report 86:92 May 21, 79)

Jong, Erica. I cannibalized real life. (Newsweek 85:71 May 5, 75)

Nabokov, Vladimir. Great novels are above all great fairy tales. Literature does not tell the truth but makes it up. (Newsweek 90:42 July 18, 77)

O'Connor, Flannery. For a fiction writer, to believe nothing is to see nothing. (Ms 8:39 July 79)

Singer, Isaac Bashevis. A Marxist has never written a good novel. (New York Times Magazine 42 Nov 26, 78)

Singer, Isaac Bashevis. Fiction can entertain and stir the mind; it does not direct it. (Time 112:82 July 3, 78)

Styron, William. I think a great novel could even come out of Beverly Hills. (New York Times Book Review 18 May 27, 79)

FICTION see also WRITING

FIELD, MARSHALL, V.—FAMILY

Field, Marshall, V. They all started out with nothing in those days, and the biggest crooks won. I was just lucky to come from a line of successful crooks. (Esquire 89:96 Mar 28, 78)

FIELDS, W. C.

Fields, W. C. Women are like elephants. They're nice to look at but I wouldn't want to own one. (Viva 5:26 Dec 77)

Rosten, Leo. Any man who hates dogs and babies can't be all bad (about W. C. Fields). (TV Guide 26:29 Dec 30, 78)

FINANCE, PERSONAL

Cameron, John. In order to get a loan you

must first prove you don't need it. (Washingtonian 14:154 Nov 78)

Lance, Thomas Bertram. Folks are serious about three things—their religion, their family, and most of all, their money. (Time 108:20 Dec 6, 76)

Mailer, Norman. My talent is making money, not managing it. (Kansas City Times 111:2A Jan 25, 79)

Parker, Charlie. Romance without finance ain't got no chance. (The Animator 4:1 Fall 76)

Stevenson, Adlai, II. There was a time when a fool and his money were soon parted, but now it happens to everybody. (New York Times 128:A19 June 11, 79)

FINLEY, CHARLES OSCAR

Finley, Charles Oscar. I've never seen so many damned idiots as the owners in sport. (Time 106:42 Aug 18, 75)

Griffith, Calvin. He's the P.T. Barnum of baseball. (about Charles Oscar Finley). (Time 106:42 Aug 18, 75)

Symington, Stuart. (Charles Finley) is one of the most disreputable characters to enter the American sports scene. (New York Times 125:2 Section 5 Sept 19, 76)

FIREARMS—LAWS AND REGULATIONS

Hansen, George. Firearms are not the problem. People are. (American Opinion 18:29 Sept 75)

Koch, Edward I. You're not a nice guy if you have a gun, even if you are a nice guy. (Time 115:63 Mar 3, 80)

Mankiewicz, Frank Fabian. Since we are not yet serious about guns, let us at least withhold the most costly target (the President). (Newsweek 86:34 Oct 6, 75)

Reagan, Ronald. Take away the arms of the citizenry and where is its defense. (Time 106:24 Nov 24, 75)

Rogers, Roy. They'll have to shoot me first to take my gun. (Time 120:61 Aug 2, 82)

Thompson, Hunter S. I don't plan to give up any of my guns until the cops give up theirs. (The California Aggie 96:6 Mar 2, 78)

FISHER, M. F. K.

Auden, Wystan Hugh. I do not know of anyone in the United States who writes better prose (about M. F. K. Fisher). (Bon Appetit 23:127 Nov 78)

FISHERMEN

Apollonio, Spencer. When four fishermen get together, there's always a fifth. (Down East 22:108 Dec 31, 75)

FISHING

Talbert, Diron. There ain't but one time to go fishin' and that's whenever you can. (Washingtonian 11:116 Sept 76)

FITZGERALD, F. SCOTT

Fitzgerald, F. Scott. I talk with the authority of failure—Ernest (Hemingway) with the authority of success. (Time 111:89 April 3, 78)

FITZGERALD, ZELDA

Fitzgerald, Zelda. A vacuum can only exist, I imagine, by the things which enclose it. (Chicago Tribune 176:2 Section 2 June 25, 78)

FLAGS—MUTILATION, DEFACEMENT, ETC.

Brennan, William. We do not consecrate the flag by punishing its descration for in doing so we dilute the freedom that this cherished emblem represents. (Newsweek 114:20 July 3, 89)

Bush, George. Flag burning is wrong—dead wrong. (Time 134:15 July 3, 89)

Cole, David. If free expression is to exist in this country, people must be as free to burn the flag as they are to wave it. (Time 134:15 July 3, 89)

FLANNER, JANET

Flanner, Janet. I'm not one of those journalists with a staff. I don't even have a secretary. I act as a sponge. I soak it up and squeeze it out in ink every two weeks. (New York Times 28:B10 Nov 8, 78)

FLATTERY

Lindsay, John Vliet. Flattery isn't harmful unless inhaled. (Chicago Tribune 22:1 Section 2 Jan 22, 78)

FLIGHT

Dickey, James. Flight is the only truly new sensation that men have achieved in modern history. (New York Times Book Review 15 July 15, 79)

FLOREZ, ELISA (MISSY)

Florez, Elisa (Missy). When you start getting paid big money to take your clothes off, and people tell you look good, it does wonders for you. (Washingtonian 22:24 April 87)

FLORIDA see also MIAMI

FLY FISHING

Maclean, Norman. In our family, there was no clear line between religion and fly fishing. (Lawrence (Kansas) Journal-World 130:2C June 12, 88)

FLYNT, LARRY

Flynt, Larry. If you ask me, yes, I am a born-again Christian. But I am going to continue publishing pornography, and anybody who doesn't like it can go kiss a rope. (New York Times 127:A16 Feb 2, 78)

FOLK ART see also PIPPIN, HORACE

FONDA, PETER

Fonda, Peter. I'm heir to nothing but a legend, which is full of ...air. (Chicago Tribune Magazine 70 Nov 6, 77)

FOOD

Curtis, Carl Thomas. In the whole history of the world, whenever a meateating race has gone to war against a non-meateating race, the meat eaters won. It produces superior people. (Washingtonian 11:22-23 Dec 75)

FOOD, HEALTH

Child, Julia. I just hate health food. (San Francisco 25:32 Aug 83)

Redford, Robert. Health food may be good for the conscience, but Oreos taste a hell of a lot better. (Chicago Tribune 27:12 Jan 27, 78)

FOOTBALL

Dodds, Deloss. Football is one of the single most important things in people's lives. (Chicago Tribune 187:9 Section 3 July 6, 87)

Dundes, Alan. Football is a healthy outlet for male-to-male affections just as spin the bottle and post office are healthy outlets for adolescent heterosexual needs. (Time 112:112 Nov 13, 78)

Hayes, Woody. Football is about the only unifying force left in America today. (Life 2:87 Dec 79)

Jones, Bertram Hays. Football plays are like accounting problems. They baffle you at first, but once you've learned the system they're easy. (People Weekly 6:36 Dec 27/Jan 3, 77)

Kemp, Jack. Whether it's politics or football, winning is like shaving: you do it every day or you wind up looking like a bum. (The Sporting News 202:12 Aug 4, 86)

McLuhan, Marshall. Football is itself the biggest dramatization of American business ever invented. (Inside Sports 3:70 Jan 31, 81)

Mills, Chuck. When it comes to football, God is prejudiced—toward big, fast kids (commenting on religion and football). (New York Times 125:3 Feb 1, 76)

FOOTBALL, COLLEGE

Mason, Tony. The thing is that 90% of the colleges are abiding by the rules, doing things right. The other 10%, they're going to the bowl games. (Sports Illustrated 43:14 Oct 27, 75)

Rockne, Knute. You show me a good and gracious loser, and I'll show you a failure! (Argosy 384:15 Nov 76)

FOOTBALL, COLLEGE—COACHES

Bryant, Paul W. (Bear). No coach ever won a game by what he knows; it's what his players have learned. (Time 118:68 Dec 7, 81)

Daugherty, Duffy. All of those football coaches who hold dressing room prayers before a game should be forced to attend church once a week. (Kansas City Star 106:1C Jan 8, 86)

FOOTBALL, PROFESSIONAL

Landry, Tom. Nothing funny ever happens on the football field. (Time 111:75 Jan 16, 78)

Payton, Walter. I don't watch much football. It's boring. (US 3:17 Nov 3, 86)

Wiley, Ralph. A National Football League center once said that potential is a French word meaning you aren't worth a damn yet. (Sports Illustrated 65:27 Oct 6, 86)

**FOOTBALL, PROFESSIONAL—
QUARTERBACKS**

Walker, Doak. He was the greatest two-minute quarterback ever. Bobby Layne simply never lost a game. Sometimes, time just ran out on him. (The Sporting News 202:61 Dec 15, 86)

FOOTBALL—GAMBLING

Rozelle, Pete. The world knows no less rational person than a losing bettor (commenting in opposition to efforts to legalize betting on professional football). (Time 108:69 Sept 20, 76)

FOOTBALL—TEXAS

Wood, Gordon. People in Texas believe in slow-talking football coaches more than they believe in fast-talking politicians. (Chicago Tribune 67:6 Mar 8, 87)

FORD, EDSEL, II

Ford, Edsel, II. I've got engines in my blood. (W 12A:8 July 29, 83)

FORD, GERALD RUDOLPH

Abzug, Bella. Richard Nixon self-impeached himself. He gave us Gerald Ford as his revenge. (Rolling Stone 227:43 Dec 2, 76)

Ford, Gerald Rudolph. Having become Vice President and President without expecting or seeking either, I have a special feeling toward these high offices. To me, the presidency and vice presidency were not prizes to be won, but a duty to be done. (Time 108:22 Aug 30, 76)

Ford, Gerald Rudolph. I learned a long time ago in politics, never say never. (New York Times 128:17 April 22, 79)

Ford, Gerald Rudolph. I'm a better President than a campaigner. (Time 107:16 June 28, 76)

Ford, Gerald Rudolph. My motto towards the Congress is communication, conciliation, compromise and cooperation. (Time 104:27 Dec 2, 74)

Goodwin, Richard N. He's not even an accidental president. He's a double-misfortune president—president

by grace of the criminal code and modern electronics (about Gerald R. Ford). (New York 8:43 Aug 18, 75)

Safire, William. Gerald Ford's Presidency was unique in this century for not producing a single memorable phrase. (New York Times Magazine 90 Nov 19, 78)

Swayduck, Edward. When we examine Ford's political and legislative record, we must ask the crucial question: Is Ford really an Edsel. (Washingtonian 11:294 Dec 75)

FORD, GERALD RUDOLPH—STAFF

Nessen, Ron. Press conferences force more policy decisions than anything else. (Time 106:32 May 5, 75)

FORD, GERALD RUDOLPH—THOUGHT AND THINKING

Ford, Gerald Rudolph. Things are more like they are now than they've ever been. (The Nation 237:385 Oct 29, 83)

FORD, HENRY, II

Bundy, McGeorge. One of the things we've always valued about Henry Ford is candor. (Harper's 254:32 Mar 77)

FORECASTING

Kojak, Theo. Hindsight is the only exact science. (Philadelphia 68:113 July 77)

FOREMAN, GEORGE

Foreman, George. Boxing is like jazz. The better it is, the less people appreciate it. (Sepia 25:12 Sept 76)

FOREST CONSERVATION

Reagan, Ronald. Once you've seen one redwood, you've seen them all. (New York Times Magazine 71 July 4, 76)

FORM

Oldenburg, Claes. To give birth to form is the only act of man that has any consequence. (Chicago 25:18 Nov 76)

FORSTER, E. M.

Forster, E. M. If I had to choose between betraying my country and betraying my friend, I hope I should have the guts to betray my country. (Time 115:78 June 2, 80)

FRANCE

Bell, Helen Choate. The French are a low lot. Give them two more legs and a tail, and there you are. (New York 10:88 Jan 31, 77)

Wilder, Billy. France is a country where the money falls apart in your hands and you can't tear the toilet paper. (New York 8:43 Nov 24, 75)

FRANCE see also ATOMIC POWER—FRANCE;
  CHARACTERS AND CHARACTERISTICS—FRANCE

FRANCE—POLITICS AND GOVERNMENT

Anonymous. The right governs, the left thinks (about French politics). (Time

114:31 Aug 13, 79)
Giscard d'Estaing, Valery. Nuclear energy is at the crossroads of the two independences of France: the independence of her defense and the independence of her energy supply. (Time 110:31 Aug 15, 77)

Pasqua, Charles (French interior minister). Democracy ends where the interest of the State begins. (The Progressive 51:10 July 87)

FRANCE—POLITICS AND GOVERNMENT
see also DE GAULLE, CHARLES

FRANCO, FRANCISCO
Aregood, Richard. They say only the good die young. Generalissimo Francisco Franco was 82. Seems about right. (More 6:55 July/Aug 76)

FRANKEL'S LAW (QUOTATION)
Frankel, Charles. Whatever happens in government could have happened differently, and it usually would have been better if it had. (The Reader (Chicago's Free Weekly) 5:2 May 28, 76)

FRANKLIN, BENJAMIN
Comins, David H. People will accept your idea more readily if you tell them Benjamin Franklin said it first. (Washingtonian 14:152 Nov 78)

FREE ENTERPRISE
Iacocca, Lee A. The free-enterprise system has gone to hell. (Time 114:74 Oct 8, 79)

Kahn, J. Kesner. Free market competition, freely advertised, is consumerism at its best. (American Opinion 18:18 June 75)

Ray, Dixie Lee. Anything that the private sector can do, government can do it worse. (Mother Jones 2:31 May 77)

FREE PRESS see FREEDOM OF THE PRESS

FREE SPEECH
Fleishman, Stanley. There are more citizens in jail in the United States today for publishing books, magazines, newspapers, and films than there are in all the countries of the world put together. (American Film 2:4 June 77)

Lumbard, J. Edward. In areas of doubt and conflicting considerations, it is thought better to err on the side of free speech. (American Legion Magazine 102:22 June 77)

Moynihan, Daniel Patrick. There is no nation so poor that it cannot afford free speech, but there are few elites which will put up with the bother of it. (Time 107:28 Jan 26, 76)

FREE TRADE AND PROTECTION
Hyland, William G. Protectionism is the ally of isolationism, and isolationism is the Dracula of American foreign policy. (New York Times 136:2 May 17, 87)

FREEDOM see LIBERTY

FREEDOM OF THE PRESS
Buchwald, Art. In 80 percent of the countries in the world today, guys like myself would be in jail. (Book Digest 4:27 Sept 77)

Douglas, William Orville. The press has a preferred position in our constitutional scheme not to enable it to make money, not to set newsmen apart as a favored class, but to bring fulfillment to the public's right to know. (New York Times 127:2 Section 4 Aug 6, 78)

Gurfein, Murray. A cantankerous press must be suffered by those in authority in order to preserve freedom of expression and the right of the people to know. (Time 114:59 Dec 31, 79)

Irani, C. R. The only protection for a free press is the courage to demand it. (Chicago Tribune 233:4 Section 2 Aug 21, 77)

Kennedy, Edward Moore. If and when needed, anti-trust laws are ready and able to promote a diverse and competitive press. (Esquire 91:6 Feb 27, 79)

Liebling, A. J. Freedom of the press belongs to those who own one. (American Film 3:67 July/Aug 78)

Lippmann, Walter. The theory of a free press is that the truth will emerge from free reporting and free discussions, not that it is presented perfectly and instantly in any one account. (Chicago Tribune 57:2 Section 5 Feb 26, 89)

Moynihan, Daniel Patrick. When a person goes to a country and finds their newspapers filled with nothing but good news, he can bet there are good men in jail. (University Daily Kansan 87:4 Feb 16, 77)

Nader, Ralph. Information is the currency of democracy. (Chicago Tribune 258:3 Sept 15, 89)

FRENCH
Barenboim, Daniel. When they want to be difficult, the French can seem impossible. But when they decide to get something done, there's no one better. (Time 125:65 June 17, 85)

FREUD, SIGMUND
Freud, Sigmund. My cigar is not a symbol. It is only a cigar. (Washingtonian 12:112 April 77)

FRIEDMAN, MILTON
Friedman, Milton. There is no such thing as a free lunch. That is the sum of my economic theory. The rest is elaboration. (Reader's Digest 112:190 Feb 78)

FRIENDSHIP
Carter, Hodding, III. The thing you have to remember about Southerners is that we're

always generous and forgiving—with our friends. (New York 9:28 July 26, 76)

Eastwood, Clint. Everybody talks about love, but the thing that keeps marriage together for me is friendship. (Chicago Tribune Magazine 174:25 Aug 1, 76)

Forster, E. M. If I had to choose between betraying my country and betraying my friend, I hope I should have the guts to betray my country. (Time 115:78 June 2, 80)

Gentry, Dave Tyson. True friendship comes when silence between two people is comfortable. (Reader's Digest 107:56B Sept 75)

Humphrey, Hubert Horatio. The greatest gift of life is friendship and I have received it. (Time 110:23 Nov 7, 77)

Jones, Thomas. Friends may come and go, but enemies accumulate. (Washingtonian 14:155 Nov 78)

Truman, Harry S. You want a friend in this life, get a dog. (New West 3:33 Dec 4, 78)

FUEL INDUSTRY

Nader, Ralph. There is not an energy crisis. There is an energy monopoly crisis, too many of the energy decisions are being made by a few large corporations instead of by a broader aggregate of consumer determinants. (Meet the Press 21:3 April 17, 77)

Penden, Bill. Atomic energy is a future idea whose time is past. Renewable energy is a future idea whose time has come. (Atlas World Press Review 24:38 April 77)

FUEL INDUSTRY—WESTERN STATES

Apodaca, Jerry. Let there be no mistake, the West will not become an energy colony for the rest of the nation. (Newsweek 85:65 May 5, 75)

FUND RAISING

Shapiro, Joseph H. Nowhere is a man's imagination so fertile as in the discovery of new ways to say no to a man who asks for money. (Chicago 26:178 Sept 77)

FUNERALS

Ray, Man. I would like to go to only one funeral, mine. (Andy Warhol's Interview 7:23 Feb 76)

FUR BEARING ANIMALS

Moore, Mary Tyler. Behind each beautiful wild fur there is an ugly story. It is a brutal, bloody and barbaric story. The animal is not killed—it is tortured. I don't think a fur coat is worth it. (Chicago Sun-Times 28:3 Nov 18, 75)

FUR COATS, WRAPS, ETC.

Moore, Mary Tyler. Behind each beautiful wild fur there is an ugly story. It is a brutal, bloody and barbaric story. The animal is not killed—it is tortured. I don't think a fur coat is worth it. (Chicago Sun-Times 28:3 Nov 18, 75)

FUTURE

Brecht, Bertolt. Because things are the way they are things will not stay the way they are. (Philadelphia Magazine 68:305 Nov 77)

Brown, Edmund Gerald, Jr. We must sacrifice for the future, or else we steal from it. (The Tennessean 74:6 April 11, 79)

Buck, Pearl. One faces the future with one's past. (Chicago Tribune 176:2 Section 2 June 25, 78)

Clarke, Arthur C. The facts of the future can hardly be imagined ab initio by those who are unfamiliar with the fantasies of the past. (Omni 2:94 April 80)

Dyson, Freeman. The only certainty in (the) remote future is that radically new things will be happening. (Omni 2:40 June 80)

Eiseley, Loren. There is but one way into the future: the technological way. (Time 110:61 July 25, 77)

Fuller, R. Buckminster. The future is a choice between Utopia and oblivion. (Analog Science Fiction/Science Fact 99:97 Oct 79)

Orwell, George. If you want a picture of the future, imagine a boot stamping on the human face—forever...and remember that it is forever. (Omni 2:94 April 80)

Sanchez, Robert. In looking backward, we must renew our faith in God. In looking forward, we must renew our faith in men. (National Catholic Reporter 12:8 July 2, 76)

Stengel, Charles Dillon (Casey). Never make predictions, especially about the future. (New York 18:20 June 3, 85)

Warhol, Andy. In the future everybody will be world famous for at least 15 minutes. (Time 107:8 May 31, 76)

GABLE, CLARK

Lombard, Carole. You know how much I love Pappy, but to tell you the honest truth, he isn't such a hell of a good lay (about Clark Gable). (Cosmopolitan 197:190 Mar 84)

GABOR, ZSA ZSA

Gabor, Zsa Zsa. I have never hated a man enough to give his diamonds back. (Cosmopolitan 188:268 Feb 80)

GAMBLING see also FOOTBALL—GAMBLING

GAMES

Harris, Sidney J. The paradox in games is that most games are no fun unless you take them seriously; but when you take them seriously, they cease being games. (Chicago Daily News 8 May 5, 77)

GARDENING

Pereire, Anita. Gardening is a combination of being an architect and an interior designer. (W 15:29 June 16, 86)

GARLAND, JUDY

Garland, Judy. I have gone through hell, I tell you, a hell no one, no person, no man, no beast, not even a fire hydrant could endure. (Newsweek 85:52 May 26, 75)

GARN, JAKE

Garn, Jake. I frankly don't give a damn if a 14-legged bug or the woundfin minnow live or die. (Outside 1:10 July 78)

GASTRONOMY

Claiborne, Craig. I think that some people, and I suspect a great number of people, are born with the gustatory equivalent of perfect pitch. (New York Times 126:C6 Nov 22, 76)

GEMS

Earhart, Amelia. There are two kinds of stones, as everyone knows, one of which rolls. (Chicago Tribune 176:2 Section 2 June 25, 78)

GENERAL MOTORS CORPORATION

Perot, H. Ross. We've got to nuke the GM system. (Kansas City Times 120:A-2 Jan 30, 88)

Smith, Roger. I'd rather be remembered as the guy that lost market share and increased profits than the guy who increased market share and lost profits. (Chicago Tribune 215:21 Section 1 Aug 3, 90)

GENERALIZATIONS

Pitman, Keith A. All generalizations are untrue. (Washingtonian 14:26 Dec 78)

GENERATION GAP see CONFLICT OF GENERATIONS

GEORGIA—POLITICS AND GOVERNMENT

Young, Andrew. Georgia is more liberal than New York. (Atlanta 19:60 Nov 79)

GERMAN REUNIFICATION QUESTION

Andreotti, Giulio. There are two German states, and there must remain two German states. (Time 134:34 Sept 11, 89)

Brandt, Willy. Unity is only a question of time. (Chicago Tribune 361:19 Section 1 Dec 27, 89)

Kohl, Helmut. We have less reason than ever to be resigned to the long-term division of Germany into two states. (New York Times 139:2 Nov 9, 89)

Walesa, Lech. We should leave the political situation as it is now (1989). (Newsweek 104:35 Nov 27, 89)

GERMANY (FEDERAL REPUBLIC)— FOREIGN RELATIONS

Schmidt, Helmut. We Germans are in the heart of Europe. In any new war, we have everything to lose and nothing to gain. (Newsweek 96:37 July 14, 80)

GERMANY (FEDERAL REPUBLIC)— POLITICS AND GOVERNMENT see also SCHMIDT, HELMUT

GETTY, GORDON PETER

Getty, Gordon Peter. I think I will be remembered not for my music, but for my economic theories. (Chicago Tribune 50:14B Section 7 Feb 19, 89)

GETTY, JEAN PAUL

Getty, Jean Paul. I suffer no guilt complexes or conscience pangs about my wealth. The Lord may have been disproportionate, but that is how He—or nature, if you like—operates. (Time 107:41 May 24, 76)

Getty, Jean Paul. If you can count your money, you don't have a billion dollars. (Newsweek 87:55 June 14, 76)

GIFTS

Gibbs, Philip. It's better to give than to lend, and it costs about the same. (Kansas City Star 97:38 July 14, 77)

GILLESPIE, DIZZY

Gillespie, Dizzy. It took me all my life to learn the biggest music lesson of them all— what not to play. (Sepia 25:10 Dec 76)

GILMORE, GARY MARK

Gilmore, Gary Mark. Death is the only inescapable, unavoidable, sure thing. We are sentenced to die the day we're born. (Chicago Sun-Times 29:2 Nov 17, 76)

GINGRICH, NEWT

Alexander, Bill. Mr. Gingrich is a congressional Jimmy Swaggart, who condemns sin while committing hypocrisy. (Village Voice 33:18 May 9, 89)

Gingrich, Newt. I am now a famous person (1985). (Washingtonian 20:5 July 85)

GINSBERG, ALLEN

Ginsberg, Allen. I like a varied audience— little old ladies, homosexuals, weirdos. (Time 113:81 Mar 5, 79)

GIONO, JEAN

Giono, Jean. Reality pushed to its extreme ends in unreality. (Village Voice 21:93 Sept 27, 76)

GISH, LILLIAN

Gish, Lillian. I've had the best life of anyone I know, or knew, Dear. And I knew some amazing people. (Guardian Weekly 120:19 May 6, 79)

GIULINI, CARLO MARIA

Giulini, Carlo Maria. I always think I am a very small man. When I shave myself, I look in the mirror and see behind me Beethoven and Brahms. (Time 111:63 April 3, 78)

GIVENCHY, HUBERT DE

Givenchy, Hubert De. After I open a collection and see people trying on my clothes and treating them roughly, I suffer. My dresses are like my family. (Time 110:67 Sept 26, 77)

THE GLASS MENAGERIE (THEATRICAL PRODUCTION)

Williams, Tennessee. They teach it (The Glass Menagerie) in college now, and everybody approaches it as though it were a place of worship. Frankly, I fall asleep at times. (Time 106:31 Dec 29, 75)

GLEASON, JACKIE

Gleason, Jackie. How sweet it is! (Time 13:58 Dec 28, 87)

Gleason, Jackie. I drank because it removed the warts and blemishes. Not from me but from the people I associated with. It sort of dimmed the lights. (Chicago Tribune Magazine 17 Mar 26, 78)

GOD

Barth, John. God was a pretty good novelist; the only trouble was that He was a realist. (New York Times Book Review 33 April 1, 79)

Beauvoir, Simone De. I cannot be angry at God, in whom I do not believe. (The Observer 9776:10 Jan 7, 79)

Bryant, Anita. God says that someone who practices homosexuality shall not inherit the Kingdom of God. God is very plain on that. (Ms 6:50 July 77)

Caddell, Patrick. Clearly, God is a Democrat. (Boston 68:115 Sept 76)

Charles, Prince of Wales. Our protection depends, I believe, on the mystical power which from time immemorial has been called God. (The Observer 9937:13 Feb 14, 82)

Einstein, Albert. God may be subtle, but He isn't mean. (The Observer 9785:9 Mar 11, 79)

Fuller, R. Buckminster. Sometimes I think we're alone. Sometimes I think we're not. In either case, the thought is quite staggering. (Omni 2:39 April 80)

Galbraith, John Kenneth. I reserve judgment on whether God is a conservative or not. (Life 5:58 Jan 82)

Gallup, George. I could prove God statistically. (Omni 2:42 Nov 79)

Ionesco, Eugene. Basically I think it is stupid not to believe in God. (Harvard Magazine 89:24 Nov 86)

King, Martin Luther, Jr. I'm not fearing any man. Mine eyes have seen the glory of the coming of the Lord. (Playboy 23:127 June 76)

Knight, Damon. If there is a universal mind, must it be sane? (Village Voice 23:37 Aug 21, 78)

Landry, Tom. God doesn't make any losers. (Chicago Sun-Times 32:32 April 21, 79)

Lebowitz, Fran. If God had meant for everything to happen at once, he would not have invented desk calendars. (Time 111:K3 May 29, 78)

Lewis, C. S. A young man who wishes to remain a sound atheist cannot be too careful of his reading. God is, if I may say it, very unscrupulous. (New York Times 126:B1 Dec 20, 76)

Orlans, Harold. Logic is a game men play as cats play with balls of string, whereas reality is a game the gods play with us. (Change 9:34 April 77)

Sanchez, Robert. In looking backward, we must renew our faith in God. In looking forward, we must renew our faith in men. (National Catholic Reporter 12:8 July 2, 76)

Sandburg, Carl. A baby is God's opinion that the world should go on. (Kansas City Star 97:2D Feb 20, 77)

Shaffer, Floyd. I believe it would be healthier if the church could laugh because I believe that God laughs. (Newsweek 86:64 Sept 29, 75)

Tanner, Jack. When God created the world, He said it was good. That was His second mistake. (Challenge 19:5 Mar/April 76)

Updike, John. I've never been able to take sins of the flesh awfully seriously, nor do I believe that God takes them terribly seriously. (Kansas City Star 119:4C Oct 14, 86)

Voznesensky, Andrei. When Man put on clothes for the first time, he challenged the Lord and became His equal. (Vogue 168:193 Feb 78)

White, Theodore. If you go back through 2000 years, I guess luck, Marx, and God have made history, the three of them together. (Firing Line 15 July 26, 75)

GOLD

Henshaw, Paul C. Gold is how you survive when everything else is down the drain. (New West 1:11 July 5, 76)

GOLDWATER, BARRY MORRIS

Goldwater, Barry Morris. I don't care if I'm called a Democrat or a Republican as long as I'm in bed with people of the same thinking. (Rolling Stone 227:43 Dec 2, 76)

Goldwater, Barry Morris. I don't object to a woman doing anything in combat as long as she gets home in time to cook dinner. (Viva 5:29 Oct 77)

Goldwater, Barry Morris. This is a great country where anybody can grow up to be President—except me. (Chicago Tribune 245:20 Sept 2, 77)

GOLDWYN, SAMUEL
Goldwyn, Samuel. If ya wanna send a message, call Western Union. (Mother Jones 2:61 Sept 77)

GOLF
Carter, Don. One of the advantages bowling has over golf is that you seldom lose a bowling ball. (Sports Illustrated 43:8 Aug 11, 75)

Trevino, Lee. Pressure is playing for ten dollars when you don't have a dime in your pocket. (Esquire 93:44 Jan 31, 80)

GOODMAN, BENNY
Goodman, Benny. Everything I own, whatever I have accomplished, all that I am, really, I owe to music. (People Weekly 9:80 Jan 23, 78)

GOODWIN, RICHARD N.
Moyers, Bill D. Dick Goodwin was no saint, not close, but if there's a hereafter, I'd rather spend it with Goodwin than with Gabriel. (New York 8:38 Aug 18, 75)

GORBACHEV, MIKHAIL
Reagan, Ronald. I don't resent his (Mikhail Gorbachev) popularity or anything else. Good Lord, I costarred with Errol Flynn once. (Chicago Tribune 342:17 Dec 8, 87)

Sakharov, Andrei Dmitrievich. There is, of course, no alternative to Mikhail Gorbachev as leader of the Soviet Union at this decisive moment in its history. (Chicago Tribune 365:5 Section 1 Dec 31, 89)

GOSSIP
Dempster, Nigel. If you can't take it (gossip), then don't give it. (Viva 4:105 Oct 76)

Korda, Michael. Gossip, unlike river water, flows both ways. (Reader's Digest 106:114 June 76)

Lilly, Doris. Gossip and manure are only good for one thing—and that's spreading. Gossip doesn't mean a damn thing unless you spread it around. (W 4:2 Aug 22, 75)

GOSSIP see also LEAR, AMANDA

GOURMETS see GASTRONOMY

GOVERNMENT ADMINISTRATIVE EFFICIENCY see EFFICIENCY, ADMINISTRATIVE

GOVERNMENT AND THE PRESS
Anderson, Jack. The founding fathers intended us to be watchdogs, not lapdogs. (Time 106:78 Nov 24, 75)

Cline, Ray S. The only unrestricted intelligence organization in this country is the American press. (Time 106:10 Aug 4, 75)

Fulbright, James William. If once the press was excessively orthodox and unquestioning of Government policy, it has now become almost sweepingly iconoclastic. (Time 106:78 Nov 24, 75)

Nessen, Ron. Press conferences force more policy decisions than anything else. (Time 106:32 May 5, 75)

Nixon, Richard Milhous. When news is concerned, nobody in the press is a friend—they are all enemies. (Time 111:104 April 17, 78)

GOVERNMENT AND THE PRESS— GREAT BRITAIN
Knight, Andrew (Editor of The Economist, London). We are a government of opposition, no matter who is in power. (W 4:2 Sept 19, 75)

GOVERNMENT EMPLOYEES
Bush, George. Government should be an opportunity for public service, not for public gain. (Chicago Tribune 36:6 Section 4 Feb 5, 89)

Strauss, Robert S. Everybody in government is like a bunch of ants on a log floating down a river. Each one thinks he is guiding the log, but it's really just going with the flow. (Time 111:47 April 17, 78)

GOVERNMENT SPENDING POLICY
Jarvis, Howard. The only way to cut Government spending is not to give them the money to spend in the first place. (New West 3:32 July 3, 78)

GOVERNMENTAL DECISION MAKING see DECISION MAKING (POLITICAL SCIENCE)

GOVERNORS
Brown, Edmund Gerald, Jr. The power of the executive is like a chess game; there are very few moves that one can make. (Gold Coast Pictorial 13:9 Feb 77)

GRABLE, BETTY
Grable, Betty. There are only two reasons for my success, and I'm standing on them. (New Orleans 10:108 July 31, 76)

GRAFT IN POLITICS see POLITICS, CORRUPTION IN

GRAHAM, BILLY
Graham, Billy. I believe I have demonic forces opposed to me wherever I preach. (The Observer 9832:9 Feb 3, 80)

Graham, Billy. Nixon in my judgement was a true intellectual. (Chicago Tribune Magazine 46 Nov 6, 77)

Graham, Billy. The pressures of being a well-known clergyman are unbelievable, and I'd like to escape to heaven if I could. (Chicago Tribune Magazine 32 Nov 6, 77)

GRAND JURY
Campbell, William J. The grand jury is the total captive of the prosecutor, who, if he is candid, will concede that he can indict anybody, at any time, for almost anything, before any grand jury. (Time 110:61 July 4, 77)

GRANT, CARY
Grant, Cary. My formula for living is quite simple. I get up in the morning and go to bed at night. In between times, I occupy myself as best I can. (Los Angeles Times Calendar 39 June 11, 78)

GRATITUDE
Lindsay, John Vliet. If you want gratitude, get yourself a dog. (Chicago Tribune 22:2 Section 2 Jan 22, 78)

GRAVES, ROBERT
Spender, Stephen. He (Robert Graves) was one of those rare people whom, whatever their foibles, one knows to be ultimately true and good. (Manchester Guardian Weekly 133:5 Dec 15, 85)

GREAT BRITAIN see also BUSINESSMEN—GREAT BRITAIN; CHARACTERS AND CHARACTERISTICS—GREAT BRITAIN; GOVERNMENT AND THE PRESS—GREAT BRITAIN; SOCIALISM—GREAT BRITAIN

GREAT BRITAIN—DESCRIPTION
Baldwin, James. The range (and rein) of accents on that damp little island make England coherent for the English and totally incomprehensible for everyone else. (Saturday Review 6:14 Oct 13, 79)
Goldsmith, James. We (British) have reached the state where the private sector is that part of the economy the Government controls and the public sector is the part that nobody controls. (The Observer 9787:11 Mar 25, 79)

GREAT BRITAIN—ECONOMIC CONDITIONS
Thatcher, Margaret Hilda. You cannot have national welfare before someone has created national wealth. (Time 112:61 Sept 11, 78)

GREAT BRITAIN—ECONOMIC POLICY
Healey, Denis. Mrs. Thatcher is doing for monetarism what the Boston Strangler did for door-to-door salesmen. (The Observer 9825:10 Dec 16, 79)

GREAT BRITAIN—FOREIGN POLICY
Thatcher, Margaret Hilda. Foreign policy is simply a matter of national self-interest. (New York Times Magazine 56 April 29, 79)

GREAT BRITAIN—FOREIGN RELATIONS
Macmillan, Harold. A foreign secretary is forever poised between a cliche and an indiscretion. (Kansas City Star 97:4B Jan 30, 77)

GREAT BRITAIN—POLITICS AND GOVERNMENT
Cockburn, Alexander. A nation that love Hailsham and re-elects Thatcher deserves everything it gets. (Village Voice 28:15 June 14, 83)

Heal, Sylvia. The dark age of Thatcherism is drawing to a close (1990). (Newsweek 115:31 April 2, 90)
Howe, Sir Geoffrey. Finance must determine expenditure; expenditure must not determine finance. (The Observer 9799:9 June 17, 79)
Thatcher, Margaret Hilda. Britain's progress toward socialism has been an alternation of two steps forward with half a step back. (Time 105:30 Feb 10, 75)
Thatcher, Margaret Hilda. I never read books. (The Observer 9774:7 Dec 24, 79)
Thatcher, Margaret Hilda. If a Tory does not believe that private property is one of the main bulwarks of individual freedom, then he had better become a socialist and have done with it. (Time 105:30-31 Feb 24, 75)
Thatcher, Margaret Hilda. It is important not to be so obsessed with yesterday's danger that we fail to detect today's. (The Observer 9822:9 Nov 25, 79)
Thatcher, Margaret Hilda. We are not short of summits. The only thing we are short of is the results from summits. (The Observer 9723:11 Dec 18, 77)
Thatcher, Margaret Hilda. What Britain needs is an iron lady. (Newsweek 93:50 May 14, 79)

GREAT BRITAIN—POLITICS AND GOVERNMENT see also HEATH, EDWARD; THATCHER, MARGARET HILDA

GREAT BRITAIN—SOCIAL LIFE AND CUSTOMS
Balanchine, George. In England you have to be dignified; if you are awake it is already vulgar. (The Observer 9813:14 Sept 23, 79)

GREECE—POLITICS AND GOVERNMENT
Caramanlis, Constantine. So we Greeks have been from ancient times: we are skillful at making idols, not that we may worship them, but that we may have the pleasure of destroying them. (Time 110:51 Dec 5, 77)

GREENE, GAEL
Breslin, Jimmy. If this is what happens when you let them out of the kitchen, I'm all for it (commenting on Gael Greene's first novel Blue Skies, No Candy). (New York Times 126:52 Nov 16, 76)

GREENE, GRAHAM
O'Connor, Flannery. What (Graham Greene) does, I think, is try to make religion respectable to the modern unbeliever by making it seedy. (Time 113:86 Mar 5, 79)

GREENMAIL
Epstein, Edward Jay. Corporate America is the perpetrator, not the victim, of greenmail. (Manhattan, Inc. 4:26 Feb 87)

GREENSPAN, ALAN

Greenspan, Alan. When I met Ayn Rand, I was a free enterpriser in the Adam Smith sense, impressed with the theoretical structure and efficiency of markets. What she did was to make me see that capitalism is not only efficient and practical, but also moral. (Newsweek 85:61 Feb 24, 75)

GREER, GERMAINE

Greer, Germaine. Everyone I know is either married or dotty. (The Observer 9790:10 April 15, 79)

Greer, Germaine. I love men like some people like good food or wine. (The Observer 9782:10 Feb 18, 79)

GRETZKY, WAYNE

Brodeur, Richard (goalie for Vancouver Canucks). What he does best is make you look bad (commenting on Wayne Gretzky). (The Sporting News 193:8 Jan 30, 82)

GUCCI (DEPARTMENT STORE)

Gucci, Aldo. We are not businessmen, we are poets. (Town & Country 131:193 Dec 77)

GUGGENHEIM, PEGGY

Guggenheim, Peggy. I don't like art today, I think it has gone to hell. (W 8:24 Oct 12, 79)

GUILT

Beckett, Samuel. There's man all over for you, blaming his boots for the faults of his feet. (Philadelphia 69:187 Sept 78)

Jong, Erica. You don't have to beat a woman if you can make her feel guilty. (Viva 4:28 April 77)

Smith, Patti. Jesus died for somebody's sins but not mine. (Philadelphia 69:185 Sept 78)

GUINNESS, SIR ALEC

Bujold, Genevieve. Caesar was Cleopatra's guru and Guinness was mine. (Newsweek 85:32 Jan 6, 76)

GUMBEL, BRYANT

Gumbel, Bryant. I love to gamble, it's a real weakness. (US 3:64 Sept 9, 85)

GUTHRIE, ARLO

Guthrie, Arlo. The world has shown me what it has to offer...It's a nice plce to visit, but I wouldn't want to live there. (Rolling Stone 268:36 June 29, 78)

HABIT

Maugham, William Somerset. The unfortunate thing about this world is that good habits are so much easier to get out of than bad ones. (Kansas City Times 109:14C Jan 22, 77)

HAGGARD, MERLE

Haggard, Merle. I was born the running

kind, with leaving always on my mind. (Village Voice 25:8 July 2, 80)

HAHN, JESSICA

Hahn, Jessica. I spoke with God and asked for a miracle. The next day, Playboy called. (Chicago Tribune 54:22 Section 1 Feb 23, 89)

HAIG, ALEXANDER M.

Kissinger, Henry Alfred. One thing I don't want around me is a military intellectual. I don't have to worry about you on that score (to Alexander Haig). (Look 1:58 June 11, 79)

Nixon, Richard Malhous. When he is in top form, he can make the eagles scream. (Newsweek 110:21 Sept 21, 87)

HAIR—CARE

Polykoff, Shirley. If I've only one life, let me live it as a blonde! (advertising slogan). (New York 9:37 Aug 23, 76)

HAITI

Allman, T. D. Haiti is to this hemisphere what black holes are to outer space. (Vanity Fair 52:8 Jan 89)

HAITI—ECONOMIC CONDITIONS

Darbouze, Father. Dying of hunger and being executed by the government are the same thing. (Newsweek 96:31 July 7, 80)

HAITI—POLITICS AND GOVERNMENT

Darbouze, Father. Dying of hunger and being executed by the government are the same thing. (Newsweek 96:31 July 7, 80)

HALDEMAN, HARRY ROBBINS

Haldeman, Harry Robbins. I'll approve of whatever will work and am concerned with results—not methods. (Time 103:12 Mar 11, 74)

HALEY, JACK

Haley, Jack. I don't believe there's no business like show business. (Newsweek 93:90 June 18, 79)

HALL, JERRY

Hall, Jerry. Often I think the main point of life is having something to talk about at dinner. (US 3:64 July 1, 85)

HAMMER, ARMAND

Hammer, Armand. Having spent my lifetime fighting injustice, this vindication reinforces my abiding faith in the American system of justice (upon being pardoned for illegal campaign contributions to Richard Nixon's 1972 presidential campaign). (Chicago Tribune 243:27 Aug 31, 89)

HAMMER, MIKE (LITERARY CHARACTER)

Spillane, Mickey. Mike Hammer drinks beer, not cognac, because I can't spell cognac. (American Bookseller 11:23 Dec 87)

HAPPINESS

Christie, Agatha. The happy people are failures because they are on such good terms with themselves that they don't give a damn. (Lawrence (Kansas) Journal-World 127:3D Oct 28, 84)

Gunther, John. All happiness depends on a leisurely breakfast. (Washingtonian 14:154 Nov 78)

Levant, Oscar. Happiness is not a thing you experience, but something you remember. (Chicago 31:22 July 31, 82)

Rubinstein, Artur. Most people ask for happiness on condition. Happiness can only be felt if you don't set any condition. (Kansas City Star 97:15C Sept 22, 76)

HARDING, WARREN GAMALIEL

Harding, Warren Gamaliel. Our most dangerous tendency is to expect too much of government, and at the same time to do for it too little (inaugural address—1921). (Christian Science Monitor 69:14 Jan 20, 77)

HARRIMAN, AVERELL

Harriman, Averell. The Russians are not nuts, they are not crazy people, they're not Hitler. But they are trying to dominate the world by their ideology and we are killing the one instrument which we have to fight that ideology, the CIA. (W 4:16 Nov 16, 75)

HARRIS, FRED

Harris, Fred. The basic issue in 1976 is privilege. It's time to take the rich off welfare. (Newsweek 86:24 Dec 22, 75)

HARRISON, REX

Harrison, Elizabeth (former wife of Rex Harrison). Rex is the only man in the world who would disdainfully send back the wine in his own home. (Time 106:41 Dec 29, 75)

HART, GARY

Hart, Gary. I think it's time we as Americans kind of grow up...and instead of expecting our leaders to be perfect, we are going to have to expect them to be human. (Lawrence (Kansas) Journal-World 130:1A Jan 8, 87)

HARVARD UNIVERSITY. SCHOOL OF LAW

Morgan, Charles, Jr. If Moses had gone to Harvard Law School and spent three years working on the Hill, he would have written the Ten Commandments with three exceptions and a savings clause. (Rolling Stone 205:30 Jan 15, 76)

HATE

Connolly, Cyril. Nothing dates like hate. (Village Voice 22:52 Oct 31, 77)

Davis, Bette. You've got to know someone pretty well to hate them. (Village Voice 21:105 July 19, 76)

Myerson, Bess. You can't be beautiful and hate. (Forbes 122:200 Oct 30, 78)

HAUPTMANN, BRUNO RICHARD

Hauptmann, Bruno Richard. I have said it all, I am innocent. There is nothing else I could tell. (New York 9:76 Nov 22, 76)

HAVEL, VACLAV

Miller, Arthur. I welcome him as the world's first avant-garge president. (Newsweek 115:28 Mar 5, 90)

HAWKINS, PAULA

Hawkins, Paula. Nicaragua is involved in an insidious plot to cripple our youth in America (1985). (Mother Jones 10:11 Aug 85)

HAYDEN, THOMAS

Hayden, Thomas. During the 1960s, we fought the pigs. Now we fight the high price of bacon. (Newsweek 90:36 Nov 7, 77)

Hayden, Thomas. I don't believe that any defense contract ought to be cut in the face of mass unemployment. (US News & World Report 18:12 Nov 3, 75)

Hayden, Thomas. If it weren't for the Bill of Rights people like me would be in jail instead of running for office (commenting on his bid for the Senate). (Los Angeles Times 95:3 Part 1 Jan 5, 76)

HAZARDOUS SUBSTANCES—DISPOSAL

Brown, Michael. We have planted thousands of toxic time bombs; it is only a question of time before they explode (commenting on U. S. chemical dumps). (Life 4:21 Jan 81)

HEARST, PATRICIA CAMPBELL

Welles, Orson. Patty Hearst is the central victim of our time...the best human story in the last thirty years—better than Kane. (Esquire 91:38 Feb 27, 79)

HEATH, EDWARD

Heath, Edward. I started out studying music but very quickly went downhill and into politics. (Time 116:93 Sept 15, 80)

HEFNER, HUGH MARSTON

Hefner, Hugh Marston. I am an incurable romantic. (US 3:6 May 2, 88)

Hefner, Hugh Marston. I'm not primarily an entrepreneurial businessman. I'm primarily a playboy philosopher. (Chicago Tribune 124:1 Section 1 May 3, 76)

Hefner, Hugh Marston. I've had a bachelor party for 30 years, why do I need one now (upon his marriage in 1989). (Chicago Tribune 183:8 Section 1 July 2, 89)

Morton, Arnie (attributed by Victor Lownes). He's (Hugh Hefner) the nicest, kindest, most selfish man I've ever met. (USA Today 1:50 June 30, 83)

HEIDE, WILMA SCOTT

Heide, Wilma Scott. I do not refer to myself as a housewife for the reason that I did not marry a house. (Viva 4:26 Aug 77)

HEIDEGGER, MARTIN

Heidegger, Martin. He who does not know what homesickness is, cannot philosophize. (Time 107:59 June 7, 76)

HELL

Friedman, Milton. In this day and age, we need to revise the old saying to read, Hell hath no fury like a bureaucrat scorned. (Newsweek 86:47 Dec 29, 75)

Hales, E. E. Y. Hell is where you are free to be yourself, and nothing but yourself (commenting in his novel Chariot of Fire). (Time 109:92 Mar 7, 77)

HELLER, JOSEPH

Heller, Joseph. If I could be clever on demand, I'd still be in advertising. (Life 2:16 June 79)

Puzo, Mario. I never knew anybody so determined to be unhappy (about Joseph Heller). (New York Times 128:16 Section 6 Mar 4, 79)

HELLMAN, LILLIAN

Hellman, Lillian. I would like to have had the courage to do what I wrote about. (American Theatre 1:13 May 84)

Hellman, Lillian. If I had to give young writers advice, I would say, Don't listen to writers talking about writing or about themselves. (Time 110:40 Sept 5, 77)

HELM, LEVON

Helm, Levon. Music is medicine, and if the doctor is going to make house calls, he better know how to play. (Newsweek 90:102 Oct 31, 77)

HELMS, JESSE

Helms, Jesse. If Environmental Action had its way, the American people would starve and freeze to death in the dark. (Chicago Sun-Times 31:2 June 5, 78)

Woods, Mike. If Jesse Helms ran against Jesus Christ, I think Jesus Christ would win by a very slim margin. (Southpoint 2:8 May 90)

HELMS, RICHARD MCGARRAH

Helms, Richard McGarrah. If I ever do decide to talk, there are going to be some very embarrassed people in this town, you can bet on that (commenting after testifying to the Watergate Committee on CIA involvement in domestic intelligence operations). (Newsweek 85:21 Feb 24, 75)

HEMINGWAY, ERNEST

Fitzgerald, F. Scott. I talk with the authority of failure—Ernest (Hemingway) with the authority of success. (Time 111:89 April 3, 78)

Hemingway, Ernest. I know it means I will never have any dough but I know I shouldn't work in pictures when I go well enough in books. (American Film 6:12 May 81)

Steinbeck, John. Competing with Hemingway isn't my idea of good business. (Time 106:48 Dec 1, 75)

HEMINGWAY, MARY

Hemingway, Mary. I'm too old to waste my time being sentimental. (Time 110:41 July 25, 77)

HEROES

Caputo, Philip J. The impetus or the impulse that makes people heroic in wars is the very thing that can make them monsters. (Chicago Tribune Magazine 23 Mar 19, 78)

Einstein, Albert. The world needs heroes and it's better they be harmless men like me than villains like Hitler. (Newsweek 92:43 Nov 27, 78)

Lennon, John. A working class hero is something to be. (Sports Illustrated 65:77 Oct 27, 86)

McCarthy, Mary. It really takes a hero to live any kind of spiritual life without religious belief. (The Observer 9816:35 Oct 14, 79)

Price, Reynolds. The classical world decided wisely that any human accorded the honors of a hero must be, above all, dead. (Saturday Review 5:17 Dec 78)

HEROIN

Johnson, Sterling. In the heroin business, the Mexicans are the short-order cooks. The French are the chefs. (Rolling Stone 204:30 Jan 15, 76)

Rappolt, Richard T. It's easier to get people off of heroin than coffee. (Rolling Stone 234:39 Mar 10, 77)

HESTON, CHARLTON

Heston, Charlton. Truly, I would rather play a senator than be one. (US 3:64 Aug 26, 85)

HIGH SCHOOLS

Zappa, Frank. High school isn't a time and a place. It's a state of mind. (Human Behavior 5:65 Aug 76)

HINDSIGHT

Kojak, Theo. Hindsight is the only exact science. (Philadelphia 68:113 July 77)

HIPPIES

Nash, Graham. Serious musicians who read music don't understand what goes on with hippies. (People Weekly 8:57 Dec 12, 77)

HISTORY

Adenauer, Konrad. History is the sum total of the things that could have been avoided. (Kansas City Times 109:12H Dec 9, 76)

Cockburn, Alexander. History is the propaganda of the victors. (The Nation 251:190 Sept 3, 90)

Commager, Henry Steele. History is what you make of it. (Geo 6:20 June 84)

Cousins, Norman. History is an accumulation of error. (Saturday Review 5:13 April 15, 78)

Faulkner, William. The past is never dead; it is not even past. (Newsweek 89:87 Feb 21, 77)

Ford, Henry. History is more or less bunk. (Time 111:74 Jan 9, 78)

Kelley, Ken. But history is nothing but a chronology of oppressors oppressing the oppressed. (Rolling Stone 216:38 July 1, 76)

Malinowski, Bronislaw. Every historical change creates its mythology. (Time 109:86 May 23, 77)

McLuhan, Marshall. Only the vanquished remember history. (Forbes 120:120 Aug 15, 77)

Schlesinger, Arthur, Jr. History can be a high-risk occupation. (The Observer 9769:13 Nov 19, 78)

Singer, Isaac Bashevis. The whole human history is a holocaust. (Chicago Tribune 174:3 Section 5 June 23, 87)

West, Rebecca. There are jungles of people, and jungles of facts—which make it harder to recognize the great things when they do happen. (New York Times Book Review 14 Oct 2, 77)

White, Theodore. If you go back through 2000 years, I guess luck, Marx, and God have made history, the three of them together. (Firing Line 15 July 26, 75)

HISTORY see also PROGRESS

HITCHCOCK, ALFRED JOSEPH

Hitchcock, Alfred Joseph. Most people make mystery films. I don't. I make films of suspense. A surprise in a film takes 10 seconds, suspense takes up an hour. (Chicago Daily News 92:29 April 9, 76)

HITCHENS, IVON

Hitchens, Ivon. My pictures are painted to be listened to. (The Observer 9787:14 Mar 25, 79)

HITLER, ADOLF

Wagner, Winifred. If Hitler walked through the door today, I would be just as glad and happy to see and have him here as ever. (Time 106:33 Aug 18, 75)

HOCKNEY, DAVID

Hockney, David. I'm a Puritan at heart. I also think I'm the world's most overrated, overpaid artist. (Newsweek 90:73 Nov 14, 77)

Hockney, David. Three hundred homosexuals rule the world and I know

every one of them. (Manchester Guardian Weekly 140:29 May 21, 89)

HOFFA, JAMES RIDDLE

Hoffa, James Riddle. I don't cheat nobody. I don't lie about nobody. I don't frame nobody. I don't talk bad about people. If I do, I tell 'em. So what the hell's people gonna try to kill me for? (Playboy 22:73 Dec 75)

Hoffa, James Riddle. The only guy who needs a bodyguard is a liar, a cheat, a guy who betrays friendship. (Time 106:63 Nov 24, 75)

HOFFA, JIMMY see HOFFA, JAMES RIDDLE

HOFFER, ERIC

Hoffer, Eric. I hang onto my prejudices. They are the testicles of my mind. (New York Times 128:9 Section 7 Jan 28, 79)

HOFFMAN, ABBIE

Hoffman, Jack. He didn't die with a Rolex. He died with a full heart (about Abbie Hoffman). (Chicago Tribune 109:3 Section 1 April 19, 89)

HOFFMAN, DUSTIN

Malkovich, John. He's (Dustin Hoffman) the quintessential terminal juvenile. (American Film 11:28 Oct 85)

HOLLYWOOD, CALIFORNIA

Antonioni, Michelangelo. Hollywood is like being nowhere and talking to nobody about nothing. (Chicago Tribune Magazine 6 Oct 16, 83)

Dunne, John Gregory. Hollywood is the only place where you fail upwards. (US 1:12 Feb 21, 78)

Lear, Norman. When I give advice to rising starlets I say, just remember, Hollywood is the land of the definite maybe. (US 1:81 June 14, 77)

Pisier, Marie-France. People wear resort clothes but actually Hollywood is an enormous factory. People work ten times harder than anywhere else. (Newsweek 89:47 May 16, 77)

Prinze, Freddie. Hollywood is one big whore. It breeds decadence. (Playboy 24:110 June 77)

Tartikoff, Brandon. Hollywood is like Harvard. Once you're accepted, you can't flunk out. (New Times 10:31 Jan 9, 78)

HOLLYWOOD, CALIFORNIA— DESCRIPTION

Allen, Fred. Hollywood is a place where people from Iowa mistake each other for stars. (Chicago Tribune Magazine 6 Oct 16, 83)

Reed, Rex. In Hollywood, if you don't have happiness, you send out for it. (Chicago Tribune Magazine 6 Oct 16, 83)

HOLOCAUST, JEWISH (1939-1945) see also AUSCHWITZ CONCENTRATION CAMP

HOLOCAUSTS

Singer, Isaac Bashevis. The whole human history is a holocaust. (Chicago Tribune 174:3 Section 5 June 23, 87)

HOME

Frost, Robert. Home is the place where when you have to go there, they have to take you in. (Rocky Mountain News 134:44 Sept 3, 79)

Larkin, Philip. Generally speaking, the further one gets from home, the greater the misery. (New York 17:22 June 11, 84)

Luce, Clare Boothe. A man's home may seem to be his castle on the outside; inside it is more often his nursery. (Cosmopolitan 196:332 Oct 83)

HOMOSEXUALITY

Bryant, Anita. God says that someone who practices homosexuality shall not inherit the Kingdom of God. God is very plain on that. (Ms 6:50 July 77)

Dannemeyer, William. God's plan for man was Adam and Eve, not Adam and Steve. (Lawrence (Kansas) Journal-World 127:2 Oct 3, 85)

Fierstein, Harvey. I assume everyone is gay unless I'm told otherwise. (Life 7:40 Jan 84)

Loos, Anita. Gentlemen don't prefer blondes. If I were writing that book today, I'd call it 'Gentlemen Prefer Gentlemen'. (Newsweek 85:72 May 12, 75)

Matlovich, Leonard P. They gave me a medal for killing two men and discharged me for loving one. (Chicago Sun-Times 28:36 Aug 18, 75)

Schlesinger, Arthur, Jr. 'Gay' used to be one of the most agreeable words in the language. Its appropriation by a notably morose group is an act of piracy. (Time 111:36 Jan 2, 78)

HOMOSEXUALS—CIVIL RIGHTS— CALIFORNIA

Briggs, John. When it comes to politics, anything is fair. (Village Voice 23:62 Oct 16, 78)

HONESTY

Cameron, Simon. An honest politician is one who, when he is bought, will stay bought. (Village Voice 21:16 Nov 8, 76)

Hunt, Everette Howard. No one is entitled to the truth. (Rolling Stone 239:40 May 19, 77)

Jennings, Waylon. Honesty is something you can't wear out. (Country Music 7:55 Jan 79)

McNulty, Franklin L. With adequate integrity, guts can be located. (Parade 4 May 27, 79)

HOOVER, JOHN EDGAR

Hoover, John Edgar. The cure for crime is not the electric chair but the high chair. (Chicago Sun-Times 29:76 July 9, 76)

Johnson, Lyndon Baines. I'd druther have him (J. Edgar Hoover) inside the tent pissin' out than outside pissin' in. (Washingtonian 13:221 Mar 78)

HOPE

Borges, Jorge Luis. America is still the best hope. But the Americans themselves will have to be the best hope too. (Time 107:51 July 5, 76)

Jenkins, Robin. It is not the goodness of saints that makes us feel there is hope for humanity: it is the goodness of obscure men. (New York Times Book Review 14 Feb 3, 80)

Spark, Muriel. People who have hope are sad because they are so often disappointed. (New York Times Book Review 47 May 20, 79)

HOPE, BOB

Hope, Bob. I don't think I'd do anything if it were a sacrifice. (Rolling Stone 311:47 Mar 20, 80)

HOROWITZ, VLADIMIR

Horowitz, Vladimir. You can't be serious 24 hours a day. You have to take half an hour or an hour a day to be childish. (Time 112:88 Oct 16, 78)

HORSES

Reagan, Ronald. There is nothing better for the inside of a man than the outside of a horse. (Time 130:52 Dec 28, 87)

HOSPITALITY

Capone, Alphonse. When I sell liquor, it's called bootlegging; when my patrons serve it on silver trays on Lake Shore Drive, it's called hospitality. (Aspen 3:43 Spring 77)

HOSPITALS

Cousins, Norman. A hospital is no place for a person who is seriously ill. (Time 115:71 June 30, 80)

Thomson, Campbell. If it ever was true that a hospital was a charity organization, it no longer is true. (San Francisco Examiner 1977:1 May 1, 77)

HOSTAGES, AMERICAN—IRAQ

Bush, George. They are, in fact, hostages (August 20, 1990). (Chicago Tribune 233:1 Section 1 Aug 21, 90)

HOSTAGES, AMERICAN—KUWAIT

Bush, George. They are, in fact, hostages (August 20, 1990). (Chicago Tribune 233:1 Section 1 Aug 21, 90)

HOUSE DECORATION

Stone, Richard. One privilege of home ownership is the right to have lousy taste and display it. (Time 111:24 April 17, 78)

HOUSTON

Graham, Billy. Most Houstonians will spend eternity in Hell. (Texas Monthly 6:154 Feb 78)

HOWE, TINA

Howe, Tina. I'm not identified as a feminist writer, yet I'm convinced I am one—and one of the fiercer ones, to boot. (American Theatre 2:12 Sept 85)

HUBBARD, L. RON

Hubbard, L. Ron. If a man really wants to make a million dollars, the best way would be to start his own religion. (Time 127:86 Feb 10, 86)

HUGHES, HOWARD ROBARD

Kane, Walter. It is tragic that Howard Hughes had to die to prove that he was alive. (Newsweek 87:25 April 19, 76)

HUMAN NATURE see MAN

HUMAN RIGHTS see CIVIL RIGHTS

HUMOR

Feldman, Marty. Humor is like sex. Those who do it don't talk about it. (People Weekly 6:103 Dec 27/Jan 3, 77)

Landon, Melville. Levity is the soul of wit. (San Francisco Chronicle This World 1978:40 Jan 29, 78)

Rogers, Will. Everything is funny as long as it is happening to somebody else. (Kansas City Star 97:2A April 10, 77)

White, E. B. Humor can be dissected, as a frog can, but the thing dies in the process and the innards are discouraging to any but the pure scientific mind. (New York Times Magazine 70 Dec 2, 79)

HUMPHREY, HUBERT HORATIO

Humphrey, Hubert Horatio. A man with no tears is a man with no heart. (Chicago Tribune 263:2 Sept 20, 77)

Humphrey, Hubert Horatio. I would rather be honestly wrong than to be a deliberate hypocrite. (New Times 10:72 Feb 6, 78)

Humphrey, Hubert Horatio. Life was not meant to be endured, but enjoyed. (New Times 10:51 Feb 6, 78)

Humphrey, Hubert Horatio. The greatest gift of life is friendship and I have received it. (Time 110:23 Nov 7, 77)

Humphrey, Hubert Horatio. The hardest job for a politician today is to have the courage to be moderate. (Time 111:22-24 Jan 23, 78)

Stevenson, Adlai, II. He's (Hubert Humphrey) a politician with more solutions than there are problems. (Washingtonian 16:22 June 81)

HUNGER—UNITED STATES

Leland, Mickey. It's a white mark on America's history for us to have hungry children in our society. (The New Yorker 65:31 Sept 11, 89)

HUNT FAMILY

Hunt, Nelson Bunker. Money never meant anything to us. It was just sort of how we kept score. (Dun's Business Month 127:50 Feb 86)

HUNT, EVERETTE HOWARD

Hunt, Everette Howard. No one is entitled to the truth. (Rolling Stone 239:40 May 19, 77)

HUNT, HAROLDSON LAFAYETTE

Hunt, Haroldson Lafayette. Money is just something to make bookkeeping convenient. (Time 104:44 Dec 9, 74)

HUNTER, ALBERTA

Blake, Eubie. When she (Alberta Hunter) sang the blues, you felt so sorry for her you would want to kill the guy she was singing about. (Newsweek 90:101 Oct 31, 77)

HUTTON, BARBARA

Hutton, Barbara. All the unhappiness in my life has been caused by men. (New York Times 128:1 May 13, 79)

IDEA (PHILOSOPHY)

Kahn, Herman. Think the unthinkable. (National Catholic Reporter 21:26 Dec 21, 84)

IDEAS

Comins, David H. People will accept your idea more readily if you tell them Benjamin Franklin said it first. (Washingtonian 14:152 Nov 78)

Harden, Frank. Every time you come up with a terrific idea, you find that someone else thought of it first. (Washingtonian 14:154 Nov 78)

Wattenberg, Ben. There is nothing so powerful as an old idea whose time has come again. (Washingtonian 15:143 Nov 79)

IDENTITY (PSYCHOLOGY)

Theroux, Paul. You are not what you eat; but where you eat is who you are. (Travel & Leisure 7:76 July 31, 77)

IGNORANCE

Paulucci, Jeno F. It pays to be ignorant, for when you're smart you already know it can't be done. (New York Times 126:5 Section 3 Nov 7, 76)

ILLINOIS see also POLITICS, CORRUPTION IN—ILLINOIS

ILLINOIS—POLITICS AND GOVERNMENT see also STEVENSON, ADLAI

IMAGINATION

Hugo, Richard. In the world of imagination, all things belong. (New York Times Book Review 11 Mar 25, 79)

INCOME

Parkinson, C. Northcote. Expenditure rises to meet income. (Washingtonian 14:155 Nov 78)

INCOME TAX

Gibbs, Lawrence. A taxpaying public that doesn't understand the law is a taxpaying public that can't comply with the law. (Chicago Tribune 79:19 Mar 20, 87)

Meese, Edwin. The progressive income tax is immoral. (USA Today 1:8A July 22, 83)

Reagan, Ronald. The entire graduated-income-tax structure was created by Karl Marx. (New York 13:28 April 28, 80)

INCOME TAX—RETURNS see TAX RETURNS

INDIA—POLITICS AND GOVERNMENT

Gandhi, Indira (Nehru). The freedom of the people cannot be allowed to come in the way of the freedom of the masses. (People Weekly 4:33 Dec 29/Jan 5, 76)

Gandhi, Indira (Nehru). We should be vigilant to see that our march to progress is not hampered in the name of the Constitution. (New York Times 125:5 Section 1 Dec 28, 75)

Singh, Vishwanath Pratap. This is a government of the poor, for the poor (about India). (Chicago Tribune 344:22 Section 1 Sept 10, 89)

INDIANA. UNIVERSITY (BASKETBALL)

Cosell, Howard. Indiana should be No. 1. They probably have a bigger payroll than the New York Knicks (1976). (Chicago Tribune 123:3 Section 3 May 2, 76)

INDIANS OF NORTH AMERICA

Black Elk. Sometimes I think it might have been better if we had stayed together and made them kill us all. (Quest/78 2:113 Sept/Oct 78)

Hollow, Norman. In the olden days the Indian peoples defended themselves with bows and arrows. Now, politics is the only way our rights can be developed. (New York Times 125:1 Section 1 Dec 21, 75)

INDIANS OF NORTH AMERICA see also UNITED STATES. BUREAU OF INDIAN AFFAIRS

INDIVIDUAL AND SOCIETY

Borges, Jorge Luis. I think most people are more important than their opinions. (The Times 8067:39 Feb 5, 78)

Gentry, Charles B. Unrestrained individualism is incompatible with civilization. (The Atlantic 266:6 Sept 90)

INDIVIDUALISM

Leschak, Peter M. Whenever an individual is ostracized from society, suspect society first. (Mpls/St. Paul 15:228 Mar 87)

INFANTS

Sandburg, Carl. A baby is God's opinion that the world should go on. (Kansas City Star 97:2D Feb 20, 77)

INFINITY

Cousins, Norman. Infinity converts the possible into the inevitable. (Saturday Review 5:18 April 15, 78)

INFLATION (FINANCE)

Abboud, A. Robert. Inflation is a product of—and can only be cured by—the people. (New Republic 180:8 June 30, 79)

Berra, Yogi. A nickel ain't worth a dime anymore. (Duns Business Month 127:50 Jan 31, 86)

Burns, Arthur Frank. The ultimate consequence of inflation could well be a significant decline of economic and political freedom for the American people. (Time 111:33 Jan 9, 78)

Carter, James Earl. Inflation has become embedded in the very tissue of our economy (1978). (Time 111:66 April 24, 78)

Friedman, Milton. Inflation is the one form of taxation that can be imposed without legislation. (American Opinion 18:37 April 75)

Hayden, Thomas. During the 1960s, we fought the pigs. Now we fight the high price of bacon. (Newsweek 90:36 Nov 7, 77)

Lowrey, Bette. Inflation is just a high priced depression. (Cleveland 4:15 May 75)

Meany, George. The fight against inflation must be on the basis of the equality of sacrifice, not the sacrifice of equality. (Time 113:9 Feb 5, 79)

Miller, George William. Inflation (is) a clear and present danger. (New York Times 128:10 Section 4 Aug 12, 79)

Scammon, Richard. There's nothing wrong with the Republican Party that double-digit inflation won't cure. (Guardian Weekly 119:17 Nov 12, 78)

Will, George F. Inflation is a great conservatizing issue. (Newsweek 90:36 Nov 7, 77)

INFLUENCE

Young, Andrew. Influence is like a savings account. The less you use it, the more you've got. (People Weekly 6:30 Dec 27/Jan 3, 1977)

INFORMATION

Stein, Gertrude. Everybody gets so much information all day long that they lose their common sense. (Chicago Tribune 176:2 Section 2 June 25, 78)

INFORMATION THEORY

Vallee, Jacques. The theory of space and time is a cultural artifact made possible by the invention of graph paper. (CoEvolution Quarterly 16:82 Winter 77/78)

INNOCENCE

Guare, John. Innocence is ignorance where you're not getting caught. (Village Voice 22:35 Aug 15, 77)

INSANITY

Menninger, Karl. 'Insane' is an expression we psychiatrists don't use until we get to court. Insanity is a question of public opinion. (Time 106:57 Oct 20, 75)

INSECURITY see SECURITY (PSYCHOLOGY)

INSTITUTIONS

Drucker, Peter F. The wonder of modern institutions is not that they work so badly, but that anything works at all. (The Wharton Magazine 1:14 Fall 76)

INSURANCE COMPANIES

Belli, Melvin. I'd rather have Adolf Hitler as the executor of my will than the president of an insurance company. (Chicago Sun-Times 35:16 Mar 10, 82)

INTEGRATION

Gruber, Jack. Integration is not something you win at, it's something you work at. (Time 110:21 Oct 31, 77)

INTELLECT

Miller, Henry. To the person who thinks with his head, life is a comedy. To those who think with their feelings, or work through their feelings, life is a tragedy. (Soho News 5:3 Jan 26, 78)

INTELLECTUALS

Aron, Raymond. Marxism is the opium of the intellectuals. (Time 114:41 July 9, 79)

Kissinger, Henry Alfred. Intellectuals condemn society for materialism when it is prosperous and for injustice when it fails to ensure prosperity. (Time 107:49 June 20, 77)

Laughlin, Tom. Never trust a man with ideas. (New York 8:51 Aug 4, 75)

Snow, C. P. Literary intellectuals at one pole—at the other, scientists...Between the two a gulf of mutual incomprehension. (Omni 1:39 Mar 79)

INTELLIGENCE SERVICE—UNITED STATES

Colby, William Egan. I'm convinced it's possible to run a secret agency as part of a constitutional society. (Time 107:17 Jan 19, 75)

Kissinger, Henry Alfred. We must resist the myth that government is a gigantic conspiracy. We cannot allow the intelligence services of the country to be dismantled. (Washington Post 355:1 Nov 25, 75)

Mondale, Walter Frederick. There must be some fundamental changes in America's intelligence activities or they will fundamentally change America. (Foreign Policy 23:58 Summer 76)

Stone, Isidor Feinstein. The biggest menace to American freedom is the intelligence community. (Wilson Library Bulletin 51:25 Sept 76)

United States. Congress. Senate. Select Committee On Intelligence Operations. There is no inherent Constitutional authority for the President or any intelligence agency to violate the law. (New York Times 125:14 Section 4 May 2, 76)

INTERIOR DECORATION

Rowen, Phyllis. When you grow as a designer, you realize that nothing is forever. (Architectural Digest 32:122 Nov 75)

INTERIOR DECORATORS see also ROWEN, PHYLLIS

INTERNATIONAL BROTHERHOOD OF TEAMSTERS, CHAUFFEURS, WAREHOUSEMEN AND HELPERS OF AMERICA

Fitzsimmons, Frank E. The Teamsters are without peer as an organization dedicated to the service of mankind. (New York Times Magazine 31 Nov 7, 76)

INTERNATIONAL RELATIONS

Einstein, Albert. An empty stomach is not a good political adviser. (Kansas City Times 109:14B May 11, 77)

Goldberg, Arthur Joseph. We need a world in which it is safe to be human. (Kansas City Times 109:28 Jan 4, 77)

INTERPERSONAL RELATIONS

Nova, Leo. The other person's attitude depends on which direction the money moves between you. (Omni 1:131-32 May 79)

Ono, Yoko. Keep your intentions in a clear bottle and leave it on the shelf when you rap. (Chicago Tribune 176:2 Section 2 June 25, 78)

INTERVIEWING

Wallace, Mike. There are no indiscreet questions, there are only indiscreet answers. (Washington Post 190:L2 June 10, 79)

INVENTORS see also EDISON, THOMAS ALVA; LAND, EDWIN

INVESTMENT ADVISERS

Drucker, Peter F. Capital formation is shifting from the entrepreneur who invests in the future to the pension trustee who invests in the past. (New York Times 125:15 Section 3 May 16, 76)

INVESTMENT, AMERICAN—MEXICO

Cavazos, Agapito Gonzales. They come to exploit us, they do not come to help us (about the maquiladora industry). (Chicago Tribune 126:11D Section 7 May 6, 90)

INVESTMENTS

Boesky, Ivan F. It's OK to make money. It's good thing. You go to heaven if you do it. (Kansas Cith Star 107:8A Nov 18, 86)

LeFevre, William M. Fears expressed by the majority of investors are very often like bad dreams—they rarely come true in real life. (Kansas City Star 106:5A Dec 30, 85)

Nakagama, Sam. I would say that you can discount almost anything you read in the Wall Street Journal. (Manhattan, Inc. 5:56 Nov 88)

Rose, Billy. Never invest your money in anything that eats or needs repairing. (Duns Business Month 127:50 Feb 86)

Skodack, Debra. A person is not an investor until he has delt with a bad stock market. (Kansas City Times 120:D-3 Oct 22, 87)

Taylor, Francis H. The trick is to buy the right thing at the wrong time (about collecting). (Philadelphia 75:153 Sept 84)

IONESCO, EUGENE

Ionesco, Eugene. Basically I think it is stupid not to believe in God. (Harvard Magazine 89:24 Nov 86)

IRAN—FOREIGN RELATIONS—UNITED STATES

Banisadr, Abolhassan. In our campaign against the U.S., the hostages are our weakness, not our strength. (Time 115:31 Mar 21, 80)

Khomeini, Ayatollah Ali. Anyone who fights America's aggression has engaged in a holy war in the cause of Allah, and anyone who is killed on that path is a martyr. (Time 136:32 Sept 24, 89)

IRAN—POLITICS AND GOVERNMENT

Bakhtiar, Shapour. We have replaced an old and corrupt dictatorship with a dictatorship accompanied by anarchy. (The Observer 9787:1 Mar 25, 79)

Fahd, King of Saudi Arabia. If Iran goes, God help us. (The Observer 9777:11 Jan 14, 79)

Khomeini, Ayatollah Ruhollah. As long as I am alive, I will not let the State (Iran) fall into the hands of liberals. (Chicago Tribune 54:2 Section 1 Feb 23, 89)

Khomeini, Ayatollah Ruhollah. The people of Iran want to be martyrs. (The Observer 9826:9 Dec 23, 79)

IRAN-CONTRA AFFAIR

Hamilton, Lee. Those involved, whether public official or private citizen, had no doubt they were acting on the authority of the President of the United States. (Kansas City Star 107:6B June 10, 87)

Inouye, Daniel. I see it as a chilling story, a story of deceit and duplicity and the arrogant disregard of the rule of law. (Kansas City Star 107:5A Aug 4, 86)

North, Oliver L., Jr. I assumed that the President was aware of what I was doing and had, through my superiors, approved. (Time 130:40 Dec 28, 87)

Reagan, Maureen. A member of the United States military who lies to the commander-in-chief is guilty of treason and should be court-martialed (about Oliver North and John Poindexter). (Chicago Tribune 79:19 Mar 20, 87)

Wilson, Edwin. If I wasn't in jail, I'd have headed up this (Iran-contra aid) operation. (Newsweek 109:22 May 11, 87)

IRANIAN-IRAQI WAR, 1980-1988

Kissinger, Henry Alfred. The tragedy of this war (the Iranian-Iraqi war) is that it has to end someday. (Manhattan, Inc. 5:46 Sept 88)

IRAQ—FOREIGN RELATIONS

Hussein, Saddam. We would rather die than be humiliated, and we will pluck out the eyes of those who attack the Arab nation. (Chicago Tribune 227:17 Section 1 Aug 15, 90)

IRAQ—FOREIGN RELATIONS—KUWAIT

Hussein, Saddam. Kuwait belongs to Iraq, and we will never give it up even if we have to fight over it for one thousand years. (Time 136:26 Oct 8, 90)

IRELAND see also CHARACTERS AND CHARACTERISTICS—IRELAND; NORTHERN IRELAND; SUCCESS—IRELAND

IRISH

Byrne, Jane. With the Irish, you know, only the strongest survive. (New York Times Magazine 77 Mar 9, 80)

Flanagan, Fionnula. The one thing you must not commit with the Irish is to succeed. (TV Guide 26:22 April 29, 78)

Moynihan, Daniel Patrick. I don't think there's any point in being Irish if you don't know that the world is going to break your heart eventually. (New York Times Book Review 15 April 30, 78)

IRISH REPUBLICAN ARMY

O'Connell, David (IRA tactician). Put your faith in the Provos and Ireland will be free. We will abolish British rule, we will smash it. (New York Times 125:7 April 26, 76)

IRVING, JOHN

Irving, John. Let no one forget that when I say I'm only a storyteller, I'm not being humble. (New York Times 138:16 April 25, 89)

ISOLATIONISM (UNITED STATES)

Hyland, William G. Protectionism is the ally of isolationism, and isolationism is the Dracula of American foreign policy. (New York Times 136:2 May 17, 87)

ISRAEL

Carter, James Earl. The survival of Israel is not a political issue. It is a moral imperative. (Time 107:13 June 21, 76)

Eban, Abba Solomon. Better to be disliked than pitied. (New York 9:38 July 26, 76)

ISRAEL—ECONOMIC CONDITIONS

Arnon, Jacob (Former Israeli Finance Ministry director). There comes a point when defense spending becomes so enormous that it presents just as much danger to our survival as do our Arab enemies. (Time 107:49 Jan 5, 76)

ISRAEL—FOREIGN POLICY

Fein, Leonard. Israel is squandering recklessly its most critical and natural resource—the good will that many people around the world, and in this country in particular, feel for this gutsy country. (Time 114:43 July 23, 79)

ISRAEL—FOREIGN RELATIONS—ARAB STATES

Arnon, Jacob (Former Israeli Finance Ministry director). There comes a point when defense spending becomes so enormous that it presents just as much danger to our survival as do our Arab enemies. (Time 107:49 Jan 5, 76)

ISRAEL—MILITARY POLICY

Begin, Menachem. Europe's rivers are still red with Jewish blood. This Europe cannot teach us how to maintain our security. (Christian Science Monitor 70:5 Dec 2, 77)

ISRAEL—POLITICS AND GOVERNMENT

Dayan, Moshe. I, Moshe Dayan, as an individual am not a coward. But as a Jew I am a very frightened man. (Time 110:30 Oct 17, 77)

Fleener, Terre. What the Jewish people endured does not give them the right to visit violence on other people. (Chicago Sun-Times 32:100 July 1, 79)

Kadishai, Yechiel. We want to settle so many Jews that the West Bank and Gaza can't be given back to the Arabs. (USA Today 1:10A April 11, 83)

Meir, Golda. I wouldn't accept the West Bank and Gaza as part of Israel if they were offered on a silver platter. (Village Voice 25:8 Oct 8, 80)

Sharon, Ariel. In order to overcome our problems, the first thing to do is to eliminate the heads of the terrorist organizations, and the first one is Yasir Arafat. (Chicago Tribune 208:27 Section 1 July 27, 89)

ISRAEL—POLITICS AND GOVERNMENT

see also JERUSALEM

ISRAEL—PUBLIC RELATIONS

Podhoretz, Norman. The role of Jews who write in both the Jewish and general press is to defend Israel, and not join in the attacks on Israel. (Mother Jones 12:21 Mar/April 87)

ITALIANS

West, Morris. In discourse the Italians are the most eloquent people in the world. In action they are either apathetic or impulsive to the point of insanity. (Esquire 89:81 April 25, 78)

ITALY see also ROME; STRIKES—ITALY; TRADE UNIONS—ITALY

ITALY—DESCRIPTION

Anselmi, Tina (first Italian woman cabinet member). If people outside Italy have the impression that Italy is always on strike, that is because it is. (New York Times 126:21 Section 1 Oct 10, 76)

Gardner, Richard. Italy is a poor country full of right people. (The Observer 9931:13 Jan 3, 82)

ITALY—POLITICS AND GOVERNMENT

Andreotti, Giulio. In politics there is a clause that is always valid: rebus sic stantibus (circumstances being what they are). (Time 108:54 Dec 13, 76)

Barzini, Luigi. We (Italians) might be the first developed country to turn itself back into an underdeveloped country. (Time 111:63 April 3, 78)

Crespi, Consuelo. In Italy now you want to feel rich and look poor. (Time 111:53 May 15, 78)

JACKSON, REGGIE

Jackson, Reggie. Hitting is better than sex. (Esquire 89:98 Mar 1, 78)

Jackson, Reggie. I don't mind getting beaten, but I hate to lose. (Sepia 26:10 Mar 77)

JACOBS, ANDREW, JR.

Jacobs, Andrew, Jr. (Ralph) Nader has become a legend in his own mind. (Time 112:21 Aug 7, 78)

JAGGER, BIANCA

Jagger, Bianca. What do I really want as a woman? I want it all. (Playboy 26:186 Jan 79)

JAGGER, MICK

Jagger, Mick. I'd rather be dead than sing Satisfaction when I'm 45. (People Weekly 7:58 May 2, 77)

Jagger, Mick. Keith and I are two of the nicest people we know. (Creem 10:55 Jan 78)

JAMES, HENRY

Will, George F. Eighty years ago, Henry James defined journalism as the science of beating the sense out of words. (Lawrence (Kansas) Journal-World 126:5A Sept 23, 84)

JAMISON, JUDITH

Jamison, Judith. Every dancer lives on the threshold of chucking it. (New York Times Magazine 148 Dec 5, 76)

JAPAN—COMMERCE—UNITED STATES

Izawa, Osamu. The irony is that no matter how much the American companies claim their products are better than the Japanese, the American public may not believe so. (Newsweek 99:69 April 12, 82)

JAPAN—POLITICS AND GOVERNMENT

Nosaka, Akiyuke. There is no doubt in my mind that Japan wants to rule Asia again, but this time it wants to do it as an American subcontractor. (Chicago Tribune 14:21 Jan 14, 87)

JEFFERSON, THOMAS

Lapham, Lewis H. I take for granted Jefferson's dictum that money, not morality, constitutes the principle of commercial nations. (Harper's 254:32 Feb 77)

JERUSALEM

Begin, Menachem. Jerusalem will remain undivided for all generations until the end of the world. (The Observer 9762:15 Oct 1, 78)

JESUS CHRIST

Mother Teresa. Jesus said love one another. He didn't say love the whole world. (The Observer 9836:9 Mar 2, 80)

Peale, Norman Vincent. If Jesus were alive today he would be at the Super Bowl. (Time 119:82 Feb 8, 82)

Smith, Patti. Jesus died for somebody's sins but not mine. (Philadelphia 69:185 Sept 78)

JEWELRY—MEN

Hoving, Walter. It is in poor taste for a man to wear a diamond ring. (W Supplement 131 July 27, 87)

JEWISH-ARAB RELATIONS

Rabin, Yitzhak. For me, peace means reconciliation of the Arab countries with the existence of Israel as a Jewish state. (Newsweek 88:47 Dec 20, 76)

JEWS—IRAN

Khomeini, Ayatollah Ruhollah. From its very inception, Islam has been afflicted by the Jews. (Newsweek 93:42 Jan 29, 79)

JOBS

Becker, Jules. It is much harder to find a job than to keep one. (Washingtonian 14:152 Nov 78)

McGovern, George Stanley. The longer the title, the less important the job . (Town & Country 133:141 May 79)

JOHN PAUL I, POPE

John Paul I, Pope. If I hadn't been a bishop, I would have wanted to be a journalist. (Time 112:80 Sept 11, 78)

John Paul I, Pope. If someone had told me I would be Pope one day, I would have

studied harder. (The Observer 9761:14 Sept 24, 78)

JOHN PAUL II, POPE

John Paul II, Pope. Social injustice and unjust social structures exist only because individuals and groups of individuals deliberately maintain or tolerate them. (Kansas City Star 107:10A Sept 14, 87)

Wills, Garry. (John Paul II's) theological conservatism undercuts his political liberalism. (Time 114:35 Oct 15, 79)

JOHNS, GLYNNIS

Johns, Glynnis. For me, most relationships with men have been like pregnancies—they last about nine months. (Chicago Tribune 226:2 Section 5 Aug 14, 77)

JOHNSON, LYNDON BAINES

Ball, George W. (Lyndon Johnson) did not suffer from a poor education, he suffered from the belief that he had a poor education. (Washingtonian 11:102 June 76)

Johnson, Lyndon Baines. Boys, it is just like the Alamo. Somebody should have by God helped those Texans. I'm going to Viet Nam. (Time 105:28 May 12, 75)

Johnson, Lyndon Baines. I never believed that Oswald acted alone, although I can accept that he pulled the trigger. (Skeptic 9:55 Sept 75)

Johnson, Lyndon Baines. I never trust a man unless I've got his pecker in my pocket. (Village Voice 21:16 Nov 8, 76)

Johnson, Lyndon Baines. I'm not going to be the first President to lose a war. (Time 105:28 May 12, 75)

McCarthy, Eugene Joseph (attributed by Daniel Patrick Moynihan). No one ever was associated with (Lyndon Johnson) who was not in the end somehow diminished. (The Observer 9796:34 May 27, 79)

Mitchell, Clarence M., Jr. Lyndon B. Johnson was the greatest American President on civil rights. (New York Times 128:28 April 15, 79)

Sherrill, Robert. No politician ever deserved our hatred more than (Lyndon) Johnson because, simply, no politician ever did more than he to destroy the country. (Texas Observer 82:14 April 6, 90)

JOHNSON, PHILIP

Johnson, Philip. Houston is only more interesting than Dallas because I've built more there. (Texas Homes 9:85 May 85)

JONES, JAMES

Hemingway, Ernest. I wish him (James Jones) no luck at all and hope he goes out and hangs himself as soon as plausible. (Kansas City Star 106:1K Dec 29, 85)

JONES, JAMES THURMAN

Jones, James Thurman. I am God; there is no other God and religion is the opium of the people. (New York Times 128:A17 Nov 21, 78)

JORDAN

Sharon, Ariel. Jordan is the Palestinian state. (USA Today 1:8A Dec 22, 82)

JOURNALISM

Albert, Claude. You have to love the business (journalism) for what it is, not for what you'd like it to be. (Connecticut 41:32 Feb 78)

Alexander, Shana. (Journalism) offers the maximum of vicarious living with a minimum of emotional involvement. (New York Times Book Review 3 May 6, 79)

Buchwald, Art. In this country, when you attack the Establishment, they don't put you in jail or a mental institution. They do something worse. They make you a member of the Establishment. (Time 110:67 Dec 5, 77)

Cohen, Richard. The best stories never check out. (The Nation 231:663 Dec 20, 80)

Cronkite, Walter. It is not the reporter's job to be a patriot or to presume to determine where patriotism lies. His job is to relate the facts. (Time 115:60 Feb 11, 80)

Dornfeld, Arnold (attributed by Mike Royko). If your mother says she loves you, check it out (on the journalist's responsibility). (Town & Country 132:173 Sept 78)

Fairlie, Henry. Celebrity has become the main threat to journalism, especially in Washington. (Washingtonian 24:119 April 89)

John Paul I, Pope. If St. Paul returned to the world now as a journalist he would not only direct Reuters but seek time on television. (The Observer 9758:9 Sept 3, 78)

Krause, Charles. In the jungle, a press card is just another piece of paper. (Washingtonian 15:142 Nov 79)

Moyers, Bill D. Of all the myths of journalism, objectivity is the greatest. (National Review 31:1021 Aug 12, 79)

Muggeridge, Malcolm. (Journalism) is the ideal profession for those who find power fascinating and its exercise abhorrent. (Time 114:73 Aug 13, 79)

Nicholas, N. J. The journalism business has very much become as much entertainment as it is journalism. (Manhattan, Inc. 6:76 May 89)

Schorr, Daniel. All news is an exaggeration of life. (Village Voice 20:134 May 26, 75)

Thompson, Hunter S. There's no such thing as a 'nice' reporter. That's like saying somebody's a nice liberal. (W 5:11 Sept 3, 76)

Will, George F. Eighty years ago, Henry James defined journalism as the science of beating the sense out of words. (Lawrence (Kansas) Journal-World 126:5A Sept 23, 84)

JOURNALISM see also EDITORS AND EDITING; SPORTS JOURNALISM

JOURNALISM—WASHINGTON, D. C.

Fairlie, Henry. Celebrity has become the main threat to journalism, especially in Washington. (Washingtonian 24:119 April 89)

JOURNALISTIC ETHICS

Nixon, Richard Milhous. When news is concerned, nobody in the press is a friend—they are all enemies. (Time 111:104 April 17, 78)

Rosenthal, A. M. I don't care if you screw an elephant, just don't cover the circus. (New West 4:17 Mar 26, 79)

Scheer, Robert. The journalist's job is to get the story by breaking into their offices, by bribing, by seducing people, by lying, by anything else to break through that palace guard. (Time 107:56 April 4, 77)

Schorr, Daniel. To betray a source would be to betray myself, my career and my life. I cannot do it (commenting in his testimony before the Pike committee). (Time 108:76 Oct 11, 76)

JOURNALISTIC ETHICS see also SCHORR, DANIEL

JOURNALISTS

Beatty, Warren. When a reporter enters the room, your privacy ends and his begins. (Life 7:40 Jan 84)

Breslin, Catherine. A freelancer lives at the end of a sawed-off limb. (Time 111:77 April 10, 78)

Dorfman, Dan. To lie to the press on a public matter is, in effect, to lie to the people. (New York 10:9 May 9, 77)

Eisenhower, David. Journalists aren't nearly as interesting as they think they are. (Esquire 87:35 June 30, 77)

Kovar, Jay. Journalists today are more into jogging than drinking. (Chicago 34:16 July 85)

JOURNALISTS see also DEAN, JOHN WESLEY, III; FLANNER, JANET; LIEBLING, A. J.; SAFIRE, WILLIAM; SCHEER, ROBERT; SCHORR, DANIEL; WOODWARD, BOB

JUDGES

Burger, Warren Earl. We may be well on our way to a society overrun by hordes of lawyers, hungry as locusts, and brigades of judges in numbers never before contemplated. (Time 109:40 June 27, 77)

Dershowitz, Alan M. Judges are the weakest link in our system of justice, and they are also the most protected. (Newsweek 91:76 Feb 20, 78)

Douglas, William Orville. A lifetime diet of the law alone turns judges into dull, dry husks. (Newsweek 86:46 Nov 24, 75)

Kaufman, Irving. It is not enough for justice to be declared. The judge must assure that justice is done. (Time 113:92 Jan 22, 79)

Rifkind, Simon. (Judicial) impartiality is an acquired taste, like olives. You have to be habituated to it. (Time 114:49 Aug 20, 79)

Stevens, John Paul. Judges should impose on themselves the discipline of deciding no more than is before them. (American Legion Magazine 100:9 Feb 76)

Warren, Earl. A jurist's mind cannot operate in a vacuum. (Christian Science Monitor 69:27 Aug 3, 77)

JUDGES see also **STEVENS, JOHN PAUL**

JUDGES—CHICAGO

Anonymous. Get behind a judge on Monday in case you find yourself in front of him on Tuesday (about Chicago). (Los Angeles Times 97:1 Part 1 Nov 29, 78)

JUSTICE

Bennett, Arnold. The price of justice is eternal publicity. (Time 113:85 April 30, 79)

JUSTICE, ADMINISTRATION OF

Dershowitz, Alan M. Judges are the weakest link in our system of justice, and they are also the most protected. (Newsweek 91:76 Feb 20, 78)

Hoover, John Edgar. Justice is incidental to law and order. (USA Today 1:8A Mar 15, 83)

Kaufman, Irving. It is not enough for justice to be declared. The judge must assure that justice is done. (Time 113:92 Jan 22, 79)

McKay, Robert. If war is too important to be left to the generals, surely justice is too important to be left to lawyers. (Time 111:66 April 10, 78)

Newfield, Jack. Justice is a meat grinder. (Chicago Tribune 46:1 Section 7 Feb 15, 76)

Rifkind, Simon. (Judicial) impartiality is an acquired taste, like olives. You have to be habituated to it. (Time 114:49 Aug 20, 79)

Spence, Gary. There is no justice in seeking justice anymore. (W 4:86 April 87)

JUSTICE, ADMINISTRATION OF— UNITED STATES

Burger, Warren Earl. We may be well on our way to a society overrun by hordes of lawyers, hungry as locusts, and brigades of judges in numbers never before contemplated. (Time 109:40 June 27, 77)

Liddy, G. Gordon. Before going to prison I

believed that criticism of the criminal justice system for its treatment of the poor was so much liberal bleating and bunk. I was wrong. (Connecticut 40:48 Feb 77)

KAFKA, FRANZ

Auden, Wystan Hugh. Had one to name the author who comes nearest to bearing the same kind of relation to our age as Dante, Shakespeare and Goethe bore to theirs, Kafka is the first one would think of. (Time 111:80 Jan 30, 78)

KAHN, ALFRED

Kahn, Alfred. If you can't explain what you're doing in simple English, you are probably doing something wrong. (Time 111:63 May 8, 78)

KANSAS CITY, MISSOURI—POLITICS AND GOVERNMENT

Prendergast, George Washington. I never took a dime from the public till; it's all been honest graft. (Change 8:60 Aug 76)

KAROL, PAMALA (LA LOCA)

Karol, Pamala (La Loca). My work is sort of a psychic vomit that comes from within. (Los Angeles 35:20 April 90)

KEMP, JACK

Kemp, Jack. I want it known that you cannot balance the budget off the backs of the poor. (Lawrence (Kansas) Journal-World 130:1A Dec 20, 88)

KENNEDY FAMILY

Kennedy, Edward Moore. Whatever contributions the Kennedys have made are very much tied into the incredible importance and power of that force in our lives, the family. (New York Times Magazine 15 June 17, 79)

KENNEDY, EDWARD MOORE

Carey, Hugh. A hard worker but he is perceived otherwise (about Ted Kennedy). (New York Times 128:A18 Nov 22, 78)

Kennedy, Edward Moore. My father always said: 'If it's on the table, eat it'. (The Observer 9813:9 Sept 23, 79)

KENNEDY, JOHN FITZGERALD

Dudney, Bob. The country would have recovered from the death of John Kennedy, but it hasn't recovered yet from the death of Lee Harvey Oswald and probably never will. (Esquire 85:62 Feb 76)

Kennedy, John Fitzgerald. And so, my fellow Americans, ask not what your country can do for you; ask what you can do for your country (inaugural address—1961). (Christian Science Monitor 69:14 Jan 20, 77)

Kennedy, John Fitzgerald. The worse I do, the more popular I get. (Time 115:31 May 5, 80)

Kennedy, Robert Francis (attributed by Bill Moyers). I have myself wondered if we did not pay a very great price for being more energetic than wise about a lot of things, especially Cuba. (Washington Post 228:A5 July 21, 77)

Monroe, Marilyn. I think I made his back feel better (about John F. Kennedy). (Time 106:11 Dec 29, 75)

Schlesinger, Arthur, Jr. John Kennedy was a realist brilliantly disguised as a romantic; Robert Kennedy, a romantic stubbornly disguised as a realist. (Newsweek 92:78 Sept 4, 78)

Truman, Harry S. (John Kennedy) had his ear so close to the ground it was full of grasshoppers. (Time 111:89 Mar 20, 78)

**KENNEDY, JOHN FITZGERALD—
ASSASSINATION**

Hill, Clinton J. If I had reacted just a little bit quicker, I could have (saved Kennedy), I guess, and I'll live with that to my grave. (Chicago Tribune 341:16 Section 1 Dec 7, 75)

Johnson, Lyndon Baines. I never believed that Oswald acted alone, although I can accept that he pulled the trigger. (Skeptic 9:55 Sept 75)

Kennedy, John Fitzgerald. If somebody is going to kill me, they are going to kill me. (New Leader 61:15 Nov 6, 78)

Moynihan, Daniel Patrick. I don't think there's any point in being Irish if you don't know that the world is going to break your heart eventually. (New York Times Book Review 15 April 30, 78)

Shriver, Eunice. Mistakes were obviously made in terms of the investigation, but I'm satisfied with their conclusions (on the Warren Commission). (Christian Science Monitor 68:8 Dec 3, 75)

KENNEDY, JOSEPH P., III

Kennedy, Joseph P., III. There's no question being a Kennedy can open a lot of doors, but it's also opened a few I didn't want to walk through. (Newsweek 88:24 July 12, 76)

KENNEDY, ROBERT FRANCIS

Schlesinger, Arthur, Jr. John Kennedy was a realist brilliantly disguised as a romantic; Robert Kennedy, a romantic stubbornly disguised as a realist. (Newsweek 92:78 Sept 4, 78)

KEROUAC, JACK

Capote, Truman. It is not writing; it is only typing (about Jack Kerouac). (Village Voice 22:52 Oct 31, 77)

KEYNES, JOHN MAYNARD

Keynes, John Maynard. My only regret in life is that I did not drink more champagne. (Money 5:53 April 76)

KHMER ROUGE see REVOLUTIONISTS, CAMBODIAN

KHOMEINI, AYATOLLAH RUHOLLAH

Khomeini, Ayatollah Ruhollah. We have the ideology to distinguish right from wrong, and we should not hesitate to tell misguided people, here and abroad, what is wrong with them. (Time 114:25 Dec 10, 79)

KIDD, BRUCE

Kidd, Bruce. We should stop preaching about sport's moral values. Sport, after all, isn't Lent. It's a pleasure of the flesh. (Chicago Tribune 76:1 Section 2 Mar 17, 78)

KIDNAPPING see also HAUPTMANN, BRUNO RICHARD; LINDBERG, CHARLES AUGUSTUS— KIDNAPPING CASE

KING'S LAW (QUOTATION)

King, Larry L. One receives an inverse ratio of romantic opportunities to that which one needs. (Viva 4:72 Dec 76)

KING, DONALD

King, Donald. I have risen to the top in the promotion business just as I climbed to the top in the numbers game: by wits and grits and bullshit. (Cleveland 4:90 Nov 75)

KING, MARTIN LUTHER, JR.

King, Martin Luther, Jr. I'm not fearing any man. Mine eyes have seen the glory of the coming of the Lord. (Playboy 23:127 June 76)

**KING, MARTIN LUTHER, JR.—
ASSASSINATION**

King, Coretta Scott. I don't have the facts, but at this stage I say it appears there was a conspiracy in the death of my husband. (Los Angeles Times 94:12 Part 1 Nov 28, 75)

KINGMAN, DAVID ARTHUR

Kingman, David Arthur. There's no way to be a nice guy and play professional athletics. You have to just go out and be mean. (Chicago Tribune Magazine 21 April 19, 78)

KIRKLAND, GELSEY

Kirkland, Gelsey. My brain was the last of my muscles to develop. (US 3:17 Feb 9, 87)

KIRKPATRICK, JEANE

Kirkpatrick, Jeane. I have absolutely no intention of running for office—ever. (Chicago Tribune 6:5 Section 1 Mar 27, 85)

KISSING

Bergman, Ingrid. A kiss is a lovely trick designed by nature to stop speech when words become superfluous. (Viva 4:26 May 77)

KISSINGER, HENRY ALFRED

Kissinger, Henry Alfred. Among the many claims on American resources, I would put those of Vietnam in alphabetical order. (Newsweek 89:47 May 16, 77)

Kissinger, Henry Alfred. I have always thought of foreign policy as bipartisan. (Chicago Tribune 233:6 Section 2 Aug 21, 77)

Kissinger, Henry Alfred. I think Metternich was an extremely skilled diplomat, but not very creative. (Time 107:33 Jan 12, 76)

Kissinger, Henry Alfred. Power is the greatest aphrodisiac of all. (Maclean's 91:72 Mar 6, 78)

Kissinger, Henry Alfred. The longer I am out of office, the more infallible I appear to myself. (San Francisco Chronicle This World 1977:2 Oct 16, 77)

Kissinger, Henry Alfred. The main point...in the mechanics of my success comes from the fact that I have acted alone. (Esquire 89:41-42 Mar 14, 78)

Kissinger, Henry Alfred. Two years from now nobody will give a damn if I am up, down or sideways. (Time 106:29 Nov 17, 75)

Kissinger, Henry Alfred. We are all the president's men, and have got to behave that way. (Meet the Press 20:6 April 18, 76)

Lehrer, Tom. When Henry Kissinger can get the Nobel Peace Prize, what is there left for satire? (Chicago Sun-Times 33:76 July 9, 80)

McCarthy, Eugene Joseph. Kissinger won a Nobel Peace Prize for watching a war end that he was for. (New York Times Magazine 100 Oct 24, 76)

Meany, George. Foreign policy is too damned important to be left to the Secretary of State. (Time 106:7 Sept 8, 75)

Nixon, Richard Milhous. Henry (Kissinger) likes to say outrageous things....he was fascinated by the celebrity set and he liked being one himself. (Time 109:41 May 23, 77)

Reagan, Ronald. I worry about Kissinger. He needed someone like Nixon to keep him on that tough track. He has to have someone around who can keep him from giving away the store. (Time 106:22 Nov 17, 75)

Thomson, Meldrim. Henry Kissinger is the cunning architect of America's planned destruction. (American Opinion 18:27 Oct 75)

KISSLING, FRANCES

Kissling, Frances. God put me on earth to give the Pope a hard time. (Village Voice 32:24 Jan 27, 87)

KLUGE, ALEXANDER

Kluge, Alexander. German (movie) directors are like airplanes always circling the airport but never landing. (Time 111:53 Mar 20, 78)

KNOPF, ALFRED A.

Knopf, Alfred A. It's peculiar. The older I become the more radical I become. (W 4:2 Oct 31, 75)

KNOWLEDGE

Armstrong, Louis. There are some things which, if there ain't nobody said them, there must be a reason. (Chicago 16:57 July 81)

Butler, Nicholas Murray. An expert is one who knows more and more about less and less. (Kansas City Times 109:14B July 8, 77)

Clarke, Arthur C. The only way to find the limits of the possible is by going beyond them to the impossible. (Omni 2:85 April 80)

Condon, Richard. When you don't know the whole truth, the worst you can imagine is probably close. (D Magazine 15:38 April 88)

Guare, John. Innocence is ignorance where you're not getting caught. (Village Voice 22:35 Aug 15, 77)

Mayer, Jean. The ability to arrive at complex decisions is the hallmark of the educated person. (People Weekly 6:44 Nov 15, 76)

Paulucci, Jeno F. It pays to be ignorant, for when you're smart you already know it can't be done. (New York Times 126:5 Section 3 Nov 7, 76)

Perls, Fritz. Learning is discovering that something is possible. (Omni 2:36 Nov 79)

Santayana, George. Our dignity is not in what we do, but in what we understand. (Kansas City Star 97:4B Oct 10, 76)

Singer, Isaac Bashevis. The supernatural is like the ocean, while the so-called natural is only a little island on it. And even this little island is a great riddle. (New York Times 128:18 Section 4 Dec 3, 78)

Spock, Benjamin. You know more than you think you do. (Yankee 48:75 Dec 84)

Truman, Harry S. The only things worth learning are the things you learn after you know it all. (Reader's Digest 106:145 April 75)

Wicker, Tom. To know things as they are is better than to believe things as they seem. (Reader's Digest 107:121 July 75)

KNOWLEDGE see also LEARNING AND SCHOLARSHIP

KNOWLEDGE, SOCIOLOGY OF

Snow, C. P. Literary intellectuals at one pole—at the other, scientists...Between the two a gulf of mutual incomprehension. (Omni 1:39 Mar 79)

KNOWLEDGE, THEORY OF

Kahn, Herman. Think the unthinkable. (National Catholic Reporter 21:26 Dec 21, 84)

KOCH, EDWARD I.

Giuliani, Rudolph W. Ed Koch has always taken the low road. (New York Times 138:14 May 25, 89)

Koch, Edward I. I always run for office with the humility of an adopted child. (US 3:64 Feb 10, 86)

Koch, Edward I. My experience with blacks is that they are basically anti-Semitic. (Village Voice 27:12 Mar 9, 82)

Morgan, Thomas B. Koch had the opportunity to be the national urban leader, but he fled from it. (Manhattan, Inc. 6:9 Jan 89)

KOJAK, THEO (TELEVISION CHARACTER)

Kojak, Theo. Hindsight is the only exact science. (Philadelphia 68:113 July 77)

KORDA, MICHAEL

Korda, Michael. Accuracy has never been my strongest point. (Chicago Tribune 332:1 Section 3 Nov 28, 79)

KOVIC, RON

Kovic, Ron. The government took the best years of my life away from me and millions of other young men. I just think they're lucky I wrote a book instead of buying a gun. (People Weekly 6:58 Dec 27/Jan 3, 77)

KU KLUX KLAN

Duke, David. Black people have organizations that fight for black power, and Jews look out for each other. But there isn't anyone except the Klan who will fight for the rights of white people. (Newsweek 90:45 Nov 14, 77)

Marshall, Thurgood. The Ku Klux Klan never dies. They just stop wearing sheets because sheets cost too much. (Time 112:91 Dec 4, 78)

KUBRICK, STANLEY

Kubrick, Stanley. The essence of dramatic form is to let an idea come over people without its being plainly stated. (Time 106:72 Dec 15, 75)

KUWAIT see also IRAQ—FOREIGN RELATIONS— KUWAIT

LA PASIONARIA see IBARRURI, DOLORES

LABOR AND LABORING CLASSES

Lennon, John. A working class hero is something to be. (Sports Illustrated 65:77 Oct 27, 86)

LABOR AND LABORING CLASSES see also INTERNATIONAL BROTHERHOOD OF TEAMSTERS, CHAUFFEURS, WAREHOUSEMEN AND HELPERS OF AMERICA; STRIKES

LABOR AND LABORING CLASSES— RUSSIA

Anonymous. As long as the bosses pretend they are paying us a decent wage, we will pretend that we are working (Soviet worker's saying). (New York Times 126:25 Section 12 Jan 30, 77)

LAND, EDWIN

Land, Edwin. I am addicted to at least one good experiment a day. (Time 115:68 Mar 17, 80)

LANGE, JESSICA

Nicholson, Jack. She's like a delicate fawn crossed with a Buick (about Jessia Lange). (Vanity Fair 47:72 Oct 84)

LANGLOIS, HENRI

Langlois, Henri. Most people advance through life walking backward. Those artists who face forward are likely to be put in jail—or the madhouse. (New York Times 126:D13 Jan 23, 77)

LANGUAGE AND LANGUAGES

Baldwin, James. It (language) is the most vivid and crucial key to identity. (Saturday Review 6:14 Oct 13, 79)

LAROUCHE, LYNDON

LaRouche, Lyndon. I am the leading economist of the century. (Inquiry 6:21 Feb 28, 83)

LASORDA, TOM

Garagiola, Joe. You could plant two thousand rows of corn with the fertilizer he spreads around (commenting on Tom Lasorda, manager of the L. A. Dodgers). (The Sporting News 193:10 May 3, 82)

LASSER, LOUISE

Lasser, Louise. When you are a celebrity, you are totally a victim. (Time 111:56 June 19, 78)

LAUGHTER

Auden, Wystan Hugh. Among those whom I like, I can find no common denominator; but among those whom I love, I can: all of them make me laugh. (Reader's Digest 107:78 Nov 75)

LAUREN, RALPH

Lauren, Ralph. I can do anything I want. (W 7:8 Dec 8, 79)

LAW

Bell, Griffin. I think we have too many crimes, and I definitely have the view that we have too many laws. (Time 108:16 Dec 27, 76)

Harris, Sydney J. It is not criminals, but laws that are the worst enemy of Law. (Chicago Daily News 8 May 5, 77)

Roosevelt, Franklin Delano. Obedience to the law is demanded as a right, not asked as a favor. (The Oklahoma Observer 16:13 Jan 25, 84)

Silberman, Laurence. The legal process, because of its unbridled growth, has become a cancer which threatens the vitality of our forms of capitalism and democracy. (Time 111:56 April 10, 78)

LAW—PRACTICE—UNITED STATES

Countryman, Vernon (Harvard professor). The bar is still dominated by shortsightedness and self-interest. Spotting change there is like watching a glacier move. (Time 110:52 Aug 8, 77)

Foreman, Percy. You don't approach a case with the philosophy of applying abstract justice—you go in to win. (USA Today 1:10A May 5, 83)

Green, Mark. While piously proclaiming an interest in the public good, the bar's Canons of Ethics have operated as Canons of Profits. (Time 110:52 Aug 8, 77)

LAWYERS

Auerbach, Jerold S. Equal justice under law (often means) unequal justice under lawyers. (Time 111:59 April 10, 78)

Burger, Warren Earl. We may be well on our way to a society overrun by hordes of lawyers, hungry as locusts, and brigades of judges in numbers never before contemplated. (Time 109:40 June 27, 77)

Clancy, Tom. A lawyer is just like an attack dog, only without a conscience. (Chicago Tribune 222:15 Section 1 Aug 9, 88)

Countryman, Vernon (Harvard professor). The bar is still dominated by shortsightedness and self-interest. Spotting change there is like watching a glacier move. (Time 110:52 Aug 8, 77)

Dutton, Fred. Lawyers have become secular priests. (Time 111:58 April 10, 78)

Green, Mark. While piously proclaiming an interest in the public good, the bar's Canons of Ethics have operated as Canons of Profits. (Time 110:52 Aug 8, 77)

Hundley, William G. The worst defense lawyers I know are those who become convinced their clients are innocent. (Time 111:89 Mar 6, 78)

Kennedy, Florynce Rae. Most lawyers are like whores. They serve the client who puts the highest fee on the table. (Ms 1:89 Mar 73)

Lebowitz, Fran. A dog who thinks he is a man's best friend is a dog who obviously has never met a tax lawyer. (Book World 11:5 Sept 81)

McKay, Robert. If war is too important to be left to the generals, surely justice is too important to be left to lawyers. (Time 111:66 April 10, 78)

Nolan, John T. If you outsmart your own lawyer, you've got the wrong lawyer. (Washingtonian 15:142 Nov 79)

Reuben, Don. Lawyers are impossible to manage, they are contemptious and egotistical. (American Lawyer 10:15 July/Aug 88)

Spence, Gary. There is no justice in seeking justice anymore. (W 4:86 April 87)

Sutton, Willie. I always figured that being a good robber was like being a good lawyer. (Village Voice 21:118 Sept 13, 76)

Warren, Earl. A jurist's mind cannot operate in a vacuum. (Christian Science Monitor 69:27 Aug 3, 77)

LAWYERS see also BAILEY, F. LEE

LAYNE, BOBBY

Walker, Doak. He was the greatest two-minute quarterback ever. Bobby Layne simply never lost a game. Sometimes, time just ran out on him. (The Sporting News 202:61 Dec 15, 86)

LEADBELLY see LEDBETTER, HUDDIE

LEADERSHIP

Clark, Joseph. A leader should not get too far in front of his troops or he will be shot in the ass. (Washingtonian 15:140 Nov 79)

Gorbachev, Mikhail S. History punishes those who come late. (Vanity Fair 53:189 Feb 90)

Kilpatrick, James J. Find out where the people want to go, then hustle yourself around in front of them. (Washingtonian 15:143 Nov 79)

Lippmann, Walter. The final test of a leader is that he leaves behind him in other men the conviction and the will to carry on. (Sports Illustrated 65:66 Oct 6, 86)

Nader, Ralph. I start with the premise that the function of leadership is to produce more leaders, not more followers. (Time 108:41 Nov 8, 76)

Qaddafi, Muammar. People are getting killed everywhere by their leaders. (The Observer 9799:9 June 17, 79)

Riesman, David. The question is not whether leadership is obsolete but whether democracy is governable. (Time 114:26 Aug 6, 79)

Truman, Harry S. The C students run the world. (Time 108:32 Nov 8, 76)

White, Kevin Hagen. Charismatic leadership is hungered for, but at the same time we fear it. (Time 107:10 Feb 9, 76)

White, Theodore. Class is a matter of style in leadership. It is the magic that translates the language of the street into the language of history. (Time 111:20 Mar 6, 78)

LEAR, AMANDA
Lear, Amanda. I hate to spread rumors, but what else can you do with them. (Interview 8:32 Mar 78)

LEARNING AND SCHOLARSHIP
Frankel, Charles. Scholarship must be free to follow crooked paths to unexpected conclusions. (Time 113:8 May 14, 79)

Lollobrigida, Gina. Whatever we learn, we learn too late. (Chicago Tribune Magazine 2 July 5, 87)

Truman, Harry S. The only things worth learning are the things you learn after you know it all. (Reader's Digest 106:145 April 75)

LEBANON
Salem, Elie. Whatever the target, Lebanon is always the victim. (Life 7:114 Jan 84)

LEBOWITZ, FRAN
Lebowitz, Fran. I can't write if there's another person in the building. (W 17:52 Sept 19, 88)

LEBRON, LOLITA
Lebron, Lolita. Until my last breath I will fight for the liberation and freedom of Puerto Rico. (New York Times 128:1 Sept 12, 79)

LEDBETTER, HUDDIE
Parks, Gordon. Huddie (Ledbetter) was meant for music and born for trouble. (New York 9:66 May 10, 76)

LEFEBVRE, MARCEL
Lefebvre, Marcel. Rome, and not I, is in error. (Guardian Weekly 120:6 Jan 28, 79)

LEFT WING POLITICS
Barry, Lynda. The problem with the left is that they don't realize that people have genitals. (In These Times 14:15 Oct 24, 90)

Carmichael, Stokely. The only position for women in the movement is prone. (New York Times Magazine 91 April 10, 77)

Hoffman, Abbie. The movie isn't over yet (1989). (Chicago Tribune 104:10 Section 2 April 14, 89)

Lasch, Christopher. Radicalism in the United States has no great triumphs to record. (Time 110:67 Aug 15, 77)

Von Hoffman, Nicholas. It's getting so this society has no left, except in baseball. (Chicago Tribune 86:19 Section 1 Mar 27, 85)

LEGISLATION
Talmadge, Betty. If you love the law and you love good sausage, don't watch either of them being made. (The Reader (Chicago's Free Weekly) 7:23 Nov 25, 77)

LEISURE
Jerome, Jerome K. It is impossible to enjoy idling thoroughly unless one has plenty of work to do. (Rocky Mountain News 79:86 July 10, 80)

Wilson, Sloan. A man who wants time to read and write must let the grass grow long. (New York 9:46 May 24, 76)

LESBIANISM
Johnston, Jill. All women are lesbians except those who don't know it yet. (Ms 4:80 Nov 75)

Johnston, Jill. Feminism at heart is a massive complaint. Lesbianism is the solution. (Time 106:39 Sept 8, 75)

Lowell, Robert. Almost all good women poets are either divorced or lesbian. (San Francisco Chronicle 111:19 May 25, 77)

LETTERS
Stimson, Henry. Gentlemen do not read each other's mail. (Maclean's 89:72 April 5, 76)

Woolf, Virginia. The best letters of our times are those that can never be published. (Village Voice 27:25 July 6, 82)

LEVANT, OSCAR
Levant, Oscar. I never read bad reviews about myself because my best friends invaribly tell me about them. (Chicago 31:22 July 31, 82)

LEWIS, JOHN L.
Longworth, Alice Roosevelt. He was the best company there ever was (about John L. Lewis). (New York Times 124:15 Section 4 Aug 17, 75)

LIBERALISM
Frost, Robert. A liberal is a man who can't take his own side in an argument. (Harvard Magazine 87:68 Sept 84)

Mikva, Abner J. My definition of a liberal is someone who can look at an idea and see that it doesn't work, even if it was a liberal idea. (Chicago Tribune 222:4 Section 3 Aug 10, 78)

Rockefeller, Nelson Aldrich. One thing I can't stand is a goddamned bleeding heart. (American Spectator 15:22 Oct 82)

Rosenblatt, Roger. Liberals are radicals with assets. (US 3:14 Dec 2, 85)

Rutler, George William. Anti-Catholicism has become the Anti-Semitism of the liberals. (Chicago Tribune 68:16 Mar 9, 86)

Thompson, Hunter S. There's no such thing as a 'nice' reporter. That's like saying somebody's a nice liberal. (W 5:11 Sept 3, 76)

Tonsor, Stephen. New Deal liberals are as dead as a dodo. The only problem is they don't know it. (Newsweek 90:34 Nov 7, 77)

Wilson, James Q. There aren't any liberals left in New York. They've all been mugged by now. (American Spectator 18:18 April 85)

LIBERATION THEOLOGY
Esquerra, Maria Antonia (Chicana nun). The

theology of liberation in North America will be written by the oppressed. (Time 106:34 Sept 1, 75)

LIBERTY

Burger, Warren Earl. The very discussion of independence reminds us how much each freedom is dependent on other freedoms. (American Legion Magazine 99:36 Nov 75)

Friedman, Milton. Let me propose that we take as our major motto what I would like to see as an 11th commandment: that everyone shall be free to do good at his own expense. (American Legion Magazine 103:12 Aug 77)

Gandhi, Indira (Nehru). The freedom of the people cannot be allowed to come in the way of the freedom of the masses. (People Weekly 4:33 Dec 29/Jan 5, 76)

Giscard d'Estaing, Valery. You do not fear freedom for yourself, do not then fear it for your friends and allies. (New York Times 125:2 May 19, 76)

Goldwater, Barry Morris. Eternal vigilance is the price of liberty. (Texas Observer 70:2 Aug 11, 78)

MacLeish, Archibald. Freedom is still the last great revolutionary cause. (Chicago Tribune 163:2 Section 2 June 11, 78)

Safire, William. I think that one of Nixon's great contributions to civil liberties was getting caught doing what the two presidents before him got away with. (Book Digest 4:28 July 77)

Sheen, Fulton J. Freedom is the right to do what you ought to do. (Time 114:84 Dec 24, 79)

Stevenson, Adlai, II. A free society is one where it is safe to be unpopular. (Human Behavior 7:68 May 78)

Stravinsky, Igor Fedorovich. If everything would be permitted to me, I would feel lost in this abyss of freedom. (New York Times 126:D25 Sept 11, 77)

Thatcher, Margaret Hilda. There can be no liberty unless there is economic liberty. (Village Voice 24:35 May 14, 79)

Von Hayek, Friedrich. You can have economic freedom without political freedom, but you cannot have political freedom without economic freedom. (Village Voice 24:35 May 14, 79)

LIBRARIANS

Clark, Alan. Librarians are standing in their graves. (New York Times 128:26 April 8, 79)

Fremont-Smith, Eliot. Booksellers are good at drinking; librarians are better. (Village Voice 20:49 June 9, 75)

LIBRARIES

Clark, Alan. Librarians are standing in their graves. (New York Times 128:26 April 8, 79)

Fleming, John. Show me your books, and I'll tell you who you are. (Esquire 89:71 Jan 31, 78)

Kohler, Jerry. I'd just as soon die in Vietnam as in the library. (Salina (Kansas) Journal 10 May 27, 76)

LIBRARIES AND PUBLISHERS

Shields, Gerald R. It is obvious that the photocopying issue is to be decided soon and that the odds favor turning libraries into some sort of reprint warehouse for publisher's products. (Library Journal 100:2307 Dec 15, 75)

LIDDY, G. GORDON

Liddy, G. Gordon. Before going to prison I believed that criticism of the criminal justice system for its treatment of the poor was so much liberal bleating and bunk. I was wrong. (Connecticut 40:48 Feb 77)

LIEBLING, A. J.

Shawn, William (attributed by Brendan Gill). Liebling wants to live like a stockbroker, but he doesn't want to be a stockbroker. (Andy Warhol's Interview 8:60 Dec 78)

LIFE

Adjani, Isabelle. Life is worth being lived but not worth being discussed all the time. (Time 113:67 Feb 12, 79)

Allen, Woody. The meaning of life is that nobody knows the meaning of life. (Rolling Stone 216:88 July 1, 76)

Allen, Woody (attributed by Marshall Brickman). Showing up is 80 percent of life. (New York Times 126:11 Section 2 Aug 21, 77)

Anonymous (Haight-Ashbury Diggers slogan). Today is the first day of the rest of your life. (New Times 9:68 Aug 19, 77)

Ayckbourn, Alan. There are very few people on top of life, and the rest of us don't like them very much. (Newsweek 128:4 Mar 25, 79)

Berry, Chuck. The minute you toot your horn, it seems like society will try and disconnect your battery. (US 3:6 Nov 16, 87)

Burroughs, William S. Life is a cut-up. (University Daily Kansan 93:11 April 25, 83)

Camus, Albert. Not only is there no solution but there aren't even any problems. (Time 112:74 July 10, 78)

Carter, James Earl. There are many things in life that are not fair. (Village Voice 23:11 Jan 2, 78)

Chaplin, Charles Spencer. In the end, everything is a gag. (Newsweek 102:79 July 11, 83)

Chaplin, Charles Spencer. Life is a tragedy

when seen in close-up, but a comedy in long-shot. (Guardian Weekly 118:5 Jan 1, 78)

Child, Julia. Life itself is the proper binge. (Cosmopolitan 180:178 May 76)

Cousins, Norman. Life is an adventure in forgiveness. (Saturday Review 5:12 April 15, 78)

Daniels, Billy. Life is a lot like a good song; take is slow and easy, the music will carry you through. (Chicago Tribune 290:2 Section 13 Oct 16, 88)

Eaton, Richard. Life is subject to change without notice. (More 8:9 June 78)

Gonick, Jean. For women, life is a series of leaking tampons. (GQ 57:99 May 87)

Goodman, Ellen. It has begun to occur to me that life is a stage I'm going through. (Time 114:125 Dec 10, 79)

Guevara, Nacha. In life the things you want always arrive after you've stopped waiting. (Chicago Sun-Times 32:8 Section 4 July 1, 79)

Hendrix, Jimi. It's funny the way most people love the dead. Once you are dead, you are made for life. (Rolling Stone 227:81 Dec 2, 76)

Kahn, Alfred. All life is a concatenation of ephemeralities. (Barron's 59:5 Feb 19, 79)

Khrushchev, Nikita Sergeevich. Life is short. Live it up. (Viva 4:25 July 77)

Kristol, Irving. Being frustrated is disagreeable, but the real disasters of life begin when you get what you want. (Book Digest 6:28 Dec 79)

Larkin, Philip. I see life more as an affair of solitude diversified by company than as an affair of company diversified by solitude. (The Observer 9825:35 Dec 16, 79)

Lindbergh, Anne Morrow (attributed by Julie Nixon Eisenhower). Life is a gift, given in trust—like a child. (Christian Science Monitor 69:21 June 23, 77)

Lindbergh, Charles Augustus. Life is like a landscape. You live in the midst of it, but can describe it only from the vantage point of distance. (Washington Post 161:G2 May 15, 77)

Martin, Judith. Life is full of situations that cry out not to be commented upon. (Kansas City Times 117:A-23 Oct 25, 84)

Millay, Edna St. Vincent. It is not true that life is one damn thing after another; it's one damn thing over and over. (Viva 4:25 July 77)

Miller, Henry. To the person who thinks with his head, life is a comedy. To those who think with their feelings, or work through their feelings, life is a tragedy. (Soho News 5:3 Jan 26, 78)

O'Malley, Frank Ward. Life is just one damned thing after another. (Viva 4:25 July 77)

O'Neill, Eugene. Life is a tragedy, hurrah. (New York Times 128:15 Section 6 Mar 4, 79)

Olivier, Laurence. Living is strife and torment, disappointment and love and sacrifice, golden sunsets and black storms. (Los Angeles Times Calendar 35 Feb 26, 78)

Orwell, George. Any life when viewed from the inside is simply a series of defeats. (Toronto Globe and Mail 136:5 Section 5 Nov 17, 79)

Pirandello, Luigi. Life is little more than a loan shark: it exacts a very high rate of interest for the few pleasures it concedes. (The Reader (Chicago's Free Weekly) 7:2 Dec 23, 77)

Rattigan, Terrence. What a lovely world we're in, if only we'd let ourselves see it. (Guardian Weekly 117:4 Dec 11, 77)

Runyon, Damon. All life is six-to-five against. (New York 9:36 Nov 1, 76)

Shepard, Sam. If you can stay right in the middle of a contradiction, that's where life is. (Interview 18:76 Sept 88)

Sontag, Susan. There are some elements in life—above all, sexual pleasure—about which it isn't necessary to have a position. (Village Voice 21:77 Mar 22, 76)

Ullmann, Liv. You must put more in your life than a man. (Time 113:65 Jan 29, 79)

Vallee, Rudy. I thought my freshman English instructor at Yale was crazy when he said life was cold, cruel, rotten, hard and it stinks. But I found out he was right. (Washington Post 333:B7 Nov 3, 75)

Vreeland, Diana. Either one's life is attractive or it isn't. (Town & Country 129:79 June 75)

Woods, Rose Mary. There's more to life than money. (W 12:4 April 23, 82)

LIFE ON OTHER PLANETS

Soffer, Gerald. All the signs suggest that life exists on Mars, but we can't find any bodies. (Omni 2:40 April 80)

LINDBERGH, CHARLES AUGUSTUS

Lindbergh, Charles Augustus. I've had enough fame for a dozen lives; it's not what it's cracked up to be. (New York Times Magazine 12 May 8, 77)

LINDBERGH, CHARLES AUGUSTUS— KIDNAPPING CASE

Hauptmann, Bruno Richard. I have said it all, I am innocent. There is nothing else I could tell. (New York 9:76 Nov 22, 76)

LINDSAY, JOHN VLIET

Moses, Robert. If you elect a matinee idol as

mayor, you get a musical-comedy administration. (New York 10:58 Sept 5, 77)

LIQUOR TRAFFIC—CHICAGO—PROHIBITION

Capone, Alphonse. When I sell liquor, it's called bootlegging; when my patrons serve it on silver trays on Lake Shore Drive, it's called hospitality. (Aspen 3:43 Spring 77)

LITERATURE

Blackmur, R. P. Literature exists to remind the powers that be, simple and corrupt as they are, of the turbulence they have to control. (New York Times Book Review 32 Sept 23, 79)

Cheever, John. Literature is much more a conversation than a discourse. (US News & World Report 86:92 May 21, 79)

Nabokov, Vladimir. Great novels are above all great fairy tales. Literature does not tell the truth but makes it up. (Newsweek 90:42 July 18, 77)

Singer, Isaac Bashevis. Literature is the memory of humanity. (US News & World Report 85:60 Nov 6, 78)

LITERATURE—AWARDS, PRIZES, ETC.

Auchincloss, Louis. Prizes are for the birds. They fill the head of one author with vanity and 30 others with misery. (Time 118:61 Sept 21, 81)

LITERATURE—CRITICISM

Steinbeck, John (attributed by John Kenneth Galbraith). Unless the bastards have the courage to give you unqualified praise, I say ignore them. (Esquire 99:88 April 30, 83)

LITTLE RICHARD

Little Richard. If there was anything I loved better than a big penis it was a bigger penis. (Spin 2:12 Mar 87)

LOBBYING

Lipsen, Chuck. Folklore has it that the oldest profession is prostitution. I always thought it was lobbying. (W 6:2 Sept 16, 77)

LOGIC

Mencken, Henry Louis. One horse laugh is worth ten thousand syllogisms. (New York Times Book Review 27 Sept 7, 80)

Orlans, Harold. Logic is a game men play as cats play with balls of string, whereas reality is a game the gods play with us. (Change 9:34 April 77)

LOMBARDO, GUY

Lombardo, Guy. When I go, I'll take New Year's Eve with me. (Newsweek 90:126 Nov 14, 77)

LONELINESS

Lynch, James. If we do not live together, we will die—prematurely—alone. (Guardian Weekly 117:17 Sept 18, 77)

Mother Teresa. Loneliness and the feeling of being unwanted is the most terrible poverty. (Time 106:49 Dec 29, 75)

Wharton, William. After I muddle in other people's puddles, I find out it's all one, big lonesome ocean. (National Catholic Reporter 21:13 May 17, 85)

LONGEVITY

Burns, George. The secret to longevity is three martini's before dinner and always dance close. (W Supplement 131 July 27, 87)

Stone, Isidor Feinstein. If you live long enough, you get accused of things you never did and praised for virtues you never had. (American Spectator 17:17 July 84)

LOREN, SOPHIA

Loren, Sophia. I will be a very wise and serene old lady. As I get older, I get quieter, because now I know myself better. (Chicago Tribune 15:33 Jan 15, 78)

LOS ANGELES

Blass, Bill. L. A. stinks, and I can say that because I'm not running for anything. (Time 122:49 Sept 12, 83)

Medlin, James. The most healthy thing in L.A. is to do nothing. (New West 3:Oct 9, 78

LOSING

Rockne, Knute. You show me a good and gracious loser, and I'll show you a failure! (Argosy 384:15 Nov 76)

LOVE

Auden, Wystan Hugh. Among those whom I like, I can find no common denominator; but among those whom I love, I can: all of them make me laugh. (Reader's Digest 107:78 Nov 75)

Baldwin, James. Love does not begin and end the way we seem to think it does. Love is a battle, love is a war; love is a growing up. (Cosmopolitan 188:268 Feb 80)

Bombeck, Erma. A child needs your love most when he deserves it the least. (Family Circle 97:14 Jan 3, 84)

Brenan, Gerald. When the coin is tossed, either love or lust will fall uppermost. But if the metal is right, under the one will always lie the other. (Time 113:147-48 Feb 5, 79)

Brooks, Mel. Everything we do in life is based on fear, especially love. (Playboy 26:26 Oct 79)

Brown, Rita Mae. Love is the wild card of existence. (Chicago Sun-Times 34:53 Sept 2, 81)

Ciardi, John. Love is the word used to label the sexual excitement of the young, the habituation of the middle-aged, and the mutual dependence of the old. (Chicago Tribune 212:1 Section 2 July 31, 78)

Fiedler, Leslie. There can be no terror without the hope for love and love's defeat. (New York Arts Journal 9:15 April 78)

Freud, Sigmund. One is very crazy when in love. (Playboy 26:26 Oct 79)

Gurley, George H., Jr. The omnipresence of vulgar sexual imagery reflects our taste in love in the same way that Chicken McNuggets represent our taste in food. (Kansas City Times 120:1B Nov 3, 87)

Janeway, Eliot. The thrill of making a fast buck follows only the thrill of love at first sight. Everyone needs to take an occasional fling with money...and with love. (Chicago Tribune 95:14 April 5, 77)

Landers, Ann. Love is the most precious thing in all the world. Whatever figures in second place doesn't even come close. (New York 9:68 Feb 16, 76)

McCarthy, Mary. One has to believe that love is eternal, even if one knows it is not. (The Observer 9816:35 Oct 14, 79)

McCarthy, Mary. You mustn't force sex to do the work of love or love to do the work of sex. (Cosmopolitan 197:274 Mar 84)

Moreau, Jeanne. Age does not protect you from love. But love, to some extent, protects you from age. (People Weekly 3:66 Feb 3, 75)

Mother Teresa. Jesus said love one another. He didn't say love the whole world. (The Observer 9836:9 Mar 2, 80)

Munro, Alice. Love is not kind or honest and does not contribute to happiness in any reliable way. (California 10:71 Sept 85)

Patton, George S. In war, just as in loving, you've got to keep on shoving. (Playboy 26:26 Oct 79)

Russell, Bertrand. I believe myself that romantic love is the source of the most intense delights that life has to offer. (Chicago Tribune 212:1 Section 2 July 31, 78)

Tomlin, Lily. If love is the answer, could you rephrase the question? (Cosmopolitan 188:268 Feb 80)

Truffaut, Francois. In love, women are professionals, men are amateurs. (Rolling Stone 293:43 June 14, 79)

Viorst, Judith. Brevity may be the soul of wit, but not when someone's saying 'I love you'. (Chicago Tribune 176:2 Section 2 June 25, 78)

LOVE see also ROMANCE

LOWER CLASSES—GREAT BRITAIN

Waugh, Evelyn. It is impudent and exorbitant to demand truth from the lower classes. (Time 110:102 Oct 17, 77)

LUBBOCK, TEXAS

Layne, Bobby. Living in a small town (Lubbock) in Texas ain't half bad—if you own it. (Kansas City Times 111:10 Nov 17, 78)

LUCAS, GEORGE

Lucas, George. I'm not out to be thought of as a great artist. It's a big world and everybody doesn't have to be significant. (Time 115:73 May 19, 80)

LUCE, CLARE BOOTHE

Fadiman, Clifton. No woman of our time has gone further with less mental equipment (Clare Boothe Luce). (New York 15:70 Mar 1, 82)

LUCE, HENRY

Luce, Henry. Make money, be proud of it; make more money, be prouder of it. (Washington Journalism Review 1:22 April 78)

LUCK

Bohr, Niels. But horseshoes have a way of bringing you luck even when you don't believe in them. (Village Voice 21:25 June 28, 76)

Hammer, Armand. Luck seems to come to the guy who works 14 hours a day, seven days a week. (Kansas City Star 108:1F Dec 27, 87)

Rickey, Branch. Luck is the residue of design. (Toronto Life 22 May 84)

LUDLAM, CHARLES

Ludlam, Charles. My work is eclectic not ethnocentric. It is a Rosetta Stone of theatrical conventions. (Village Voice 20:120 Nov 17, 75)

LYING

Jerome, Jerome K. It is always the best policy to speak the truth, unless of course you are an exceptionally good liar. (Kansas City Star 97:26 May 2, 77)

LYING see also CAPOTE, TRUMAN

MACARTHUR, DOUGLAS

MacArthur, Douglas. It's the orders you disobey that make you famous. (Time 112:89 Sept 11, 78)

MACARTHUR, JOHN D.

MacArthur, John D. Anybody who knows what he's worth, isn't worth very much (upon being asked how much he was worth). (Chicago Tribune 340:2 Section 1 Dec 5, 76)

MACHISMO

Gabor, Zsa Zsa. Macho does not prove mucho. (Washingtonian 15:143 Nov 79)

MACLAINE, SHIRLEY

MacLaine, Shirley. When you know who you are and you realize what you can do, you can do things better at 40 than when you're 20. (Time 107:39 Feb 16, 76)

MADONNA (ROCK MUSICIAN)

Madonna, (rock musician). I'm just a midwestern girl in a bustier. (US 3:6 July 11, 88)

MAFIA

Lansky, Meyer. We're bigger than U. S. Steel. (Playboy 31:22 May 84)

MAHFOUZ, NAGUIB

Mahfouz, Naguib. If the rage to write should ever leave me, I want that day to be my last. (Chicago Tribune 300:23 Section 1 Oct 26, 88)

MAILER, NORMAN

Mailer, Norman. I don't pretend I'm typical, but I've always found promiscuous women interesting. I suspect I would have been promiscuous if I'd been a woman. I certainly have been as a man. (Kansas City Star 110:D-1 May 7, 90)

Mailer, Norman. I've made an ass of myself so many times I often wonder if I am one. (New York Times Magazine 53 Sept 9, 79)

MALAMUD, BERNARD

Malamud, Bernard. I write to know the next room of my fate. (Time 114:86 July 2, 79)

MALCOLM X

Malcolm X. This thing with me will be resolved by death and violence. (Playboy 23:127 June 76)

MALLE, LOUIS

Malle, Louis. Being a director is like being a thief. You steal bits and pieces of the lives around you, and you put them into a movie. (New York Times 126:C6 Nov 19, 76)

MAMET, DAVID

Mamet, David. I want to change the future of American theatre. (Village Voice 21:101 July 5, 76)

MAN

Asimov, Isaac. We are the only creatures ever to inhabit the Earth who have truly seen the stars. (Omni 2:90 April 80)

Beckett, Samuel. There's man all over for you, blaming his boots for the faults of his feet. (Philadelphia 69:187 Sept 78)

Camus, Albert. Alas, after a certain age every man is responsible for his face. (CoEvolution Quarterly 17:30 Spring 78)

Castro, Fidel. Men are very fragile. We disappear and go up in smoke for almost any reason. (Time 107:51 Jan 5, 76)

DeVries, Peter. Man is vile, I know, but people are wonderful. (Chicago 31:24 Sept 82)

Eliot, Thomas Stearns. Humankind cannot bear very much reality. (Chicago Tribune Magazine 6 Aug 19, 84)

Faulkner, William. I believe that man will not merely endure: he will prevail (commenting in his 1950 Nobel Prize acceptance speech). (New York Times Magazine 42 Dec 5, 76)

Foreman, Percy. Man's inhumanity to man is only exceeded by woman's inhumanity to woman. (Newsweek 88:93 Nov 8, 76)

Fulbright, James William. It is one of the perversities of human nature that people have a far greater capacity for enduring disasters than for preventing them, even when the danger is plain and imminent. (American Legion Magazine 98:20 Jan 75)

Gingrich, Arnold. To stand out, for a man or a magazine, it is necessary to stand for something. Otherwise you stand still. (Newsweek 88:78 July 19, 76)

Humphrey, Hubert Horatio. A man with no tears is a man with no heart. (Chicago Tribune 263:2 Sept 20, 77)

Jones, David. Man is the only maker, neither beast nor angel share this dignity with him. (New York Times 128:9 Section 7 Feb 18, 79)

Kraus, Karl. The devil is an optimist if he thinks he can make people worse than they are. (Inquiry 1:25 Jan 23, 78)

Landor, Walter Savage. Men cannot bear to be deprived of anything they are used to; not even of their fears. (Kansas City Star 97:4B Oct 10, 76)

Laszlo, Ervin. The materialistic growth ethic is not an immutable expression of human nature. (Time 107:56 April 26, 76)

Le Carre, John. People are very secretive creatures—secret even from themselves. (The Observer 9833:9 Feb 10, 80)

Lodge, John Davis. Man is born into the world as a pig and is civilized by women. (W 6:2 Feb 18, 77)

Malraux, Andre. There cannot be another Michelangelo in today's society because our faith in man is too weak. (Time 105:40 May 12, 75)

Morris, Richard B. The United States is still the last best hope of man. (US News & World Report 81:73 July 5, 76)

Morrison, Toni. What is curious to me is that bestial treatment of human beings never produces a race of beasts. (New York Times Magazine 40 May 20, 79)

Muggeridge, Malcolm. It is only believers in the Fall of Man who can really appreciate how funny men are. (The Observer 9762:15 Oct 1, 78)

Oldenburg, Claes. To give birth to form is the only act of man that has any consequence. (Chicago 25:18 Nov 76)

Orlans, Harold. Logic is a game men play as cats play with balls of string, whereas reality is a game the gods play with us. (Change 9:34 April 77)

Pogo, (Cartoon Character). We have met the enemy and they is us. (Philadelphia 69:188 Sept 78)

Sanchez, Robert. In looking backward, we must renew our faith in God. In looking forward, we must renew our faith in men. (National Catholic Reporter 12:8 July 2, 76)

Santayana, George. Our dignity is not in what we do, but in what we understand. (Kansas City Star 97:4B Oct 10, 76)

Thomas, Lewis. We do not, in any real way, run the (world). It runs itself, and we are part of the running. (Time 111:85 May 29, 78)

Valli, Frankie. There's nothing wrong with the world, only the people in it. And the same goes for music. (New York 8:62 Aug 4, 75)

Voznesensky, Andrei. When Man put on clothes for the first time, he challenged the Lord and became His equal. (Vogue 168:193 Feb 78)

Warren, Robert Penn. What is man but his passion? (Saturday Review 5:19 Dec 78)

MAN AND NATURE see MAN—INFLUENCE ON NATURE

MAN RAY see RAY, MAN

MAN—INFLUENCE ON NATURE

Beston, Henry. Peace with the earth is the first peace. (Blair & Ketchum's Country Journal 3:88 Aug 76)

MANAGEMENT

Lidberg, A. A. Distribute dissatisfaction uniformly. (Washingtonian 15:140 Nov 79)

MANDELA, NELSON

Tutu, Desmond. Mandela has become the symbol of our people. (Chicago Tribune 182:13 Section 1 July 1, 90)

MANNERS AND CUSTOMS

Guest, Lucy Cochrane (C.Z.). I think manners are the most important thing in life. (Mother Jones 2:10 Aug 77)

MAO, TSE-TUNG

Mao, Tse-Tung. (I am) only a lone monk walking the world with a leaky umbrella. (Time 108:37 Sept 20, 76)

Mao, Tse-Tung. Every Communist must grasp the truth: political power grown out of the barrel of a gun. Our principle is that the party commands the gun and the gun must never be allowed to command the party. (Newsweek 88:40 Sept 20, 76)

Mao, Tse-Tung. I am alone with the masses. (Time 108:38 Sept 20, 76)

MARCEAU, MARCEL

Marceau, Marcel. I am a silent witness of my time. (Christian Science Monitor 69:22 Feb 2, 77)

MARCOS, FERDINAND

Bush, George. We love your adherence to democratic principles—and to the democratic process (about Ferdinand Marcos). (Mother Jones 7:28 Feb 82)

MARINE POLLUTION

Cousteau, Jacques Yves. Today I don't swim at all because I haven't the time to go 10 to 12 miles offshore to find clean water. (Washington Post 226:B2 July 19, 77)

MARKETING

Golembo, Eri. People will buy any product that has been made smaller if it retains the functionality of the larger product and has a handle. (PC Magazine 5:148 Mar 25, 86)

Paulucci, Jeno F. The meek have to inherit the earth—they sure don't know how to market it. (New York Times 126:5 Section 3 Nov 7, 76)

MARRIAGE

Astor, Nancy. I married beneath me. All women do. (The Observer 9822:35 Nov 25, 79)

Aumont, Jean-Pierre. Marriages are not eternal, so why should divorce be? (W 6:2 July 8, 77)

Brickman, Marshall. Open marriage is nature's way of telling you you need a divorce. (Cosmopolitan 188:268 Feb 80)

Carter, Lillian. Marriage ain't but nothing that's worth much ever is. (Chicago Sun-Times 32:33 July 16, 79)

DeVries, Peter. Marriage has driven more than one man to sex. (Penthouse 16:152 Nov 84)

Faulkner, William. You can cure human beings of almost anything except marrying. (Playboy 32:130 Jan 85)

Gabor, Zsa Zsa. A man in love is incomplete until he has married. Then he's finished. (Village Voice 22:20 Dec 26, 77)

Gish, Lillian. I don't think actresses have the right to marry and ruin a man's life. (Chicago Sun-Times 32:33 Nov 30, 98)

Hefferan, Colien. The woman who once saw marriage as a form of security now finds that she can provide her own security. (US News & World Report 85:83 Nov 27, 78)

Heide, Wilma Scott. I do not refer to myself as a housewife for the reason that I did not marry a house. (Viva 4:26 Aug 77)

Kerr, Jean. Marrying a man is like buying something you've been admiring for a long time in a shop window. You may love it when you get it home, but it doesn't always go with everything else in the house. (Chicago Tribune 65:1 Section 5 Mar 5, 78)

Luce, Clare Boothe. Widowhood is a fringe

benefit of marriage. (Washingtonian 21:121 Jan 85)

O'Brian, Hugh. There is quite enough grief when one is alone. Why compound it by getting married? (upon his founding Marriage Anonymous). (People Weekly 5:72 Jan 26, 76)

Parton, Dolly. A real important thing is that, though I rely on my husband for love, I rely on myself for strength. (Chicago Sun-Times 32:33 July 16, 79)

Richard, Cliff. Just because someone isn't married doesn't mean he's homosexual. (People Weekly 13:55 Feb 18, 80)

Saint James, Margo. (We've already) got legalized prostitution: marriage. (Washington Post 138:B7 April 21, 76)

Shepherd, Cybill. It's divorce that's the problem with marriage. (US 3:4 May 4, 87)

Steinem, Gloria. Today a woman without a man is like a fish without a bicycle. (New York 9:26 Aug 9, 76)

Trudeau, Margaret. It takes two to destroy a marriage. (Cosmopolitan 188:268 Feb 80)

West, Mae. Marriage is a great institution, but I'm not ready for an institution yet. (American Spectator 15:34 Feb 82)

West, Mae. You should marry for sex or money and you're really lucky if you can get both. (Chicago Tribune 64:1 Section 5 Mar 5, 78)

MARS (PLANET)

Soffer, Gerald. All the signs suggest that life exists on Mars, but we can't find any bodies. (Omni 2:40 April 80)

MARTINIS

Thurber, James. One martini is all right, two is too many, three is not enough. (Rocky Mountain News 327:86 Mar 14, 80)

MARTYRDOM

Schorr, Daniel. The joys of martyrdom are considerably overrated. (Time 107:62 Mar 8, 76)

MARX, GROUCHO

Marx, Groucho. I never forget a face, but in your case I'll make an exception. (Viva 5:80 Sept 77)

Marx, Groucho. I wouldn't belong to any club that would have me for a member. (New York Times 126:40 Aug 21, 77)

MARX, KARL

White, Theodore. If you go back through 2000 years, I guess luck, Marx, and God have made history, the three of them together. (Firing Line 15 July 26, 75)

MARXISM

Fang Lizhi. It (Marxism) is a thing of the past...and like a worn-out dress it should be discarded. (Fame 1:50 Mar 90)

Singer, Isaac Bashevis. A Marxist has never written a good novel. (New York Times Magazine 42 Nov 26, 78)

MASS MEDIA

Clay, William. Whenever I see certain elements in the press show favoritism to a Black man running for a position of power, I know there's a nigger in the woodpile somewhere. (Sepia 26:10 May 76)

Page, Clarence. Any concept can be sold to the media as long as it can be described in two words. (Chicago Tribune 5:17 Section 4 Jan 5, 85)

Quayle, Marilyn. Regular people are not equipped to deal with the viciousness of the media. (W 17:18 Nov 14, 88)

MASS MEDIA—UNITED STATES

Ravitz, Justin Charles. I understand the function of American media. Essentially, they exist to please their advertisers. (Mother Jones 2:51 Sept 77)

MASTURBATION

Capote, Truman. The good thing about masturbation is that you don't have to dress up for it. (Playboy 32:16 Feb 85)

MATERIALISM

Laszlo, Ervin. The materialistic growth ethic is not an immutable expression of human nature. (Time 107:56 April 26, 76)

MATTER

Elgin, Duane S (futurologist). Once you discover that space doesn't matter, or that time can be traveled through at will so that time doesn't matter, and that matter can be moved by consciousness so that matter doesn't matter—well, you can't go home again. (New York 10:55 Dec 27, 76)

MAUGHAM, WILLIAM SOMERSET

Churchill, Sir Winston (attributed by Michael Korda). Willie (W. Somerset Maugham) may be an old bugger, but by God, he's never tried to bugger me. (Newsweek 94:105 Nov 5, 79)

MAXWELL, ELSA

Flanner, Janet. She (Elsa Maxwell) was built for crowds. She has never come any closer to life than the dinner table. (New York Times 128:B10 Nov 8, 78)

MAYS, WILLIE

Mays, Willie. I think I was the best baseball player I ever saw. (Newsweek 93:68 Feb 5, 79)

MCCARTHY, JOSEPH RAYMOND

Chambers, Whittaker (attributed by Ralph de Toledano). Joe McCarthy's a rascal, but he's our rascal. (Chicago Tribune 22:11 Section 5 Jan 22, 86)

Hellman, Lillian. I think (Watergate and the McCarthy Era) are deeply connected, with Mr. Nixon being the connection, the rope that carries it all through. (New York Times 125:28 Nov 7, 75)

Wayne, John. In my opinion Senator Joseph McCarthy was one of the greatest Americans that ever lived. (Guardian Weekly 120:6 June 17, 79)

MCCARTNEY, PAUL

McCartney, Linda. Our kids keep asking, what is Daddy going to do when he grows up? (People Weekly 5:35 June 7, 76)

MCCULLERS, CARSON

McCullers, Carson. I have more to say than Hemingway, and, God knows, I say it better than Faulkner. (Time 106:E3 July 21, 75)

MCGOVERN, GEORGE STANLEY

Dole, Robert J. Jimmy Carter is chicken-fried McGovern. (Washingtonian 20:111 Sept 30, 84)

MCKUEN, ROD

McKuen, Rod. Having been born a bastard, I feel it has given me a head start on all those people who have spent their lives becoming one. (Time 106:30 Dec 29, 75)

MCLUHAN, MARSHALL

McLuhan, Marshall. Most clear writing is a sign that there is no exploration going on. Clear prose indicates an absence of thought. (Time 106:36 Aug 25, 75)

MEAD, MARGARET

Bohannan, Paul. Margaret Mead was, in fact, a centipede; she had that many shoes. (Time 112:57 Nov 27, 78)

Mead, Margaret. I expect to die someday but I'll never retire. (Change 9:12 Sept 77)

MEANY, GEORGE

Dole, Robert J. George Meany could run for President. But why should he step down? (Wall Street Journal 56:1 Sept 7, 76)

MEDICAL SERVICE

Barnard, Christiaan. There is one message I would give to young doctors and that is that the goal of medicine is not to prolong life. It is to alleviate suffering and improve the quality of life. (Chicago Tribune 64:14 Mar 5, 78)

MEDICAL SERVICE, COST OF

Thomson, Campbell. If it ever was true that a hospital was a charity organization, it no longer is true. (San Francisco Examiner 1977:1 May 1, 77)

MEDICAL SERVICE—UNITED STATES

Anonymous. The socialization of medicine is coming...the time now is here for the medical profession to acknowledge that it is tired of the eternal struggle for advantage over one's neighbor (editorial comment in the Journal of the American Medical Association, 1914). (New York Times Magazine 12 Jan 9, 77)

Califano, Joseph A., Jr. No just society can deny the right of its citizens to the health care they need. We are the only industrial society that does. (New York Times 136:2 Jan 13, 87)

Cousins, Norman. A hospital is no place for a person who is seriously ill. (Time 115:71 June 30, 80)

Crichton, Michael. I think we can all agree that American medicine, the way it is now, is not successful. But there's no evidence that the Government can run anything. If you like the Post Office, you'll like socialized medicine. (Time 111:91 Jan 9, 78)

MEDIOCRITY

Miller, George William. Don't rationalize mediocrity. (Time 112:62 July 17, 78)

MEDITATION

Elgin, Duane S (futurologist). Once you discover that space doesn't matter, or that time can be traveled through at will so that time doesn't matter, and that matter can be moved by consciousness so that matter doesn't matter—well, you can't go home again. (New York 10:55 Dec 27, 76)

Van De Wetering, Janwillem. I've meditated for thousands of hours now, and I still don't know nothing. It's disgusting. (Chicago Tribune 291:1 Section 2 Oct 18, 79)

MEDITATION see also TRANSCENDENTAL MEDITATION

MEEKNESS

Allen, Woody. The lion and the calf shall lie down together, but the calf won't get much sleep. (Time 113:25 Feb 26, 79)

Getty, Jean Paul. The meek shall inherit the earth, but not its mineral rights. (Time 113:25 Feb 26, 79)

MEIR, GOLDA

Meir, Golda. I may not have been a great prime minister, but I would have been a great farmer. (Chicago Tribune 306:18 Nov 2, 77)

MEKAS, JONAS

Mekas, Jonas. I am minister of interior for independent filmmakers. (Elle 2:46 Nov 86)

MEMORY

Cabell, James Branch. There is no memory with less satisfaction in it than the memory of some temptation we resisted. (Forbes 120:100 July 15, 77)

MEN

Addams, Jane. I do not believe that women are better than men. We have not wrecked railroads, nor corrupted legislatures, nor done many unholy things that men have done; but then we must remember that we have not had the chance. (Working Woman 1:8 Nov 76)

Bardot, Brigitte. Men are beasts and even beasts don't behave as they do. (Viva 4:26 Feb 77)

Castro, Fidel. Men are very fragile. We disappear and go up in smoke for almost any reason. (Time 107:51 Jan 5, 76)

Diana, Princess of Wales. If men had to have babies, they would have only one each. (Life 8:102 Jan 85)

Luce, Clare Boothe. There aren't many women now I'd like to see as President—but there are fewer men. (Newsweek 94:95 Oct 22, 79)

Needham, Richard J. Men are foolish, they think money should be taken from the rich and given to the poor. Women are sensible, they think money should be taken from the rich and given to them. (Toronto Globe and Mail 134:6 July 13, 77)

Nureev, Rudolf. Men are better at everything. (Chicago Tribune 349:11 Section 5 Dec 15, 83)

Peterson, Esther. If a man fights his adversaries, he's called determined. If a woman does it, she's frustrated. (National Observer 16:18 June 13, 77)

Reagan, Ronald. I happen to be one who believes that it it wasn't for women, us men would still be walking around in skin suits carrying clubs. (Life 7:172 Jan 84)

Sanchez, Robert. In looking backward, we must renew our faith in God. In looking forward, we must renew our faith in men. (National Catholic Reporter 12:8 July 2, 76)

Schreiner, Olive. We are men or women in the second place, human beings in the first. (Ms 6:94 Aug 77)

Thatcher, Margaret Hilda. If you want anything said, ask a man; if you want anything done, ask a woman. (New York Times Magazine 52 April 29, 79)

Updike, John. Every man is a failed boy. (Village Voice Literary Supplement 29:8 Sept 30, 84)

Williams, Tennessee. Men are rather inscrutable to me. (W 8:14 April 13, 79)

MEN see also BEAUTY, PERSONAL—MEN; WOMEN AND MEN

MEN—BEHAVIOR

Stevenson, Adlai, II. Man does not live by words alone, despite the fact that sometimes he has to eat them. (Human Behavior 7:69 May 78)

MEN—BEHAVIOR (PSYCHOLOGY)

DeVore, Irven. Males are a vast breeding experiment run by females. (Time 110:63 Aug 1, 77)

MEN—PSYCHOLOGY

Alsop, Stewart. A fashionable gentleman who much concerns himself with the fashions of gentlemen is neither fashionable nor a gentleman. (Newsweek 83:108 April 15, 74)

Gabor, Zsa Zsa. A man in love is incomplete until he has married. Then he's finished. (Village Voice 22:20 Dec 26, 77)

Gabor, Zsa Zsa. Macho does not prove mucho. (Washingtonian 15:143 Nov 79)

Hufstedler, Shirley. A man cannot be very kind unless he is also very strong. (New York Times Magazine 104 June 8, 80)

Mead, Margaret. Women, it is true, make human beings, but only men can make men. (Chicago Tribune 176:2 Section 2 June 25, 78)

MENTAL HEALTH see MENTAL HYGIENE

MENTAL HYGIENE

Janov, Arthur. The world is having a nervous breakdown. Valium is the only glue that holds it together. (Rolling Stone 219:19 Aug 12, 76)

MENTAL HYGIENE see also CRIME AND CRIMINALS—RELATIONS—MENTAL HYGIENE

MERCOURI, MELINA

Mercouri, Melina. I have been playing a woman with a past since I was five years old. (Time 107:93 June 6, 77)

MERMAN, ETHEL

Merman, Ethel. Broadway has been very good to me—but then, I've been very good to Broadway. (Time 124:47 Dec 31, 84)

METTERNICH, KLEMENS WENZEL NEPOMUK LOTHAR, VON, PRINCE

Kissinger, Henry Alfred. I think Metternich was an extremely skilled diplomat, but not very creative. (Time 107:33 Jan 12, 76)

MEXICO

Fuentes, Carlos. Mexicans have always asked themselves why a people so close to God should be so near the United States. (W 5:9 Oct 29, 76)

MEXICO—DESCRIPTION

Gortazar, Jesus. The bullfight is the only thing that really begins on time in Mexico. (Western Houseman 52:24 April 87)

MEXICO—POLITICS AND GOVERNMENT

Riding, Alan. Never commit yourself fully to anyone; always leave numerous options open; be all things to all men, and, keep your true sentiments well hidden (rule number 1 of long-term survival in Mexican politics). (New York Times Magazine 130 Sept 16, 79)

MEYER, RUSS

Meyer, Russ. My films are like a reptile you beat with a club. You think you've killed it, but then you turn around and it gets you in the ankle. (Washington Post 340:B1 Nov 9, 76)

MIAMI

Benes, Bernardo. God gave us our geography and Fidel Castro gave us our biculturalism (about Miami). (Miami Magazine 27:27 Nov 75)

MIAMI—DESCRIPTION

Arboleya, Carlos. History will write Miami's future in Spanish and English. (Time 112:48 Oct 16, 78)

MIDDLE AGE

Dundee, Chris. Middle age is when you start for home about the same time you used to start for somewhere else. (Sports Illustrated 44:10 Mar 29, 76)

MacLaine, Shirley. When you know who you are and you realize what you can do, you can do things better at 40 than when you're 20. (Time 107:39 Feb 16, 76)

Reagan, Ronald. Middle age is when you're faced with two temptations and you choose the one that will get you home by 9:30 (commenting on the 27th anniversary of his 39th birthday). (Washington Post 65:C6 Feb 8, 77)

Wilson, Earl. Middle age is when your clothes no longer fit, and it's you who need the alterations. (Reader's Digest 108:146 Feb 76)

MIDDLE EAST

Begin, Menachem. This region isn't Switzerland. (The Observer 9795:9 May 20, 79)

MIDDLE EAST see also PEACE—MIDDLE EAST; RUSSIA—FOREIGN RELATIONS—MIDDLE EAST; UNITED STATES—FOREIGN RELATIONS—MIDDLE EAST

MIDDLE EAST—POLITICS AND GOVERNMENT

Anonymous. The Arabs cannot make war without the Egyptians, but they cannot make peace without the Palestinians. (Time 111:35 Mar 27, 78)

Arafat, Yasir. I have very few cards, but I have the strongest cards. (Time 114:27 Aug 20, 79)

Arafat, Yasir. Palestine is the cement that holds the Arab world together, or it is the explosive that blows it apart. (Time 104:27 Nov 11, 74)

Assad, Hafez. Step-by-step might be all right if the steps were giant steps, but they are tortoise steps. (Time 106:29 Dec 8, 75)

Carter, James Earl. I have never met an Arab leader that in private professed the desire for an independent Palestinian state. (New York Times 128:21 Sept 1, 79)

Dayan, Moshe. You cannot get the Arab opinion by sitting and talking to Jews. (The Observer 9810:10 Sept 2, 79)

Eban, Abba Solomon. You cannot have peace without risks. (Time 111:37 Mar 6, 78)

Hussein, King of Jordan. It's amusing. The Americans have changed Presidents six times since I've been King. And they talk to the Arabs about stability? (People Weekly 6:122 Dec 13, 76)

MIDLER, BETTE

Midler, Bette. (Fans) make me think that maybe there's more to me than I know. (Newsweek 94:37 July 2, 79)

Midler, Bette. I want to be a legend. (TV Guide 25:22 Dec 3, 77)

Midler, Bette. The worst part of having success is to try finding someone who is happy for you. (Chicago Sun-Times 29:32 Mar 3, 76)

MIKULSKI, BARBARA A.

Mikulski, Barbara A. Some people like to raise flowers; I like to raise hell, I want to be the Amelia Earhart of Congress. I want to fly into the areas of the unknown, like she did, for the fun of it. (Time 108:48 Nov 15, 76)

MILITARY ASSISTANCE

Sakata, Michita. Security is like sun, water or air. When they are plentiful you don't appreciate their value. (Newsweek 86:53 Oct 6, 75)

MILITARY ASSISTANCE, AMERICAN—NICARAGUA

Gorman, Paul (Former commander of U. S. Southern Command). You're not going to knock off the Sandinistas with a conventional force, and that's what the Contras are. (Chicago Tribune 67:30 Section 1 Mar 8, 87)

MILITARY HISTORY

Spiller, Roger. Military history is the laboratory of the professional officer in time of peace. (Chicago Tribune 104:19 Section 1 April 14, 89)

MILITARY INTELLIGENCE

Marx, Groucho. Military intelligence is a contradiction in terms. (San Francisco Chronicle This World 1978:40 Jan 29, 78)

MILITARY SERVICE AS A PROFESSION

Haig, Alexander M. Military service and public service are not unakin. (The Observer 9776:10 Jan 7, 79)

MILITARY-INDUSTRIAL COMPLEX

Metzenbaum, Howard. The President can't stand up to the military-industrial complex, and neither can Congress. (Penthouse 14:175 Oct 82)

White, Donald (President of Hughes Aircraft Company). If you did a survey on whether the American public can trust military-defense contractors, I'm afraid the score would not be too high. (Los Angeles 34:131 Mar 89)

Zappa, Frank. The biggest dangers we face today don't even need to sneak past our billion-dollar defense system. They issue the contracts for them. (Rolling Stone 205:22 Jan 29, 76)

MILLER, ANN

Miller, Ann. All my life I've tried to be an eight-by-ten glossy. (Newsweek 85:52 May 26, 75)

MILLER, ARTHUR

Miller, Arthur. I've always written in the back of my head for the great unwashed. (New York Times 128:6 Section 2 June 17, 79)

Miller, Arthur. Part of being a playwright is being an actor. One way or another, whether surreptitiously or not, a good playwright is an actor. (Connecticut 41:115 Jan 78)

MILLER, GEORGE WILLIAM

Miller, George William. There is no penalty for overachievement. (Time 112:62 July 17, 78)

MILLER, HENRY

Miller, Henry. I'm going to beat those bastards (when asked how he would write his epitaph). (People Weekly 10:62 Aug 21, 78)

MILLIONAIRES

Shor, Toots. I don't want to be a millionaire, I just want to live like one. (New York Times 126:36 Jan 25, 77)

MILNES, RICHARD MONCKTON

Milnes, Richard Monckton. My exit is the result of too many entrees. (Writer's Digest 58:11 Oct 78)

MIME see also MARCEAU, MARCEL

MIND

Knight, Damon. If there is a universal mind, must it be sane? (Village Voice 23:37 Aug 21, 78)

MINELLI, LIZA

Simon, John. I always thought Miss (Liza) Minelli's face deserving—of first prize in the beagle category. (Time 110:34 Dec 26, 77)

MINERAL RIGHTS

Getty, Jean Paul. The meek shall inherit the earth, but not its mineral rights. (Time 113:25 Feb 26, 79)

MINGUS, CHARLES

Mingus, Charles. Don't call me a jazz musician. The word jazz means nigger, discrimination, second-class citizenship, the back-of-the-bus bit. (Time 113:77 Jan 22, 79)

MINIMUM WAGE

Reagan, Ronald. The minimum wage has caused more misery and unemployment than anything since the Great Depression. (Time 116:11 Sept 1, 80)

MINORITIES—EQUAL RIGHTS

Henderson, Vivian Wilson. We have programs for combatting racial discrimination, but not for combatting economic class distinctions. (Time 107:71 Feb 9, 76)

MIRACLES

Brenan, Gerald. Miracles are like jokes. They relieve our tension suddenly by setting us free from the chain of cause and effect. (Time 113:147 Feb 5, 79)

MISERY

Baker, Russell. Misery no longer loves company. Nowadays it insists upon it. (Washingtonian 14:152 Nov 78)

MISTAKES

Peter, Laurence J. In the country of the blind, the one-eyed King can still goof up. (San Francisco Chronicle This World 1978:40 Jan 29, 78)

MITCHELL, MARTHA

Nixon, Richard Milhous. If it hadn't been for Martha (Mitchell), there'd have been no Watergate. (Washingtonian 13:11 Nov 77)

MITCHUM, ROBERT

Mitchum, Robert. I do films for the greatest return, for the least effort. (The Times 8042:3 Aug 7, 77)

MOBS—PSYCHOLOGY

Houde, Camillien. A mob is like a river—it never runs uphill. (Macleans 90:63 July 11, 77)

MODERATION

Kissinger, Henry Alfred. Moderation is a virtue only in those who are thought to have an alternative. (The Observer 9934:13 Jan 24, 82)

MODESTY

Galbraith, John Kenneth. Modesty is a vastly overrated virtue. (Washingtonian 18:127 Sept 83)

MOHAMMED REZA PAHLEVI, SHAH OF IRAN

Kissinger, Henry Alfred. The Shah (of Iran) was—despite the travesties of retroactive myth—a dedicated reformer. (Time 114:77 Oct 15, 79)

Mohammed Reza Pahlevi, Shah of Iran. I'm not just another dictator. I'm a hereditary monarch. (Village Voice 23:19 Aug 21, 78)

Mohammed Reza Pahlevi, Shah of Iran. Nobody can overthrow me—I have the power. (US News & World Report 84:37 June 26, 78)

Nixon, Richard Milhous. If the United States doesn't stand up for our friends when they are in trouble, we're going to wind up

without any friends. (New York Times
128:B6 July 12, 79)

MONDALE, WALTER FREDERICK

McCarthy, Eugene Joseph. He (Fritz
Mondale) has the soul of a vice-president.
(Village Voice 21:14 Oct 11, 76)

MONEY

Ashley, Elizabeth. Money is the long hair of
the Eighties. (Life 5:142 Jan 82)

George, Phyllis. The most popular
labor-saving device is still money.
(Cosmopolitan 196:332 Oct 83)

Hunt, Haroldson Lafayette. Money is just
something to make bookkeeping
convenient. (Time 104:44 Dec 9, 74)

Janeway, Eliot. The thrill of making a fast
buck follows only the thrill of love at first
sight. Everyone needs to take an
occasional fling with money...and with
love. (Chicago Tribune 95:14 April 5, 77)

Luce, Henry. Make money, be proud of it;
make more money, be prouder of it.
(Washington Journalism Review 1:22 April
78)

Peck, Bernice. Money isn't everything, but
you can buy the rest. (Village Voice 31:43
Jan 7, 86)

Ringer, Robert J. Everything worthwhile has
a price. (Playboy 28:97 Sept 81)

Smathers, George. They say life is a game,
but you keep score in money.
(Washingtonian 17:66 Aug 82)

Snow, C. P. Money is not so important as a
pat on the head. (The Observer 9723:11
Dec 18, 77)

Stein, Gertrude. Money is always there but
the pockets change; it is not in the same
pockets after a change, and that is all
there is to say about money. (Time
106:E8 Oct 13, 75)

Wallace, Clinton. Money is the means by
which you can purchase everything but
happiness and health, and will pay your
ticket to all places but Heaven. (National
Review 30:282 Mar 3, 78)

Woods, Rose Mary. There's more to life than
money. (W 12:4 April 23, 82)

MONROE, MARILYN

James, Clive. She (Marilyn Monroe) was
good at playing abstract confusion in the
same way a midget is good at being
short. (Details 8:25 Oct 89)

Monroe, Marilyn. I think I made his back feel
better (about John F. Kennedy). (Time
106:11 Dec 29, 75)

MOON, KEITH

Moon, Keith. Some of the things I've done, I
couldn't have anything but the reputation
of being a lunatic. (Newsweek 92:93 Sept
18, 78)

MOON, SUN MYUNG

Moon, Sun Myung. God has been very
good to me. (Newsweek 92:81 Dec 4, 78)

Moon, Sun Myung. God sent me to America
in the role of a doctor. (People Weekly
6:35 Dec 27, 76)

Moon, Sun Myung. The time will come when
my words will serve as law. (New York
10:97 Mar 7, 77)

Moon, Sun Myung. Without me, on earth
everything will be nullified. (New West
4:62 Jan 29, 79)

MOON—EXPLORATION

Armstrong, Neil A. That's one small step for
man, one giant leap for mankind (upon
stepping on the Moon). (New York Times
128:A12 July 20, 79)

MOORE, HENRY

Moore, Henry. Some people ask me why I
live and work in the country. Space, light
and distance are three good reasons.
(Mankind 6:10 May 78)

MOORE, MARIANNE

Moore, Marianne. A writer is unfair when he
is unable to be hard on himself. (Writer's
Digest 58:6 Feb 78)

MOORE, ROGER

Moore, Roger. My real attitude toward
women is this, and it hasn't changed
because of any movement or anything:
basically, women like to be treated as sex
objects. (Playboy 25:102 May 78)

MORAL ATTITUDES see also CHARACTER

MOSES

Morgan, Charles, Jr. If Moses had gone to
Harvard Law School and spent three
years working on the Hill, he would have
written the Ten Commandments with three
exceptions and a savings clause. (Rolling
Stone 205:30 Jan 15, 76)

MOSES, ROBERT

Moses, Robert. Nothing I have ever done
has been tinged with legality. (New York
Times 130:11 July 30, 81)

Moses, Robert. Those who can, build.
Those who can't, criticize. (New York
Times 130:1 July 30, 81)

MOTHER TERESA

Mother Teresa. I am unworthy (upon
winning the Nobel Peace Prize). (New
York Times 129:1 Oct 18, 79)

MOTHERS

Duncan, Isadora. With what a price we pay
for the glory of motherhood. (Chicago
Tribune 176:2 Section 2 June 25, 78)

Lasch, Christopher. The mother's power
originates in the imposition of her own
madness on everybody else. (New York
Times Magazine 14 May 13, 79)

MOVING PICTURE ACTORS AND

ACTRESSES

Chambers, Marilyn. In straight films you have to do it to get a part. In porno films, you do it after you sign the contract. (Connecticut 47:11 Sept 30, 84)

Lear, Norman. When I give advice to rising starlets I say, just remember, Hollywood is the land of the definite maybe. (US 1:81 June 14, 77)

Loren, Sophia. The mob that adores you is the most wonderful tribute there can be. (Newsweek 96:63 Oct 6, 80)

Scott, George C. The actor is never rewarded in film. Film stardom is a peripheral and distorted kind of fulfillment. (New York Times Magazine 12 Jan 23, 77)

MOVING PICTURE AUDIENCES

Chabrol, Claude. I ask audiences to contemplate a character, not identify with him. (Time 106:76 Sept 29, 75)

Winner, Michael. Film audiences are people who are seeking light relief in a dark room for an hour and a half. (Chicago Tribune 324:22 Section 6 Nov 20, 77)

MOVING PICTURE AUTHORSHIP

Hemingway, Ernest. I know it means I will never have any dough but I know I shouldn't work in pictures when I go well enough in books. (American Film 6:12 May 81)

Puzo, Mario. (Film writing) is the most crooked business that I've ever had any experience with. You can get a better shake in Vegas than you can in Hollywood. (Time 112:72 Aug 28, 78)

MOVING PICTURE INDUSTRY

Chandler, Raymond. People who make pictures are not all idiots. They just behave as if they were. (Westways 74:67 Jan 82)

Dunne, John Gregory. Hollywood is the only place where you fail upwards. (US 1:12 Feb 21, 78)

Guber, Peter. In Hollywood, it's all just the size of your dick. (Vanity Fair 53:194 Feb 90)

Kael, Pauline. Hollywood is the only place where you can die of encouragement. (After Dark 13:20 Sept 80)

Lear, Norman. When I give advice to rising starlets I say, just remember, Hollywood is the land of the definite maybe. (US 1:81 June 14, 77)

McClintick, David. There is only one law of the Hollywood jungle, and it is box office. (Time 120:47 July 26, 82)

Mekas, Jonas. Avant-garde film doesn't want to and can't be part of any business. (Village Voice 20:72 July 7, 75)

Sellers, Peter. The older I get, the less I like the film industry and the people in it. In fact, I'm at a stage where I almost loathe them. (Time 115:73 Mar 3, 80)

Tanen, Ned (former Hollywood agent). There's no orphan like the movie that doesn't work; a hit movie has 90 fathers. (New York Times Magazine 18 Aug 7, 77)

MOVING PICTURE INDUSTRY see also
GOLDWYN, SAMUEL; ZUKOR, ADOLPH

MOVING PICTURE INDUSTRY—GREAT BRITAIN

Truffaut, Francois. The words British cinema are a contradiction in terms. (The Reader (Chicago's Free Weekly) 12:14 April 22, 83)

MOVING PICTURE INDUSTRY—WAGES

Hunter, Ross. Every one of us in Hollywood is overpaid. (W 8:2 Mar 16, 79)

MOVING PICTURES

Anger, Kenneth. I have always considered movies evil. (Chicago Tribune 295:15E Section 5 Oct 23, 86)

Babenco, Hector. I think a people without a cinema is like a person without a mirror. (American Film 10:72 Oct 84)

Burton, Richard. I only see a movie when I can't avoid it. (W 5:16 July 23, 76)

Costa-Gavras. Film is the only way now to reach out to people all around the world. The time of the book is over. (Village Voice 20:106 Dec 8, 75)

Davis, Bette. My contention is that producers won't make repulsive films if the public don't go to see them. (The Observer 9813:9 Sept 23, 79)

De Laurentiis, Dino. To make a movie is not like to make a book. A movie is much, much more—not just pushing a pencil in a room. (Los Angeles Times Calendar 60 Nov 28, 76)

Fassbinder, Rainer Werner. I long for a little naivete but there's none around. (Film Comment 12:2 Jan 75)

Fonda, Jane. I think that every movie is political. (New Times 10:58 Mar 20, 78)

Gish, Lillian. Films are the greatest force ever to move the hearts and minds of the world. (The Observer 9772:10 Oct 31, 78)

Gish, Lillian. Movies have to answer a great deal for what the world is today. (Time 105:44 Feb 3, 75)

Greenfeld, Josh. Cinema is a form of Danish. (Time 111:97 April 10, 78)

Herzog, Werner. You should look straight at a film; that's the only way to see one. Film is not the art of scholars but of illiterates. (New York Times 126:D19 Sept 11, 77)

Hitchcock, Alfred Joseph. Most people make mystery films. I don't. I make films of suspense. A surprise in a film takes 10 seconds, suspense takes up an hour. (Chicago Daily News 92:29 April 9, 76)

Monaco, James. Film has come of age as

an art, probably because television now receives the brunt of contempt from the remaining proponents of an elite culture. (New York Times Book Review 11 April 1, 79)

Newman, Susan. Making movies has nothing to do with acting. (Time 111:52 Feb 6, 78)

Rossellini, Roberto. I believe that the cinema has failed in its mission of being the art of our century. (Newsweek 89:75 July 13, 77)

Stein, Gertrude. One of the great things about not going to movies is that you get lots of surprises. (Film Comment 12:2 Jan 76)

Truffaut, Francois. They (tomorrow's films) will resemble the men who make them, and the number of spectators will be about equal to the number of the director's friends. They will be an act of love. (Print 30:85 May/June 77)

Vidor, King. Good films, like good wine, improve with age. (New York Times 126:C6 Jan 14, 77)

Warhol, Andy. Movies are the new novels. No one is going to read anymore. Everyone is going to do movies, because movies are easier to do. (Texas Monthly 4:42 Aug 76)

Wiseman, Frederick. The final film is a theory about the event, about the subject in the film. (Film Quarterly 31:15 Spring 78)

Zukor, Adolph. Look ahead a little and gamble a lot (a formula for success). (Time 107:55 June 21, 76)

MOVING PICTURES, EXPERIMENTAL

Mekas, Jonas. Avant-garde film doesn't want to and can't be part of any business. (Village Voice 20:72 July 7, 75)

MOVING PICTURES—COLLECTORS AND COLLECTING see also LANGLOIS, HENRI

MOVING PICTURES—DIRECTORS

Bertolucci, Bernardo. To make a film it is not necessary to know anything technical at all. It will all come with time. (Texas Monthly 4:40 Aug 76)

Cukor, George. If you live long enough you get rediscovered. (Toronto Star C3 Jan 30, 83)

Kluge, Alexander. German (movie) directors are like airplanes always circling the airport but never landing. (Time 111:53 Mar 20, 78)

Mekas, Jonas. I am minister of interior for independent filmmakers. (Elle 2:46 Nov 86)

Spielberg, Steven. My advice to anyone who wants to be a movie director is to make home movies. I started out by shooting 8

millimeter home movies with neighbors and friends. (Texas Monthly 4:38 Aug 76)

Ullmann, Liv. A good director is the same all over the world. A good director is one who provides the inspiration and courage for you to use what is inside you. (Washington Post 77:K9 Feb 20, 77)

Waters, John. I always wanted to sell out, but nobody would buy me. (University Daily Kansan 98:3 Nov 17, 87)

Welles, Orson. The director is the most overrated artist in the world. (Time 119:69 Mar 8, 82)

MOVING PICTURES—DIRECTORS see also BERGMAN, INGMAR; CHABROL, CLAUDE; COSTA-GAVRAS; FELLINI, FEDERICO; HITCHCOCK, ALFRED JOSEPH; KUBRICK, STANLEY; LUCAS, GEORGE; MALLE, LOUIS; MEYER, RUSS; SPIELBERG, STEVEN; WILDER, BILLY; WISEMAN, FREDERICK; ZUKOR, ADOLPH

MOVING PICTURES—FINANCE

Hitchcock, Alfred Joseph. I wouldn't be able to sleep nights if I thought I had to spend even $10 million on a picture...When you work with a smaller budget, you're forced to use ingenuity and imagination and you almost always come up with a better picture. (Chicago Tribune 339:16 Dec 5, 77)

MOVING PICTURES—PORNOGRAPHY

Goldstein, Al. Most porn films I've seen are a wonderful argument in favor of blindness. (TV Guide 32:38 June 30, 84)

Hope, Bob. I think we're running out of perversions to put in film, and I'm looking forward to it (on pornographic movies). (Los Angeles Times 96:2 Part 1 Dec 30, 76)

MOVING PICTURES—PRODUCTION AND DIRECTION

Altman, Robert. Every time you make a film, you live a full lifetime. (Newsweek 85:46 June 30, 75)

Altman, Robert. Making movies is like playing baseball—the fun is the playing. (Time 105:68 June 16, 75)

Anonymous. In Cannes, a producer is what any man calls himself if he owns a suit, a tie, and hasn't recently been employed as a pimp. (Village Voice 22:26 June 6, 77)

Hitchcock, Alfred Joseph. Always make an audience suffer as much as possible. (Family Circle 44 Jan 12, 82)

Lehman, Ernest. Very few people realize, when they go to a movie theatre and want to be entertained, what sort of blood has flowed in order that they might have a good time. (Chicago Tribune 282:18 Section 6 Oct 9, 77)

Malle, Louis. Being a director is like being a thief. You steal bits and pieces of the lives around you, and you put them into a movie. (New York Times 126:C6 Nov 19, 76)

Nordern, Michael. Making a movie is rather like warfare—99 percent boredom and 1 percent terror. (New York Times 132:22 Section 2 Jan 9, 82)

Tati, Jacques. Comedians speak with their legs. (Times Literary Supplement 3969:460 April 28, 78)

Towne, Robert. Directing a script you wrote is somewhere between shooting yourself in the foot, shooting yourself in the head, and shooting yourself in the nuts. (Vanity Fair 52:40 Jan 89)

Wilder, Billy. As soon as you have chosen a subject for a film, you have already made a success or a failure. (New York 8:43 Nov 24, 75)

Wilder, Gene. It has been my experience that a producer gets more money than anyone else for what is essentially a $6.50-an-hour job. (The Star 4:2 July 26, 77)

Zeffirelli, Franco. You must be as tough as rubber and as soft as steel. (Times Literary Supplement 3969:460 April 28, 78)

MOVING PICTURES—WESTERN FILMS
see WESTERN FILMS

MOWAT, FARLEY

Mowat, Farley. Everything outrages me that outrages nature—and most of what modern man does outrages nature. (People Weekly 13:65 Mar 31, 80)

MOYERS, BILL D.

Moyers, Bill D. Dick Goodwin was no saint, not close, but if there's a hereafter, I'd rather spend it with Goodwin than with Gabriel. (New York 8:38 Aug 18, 75)

MOZAMBIQUE—POLITICS AND GOVERNMENT

Machel, Samora. We cannot tolerate a bourgeoisie in Mozambique, even a black one. (Time 107:26 May 3, 76)

MUHAMMAD, WALLACE D.

Muhammad, Wallace D. I doubt if the Pope knows as much about Scripture as I do. I may not be the best orator, I may not have gone very far in school, but I am the boldest nigger you ever saw. (Newsweek 85:71 June 30, 75)

MUNITIONS

Cummings, Sam. The arms business is founded on human folly. That is why its depths will never be plumbed, and why it will go on forever. (Esquire 90:64 Mar 1, 78)

Haig, Alexander M. The arms race is the only game in town. (Esquire 90:31 Sept 26, 78)

MURDOCH, IRIS

Murdoch, Iris. A bad review is even less important than whether it is raining in Patagonia. (The Observer 9770:12 Nov 26, 78)

MURDOCH, RUPERT

Murdoch, Rupert. I cannot avoid the temptation of wondering whether there is any other industry (than newspaper publishing) in this country which seeks to presume so completely to give the customer what he does not want. (Time 107:46 May 30, 77)

Murdoch, Rupert. We will never be boring (about his newspapers). (M 7:95 Feb 90)

MURPHY'S LAW (QUOTATION)

Allen, Agnes. Almost anything is easier to get into than to get out of. (Omni 1:131 May 79)

Anonymous (Corollary to Murphy's Law). Everything will take longer than you think it will. (The Reader (Chicago's Free Weekly) 5:2 May 28, 76)

Anonymous (Corollary to Murphy's Law). If everything appears to be going well, you have obviously overlooked something. (Washingtonian 13:7 Dec 77)

Anonymous (Corollary to Murphy's Law). If there is a possibility of several things going wrong, the one that will go wrong is the one that will do the most damage. (Washingtonian 13:7 Dec 77)

Anonymous (Corollary to Murphy's Law). Nothing is as easy as it looks. (The Reader (Chicago's Free Weekly) 5:2 May 28, 76)

Anonymous (Murphy's Law). If anything can go wrong, eventually it will. (The Reader (Chicago's Free Weekly) 5:2 May 28, 76)

Carswell, James. Whenever man comes up with a better mousetrap, nature invariably comes up with a better mouse. (Omni 1:132 May 79)

Duffy, Sean. The chance of a meaningful relationship with a member of the opposite sex is inversely proportional to their amount of beauty. (Omni 1:132 May 79)

Emerson, Eric. The second is never as good as the first. (Omni 1:131 May 79)

Epstein, Thomas A. With extremely few exceptions, nothing is worth the trouble. (Omni 1:131 May 79)

Felix, Virginia. Decision makers are those who have the greatest vested interest in the decision. (Omni 1:132 May 79)

Mathis, Andrew W. It's bad luck to be superstitious. (Omni 1:131 May 79)

Nova, Leo. The other person's attitude depends on which direction the money moves between you. (Omni 1:131-32

May 79)

Sproles, Judy. If there is an opinion, facts will be found to support it. (Omni 1:132 May 79)

Teague, Freeman, Jr. Nothing is so simple it cannot be misunderstood. (Omni 1:132 May 79)

MUSIC

Arrau, Claudio. Every concert must be an event, never a routine. (Horizon 20:9 Dec 77)

Fela, 1938-. Music is the weapon of the future. (Newsweek 106:67 July 15, 85)

Nyiregyhazi, Ervin. Music is a wonderful way of life but a terrible career. (Stereo Review 41:61 July 78)

Rubinstein, Artur. It's more important to play the wrong note right than the right note wrong. (High Fidelity (Musical America Edition) 35:17 May 85)

Schnabel, Artur. Great music is music that is written better than it can be played. (Chicago Sun-Times 39:17 Dec 30, 85)

Schuman, William. The simple is not easy (about Virgil Thomson). (Village Voice 31:112 Dec 16, 86)

Stokowski, Leopold. Music appeals to me for what can be done with it. (Time 110:54 Sept 26, 77)

Valli, Frankie. There's nothing wrong with the world, only the people in it. And the same goes for music. (New York 8:62 Aug 4, 75)

MUSIC APPRECIATION see MUSIC— APPRECIATION

MUSIC, BLUES

Standish, David. The blues hasn't died out; it's turned white. (Chicago 27:236 Jan 78)

MUSIC, BLUES see also HUNTER, ALBERTA

MUSIC, CALYPSO

Black Stalin (singer). In Calypso, there is no retirement plan. (Spin 3:12 Dec 87)

MUSIC, CLASSICAL

Zelzer, Harry. Good music is not as bad as it sounds. (Chicago 27:12 Oct 78)

MUSIC, COUNTRY AND WESTERN see also CASH, JOHNNY; HAGGARD, MERLE; PARTON, DOLLY; PIERCE, WEBB; RONSTADT, LINDA

MUSIC, FOLK

Broonzy, Bill (Big). It's all folk music, cause horses don't sing (in response to Studs Terkel's question, are the Blues folk music). (Stereo Review 37:62 July 76)

MUSIC, JAZZ

Broonzy, Bill (Big). It's all folk music, cause horses don't sing (in response to Studs Terkel's question, are the Blues folk music). (Stereo Review 37:62 July 76)

Foreman, George. Boxing is like jazz. The better it is, the less people appreciate it. (Sepia 25:12 Sept 76)

Rollins, Sonny. Music is an open sky. (Soho Weekly News 6:27 Nov 2, 78)

Simone, Nina. Jazz lets black people know, everytime they hear it, that they have their hands on the pulse of life. (Sepia 26:10 June 77)

MUSIC, JAZZ see also CALLOWAY, CAB; GILLESPIE, DIZZY; MINGUS, CHARLES; ROLLINS, SONNY

MUSIC, JAZZ—WOMEN

Simon, George T. Only God can make a tree and only men can play good jazz. (National NOW Times 11:12 Aug 78)

MUSIC, POPULAR

Stokowski, Leopold. The history of popular music shows that it is the true art form of the people. (Newsweek 90:94 Sept 26, 77)

MUSIC, RAP

Nixon, Richard Milhous. I have often thought that if there had been a good rap group around in those days I might have chosen a career in music instead of politics. (Newsweek 116:13 July 30, 90)

MUSIC, ROCK

Dylan, Bob. Rock and roll ended with Little Anthony and the Imperials. (Rolling Stone 257:42 Jan 26, 78)

Nash, Graham. Serious musicians who read music don't understand what goes on with hippies. (People Weekly 8:57 Dec 12, 77)

Smith, Patti. Not even boot camp is as tough as being in rock and roll. (Chicago Tribune 340:3 Section 6 Dec 13, 76)

MUSIC, ROCK see also DYLAN, BOB; HELM, LEVON; JAGGER, MICK; MOON, KEITH; PRESLEY, ELVIS; REED, LOU; RICHARD, KEITH; RONSTADT, LINDA; SLICK, GRACE

MUSIC, ROCK—JOURNALISM

Zappa, Frank. Most rock journalism is people who can't write, interviewing people who can't talk, for people who can't read. (Chicago Tribune 18:12 Jan 18, 78)

MUSIC—APPRECIATION

Copland, Aaron. The ideal listener, above all else, possesses the ability to lend himself to the power of music. (Washington Post 352:G1 Nov 21, 76)

Reich, Steve. You must love music or be a duck. (Ear 4:8 Feb 78)

TeKanawa, Kiri. Nothing is worse than a musical snob. (W 12A:13 July 29, 83)

Thomson, Virgil. Music in any generation is not what the public thinks of it but what the musicians make of it. (New York Times 127:13 Section 2 July 2, 78)

MUSIC—CRITICISM

Thomson, Virgil. It's (musical criticism) a minor art best practiced by composers. (Newsweek 98:84 Dec 7, 81)

MUSICAL COMEDIES, REVUES, ETC.

Sondheim, Stephen. Books are what the musical theater is about. (Los Angeles 30:46 Nov 85)

MUSICIANS

Nyiregyhazi, Ervin. Music is a wonderful way of life but a terrible career. (Stereo Review 41:61 July 78)

MUSICIANS, ROCK

Hall, Daryl. It's socially immoral for a white person to act like a black person. (Creem 9:34 Aug 77)

Perry, Joe. The only aging rock star is a dead one. (Creem 10:30 Dec 78)

Plant, Robert. The lifestyle of rock 'n' roll is to live well and take a good woman. (Creem 9:49 July 77)

Sting, (Musician). When you're a rock star, you're allowed to be a petulant child and many other things you'r supposed to grow out of. (Life 7:40 Jan 83)

Taupin, Bernie. We've all made assholes of ourselves. (Playboy 31:90 April 84)

MUSICIANS—CONDUCT OF LIFE

Segovia, Andres. Artists who say they practice eight hours a day are liars or asses. (The Observer 9839:10 Mar 23, 80)

MYTHOLOGY

Tanner, Jack. What is counted as truth in one age is counted as myth in the next. (Challenge 19:4 Mar/April 76)

NABOKOV, VLADIMIR

Nabokov, Vladimir. I am an American writer, born in Russia and educated in England, where I studied French literature before spending 15 years in Germany. (Washington Post 212:C4 July 5, 77)

NADER, RALPH

Jacobs, Andrew, Jr. (Ralph) Nader has become a legend in his own mind. (Time 112:21 Aug 7, 78)

NAIVETE

Fassbinder, Rainer Werner. I long for a little naivete but there's none around. (Film Comment 12:2 Jan 75)

NARCOTICS

Ehrlichman, John D. Narcotics suppression is a very sexy political issue. (Playboy 23:174 Nov 76)

NARCOTICS see also HEROIN

NATIONAL COLLEGIATE ATHLETIC ASSOCIATION

Brown, Dale. If you don't violate NCAA rules, you're in a coma or in a crematorium. (Lawrence (Kansas) Journal-World 129:5B Mar 25, 87)

NATIONALISM

Einstein, Albert. Nationalism is an infantile disease. It is the measles of mankind. (Chicago Tribune 281:2 Section 2 Oct 8, 78)

Will, George F. Nationalism is another supposed anachronism whose time has come 'round again. (Kansas City Times 115:A-15 Feb 15, 83)

NAVRATILOVA, MARTINA

Navratilova, Martina. When I win, it is routine. When I lose, life comes to an end. (Life 7:141 Jan 83)

NECESSITY

Hall, Keith W. The word 'necessary' seldom is. (Washingtonian 15:141-42 Nov 79)

NEED (PSYCHOLOGY)

Kirkup, Jon. The sun goes down just when you need it the most. (Washingtonian 14:154 Nov 78)

NEIGHBORS

Will, George F. People do not want to be equal to their neighbors. They want to be richer than their neighbors. (Kansas City Times 119:A-7 Mar 17, 87)

NELSON, WILLIE

Nelson, Willie. To write songs, I usually need a reason. Like not having any money. (Newsweek 92:53 Aug 14, 78)

NEUROSES

Clark, Alex. It's always darkest just before the lights go out. (Washingtonian 14:152 Nov 78)

NEW JERSEY—DESCRIPTION

Greenfeld, Josh. New Jersey looks like the back of an old radio. (Time 111:97 April 10, 78)

NEW ORLEANS—DESCRIPTION

Monaghan, Jim. I guess every day in New Orleans is like a B-movie. (New Orleans 10:30 Jan 75)

NEW YORK (CITY)

Anonymous. If you're bored in New York, you're boring. (Chicago Tribune 193:1 July 11, 76)

Charles, Ray (attributed by Arthur Ashe). When you leave New York, you ain't goin' nowhere. (Travel & Leisure 13:164 June 83)

Emerson, William A., Jr. New Yorkers are an endangered species. (Newsweek 86:9 Dec 29, 75)

Gannett, Lewis. The great days in New York were just before you got there. (Country Journal 5:10 Dec 78)

Goldberger, Paul. Other cities consume culture, New York creates it. (Town & Country 131:14 Sept 77)

Korda, Michael. New York—it's a fun place, but by and large, people are here because this is where success matters the most and this where it pays off the most. (New York 19:54 Dec 22, 86)

Vreeland, Diana. New York City is the leading light of the Twentieth Century. (New York 17:27 Dec 24, 84)

White, E. B. New Yorkers temperamentally do not crave comfort and convenience. If they did, they would live elsewhere. (Time 112:20 Aug 21, 78)

Wolfe, Tom. There's not too much reason to come to Manhattan unless you're ambitious. (Kansas City Times 116:A-2 June 29, 84)

NEW YORK (CITY)—DESCRIPTION

Dryansky, G. Y. Paris is becoming more vulgar, New York more refined. (W 8:8 Jan 19, 79)

NEW YORK (CITY)—HARLEM—DESCRIPTION

Washington, Booker T., III. Being the sensitive man he was about his race, I think the present day Harlem scene would bring tears to my grandfather's eyes. (Sepia 26:10 Feb 77)

NEW YORK (CITY)—POLITICS AND GOVERNMENT

Esposito, Meade H. If I wrote a book, no one would come to my wake. (New York Times 133:2 Jan 27, 84)

Reeves, Richard. The people of New York have no political leader. (New York 8:33 Aug 4, 75)

NEW YORK (CITY)—POLITICS AND GOVERNMENT see also LINDSAY, JOHN VLIET

NEW YORK (CITY). BASEBALL CLUB (AMERICAN LEAGUE)

Auerbach, Red. There are only three teams in sports that have achieved true national status. The old Yankees, the Dallas Cowboys and us. That's not ego, that's just fact. (Sports Illustrated 67:73 Nov 9, 87)

NEW YORK (STATE)—POLITICS AND GOVERNMENT

Fink, Stanley. There are times when reasonable people come to no solution. (New York 10:9 July 25, 77)

Moses, Robert. As long as you're on the side of parks, you're on the side of the angels. (New York Times 130:11 July 30, 81)

Reeves, Richard. The people of New York have no political leader. (New York 8:33 Aug 4, 75)

Young, Andrew. Georgia is more liberal than New York. (Atlanta 19:60 Nov 79)

NEW YORK TIMES

Eder, Richard. A critic may write for an institution, but he shouldn't be one. (Village Voice 22:97 Mar 28, 77)

Ochs, Adolph Simon. When a tabloid prints it, that's smut. When the Times prints it,

that's sociology. (Time 110:75 Aug 15, 77)

Sarris, Andrew. We New Yorkers are the most naive and provincial people in the world to put so much faith not in princes and priests, but in a mere publication (about the New York Times). (Village Voice 20:63 Aug 11, 75)

NEW YORKER (PERIODICAL)

Gottlieb, Robert. The editor of the New Yorker is treated as a living god. (Manhattan, Inc. 7:57 June 90)

NEW YORKERS

Buckley, Pat. A New Yorker is anyone possessing a Green Card. (W 13:9 Feb 10, 84)

NEWMAN, PAUL

Newman, Paul. I figure that on my tombstone, it's going to say, 'He was a terrific actor until one day his eyes turned brown'. (Chicago Tribune 319:31 Section 1 Nov 14, 76)

Newman, Paul. There's no way that what people see on celluloid has anything to do with me. (Chicago 25:86 July 76)

NEWSPAPER EDITORS AND EDITING

Catledge, Turner. When in doubt, do it. (Newsweek 101:76 May 9, 83)

NEWSPAPER PUBLISHERS AND PUBLISHING

Charles, Prince of Wales. The thing that appalls me about the newspaper business is the number of trees it consumes. (Kansas City Times 107:B-8 Nov 2, 87)

Ingersoll, Ralph. The owners of newspapers don't give a damn who's president. (Progressive 49:50 June 30, 85)

Murdoch, Rupert. I cannot avoid the temptation of wondering whether there is any other industry (than newspaper publishing) in this country which seeks to presume so completely to give the customer what he does not want. (Time 107:46 May 30, 77)

Wicker, Tom. A reporter should write and his newspaper should print what they know. (Texas Observer 70:9 April 28, 78)

NEWSPAPER PUBLISHERS AND PUBLISHING see also MURDOCH, RUPERT; THOMPSON, LORD ROY HERBERT

NEWSPAPERS

Bagnold, Enid. The state of the world depends on one's newspaper. (Washington Post 351:C1 Nov 21, 75)

Cockburn, Alexander. Descriptions of sin are what we want at the breakfast table, not admonitions against it. (Village Voice 23:13 Jan 9, 77)

Daley, Richard J. But then you can never go as low as a newspaper. A newspaper is the lowest thing there is. (Newsweek

85:55 May 5, 75)

Gold, Herbert. Never trust a newspaper over 10. (New West 4:52 Jan 1, 79)

Moynihan, Daniel Patrick. When a person goes to a country and finds their newspapers filled with nothing but good news, he can bet there are good men in jail. (University Daily Kansan 87:4 Feb 16, 77)

Spaulding, Jim. When newspapers write about themselves, they lie. (New West 3:65 Jan 16, 78)

NEWSPAPERS see also NEW YORK TIMES

NEWSPAPERS AND TELEVISION

Chancellor, John. Television is good at the transmission of experience. Print is better at the transmission of facts. (Time 115:71 Feb 25, 80)

NEWSPAPERS—PHILADELPHIA

Rizzo, Frank Lazzaro. If you want fiction, read the news pages; if you want facts, read the comic pages. (Philadelphia Magazine 69:253 Nov 78)

NEWSPAPERS—SOUTH AFRICA

Nel, Louis. We do not have censorship. What we have is a limitation on what newspapers can report (in South Africa). (New York Times 135:A3 June 26, 86)

NICARAGUA—POLITICS AND GOVERNMENT

Ortega Saavedra, Daniel. We do not consider it an acceptable cease-fire when we cease and the Contras fire. (Time 134:49 Nov 13, 89)

Wright, Jim. The Sandinistas have had a history of snatching defeat from the jaws of victory. (Kansas City Star 108:6A Dec 15, 87)

NIGERIA—POLITICS AND GOVERNMENT

Fela, 1938-. Music is the weapon of the future. (Newsweek 106:67 July 15, 85)

NIGHT LIFE

Rose, Billy. Sun is for apricots and exercise is for horses. (Food & Wine 10:64 Feb 87)

1960'S

Brand, Stewart. I thought the sixties went on too long. (Outside 1:68 Dec 77)

Brand, Stewart. While we were out in the streets marching, the real revolutionaries were in the computer labs. (Inc 7:53 July 85)

Dickstein, Morris. The history of the sixties was written as much in the Berkeley Barb as in the New York Times. (New West 4:52 Jan 1, 79)

1970'S

Epstein, Joseph. A few things ought to be said on behalf of the 1970's—not the least among them that they weren't the 1960's. (Time 115:39 Jan 7, 80)

1980'S

Daley, Steve. In the age of television, history bores us. That's why everything is a surprise. (Chicago Tribune 84:1 Section 5 Mar 24, 88)

Klein, Calvin. We live in an age of obsession: obsession with work, obsession with romance. (Interview 14:135 June 85)

1980'S

Thompson, Hunter S. Huge brains, small necks, weak muscles, and fat wallets— these are the dominant characteristics of the 80s—the generation of swine. (Spin 2:50 April 30, 86)

1990S

Trump, Donald. The 1990s sure aren't like the 1980s'. (Newsweek 115:June 18, 90)

Wavy Gravy. The nineties will be the sixties standing on your head. (California 14:83 Dec 89)

1970'S

Salmore, Stephen. In the 1960s, the burden of proof against change rested with those accepting the status quo. In the 1970s, the burden of proof rests with those who want change. (US News & World Report 84:25 Jan 23, 78)

1960'S

Salmore, Stephen. In the 1960s, the burden of proof against change rested with those accepting the status quo. In the 1970s, the burden of proof rests with those who want change. (US News & World Report 84:25 Jan 23, 78)

NIXON, PATRICIA RYAN

Nixon, Patricia Ryan. I gave up everything I've ever loved (commenting in 1960 on the price of political life). (Good Housekeeping 187:158 Aug 78)

NIXON, RICHARD MILHOUS

Abzug, Bella. Richard Nixon self-impeached himself. He gave us Gerald Ford as his revenge. (Rolling Stone 227:43 Dec 2, 76)

Beard, Peter. Nixon is what America deserved and Nixon is what America got. (Photograph 5:5 April 78)

Cohen, Richard. His (Richard Nixon) career is blemished only by his time in public office. (Kansas City Times 121:A-8 May 22, 89)

De Gaulle, Sandra. Everyone in the world loves him except the Americans (about Richard Nixon). (W 9:4 Dec 5, 80)

Dean, John Wesley, III. He's running for the office of ex-president and he's won (about Richard Nixon). (US 3:64 June 30, 86)

Dole, Robert J. If you liked Richard Nixon, you'll love Bob Dole. (Christian Science Monitor 68:17 Sept 10, 76)

Ehrlichman, John D. I have done my time. I don't think he (Richard Nixon) is ever going to stop doing his time. (Time 111:67 May 15, 78)

Ervin, Samuel James. Nobody I know wanted to see Nixon go to jail, (but) there's an old saying that mercy but murders, pardoning those that kill. (Newsweek 85:24 Jan 13, 75)

Goldwater, Barry Morris. I have no use for Nixon. I call him the world's biggest liar, and he's never done anything to disprove that. (New York Times 138:12 Oct 4, 88)

Goldwater, Barry Morris. If he (Richard Nixon) wants to do this country a favor, he might stay in China. (Family Weekly 4 Dec 30, 84)

Goldwater, Barry Morris. There are only so many lies you can take, and now there has been one too many. Nixon should get his ass out of the White House—today (after leaving a conference with Nixon before his resignation as president). (Time 104:21 Aug 19, 74)

Graham, Billy. Nixon in my judgement was a true intellectual. (Chicago Tribune Magazine 46 Nov 6, 77)

Hellman, Lillian. I think (Watergate and the McCarthy Era) are deeply connected, with Mr. Nixon being the connection, the rope that carries it all through. (New York Times 125:28 Nov 7, 75)

Jackson, Maynard. If Richard Nixon were black, he would be catching so much hell, he would rather be in jail. (Sepia 24:10 Jan 75)

Kennedy, John Fitzgerald. He's got no class (about Richard Nixon). (Time 111:20 Mar 6, 78)

Kennedy, Robert F. Richard Nixon represents the dark side of the American spirit. (Village Voice Literary Supplement 58:14 Sept 87)

Kissinger, Henry Alfred. It was hard to avoid the impression that Nixon, who thrived on crisis, also craved disasters. (Time 114:59 Oct 1, 79)

Kissinger, Henry Alfred. We are all the president's men, and have got to behave that way. (Meet the Press 20:6 April 18, 76)

Kutler, Stanley. Richard Nixon is struggling for the soul of history and for the souls of historians. Historians ought to worry about theirs. (Chicago Tribune 342:17 Dec 8, 87)

Laxalt, Paul D. If there's an elder statesman in our party right now, it's Richard Nixon. (Newsweek 107:27 May 19, 86)

Moyers, Bill D. Nixon systematically robbed the country of its ability and willingness to trust the President. (Newsweek 83:80 April 15, 74)

Moynihan, Daniel Patrick. Nixon understood more about liberals than liberals ever understood about him. (The Observer 9796:33 May 27, 79)

Nixon, Richard Milhous. (Watergate) was worse than a crime, it was a blunder. (The Observer 9771:14 Dec 3, 78)

Nixon, Richard Milhous. A man is not finished when he is defeated, he is defeated when he quits. (Fame 1:94 Mar 90)

Nixon, Richard Milhous. From a personal standpoint, what I would prefer to be remembered for is the example I set for surviving and coming back from adversity. (Fame 1:97 Mar 90)

Nixon, Richard Milhous. I brought myself down. I have impeached myself. (New York Times 127:38 April 30, 78)

Nixon, Richard Milhous. I have often thought that if there had been a good rap group around in those days I might have chosen a career in music instead of politics. (Newsweek 116:13 July 30, 90)

Nixon, Richard Milhous. I would have made a good Pope. (US 3:64 Mar 10, 86)

Nixon, Richard Milhous. I'd like to see people, instead of spending so much time on the ethical problem, get after the problems that really affect the people of this country. (Newsweek 114:15 July 10, 89)

Nixon, Richard Milhous. In our own lives, let each of us ask—not just what will government do for me, but what can I do for myself (inaugural address—1973). (Christian Science Monitor 69:14 Jan 20, 77)

Nixon, Richard Milhous. My political life is over (1978). (New York Times 128:A5 Dec 1, 78)

Nixon, Richard Milhous. One thing I really hate is exercise for exercise's sake. (Philadelphia 69:131 April 78)

Nixon, Richard Milhous. Won some, lost some, all interesting (commenting on his political career). (Chicago Tribune 206:13 Section 1 July 25, 90)

Nixon, Richard Milhous. Writing is the toughest thing I've ever done. (Rolling Stone 227:43 Dec 2, 76)

Rockwell, Geo. Making something perfectly clear only confuses everybody. (Down East 22:108 Jan 76)

Safire, William. I think that one of Nixon's great contributions to civil liberties was getting caught doing what the two presidents before him got away with. (Book Digest 4:28 July 77)

Sirica, John J. I hope no political party will ever stoop so low as to embrace the likes of Richard Nixon again. (The Tennessean 74:10 Section F May 13, 79)

Sirica, John J. Nixon should have been indicted. (Chicago Tribune 119:2 Section 2 April 29, 79)

Stevenson, Adlai, II. Nixon is the kind of politician who would cut down a redwood tree, then mount the stump for a speech on conservation. (Human Behavior 7:68 May 78)

Truman, Harry S. That Richard Nixon, boys, is a no-good lying son of a bitch (commenting during one of his Presidential press conferences). (Newsweek 85:89 May 12, 75)

Warren, Earl. Tricky (Richard Nixon) is perhaps the most despicable President this nation has ever had. He was a cheat, a liar and a crook, and he brought my country, which I love, into disrepute. Even worse than abusing his office, he abused the American people. (Esquire 83:83 Mar 31, 75)

White, Theodore. The true crime of Richard Nixon was simple: he destroyed the myth that binds America together, and for this he was driven from power. (Esquire 91:34 Feb 27, 79)

NIXON, RICHARD MILHOUS—CONDUCT OF LIFE

Peter, Laurence J. If two wrongs don't make a right, try three (Nixon's principle). (Washingtonian 14:155 Nov 78)

NIXON, RICHARD MILHOUS—STAFF

Colson, Charles Wendell. I would do anything that Richard Nixon asks me to do. (Time 103:13 Mar 11, 74)

Connally, John Bowden. I don't subscribe to the notion that everyone around President Nixon was tarnished. (New York 12:8 July 9, 79)

Douglas, William Orville. I forgot to tell you that this gang in power (the Nixon administration) is not just in search of the truth. They are 'search and destroy' people. (Kansas City Star 108:1A Nov 27, 87)

Haldeman, Harry Robbins. I'll approve of whatever will work and am concerned with results—not methods. (Time 103:12 Mar 11, 74)

Ziegler, Ronald Louis. I never knowingly lied, but certainly history shows that many things I said were incorrect. (Newsweek 91:22 April 17, 78)

NIXON, RICHARD MILHOUS—STAFF see also COLSON, CHARLES WENDELL; HALDEMAN, HARRY ROBBINS; ZIEGLER, RONALD LOUIS

NKOMO, JOSHUA

Nkomo, Joshua. There's no such thing to me as whites. (The Observer 9760:13 Sept 17, 78)

NOBEL PRIZES

Gorbachev, Mikhail S. It is now clear that he deserved the Nobel Prize (about Andrei Sakharov). (Chicago Tribune 341:14 Section 1 Dec 19, 89)

McCarthy, Eugene Joseph. Kissinger won a Nobel Peace Prize for watching a war end that he was for. (New York Times Magazine 100 Oct 24, 76)

Mother Teresa. I am unworthy (upon winning the Nobel Peace Prize). (New York Times 129:1 Oct 18, 79)

Paz, Octavio. The prize is not a passport to immortality, but it does give a poet the possibility of a wider audience, and every writer needs a wider audience. (Chicago Tribune 288:11 Section 1 Oct 15, 90)

Sakharov, Andrei Dmitrievich. I hope this prize is not only an acknowledgement of my personal merits, but of the merits of all those who fight for human rights (commenting on his Nobel Peace Prize). (People Weekly 4:26 Oct 27, 75)

Tiselius, Arne. The world is full of people who should get the Nobel Prize but haven't got it and won't get it. (Time 112:81 Sept 25, 78)

NOBEL PRIZES see also MOTHER TERESA; SAKHAROV, ANDREI DMITRIEVICH

NOGUCHI, ISAMU

Noguchi, Isamu. Stones are like people, some more alive than others. (Chicago Tribune 366:1 Dec 31, 88)

NORODOM SIHANOUK, KING OF CAMBODIA (ABDICATED 1955)

Norodom Sihanouk, King Of Cambodia (Abdicated 1955). When they no longer need me, they will spit me out like a cherry pit (about the Khmer Rouge). (Time 106:38 Sept 22, 75)

NORTH AMERICA

McLuhan, Marshall. North America looks, as usual, grim. (Mother Jones 1:9 Nov 76)

NORTH CAROLINA—POLITICS AND GOVERNMENT

Woods, Mike. If Jesse Helms ran against Jesus Christ, I think Jesus Christ would win by a very slim margin. (Southpoint 2:8 May 90)

NORTH CAROLINA—POLITICS AND GOVERNMENT see also HELMS, JESSE

NORTH, OLIVER L., JR.

Buchanan, Patrick J. The day the United States ceases to produce soldiers of the kidney and spleen and heart and soul of Oliver North is the day this country enters on its irreversible decline. (Washington Post National Weekly Edition 4:5 Dec 29, 86)

Durenberger, David. I wouldn't trust Elliott Abrams any further than I could throw Oliver North. (Village Voice 32:20 Mar 3, 87)

Keker, John W. The evidence will show that when the time came for Oliver North to tell the truth, he lied. When the time came for Oliver North to come clean he shreded, he erased, he altered. When the time came for Oliver North to let the light shine in, he covered up. (New York Times 138:2 Feb 22, 89)

North, Oliver L., Jr. I never carried out a single act, not one, in which I did not have authority from my superiors. (Kansas City Star 107:6A July 8, 86)

North, Oliver L., Jr. Those accusations (Iran-Contra indictments) are not a brand. They are a badge of honor. (Chicago Tribune 130:15 Section 1 May 9, 88)

Reagan, Maureen. A member of the United States military who lies to the commander-in-chief is guilty of treason and should be court-martialed (about Oliver North and John Poindexter). (Chicago Tribune 79:19 Mar 20, 87)

Reagan, Ronald. He (Oliver North) is a national hero. (Chicago Tribune 67:7 Section 5 Mar 8, 87)

NORTHERN IRELAND
O'Connell, David (IRA tactician). Put your faith in the Provos and Ireland will be free. We will abolish British rule, we will smash it. (New York Times 125:7 April 26, 76)

NORTHERN IRELAND—DESCRIPTION
Holland, Jack. The tragedy of Northern Ireland is that it is now a society in which the dead console the living. (New York Times Magazine 39 July 15, 79)

NORTHERN IRELAND—POLITICS AND GOVERNMENT
Anonymous. Northern Ireland has too many Catholics and twice as many Protestants, but very few Christians. (Time 104:30 Dec 30, 74)

Rose, Richard. Even an atheist must be a Protestant atheist or Catholic atheist in order to have status in the society (commenting on life in Northern Ireland). (Time 104:30 Dec 30, 74)

NORTHERN IRELAND—RELIGION
Anonymous. Northern Ireland has too many Catholics and twice as many Protestants, but very few Christians. (Time 104:30 Dec 30, 74)

NOTHING (PHILOSOPHY)
Durant, Will. One of the lessons of history is that nothing is often a good thing to do and always a clever thing to say. (Washingtonian 14:153 Nov 78)

NOUVELLE CUISINE
Bocuse, Paul. Nothing is on the plate and everything is on the bill (about nouvelle cuisine). (Chicago 38:276 Dec 89)

NOVELS see FICTION

NUCLEAR WARFARE see ATOMIC WARFARE

NUNN, SAM
Nunn, Sam. I've never gotten up in the morning, looked in the mirror, and seen a president staring me in the face. (Newsweek 108:30 Oct 27, 86)

NUREEV, RUDOLF
Nureev, Rudolf. I do not try to dance better than anyone else. I only try to dance better than myself. (Newsweek 85:32 Jan 6, 76)

NUREYEV, RUDOLF see NUREEV, RUDOLF

NYIREGYHAZI, ERVIN
Nyiregyhazi, Ervin. Music is a wonderful way of life but a terrible career. (Stereo Review 41:61 July 78)

O'KEEFFE, GEORGIA
O'Keeffe, Georgia. I am not a woman artist. (New York Times 138:19 Nov 18, 88)

O'Keeffe, Georgia. I'll paint what I see but I'll paint it big to say what is to me the wideness and wonder of the world as I live it. (Newsweek 88:76 Nov 22, 76)

O'NEILL, EUGENE
O'Neill, Eugene. Born in a hotel room—and God damn it—died in a hotel room. (New York Times 128:5 Section D Nov 26, 78)

O'ROURKE, P. J.
O'Rourke, P. J. All I really do is say in print what all the other reporters say at 10 at night in the bar. (Washington Journalism Review 10:22 Sept 88)

OATES, JOYCE CAROL
Oates, Joyce Carol. Sometimes my work is very savage, very harsh. But so is life. My material is not sordid, it's just a realistic reflection of a society that is in turmoil. (People Weekly 6:66 Nov 15, 76)

OBESITY
Connolly, Cyril. Imprisoned in every fat man a thin one is wildly signalling to be let out. (Newsweek 85:74B Jan 20, 75)

Gleason, Jackie. Thin people are beautiful, but fat people are adorable. (People Weekly 5:29 May 3, 76)

Leachman, Cloris. Fat people pollute the esthetic environment. (People Weekly 5:29 May 3, 76)

Outhier, Louis. You don't get fat from a good kitchen—only from a bad one. (W 4:11 Nov 28, 75)

OBEY, DAVID R.
Obey, David R. Joe McCarthy made me an independent, Stevenson made me a Liberal, and Eisenhower made me a

Democrat. (New York Times 128:B20 Mar 1, 79)

OBSCENITY (LAW)

Fleishman, Stanley. There are more citizens in jail in the United States today for publishing books, magazines, newspapers, and films than there are in all the countries of the world put together. (American Film 2:4 June 77)

Stevens, John Paul. One of the strongest arguments against regulating obscenity through criminal law is the inherent vagueness of the obscenity concept. (Chicago Tribune 161:12 Section 1 June 10, 77)

OCCUPATIONS

Becker, Jules. It is much harder to find a job than to keep one. (Washingtonian 14:152 Nov 78)

Perot, H. Ross. T There's only two places a 28-year-old can make a half million dollars—Wall Street and dealing dope. (Newsweek 112:143 July 11, 88)

OFFICES—ETIQUETTE

McArthur, Robert. Never imply that they care whether your socks match; and never forget that they do. (Washingtonian 14:46 Jan 78)

OFFICIAL SECRETS

Anderson, Thomas J. The only secrets the American government has are the secrets it keeps from its own people. (American Opinion 18:17 June 75)

Chiles, Lawton M., Jr. Secrecy in government has become synonymous, in the public mind, with deception by the government. (Christian Science Monitor 67:3 Nov 4, 75)

Seale, Bobby. Those who know don't talk; and those who talk don't know. (New York Times Magazine 53 Nov 20, 77)

OHIO. KENT STATE UNIVERSITY, KENT

Capp, Al. The martyrs at Kent State were the kids in National Guard uniforms. (Newsweek 90:50 Oct 17, 77)

OKLAHOMA. UNIVERSITY—FOOTBALL

Cross, George L. We want to build a university the football team can be proud of (about the University of Oklahoma). (Chicago Sun-Times 32:69 Nov 8, 79)

OLIVIER, LAURENCE

Glenville, Peter. Compared to ordinary men with ordinary ambitions, Larry (Olivier) was a sea monster. (New York Times Magazine 62 Mar 25, 79)

Olivier, Laurence. I am an actor because that is all I am qualified to do. (Los Angeles Times Calendar 33 Feb 26, 78)

Olivier, Laurence. I love comedy every bit as much as tragedy, perhaps more, because the whole scene of humanity is under its roof. (New York Times Magazine 60 Mar 25, 79)

Olivier, Laurence. I'm not sure what I'm like and I'm not sure I want to know. (New York Times Magazine 56 Mar 25, 79)

Olivier, Laurence. Probably every great actor in history was the son of a clergyman. (Chicago Tribune 201:20 July 20, 79)

OMNISCIENCE

Santayana, George. Fanatics are those people who know what they are doing is what God would be doing if He only had all the facts. (Time 112:94 Oct 9, 78)

ONASSIS, JACQUELINE LEE (BOUVIER) KENNEDY

Jong, Erica. If Jackie Kennedy did not exist, the press would have to invent her. (In The Know 1:9 Nov 75)

Onassis, Jacqueline Lee (Bouvier) Kennedy. I always wanted to be some kind of writer or newspaper reporter. But after college—I did other things. (New York Times 126:A10 Jan 14, 77)

OPERA

Liebermann, Rolf. Running an opera is like running a restaurant. If the boss is not there, the food gets bad and the service even worse. (Time 108:58 Sept 20, 76)

Pekar, Harvey. A person who can't relate to comic books is like somebody who can't relate to opera. They're both culturally deprived. (Cleveland 5:153 July 76)

OPERA SINGERS

Callas, Maria. To be an opera singer, you have to be an actress. (Newsweek 90:67 Nov 7, 77)

Tourel, Jennie. You see, it isn't just boiled potatoes, what I do. (Stereo Review 35:80 Nov 75)

OPERA SINGERS see also TOUREL, JENNIE

OPPORTUNITY

Thatcher, Margaret Hilda. Opportunity means nothing unless it includes the right to be unequal. (The Illustrated London News 263:26 Oct 31, 75)

OPPRESSION

Kelley, Ken. But history is nothing but a chronology of oppressors oppressing the oppressed. (Rolling Stone 216:38 July 1, 76)

OPTIMISM

Martin, Abe. Being an optimist after you've got everything you want doesn't count. (Human Behavior 7:70 Sept 78)

Oppenheimer, J. Robert. The optimist thinks this is the best of all possible worlds, and the pessimist knows it. (Town & Country 133:141 May 79)

Ustinov, Peter. An optimist is someone who knows exactly how sad and bad the world can be. (The Observer 9826:9 Dec 23, 79)

ORAL SEX see also UNITED STATES. FEDERAL BUREAU OF INVESTIGATION—RELATIONS—ORAL SEX

ORGANIZATIONS

Drucker, Peter F. The only things that evolve by themselves in an organization are disorder, friction and malperformance. (The Wharton Magazine 1:14 Fall 76)

OSWALD, LEE HARVEY

Dudney, Bob. The country would have recovered from the death of John Kennedy, but it hasn't recovered yet from the death of Lee Harvey Oswald and probably never will. (Esquire 85:62 Feb 76)

Johnson, Lyndon Baines. I never believed that Oswald acted alone, although I can accept that he pulled the trigger. (Skeptic 9:55 Sept 75)

PACIFISM

Criswell, W. A. In order to uphold the idea of communism, the idea of pacifism was conceived (1954). (Texas Monthly 12:166 Oct 84)

PAGE, GERALDINE

Page, Geraldine. The sadness I feel is that half my life or more is over, the list of films so short, and the people won't see all of what I could have shown them (1978). (Los Angeles Times Calendar 27 Sept 3, 78)

PAINTING

Delacroix, Eugene. A taste for simplicity cannot endure for long. (Time 113:57 Jan 8, 79)

Duchamp, Marcel. I was interested in ideas—not in merely visual products. I wanted to put painting once again at the service of the mind. (New York Times 128:1 Section 7 Feb 11, 79)

Motherwell, Robert. Every intelligent painter carries the whole culture of modern painting in his head. It is his real subject, of which anything he paints is both an homage and a critique. (Los Angeles Times Calendar 96:86 July 31, 77)

Paschke, Ed. Painting is like rock 'n' roll. It should never get safe. (Chicago Tribune 259:23 Section 10 Sept 16, 90)

Rothko, Mark. There is no such thing as a good painting about nothing. (Texas Monthly 7:166 April 79)

PAINTING—REALISM

Wyeth, Andrew. True reality goes beyond reality itself. (Christian Science Monitor 70:24 Sept 28, 78)

PAKISTAN—POLITICS AND GOVERNMENT

Zia Ul-Haq, Mohammad. The army is the only stable institution in Pakistan. (The Observer 9701:13 July 17, 77)

PALESTINE

Arafat, Yasir. Palestine is the cement that holds the Arab world together, or it is the explosive that blows it apart. (Time 104:27 Nov 11, 74)

Arafat, Yasir. There is nothing greater than to die for Palestine's return. (Time 111:36 Mar 27, 78)

PALESTINE LIBERATION ORGANIZATION

Arafat, Yasir. I have come bearing an olive branch and a freedom fighter's gun. Do not let the olive branch fall from my hand (addressing the United Nations (1974)). (Time 104:43 Nov 25, 74)

Arafat, Yasir. I have very few cards, but I have the strongest cards. (Time 114:27 Aug 20, 79)

Hawatmeh, Nayef. The Palestine Liberation Organization is returning to the golden age of unity, and the phase of divisiveness is gone forever (1987). (Chicago Tribune 110:9 April 20, 87)

Peres, Shimon. Stroking a tiger (the P.L.O.) will not make it a pussycat. (Time 109:24 April 18, 77)

PALESTINE LIBERATION ORGANIZATION see also ARAFAT, YASIR

PALESTINIAN ARABS

Arafat, Yasir. Palestine is the cement that holds the Arab world together, or it is the explosive that blows it apart. (Time 104:27 Nov 11, 74)

Arafat, Yasir. Until I return to my homeland in Palestine, every Arab country is a temporary home for me and my people. (USA Today 1:10A April 11, 83)

Carter, James Earl. I have never met an Arab leader that in private professed the desire for an independent Palestinian state. (New York Times 128:21 Sept 1, 79)

Tawil, Raymonde. We (Palestinians) are like grass. The more you cut it, the more it will grow. (Time 111:36 Mar 27, 78)

PALEY, WILLIAM S.

Von Hoffman, Nicholas. If he (William Paley) is remembered at all, it will be as the man who gave America 'Hee Haw'. (New York 12:109 April 30, 79)

PANAMA CANAL

Buckley, William Frank, Jr. We should be big enough to grant a little people what we ourselves fought for 200 years ago (commenting on the Panama Canal). (San Francisco Chronicle This World 1978:2 Jan 22, 78)

Reagan, Ronald. Treaties invite nationalization (about the Panama Canal). (Time 107:19 May 17, 76)

Roosevelt, James. My uncle Teddy stole it, my father Franklin kept it going, and as far as I'm concerned they can now give it back (commenting on the Panama Canal). (Rolling Stone 262:36 April 6, 78)

PANAMA—FOREIGN RELATIONS—UNITED STATES

Torrijos, Omar. In truth, the (Panama Canal Zone) treaty is like a little pebble which we shall be able to carry in our shoe for 23 years, and that is better than the stake we have had to carry in our hearts. (Time 110:10 Aug 22, 77)

PARAGUAY see also CIVIL RIGHTS—PARAGUAY

PARANOIA

Sanders, Ed. Just because you're paranoid doesn't mean they're not trying to get you. (The Reader (Chicago's Free Weekly) 7:4 Section 1 April 7, 78)

Schott, Phil. Paranoia among politicians is simply a state of heightened awareness. (San Diego Magazine 35:168 Sept 83)

PARENT-CHILD RELATIONSHIP

Bombeck, Erma. A child needs your love most when he deserves it the least. (Family Circle 97:14 Jan 3, 84)

Colette, Sidonie Gabrielle Claudine. It is not a bad thing that children should occasionally, and politely, put parents in their place. (Chicago Tribune 176:2 Section 2 June 25, 78)

Irving, John. I think those of us who into our adult lives maintain good relations with our parents probably do it at the expense of total honesty. (New York Times Book Review 3 Aug 16, 81)

Jung, Carl Gustav. Nothing has a stronger influence on their children than the unlived lives of the parents. (Boston 70:97 June 78)

Levenson, Sam. The reason grandparents and grandchildren get along so well is that they have a common enemy. (Cosmopolitan 197:184 Sept 84)

Needham, Richard J. You should treat your children as strangers whom you happen to like. If, that is, you happen to like them. (Toronto Globe and Mail 134:6 July 13, 77)

PARIS—DESCRIPTION

Anonymous (French politician). It seems that the more Paris resembles New York, the more anti-American we become. (Christian Science Monitor 71:7 Aug 14, 79)

Dryansky, G. Y. Paris is becoming more vulgar, New York more refined. (W 8:8 Jan 19, 79)

Harriss, Joseph. Parisians have always recognized the human need for the superfluous. (Time 110:38 July 18, 77)

PARKINSON'S LAW (QUOTATION)

Parkinson, C. Northcote. Work expands to fill the time allotted to it, or, conversely, the amount of work completed is in inverse proportion to the number of people employed. (The Reader (Chicago's Free Weekly) 5:2 May 28, 76)

PARKINSON'S LAW (QUOTATION)—COROLLARY

Johnson, Haynes. As work and space expand and collide they breed their own reaction. (Washington Post 252:A3 Aug 14, 77)

Parkinson, C. Northcote. Nonsense expands so as to fill the space available (Corollary to Parkinson's Law). (Wilson Library Bulletin 52:219 Nov 77)

PARKS

Moses, Robert. As long as you're on the side of parks, you're on the side of the angels. (New York Times 130:11 July 30, 81)

PARTON, DOLLY

Parton, Dolly. If people think I'm a dumb blonde because of the way I look, then they're dumber than they think I am. (Ms 7:16 June 79)

Parton, Dolly. When I sit back in my rocker, I want to have done it all. (Time 109:73 April 18, 77)

PARTRIDGE, ERIC

Partridge, Eric. I always wanted to become a writer, and I consider myself to be one. (Time 110:76 Oct 17, 77)

PAST (TIME)

Faulkner, William. The past is never dead; it is not even past. (Newsweek 89:87 Feb 21, 77)

PATRIOTISM

Axelson, Walter. If a man is reluctant to pay the taxes levied by his democratically elected government, he does not love his country, he loves money. (Chicago Tribune 289:10 Oct 15, 88)

PAUL, SAINT

John Paul I, Pope. If St. Paul returned to the world now as a journalist he would not only direct Reuters but seek time on television. (The Observer 9758:9 Sept 3, 78)

PAYTON, WALTER

Payton, Walter. I don't watch much football. It's boring. (US 3:17 Nov 3, 86)

PEACE

Beston, Henry. Peace with the earth is the first peace. (Blair & Ketchum's Country Journal 3:88 Aug 76)

Carter, James Earl. In war, we offer our very lives as a matter of routine. We must be no less daring, no less steadfast, in the pursuit of peace. (Time 113:12 Mar 26, 79)

Hua, Kuo-Feng. Peace cannot be got by begging. War cannot be averted by yielding. (The Observer 9819:9 Nov 4, 79)

Paul VI, Pope. If you want peace, work for justice. (National Catholic Reporter 22:1 April 25, 86)

Stevenson, Adlai, II. The journey of a thousand leagues begins with a single step. So we must never neglect any work of peace within our reach, however small. (Human Behavior 7:69 May 78)

West, Mae. I'm for peace. I have yet to wake up in the morning and hear a man say, I've just had a good war. (Viva 4:26 Aug 77)

PEACE—MIDDLE EAST

Anonymous. The Arabs cannot make war without the Egyptians, but they cannot make peace without the Palestinians. (Time 111:35 Mar 27, 78)

Eban, Abba Solomon. You cannot have peace without risks. (Time 111:37 Mar 6, 78)

Kissinger, Henry Alfred. The absence of alternatives (in the Middle East) clears the mind marvelously. (Time 111:35 Jan 2, 78)

Rabin, Yitzhak. For me, peace means reconciliation of the Arab countries with the existence of Israel as a Jewish state. (Newsweek 88:47 Dec 20, 76)

PEREZ, MANUEL BENITEZ

Perez, Manuel Benitez. Bullfighting is an animal inside me, and it is one that I cannot dominate—it dominates me. (Newsweek 96:12 Sept 8, 80)

PERFECTION

Whitehead, Alfred North. Even perfection will not bear the tedium of indefinite repetition. (The Atlantic 244:29 Sept 79)

PERIODICAL EDITORS AND EDITING

Gottlieb, Robert. The editor of the New Yorker is treated as a living god. (Manhattan, Inc. 7:57 June 90)

PERIODICALS

Gingrich, Arnold. To stand out, for a man or a magazine, it is necessary to stand for something. Otherwise you stand still. (Newsweek 88:78 July 19, 76)

PERIODICALS see also PLAYBOY

PERIODICALS—COVERS

Stolley, Richard. Young sells better than old, pretty sells better than ugly, music sells better than television, television better than movies, and politics doesn't sell at all. (New York 10:15 Sept 12, 77)

PERKINS, MAXWELL

Perkins, Maxwell. You have to throw yourself away when you write (to Elizabeth

Lemmon). (Esquire 89:65 July 18, 78)

PEROT, H. ROSS

Perot, H. Ross. This country has enough problems without inflicting me on it. (Chicago Tribune 72:21 Mar 13, 87)

PERSONALITY

Erhard, Werner. You are perfect exactly the way you are. (Life 2:86 Dec 79)

Pagnol, Marcel. The most difficult secret for a man to keep is the opinion he has of himself. (Reader's Digest 107:166 Oct 75)

Read, David H. C. The worst sin is dullness. (Time 114:65 Dec 31, 79)

Schwab, Charles M. Personality is to a man what perfume is to a flower. (Kansas City Times 109:1 April 15, 77)

PERSONALITY AND CULTURE

Hayakawa, Samuel Ichiye. If you see in any given situation only what everyone else can see, you can be said to be so much a representative of your culture that you are a victim of it. (Phoenix 18:94 April 83)

PERSUASION (PSYCHOLOGY)

Comins, David H. People will accept your idea more readily if you tell them Benjamin Franklin said it first. (Washingtonian 14:152 Nov 78)

PERSUASION (RHETORIC)

Comins, David H. People will accept your idea more readily if you tell them Benjamin Franklin said it first. (Washingtonian 14:152 Nov 78)

PESSIMISM

Brzezinski, Zbigniew. Pessimism is a luxury that policymakers can't afford because pessimism, on the part of people who try to shape events, can become a self-fulfilling prophecy. (Time 112:26 Aug 21, 78)

Cousins, Norman. I am no pessimist. I doubt that any man knows enough to be a pessimist. (Saturday Review 5:12 April 15, 78)

Oppenheimer, J. Robert. The optimist thinks this is the best of all possible worlds, and the pessimist knows it. (Town & Country 133:141 May 79)

PETER PRINCIPLE (QUOTATION)

Peter, Laurence J. In a hierarchy, every employee tends to rise to the level of his own incompetence. (The Reader (Chicago's Free Weekly) 5:2 May 28, 76)

Peter, Laurence J. Most hierarchies were established by men who now occupy the upper levels, thus depriving women of an equal opportunity to achieve their levels of incompetence. (San Francisco Chronicle This World 1978:40 Jan 29, 78)

Peter, Laurence J. The cream rises until it sours. (San Francisco Chronicle This

World 1978:40 Jan 29, 78)

PETROLEUM INDUSTRY

Adams, Cecil. The average oilman has the moral development of a newt. (The Reader (Chicago's Free Weekly) 8:2 April 27, 79)

Bayh, Birch Evans. If there is one symbol of the Establishment ripping off the people, it is the oil companies. (Time 107:56 June 28, 76)

Carter, James Earl. As is the case in time of war there is potential war profiteering in the impending energy crisis. This could develop with the passing months as the biggest rip-off in history (1977). (New York Times 126:A16 Oct 14, 77)

Dirksen, Everett McKinley. The oil can is mightier than the sword. (Washingtonian 14:153 Nov 78)

Ehrlich, Paul. The petrochemical industry is at about the intellectual and moral level of the people who sell heroin to high school kids. (Outside 1:10 July 78)

Glenn, John. Our objective is to prevent the people of this country from getting economically raped (arguing against the decontrol of petroleum prices). (Time 106:61 Oct 13, 75)

Long, Russell. Those who defame us, curse us, abuse us and lie about us, would be in one hell of a fix without us (about energy producers). (Time 114:84 Nov 26, 79)

Rockefeller, John Davison, III. I don't have a whole lot of faith in what the oil companies say. (Time 114:61 July 16, 79)

PETROLEUM SUPPLY

O'Leary, John. There isn't a gasoline shortage. There's a driving surplus (1979). (Time 113:66 June 25, 79)

Wagner, Robert. A person's state of happiness is almost directly related to the amount of gas in his tank (1979). (New York Times 128:A10 July 13, 79)

PETROLEUM SUPPLY—TEXAS

Hubbard, Harry. Making Texans stand in line for gas is like making Kansans stand in line for wheat (1979). (Newsweek 94:22 July 2, 79)

PETROLEUM—PRICES

Bayh, Birch Evans. If there is one symbol of the Establishment ripping off the people, it is the oil companies. (Time 107:56 June 28, 76)

PHILADELPHIA see also NEWSPAPERS— PHILADELPHIA

PHILADELPHIA ORCHESTRA

Ormandy, Eugene. The Philadelphia sound—its me. (Time 127:57 Dec 30, 85)

PHILANTROPHY

Gund, Gordon. The greatest satisfactions in life come from endeavors which directly or indirectly have a positive impact on others at the same time they impact on you. (Town & Country 143:161 Dec 89)

PHILIPPINES—FOREIGN RELATIONS— UNITED STATES

Marcos, Imelda. The Americans need us more than we need them. (USA Today 1:8A Aug 23, 83)

PHILIPPINES—POLITICS AND GOVERNMENT

Marcos, Ferdinand E. I would like to return the Filipino to what he was before he was altered and modified by the softness of Western and other ways. (Time 107:21 Jan 5, 76)

PHILLIPS, MICHELLE

Phillips, Michelle. Deep down, I may be a very shallow person. (US 3:59 Dec 15, 86)

PHILOSOPHERS see also HEIDEGGER, MARTIN

PHILOSOPHY

Adler, Mortimer. Philosophy is everybody's business. (Time 110:57 July 25, 77)

Harris, Sydney J. Any philosophy that can be 'put in a nutshell' belongs there. (Washingtonian 14:154 Nov 78)

Panza di Biumo, Giuseppe. For me, art is the visualization of philosophy. (Newsweek 86:69 Aug 11, 75)

PHOBIAS

Clark, Alex. It's always darkest just before the lights go out. (Washingtonian 14:152 Nov 78)

PHONOGRAPH RECORD INDUSTRY

Horn, Trevor. Kids want to buy records by people they want to mate with. (New York 17:22 Aug 20, 84)

PHOTOGRAPHERS

Abbott, Berenice. You have to have the courage to be poor (about photography as a profession). (Life 5:126 May 82)

Ray, Man. The streets are full of admirable craftsmen, but so few practical dreamers. (ARTnews 76:52 Jan 76)

PHOTOGRAPHERS see also ARBUS, DIANE; CARTIER-BRESSON, HENRI; RAY, MAN; SMITH, W. EUGENE

PHOTOGRAPHY

Adams, Ansel. You don't take a photograph, you make it. (Time 124:46 Dec 31, 84)

Bourke-White, Margaret. Know your subject thoroughly, saturate yourself with your subject, and your camera will take you by the hand. (Blair & Ketchum's Country Journal 4:78 June 77)

Cartier-Bresson, Henri. For me the camera is an instrument of intuition and spontaneity, the master of the instant. (The Times 8104:5 Nov 5, 78)

Evans, Walker. Photography isn't a matter of taking pictures. It's a matter of having an eye. (Chicago Tribune 226:2 Section 6 Aug 14, 77)

Giono, Jean. Reality pushed to its extreme ends in unreality. (Village Voice 21:93 Sept 27, 76)

Ray, Man. I have always preferred inspiration to information (commenting on photography). (ARTnews 76:52 Jan 76)

Rivers, Larry. Is photography art? Art is everything. (Andy Warhol's Interview 7:12 Nov 75)

Sontag, Susan. Nobody ever discovered ugliness through photographs. But many, through photographs, have discovered beauty. (Vogue 168:185 June 78)

Steichen, Edward. The mission of photography is to explain man to man and each man to himself. (Camera 35 20:37 July 76)

Stieglitz, Alfred. Photography is photography, neither more nor less. (American Photographer 22:7 Mar 89)

PHYSICIAN AND PATIENT

Schweitzer, Albert (attributed by Norman Cousins). We are at our best when we give the doctor who resides within each patient a chance to go to work. (Newsweek 94:99 Sept 24, 79)

West, Tom. Every patient that every doctor has is going to die. (Lawrence (Kansas) Journal-World 130:5A Dec 20, 88)

PHYSICIANS—PSYCHOLOGY

Cooley, Denton. A successful surgeon should be a man who, when asked to name the three best surgeons in the world, would have difficulty deciding on the other two. (The Atlantic 244:56 Sept 79)

PHYSICS

Bohr, Niels. When it comes to atoms, language can be used only as in poetry. (Discover 3:70 Dec 82)

PIANISTS

Rubinstein, Artur. It's more important to play the wrong note right than the right note wrong. (High Fidelity (Musical America Edition) 35:17 May 85)

PIANISTS see also ARRAU, CLAUDIO; HOROWITZ, VLADIMIR; NYIREGYHAZI, ERVIN

PICASSO, PABLO

Picasso, Jacqueline. Living with Picasso was like living with a blowtorch; he was a consuming flame. (Time 108:70 Nov 8, 76)

Picasso, Pablo. Every child is an artist. The problem is how to remain an artist once he grows up. (Time 108:68 Oct 4, 76)

Picasso, Pablo. For me there are only two kinds of women—goddesses and doormats. (People Weekly 13:37 May 26, 80)

Picasso, Pablo. I paint forms as I think them, not as I see them. (Art & Antiques 1:53 Sept 84)

Rivera, Diego. I have never believed in God, but I believe in Picasso. (Connoisseur 214:28 Mar 84)

PIERCE, WEBB

Pierce, Webb. One drink is too many and a million is not enough. (Country Music 5:63 April 77)

PINERO, MIGUEL

Pinero, Miguel. I'd like to die with my back against the wall and two guns smokin'. (Andy Warhol's Interview 7:27 Nov 77)

PIPPIN, HORACE

Pippin, Horace (folk artist). Pictures just come to my mind and then I tell my heart to go ahead. (Newsweek 90:60 Aug 22, 77)

PITCHING (BASEBALL)

Gomez, Lefty. If you don't throw it, they can't hit it. (Washingtonian 15:141 Nov 79)

PITY

Eban, Abba Solomon. Better to be disliked than pitied. (New York 9:38 July 26, 76)

Ryan, Cornelius. The mathematics of self-pity can be raised to infinity. (Time 114:83 Aug 6, 79)

PLANNING

Augustine, Norman. If today were half as good as tomorrow is supposed to be, it would probably be twice as good as yesterday was. (Business Month 129:30 June 87)

Brown, Edmund Gerald, Jr. The reason why everybody likes planning is because nobody has to do anything. (The Coevolution Quarterly 10:23 Summer 76)

Feather, William. No plan is worth a damn unless somebody makes it work. (Forbes 120:186 Oct 15, 77)

Leopold, Aldo. The first prerequisite of intelligent tinkering is to save all the pieces. (Washingtonian 13:149 Sept 78)

Peter, Laurence J. If you don't know where you are going, you will probably end up somewhere else. (San Francisco Chronicle This World 1978:40 Jan 29, 78)

Van Derbur, Marilyn (former Miss America). The vital, successful people I have met all had one common characteristic. They had a plan. (People Weekly 6:23 Dec 13, 76)

PLAYBOY (PERIODICAL)

Hefner, Hugh Marston. If I told you, for example that Playboy, in its 22 years, was one of the major things that contributed to the women's movement, you might find it a mindboggler, but it happens to be true. (Chicago Tribune 124:1 Section 1 May 3, 76)

PLO see PALESTINE LIBERATION ORGANIZATION

POETRY

Auden, Wystan Hugh. Poetry makes nothing happen. (Washingtonian 13:166 Dec 77)

Bishop, Elizabeth. Poetry shouldn't be used as a vehicle for any personal philosophy. (Chicago Tribune 155:1 Section 5 June 4, 78)

Kavanagh, Patrick. Whatever will live must touch the heart of the mob in some way. (Washington Post 102:A17 Mar 17, 77)

Marsh, Jean. I think poetry is like a diary: people don't tend to write anything in it until something awful happens. (Newsweek 91:32 Feb 13, 78)

POETS

Ashbery, John. If one is a famous poet, one still isn't famous. (Details 6:99 Mar 88)

Fowles, John. Cherish the poet; there seemed many great auks till the last one died. (The American Book Review 1:21 Dec 77)

Jong, Erica. I want to set an example of a woman poet who doesn't kill herself. (Kansas City Star 117:6B Dec 3, 84)

Papp, Joseph. The true dramatist of our time is a poet; the true poet, a dramatist. (New York Times 128:C24 Dec 1, 78)

Pritchett, V. S. It is the role of the poet to look at what is happening in the world and to know that quite other things are happening. (New York Times Book Review 50 June 3, 79)

Sexton, Anne. I wonder if the artist ever lives his life—he is so busy recreating it. (The American Book Review 1:4 Dec 77)

Varese, Edgar. Scientists are the poets of today. (Artspace 9:30 Fall 85)

Wagner, Richard. A poet is nothing if not someone who knows without having made a study. (New York Times Book Review 9 April 1, 79)

POETS see also WOMEN AS POETS

POETS, AMERICAN see also GINSBERG, ALLEN; KAROL, PAMALA (LA LOCA); MOORE, MARIANNE

POETS, ENGLISH see also AUDEN, WYSTAN HUGH

POETS, FRENCH see also RIMBAUD, ARTHUR

POETS, WELSH see also THOMAS, DYLAN

POINDEXTER, JOHN M.

Reagan, Maureen. A member of the United States military who lies to the commander-in-chief is guilty of treason and should be court-martialed (about Oliver North and John Poindexter). (Chicago Tribune 79:19 Mar 20, 87)

POLAND—POLITICS AND GOVERNMENT

Jaruzelski, Wojciech. Our country is on the edge of the abyss (declaring martial law). (Newsweek 99:49 Jan 4, 82)

Pruszynska, Elzbieta. In Poland, it seems it's a rule that whoever is in power is ruining us. (Chicago Tribune 161:1 Section 4 June 10, 90)

Wattenberg, Ben. Poland is one of those great events that happen once in a generation to unmask the truth. (Time 119:20 Jan 11, 83)

POLICE

Behan, Brendan. I have never seen a situation so dismal that a policeman couldn't make it worse. (Cleveland 4:118 Aug 75)

Cleaver, Eldridge. A black pig, a white pig, a yellow pig, a pink pig—a dead pig is the best pig of all. We encourage people to kill them (in 1970). (Newsweek 85:40 Mar 17, 75)

Fernandes, Millor (Brazilian playwright). In a democracy we are all equal before the law. In a dictatorship we are all equal before the police. (New York Times 126:8 May 24, 77)

Mark, Sir Robert (chief of London's police force). The real art of policing a free society or a democracy is to win by appearing to lose or at least to win by not appearing to win. (The Observer 9701:13 July 17, 77)

Thompson, Hunter S. Today's pig is tomorrow's bacon. (Kansas City Star 110:A-6 May 23, 90)

POLICE see also CHICAGO—POLICE

POLITICAL PRISONERS

Moynihan, Daniel Patrick. When a person goes to a country and finds their newspapers filled with nothing but good news, he can bet there are good men in jail. (University Daily Kansan 87:4 Feb 16, 77)

POLITICIANS

Abourezk, James. If you want to curry favor with a politician, give him credit for something someone else did. (Washingtonian 15:140 Nov 79)

Alda, Alan. If I were a politician, I'd be a decent politician. (Newsweek 94:62 Aug 27, 79)

Anonymous. A statesman is a dead politician. (Newsweek 94:35 July 2, 79)

Bhutto, Zulfikar Ali. A politician is like a spring flower: he blossoms, he blooms, and a time comes for him to fade. (Time 107:38 May 2, 77)

Burgess, Anthony. We need beauty queens more than politicians. (The Observer 9809:10 Aug 26, 79)

Caddell, Patrick. I don't know any politicians in America who could run against himself and win. (Time 115:18 April 7, 80)

Cameron, Simon. An honest politician is one who, when he is bought, will stay bought. (Village Voice 21:16 Nov 8, 76)

Condon, Richard. If you are writing about politicians, you are writing about marshmallows and smoke. (International Herald Tribune 33367:24 June 7, 90)

Eckhardt, Nadine. Most politicians are just little men who couldn't get it up in high school. (Newsweek 86:38 Oct 13, 75)

Fahrenkopf, Frank. Every time a Democrat gets into trouble, it's sex, every time a Republican does, it's money. (Washingtonian 22:99 July 87)

Greenfield, Jeff. You will get what you want if you vote for the candidate who says exactly the opposite of what you most deeply believe. (Penthouse 10:123 Nov 78)

Johnson, Claudia Alta (Taylor). A politician ought to be born a foundling and remain a bachelor. (Time 106:56 Dec 1, 75)

Johnson, Lyndon Baines. I never trust a man unless I've got his pecker in my pocket. (Village Voice 21:16 Nov 8, 76)

Kahn, J. Kesner. When politicians come up with a solution for your problem, you have two problems. (American Opinion 18:21 May 75)

Khrushchev, Nikita Sergeevich. Politicians are the same the world over: they promise to build a bridge even where there is no river. (Village Voice 22:23 Aug 29, 77)

Menninger, Karl. The jail is a horrible institution manned by amateurs and politicians. (Los Angeles Times 96:2 Part 1 Oct 2, 77)

Moynihan, Daniel Patrick. Most politicians have a right to feel morally superior to their constituencies. (Rolling Stone 219:43 Aug 12, 76)

Nixon, Richard Milhous. The worst thing a politician can be is dull. (Newsweek 107:32 May 19, 86)

Rickover, Hyman G. Politics is to government like sex is to conception. (University Daily Kansan 94:1 Sept 30, 83)

Ridgeway, Matthew B. Candidates are no better or worse than those who choose and elect them, and therein lies the answer to what we are to become. (American Legion Magazine 101:21 Aug 76)

Roth, William V., Jr. Public confidence and trust in the federal government are low not only because of Watergate or our experience in Vietnam, but also because too many politicians have promised more than the government can deliver. (Chicago Tribune 311:1 Section 1 Nov 7, 75)

Schott, Phil. Paranoia among politicians is simply a state of heightened awareness. (San Diego Magazine 35:168 Sept 83)

Simon, William E. Bad politicians are sent to Washington by good people who don't vote. (Atlanta 16:130 Aug 76)

Stone, Isidor Feinstein. Every government is run by liars. Nothing they say should be believed. (The Progressive 53:4 Aug 89)

Strauss, Robert S. If you're in politics, you're a whore anyhow. It doesn't make any difference who you sleep with. (Texas Monthly 6:132 Feb 78)

Truman, Harry S. The C students run the world. (Time 108:32 Nov 8, 76)

Unruh, Jesse. If I had slain all my political enemies, I wouldn't have any friends today. (New West 1:8 Sept 13, 76)

Wills, Garry. Politicians fascinate because they constitute such a paradox: they are an elite that accomplishes mediocrity for the public good. (Time 113:86 April 23, 79)

Youngquist, Wayne. People want leaders with vision rather than programs. Even if conservatism is overtaking liberalism and individualism is prized over collective action, vision is always in demand and often rewarded at the polls. (Time 112:23 Oct 23, 78)

POLITICIANS see also **BLACK POLITICIANS**

POLITICIANS—FUND RAISING

Farmer, Robert. The main reason people give to political campaigns is because they don't want to say no to the person who asked them. (New England Monthly 5:38 July 88)

POLITICIANS—RELATION WITH THE PRESS

Dorfman, Dan. To lie to the press on a public matter is, in effect, to lie to the people. (New York 10:9 May 9, 77)

POLITICIANS—SEXUAL BEHAVIOR

Wright, Jim. The Wright broad rule is that broads ought to be able to type (commenting when asked to state a broad rule for avoiding Congressional sex scandals). (Wall Street Journal 57:1 Dec 31, 76)

POLITICIANS—UNITED STATES

Burns, George. Too bad that all the people who know how to run the country are busy driving taxicabs and cutting hair. (Life 2:117 Dec 79)

POLITICIANS—WIVES

Johnson, Claudia Alta (Taylor). A politician ought to be born a foundling and remain a bachelor. (Time 106:56 Dec 1, 75)

Nixon, Patricia Ryan. I gave up everything I've ever loved (commenting in 1960 on the price of political life). (Good Housekeeping 187:158 Aug 78)

POLITICS

Abourezk, James. Don't worry about your enemies, it's your allies who will do you in (in politics). (Playboy 26:106 Mar 79)

Abourezk, James. In politics, people will do whatever is necessary to get their way. (Playboy 26:106 Mar 79)

Abourezk, James. Politics is like the farmer's dog. If you run too fast you get nipped in the ass. If you stand still too long you get screwed. (Politicks & Other Human Interests 1:17 April 25, 78)

Andreotti, Giulio. In politics there is a clause that is always valid: rebus sic stantibus (circumstances being what they are). (Time 108:54 Dec 13, 76)

Anonymous. To err is human; to blame it on the other party is politics. (Washingtonian 15:142 Nov 79)

Barkley, Alben. Three months is a generation in politics. (Time 106:9 July 14, 75)

Bellow, Saul. I see politics—ultimately—as a buzzing preoccupation that swallows up art and the life of the spirit. (Newsweek 86:39 Sept 1, 75)

Briggs, John. When it comes to politics, anything is fair. (Village Voice 23:62 Oct 16, 78)

Brown, Edmund Gerald, Jr. Issues are the last refuges of scoundrels. (Washingtonian 15:140 Nov 79)

Brown, Edmund Gerald, Jr. The first rule of politics is to be different. (Newsweek 93:24 April 23, 79)

Brown, Edmund Gerald, Jr. You lean a little to the left and then a little to the right in order to always move straight ahead (on the art of governing). (Time 112:89 Oct 2, 78)

Brown, Sam. Never offend people with style when you can offend them with substance. (Washingtonian 14:152 Nov 78)

Cohen, Mark B. Nothing can so alienate a voter from the political system as backing a winning candidate. (Washingtonian 14:152 Nov 78)

Connally, John Bowden (attributed by Henry Alfred Kissinger). You will be measured in (Washington D.C.) by the enemies you destroy. The bigger they are, the bigger you are. (Time 114:45 Oct 8, 79)

Crane, Philip. It's always better to stand on your principles and lose than to lose your principles and win. (Newsweek 93:37 Mar 19, 79)

Drinan, Robert. Politics is the formation of public morality. (Chicago Tribune 261:20

Sept 17, 80)

Edwards, Shelton. The way to get somewhere in politics is to find a crowd that's going some place and get in front of it. (Time 112:16 Aug 28, 78)

Ford, Gerald Rudolph. I learned a long time ago in politics, never say never. (New York Times 128:17 April 22, 79)

Goldwater, Barry Morris. Sex and politics are a lot alike. You don't have to be good at them to enjoy them. (University Daily Kansan 94:9 Jan 25, 84)

Heller, Joseph. No one governs. Everyone performs. Politics has become a social world. (New York Times 128:15 Section 6 Mar 4, 79)

Hillman, Sidney. Politics is the science of how who gets what, when and why. (Rocky Mountain News 62:36 June 23, 80)

Horowitz, Rachel. If you're a public employee and your job depends on public officials, you have to be in politics. (Newsweek 96:27 July 14, 80)

Humphrey, Hubert Horatio. Politics isn't a matter of making love. It's making choices. (Newsweek 91:22 Jan 23, 78)

Humphrey, Hubert Horatio. The biggest corruption in politics, friends, is not money. It's publicity. (New York 9:100 May 10, 76)

Jagger, Mick. Politics, like the legal system, is dominated by old men. (Life 2:117 Dec 79)

Kapiloff, Larry. I believe that politics is 90 percent the profession of cowards. (San Diego Magazine 31:88 May 79)

Kelley, Stanley. Last guys don't finish nice. (Town & Country 133:140 May 79)

Kemp, Jack. Whether it's politics or football, winning is like shaving: you do it every day or you wind up looking like a bum. (The Sporting News 202:12 Aug 4, 86)

Kennedy, Florynce Rae. If the ass is protecting the system, ass-kicking should be undertaken regardless of the sex, ethnicity, or charm of the ass involved. (Ms 1:89 Mar 73)

Kissinger, Henry Alfred. Competing pressures tempt one to believe that an issue deferred is a problem avoided; more often it is a crisis invited. (Time 114:82 Oct 15, 79)

Kissinger, Henry Alfred. I have always thought of foreign policy as bipartisan. (Chicago Tribune 233:6 Section 2 Aug 21, 77)

Koch, Edward I. It happens that intellectual honesty is not the coin of the realm in politics. (New York Times 129:B1 Oct 23, 79)

Mathias, Charles McCurdy. People tend to want to follow the beaten path. The difficulty is that the beaten path doesn't seem to be leading anywhere. (Time 106:12 Dec 8, 75)

McGovern, George Stanley. Marching in mindless lockstep is the lowest form of party loyalty. (Village Voice 22:34 May 16, 77)

Mikva, Abner J. Someone once said that politics is like poker—it's only fun when you play for a trifle more than you can afford to lose. (Chicago Sun-Times 31:5 Nov 9, 78)

Nixon, Patricia Ryan. I gave up everything I've ever loved (commenting in 1960 on the price of political life). (Good Housekeeping 187:158 Aug 78)

Nixon, Richard Milhous. There is one thing solid and fundamental in politics—the law of change. What's up today is down tomorrow. (Time 104:40 Aug 19, 74)

Okun, Arthur M. The world is not safe for incumbents. (New York Times 128:15 Section 3 June 24, 79)

Pannenberg, Wolfhart. The greatest deception (of our era is the idea that) political change can satisfy a religious need. (Time 107:65 Mar 8, 76)

Rayburn, Sam. A whore's vote is just as good as a debutante's. (D Magazine 6:86 June 79)

Reagan, Ronald. I finally figured out this politics. It's like show business. You start with a big opening act, coast, and close with a great crescendo. (Time 106:16 Nov 24, 75)

Reagan, Ronald. You know, politics has been called the second oldest profession. Sometimes there is a similarity to the first. (Chicago Tribune 323:1 Section 1 Nov 19, 75)

Reeves, Richard. Politics is sex in a hula-hoop. (New York 9:99 June 14, 76)

Roosevelt, Franklin Delano. Nothing just happens in politics. If something happens you can be sure it was planned that way. (Oui 7:107 May 78)

Rostenkowski, Dan. The art of politics is finding the center. (Washington Post National Weekly Edition 3:5 Dec 9, 85)

Rumsfeld, Donald. If you try to please everybody, somebody is not going to like it. (Washingtonian 12:107 Feb 77)

Sears, John. Politics is motion and excitement. (Time 114:22 Nov 12, 79)

Sears, John. You never really win anything in politics. All you get is a chance to play for higher stakes and perform at a higher level. (Time 115:32 Jan 21, 80)

Stevenson, Adlai, II. Good government cannot exist side by side with bad politics: the best government is the best politics. (Kansas City Star 97:4B Jan 30, 77)

Stevenson, Adlai, III. I don't think ideas are incompatible with political reality. (Time 113:18 Feb 26, 79)

Stolley, Richard. Young sells better than old, pretty sells better than ugly, music sells better than television, television better than movies, and politics doesn't sell at all. (New York 10:15 Sept 12, 77)

Talmadge, Betty. There's not much difference between selling a ham and selling a political idea. (Time 112:23 July 31, 78)

Thalberg, Irving. Nothing is unfair in politics. (The Nation 239:77 Aug 4, 84)

Thompson, James. It is better to make fun of yourself than let your opponent do it for you. (San Francisco Chronicle This World 1977:2 Oct 16, 77)

Unruh, Jesse. Money is the mother's milk of politics. (US News & World Report 85:50 Sept 18, 78)

Vidal, Gore. In writing and politicking, it's best not to think about it, just do it. (Bookviews 1:24 June 78)

Voigt, Jon. Things don't have to be about politics to be political. (Rolling Stone 292:50 May 31, 79)

Walker, Jimmy. A reformer is a guy who rides through a sewer in a glass-bottomed boat. (New York Times 129:A15 July 7, 80)

White, Kevin Hagen. Charismatic leadership is hungered for, but at the same time we fear it. (Time 107:10 Feb 9, 76)

White, Theodore. Politics in America is the binding secular religion. (Firing Line 5 July 26, 75)

Will, George F. Politics is more difficult than you think. (Gentlemen's Quarterly 56:68 May 86)

POLITICS see also PRESIDENTIAL CAMPAIGNS; UNITED STATES—POLITICS AND GOVERNMENT; UNITED STATES. CONGRESS; VICE-PRESIDENTS; WORLD POLITICS

POLITICS, CORRUPTION IN

Cameron, Simon. An honest politician is one who, when he is bought, will stay bought. (Village Voice 21:16 Nov 8, 76)

POLITICS, CORRUPTION IN—ILLINOIS

Powell, Paul. I can smell the meat a-cookin'. If you can't get a meal, take a sandwich (advice to lawmakers). (Chicago 27:11 June 78)

POLITICS, CORRUPTION IN—KANSAS CITY, MISSOURI

Prendergast, George Washington. I never took a dime from the public till; it's all been honest graft. (Change 8:60 Aug 76)

POLITICS—SOUTH

Allen, Maryon. People in the South love their politics better than their food on the table. (Time 112:32 Oct 9, 78)

POLLOCK, JACKSON

Warhol, Andy. I wish I were as rich as Jackson Pollock. (Art & Antiques 87 Oct 84)

POLLUTION

Gardner, Brian. Polluters must be made to pay so much that the fines—continuously leveled until the pollution stops—are so high that not to pollute is a cheaper alternative. (New Scientist 76:516 Nov 24, 77)

POLO

Stallone, Sylvester. Playing polo is a lot like trying to hit a golf ball during an earthquake. (Metro 5:68 1990)

POOR

Churchill, Sir Winston. You don't make the poor richer by making the rich poorer. (To The Point International 3:39 Nov 1, 76)

Liddy, G. Gordon. Before going to prison I believed that criticism of the criminal justice system for its treatment of the poor was so much liberal bleating and bunk. I was wrong. (Connecticut 40:48 Feb 77)

Pendleton, Clarence. The best way to help poor folks is not to be one. (Mother Jones 7:25 Feb 82)

Poirot, Paul L. Multiplying wealth is by far the fastest way to help the poor. Dividing the wealth and subsidizing poverty is the fastest way to starve everyone. (American Opinion 18:29 Nov 75)

Smith, Charles Merrill. In a democracy you can be respected though poor, but don't count on it. (Time 113:25 Feb 26, 79)

POPULAR CULTURE

Hayakawa, Samuel Ichiye. If you see in any given situation only what everyone else can see, you can be said to be so much a representative of your culture that you are a victim of it. (Phoenix 18:94 April 83)

Price, Roger. If everybody doesn't want it, nobody gets it. (Texas Observer 76:22 Nov 23, 84)

PORNOGRAPHY

Goldstein, Al. When it comes to pornography, I know two kinds of people: those who don't know what they're talking about, and those who don't know what they're missing. (Washington Post 353:D3 Nov 22, 76)

Wallace, George Corley. The Supreme Court has to write a hundred pages on what pornography is. The average man who works in a steel mill can tell you right off whether that's filth or not. (Newsweek 85:44 April 21, 75)

PORTER, COLE

Merman, Ethel. (Cole Porter) sang like a hinge. (Time 114:97 Oct 1, 79)

POSTAL SERVICE—UNITED STATES

Goldwater, Barry Morris. A book should not be charged the same rate for mailing as a brick. (New York Times 126:16 Section 4 Jan 30, 77)

POSTEMA, PAM

Knepper, Bob. You can be a woman umpire if you want, but that doesn't mean it's right. (The Sporting News 205:36 Mar 28, 88)

POTENTIAL

Wiley, Ralph. A National Football League center once said that potential is a French word meaning you aren't worth a damn yet. (Sports Illustrated 65:27 Oct 6, 86)

POUND, EZRA

Pound, Ezra. At seventy, I realized that instead of being a lunatic, I was a moron. (Horizon 21:96 Mar 78)

POVERTY

Ali, Muhammad. Wars on nations are fought to change maps, but wars on poverty are fought to map change. (Playboy 22:68 Nov 75)

Harris, Patricia Roberts. Poverty is not so much the absence of money as the absence of aspiration, of the knowledge that it is possible to go anywhere else. (Skeptic 19:10 May 77)

Mother Teresa. Loneliness and the feeling of being unwanted is the most terrible poverty. (Time 106:49 Dec 29, 75)

Poirot, Paul L. Multiplying wealth is by far the fastest way to help the poor. Dividing the wealth and subsidizing poverty is the fastest way to starve everyone. (American Opinion 18:29 Nov 75)

POWELL, PAUL

Powell, Paul. I can smell the meat a-cookin'. If you can't get a meal, take a sandwich (advice to lawmakers). (Chicago 27:11 June 78)

POWER (SOCIAL SCIENCES)

Abe, Kobo. In the love for the weak there is always an intent to kill. (New York Times Magazine 86 April 29, 79)

Addams, Jane. I do not believe that women are better than men. We have not wrecked railroads, nor corrupted legislatures, nor done many unholy things that men have done; but then we must remember that we have not had the chance. (Working Woman 1:8 Nov 76)

Allen, Woody. The lion and the calf shall lie down together, but the calf won't get much sleep. (Time 113:25 Feb 26, 79)

Brown, Edmund Gerald, Jr. The power of the executive is like a chess game; there are very few moves that one can make. (Gold Coast Pictorial 13:9 Feb 77)

Canetti, Elias. To be the last man to remain alive is the deepest urge of every real seeker after power. (New York Times Book Review 58 April 29, 79)

Carr, Jesse. Being powerful is like being a lady. If you have to tell people you are, you ain't. (Newsweek 88:77 Sept 27, 76)

Cater, Douglass. If power corrupts, being out of power corrupts absolutely. (Book Digest 6:32 Dec 79)

Evans, Medford. It usually takes disciplined organization to dislodge entrenched power. (American Opinion 18:29 Nov 75)

Hockney, David. Three hundred homosexuals rule the world and I know every one of them. (Manchester Guardian Weekly 140:29 May 21, 89)

Kissinger, Henry Alfred. Power is the greatest aphrodisiac of all. (Maclean's 91:72 Mar 6, 78)

Novick, Julius. It is a well-known and infuriating fact of life that in any relationship, if one party really and truly does not give a damn, that party will inevitably have the upper hand. Indifference is power (ask any cat). (Village Voice 21:81 Feb 14, 77)

Shanker, Albert. Power is a good thing. It is better than powerlessness. (Time 106:17 Sept 22, 75)

Vidal, Gore. Power is far more exciting than sex. (Chicago Tribune 173:3 Section 5 June 22, 87)

Young, Andrew. Influence is like a savings account. The less you use it, the more you've got. (People Weekly 6:30 Dec 27/Jan 3, 1977)

POWER RESOURCES

Adelman, Morris A. (economist). The (energy) gap is like the horizon, always receding as you walk, ride, or fly toward it. (Time 110:61 Oct 10, 77)

Carter, James Earl. No one should mistake the energy problem for what it is—a fundamental crisis that threatens Americans and America's way of life. (Time 109:63 May 23, 77)

Laird, Melvin. Conservation alone is a slow walk down a dead-end street. (Time 110:62 Oct 10, 77)

Nader, Ralph. There is not an energy crisis. There is an energy monopoly crisis, too many of the energy decisions are being made by a few large corporations instead of by a broader aggregate of consumer determinants. (Meet the Press 21:3 April 17, 77)

Penden, Bill. Atomic energy is a future idea whose time is past. Renewable energy is a future idea whose time has come. (Atlas World Press Review 24:38 April 77)

Reagan, Ronald. The problem isn't a shortage of fuel, it's a surplus of government. (Newsweek 94:21 Oct 1, 79)

PRAISE

Nabokov, Vladimir. Anonymous praise hurts nobody. (New York Times Book Review 27 July 31, 77)

Post, Emily. An overdose of praise is like 10 lumps of sugar in coffee; only a very few people can swallow it. (Kansas City Times 109:14C Jan 22, 77)

PRAYER IN THE SCHOOLS see PUBLIC SCHOOLS AND RELIGION

PREDICTION see FORECASTING

PREJUDICE

Comfort, Alex. Nobody is safe being prejudiced against what they themselves are going to become (commenting on aging). (New York Times 126:24 Oct 25, 76)

PRESENT (TIME)

Boorstin, Daniel J. The contemporary time is always the best time to live. It is a mistake to say the best age is one without problems. (Time 106:53 Sept 1, 75)

Faulkner, William. The past is never dead; it is not even past. (Newsweek 89:87 Feb 21, 77)

PRESIDENTIAL CAMPAIGNS

Broder, David S. Anybody who wants the presidency so much that he'll spend two years organizing and campaigning for it is not to be trusted with the office. (Time 113:25 Feb 26, 79)

Brown, Edmund Gerald, Jr. In this business (politics) a little vagueness goes a long way. (New Times 6:18 May 28, 76)

Byrd, Robert. Do not run a campaign that would embarrass your mother. (Kansas City Times 120:A-9 Oct 13, 87)

Thompson, Mike. Franklin Roosevelt couldn't be nominated today. A Bruce Jenner could beat him. (Time 115:26 Jan 28, 80)

PRESIDENTIAL CAMPAIGNS—1980

Kennedy, Edward Moore. I think Mr. Carter has created Ronald Reagan. (The Observer 9856:12 July 20, 80)

Reagan, Ronald. This is not a campaign; it's a crusade. (Tennessean 75:7 July 16, 80)

PRESIDENTIAL CAMPAIGNS—1984

Sarbanes, Paul. A working man voting for Reagan is like a chicken voting for Colonel Sanders. (Washingtonian 20:328 Nov 84)

PRESIDENTIAL CAMPAIGNS—1988 see also BUSH, GEORGE—PRESIDENTIAL CAMPAIGN—1988

PRESIDENTIAL CAMPAIGNS—1976

Ford, Gerald Rudolph. There is no Soviet

domination of Eastern Europe and there never will be under a Ford Administration. (Chicago Sun-Times 29:2 Oct 8, 76)

PRESIDENTIAL CANDIDATES

Byrd, Robert. Do not run a campaign that would embarrass your mother. (Kansas City Times 120:A-9 Oct 13, 87)

PRESIDENTIAL CANDIDATES see also
BROWN, EDMUND GERALD, JR.; BUSH, GEORGE; CARTER, JAMES EARL; EISENHOWER, DWIGHT DAVID; HARRIS, FRED; REAGAN, RONALD; STEVENSON, ADLAI, II; THURMOND, STROM

PRESIDENTIAL CANDIDATES— CONDUCT OF LIFE

Hart, Gary. Follow me around. I don't care. I'm serious. If anybody wants to put a tail on me, go ahead. They'd be very bored. (Kansas City Star 107:1B May 10, 87)

PRESIDENTS—INAUGURAL ADDRESSES—1921

Harding, Warren Gamaliel. Our most dangerous tendency is to expect too much of government, and at the same time to do for it too little (inaugural address—1921). (Christian Science Monitor 69:14 Jan 20, 77)

PRESIDENTS—INAUGURAL ADDRESSES—1933

Roosevelt, Franklin Delano. Our true destiny is not to be ministered into but to minister to ourselves and to our fellow men (inaugural address—1933). (Christian Science Monitor 69:14 Jan 20, 77)

PRESIDENTS—INAUGURAL ADDRESSES—1961

Kennedy, John Fitzgerald. And so, my fellow Americans, ask not what your country can do for you; ask what you can do for your country (inaugural address—1961). (Christian Science Monitor 69:14 Jan 20, 77)

PRESIDENTS—INAUGURAL ADDRESSES—1973

Nixon, Richard Milhous. In our own lives, let each of us ask—not just what will government do for me, but what can I do for myself (inaugural address—1973). (Christian Science Monitor 69:14 Jan 20, 77)

PRESIDENTS—UNITED STATES

Adams, Sherman. I believe that a president should above all understand his own prejudices. (Time 119:12 April 5, 82)

Broder, David S. Anybody who wants the presidency so much that he'll spend two years organizing and campaigning for it is not to be trusted with the office. (Time 113:25 Feb 26, 79)

Bush, George. The single most important job of the President is the national security

of the United States. (Time 136:20 Aug 20, 90)

Carter, James Earl. I think the President is the only person who can change the direction or attitude of our nation. (Encore American & Worldwide News 5:4 June 21, 76)

Church, Frank. The Presidency is no place for on-the-job training. I've always advocated the politics of substance, not the politics of style. (Encore American & Worldwide News 5:4 June 21, 76)

Fallows, James. I'm inclined to doubt this government can be changed, by Carter or any other President. (Time 112:91 Dec 4, 78)

Ford, Gerald Rudolph. Most of the important things that happen in the world happen in the middle of the night. (San Francisco Chronicle This World 1978:2 Feb 26, 78)

Harlow, Bryce N. Our only protection against the presidency is the character of the president. (Washingtonian 11:103 June 76)

Hussein, King of Jordan. It's amusing. The Americans have changed Presidents six times since I've been King. And they talk to the Arabs about stability? (People Weekly 6:122 Dec 13, 76)

Kennedy, John Fitzgerald. I know that when things don't go well, they like to blame the President, and that is one of the things presidents are paid for. (Rocky Mountain News 185:60 Oct 24, 79)

Luce, Clare Boothe. There aren't many women now I'd like to see as President— but there are fewer men. (Newsweek 94:95 Oct 22, 79)

Moyers, Bill D. It isn't wisdom or intelligence that influences a President, it's opportunity. (Newsweek 91:22 April 17, 78)

Nixon, Richard Milhous. Knowing a little about everything won't work. Knowing a great deal about important things is essential (for Presidents). (Time 112:16 Aug 28, 78)

Nixon, Richard Milhous. The next President's qualifications should be tested against foreign policy. If he fails there, we all fail. (Time 114:27 Sept 10, 79)

Reagan, Ronald. A president should never say never. (Life 7:113 Jan 83)

Reagan, Ronald. If I were really lucky, I wouldn't have this job. (US 3:64 May 5, 86)

Reston, James. Old men running for the Presidency of the United States are like old men who take young brides. It's an exciting idea for a while but it seldom works. (New York Times 128:25 Jan 26, 79)

Safire, William. I think that one of Nixon's great contributions to civil liberties was getting caught doing what the two presidents before him got away with. (Book Digest 4:28 July 77)

Stevenson, Adlai, II. By the time a man is nominated for the Presidency of the United States, he is no longer worthy to hold the office. (Washingtonian 15:143 Nov 79)

Stoessinger, John G. The President holds our future in his hands. His personality may be our destiny. (Time 114:20 Dec 31, 79)

Strauss, Robert S. There ain't but one good job in this government, and you got it (to Jimmy Carter). (Time 116:12 Sept 22, 80)

Thompson, Hunter S. I don't think incompetence is any excuse for being a dumb President. (The California Aggie 96:6 Mar 2, 78)

Thompson, Mike. Franklin Roosevelt couldn't be nominated today. A Bruce Jenner could beat him. (Time 115:26 Jan 28, 80)

United States. Congress. Senate. Select Committee On Intelligence Operations. There is no inherent Constitutional authority for the President or any intelligence agency to violate the law. (New York Times 125:14 Section 4 May 2, 76)

Vidal, Gore. Any man who can win a contemporary presidential campaign ought not to be President. (Rolling Stone 319:42 May 15, 80)

Vidal, Gore. As now set up, the best one can hope for in a President is that he not be entirely insane. (Rolling Stone 319:42 May 15, 80)

Welch, Robert (founder of the John Birch Society). Every President since Theodore Roosevelt has committed a treasonable act except—maybe—Warren G. Harding, Calvin Coolidge, and Herbert Hoover. (Chicago Tribune 194:14 July 13, 77)

PRESIDENTS—UNITED STATES see also
CARTER, JAMES EARL; EISENHOWER, DWIGHT DAVID; HARDING, WARREN GAMALIEL; NIXON, RICHARD MILHOUS; REAGAN, RONALD; ROOSEVELT, FRANKLIN DELANO; TRUMAN, HARRY S.

PRESIDENTS—UNITED STATES— POWERS AND DUTIES

Brown, Edmund Gerald, Jr. You don't have to do things. Maybe by avoiding doing things you accomplish a lot. (New York Times 125:17 April 26, 76)

Ford, Gerald Rudolph. A President should never promise more than he can deliver

and a President should always deliver everything that he's promised. (Time 108:15 Oct 4, 76)

Rockefeller, Nelson Aldrich. Congressional actions in the past few years, however well intentioned, have hamstrung the presidency and usurped the presidential prerogative in the conduct of foreign affairs. (Christian Science Monitor 68:2 May 11, 76)

PRESIDENTS—UNITED STATES— PROTECTION

Mankiewicz, Frank Fabian. Since we are not yet serious about guns, let us at least withhold the most costly target (the President). (Newsweek 86:34 Oct 6, 75)

PRESIDENTS—UNITED STATES— PUBLIC RELATIONS

Califano, Joseph A., Jr. No just society can deny the right of its citizens to the health care they need. We are the only industrial society that does. (New York Times 136:2 Jan 13, 87)

PRESIDENTS—UNITED STATES—WIVES

Johnson, Claudia Alta (Taylor). The First Lady is an unpaid public servant elected by one person: her husband. (Washington Post 266:K7 Aug 28, 77)

PRESLEY, ELVIS

Jarvis, Felton (Elvis Presly's producer). It's like someone just came up and told me there aren't going to be any more cheeseburgers in the world (commenting on Elvis Presley's death). (Country Music 7:36 Dec 77)

Lewis, Jerry Lee. That dead son of a gun is still riding on my coattails (about Elvis Presley). (New York Times Magazine 45 Mar 25, 79)

Presley, Elvis. I don't know anything about music. In my line I don't have to. (Creem 11:30 Feb 80)

Smith, Sam. He stood on his own (about Elvis Presley). (New York Times Magazine 45 Mar 25, 79)

PRESS

Bird, Rose. The press has become the modern equivalent of peer group pressure. (Wilson Library Bulletin 62:21 Sept 87)

Nelson, Jack. I think there is a real contempt for the press within the Reagan Administration, and I think it starts at the top. (Time 128:88 Nov 17, 86)

Nixon, Richard Milhous. When news is concerned, nobody in the press is a friend—they are all enemies. (Time 111:104 April 17, 78)

Reagan, Ronald. I'd like to go back to those days when the press never quoted the President without permission. (SA Today

1:4A Jan 12, 83)

PRIESTS

John Paul II, Pope. Priesthood is forever—
we do not return the gift once given.
(Time 114:21 Oct 15, 79)

PRINCE (MUSICIAN)

Little Richard. Prince is me in this
generation. (US 3:4 April 6, 87)

PRINCETON, NEW JERSEY

Einstein, Albert. Princeton is a wonderful
little spot. A quaint and ceremonious
village of puny demigods on stilts.
(Philadelphia Magazine 66:116 Aug 75)

PRISONS

Day, Samuel H., Jr. While prison is the
proper place for those who break the law
in the interest of peace and justice, it is no
place at all for most of the remaining 99.9
per cent who find themselves incarcerated
today. (Progressive 54:28 Jan 90)

Dean, John Wesley, III. Prisons are
emotional zoos filled with paranoids,
manic depressives, homosexuals,
schizophrenics and assorted fruits and
vegetables without labels. (Newsweek
40:9 July 4, 77)

Menninger, Karl. The jail is a horrible
institution manned by amateurs and
politicians. (Los Angeles Times 96:2 Part
1 Oct 2, 77)

PRIVACY, RIGHT OF

Goldwater, Barry Morris, Jr. Without a sense
of privacy, the Bill of Rights' guarantees
cease to function. (Time 110:17 July 18,
77)

Stimson, Henry. Gentlemen do not read
each other's mail. (Maclean's 89:72 April
5, 76)

PRIVATE ENTERPRISE see FREE ENTERPRISE

PROBLEM SOLVING

Anderson, Paul. I have yet to see any
problem, however complicated, which,
when you looked at it in the right way, did
not become still more complicated.
(Washingtonian 14:152 Nov 78)

Mencken, Henry Louis. For every human
problem, there is a neat, plain solution—
and it is always wrong. (Washingtonian
14:155 Nov 78)

Paulucci, Jeno F. It pays to be ignorant, for
when you're smart you already know it
can't be done. (New York Times 126:5
Section 3 Nov 7, 76)

Sevareid, Eric. The chief cause of problems
is solutions. (Town & Country 133:141
May 79)

PRODUCTION STANDARDS

Schultze, Charles. If you can't measure
output, then you measure input.
(Washingtonian 14:155 Nov 78)

PROFESSIONALISM

Von Hoffman, Nicholas. Professionalism is a
cheap and easy way of disciplining labor.
(More 8:25 Feb 78)

PROFIT

Brooks, Jim. Businessmen commit a fraud
when they say they're interested in
anything but profit. (New West 1:17 Dec
20, 76)

Janeway, Eliot. The thrill of making a fast
buck follows only the thrill of love at first
sight. Everyone needs to take an
occasional fling with money...and with
love. (Chicago Tribune 95:14 April 5, 77)

PROGRESS

Adenauer, Konrad. History is the sum total of
the things that could have been avoided.
(Kansas City Times 109:12H Dec 9, 76)

Bowles, Paul. Everything gets worse.
(Vanity Fair 48:131 Sept 85)

Eiseley, Loren. There is but one way into the
future: the technological way. (Time
110:61 July 25, 77)

Jenkins, Robin. It is not the goodness of
saints that makes us feel there is hope for
humanity: it is the goodness of obscure
men. (New York Times Book Review 14
Feb 3, 80)

King, Coretta Scott. There is a spirit and a
need and a man at the beginning of every
great human advance. Each of these
must be right for that particular moment of
history, or nothing happens. (Chicago
Tribune 176:2 Section 2 June 25, 78)

Nash, Ogden. Progress might have been all
right once, but it's gone on too long.
(Reader's Digest 106:98 Feb 75)

Rogers, Will. Any man who thinks civilization
has advanced is an egoist. (Time 104:92
Oct 7, 74)

PRONUNCIATION

Broun, Heywood Hale. If anyone corrects
your pronunciation of a word in a public
place, you have every right to punch him
in the nose. (Kansas City Times 109:14B
July 8, 77)

PROPERTY

Didion, Joan. I think nobody owns land until
their dead are in it. (Chicago Tribune
176:2 Section 2 June 25, 78)

Wolfe, Tom. Rental property should sell for
100 times the monthly rental income.
(CoEvolution Quarterly 35:5 Fall 82)

PROSTITUTION

Lipsen, Chuck. Folklore has it that the oldest
profession is prostitution. I always thought
it was lobbying. (W 6:2 Sept 16, 77)

Reagan, Ronald. You know, politics has
been called the second oldest profession.
Sometimes there is a similarity to the first.
(Chicago Tribune 323:1 Section 1 Nov 19, 75)

Saint James, Margo. (We've already) got legalized prostitution: marriage. (Washington Post 138:B7 April 21, 76)

PSYCHIATRISTS

Brando, Marlon. The principal benefit acting has offered me is the money to pay my psychiatrists. (Los Angeles 23:181 Nov 78)

Montagu, Ashley. Most psychiatrists need to have their heads examined. Analysis, it has been said, is the study of the id by the odd. (Chicago Tribune 142:3 Section 5 May 22, 77)

Spillane, Mickey. Freud's stupid. I didn't like Jung or Adler, either. I go along with Samuel Goldwyn: he said anybody who has to see a psychiatrist ought to have to have his head examined. (Gentlemen's Quarterly 55:327 Oct 85)

PSYCHIATRISTS see also **FREUD, SIGMUND**

PSYCHIATRY

Greenberg, David. An oldtimer is someone who can remember when a naughty child was taken to the woodshed instead of to a psychiatrist. (American Opinion 18:29 Nov 75)

Montagu, Ashley. Most psychiatrists need to have their heads examined. Analysis, it has been said, is the study of the id by the odd. (Chicago Tribune 142:3 Section 5 May 22, 77)

PSYCHOLOGY

Wharton, William. After I muddle in other people's puddles, I find out it's all one, big lonesome ocean. (National Catholic Reporter 21:13 May 17, 85)

PSYCHOTHERAPY

Spillane, Mickey. Freud's stupid. I didn't like Jung or Adler, either. I go along with Samuel Goldwyn: he said anybody who has to see a psychiatrist ought to have to have his head examined. (Gentlemen's Quarterly 55:327 Oct 85)

PUBLIC OFFICE

Kissinger, Henry Alfred. High office teaches decision making, not substance. It consumes intellectual capital; it does not create it. (Time 114:81 Oct 15, 79)

PUBLIC OFFICERS

Baker, Russell. In Washington when you cash in your public service for a big payday, the trick is not to offend anybody important on the way to the bank. (New York Times 135:27 April 30, 86)

PUBLIC OFFICERS—SALARIES, PENSIONS, ETC.

Wilson, Helen S. One cannot buy wisdom in the marketplace. (Chicago Tribune 362:1 Section 7 Dec 2, 86)

PUBLIC OPINION

Brown, Sam. Never offend people with style when you can offend them with substance. (Washingtonian 14:152 Nov 78)

Roth, William V., Jr. Public confidence and trust in the federal government are low not only because of Watergate or our experience in Vietnam, but also because too many politicians have promised more than the government can deliver. (Chicago Tribune 311:1 Section 1 Nov 7, 75)

Rowse, A. L. Most people's opinions are of no value at all. (The Observer 9809:10 Aug 26, 79)

PUBLIC RELATIONS INDUSTRY

Speakes, Larry. If you tell the same story five times, it's true. (Spy 32:June 89

PUBLIC SCHOOLS AND RELIGION

Reagan, Ronald. If we get the federal government out of the classroom, maybe we'll get God back in. (The Washingtonian 11:97 July 76)

PUBLIC SCHOOLS—DESEGREGATION

Clark, Kenneth. Integration is a painful job. It is social therapy, and like personal therapy it is not easy. (Time 106:14 Sept 22, 75)

Eisenhower, Dwight David. These are not bad people... All they are concerned about is to see that their sweet little girls are not required to sit in schools alongside some big overgrown Negroes. (Time 109:66 Mar 28, 77)

Wallace, George Corley. I draw the line in the dust and toss the gauntlet before the feet of tyranny. And I say, segregation now. Segregation tomorrow. Segregation forever. (New York 8:36 July 28, 75)

Wallace, George Corley. Segregation is a moot question, and integration is the law of the land. It is a moot question, and therefore we don't want to go back, nor make any attempt to change what is now a fact accomplished. (Meet the Press 20:5 Mar 28, 76)

PUBLIC SCHOOLS—PHILADELPHIA

Rizzo, Frank Lazzaro. We need excellence in public education and if the teachers can't do it, we'll send in a couple of policemen. (Time 110:40 Oct 24, 77)

PUBLIC SERVICE

Schlesinger, Arthur, Jr. The higher loyalty, it has always seemed to me, is to truth, public enlightenment, and history. (The Atlantic 244:28 Aug 79)

PUBLISHERS AND PUBLISHING

Bork, Robert. I don't care how free enterprise you are, once you deal with a publisher you'll want to nationalize the industry. (Chicago Tribune 82:13 Section 1 Mar 22, 88)

Coover, Robert. You make a million or you don't even get printed. (New Times 8:53 Aug 19, 77)

Costa-Gavras. Film is the only way now to reach out to people all around the world. The time of the book is over. (Village Voice 20:106 Dec 8, 75)

Evans, Harold. Publishing is: Talk softly and carry a big stick, but don't let them see the big stick. (Chicago Tribune 316:5 Section 5 Nov 12, 90)

Hochmann, John L. After all, publishing is a business, literature is a happy accident. (New York Times Book Review 35 July 30, 78)

Lazar, Irving L (Swifty). Dostoevsky couldn't get a publisher today. (Chicago Tribune 40:18 Section 1 Feb 9, 82)

Talese, Gay. Lawyers have become the third force in publishing. I see them as the new enemy. (Time 115:51 Mar 17, 80)

Townshend, Peter. It isn't enough any more to write books: publishers expect you to sell them. (W 7:39 Nov 10, 78)

PUERTO RICO—POLITICS AND GOVERNMENT see also LEBRON, LOLITA

PUNCTUALITY

Waugh, Evelyn. Punctuality is the virtue of the bored. (Time 110:102 Oct 17, 77)

PURCHASING

Allen, Marty. A study of economics usually reveals that the best time to buy anything is last year. (Atlanta 15:26 Jan 75)

QADDAFI, MUAMMAR

Qaddafi, Muammar. From time to time, I weep, but only when I am alone. (Time 127:29 April 21, 86)

Qaddafi, Muammar. My people have the right to liquidate opponents inside and outside the country even under broad daylight. (Time 127:29 April 21, 86)

QUALITY

Block, Herbert L. If it's good, they'll stop making it. (Time 113:25 Feb 26, 79)

QUAYLE, DAN

Bentsen, Lloyd. Jack Kennedy was a friend of mine. Senator, you're no Jack Kennedy (to Dan Quayle). (Chicago Tribune 280:1 Oct 6, 88)

Bush, George. He's (Dan Quayle) going to be one of the greatest vice presidents. You watch him closely, America, because you're going to respect what you see. (Chicago Tribune 315:16 Section 1 Nov 10, 88)

Canzeri, Joseph. Ask him (Dan Quayle) to turn off a light, and by the time he gets to the switch, he's forgotten what he went for. (Chicago Tribune 200:3 Section 1 July 19, 89)

Donaldson, Sam. George Bush picked Dan Quayle because he wanted a nonentity that would not threaten him in any way, shape or form. (M 6:127 Sept 89)

Fisher, Carrie. Show me a child with a simple, happy, uncomplicated childhood, and I'll show you Dan Quayle. (Chicago Tribune 288:11 Section 1 Oct 15, 90)

Mahe, Edward, Jr. Everything Quayle does—or doesn't do—will reflect on George Bush's judgement. (Newsweek 112:13 Nov 21, 88)

Quayle, Dan. I'm going to be a vice-president very much like George Bush was. (New York 22:49 Mar 13, 89)

Quayle, Dan. You won't see me being the so-called spear carrier for all the so-called conservative issues. (Chicago Tribune 142:10 Section 1 Dec 1, 88)

QUAYLE, MARILYN

Quayle, Marilyn. I believe in creationism. I think the Bible is correct in that. (Chicago Tribune 15:8 Section 5 Jan 15, 89)

QUOTATIONS

Chapman, Robert W. A quotation, like a pun, should come unsought, and then be welcomed only for some propriety or felicity justifying the intrusion (from "The Art of Quotation"). (Writer's Digest 57:11 May 77)

RACE DISCRIMINATION

Carter, James Earl. I can't resign from the human race because there's discrimination, and I don't intend to resign from my own church because there's discrimination. (Time 108:22 Nov 22, 76)

RACE DISCRIMINATION see also RHODESIA—RACE QUESTION; SOUTH AFRICA—RACE QUESTION; UNITED STATES—RACE QUESTION

RACE RELATIONS

Gruber, Jack. Integration is not something you win at, it's something you work at. (Time 110:21 Oct 31, 77)

RADICALISM

Lasch, Christopher. Radicalism in the United States has no great triumphs to record. (Time 110:67 Aug 15, 77)

RADIO BROADCASTING

Newman, Edwin. I believe some silence is helpful to thought. And I believe to some extent radio and television discourage thought and reflection. (Chicago Tribune 1:23 Jan 1, 78)

RAFKO, KAYE LANI RAE

Rafko, Kaye Lani Rae (Miss America). I'm a professional individual. (US 3:6 Nov 2, 87)

RAM DASS

Ram Dass. If I'm saving the whale, why am I

eating tuna fish? (New Times 11:39 Sept 4, 78)

RAND, AYN

Greenspan, Alan. When I met Ayn Rand, I was a free enterpriser in the Adam Smith sense, impressed with the theoretical structure and efficiency of markets. What she did was to make me see that capitalism is not only efficient and practical, but also moral. (Newsweek 85:61 Feb 24, 75)

RAPE

Brownmiller, Susan. It (rape) is nothing more or less than a conscious process of intimidation by which all men keep all women in a state of fear. (Time 106:48 Oct 13, 75)

RARE ANIMALS

Watt, James. We don't have to worry about endangered species—why, we can't even get rid of the cockroach. (Life 5:33 Jan 81)

RATHER, DAN

Rather, Dan. I'm at my relaxed and effective best when I'm reporting stories. (Newsweek 111:17 Feb 1, 88)

RATTIGAN, TERRENCE

Rattigan, Terrence. I could never see why craftsmanship should be equated with insincerity. (The Times 8059:35 Dec 4, 77)

Rattigan, Terrence. What a lovely world we're in, if only we'd let ourselves see it. (Guardian Weekly 117:4 Dec 11, 77)

RAUSCHENBERG, ROBERT

Rauschenberg, Robert. Painting relates to both art and life. I try to act in the gap between the two. (Chicago 26:112 Dec 77)

RAY, MAN

Ray, Man. I would like to go to only one funeral, mine. (Andy Warhol's Interview 7:23 Feb 76)

Ray, Man. The pursuit of liberty and the pursuit of pleasure—that takes care of my whole art. (Newsweek 88:53 Nov 29, 76)

REACTIONARIES

Mao, Tse-Tung. All reactionaries are paper tigers. (Newsweek 88:45 Sept 20, 76)

READING

Lewis, C. S. A young man who wishes to remain a sound atheist cannot be too careful of his reading. God is, if I may say it, very unscrupulous. (New York Times 126:B1 Dec 20, 76)

Puzo, Mario. I find that the only thing that really stands up, better than gambling, better than booze, better than women, is reading. (Time 111:72 June 26, 78)

Warhol, Andy. Movies are the new novels. No one is going to read anymore. Everyone is going to do movies, because movies are easier to do. (Texas Monthly 4:42 Aug 76)

REAGAN, NANCY

Reagan, Nancy. My life began with Ronnie. (Newsweek 86:38 Oct 13, 75)

Reagan, Ronald. As a matter of fact, Nancy never had any interest in politics or anything else when we got married (denying charges that his wife is the real political power in the family). (Rolling Stone 219:19 Aug 12, 76)

REAGAN, RONALD

Brock, Bill. Reagan has this remarkable ability to project decency, a sense of knowing where he is and where he is going. (Time 116:13 July 28, 80)

Bush, George. I'll prevail over Reagan because it is right that I prevail (1980). (New York 13:44 Jan 21, 80)

Carter, James Earl. I cannot think of a single international or diplomatic achievement that's been realized by Ronald Reagan. (Chicago Tribune 273:2 Sept 30, 86)

Carter, James Earl. In trying to brief him on matters of supreme importance, I was very disturbed at his lack of interest (about Ronald Reagan). (Kansas City Times 115:D1 Jan 1, 83)

Derrow, Martin. Ronald Reagan is the prototype American politician of the '70s: mindless, witless, positionless and worthless. (Time 106:4 Dec 15, 75)

Haig, Alexander M. If you knew the true story, it would make your hair stand on end (on President Reagan's illness following the 1981 assassination attempt on his life). (Chicago Tribune 282:27 Oct 9, 87)

Hinckley, John W., Jr. I helped his presidency. After I shot him his polls went up 20 percent (about Ronald Reagan). (Kansas City Times 115:D1 Jan 1, 84)

Kennedy, Edward Moore. I think Mr. Carter has created Ronald Reagan. (The Observer 9856:12 July 20, 80)

MacLaine, Shirley. He (Ronald Reagan) is a true velvet fascist, really smooth. (Chicago Sun-Times 29:12 Feb 17, 76)

Nelson, Jack. I think there is a real contempt for the press within the Reagan Administration, and I think it starts at the top. (Time 128:88 Nov 17, 86)

Novak, Michael. Reagan has done more to help the poor than Carter. (USA Today 2:10A Nov 7, 83)

O'Neill, Thomas P. (Tip). When it comes to giving tax breaks to the wealthy of this country, the President has a heart of gold.

(Life 5:33 Jan 81)

O'Neill, Thomas P.(Tip). I hate to say it about such an agreeable man, but it was sinful that Ronald Reagan ever became president. (University Daily Kansan 98:7B Aug 26, 87)

Reagan, Ronald. A president should never say never. (Life 7:113 Jan 83)

Reagan, Ronald. I always grew up believing that if you build a better mousetrap, the world will beat a path to your door. Now if you build a better mousetrap the government comes along with a better mouse. (Chicago Tribune 323:1 Section 1 Nov 19, 75)

Reagan, Ronald. I do not think it (the Iran arms sale) was a mistake. (Time 128:18 Dec 8, 86)

Reagan, Ronald. I don't resent his (Mikhail Gorbachev) popularity or anything else. Good Lord, I costarred with Errol Flynn once. (Chicago Tribune 342:17 Dec 8, 87)

Reagan, Ronald. I think we took the only action we could have in Iran (1986). (Time 128:18 Dec 8, 86)

Reagan, Ronald. I was not fully informed (about Iran arms sales). (Time 128:16 Dec 8, 86)

Reagan, Ronald. I wasn't a Great Communicator, but I communicated great things. (New York Times 138:8 Jan 12, 89)

Reagan, Ronald. If I were really lucky, I wouldn't have this job. (US 3:64 May 5, 86)

Reagan, Ronald. No policy or decision in my mind has ever been influenced by astrology. (Kansas City Star 108:8c May 4, 88)

Reagan, Ronald. Once you've seen one redwood, you've seen them all. (New York Times Magazine 71 July 4, 76)

Reagan, Ronald. The deficit is big enough to take care of itself. (Newsweek 112:29 Nov 21, 88)

Reagan, Ronald. There ain't no smoking gun (about the Iran Arms-Contra Aid Case). (Newsweek 109:19 June 29, 87)

Reagan, Ronald. Thou shalt not criticize other Republicans. (Time 116:13 July 28, 80)

Sarbanes, Paul. A working man voting for Reagan is like a chicken voting for Colonel Sanders. (Washingtonian 20:328 Nov 84)

Sasser, Jim. He's (Ronald Reagan) become a kindly old relative that you don't have to pay much attention to. He's just run his course (1987). (Newsweek 109:19 June 29, 87)

Smith, Howard K. The trouble with Ronald Reagan is that he thinks the whole world began in Dixon, Illinois. (USA Today 1:2D Jan 3, 83)

Unruh, Jesse. As a Governor, Reagan was better than most Democrats would concede, though not nearly as good as most Republicans like to think. (Time 106:19 Nov 24, 75)

Will, George F. Reagan's policy is detente without intellect. (Time 119:51 April 19, 82)

REAGAN, RONALD—ECONOMIC POLICY

Heller, Walter. Only an ostrich could have missed the contradictions in Reaganomics. (Life 5:33 Jan 82)

Heller, Walter. Waiting for supply-side economics to work is like leaving the landing lights on for Amelia Earhart. (Dun's Business Month 127:51 Feb 86)

Jacob, John. Reaganomics is giving voodoo a bad name. (Lawrence (Kansas) Journal-World 124:5A Nov 7, 82)

REAGAN, RONALD—RELATIONS—LEFT WING POLITICS

Viguerie, Richard. Defunding the Left should be a principal priority of the Reagan administration. (Mother Jones 8:7 Jan 82)

REAGAN, RONALD—STAFF

Adams, Ansel. They (Ronald Reagan's staff) know the cost of everything but the value of nothing. (California 8:54 Sept 83)

Iacocca, Lee A. Don Regan shouldn't be president of the U.S.—and he is. Make no mistake about it. (US 3:17 Sept 22, 86)

REAL ESTATE DEVELOPMENT

Cooper, Alexander. Scratch any real estate developer and you'll find an anarchist. (M 4:73 Mar 87)

Koch, Edward I. Gentrification isn't a dirty word. (Village Voice 31:32 Dec 9, 86)

REAL ESTATE INVESTMENT

Koslow, Ron. What marijuana was to the Sixties, real estate is to the Seventies. (Esquire 93:17 Feb 80)

Sterling, Donald T. Buy it. Improve it. Keep it...forever. (California 14:60 July 89)

REALITY

Baker, Russell. Inanimate objects are classified scientifically into three major categories—those that don't work, those that break down; and those that get lost. (Washingtonian 15:140 Nov 79)

Cohodas, Howard L. If it looks too good to be true, it is too good to be true. (Washingtonian 15:151 Nov 79)

De Vries, Peter. Reality is impossible to take neat, we must dilute it with alcohol. (Writer's Digest 58:29 Oct 78)

Giono, Jean. Reality pushed to its extreme ends in unreality. (Village Voice 21:93

Sept 27, 76)

Orlans, Harold. Logic is a game men play as cats play with balls of string, whereas reality is a game the gods play with us. (Change 9:34 April 77)

Waits, Tom. Reality is for those who can't face drugs. (Playboy 26:26 Oct 79)

Wyeth, Andrew. True reality goes beyond reality itself. (Christian Science Monitor 70:24 Sept 28, 78)

REASON

Fink, Stanley. There are times when reasonable people come to no solution. (New York 10:9 July 25, 77)

REDDY, HELEN

Wald, Jeffrey. I don't think I made her a star. I know I did (about Helen Reddy). (People Weekly 3:64 May 12, 75)

REDFORD, ROBERT

Fonda, Jane. (Robert Redford) is, and remains, a bourgeois in the worst sense of the word. (Chicago Tribune 314:28 Nov 10, 77)

Newman, Paul. He makes the Sphinx look like a blabber-mouth (about Robert Redford). (Newsweek 103:75 May 28, 84)

Redford, Robert. Health food may be good for the conscience, but Oreos taste a hell of a lot better. (Chicago Tribune 27:12 Jan 27, 78)

Redford, Robert. I spent most of my life feeling like an academic failure—largely because I was. (US 3:4 Mar 23, 87)

Redford, Robert. I've always had a very low regard for cynicism; I think it is the beginning of dying. (Time 107:55 Mar 29, 76)

REED, LOU

Reed, Lou. I'm like an Elvis Presley with brains, or Bob Dylan with looks. (Time 111:79 April 24, 78)

REEVE, CHRISTOPHER

Reeve, Christopher. Women keep asking me if I really am Superman. My reply to them is, 'only if you're Lois Lane'. (W 7:33 Nov 10, 78)

REFORM

Carter, James Earl. I think the President is the only person who can change the direction or attitude of our nation. (Encore American & Worldwide News 5:4 June 21, 76)

REFUGEES, VIETNAMESE

Hung, Tran Van (Vietnamese refugee). We are shrubs, planted in a new place, needing care and water to grow again. (Newsweek 94:52 July 2, 79)

REGAN, DON

Iacocca, Lee A. Don Regan shouldn't be president of the U.S.—and he is. Make no mistake about it. (US 3:17 Sept 22, 86)

REGULATION

Emery, Fred J. Regulation is the substitution of error for chance. (Washingtonian 15:141 Nov 79)

RELATIVITY THEORY

Einstein, Albert. Sit with a pretty girl for an hour, and it seems like a minute; sit on a hot stove for a minute, and it seems like an hour—that's relativity. (Rocky Mountain News 235:104 Dec 13, 79)

RELIGION

Fairlie, Henry. Where there is no theology, there is no religion. (Chicago Tribune 123:3 May 3, 87)

Hubbard, L. Ron. If a man really wants to make a million dollars, the best way would be to start his own religion. (Time 127:86 Feb 10, 86)

Lance, Thomas Bertram. Folks are serious about three things—their religion, their family, and most of all, their money. (Time 108:20 Dec 6, 76)

McCarthy, Mary. It really takes a hero to live any kind of spiritual life without religious belief. (The Observer 9816:35 Oct 14, 79)

Pannenberg, Wolfhart. The greatest deception (of our era is the idea that) political change can satisfy a religious need. (Time 107:65 Mar 8, 76)

Schuller, Robert. The church is in the business of retailing religion. (Time 105:38 Feb 24, 75)

Shaffer, Floyd. I believe it would be healthier if the church could laugh because I believe that God laughs. (Newsweek 86:64 Sept 29, 75)

White, Theodore. Politics in America is the binding secular religion. (Firing Line 5 July 26, 75)

Zappa, Frank. A wise man once said that the only difference between a cult and a religion is the amount of real estate they own. (National Catholic Reporter 23:10 Aug 14, 87)

RELIGION see also ATHEISM; CARTER, JAMES EARL—RELATIONS—RELIGION

RELIGION—UNITED STATES

Fairlie, Henry. Religion in America leaves me, especially a European, with the impression that in place of churches there are only Do-It-Yourself God Kits. (Chicago Tribune 123:3 May 3, 87)

REPORTERS AND REPORTING

Wicker, Tom. A reporter should write and his newspaper should print what they know. (Texas Observer 70:9 April 28, 78)

REPUBLICAN PARTY

Anderson, John B. We (Republicans) are a staid and proper bunch. (Rolling Stone 315:48 April 17, 80)

Atwater, Harvey Lee. I really had two goals in life: one, to manage a presidential campaign, and to be chairman of my party. (New York Times 138:9 Nov 18, 88)

Brock, Bill. This (Republican) party is a new party—we are on our way up (1980). (Time 116:10 July 28, 80)

Brown, Ron. It is disingenuous for the people who ran the Willie Horton ads to express shock and dismay over David Duke. (Time 133:29 Mar 6, 89)

Carter, James Earl. (Republicans are) men of narrow vision who are afraid of the future and whose leaders are inclined to shoot from the hip. (Time 116:13 July 28, 80)

Dolan, Terry. The Republican Party is a fraud. It's a social club where rich people go to pick their noses. (Time 114:21 Aug 20, 79)

Dole, Robert J. A Republican has to have a sense of humor because there are so few of us. (Time 108:26 Aug 30, 76)

Dole, Robert J. With all respect, Connally, Goldwater and Rockefeller are great men but they don't indicate any forward thrust in our party. We've got to start building from the bottom up instead of the top down. (Time 108:30 Aug 30, 76)

Duke, David. I feel more comfortable in the Republican Party. (Time 133:29 Mar 6, 89)

Fitzhugh, Gilbert W. The Republicans fight like cats and go home and sulk. The Democrats fight like cats, and suddenly there are more cats. (Time 107:11 Aug 23, 76)

From, Al. The Republicans win when they draw the line between the poor and the rest of us. The Democrats win when we draw the line between the rich and the rest of us. (New York Times 138:15 Feb 19, 89)

Goldwater, Barry Morris. I don't care if I'm called a Democrat or a Republican as long as I'm in bed with people of the same thinking. (Rolling Stone 227:43 Dec 2, 76)

McCarthy, Eugene Joseph. The Republican Party is a lower form of plant life, like moss on a rock. It has very low vitality—green in the summer, slightly gray in the winter— but it never dies. If the Republicans had any decency, they'd just go away. (New York Times Magazine 13 Oct 24, 76)

Reagan, Ronald. Thou shalt not criticize other Republicans. (Time 116:13 July 28, 80)

Reagan, Ronald. We made the Republican Party into the party of the working people, the family, the neighborhood, the defense of freedom, and, yes, the American flag

and the Pledge of Allegiance. (Chicago Tribune 290:3 Section 4 Oct 16, 88)

Scammon, Richard. There's nothing wrong with the Republican Party that double-digit inflation won't cure. (Guardian Weekly 119:17 Nov 12, 78)

Scott, Ulric. An Independent-Republican is an elephant that is trying to forget. (Time 106:8 Dec 1, 75)

Stevenson, Adlai, II. I have been tempted to make a proposal to our Republican friends: that if they stop telling lies about us, we would stop telling the truth about them. (Human Behavior 7:68 May 78)

RESEARCH

Trachtenberg, Stephen. The truth is that 80 percent of research is done by 20 percent of professors who are at 10 percent of our universities. (Chicago Tribune 110:10 April 20, 87)

RESPECTABILITY

Buchan, Alastair. Respectability depends on whose side you're on. To the Turks, Lawrence of Arabia was a terrorist. (Time 104:44 Nov 25, 74)

RESTAURANTS

Algren, Nelson. Never eat at a place called Mom's. Never play cards with a man named Doc. And never lie down with a woman who's got more troubles than you. (Washingtonian 14:152 Nov 78)

Child, Julia. I just hate health food. (San Francisco 25:32 Aug 83)

RESTAURANTS—CHINA (PEOPLE'S REPUBLIC)

Cardin, Pierre. If I can put a Maxim's in Peking, I can put a Maxim's on the moon. (Life 7:142 Jan 83)

RESTAURANTS—FRANCHISE SYSTEM

Anonymous. We do it all for you (McDonald's jingle). (Life 2:86 Dec 79)

RETIREMENT

Agnelli, Giovanni. At twenty, it would be fun to retire. It's silly at sixty. At sixty, what can you do anymore? (Esquire 89:38 June 20, 78)

Burns, George. Now, they say, you should retire at 70. When I was 70 I still had pimples. (Time 112:69 Aug 7, 78)

Niven, David. Actors don't retire, they just get offered fewer parts. (W 6:18 July 8, 77)

REUBEN, DON

Nader, Ralph. No lawyer in any other city is treated with such awe and fear as Don Reuben is treated in the city of Chicago. (Chicago 31:107 Feb 82)

REVENGE

Fortas, Abe. The law of revenge has its roots in the deep recesses of the human spirit, but that is not a permissible reason for retaining capital punishment. (New York Times Magazine 9 Jan 23, 77)

REVOLUTIONISTS

Sinclair, John. You can't make a revolution if you have to make a living. (Newsweek 90:26 Sept 5, 77)

REVOLUTIONISTS, CAMBODIAN

Norodom Sihanouk, King Of Cambodia (Abdicated 1955). When they no longer need me, they will spit me out like a cherry pit (about the Khmer Rouge). (Time 106:38 Sept 22, 75)

REVOLUTIONS

Bella, Ben. It is an illusion to think you can have a revolution without prisons. (New York Times 128:3 Section 4 July 8, 79)

Castro, Fidel. I do not believe that revolution is an exportable item. (Newsweek 103:38 Jan 9, 84)

Kennedy, John Fitzgerald (attributed by David Reckford). Those who make peaceful revolution impossible make violent revolution inevitable. (The Observer 9785:13 Mar 11, 79)

Levy, Bernard-Henri. The only successful revolution of this century is totalitarianism. (Time 110:29 Sept 12, 77)

Mao, Tse-Tung. Revolution is a drama of passion. We did not win the People over by appealing to reason but by developing hope, trust, fraternity. (Time 108:41 Sept 20, 76)

Marcos, Ferdinand E. It is easier to run a revolution than a government. (Time 107:35 June 6, 77)

Marley, Bob. It takes a revolution to make a solution. (To the Point International 4:17 Sept 12, 77)

Sinclair, John. You can't make a revolution if you have to make a living. (Newsweek 90:26 Sept 5, 77)

REVOLUTIONS—AFGHANISTAN

Rahim, Abdur. The war (in Afghanistan) is like a good love affair. All the action happens at night. (Time 113:44 May 14, 79)

REVSON, CHARLES

Revson, Charles. I don't meet competition. I crush it. (Duns Business Month 127:51 Feb 86)

REWARDS, PRIZES, ETC.

Snow, C. P. Money is not so important as a pat on the head. (The Observer 9723:11 Dec 18, 77)

REYNOLDS, BURT

Reynolds, Burt. I'm trying very subtly and subliminally to ease myself away from Billy Clyde Puckett and toward Cary Grant. I may be the most unsophisticated Cary Grant in 20 years, but I'm going to get there. (Time 111:54 Jan 9, 78)

RHODESIA see also ZIMBABWE

RHODESIA—POLITICS AND GOVERNMENT

Kaunda, Kenneth. A new Zimbabwe (Rhodesia) can only be born out of the barrel of a gun. (Time 110:30 July 18, 77)

Nkomo, Joshua. I do not think the British know what genuine majority rule is. (The Observer 9806:10 Aug 5, 79)

Smith, Ian Douglas. I do not believe in black majority rule in Rhodesia—not in a thousand years. (People Weekly 5:45 June 7, 76)

Smith, Ian Douglas. I have got to admit that things haven't gone quite the way I wanted (1979). (The Observer 9797:10 June 3, 79)

RHODESIA—RACE QUESTION

Nyerere, Julius Kamberage. South Africa is no different from Rhodesia. The struggle by blacks in both countries is exactly the same—for majority rule. So what happens in Rhodesia will happen in South Africa. (People Weekly 6:40 Dec 27/Jan 3, 77)

Smith, Ian Douglas. I do not believe in black majority rule in Rhodesia—not in a thousand years. (People Weekly 5:45 June 7, 76)

RHYS, JEAN

Rhys, Jean. If you want to write the truth, you must write about yourself. (Newsweek 93:103 May 28, 79)

RICE, DONNA

Hart, Gary. It was a bad mistake. It was a damn fool mistake. But I don't think it disqualifies me from governing this country (about Donna Rice). (Chicago Tribune 6:15 Jan 6, 88)

Rice, Donna. I am not a party girl. (Washington Post National Weekly 5:9 Jan 4, 88)

RICH

Baltzell, Edward Digby, Jr. I believe in inherited wealth. Society needs to have some people who are above it all. (Town & Country 132:97 July 78)

Churchill, Sir Winston. You don't make the poor richer by making the rich poorer. (To The Point International 3:39 Nov 1, 76)

Gill, Brendan. The rich have no need to pronounce words correctly. They can leave all that to their lawyers and accountants. (Andy Warhol's Interview 8:60 Dec 78)

Harris, Fred. The basic issue in 1976 is privilege. It's time to take the rich off welfare. (Newsweek 86:24 Dec 22, 75)

MacArthur, John D. Anybody who knows what he's worth, isn't worth very much (upon being asked how much he was worth). (Chicago Tribune 340:2 Section 1

Dec 5, 76)

Poirot, Paul L. Multiplying wealth is by far the fastest way to help the poor. Dividing the wealth and subsidizing poverty is the fastest way to starve everyone. (American Opinion 18:29 Nov 75)

Shor, Toots. I don't want to be a millionaire, I just want to live like one. (New York Times 126:36 Jan 25, 77)

RICH see also GETTY, JEAN PAUL; MACARTHUR, JOHN D.; MILLIONAIRES; ROTHSCHILD, MARIE-HELENE DE

RICH, FRANK

Mamet, David. Frank Rich and John Simon are the syphilis and gonorrhea of the theater. (Newsweek 107:13 Feb 17, 86)

RICH—POLITICAL ACTIVITY

Corkey, P. J. The rich used to give us libraries, museums, universities. Now they give us themselves. (Kansas City Times 119:A-1 Oct 3, 86)

RICH—SEXUAL BEHAVIOR

Brando, Marlon. If you're rich and famous you don't have any trouble getting laid. (Players 3:32 Feb 77)

RICHARD, KEITH

Jagger, Mick. Keith and I are two of the nicest people we know. (Creem 10:55 Jan 78)

RICKOVER, HYMAN GEORGE

Rickover, Hyman G. I never start to like a man until I tell him off three or four times a day. (People Weekly 7:36 June 20, 77)

RIGHT AND WRONG

Royster, Vermont. When things go wrong somewhere, they are apt to go wrong everywhere. (Washingtonian 14:155 Nov 78)

RIGHT TO LIFE (MOVEMENT)

Frank, Barney. The anti-abortionists believe that the right to life begins at conception—and ends at birth. (Boston 73:13 Dec 81)

RIMBAUD, ARTHUR

Rimbaud, Arthur. My greatest fear is that people will see me as I see them. (Newsweek 83:103 Mar 25, 74)

RIOTS

Johnson, Lyndon Baines. Killing, rioting, and looting are contrary to the best traditions of this country. (Texas Monthly 3:93 Dec 75)

RIVERA, DIEGO

Rivera, Diego. I have never believed in God, but I believe in Picasso. (Connoisseur 214:28 Mar 84)

RIZZO, FRANK LAZZARO

Rizzo, Frank Lazzaro. I get confused about figures over 100. (Chicago Tribune 306:5 Nov 2, 86)

Rizzo, Frank Lazzaro. When I see the American flag, my blood still runs cold. (New York Times 128:29 Section 2 Jan 21, 79)

ROBBERY

Sutton, Willie. I always figured that being a good robber was like being a good lawyer. (Village Voice 21:118 Sept 13, 76)

ROBBINS, HAROLD

Robbins, Harold. I'm the best novelist in the world. (Book Digest 7:22 Aug 80)

ROBERTSON, PAT

Graham, Billy. When you say that you pray and stop a hurricane, a few things like that, it gives the press something to distort (on Pat Robertson). (Newsweek 108:23 Oct 13, 86)

Robertson, Pat. When I pray, I get answers. (Newsweek 108:13 Aug 25, 86)

ROBINSON, FRANK

Robinson, Frank. It's nice to come into town and be referred to as the manager of the Cleveland Indians instead of as the first black manager. (Sepia 26:10 Jan 75)

ROBINSON, JACKIE

Kahn, Roger. His (Jackie Robinson) race was humanity, and he did a great deal for us. (TV Guide 25:14 Aug 6, 77)

ROBINSON, JOAN

Robinson, Joan. I am an optimist by temperament, but a pessimist by intellect. (Time 122:74 Aug 22, 83)

ROCKEFELLER FAMILY

Rockefeller, David. Although I work downtown, my family does have something of a stake in a small parcel of land which abuts Fifth Avenue (commenting on Rockefeller Center and his ties to the Fifth Avenue area in New York City). (New York Times 126:A13 Oct 22, 76)

Rockefeller, Nelson Aldrich. Being a Rockefeller is like living in a goldfish bowl. The goldfish get used to it and so do we. (New York Times 128:26 Jan 28, 79)

ROCKEFELLER, JOHN DAVISON, III

Rockefeller, John Davison III (attributed by an aide). I am too rich to steal. (Time 110:81 Oct 24, 77)

Rockefeller, John Davison, III. I don't have a whole lot of faith in what the oil companies say. (Time 114:61 July 16, 79)

ROCKEFELLER, NELSON ALDRICH

Kissinger, Henry Alfred. Nelson Rockefeller was the greatest American I have ever known. (Newsweek 93:27 Feb 5, 79)

ROCKNE, KNUTE

Rockne, Knute. You show me a good and gracious loser, and I'll show you a failure! (Argosy 384:15 Nov 76)

RODGERS, RICHARD

Martin, Mary. He's (Richard Rodgers) the one person I will never, never wash out of my hair. (New York Times 128:C15 Dec 4, 78)

Rodgers, Richard. When the lyrics are right, it's easier for me to write a tune than to bend over and tie my shoelaces. (Time 115:83 Jan 14, 80)

ROLLING STONES (MUSICAL GROUP)

Jagger, Mick. We will probably be making albums until we enter some sort of future senior-citizens facility. (Time 118:61 Sept 7, 81)

ROLLINS, SONNY

Occhiogrosso, Peter. Sonny Rollins is the Vladimir Nabokov of the tenor saxophone. (Soho Weekly News 6:27 Nov 2, 78)

ROMANCE

Dubus, Andre. Romance dies hard, because its very nature is to want to live. (Boston 69:236 Dec 77)

Parker, Charlie. Romance without finance ain't got no chance. (The Animator 4:1 Fall 76)

Russell, Bertrand. I believe myself that romantic love is the source of the most intense delights that life has to offer. (Chicago Tribune 212:1 Section 2 July 31, 78)

Viorst, Judith. Brevity may be the soul of wit, but not when someone's saying 'I love you'. (Chicago Tribune 176:2 Section 2 June 25, 78)

ROME

Lebowitz, Fran. Rome is a very loony city in every respect. One needs but spend an hour or two there to realize that Fellini makes documentaries. (Andy Warhol's Interview 7:46 July 75)

RONSTADT, LINDA

Ronstadt, Linda. I'm so disorganized, what I really need is a good wife. (People Weekly 4:54 Nov 17, 75)

ROOSEVELT, FRANKLIN DELANO

Marshall, Throgood. I don't think (he) (Franklin D. Roosevelt) did much for the Negro. (Newsweek 110:21 Sept 21, 87)

Roosevelt, Franklin Delano. Our true destiny is not to be ministered unto but to minister to ourselves and to our fellow men (inaugural address—1933). (Christian Science Monitor 69:14 Jan 20, 77)

Rossiter, Clinton. The essence of (Franklin) Roosevelt's Presidency was his airy eagerness to meet the age head on. (Time 114:11 July 16, 79)

ROREM, NED

Rorem, Ned. I do my very best to say mean things about Beethoven. (Philadelphia 79:89 May 88)

Rorem, Ned. I have suffered far less from being a homosexual than I have from being a composer. (People Weekly 10:40 Aug 21, 78)

ROSE, BILLY

Rose, Billy. Sun is for apricots and exercise is for horses. (Food & Wine 10:64 Feb 87)

ROSE, PETE

Rose, Pete. I'd be willing to bet you, if I was a betting man, that I have never bet on baseball. (Time 133:85 April 3, 89)

ROSENBERG, JACK see ERHARD, WERNER

ROSSNER, JUDITH

Rossner, Judith. What is going on in my typewriter is going on in my life. (Life 6:30 Oct 83)

ROSTROPOVICH, MSTISLAV

Ozawa, Seiji. Slava (Mstislav Rostropovich) doesn't interpret, he feels. His music is really his character. He is conducting his life. (Time 110:84 Oct 24, 77)

Rostropovich, Mstislav. When I play for an audience, I feel that I am making my confession to those people. (New York Times Magazine 66 April 18, 76)

ROTHSCHILD, MARIE-HELEN DE

Rothschild, Marie-Helene De. I'm not a bit ashamed of being rich. I think it's very healthy to have big parties now and again, like they did in history. (Time 105:48 June 9, 75)

ROWEN, PHYLLIS

Rowen, Phyllis. When you grow as a designer, you realize that nothing is forever. (Architectural Digest 32:122 Nov 75)

ROWSE, A. L.

Rowse, A. L. I've always thought of myself as a parallel to D.H. Lawrence. (The Times 8062:35 Jan 1, 78)

RUBIN, JERRY

Rubin, Jerry. I'm famous. That's my job. (Christian Science Monitor 68:30 April 26, 76)

RUBINSTEIN, ARTUR

Rubinstein, Artur. I'm not a drug fiend, I'm not a drunkard, but I am the laziest man I ever met. (Time 105:39 Feb 10, 75)

Rubinstein, Artur. To get as old as I am (91) one must drink a glass of whiskey every morning, smoke a long cigar and chase beautiful girls. (People Weekly 10:144 Nov 20, 78)

RUCKLESHAUS, JILL

Ruckelshaus, Jill. It occurred to me when I was 13 and wearing white gloves and Mary Janes and going to dancing school, that no one should have to dance backwards all their lives. (Chicago Sun-Times 30:21 Jan 28, 78)

RULES

Faber, Harold. If there isn't a law, there will be. (Book Digest 6:32 Dec 79)

Jackson, Jack. No rule is ever so good, or so well written, or covers so many contingencies, that it can't be replaced by another, much better, more appropriate rule (with the exception of this rule). (Washingtonian 14:26 Dec 78)

Pitman, Keith A. All generalizations are untrue. (Washingtonian 14:26 Dec 78)

RUNNING

Sheehan, George A. To know running is to know life. (New York Times Book Review 30 Dec 3, 78)

RUSHDIE, SALMAN

Khomeini, Ayatollah Ruhollah. Even if Salman Rushdie repents and becomes the most pious man of all time, it is incumbent on every Moslem to employ everything he's got, his life and wealth, to send him to hell. (Chicago Tribune 57:3 Section 4 Feb 26, 89)

RUSHDIE, SALMAN. THE SATANIC VERSES

Rushdie, Salman. The Satanic Verses is not, in my view, an antireligious novel. (Chicago Tribune 57:3 Section 4 Feb 26, 89)

RUSSELL, ROSALIND

Russell, Rosalind. Flops are a part of life's menu, and I'm never a girl to miss out on any of the courses. (Time 108:102 Dec 13, 76)

RUSSIA

Buchwald, Art. The day you leave Russia is the happiest day of your life. (Book Digest 4:30 Sept 77)

Churchill, Sir Winston. Russia is a riddle wrapped in an enigma. (Village Voice 22:77 Nov 28, 77)

RUSSIA see also LABOR AND LABORING CLASSES—RUSSIA; WORK—RUSSIA

RUSSIA—DESCRIPTION

Greene, Graham. There is far more religious faith in Russia than in England. (The Observer 9850:13 June 8, 80)

Solzhenitsyn, Aleksandr Isaevich. For us in Russia Communism is a dead dog, while for many people in the West it is still a living lion. (The Observer 9782:10 Mar 18, 79)

Toon, Malcolm (United States Ambassador to Russia). I am not in a position to explain why the Soviets have or have not done certain things. I have never been able to explain what makes them tick. (People Weekly 6:34 Dec 13, 76)

Vidor, King. I don't think one can sum up Russia in one word, but 'grim' might do. (W 8:12 Oct 12, 79)

Voronel, Nina. Soviet life is so absurd that when I write realistically, it becomes the theatre of the absurd. (New York Times 125:28 Nov 7, 75)

RUSSIA—ECONOMIC CONDITIONS

Khrushchev, Nikita Sergeevich. Call it what you will, incentives are the only way to make people work harder (responding to a charge that the Soviet Union was becoming capitalist). (Time 106:63 July 14, 75)

RUSSIA—ECONOMIC POLICY

Tanner, Jack. Nothing could discredit capitalism more than a decision by the Russians to try it. (Challenge 19:4 Mar/April 76)

RUSSIA—FOREIGN POLICY

Yew, Lee Kuan. The Russians say that there are many different roads to socialism, and that sounds good to new nations. But the United States seems to be saying that there is only one road to democracy. (American Legion Magazine 103:12 Aug 77)

RUSSIA—FOREIGN POLICY—UNITED STATES

Brezhnev, Leonid I. Building Detente requires no little political courage. (Newsweek 93:41 Jan 22, 79)

RUSSIA—FOREIGN RELATIONS—EUROPE, EASTERN

Ford, Gerald Rudolph. There is no Soviet domination of Eastern Europe and there never will be under a Ford Administration. (Chicago Sun-Times 29:2 Oct 8, 76)

RUSSIA—FOREIGN RELATIONS—MIDDLE EAST

Kissinger, Henry Alfred. All the Russians can offer is war, but we can bring the peace (commenting on the Mideast situation). (Time 109:16 Jan 24, 77)

RUSSIA—FOREIGN RELATIONS—UNITED STATES

Noonan, Peggy. It's disorienting because it's hard to know who to assign the evil role to. (Chicago Tribune 47:19 Feb 16, 90)

Toon, Malcolm (United States Ambassador to Russia). I am not in a position to explain why the Soviets have or have not done certain things. I have never been able to explain what makes them tick. (People Weekly 6:34 Dec 13, 76)

RUSSIA—MILITARY POLICY

Aron, Raymond. There is only one field in which the Soviet Union is successful: the projection of its military power throughout the world. (US News & World Report 85:67 Nov 27, 78)

Brown, Harold. (Russia) has shown no response to U.S. restraint—when we

build, they build; when we cut, they build.
(Newsweek 93:104 June 25, 79)

Solzhenitsyn, Aleksandr Isaevich. The
Soviet Union's economy is on such a war
footing that even if it were the unanimous
opinion of all members of the Politburo
not to start a war, this would no longer be
in their power. (New York Times 125:26
Mar 3, 76)

RUSSIA—POLITICS AND GOVERNMENT

Arafat, Yasir. The Russian bear is thirsty and
he sees the water. (The Observer 9833:9
Feb 10, 80)

Ginzburg, Alexander. The Russian (people)
do not believe in Communism. (US News
& World Report 86:17 June 18, 79)

Gorbachev, Mikhail S. It is only now that the
real Perestroika begins (1990). (Time
135:29-30 Feb 19, 90)

Gorbachev, Mikhail S. The guilt of Stalin and
his immediate entourage before the party
and the people for the wholesale
repressive measures and the acts of
lawlessness is enormous and
unforgivable. This is a message for all
generations. (Kansas City Star 5C Nov 2,
87) (108)

Kendall, Donald M. If we can get the Soviet
people to enjoy good consumer goods,
they'll never be able to do without them
again. (Chicago Tribune 99:3 Section 1
April 9, 90)

Solzhenitsyn, Aleksandr Isaevich. When
changes occur in the Soviet regime, the
whole orbit of life on earth will change.
(The Observer 9783:11 Feb 25, 79)

Teng, Hsiao-Ping. You can sign all the
treaties you want, but you cannot trust the
Russians. (Chicago Tribune 38:3 Section
3 Feb 7, 79)

RUSSIA—RACE QUESTION

Young, Andrew. The Russians are the worst
racists in the world. (Life 2:117 Dec 79)

RUSSIANS

Ginzburg, Alexander. The Russian (people)
do not believe in Communism. (US News
& World Report 86:17 June 18, 79)

RYAN, NOLAN

Lopes, Davey. If he ain't struck you out, you
ain't nobody (about Nolan Ryan). (Time
134:70 Sept 4, 89)

SADAT, ANWAR

Assad, Hafez. Sadat is a traitor to his own
people and the Arab nation. (Newsweek
93:25 April 2, 79)

Kissinger, Henry Alfred. Sadat is the
greatest (statesman) since Bismarck.
(Esquire 91:30 Jan 30, 79)

Sadat, Anwar. No one ever knows what I am
thinking, not even my own family. I go
alone. (Time 111:22 Jan 2, 78)

SAFETY

Thurber, James. There is no safety in
numbers, or in anything else.
(Washingtonian 14:155 Nov 78)

SAFIRE, WILLIAM

Safire, William. My business (is) writing
informed polemics—with a satisfying zap.
(Newsweek 93:94 April 23, 79)

SAHL, MORT

Sahl, Mort. The more you stay the same, the
more they say you've changed.
(Newsweek 92:16 Dec 11, 78)

SAINTS

Marty, Martin E. A saint has to be a misfit. A
person who embodies what his culture
considers typical or normal cannot be
exemplary. (Time 106:48 Dec 29, 75)

SAINTS see also PAUL, SAINT; SETON,
ELIZABETH, SAINT

SAKHAROV, ANDREI DMITRIEVICH

Gorbachev, Mikhail S. It is now clear that he
deserved the Nobel Prize (about Andrei
Sakharov). (Chicago Tribune 341:14
Section 1 Dec 19, 89)

Le Carre, John. He (Andrei Sakharov) really
has contributed to a change in history.
(New York Times 138:15 May 22, 89)

Sakharov, Andrei Dmitrievich. I hope this
prize is not only an acknowledgment of
my personal merits, but of the merits of all
those who fight for human rights
(commenting on his Nobel Peace Prize).
(People Weekly 4:26 Oct 27, 75)

SALINGER, J. D.

Salinger, J. D. Some of my best friends are
children. In fact, all of my best friends are
children. (Washington Star 323:1 Section
D Nov 19, 78)

SALVATION

Hellman, Lillian. I don't understand personal
salvation. It seems to me a vain idea.
(Rolling Stone 233:55 Feb 24, 77)

SAN ANTONIO, TEXAS

Greenberg, Mike. Half of San Antonio's
population is of Mexican descent; the
other half just eats that way. (Chicago
24:112 Sept 75)

SAN FRANCISCO

Graham, Bill. San Francisco is not a part of
America. (Chicago Daily News Panorama
4 Dec 31, 21)

SAROYAN, WILLIAM

Saroyan, William. I would rather write, even
pompously, than celebrate
meaninglessness. (New York Times Book
Review 20 July 15, 79)

SASSOON, VIDAL

Sassoon, Vidal. I call myself a lucky barber.
(The Observer 9786:10 Mar 18, 79)

SATIRE

Kaufman, George. Satire is what closes Saturday night. (Time 107:72 Feb 2, 76)

Lehrer, Tom. When Henry Kissinger can get the Nobel Peace Prize, what is there left for satire? (Chicago Sun-Times 33:76 July 9, 80)

Trudeau, Garry. Satire has nothing to do with equal time. (Chicago Tribune 328:5 Section 13 Nov 24, 85)

SAUDI ARABIA—POLITICS AND GOVERNMENT

Bani-Assadi, Hossein. Islam has no kings. (New York Times 128:12 Feb 25, 79)

Feisal, King of Saudi Arabia. If anyone feels wrongly treated, he has only himself to blame for not telling me. What higher democracy can there be. (Time 105:22 April 7, 75)

SAVALAS, TELLY

Savalas, Telly. I am a loud, extraverted friendly person, but never rude. (Time 107:38 June 28, 76)

SAVINGS AND LOAN ASSOCIATIONS

Bush, Neil. I sleep soundly at night knowing I live an honest life. (Chicago Tribune 207:21 July 26, 90)

SCHEER, ROBERT

Scheer, Robert. The journalist's job is to get the story by breaking into their offices, by bribing, by seducing people, by lying, by anything else to break through that palace guard. (Time 107:56 April 4, 77)

SCHMIDT, HELMUT

Scheuch, Erwin. (Helmut) Schmidt is an above-average average German. (Time 113:32 June 11, 79)

SCHNEIDERMAN, DAVID

Schneiderman, David. I belong to the (Rupert) Murdoch school of journalism, er, business: When you have an idea and think you are on to something, go for it. (Washington Journalism Review 9:14 Jan/Feb 87)

SCHOOL CHILDREN— TRANSPORTATION FOR INTEGRATION

Clark, Kenneth. Integration is a painful job. It is social therapy, and like personal therapy it is not easy. (Time 106:14 Sept 22, 75)

SCHORR, DANIEL

Schorr, Daniel. The joys of martyrdom are considerably overrated. (Time 107:62 Mar 8, 76)

Schorr, Daniel. To betray a source would be to betray myself, my career and my life. I cannot do it (commenting in his testimony before the Pike committee). (Time 108:76 Oct 11, 76)

SCHRADER, PAUL

Schrader, Paul. I like to fire a movie like a bullet. Then I stay with it until it hits its target. (Chicago Sun-Times 31:1 Section 3 Mar 12, 78)

SCHROEDER, PATRICIA

Schroeder, Patricia. I am a fiscally conservative liberal. (Newsweek 110:76 Aug 17, 87)

SCHUMACHER, ERNST F.

Schumacher, Ernst F. People always called me a crank, but I didn't carry any resentment about that because it is an excellent thing, a crank. It is not expensive, it is relatively nonviolent, and it causes revolutions. (Christian Science Monitor 69:1 June 27, 77)

SCHUMAN, WILLIAM

Schuman, William. In my own music, I'm alone, absolutely alone. (New York Times 129:19 Section D Aug 3, 80)

SCIENCE

Alves, Reuben. Science is what it is, not what scientists think they do. (New York Times 128:A8 July 13, 79)

Bragg, W. L. The essence of science lies not in discovering facts but in discovering new ways of thinking about them. (Omni 1:29 April 79)

Clarke, Arthur C. When a distinguished but elderly scientist says that something is possible he is almost certainly right. When he says it is impossible, he is very probably wrong. (Omni 2:82 April 80)

Whitehead, Alfred North. The aims of scientific thought are to see the general in the particular and the eternal in the transitory. (Omni 2:41 Nov 79)

SCIENCE FICTION

Le Guin, Ursula. If science fiction becomes respectable, it may die. (Newsweek 86:74 Dec 22, 75)

Sturgeon, Theodore. Ninety percent of science fiction is crud. But then, 90 percent of everything is crud. (Kansas City Star 114:1A Dec 30, 81)

SCIENCE—RESEARCH

Einstein, Albert. When a man after long years of searching chances upon a thought which discloses something of the beauty of this mysterious universe, he should not therefore be personally celebrated. He is already sufficiently paid by his experience of seeking and finding. (New York Times 128:18 Section 4 Nov 10, 78)

SCIENTISTS

Eysenck, H. J. Scientists, especially when they leave the particular field in which they have specialized, are just as ordinary, pig-headed and unreasonable as anybody else. (Omni 2:49 Dec 79)

Snow, C. P. Literary intellectuals at one pole—at the other, scientists...Between the two a gulf of mutual incomprehension. (Omni 1:39 Mar 79)

Varese, Edgar. Scientists are the poets of today. (Artspace 9:30 Fall 85)

SCIENTISTS see also EINSTEIN, ALBERT

SCREW (PERIODICAL)

Dershowitz, Alan M. Screw is a despicable magazine, but that's what the First Amendment was designed to protect. (Newsweek 90:53 Nov 7, 77)

SCULPTURE

Moore, Henry. Looking at sculpture teaches people to use their inborn sense of form, to improve their own surroundings, to make life marvelous. (Chicago Tribune 237:1 Section 3 Aug 25, 78)

Moore, Henry. Sculpture should always at first sight have some obscurities and further meanings. People should want to go on looking and thinking. (Mankind 6:43 May 78)

Oldenburg, Claes. To give birth to form is the only act of man that has any consequence. (Chicago 25:18 Nov 76)

SECRECY IN GOVERNMENT see OFFICIAL SECRETS

SECRET SERVICE—UNITED STATES

Moore, George C. No, we never gave it a thought (in response to whether the FBI had ever discussed the constitutional or legal authority for its Cointelpro Program). (New York Times 125:1 Section 4 May 2, 76)

SECRETS

Le Carre, John. People are very secretive creatures—secret even from themselves. (The Observer 9833:9 Feb 10, 80)

Seale, Bobby. Those who know don't talk; and those who talk don't know. (New York Times Magazine 53 Nov 20, 77)

SECURITY (PSYCHOLOGY)

Greer, Germaine. Security is when everything is settled, when nothing can happen to you; security is a denial of life. (Redbook 148:57 Mar 77)

Herzberg, Donald. Never leave hold of what you've got until you've got hold of something else. (Washingtonian 14:155 Nov 78)

Rinfret, Pierre A. Consensus is the security blanket of the insecure. (Challenge 19:42 May 76)

SEGREGATION

Thurmond, Strom. There are not enough laws on the books of the nation, nor can there be enough laws, to break down segregation in the South (commenting in 1948 as he accepted the presidential nomination of the Dixiecrat Party). (Washington Post 264:A3 Aug 27, 77)

SEGREGATION see also CHURCH ATTENDANCE—SEGREGATION; PUBLIC SCHOOLS—DESEGREGATION

SEGREGATION—CHICAGO

Hauser, Philip M. (Chicago) has lace pants in the front, and soiled drawers behind. (Chicago Tribune 71:1 Mar 12, 78)

SELF EVALUATION

Bailey, Pearl. There's a period of life when we swallow a knowledge of ourselves and it becomes either good or sour inside. (Chicago Tribune 176:2 Section 2 June 25, 78)

Pagnol, Marcel. The most difficult secret for a man to keep is the opinion he has of himself. (Reader's Digest 107:166 Oct 75)

Rogers, Ginger. If you don't stand for something, you will stand for anything. (Parade 9 June 18, 78)

SELF IMAGE see SELF EVALUATION

SELF INTEREST

King, Florence. Sharing is not what America is all about; in our hearts, each of us is an only child. (Vanity Fair 47:20 Oct 84)

SELF PERCEPTION

De Gaulle, Charles. We may as well go to the moon, but that's not very far. The greatest distance we have to cover still lies within us. (Omni 2:36 April 80)

Roosevelt, Eleanor. No one can make you feel inferior without your consent. (San Francisco Chronicle This World 1978:40 Jan 29, 78)

Sartre, Jean-Paul. We can only see the somber recesses in our selves if we try to become transparent to others. (Chicago Tribune 282:4 Section 7 Oct 9, 77)

Shields, Mark. I don't think Carter and self-doubt have ever met. (Washingtonian 11:103 June 76)

Vanderbilt, Amy. One face to the world, another at home makes for misery. (Chicago Tribune 176:2 Section 2 June 25, 78)

Wicker, Tom. To know things as they are is better than to believe things as they seem. (Reader's Digest 107:121 July 75)

SELF PERCEPTION see also ARTISTS—SELF PERCEPTION

SELLECK, TOM

Selleck, Tom. In the scheme of things, I'm not as important as Dr. Jonas Salk. (Life 7:141 Jan 83)

SELLERS, PETER

Sellers, Peter. The older I get, the less I like the film industry and the people in it. In fact, I'm at a stage where I almost loathe them. (Time 115:73 Mar 3, 80)

SENATORS

Abourezk, James. When voting on the confirmation of a Presidential appointment, it's always safer to vote against the son of a bitch, because if he's confirmed, it won't be long before he proves how wise you were. (Playboy 26:106 Mar 79)

SENATORS see also AIKEN, GEORGE DAVID; BAKER, HOWARD HENRY; DOLE, ROBERT J.; GARN, JAKE; HELMS, JESSE; SIMON, PAUL

SENGHOR, LEOPOLD SEDAR

Senghor, Leopold Sedar. Africa will teach rhythm to a world dead with machinery and cannon. (Time 116:5 July 7, 80)

SERVANTS

Stotesbury, E. T. A good servant should never be in the way and never out of the way. (Town & Country 131:95 Mar 77)

SETON, ELIZABETH, SAINT

Feeney, Leonard. The first American girl who 'made good' according to God's exact standards (about Elizabeth Seton). (Time 106:53 Sept 22, 75)

SEVAREID, ERIC

Chancellor, John. Eric (Sevareid) never told people what he thought, but what he learned. (Time 110:111 Dec 12, 77)

SEX

Allen, Woody. Sex is dirty only when it's done right. (Cosmopolitan 197:288 Oct 84)

Bukowski, Charles. Sexual intercouse is kicking death in the ass while singing. (Playboy 32:16 Feb 85)

Bunuel, Luis. Sex without sin is like an egg without salt. (New Times 5:5 Nov 28, 75)

Burgess, Anthony. Women cannot help moving, and men cannot help being moved. (Playboy 24:346 Dec 77)

Carrera, Barbara. Straight men make life very difficult. (M 1:87 Mar 84)

Crisp, Quentin. For flavor, instant sex will never supercede the stuff you have to peel and cook. (Cosmopolitan 197:288 Oct 84)

Dury, Ian. Sex is about as important as a cheese sandwich. (Chicago Sun-Times 31:6 June 20, 78)

Feldman, Marty. Humor is like sex. Those who do it don't talk about it. (People Weekly 6:103 Dec 27/Jan 3, 77)

Goldstein, Al. A hard-on is its own redeeming value. (Penthouse 8:106 Jan 76)

Goldwater, Barry Morris. Sex and politics are a lot alike. You don't have to be good at them to enjoy them. (University Daily Kansan 94:9 Jan 25, 84)

Kerby, Phil. Censorship is the strongest drive in human nature. Sex is only a weak second. (Kansas City Times 117:A-6 April 22, 85)

Mailer, Norman. Sex is the reward for good work. (M 7:79 Feb 90)

McCarthy, Mary. You mustn't force sex to do the work of love or love to do the work of sex. (Cosmopolitan 197:274 Mar 84)

Menninger, Karl. Sex and sexuality never made anyone ill and never made anyone feel guilty. It is the hate and destructiveness concealed in them which produce strange aberrations and bitter regret. (Playboy 24:203 Dec 77)

Paz, Octavio. The soul has become a department of sex, and sex has become a department of politics. (Newsweek 94:137 Nov 19, 79)

Reeves, Richard. Politics is sex in a hula-hoop. (New York 9:99 June 14, 76)

Sharpe, Cornelia. I think sex is the greatest thing since Coca-Cola. (Viva 2:21 Sept 75)

Sontag, Susan. There are some elements in life—above all, sexual pleasure—about which it isn't necessary to have a position. (Village Voice 21:77 Mar 22, 76)

Thomas, Marlo. Nothing is either all masculine or all feminine except sex. (People Weekly 8:50 Dec 19, 77)

Turner, R. E. (Ted). Lots of sex for everybody, that's a solution to the world's problems. (Playboy 25:67 Aug 78)

Vidal, Gore. Power is far more exciting than sex. (Chicago Tribune 173:3 Section 5 June 22, 87)

Vidal, Gore. Sex is politics. (Playboy 26:177 Jan 77)

Vidal, Gore. There are two invitations one never turns down: sex and television. (Chicago Tribune 22:1 Section 5 Jan 22, 87)

SEX (PSYCHOLOGY)

Masters, William Howell. Males have made asses of themselves writing about female sexual experience. (Newsweek 85:74 May 5, 75)

Wetzsteon, Ross. Sex, to paraphrase Clausewitz, is the continuation of war by other means. (Village Voice 20:89 April 28, 75)

SEXUAL BEHAVIOR

Behan, Brendan. I think anything is all right provided it is done in private and doesn't frighten the horses. (Cleveland 4:118 Aug 75)

Sontag, Susan. There are some elements in life—above all, sexual pleasure—about which it isn't necessary to have a position. (Village Voice 21:77 Mar 22, 76)

Tomlin, Lily. I worry about kids today. Because of the sexual revolution they're going to grow up and never know what dirty means. (Time 109:71 Mar 28, 77)

SEXUAL BEHAVIOR see also BISEXUALITY; CELEBRITIES—SEXUAL BEHAVIOR; HOMOSEXUALITY; THE RICH—SEXUAL BEHAVIOR

SHAKESPEARE, WILLIAM

Sellars, Peter (theatrical director). We need to understand the music in Shakespeare and the Shakespeare in music. (USA Today 2:5D Oct 20, 83)

SHANKER, ALBERT

Shanker, Albert. Power is a good thing. It is better than powerlessness. (Time 106:17 Sept 22, 75)

SHANLEY, JOHN PATRICK

Shanley, John Patrick. I see no difference between writing a play and living my life. (Los Angeles 33:53 Mar 88)

SHCHARANSKY, ANATOLY

Shcharansky, Anatoly. I am happy that I have lived honestly and in peace with my conscience, and never lied even when I was threatened with death. (Guardian Weekly 119:7 July 23, 78)

SHEEN, MARTIN

Sheen, Martin. I don't believe in God, but I do believe that Mary was His mother. (Rolling Stone 303:48 Nov 1, 79)

SHEPARD, SAM

Shepard, Sam. I don't want to be a playwright. I want to be a rock 'n' roll star. (Santa Fe Reporter 8:24 Feb 24, 82)

SICILY

Dolci, Danilo. We in Sicily are still parched by the sun, plagued by poverty and milked by the Mafia. (New York Times 127:49 Oct 30, 77)

SICKNESS

Camus, Albert. Illness is a convent which has its rule, its austerity, its silences, and its inspirations. (Time 112:74 July 10, 78)

Knowles, John H. Over 99 percent of us are born healthy and made sick as a result of personal misbehavior and environmental conditions. (Time 111:65 June 12, 78)

SIHANOUK, NORODOM see NORODOM SIHANOUK

SILBER, JOHN R.

Silber, John R. I don't speak plastic like other politicians. (New York Times 139:A10 April 6, 90)

Silber, John R. I know as a (political) candidate I should kiss your ass, but I haven't learned to do that with equanimity yet (to the press). (Newsweek 115:17 Feb 5, 90)

SILENCE

Gentry, Dave Tyson. True friendship comes when silence between two people is

comfortable. (Reader's Digest 107:56B Sept 75)

SIMON, JOHN

Mamet, David. Frank Rich and John Simon are the syphilis and gonorrhea of the theater. (Newsweek 107:13 Feb 17, 86)

SIMON, PAUL

Simon, Paul. I am not a neo-anything. I'm a Democrat. (Newsweek 109:17 April 20, 87)

Simon, Paul. If money alone could do the trick, John Connally would be president. (Newsweek 111:15 Mar 14, 88)

THE SIMPSONS (TELEVISION PROGRAM)

Groening, Matt. The people who are my fans now frighten me (about The Simpsons). (Newsweek 115:June 18, 90

SINATRA, FRANK

Anka, Paul. I didn't want to find a horse's head in my bed (explaining why he allowed Frank Sinatra to first record My Way). (Rolling Stone 257:15 Jan 26, 78)

Bogart, Humphrey. Sinatra's idea of paradise is a place where there are plenty of women and no newspapermen. He doesn't know it, but he'd be better off if it were the other way 'round. (US 3:64 Dec 16, 85)

Monroe, Marilyn. After one night with Frankie, I don't have to see my analyst for weeks (about Frank Sinatra). (Cosmopolitan 197:190 Mar 84)

Sinatra, Frank. I am a symmetrical man, almost to a fault. (New York 13:32 April 28, 80)

SINCLAIR, UPTON

Sinclair, Upton. I tried to touch America's conscience and all I did was hit it in the stomach (commenting on the effect of his novel The Jungle). (Philadelphia 67:65 Nov 76)

SINGER, ISAAC BASHEVIS

Singer, Isaac Bashevis. I never forget that I am only a storyteller. (Time 112:129 Oct 16, 78)

Singer, Isaac Bashevis. I'm a pessimist with cheerfulness. It's a riddle even to me, but this is how I am. (Chicago Tribune 291:20 Oct 18, 78)

SINGERS see also BAILEY, PEARL; CALLOWAY, CAB; CROSBY, BING; GUTHRIE, ARLO; MIDLER, BETTE; REDDY, HELEN; SINATRA, FRANK; SMITH, PATTI; WATERS, ETHEL

SINGLE PEOPLE

O'Brian, Hugh. There is quite enough grief when one is alone. Why compound it by getting married? (upon his founding Marriage Anonymous). (People Weekly 5:72 Jan 26, 76)

SINS

Updike, John. I've never been able to take sins of the flesh awfully seriously, nor do I believe that God takes them terribly seriously. (Kansas City Star 119:4C Oct 14, 86)

SKIN—CARE AND HYGIENE

Swanson, Gloria. It's hereditary, all in the genes. But no one can have skin like a baby's bottom if they're going to stuff that hole in their face with chocolate and banana splits. (Chicago Tribune 320:11 Section 5 Nov 16, 75)

SKIS AND SKIING

Anonymous. If God had meant for Texans to ski, He would have made bullshit white. (Texas Observer 72:7 Sept 19, 80)

Ford, Gerald Rudolph. We skiers know that falling down isn't important; it's getting up again. (New York 10:104 Nov 14, 77)

SLANG

Sandburg, Carl. Slang is language that takes off its coat, spits on its hands, and goes to work. (Kansas City Times 109:17C July 15, 77)

SLEEP

Lebowitz, Fran. Sleep is death without the responsibility. (Time 111:K3 May 29, 78)

SLICK, GRACE

Lowe, Nick. (Grace Slick) is like somebody's mom who's had a few too many drinks at a cocktail party. (Time 111:46 June 26, 78)

SLUMS

Agnew, Spiro Theodore. If you've seen one slum, you've seen them all. (New York Times 127:1 Section 4 April 2, 78)

SMALL TOWN LIFE—TEXAS

Layne, Bobby. Living in a small town (Lubbock) in Texas ain't half bad—if you own it. (Kansas City Times 111:10 Nov 17, 78)

SMITH, IAN DOUGLAS

Smith, Ian Douglas. I do not believe in black majority rule in Rhodesia—not in a thousand years. (People Weekly 5:45 June 7, 76)

SMITH, JACLYN

Ladd, Cheryl. Jaclyn (Smith) is the only girl I know that has the body of a go-go dancer and the mind of an angel. (Chicago Tribune 76:18 Mar 17, 78)

SMITH, MAGGIE

Smith, Maggie. I'm always very relieved to be somebody else, because I'm not sure at all who I am. (New York Times 128:C26 Sept 12, 79)

SMITH, PATTI

Smith, Patti. As far as I'm concerned, being any gender is a drag. (Playboy 26:26 Oct 79)

Smith, Patti. I want every faggot, grandmother, five-year-old and Chinaman to be able to hear my music and say YEAH. (Time 107:76 Jan 5, 76)

SMITH, ROGER

Smith, Roger. I'd rather be remembered as the guy that lost market share and increased profits than the guy who increased market share and lost profits. (Chicago Tribune 215:21 Section 1 Aug 3, 90)

SMITH, W. EUGENE

Smith, W. Eugene. I carry a torch with my camera. (Life 1:56 Dec 78)

SMITH, WALTER (RED)

Smith, Walter (Red). He might have been a great athlete, except that he is small, puny, slow, inept, uncoordinated, myopic and yellow (speaking of himself). (Time 119:85 Jan 25, 82)

SMOKING

Higginson, John. We now know there are a hundred causes of cancer, and eighty of them are cigarettes. (Texas Monthly 6:174 June 76)

Shields, Brooke. Smoking can kill you, and if you've been killed, you've lost a very important part of your life. (The Atlantic 265:24 Jan 90)

SOCCER

Stewart, Rod. I'm a rock star because I couldn't be a soccer star. (Elle 2:37 Dec 86)

SOCIAL CHANGE

Bowles, Paul. Everything gets worse. (Vanity Fair 48:131 Sept 85)

Dubos, Rene. Each civilization has its own kind of pestilence and controls it only by reforming itself. (Skeptic 19:29 May 77)

Mao, Tse-Tung. All reactionaries are paper tigers. (Newsweek 88:45 Sept 20, 76)

Weizenbaum, Joseph. We are rapidly losing, have perhaps already lost, physical and mental control of our society. (Omni 2:50 Dec 79)

SOCIAL CLASSES

Lennon, John. A working class hero is something to be. (Sports Illustrated 65:77 Oct 27, 86)

Orton, Joe. All classes are criminal today. We live in an age of equality. (After Dark 11:51 Dec 78)

Switzer, Barry. Some people are born on third base and go through life thinking they hit a triple. (Kansas City Times 107:1F Nov 22, 86)

SOCIAL CLASSES—UNITED STATES

Henderson, Vivian Wilson. We have programs for combatting racial discrimination, but not for combatting economic class distinctions. (Time 107:71 Feb 9, 76)

SOCIAL INTERACTION
Fields, W. C. There comes a time in the affairs of men when you must take the bull by the tail and face the situation. (San Francisco Chronicle This World 1978:40 Jan 29, 78)

SOCIAL PROBLEMS
Junot, Philippe. Society's ills come from people having lost the taste for enjoyment. (Rolling Stone 271:16 Aug 10, 78)

SOCIAL VALUES
Eliot, Thomas Stearns. Those who say they give the public what it wants begin by underestimating public taste and end by debauching it. (American Film 5:83 Nov 79)

Ferris, Earle. There's nothing neither good nor bad that can't be made more so. (Washingtonian 15:143 Nov 79)

Loy, Myrna. Nobody seems to like each other anymore. (Viva 5:108 Oct 77)

Muggeridge, Malcolm. Western society suffers from a largely unconscious collective death wish. (Time 114:86 Sept 10, 79)

Price, Roger. If everybody doesn't want it, nobody gets it. (Texas Observer 76:22 Nov 23, 84)

Spikol, Art. The fact is that most people don't drive cars that reflect what they are: they drive the closest thing they can find to what they'd like to be. (Philadelphia Magazine 66:198 Nov 75)

SOCIALISM
Churchill, Sir Winston. The inherent vice of capitalism is the unequal sharing of the blessings; the inherent virtue of socialism is the equal sharing of the miseries. (Kansas City Star 108:1F Dec 27, 87)

Davis, Angela. I'm not pessimistic about change in this country. I'm convinced that this country will one day be socialist. (New York 11:43 April 17, 78)

Humphrey, Hubert Horatio. Compassion is not weakness and concern for the unfortunate is not socialism. (Time 111:25 Jan 23, 78)

Levy, Bernard-Henri. Between the barbarity of capitalism, which censures itself much of the time, and the barbarity of socialism, which does not, I guess I might choose capitalism. (Time 111:30 Mar 13, 78)

Mehta, Asoka. Socialism is an attractive goal, but concentration of power is as dangerous as concentration of capital. (Time 111:30 Mar 13, 78)

SOCIALISM—GREAT BRITAIN
Thatcher, Margaret Hilda. Britain's progress toward socialism has been an alternation

of two steps forward with half a step back. (Time 105:30 Feb 10, 75)

SOCIALISM—UNITED STATES
Anonymous. The socialization of medicine is coming...the time now is here for the medical profession to acknowledge that it is tired of the eternal struggle for advantage over one's neighbor (editorial comment in the Journal of the American Medical Association, 1914). (New York Times Magazine 12 Jan 9, 77)

SOCIETY
Townshend, Peter. The way all societies are is that some people get, and some people don't. (Rolling Stone 325:35 June 26, 80)

Weizenbaum, Joseph. We are rapidly losing, have perhaps already lost, physical and mental control of our society. (Omni 2:50 Dec 79) ·

SOLAR ENERGY
Porter, Sir George. If sunbeams were weapons of war, we would have had solar energy centuries ago. (Omni 2:37 June 80)

SOLDIERS
Musgrave, John. There is nothing more ruthless on the face of this earth than an 18-year-old rifleman who wants to be 19. (University Daily Kansan 97:1 Feb 26, 87)

Patton, George S. Now I want you to remember that no bastard ever won a war by dying for his country. You won it by making the other poor dumb bastard die for his country. (American West 22:22 Nov 85)

SOLITUDE
Lueders, Edward. Solitude leads to amplitude. (Country Journal 5:105 Aug 78)

SOLTI, SIR GEORG
Solti, Sir Georg. Chicago should erect a statue to me for what I have done. (Chicago 26:152 Dec 77)

SOLZHENITSYN, ALEKSANDR ISAEVICH
Boorstin, Daniel J. The courage we inherit from our Jeffersons and Lincolns and others is not the Solzhenitsyn courage of the true believer, but the courage to doubt. (Time 111:21 June 26, 78)

Levy, Bernard-Henri. Solzhenitsyn is the Shakespeare of our time, the only one who knows how to point out the monsters. (Time 110:29 Sept 12, 77)

SONGS
Guthrie, Woody. You can't write a good song about a whorehouse unless you been in one. (Los Angeles Times Calendar 82 Mar 26, 78)

SONTAG, SUSAN
Mailer, Norman. I can think of very few women who, like Susan Sontag, are first

intellectuals and then literary artists. (Village Voice 31:21 Jan 28, 86)

SOREL, EDWARD

Sorel, Edward. At what I do, I am the best there is. (Guardian Weekly 119:17 Nov 12, 78)

SOUTER, DAVID

Souter, David. I have not got any agenda on what should be done with Roe v. Wade if that case was brought before me. I have not made up my mind. (Chicago Tribune 261:19 Section 1 Sept 18, 90)

SOUTH

Carter, Hodding, III. The thing you have to remember about Southerners is that we're always generous and forgiving—with our friends. (New York 9:28 July 26, 76)

Edwards, James B. I don't believe the South will buy Jimmy Carter. He is nothing more than a Southern-talking George McGovern. (New York Times 125:51 June 29, 76)

SOUTH see also POLITICS—SOUTH

SOUTH AFRICA—POLITICS AND GOVERNMENT

Botha, Pieter W. I am going to keep order, and nobody is going to stop me. (Time 127:48 Dec 30, 85)

Buthelezi, Gatsha (Zulu Chief). South Africa is one country. It has one destiny. Those who are attempting to divide the land of our birth are attempting to stem the tide of history. (New York Times 125:4 April 23, 76)

De Klerk, F. W. The season of violence is over. The time for reconstruction and reconciliation has arrived. (Chicago Tribune 46:25 Feb 15, 90)

Jackson, Jesse. People in South Africa only have the Bible as a constitution. (Chicago Sun-Times 32:32 July 20, 79)

Lewis, Anthony. In making a prison for others, the Afrikaners have imprisoned themselves. (Chicago Daily News 14 Nov 30, 93)

Mandela, Nelson. Equality, liberty and the pursuit of happiness are fundamental human rights which are not only inalienable but must, if necessary, be defended with the weapons of war. (Chicago Tribune 178:3 Section 1 June 27, 90)

Mandela, Nelson. White South Africa has to accept that there will never be peace until the principle of majority rule is fully applied. (Time 135:27 Feb 5, 90)

Tutu, Desmond. As long as some of God's children are not free, none of God's children will be free. (Time 127:48 Dec 30, 85)

SOUTH AFRICA—POLITICS AND

GOVERNMENT see also MANDELA, NELSON

SOUTH AFRICA—RACE QUESTION

Nyerere, Julius Kamberage. South Africa is no different from Rhodesia. The struggle by blacks in both countries is exactly the same—for majority rule. So what happens in Rhodesia will happen in South Africa. (People Weekly 6:40 Dec 27/Jan 3, 77)

SOUTH AFRICA—RACE QUESTION see also APARTHEID

SOUTH CAROLINA—POLITICS AND GOVERNMENT see also THURMOND, STROM

SOUTHERNERS

Capote, Truman. All Southerners go home sooner or later, even if in a box. (Southern Magazine 2:29 May 88)

SPACE

Elgin, Duane S (futurologist). Once you discover that space doesn't matter, or that time can be traveled through at will so that time doesn't matter, and that matter can be moved by consciousness so that matter doesn't matter—well, you can't go home again. (New York 10:55 Dec 27, 76)

Joubert, Joseph. Space is to place as eternity is to time. (Omni 2:39 April 80)

Vallee, Jacques. The theory of space and time is a cultural artifact made possible by the invention of graph paper. (CoEvolution Quarterly 16:82 Winter 77/78)

SPACE EXPLORATION see SPACE, OUTER— EXPLORATION

SPACE, OUTER—EXPLORATION

Schmitt, Harrison. Space represents the kind of resource for the human spirit that North America was three hundred years ago: a new stimulus for the spirit of freedom. (Omni 2:82 June 80)

Von Braun, Werner. I look forward to the day when mankind will join hands to apply the combined technological ingenuity of all nations to the exploration and utilization of outer space for peaceful uses. (Time 109:72 June 27, 77)

SPAIN—HISTORY—CIVIL WAR, 1936-1939

Ibarruri, Dolores (Spanish Civil War activist). It is better to die on your feet than live on your knees. (Time 109:50 May 23, 77)

SPAIN—POLITICS AND GOVERNMENT

Callaghan, James. Spain's self-inflicted isolation is brought about not just by a single act of brutality, but by injustices over a generation or more. (Time 106:37 Oct 13, 75)

SPAIN—POLITICS AND GOVERNMENT see also FRANCO, FRANCISCO

SPEECH

Rayburn, Sam. No one has a finer command of language than the person who keeps his mouth shut. (Lawrence (Kansas) Daily Journal-World 120:24 Aug 29, 78)

SPIELBERG, STEVEN

Spielberg, Steven. My advice to anyone who wants to be a movie director is to make home movies. I started out by shooting 8 millimeter home movies with neighbors and friends. (Texas Monthly 4:38 Aug 76)

Spielberg, Steven. The most expensive habit in the world is celluloid, not heroin, and I need a fix every few years. (Time 113:97 April 26, 79)

SPILLANE, MICKEY

Spillane, Mickey. Hey, if Shakespeare was selling big today, I'd write like Shakespeare. (Village Voice 29:102 Feb 21, 84)

Spillane, Mickey. Mike Hammer drinks beer, not cognac, because I can't spell cognac. (American Bookseller 11:23 Dec 87)

SPORTS

Allen, George. Only winners are truly alive. Winning is living. Every time you win, you're reborn. When you lose, you die a little. (Chicago Tribune 76:1 Section 2 Mar 17, 78)

Auerbach, Red. There are only three teams in sports that have achieved true national status. The old Yankees, the Dallas Cowboys and us. That's not ego, that's just fact. (Sports Illustrated 67:73 Nov 9, 87)

Broun, Heywood Hale. Sport is a preparation for more sport and not a businessmen's ROTC. (New York Times Book Review 8 July 29, 79)

Finley, Charles Oscar. I've never seen so many damned idiots as the owners in sport. (Time 106:42 Aug 18, 75)

Garvey, Ed. When you talk about civil liberties in professional sports, it's like talking about virtue in a whorehouse. (Village Voice 20:37 Dec 8, 75)

Hemingway, Ernest. There are only three true sports: fencing, bullfighting and auto racing. Everything else is just a game. (D Magazine 11:143 June 84)

Kidd, Bruce. We should stop preaching about sport's moral values. Sport, after all, isn't Lent. It's a pleasure of the flesh. (Chicago Tribune 76:1 Section 2 Mar 17, 78)

King, Billie Jean. Amateur athletes have become the pawn of manipulators and big business. (The Nation 221:654 Dec 20, 75)

Rozelle, Pete. Sporting events give people time off from the problems of the world. (US News & World Report 85:62 Oct 16, 78)

SPORTS JOURNALISM

Sherrod, William Forrest (Blackie).

Sportswriting is just like driving a taxi. It ain't the work you enjoy. It's the people you run into. (Texas Monthly 3:93 Dec 75)

SPORTS JOURNALISTS

Paterno, Joe. If I ever need a brain transplant, I want one from a sportswriter because I know its never been used. (Chicago Tribune 273:3 Section 4 Sept 39, 90)

STAFFORD, JEAN

Stafford, Jean. I write for myself and God and a few close friends. (Time 113:78 April 9, 79)

STALIN, JOSEF V.

Gorbachev, Mikhail S. The guilt of Stalin and his immediate entourage before the party and the people for the wholesale repressive measures and the acts of lawlessness is enormous and unforgivable. This is a message for all generations. (Kansas City Star 5C Nov 2, 87)

STALLONE, SYLVESTER

Stallone, Frank. He's a frustrated musician, been that way all his life. (US 3:6 Nov 2, 87)

Stallone, Sylvester. I make my living with my mind. My muscles I consider merely machinery to carry my mind around. (Chicago Tribune 210:16 July 29, 77)

Stallone, Sylvester. Some people have skeletons in their closets, but I have a graveyard. (US 3:64 Oct 7, 85)

STALLONE, SYLVESTER—THOUGHT AND THINKING

Stallone, Sylvester. My temperature was higher than my combined SAT scores. (US 3:64 July 1, 85)

STARGELL, WILLIE

Tanner, Chuck. Having Willie Stargell on your ball club is like having a diamond ring on your finger. (Time 114:108 Oct 29, 79)

STATE GOVERNMENTS

Burns, John. We expect very little of our (state) legislatures, and they continually live up to our expectations. (Time 111:101 May 29, 78)

STATISTICS

Gallup, George. i could prove God statistically. (Omni 2:42 Nov 79)

STEEL INDUSTRY

Kennedy, John Fitzgerald. My father always told me that steel men were sons-of-bitches, but I never realized till now how right he was (in the 1962 steel-price confrontation). (Chicago Tribune 147:2 Section 2 May 29, 77)

STEINBECK, JOHN

Steinbeck, John. Competing with Hemingway isn't my idea of good business. (Time 106:48 Dec 1, 75)

STEINBERG, SAUL

Rosenberg, Harold. In linking art to the modern consciousness, no artist is more relevant than Steinberg. (Time 111:92 April 17, 78)

STEINBRENNER, GEORGE

Winfield, Dave. Everything you read about George Steinbrenner is true. That's the problem. (Kansas City Star 106:1C Jan 8, 86)

STEINEM, GLORIA

Steinem, Gloria. I can't mate in captivity. (Life 7:40 Jan 83)

STEVENS, CAT

Stevens, Cat. Nobody put a sword to my neck to make me a Moslem. (Toronto Globe and Mail 141:1 Aug 25, 84)

STEVENS, JOHN PAUL

Stevens, John Paul. It's always been my philosophy to decide cases on the narrowest grounds possible and not to reach out. (New York Times 125:1 Dec 9, 75)

Stevens, John Paul. Judges should impose on themselves the discipline of deciding no more than is before them. (American Legion Magazine 100:9 Feb 76)

STEVENSON, ADLAI, II

Stevenson, Adlai, II. I have often thought that if I had any epitaph that I would rather have more than another, it would be to say that I had disturbed the sleep of my generation. (Newsweek 90:120 Oct 24, 77)

Stevenson, Adlai, II. It is better to light one candle than to curse the darkness. (New York Times Magazine 45 July 4, 76)

STEWART, ROD

Stewart, Rod. I'm a rock star because I couldn't be a soccer star. (Elle 2:37 Dec 86)

STOCK EXCHANGES—NEW YORK EXCHANGE

Graham, Benjamin. (The stock market is) a Falstaffian joke that frequently degenerates into a madhouse. (Money 5:36 July 76)

STOCKBROKERS

Galbraith, John Kenneth. There's just a growing feeling that Wall Street is a sort of irresponsible beehive of young people who don't know what they're doing. (Kansas City Star 108:6A Oct 27, 87)

STOCKS

Levin, S. Jay. Stocks do not move unless they are pushed. (Book Digest 6:32 Dec 79)

Rogers, Jimmy. Nobody in government understands Wall Street. And very few people on Wall Street understands Wall Street. (Kansas City Star 108:6A Oct 27, 87)

Skodack, Debra. A person is not an investor until he has delt with a bad stock market. (Kansas City Times 120:D-3 Oct 22, 87)

STOKOWSKI, LEOPOLD

Stokowski, Leopold. Music appeals to me for what can be done with it. (Time 110:54 Sept 26, 77)

STONE, ISIDOR FEINSTEIN

Stone, Isidor Feinstein. I'd like to say that I never though of myself as an investigative journalist, because from my boyhood I felt that every reporter investigates what he's writing about. If he doesn't he's an idiot who just rewrites press releases. (The Nation 249:40 July 10, 89)

Terkel, Studs. He was a North Star to me (about I. F. Stone). (Chicago Tribune 170:1 June 19, 89)

STONEHENGE

Moore, Henry. Stonehenge is not a building, it is a carving. (Quest 2:26 Nov 78)

STOPPARD, TOM

Stoppard, Tom. I suppose my purpose as a playwright, if such a thing can be stated at all, has been to marry the play of ideas with comedy or farce. (Los Angeles Times Calendar 46 Jan 9, 77)

STRATEGIC ARMS LIMITATION TALKS

Biden, Joseph. Half the people don't know the difference between SALT and pepper. (Time 113:37 April 16, 79)

Brezhnev, Leonid I. God will not forgive us if we fail (about Strategic Arms Limitation Talks). (New York Times 128:1 June 17, 79)

STRATEGIC DEFENSE INITIATIVE

Cheney, Richard B. SDI is alive and well, but like everything else, it has to fit into a reduced budget. (New York Times 138:19 April 25, 89)

STRAUSS, ROBERT S.

Strauss, Robert S. I didn't come to town yesterday on a load of watermelons. (Newsweek 94:5 July 16, 79)

STRESS

Selye, Hans. Stress is the nonspecific response of the body to any demand. (Human Nature 1:58 Feb 78)

STRIKES—ITALY

Anselmi, Tina (first Italian woman cabinet member). If people outside Italy have the impression that Italy is always on strike, that is because it is. (New York Times 126:21 Section 1 Oct 10, 76)

STRIKES—NEWSPAPERS

Graham, Katharine. This company (The Washington Post) is not now and never has been antiunion. (Newsweek 86:44 Dec 22, 75)

STROUT, RICHARD

Broder, David S. He (Richard Strout) must get out of bed every day as if it's his first chance to set the world right. (Time 111:83 Mar 27, 78)

STUPIDITY

Miller, Arthur. The paranoia of stupidity is always the worst, since its fear of destruction by intelligence is reasonable. (Forbes 121:28 April 3, 78)

STYLE

Crisp, Quentin. Style is out of fashion. (Connoisseur 215:88 Nov 85)

SUCCESS

Alderson, M. H. If at first you don't succeed, you are running about average. (Reader's Digest 108:122 Feb 76)

Anonymous (Murphy's Law). If anything can go wrong, eventually it will. (The Reader (Chicago's Free Weekly) 5:2 May 28, 76)

Backus, Jim. Many a man owes his success to his first wife and his second wife to his success. (Cosmopolitan 197:184 Sept 84)

Brett, Ken. The worst curse in the world is unlimited potential. (Arkansas Times 12:67 July 86)

Bucy, Fred. Nothing is ever accomplished by a reasonable man. (Book Digest 6:30 Dec 79)

Christie, Agatha. The happy people are failures because they are on such good terms with themselves that they don't give a damn. (Lawrence (Kansas) Journal-World 127:3D Oct 28, 84)

Cozzens, James Gould. The longer I watch men and life, the surer I get that success whenever more than minor comes of luck alone. By comparison, no principles, ideas, goals, and standards of conduct matter much in an achieving of it. (New York Times 127:39 July 30, 78)

Ephron, Nora. For a lot of women, the women's movement has just given them a political rationalization for their fear of success. (Christian Science Monitor 69:2 Dec 10, 76)

Evans, Robert. Success means never have to admit you're unhappy. (Chicago Tribune Magazine 4 July 22, 84)

Goldsmith, James. Four necessary attributes for success: appetite, luck, the right people and fear. (Kansas City Star 106:5A Dec 30, 85)

Graham, Benjamin. Never having to balance your checkbook (a definition of financial success). (Money 5:37 July 76)

Hemingway, Ernest. Writing is something that you never do as well as it can be done. (D Magazine 12:168 Mar 85)

Kemp, Jack. Whether it's politics or football, winning is like shaving: you do it every day or you wind up looking like a bum. (The Sporting News 202:12 Aug 4, 86)

Kissinger, Henry Alfred. Each success only buys an admission ticket to a more difficult problem. (Wilson Library Bulletin 53:513 Mar 79)

Midler, Bette. The worst part of having success is to try finding someone who is happy for you. (Chicago Sun-Times 29:32 Mar 3, 76)

Paulucci, Jeno F. It pays to be ignorant, for when you're smart you already know it can't be done. (New York Times 126:5 Section 3 Nov 7, 76)

Simon, William E. Show me a good loser and I'll show you a loser. (Washingtonian 11:24 April 76)

Slater, Jim. As you get better at a thing it gets less interesting. (The Observer 9761:14 Sept 24, 78)

Tomlin, Lily. Sometimes I worry about being a success in a mediocre world. (New Times 9:47 Jan 9, 78)

Tomlin, Lily. Why is it we are always hearing about the tragic cases of too much, too soon? What about the rest of us? Too little, too late. (Time 109:71 Mar 28, 77)

Van Derbur, Marilyn (former Miss America). The vital, successful people I have met all had one common characteristic. They had a plan. (People Weekly 6:23 Dec 13, 76)

Vidal, Gore. It is not enough to succeed, a friend must also fail. (In The Know 1:47 June 75)

Wilson, David B. Sam Wilson used to say that any damn fool can stand adversity; but it takes real quality to stand prosperity. (Kansas City Times 119:A-7 Oct 14, 86)

Zukor, Adolph. Look ahead a little and gamble a lot (a formula for success). (Time 107:55 June 21, 76)

SUCCESS—IRELAND

Flanagan, Fionnula. The one thing you must not commit with the Irish is to succeed. (TV Guide 26:22 April 29, 78)

SUCCESS—NEW YORK (CITY)

Kriendler, Peter. If you make it in New York, you got it made. If you make it anywhere else, you've still got something to prove. (New York 108 Dec 24, 84)

SUCCESS—PSYCHOLOGICAL ASPECTS

Turner, R. E. (Ted). My desire to excel borders on the unhealthy. (Time 120:50 Aug 9, 82)

SUICIDE

Allen, Woody. There have been times when

I've thought of suicide, but with my luck it'd probably be a temporary solution. (Time 106:47 Dec 15, 75)

Jong, Erica. I want to set an example of a woman poet who doesn't kill herself. (Kansas City Star 117:6B Dec 3, 84)

Sheed, Wilfrid. Suicide is the sincerest form of criticism life gets. (The Tennessean 74:11 June 27, 79)

SULLIVAN, ED

Dylan, Bob. Somebody called me the Ed Sullivan of rock and roll. I don't know what that means, but it sounds right. (TV Guide 24:4 Sept 11, 76)

SUNUNU, JOHN H.

Bush, George. He's the right man for the job and I'm very pleased that he will lead the Bush team in the White House (about John H Sununu). (New York Times 138:8 Nov 18, 88)

SUPPLY SIDE ECONOMICS

Heller, Walter. Waiting for supply-side economics to work is like leaving the landing lights on for Amelia Earhart. (Dun's Business Month 127:51 Feb 86)

SUSANN, JACQUELINE

Susann, Jacqueline. I don't have any peers, as far as writers go. (After Dark 8:35 Aug 75)

SUTTON, WILLIE

Sutton, Willie. I always figured that being a good robber was like being a good lawyer. (Village Voice 21:118 Sept 13, 76)

SWAGGART, JIMMY LEE

Swaggart, Jimmy Lee. All I want to do is jack off awhile. (Village Voice 33:25 June 21, 88)

SWITZERLAND

Rossy, Paul (former vice chairman, Swiss Banking Commission). God, after all, created Switzerland for one purpose—to be the clearinghouse of the world. (Time 110:74 July 18, 77)

SYMPATHY

Rockefeller, Nelson Aldrich. One thing I can't stand is a goddamned bleeding heart. (American Spectator 15:22 Oct 82)

TALENT

Dean, Dizzy. It ain't bragging if you've done it. (Kansas City Times 107:A-16 April 30, 87)

Jong, Erica. Everyone has talent. What is rare is the courage to follow the talent to the dark place where it leads. (Los Angeles Times 97:6 Part 4 Feb 3, 78)

Walter, Bruno. Talent is the one real power. (Chicago 32:24 Sept 83)

TASTE (AESTHETICS)

Gurley, George H., Jr. Our problem is that we live in a culture dominated by

shameless bad taste. (Kansas City Times 120:1B Nov 3, 87)

Hall, Joyce. Good taste is good business. (Village Voice 27:15 Feb 10, 82)

Quant, Mary. Good taste is death, vulgarity life. (Life 2:83 Nov 79)

Stone, Richard. One privilege of home ownership is the right to have lousy taste and display it. (Time 111:24 April 17, 78)

Warhol, Andy. Bad taste makes the day go faster. (Houston Home/Garden 5:42 Nov 78)

TAX RETURNS

Neuman, Alfred E. Today, it takes more brains and effort to make out the Income Tax Form than it does to make the income. (Mad Magazine 175:1 June 75)

TAXATION

Bush, George. Read my lips: No new taxes (1988). (Chicago Tribune 178:1 Section 1 June 27, 90)

Dukakis, Michael. I told the truth (about taxes) and I paid the price. Mr. Bush did not and we're all now going to have to pay the price for that. (Chicago Tribune V 178:14 Section 1 June 27, 90)

Friedman, Milton. Inflation is the one form of taxation that can be imposed without legislation. (American Opinion 18:37 April 75)

Holmes, Oliver Wendell. Taxes are the price that society pays for civilization. (Time 112:60 Sept 25, 78)

Nakasone, Yasuhiro. To master the mysteries of taxation, one must learn how to shear a sheep without its bleating. (Chicago Tribune 72:21 Mar 13, 87)

Reagan, Ronald. Using taxes to cure deficits in like using leeches to cure anemia. (Chicago Tribune 174:15 June 23, 87)

Wicker, Tom. Government expands to absorb revenue—and then some. (Washingtonian 14:155 Nov 78)

TAXATION—CALIFORNIA

Jarvis, Howard. I didn't promise anybody that Prop 13 would reduce rent. (Newsweek 93:71 June 4, 79)

TAXATION—UNITED STATES

Galbraith, John Kenneth. The (tax) revolt of the affluent, which now has politicans so frightened, is not a violent thing. The response in the ghettoes if life there is allowed further to deteriorate might be different. (New York Times 128:A23 Jan 12, 79)

Simon, William E. We're going to have a taxpayers' revolt if we don't begin to make the tax system more simple, more understandable, so that everyone knows that everybody is paying his fair share. (Chicago Tribune 11:1 Section 1 Jan 11, 76)

TAYLOR, ELIZABETH

Taylor, Elizabeth. When people say: she's got everything, I've only one answer: I haven't had tomorrow. (Chicago Tribune 176:2 Section 2 June 25, 78)

TEACHERS

Adams, Henry Brooks. A teacher affects eternity; he can never tell where his influence stops. (Kansas City Star 97:15B April 6, 77)

Bennett, William J. Why don't you admit what everybody knows, which is there are a lot of teachers...who have no business in being in classrooms? (Lawrence (Kansas) Journal-World 130:1 Mar 30, 88)

Chomsky, Noam. Anybody who teaches at age fifty what he was teaching at age twenty-five had better find another profession. (Omni 6:114 Nov 83)

TEACHING

Shanker, Albert. Teaching is no longer seen as a woman's job. Teaching is seen as a tough, exciting place where things are happening. (Ms 6:85 July 77)

TECHNOLOGY AND CIVILIZATION

Clarke, Arthur C. Any sufficiently advanced technology is undistinguishable from magic. (Omni 2:87 April 80)

Clarke, Arthur C. Experience has shown that the most important results of any technological breakthrough are those that are not obvious. (American Film 2:67 Oct 76)

TELEVISION

Allen, Fred. Imitation is the sincerest form of television. (Emmy 3:46 Fall 81)

Allen, Fred. Television is a triumph of equipment over people, and the minds that control it are so small that you could put them in a gnat's navel with room left over for two caraway seeds and an agent's heart. (CoEvolution Quarterly 16:153 Winter 77/78)

Allen, Fred. Television is chewing gum for the eyes. (Playboy 23:150 June 76)

Arledge, Roone. The single biggest problem of television is that everyone talks so much. (Time 110:61 Aug 22, 77)

Arlen, Michael J. Every civilization creates its own cultural garbage and ours is television (commenting in his book The View from Highway 1). (Washington Post 352:E4 Nov 21, 76)

Arlen, Michael J. TV is a kind of language that people have learned how to read. (Time 110:44 Dec 5, 77)

Baker, Russell. Televiso ergo sum—I am televised, therefore I am. (Time 116:9 Sept 22, 80)

Canby, Vincent. Bland has always been big in television. (New York Times 126:15 Section 2 Nov 13, 77)

Chayefsky, Paddy. Television is democracy at it's ugliest. (New York Times 126:18 Section 2 Nov 14, 76)

Daley, Steve. In the age of television, history bores us. That's why everything is a surprise. (Chicago Tribune 84:1 Section 5 Mar 24, 88)

Friendly, Fred. Television makes so much money doing its worst that it can'd afford to do its best. (US 3:11 Aug 25, 86)

Garroway, Dave. Television started off mediocre and went steadily downhill. (Channels 3:53 Sept 83)

Koppel, Ted. On television, ambiguity is a virtue. (Newsweek 109:56 June 15, 87)

McLuhan, Marshall. Television is not a visual medium. (CoEvolution Quarterly 16:86 Winter 77/78)

McLuhan, Marshall. TV is addictive. It's a drug. (Washington Post 161:H1 May 15, 77)

Mead, Margaret. For the first time the young are seeing history being made before it is censored by their elders (in defense of TV). (Time 112:57 Nov 27, 78)

Minow, Newton. The most important educational institution in the country is not Harvard or Yale or Caltech—it's television. (Time 113:50 May 28, 79)

Monaco, James. Film has come of age as an art, probably because television now receives the brunt of contempt from the remaining proponents of an elite culture. (New York Times Book Review 11 April 1, 79)

Newman, Edwin. I believe some silence is helpful to thought. And I believe to some extent radio and television discourage thought and reflection. (Chicago Tribune 1:23 Jan 1, 78)

O'Connor, John J. Exposure to television is not necessarily fatal. (New York Times 127:33 Section 2 Nov 27, 77)

Reeves, Richard. Television, of course, is dangerous. But that does not mean it is necessarily bad. (Esquire 89:57 April 25, 78)

Seeger, Pete. TV must become our council fire, our town hall. (CoEvolution Quarterly 16:153 Winter 77/78)

Sevareid, Eric. On balance, TV is better for us than bad for us. (USA Today 1:10A Jan 10, 83)

Shales, Tom. People, I have found, are a poor substitute for television. (Interview 14:180 Sept 84)

Westmoreland, William Childs. Television is an instrument which can paralyze this country. (Time 119:57 April 5, 82)

TELEVISION see also VIOLENCE IN TELEVISION

TELEVISION ADVERTISING

Wald, Richard. California understands the real purpose of television is to collect a crowd of advertisers. (Esquire 89:62 Jan 31, 78)

TELEVISION AUDIENCES

Sevareid, Eric. There is an immense amount of biased listening and inaccurate listening (commenting on TV news audiences). (TV Guide 25:A55 Dec 13, 77)

TELEVISION AUTHORSHIP

Oliansky, Joel. TV writing is the country of the blind where the one-eyed man is king. (Writer's Yearbook 61 1977)

TELEVISION BROADCASTING

Arledge, Roone. The single biggest problem of television is that everyone talks so much. (Time 110:61 Aug 22, 77)

Howard, Robert T. The family hour seems to have become just another cop-out used by creative people to explain their failure. (Los Angeles Times 94:13 Part 4 Nov 4, 75)

TELEVISION BROADCASTING, NONCOMMERCIAL

Goldberg, Alan. Public TV is for the humor-impaired. (Washington Journalism Review 5:40 Nov 83)

Rich, Lee. Public broadcasting has become a joke. They spend more time fighting with each other than they do putting shows on the air. (Emmy 1:13 Winter 79)

White, E. B. Non-commercial television should address itself to the ideal of excellence, not the ideal of acceptability. (Harper's 259:78 Aug 79)

TELEVISION BROADCASTING—NEWS

Anderson, Jack. The networks don't recognize a story until it's in the New York Times. They aren't competent; they're incompetent. (TV Guide 23:7 Nov 15, 75)

Chancellor, John. Television is good at the transmission of experience. Print is better at the transmission of facts. (Time 115:71 Feb 25, 80)

Friendly, Fred. The news is the one thing networks can point to with pride. Everything else they do is crap, and they know it. (Time 115:74 Jan 14, 80)

Friendly, Fred. TV still basically indexes rather than reports the news. (Time 115:70 Feb 25, 80)

Hewitt, Don. People are finding that truth is more fascinating than fiction. (US News & World Report 85:52 Nov 20, 78)

MacNeil, Robert. TV has created a nation of news junkies who tune in every night to get their fix on the world. (Time 115:65 Feb 25, 80)

Murrow, Edward R (attributed by Charles Kuralt). Just because you speak in a voice loud enough to be heard over television by 16 million people, that doesn't make you any smarter than you were when you spoke loudly enough to be heard only at the other end of the bar. (Mpls/St. Paul 42 Jan 77)

Rather, Dan. In television news, no good deed goes unpunished. (Newsweek 112:6 Aug 22, 88)

Savitch, Jessica. The thing you need most in this business (TV journalism) is stamina. (Ms 8:86 Aug 79)

Sevareid, Eric. The problem is not so much finding out what the news is, it's making sense of it. (TV Guide 25:A55 Dec 13, 77)

TELEVISION BROADCASTING—NEWS
see also CRONKITE, WALTER

TELEVISION BROADCASTING— PROGRAMMING

Lear, Norman. TV executives don't make decisions based on their own sense of showmanship. They make decisions based on fear. (Emmy 1:12 Winter 79)

TELEVISION BROADCASTING— RELIGIOUS PROGRAMS

Bakker, Tammy. Christian television is basically very boring. (Newsweek 109:69 June 8, 87)

TELEVISION INDUSTRY see also PALEY, WILLIAM S.

TELEVISION PERFORMERS

Moyers, Bill D. TV personalities are like celluloid. They're very perishable. (Newsweek 83:80 April 15, 74)

Vidal, Gore. There are two invitations one never turns down: sex and television. (Chicago Tribune 22:1 Section 5 Jan 22, 87)

TELEVISION PROGRAMS

Hall, Monty. You can learn more about America by watching one half-hour of Let's Make a Deal than you can by watching Walter Cronkite for an entire month. (Time 115:85 Feb 18, 80)

Logan, Ben. TV is hydraulic. You push down violence and up pops exploitative sex. (Newsweek 91:54 Feb 20, 78)

Rich, Lee. People enjoy watching wealthy people with more problems than they have (about television programs). (American Film 6:28 May 81)

TELLER, EDWARD

Teller, Edward. I am forever described as the father of the H-bomb. I would much prefer to be known as the father of two wonderful children. (Outside 1:13 Oct 77)

TEMPTATION

Cabell, James Branch. There is no memory

with less satisfaction in it than the memory of some temptation we resisted. (Forbes 120:100 July 15, 77)

Talbert, Bob. Resisting temptation is easier when you think you'll probably get another chance later on. (Reader's Digest 107:166 Oct 75)

TENNIS

Anonymous. Tennis isn't a matter of life and death—it's more important than that (sign at the John Gardiner Tennis Clinic, Warren, Vermont). (New Times 5:48 Aug 8, 75)

Wilder, Roy. Tennis adds years to your life and life to your years. (New York Times 125:5 Section 5 Sept 12, 76)

TERROR

Fiedler, Leslie. There can be no terror without the hope for love and love's defeat. (New York Arts Journal 9:15 April 78)

Hitchcock, Alfred Joseph. There is no terror in a bang, only in the anticipation of it. (Village Voice 23:1 Jan 23, 78)

TERRORISM

Buchan, Alastair. Respectability depends on whose side you're on. To the Turks, Lawrence of Arabia was a terrorist. (Time 104:44 Nov 25, 74)

Ghorbal, Ashraf. Terrorism has become the lens through which the Americans look at the Middle East. (Time 127:19 June 16, 86)

John Paul II, Pope. There is but one thing more dangerous than sin: the murder of man's sense of sin. (New York Times 128:7 April 2, 79)

TERRORISM—ITALY

Crespi, Consuelo. In Italy now you want to feel rich and look poor. (Time 111:53 May 15, 78)

TEXANS

Anonymous. If God had meant for Texans to ski, He would have made bullshit white. (Texas Observer 72:7 Sept 19, 80)

Dugger, Ronnie. To be from Texas will always have a kind of gusto to it. (New York Times 129:B12 Oct 15, 79)

TEXAS

Layne, Bobby. Living in a small town (Lubbock) in Texas ain't half bad—if you own it. (Kansas City Times 111:10 Nov 17, 78)

Samuels, John S., III. Texas is sort of an opera. (New York Times 128:17 Section 2 Jan 21, 79)

TEXAS see also SAN ANTONIO, TEXAS

TEXAS—POLITICS AND GOVERNMENT

Bentsen, Lloyd. I just wasn't able to convince voters that 'Dukakis' was Greek for 'Bubba'. (Newsweek 112:15 Dec 19, 88)

Wood, Gordon. People in Texas believe in slow-talking football coaches more than they believe in fast-talking politicians. (Chicago Tribune 67:6 Mar 8, 87)

TEXAS—POLITICS AND GOVERNMENT

see also CONNALLY, JOHN BOWDEN

TEXTBOOKS

Falwell, Jerry. Textbooks are Soviet propaganda. (Kansas City Star 112:1E Dec 7, 80)

THARP, TWYLA

Tharp, Twyla. I sometimes find structure a riot. (Chicago Tribune 198:3 Section 6 July 17, 77)

THATCHER, MARGARET HILDA

Healey, Denis. Mrs. Thatcher is doing for monetarism what the Boston Strangler did for door-to-door salesmen. (The Observer 9825:10 Dec 16, 79)

Thatcher, Margaret Hilda. I am controversial. That means I stand for something. (Time 115:34 Jan 7, 80)

Thatcher, Margaret Hilda. I am extraordinary patient, provided I get my own way in the end. (The Observer 9944:8 April 4, 82)

Thatcher, Margaret Hilda. I'm not a consensus politician, or a pragmatic politician, but a conviction politician. (Newsweek 93:52 April 9, 79)

Thatcher, Margaret Hilda. Opportunity means nothing unless it includes the right to be unequal. (The Illustrated London News 263:26 Oct 31, 75)

Thatcher, Margaret Hilda. What Britain needs is an iron lady. (Newsweek 93:50 May 14, 79)

THEATER

De Mille, Agnes. The theater gives us one rule: don't be a bore. (W 6:24 Dec 9, 77)

Hayes, Helen. There is no racial or religious prejudice among people in the theater. The only prejudice is against bad actors, especially successful ones. (Time 114:85 Dec 17, 79)

Kaufman, George. Satire is what closes Saturday night. (Time 107:72 Feb 2, 76)

Mamet, David. I want to change the future of American theatre. (Village Voice 21:101 July 5, 76)

Simon, John. I love plays, but I love them in a different way. I'm not blind. I don't gush. I love the theater as it might be. (Time 110:34 Dec 26, 77)

Sondheim, Stephen. Books are what the musical theater is about. (Los Angeles 30:46 Nov 85)

Stoppard, Tom. Ambushing the audience is what theater is all about. (Newsweek 103:82 Jan 16, 84)

Stoppard, Tom. My feeling is that in the theater the emotions should be gratified as well as the intellect. (Newsweek 103:82 Jan 16, 84)

THEATRICAL PRODUCTION AND DIRECTION

Caldwell, Zoe. Acting is like being a sibling and directing is like being a parent. (W 15:30 Jan 27, 86)

Kubrick, Stanley. The essence of dramatic form is to let an idea come over people without its being plainly stated. (Time 106:72 Dec 15, 75)

Nichols, Mike. Directing is one of the few professions you can practice without knowing what it is. (American Theatre 1:32 Dec 84)

THEOLOGY

Esquerra, Maria Antonia (Chicana nun). The theology of liberation in North America will be written by the oppressed. (Time 106:34 Sept 1, 75)

Fairlie, Henry. Where there is no theology, there is no religion. (Chicago Tribune 123:3 May 3, 87)

John Paul I, Pope. Those who treat theology as a human science rather than a sacred science, or exaggerate their freedom, lack faith. (Time 112:66 Sept 4, 78)

THICKE, ALAN

Thicke, Alan. I can count my Canadian media friends on the fingers of one hand, and I express my feelings for the rest of them with one finger. (US 3:6 Mar 9, 89)

THINKING see **THOUGHT AND THINKING**

THIRD WORLD see **UNDERDEVELOPED AREAS**

THOMAS, DYLAN

Thomas, Caitlin (wife of Dylan Thomas). Dylan wanted us to be young and unwise forever—to be permanently naughty children. He managed this by killing himself with booze, but I was left to grow old. (Time 106:46 Dec 15, 75)

THOMAS, LOWELL

Thomas, Lowell. After the age of 80, everything reminds you of something else. (Time 112:62 Nov 27, 78)

THOMPSON, HUNTER S.

Thompson, Hunter S. I'm basically a lazy person. And proud of it. (The California Aggie 96:6 Mar 2, 78)

THOMPSON, JAMES

Thompson, James. If I could be president, I'd like to be president. I'm immodest enough to think that I could be a good one. (Chicago Tribune 72:21 Mar 13, 87)

THOMPSON, LORD ROY HERBERT

Thompson, Lord Roy Herbert. I am in business to make money, and I buy more newspapers to make more money to buy more newspapers. (New York Times 125:28 Aug 5, 76)

THOMSON, VIRGIL

Schuman, William. The simple is not easy (about Virgil Thomson). (Village Voice 31:112 Dec 16, 86)

THOUGHT AND ACTION

Bergson, Henri. Think like a man of action, and act like a man of thought. (Kansas City Star 97:4B Feb 6, 77)

Bruce, Lenny. I only said it, man. I didn't do it. (Oui 7:51 Feb 78)

Fitzgerald, F. Scott. The test of a first-rate intelligence is the ability to hold two opposed ideas in the mind at the same time, and still retain the ability to function. (New York Times Book Review 23 Mar 4, 79)

THOUGHT AND THINKING

Eldridge, Paul. Man is always ready to die for an idea, provided that idea is not quite clear to him. (Washingtonian 15:141 Nov 79)

Ford, Henry. Thinking is the hardest work there is—which is probably the reason why so few engage in it. (Forbes 121:96 Feb 6, 78)

Freud, Sigmund. The less a man knows about the past and the present, the more insecure must be his judgment of the future. (Kansas City Star 106:5A Dec 30, 85)

Goncalves, Vasco dos Santos. Emotion is not incompatible with lucidity. (Time 105:40 May 5, 75)

Harden, Frank. Every time you come up with a terrific idea, you find that someone else thought of it first. (Washingtonian 14:154 Nov 78)

Kahn, Alfred. Anybody who isn't schizophrenic these days isn't thinking clearly. (Life 4:21 Jan 80)

Kahn, Herman. Think the unthinkable. (National Catholic Reporter 21:26 Dec 21, 84)

Kroc, Ray. If you think small, you'll stay small. (Chicago 28:12 Mar 79)

Laker, Freddie. The man that doesn't change his mind doesn't think. (The Observer 9804:9 July 22, 79)

Lippmann, Walter. When all think alike, no one is thinking. (Book Digest 6:28 Dec 79)

Marquis, Don. If you make people think they're thinking, they'll love you; but if you really make them think, they'll hate you. (Rocky Mountain News 250:50 Dec 28, 79)

Newman, Edwin. I believe some silence is helpful to thought. And I believe to some extent radio and television discourage thought and reflection. (Chicago Tribune 1:23 Jan 1, 78)

Russell, Ken. It's possible to think three things at once. (Village Voice 26:46 Jan 21, 81)

Simmel, Marianne L. Methodology is the last refuge of a sterile mind. (Kansas City Star 109:2 F Dec 25, 88)

Skinner, B. F. The real problem is not whether machines think but whether men do. (Omni 4:36 July 82)

Whitehead, Alfred North. Nobody has a right to speak more clearly than he thinks. (Washingtonian 15:143 Nov 79)

Wilson, Robert Anton. If a man's ideas aren't frightening enough to get him imprisoned, you can be sure he's not really thinking something new and important. (Fate 30:7 Oct 77)

THURMOND, STROM

Thurmond, Strom. I admire people who have a lot of money. (W 12:9 Feb 12, 82)

Thurmond, Strom. There are not enough laws on the books of the nation, nor can there be enough laws, to break down segregation in the South (commenting in 1948 as he accepted the presidential nomination of the Dixiecrat Party). (Washington Post 264:A3 Aug 27, 77)

TIANANMEN SQUARE (CHINA) STUDENT OCCUPATION, 1989

Deng Xiaoping. In the 1960's and 1970's there were many student movements and turmoils in the United States. Did they have any other recourse but to mobilize police and troops, arrest people and shed blood. (Newsweek 114:15 July 3, 89)

Fang Lizhi. China's hope at present lies in the fact that more and more people have broken free from blind faith in the leadership (1989). (Newsweek 113:27 June 26, 89)

TIME

Elgin, Duane S (futurologist). Once you discover that space doesn't matter, or that time can be traveled through at will so that time doesn't matter, and that matter can be moved by consciousness so that matter doesn't matter—well, you can't go home again. (New York 10:55 Dec 27, 76)

Lewis, C. S. All that is not eternal is eternally out of date. (Time 110:92 Dec 5, 77)

Vallee, Jacques. The theory of space and time is a cultural artifact made possible by the invention of graph paper. (CoEvolution Quarterly 16:82 Winter 77/78)

Williams, Tennessee. Time is the longest distance between two places. (Omni 2:38 July 80)

TIME, USE OF

Rayburn, Sam. The three most important

words in the English language are 'wait a minute'. (Time 107:15 Aug 9, 76)

TINKERBELLE

Tinkerbelle. You don't need much money when the best things in life are handouts. (Vanity Fair 50:85 Jan 87)

TOMLIN, LILY

Tomlin, Lily. Sometimes I worry about being a success in a mediocre world. (New Times 9:47 Jan 9, 78)

TOSCANINI, ARTURO

Toscanini, Arturo. I kissed my first woman and smoked my first cigarette on the same day; I've never had time for tobacco since. (Kansas City Star 97:26 May 2, 77)

TOTALITARIANISM

Levy, Bernard-Henri. The only successful revolution of this century is totalitarianism. (Time 110:29 Sept 12, 77)

TOUREL, JENNIE

Tourel, Jennie. You see, it isn't just boiled potatoes, what I do. (Stereo Review 35:80 Nov 75)

TOWER, JOHN

Tower, John. I am not a mindless hawk. I am a realist. (Chicago Tribune 33:23 Section 1 Feb 2, 89)

Tower, John. I used to be a pretty good scotch drinker. (New York 22:16 Mar 13, 89)

TRADE UNIONS

Meany, George. Everything in this world that affects life, liberty and happiness is the business of the American trade union movement. (American Legion Magazine 100:9 Feb 76)

Watts, Glenn. Unions must be prepared to change with the times, or they run the risk of being run over by them. (USA Today 1:10A Sept 6, 83)

Winpisinger, William (union leader). I don't mind being called a lefty. We're being centered to death. (Time 110:52 July 11, 77)

TRADE UNIONS see also MEANY, GEORGE

TRADE UNIONS—ACTORS AND ACTRESSES

Nathan, George Jean. An artist never strikes; he leaves such things to plumbers and streetsweepers. (Village Voice 25:47 Dec 24, 80)

TRADE UNIONS—ITALY

Anselmi, Tina (first Italian woman cabinet member). If people outside Italy have the impression that Italy is always on strike, that is because it is. (New York Times 126:21 Section 1 Oct 10, 76)

TRADE UNIONS—UNITED STATES

Kirkland, Lane. All sinners belong in the church; all citizens owe fealty to their country; and all true unions belong in the

American Federation of Labor and Congress of Industrial Organizations. (New York Times 129:B1 Nov 20, 79)

TRANSCENDENTAL MEDITATION

Graham, Billy. Transcendental Meditation is evil because...it opens space within you for the devil. (Ms 6:50 July 77)

TRANSLATIONS AND TRANSLATING

Fitzgerald, Robert. Translating is writing poetry to the full extent of the product. (Connoisseur 215:83 Sept 85)

Seymour, Steven. Translations are like women. When they are pretty, chances are they won't be very faithful. (Rolling Stone 260:16 Mar 9, 78)

TRAVEL

Disraeli, Benjamin. Travel teaches toleration. (Time 110:68 Oct 10, 77)

Theroux, Paul. Travel is glamorous only in retrospect. (The Observer 9815:10 Oct 7, 79)

TRAVEL WITH CHILDREN

Benchley, Robert. Traveling with children corresponds roughly to traveling third class in Bulgaria. (Time 113:76 June 25, 79)

TREATIES

De Gaulle, Charles. Treaties fade as quickly as young girls and roses. (New York Times Magazine 42 April 27, 80)

TRILATERAL COMMISSION

Lord, Winston. The Trilateral Commission doesn't secretly run the world. The Council on Foreign Relations does that. (W 7:9 Aug 4, 78)

TRUDEAU, GARRY

Trudeau, Garry. I can't write a joke to save my ass. (Newsweek 116:61 Oct 15, 89)

Trudeau, Garry. I've been trying for some time now to develop a life-style that doesn't require my presence. (Time 118:47 July 20, 81)

TRUDEAU, MARGARET

Trudeau, Margaret. I was not so much a hippy as a failed hippy; a hippy without a cause. (Guardian Weekly 120:18 June 17, 79)

TRUMAN, HARRY S.

Truman, Harry S. I never did give anybody hell. I just told the truth, and they thought it was hell. (Time 105:45 June 9, 75)

TRUMP, DONALD

Stone, John S. Trammell Crow is the kind of person Donald Trump ought to want to be when Donald Trump grows up. (Chicago Tribune 365:1 Section 16 Dec 31, 89)

Trump, Donald. I can be very happy living in a one-bedroom apartment, believe me. (Newsweek 115:15 Mar 5, 90)

Trump, Donald. I love quality, but I don't believe in paying top price for quality. (Time 133:50 Jan 16, 89)

Trump, Donald. I'm not running for president, but if I did...I'd win. (US 3:6 Nov 2, 87)

Trump, Donald. The 1990s sure aren't like the 1980s'. (Newsweek 115:June 18, 90)

TRUST

Frain, Andy. Never trust a man with a mustache or a man who carries an umbrella. (The Reader (Chicago's Free Weekly) 7:14 Jan 27, 78)

Johnson, Lyndon Baines. I never trust a man unless I've got his pecker in my pocket. (Village Voice 21:16 Nov 8, 76)

TRUTH

Barrymore, John. There's something about a closet that makes a skeleton terribly restless. (Kansas City Times 109:14B July 8, 77)

Hazzard, Shirley. Nothing supplies the truth except the will for it. (Fame 1:38 Mar 90)

Hepburn, Katharine. I think that one terrifying thing that has happened now is that the truth has gone out of style. (Toronto Globe and Mail 138:1 Nov 28, 81)

Hunt, Everette Howard. No one is entitled to the truth. (Rolling Stone 239:40 May 19, 77)

Huxley, Thomas. It is the customary fate of new truths to begin as heresies and to end as superstitions. (Omni 2:36 June 80)

Jerome, Jerome K. It is always the best policy to speak the truth, unless of course you are an exceptionally good liar. (Kansas City Star 97:26 May 2, 77)

Keyserling, Hermann A. The greatest American superstition is belief in facts. (Kansas City Times 109:26 Jan 25, 77)

Leary, Timothy. You have to remember, the truth is funny. (Cleveland 8:17 Nov 79)

Norman, Edward. Truth does not cease because people give up believing it. (The Observer 9767:13 Nov 5, 78)

Rayburn, Sam. Son, always tell the truth. Then you'll never have to remember what you said the last time. (Chicago Sun-Times 32:32 June 28, 79)

Santayana, George. Sometimes we have to change the truth in order to remember it. (Time 106:57 July 28, 75)

Sitwell, Edith. The public will believe anything, so long as it is not founded on truth. (Kansas City Star 97:2D Feb 20, 77)

Tanner, Jack. What is counted as truth in one age is counted as myth in the next. (Challenge 19:4 Mar/April 76)

TUCHMAN, BARBARA

Tuchman, Barbara. I never became a

journalist because I wasn't pushy enough. (W Supplement 16:47 July 27, 87)

TURBEVILLE, DEBORAH

Turbeville, Deborah. I'm as far as you can get from a romantic. I'm tough, not sweet. (Mirabella 2:20 July 89)

TURNER, LANA

Shaw, Artie. If she didn't breathe by reflex, she'd probably forget to (about Lana Turner). (US 3:60 Oct 21, 85)

Turner, Lana. I never did dig sex very much. (Life 7:39 Jan 83)

TURNER, R. E. (TED)

Turner, R. E. (Ted). "If I fail" doesn't exist in my vocabulary. (TV Guide 33:7 Dec 28, 85)

Turner, R. E. (Ted). I want to be the first trillionaire. (Southpoint 2:29 April 89)

Turner, R. E. (Ted). If being against stuffiness and pompousness and bigotry is bad behavior, then I plead guilty. (Time 110:84 Sept 19, 77)

Turner, R. E. (Ted). My desire to excel borders on the unhealthy. (Time 120:50 Aug 9, 82)

TWENTIETH CENTURY

Mailer, Norman. Ego is the word of the century. (New York Times Magazine 110 Dec 2, 79)

Remarque, Erich Maria. Not to laugh at the 20th century is to shoot yourself. (Time 111:94 April 3, 78)

Rowse, A. L. This filthy 20th century. I hate its guts. (Time 112:K9 Nov 13, 78)

Solzhenitsyn, Aleksandr Isaevich. Hastiness and superficiality are the psychic disease of the 20th century. (Time 111:33 June 19, 78)

2 LIVE CREW (MUSICAL GROUP)

Rogow, Bruce. One person's vulgarity is another person's art. (Chicago Tribune 278:27 Section 1 Oct 5, 90)

UNDERDEVELOPED AREAS

Abdullah, Ismail Sabry. No nation, no matter how rich, can develop another country. (Time 106:42 Dec 22, 75)

Nam Duck Woo, (Deputy Prime Minister of South Korea). There is not one developing country in the world where Western democracy really works. (Time 107:32 June 6, 77)

UNEMPLOYMENT

Becker, Jules. It is much harder to find a job than to keep one. (Washingtonian 14:152 Nov 78)

Cohen, Jamie. The biggest industrial health problem in America today is unemployment (1986). (Southern Exposure 14:55 Sept 86)

Hayden, Thomas. I don't believe that any defense contract ought to be cut in the face of mass unemployment. (US News & World Report 18:12 Nov 3, 75)

UNEMPLOYMENT—RELIEF MEASURES

Reagan, Ronald. Unemployment insurance is a prepaid vacation plan for freeloaders. (Time 116:16 Aug 25, 80)

UNITED FARM WORKERS UNION

Chavez, Cesar. We will win in the end. We learned many years ago that the rich may have the money, but the poor have the time. (Newsweek 86:67B Sept 22, 75)

UNITED NATIONS

Koch, Edward I. If the United Nations would leave New York, nobody would ever hear of it again. (The Observer 9938:13 Feb 21, 82)

Moynihan, Daniel Patrick. If the U.N. didn't exist, it would be impossible to invent it. (Time 107:27 Jan 26, 76)

Richard, Ivor. The U.N. will not abolish sin, but it can make it more difficult for the sinner. (US News & World Report 87:62 Sept 17, 79)

UNITED STATES

Bell, Griffin. I think we have too many crimes, and I definitely have the view that we have too many laws. (Time 108:16 Dec 27, 76)

Billington, James. Violence is not only "as American as cherry pie," it is likely to remain a la mode for some time to come. (Newsweek 86:13 Oct 6, 75)

Borges, Jorge Luis. America is still the best hope. But the Americans themselves will have to be the best hope too. (Time 107:51 July 5, 76)

Brown, Edmund Gerald, Jr. People are ready to make sacrifice for the betterment of this country, but only on a basis that we all bear up the burdens and bear under them on an equal basis, and that is not happening today. (Meet The Press 19:2 Oct 5, 75)

Brown, Edmund Gerald, Jr. There is a limit to the good things we have in this country. We're coming up against those limits. It's really a very salutary exercise to learn to live with them. (Time 106:18 Dec 8, 75)

Butz, Earl Lauer. Our capitalism is no longer capitalism; it is a weakened mixture of government regulations and limited business opportunities. (American Legion Magazine 99:21 Dec 75)

Chandler, A. B. (Happy). We Americans are a peculiar people. We are for the underdog no matter how much of a dog he is. (Reader's Digest 107:78 Nov 75)

Davis, Angela. I'm not pessimistic about change in this country. I'm convinced that this country will one day be socialist. (New York 11:43 April 17, 78)

Ehrlichman, John D. We operate in this country, and in the media and the courts, on a situational ethics base. (Time 106:21 Dec 1, 75)

Falwell, Jerry. Not only should we register them (Communists), but we should stamp it on their foreheads and send them back to Russia. This is a free country. (Washington Post 275:B3 Sept 6, 77)

Ford, Henry, II. This country developed in a particular way because of the automobile, and you can't just push a button and change it. (Time 105:71 Feb 10, 75)

Fuentes, Carlos. (The U. S.) is a country in love with itself and it cares about the world only in the measure that the world cares about the United States. (Fame 3:24 Feb 90)

Fuentes, Carlos. Mexicans have always asked themselves why a people so close to God should be so near the United States. (W 5:9 Oct 29, 76)

Fuentes, Carlos. What the United States does best is to understand itself. What it does worst is understand others. (Time 127:52 June 16, 86)

Hofstadter, Richard. The United States was the only country in the world that began with perfection and aspired to progress. (Wisconsin Trails 17:5 Winter 76)

Hubbard, Elbert. This will never be a civilized country until we spend more money for books than we do for chewing gum. (Human Behavior 6:12 May 77)

Hungate, William. The electorate knows more and believes less and expresses it louder than at any time in history. (Wall Street Journal 56:1 April 28, 76)

Kennedy, John Fitzgerald. If we are strong, our strength will speak for itself. If we are weak, words will be no help. (Kansas City Times 109:28 Jan 4, 77)

Keyserling, Hermann A. The greatest American superstition is belief in facts. (Kansas City Times 109:26 Jan 25, 77)

Kissinger, Henry Alfred. The American body politic is basically healthy. Our people want to believe in their government. (Time 106:35 Oct 27, 75)

Kovic, Ron. The government took the best years of my life away from me and millions of other young men. I just think they're lucky I wrote a book instead of buying a gun. (People Weekly 6:58 Dec 27/Jan 3, 77)

Lippmann, Walter. America has always been not only a country but a dream. (American West 20:8 Nov 83)

Martin, Abe. What this country needs is a good five-cent cigar. (Human Behavior 7:70 Sept 78)

Mauldin, Bill. We have more provincialism and bigotry and superstition and prejudice per square mile than almost any other nation. (Rolling Stone 225:56 Nov 4, 76)

McGovern, George Stanley. Thoughtful Americans understand that the highest patriotism is not a blind acceptance of official policy, but a love of one's country deep enough to call her to a higher standard. (Life 2:117 Dec 79)

Montaner, Carlos Alberto. The U.S. is a neurotic Midas who homogenizes everything he touches. (Atlas World Press Review 23:39 Nov 76)

Morris, Richard B. The United States is still the last best hope of man. (US News & World Report 81:73 July 5, 76)

Moynihan, Daniel Patrick. As the lights go out in the rest of the world, they shine all the brighter here. (Time 107:28 Jan 26, 76)

Reagan, Ronald. America's best days are yet to come. You ain't seen nothin' yet (1984). (Time 124:50 Nov 19, 84)

Reagan, Ronald. I always grew up believing that if you build a better mousetrap, the world will beat a path to your door. Now if you build a better mousetrap the government comes along with a better mouse. (Chicago Tribune 323:1 Section 1 Nov 19, 75)

Reagan, Ronald. I don't know of anyone today that has less influence in this country than business. (Washington Post 353:A14 Nov 23, 75)

Sevareid, Eric. We are a turbulent society but a stable republic. The mind goes blank at the thought of a world without one such power. (Time 110:111 Dec 12, 77)

Tyrrell, R. Emmett, Jr. In America there has always been a market for a certain kind of cheap thought. (Arkansas Times 11:37 June 85) (1)

Voigt, Jon. The real dream (of America) is that with independence there is more strength and more beauty. (Rolling Stone 292:50 May 31, 79)

Wattenberg, Ben. How can a nation that believes it hasn't done anything right in the recent past even consider that it can do anything right, or bold, or creative in the immediate future. (Washington Post 72:B1 Feb 15, 77)

Will, George F. World War II was the last government program that really worked (to the Association of American Publishers). (Washingtonian 10:22 July 75)

UNITED STATES see also AMERICANS; BUDGET—UNITED STATES; DISSENTERS—UNITED

STATES; INTELLIGENCE SERVICE—UNITED
STATES; JUSTICE, ADMINISTRATION OF—UNITED
STATES; MASS MEDIA—UNITED STATES; MEDICAL
SERVICE—UNITED STATES; SOCIALISM—UNITED
STATES; TRADE UNIONS—UNITED STATES

UNITED STATES MILITARY ACADEMY, WEST POINT

MacArthur, Douglas. Duty, honor, country: Those three hallowed words reverently dictate what you want to be, what you can be, and what you will be...The long gray line has never failed us (at the U.S. Military Academy at West Point, May 12, 1962). (Washington Post 208:B1 July 1, 77)

UNITED STATES—APPROPRIATION AND EXPENDITURES

Wicker, Tom. Government expands to absorb revenue—and then some. (Washingtonian 14:155 Nov 78)

UNITED STATES—ARMED FORCES

Yarmolinsky, Adam. It is plain foolishness to have fewer and fewer well trained soldiers operating more and more complicated equipment. (USA Today 1:10A Jan 14, 83)

UNITED STATES—CONSTITUTION

Douglas, William Orville. The press has a preferred position in our constitutional scheme not to enable it to make money, not to set newsmen apart as a favored class, but to bring fulfillment to the public's right to know. (New York Times 127:2 Section 4 Aug 6, 78)

Jordan, Barbara. My faith in the Constitution is whole—complete—total. (Newsweek 88:70 July 4, 76)

Koch, Edward I. The Constitution is dumb (March 1981). (Village Voice 27:12 Mar 12, 82)

Wirin, Abraham Lincoln. The rights of all persons are wrapped in the same constitutional bundle as those of the most hated member of the community. (Time 111:94 Feb 20, 78)

UNITED STATES—CONSTITUTION—AMENDMENTS

Cline, Ray S. The First Amendment is not the central purpose of our Constitution. (More 8:21 Feb 78)

UNITED STATES—CONSTITUTION—AMENDMENTS—FIRST AMENDMENT

Brennan, William. If there is a bedrock principle underlying the First Amendment, it is that the Government may not prohibit the expression of an idea simply because society finds the idea itself offensive or disagreeable. (Time 134:14 July 3, 89)

Dershowitz, Alan M. Screw is a despicable magazine, but that's what the First Amendment was designed to protect. (Newsweek 90:53 Nov 7, 77)

UNITED STATES—CONSTITUTION—BILL OF RIGHTS

Goldwater, Barry Morris, Jr. Without a sense of privacy, the Bill of Rights' guarantees cease to function. (Time 110:17 July 18, 77)

Hayden, Thomas. If it weren't for the Bill of Rights people like me would be in jail instead of running for office (commenting on his bid for the Senate). (Los Angeles Times 95:3 Part 1 Jan 5, 76)

UNITED STATES—DEFENSES

Hart, Gary. We can't be defensive on defense. (New York 19:26 May 5, 86)

Wood, Lowell. The things most discussed in public are the ones the government is least interested in (about space weapons). (Newsweek 105:38 June 17, 85)

UNITED STATES—DESCRIPTION

Boorstin, Daniel J. We suffer primarily not from our vices or our weaknesses, but from our illusions. (Time 114:133 Nov 12, 79)

Buchwald, Art. As the economy gets better, everything else gets worse. (Book Digest 6:32 Dec 79)

Commoner, Barry. Our system today no more resembles free enterprise than a freeway resembles a dirt road. (Time 114:19 Aug 13, 79)

Douglas, William Orville. The great and invigorating influences in American life have been the unorthodox; the people who challenge an existing institution or way of life, or say and do things that make people think. (Kansas City Times 109:14C Jan 22, 77)

Eisenhower, Dwight David. It has been the tough-minded optimist whom history has proved right in America. (Newsweek 85:18 Feb 24, 75)

Erish, Andrew. America is 90 percent corn. (New York Times 128:23 Nov 25, 78)

Fairlie, Henry. The once rambunctious American spirit of innovation and adventurousness is today being paralyzed by the desire to build a risk-free society. (Time 114:71 Oct 22, 79)

Foley, Thomas S. There is a mood in this country that government action is not necessarily always the perfect solution to social problems. (US News & World Report 84:24 Jan 23, 78)

Hellman, Lillian. We have no national memory. (Time 113:28 April 23, 79)

Jordan, Hamilton. Perhaps the strongest feeling in this country today (1972) is the general distrust and disillusionment of government and politicians at all levels. (New York Times 128:A17 July 19, 79)

King, Florence. Sharing is not what America

is all about; in our hearts, each of us is an only child. (Vanity Fair 47:20 Oct 84)

Morgan, Ted. One has come to America to get a sense of life's possibilities. (Philadelphia 69:179 Nov 78)

Naipaul, V. S. Ignorant people in preppy clothes are more dangerous to America than oil embargoes. (Life 7:39 Jan 83)

Rahv, Philip. Nothing can last in America more than ten years. (Time 110:67 Aug 15, 77)

Reese, Charley. The Soviet Union has a powerful lobby in the United States which consists of Communists, socialists, greedy bankers and businessmen, pacifists, and cowards. (The Progressive 47:13 Nov 83)

Sawyer, Charles. The United States, like Atlas, is holding up the world. But who holds up Atlas? American business. (Time 113:85 April 23, 79)

Solzhenitsyn, Aleksandr Isaevich. To defend oneself, one must also be ready to die; there is little such readiness in a society raised in the cult of material well-being. (Time 111:18 June 26, 78)

Taniguchi, Yoshiko. Affluence made many Americans content with their lives. This has begun to show in their products. (Newsweek 115:19 April 2, 90)

Trudeau, Garry. America is one of the few places where the failure to promote oneself is widely regarded as arrogance. (Time 126:57 Oct 7, 85)

Vonnegut, Kurt. Life in our country has become one big TV serial. (Lawrence (Kansas) Journal-World 128:1 Oct 23, 86)

UNITED STATES—ECONOMIC CONDITIONS

Bermer, Richard. The question is no longer whether there will be a recession but how deep it will be and how long it will last (1990). (Time 136:38 Aug 20, 90)

Carter, James Earl. There is nothing for nothing. (Newsweek 96:55 July 14, 80)

Greenspan, Alan. The current level of inflation, let alone an increase, is not acceptable (1989). (Time 133:51 Mar 6, 89)

Harris, Fred. Our current economic problems are not a failure of the system, they are a failure of economic leadership. (Village Voice 20:28 July 7, 75)

Heller, Walter. By mid-year double digit inflation should be behind us (Jan 23, 1980). (Kansas City Star 102:9A Oct 12, 81)

Kurokawa, Masaaki. The United States will have to follow a set of austerity measures similar, in some sense, to those imposed by the I.M.F. on debt-ridden countries.

(New York Times 138:3 Section 3 Feb 19, 89)

Laffer, Arthur. The U.S. is the fastest 'undeveloping' country in the world. (Time 114:36 Aug 27, 79)

Nukazawa, Kazuo. The United States is over the hill, and blaming the discomfort on an easy target (Japan). (Newsweek 115:22 April 2, 90)

Volcker, Paul A. The standard of living of the average American has to decline. (New York Times 129:1 Oct 18, 79)

UNITED STATES—ECONOMIC POLICY

Friedman, Milton. In the United States the Federal Reserve has never practiced monetarism. (Washington Post 106:C4 May 29, 83)

Jacob, John. Reaganomics is giving voodoo a bad name. (Lawrence (Kansas) Journal-World 124:5A Nov 7, 82)

UNITED STATES—ECONOMIC RELATIONS—EUROPE

Rothschild, Emma. For the last 20 years, America's influence on Europe has had more to do with food and animal feed than with high politics or low diplomacy. (New York Times 127:19 Section E April 16, 78)

UNITED STATES—ECONOMIC RELATIONS—INDIANS OF NORTH AMERICA

Watt, James. If you want an example of the failure of socialism, don't go to Russia. Come to America and go to the American Indian reservations. (Life 7:176 Jan 83)

UNITED STATES—ECONOMIC RELATIONS—JAPAN

Crow, Trammell. I have yet to have one disappointment in dealing with the Japanese. (Chicago Tribune 365:1 Section 16 Dec 31, 89)

UNITED STATES—ECONOMIC RELATIONS—VIETNAM

Kissinger, Henry Alfred. Among the many claims on American resources, I would put those of Vietnam in alphabetical order. (Newsweek 89:47 May 16, 77)

UNITED STATES—FOREIGN OPINION

Morrow, Lance. It bewilders Americans to be hated. (The Observer 9829:9 Jan 13, 80)

UNITED STATES—FOREIGN POLICY

Brown, Harold. A lesson we learned from Vietnam is that we should be very cautious about intervening in any place where there's a poor political base for our presence. (Time 109:24 May 23, 77)

Brzezinski, Zbigniew. A big country like the U.S. is not like a speedboat on a lake. It can't veer suddenly to the right or left. It's like a large ship. There's continuity to its course. (Time 111:18 May 29, 78)

Brzezinski, Zbigniew. By the time we're through, the world will have been reordered. (W 7:33 Nov 10, 78)

Brzezinski, Zbigniew. Pessimism is a luxury that policymakers can't afford because pessimism, on the part of people who try to shape events, can become a self-fulfilling prophecy. (Time 112:26 Aug 21, 78)

Bush, George. I will not use food as a foreign policy weapon (1988). (Chicago Tribune 231:1 Section 4 Aug 19, 90)

Carter, James Earl. I am against any creation of a separate Palestinian state. (Chicago Sun-Times 32:3 Aug 12, 79)

Carter, James Earl. We are now free of that inordinate fear of Communism which once led us to embrace any dictator who joined us in our fear. (Time 107:9 June 6, 77)

Cline, Ray S. The most urgent task for the U. S. is to stop wars of national liberation. (Mother Jones 10:39 Aug 85)

Eaton, Cyrus S. We must either learn to live with the Communists or resign ourselves to perish with them. (Time 113:93 May 21, 79)

Giscard d'Estaing, Valery. You do not fear freedom for yourself, do not then fear it for your friends and allies. (New York Times 125:2 May 19, 76)

Guthrie, Arlo. If we want to hold hands around the world, we have to learn to use both hands. (Village Voice 26:28 Feb 18, 81)

Hyland, William G. Protectionism is the ally of isolationism, and isolationism is the Dracula of American foreign policy. (New York Times 136:2 May 17, 87)

Kennedy, Edward Moore. We cannot afford a foreign policy based on the pangs of unrequited love. (The Tennessean 74:7 Jan 30, 80)

Kennedy, John Fitzgerald. Domestic policy can only defeat us; foreign policy can kill us. (New York Times Magazine 50 Sept 9, 79)

Kissinger, Henry Alfred. I have always thought of foreign policy as bipartisan. (Chicago Tribune 233:6 Section 2 Aug 21, 77)

Meany, George. Foreign policy is too damned important to be left to the Secretary of State. (Time 106:7 Sept 8, 75)

Nixon, Richard Milhous. If the United States doesn't stand up for our friends when they are in trouble, we're going to wind up without any friends. (New York Times 128:B6 July 12, 79)

Reagan, Ronald. I'm beginning to wonder if the symbol of the United States pretty soon isn't going to be an ambassador with a flag under his arm climbing into the escape helicopter. (Time 113:11 Mar 5, 79)

Reagan, Ronald. The (Carter) administration doesn't know the difference between being a diplomat and a doormat. (US News & World Report 86:54 May 7, 79)

Reagan, Ronald. Treaties invite nationalization (about the Panama Canal). (Time 107:19 May 17, 76)

Reagan, Ronald. Walter Mondale accuses us of ad-libbing our foreign policy. Not true. We read it right off the three-by-five cards. (Washingtonian 20:113 Oct 84)

Rogers, William D. Making foreign policy is a little bit like making pornographic movies. It's more fun doing it than watching it. (Chicago Sun-Times 29:9 June 29, 76)

Schlesinger, James Rodney. The American role in maintaining a worldwide military balance is better understood in Moscow than it is in this country. (American Legion Magazine 98:20 Jan 74)

Schmidt, Helmut. He (Jimmy Carter) is making (foreign) policy from the pulpit. (Time 107:14 May 9, 77)

Weinberger, Caspar. If the movement from Cold War to detente is progress, then let me say we cannot afford much more progress. (Life 5:33 Jan 81)

Williams, William Appleman. The act of imposing one people's morality upon another people is an imperial denial of self-determination. (Chicago Tribune 71:6 Section 2 Mar 12, 90)

Yew, Lee Kuan. The Russians say that there are many different roads to socialism, and that sounds good to new nations. But the United States seems to be saying that there is only one road to democracy. (American Legion Magazine 103:12 Aug 77)

UNITED STATES—FOREIGN POLICY see also YOUNG, ANDREW

UNITED STATES—FOREIGN POLICY— 1960

Kennedy, John Fitzgerald. No future American president should be driven into a corner where his only choice is world devastation or submission (1960). (Washingtonian 19:128 Mar 84)

UNITED STATES—FOREIGN POLICY— CENTRAL AMERICA

Church, Frank. There is no reason to transform a revolution in any of the countries of Central America, regardless from where it draws its initial external support, into a security crisis for us. (The Nation 241:588 Nov 30, 85)

Schultz, George. Central America is West.

The East must get out. (New York 18:32 June 10, 84)

UNITED STATES—FOREIGN POLICY—CIVIL RIGHTS

Vance, Cyrus R. In pursuing a human rights policy, we must always keep in mind the limits of our power and of our wisdom. (New York Times 126:2 Section 1 May 1, 76)

UNITED STATES—FOREIGN POLICY—NICARAGUA

Dole, Bob. I've got a feeling a little three day invasion wouldn't make anybody unhappy down there, if you just overthrew Ortega. But that's just my guess. (Newsweek 110:21 Sept 21, 87)

Gomez, Eden Pastora. Anyone who recommends invading Nicaragua is insane. (Life 7:113 Jan 83)

Reagan, Ronald. We are not doing anything to try and overthrow the Nicaraguan government. (USA Today 1:10A April 18, 83)

UNITED STATES—FOREIGN POLICY—RELATIONS—UNITED STATES. CONGRESS

Reagan, Ronald. We have got to get to where we can run a foreign policy without a committee of 535 telling us what we can do. (New York 18:32 June 10, 84)

UNITED STATES—FOREIGN POLICY—SOUTH AFRICA

Botha, Pieter W. To both friend and foe, the United States is becoming constructively irrelevant (1987). (Chicago Tribune 14:17 Jan 14, 87)

UNITED STATES—FOREIGN POLICY—VIETNAM

Kissinger, Henry Alfred. Among the many claims on American resources, I would put those of Vietnam in alphabetical order. (Newsweek 89:47 May 16, 77)

UNITED STATES—FOREIGN RELATIONS

Ford, Gerald Rudolph. I don't think the United States should ever involve itself in the internal situation in any country. (New York 9:33 Feb 23, 76)

Giscard d'Estaing, Valery. You do not fear freedom for yourself, do not then fear it for your friends and allies. (New York Times 125:2 May 19, 76)

Harris, Fred. Sometimes it seems we are willing to prop up any two-bit dictator who can afford the price of a pair of sunglasses. (Time 106:25 Dec 22, 75)

Kissinger, Henry Alfred. We are not going around looking for opportunities to prove our manhood. (Ms 4:63 Oct 75)

Rockefeller, Nelson Aldrich. Congressional actions in the past few years, however well intentioned, have hamstrung the presidency and usurped the presidential prerogative in the conduct of foreign affairs. (Christian Science Monitor 68:2 May 11, 76)

UNITED STATES—FOREIGN RELATIONS—ANGOLA

Diggs, Charles C. As an American, I regret that the United States has allowed the Soviet Union to become identified as the principal supporter of African liberation. (New York Times 125:6 Jan 12, 76)

Kissinger, Henry Alfred. If we do not meet the Russian challenge now at modest cost we will find it necessary to do so further down the road when it will be more costly and more dangerous (commenting on why U.S. aid is needed in Angola). (Christian Science Monitor 21:9 Dec 24, 75)

UNITED STATES—FOREIGN RELATIONS—ARAB STATES

Arafat, Yasir. The future of the United States of America, the American interest in this part of the world, is with the Arab people, not with Israel. (Chicago Sun-Times 32:3 Aug 12, 79)

UNITED STATES—FOREIGN RELATIONS—BRAZIL

Nixon, Richard Milhous. As Brazil goes, so will the rest of the Latin American continent (commenting in 1971). (Time 108:30 Nov 29, 76)

UNITED STATES—FOREIGN RELATIONS—CENTRAL AMERICA

North, Oliver L., Jr. What we are facing in Central America and in Nicaragua is much more than just a regional crisis. We are fighting for our ability to survive and to prevent another world war. (Kansas City Star 107:2A July 14, 87)

UNITED STATES—FOREIGN RELATIONS—CHINA (PEOPLE'S REPUBLIC)

Aiken, George. I don't know how you go about containing an idea. I also don't know how you go about containing 700 million people. (Kansas City Times 117:A-24 Nov 22, 84)

Mao, Tse-Tung. If the Americans do not recognize us in 1,000 years, they will recognize us in 1,001 years. (New York Times 126:3 Section 4 Aug 21, 77)

Mao, Tse-Tung. Sometimes we have only to fart to stir Americans into moving a battleship or two or even a whole fleet. (Time 108:44 Sept 20, 76)

UNITED STATES—FOREIGN RELATIONS—CUBA

Kennedy, Robert Francis (attributed by Bill Moyers). I have myself wondered if we did not pay a very great price for being more energetic than wise about a lot of things, especially Cuba. (Washington Post 228:A5 July 21, 77)

UNITED STATES—FOREIGN RELATIONS—CZECHOSLOVAKIA

Havel, Vaclav. You can help us most of all if you help the Soviet Union on its irreversible but immensely complicated road to democracy. (Newsweek 115:28 Mar 5, 90)

UNITED STATES—FOREIGN RELATIONS—EUROPE

Gysi, Gregor. I have never been in America in my life, but I think it is a country that should not give up its responsibilities for Europe. (New York Times 139:1 Dec 15, 89)

UNITED STATES—FOREIGN RELATIONS—IRAQ

Bush, George. Iraq will not be permitted to annex Kuwait. That's not a threat, not a boast. That's just the way it's going to be. (Time 136:32 Sept 24, 89)

UNITED STATES—FOREIGN RELATIONS—IRAN

Janklow, William. The only way we want to give them arms is dropping them from the bay of a B-1 bomber. (Newsweek 109:17 Mar 16, 87)

Reagan, Ronald. I do not think it (the Iran arms sale) was a mistake. (Time 128:18 Dec 8, 86)

Reagan, Ronald. I think we took the only action we could have in Iran (1986). (Time 128:18 Dec 8, 86)

Reagan, Ronald. It is my desire to have the full story about Iran come out now—the alleged transfer of funds, the Swiss bank accounts, who was involved—everything. (New York Times 136:2 Dec 17, 86)

UNITED STATES—FOREIGN RELATIONS—ISRAEL

Arafat, Yasir. The future of the United States of America, the American interest in this part of the world, is with the Arab people, not with Israel. (Chicago Sun-Times 32:3 Aug 12, 79)

Carter, James Earl. I'd rather commit political suicide than hurt Israel. (Time 110:30-33 Oct 17, 77)

Carter, James Earl. The survival of Israel is not a political issue. It is a moral imperative. (Time 107:13 June 21, 76)

UNITED STATES—FOREIGN RELATIONS—LATIN AMERICA

Reagan, Ronald. The Latin American countries have a respect for macho. I think if the United States reacts with firmness and fairness, we might not earn their love, but we would earn their respect. (Time 107:12 May 17, 76)

UNITED STATES—FOREIGN RELATIONS—MEXICO

Castaneda, Jorge. We would like to see the U.S. treat us (Mexico) as an adult country capable of managing our own affairs. (Newsweek 94:26 Oct 1, 79)

Lopez Portillo, Jose. Mexico is neither on the list of United States priorities nor on that of United States respect. (New York Times 128:A8 Nov 20, 78)

UNITED STATES—FOREIGN RELATIONS—MIDDLE EAST

Kissinger, Henry Alfred. All the Russians can offer is war, but we can bring the peace (commenting on the Mideast situation). (Time 109:16 Jan 24, 77)

UNITED STATES—FOREIGN RELATIONS—RUSSIA

Ford, Gerald Rudolph. Detente means moderate and restrained behavior between two superpowers—not a license to fish in troubled waters. (American Legion Magazine 99:36 Nov 75)

Kissinger, Henry Alfred. If we do not meet the Russian challenge now at modest cost we will find it necessary to do so further down the road when it will be more costly and more dangerous (commenting on why U.S. aid is needed in Angola). (Christian Science Monitor 21:9 Dec 24, 75)

Kissinger, Henry Alfred. The cold war was not so terrible and detente was not so exalting. (The Observer 9833:9 Feb 10, 80)

Nixon, Richard Milhous. We are now in a war called peace. (Time 114:27 Sept 10, 79)

Reagan, Ronald. My fellow Americans, I'm pleased to tell you today that I've signed legislation that will outlaw Russia forever. We begin bombing in five minutes. (Life 9:72 Jan 84)

Will, George F. Reagan's policy is detente without intellect. (Time 119:51 April 19, 82)

UNITED STATES—HISTORY

Deng Xiaoping. In the 1960's and 1970's there were many student movements and turmoils in the United States. Did they have any other recourse but to mobilize police and troops, arrest people and shed blood. (Newsweek 114:15 July 3, 89)

UNITED STATES—INTELLECTUAL LIFE

Boorstin, Daniel J. The courage we inherit from our Jeffersons and Lincolns and others is not the Solzhenitsyn courage of the true believer, but the courage to doubt. (Time 111:21 June 26, 78)

Rand, Ayn. The state of today's culture is so low that I do not care to spend my time watching and discussing it. (Time 107:32

Jan 12, 76)

UNITED STATES—MILITARY POLICY

Anonymous. Any country that goes to this much trouble to account for every soldier it loses probably ought not to fight a war. (Time 109:18 Mar 28, 77)

Haig, Alexander M. The arms race is the only game in town. (Esquire 90:31 Sept 26, 78)

Hayden, Thomas. I don't believe that any defense contract ought to be cut in the face of mass unemployment. (US News & World Report 18:12 Nov 3, 75)

Kissinger, Henry Alfred. We now face the challenge of the early '80s with forces designed in the '60s. (Chicago Sun-Times 32:2 Aug 1, 79)

Kissinger, Henry Alfred. We should have bombed the hell out of them the minute we got into office (a week after the 1973 Vietnam peace agreement). (Rolling Stone 188:35 June 5, 75)

McGovern, George Stanley. He who tugs Uncle Sam's beard too hard risks reprisal from the mightiest nation on the face of this earth. (The Observer 9822:9 Nov 25, 79)

Reagan, Ronald. Of the four wars in my lifetime, none came about because the U.S. was too strong. (The Observer 9853:12 June 29, 80)

Schlesinger, James Rodney. The American role in maintaining a worldwide military balance is better understood in Moscow than it is in this country. (American Legion Magazine 98:20 Jan 74)

Schroeder, Patricia. When men talk about defense, they always claim to be protecting women and children, but they never ask the women and children what they think. (New York Times Book Review 35 Feb 17, 80)

UNITED STATES—MILITARY POLICY—IRAN

Khomeini, Ayatollah Ruhollah. We (Iran) did not need these armaments in the past; we will not be in need of them in the future (about U.S. arms). (US News & World Report 85:46 Nov 20, 78)

UNITED STATES—POLITICS AND GOVERNMENT

Abourezk, James. Anybody who really changed things for the better in this country could never be elected President anyway. (Playboy 26:105-06 Mar 79)

Armey, Dick. Demagoguery beats data every time. (Newsweek 16:22 July 16, 90)

Baker, Bobby. It's very important for the American people to know who's buying their politicians. (Chicago Sun-Times 31:8 July 7, 78)

Baron, Alan. We have divided the presidential election process from the governing process. (Time 115:27 Jan 28, 80)

Beard, Peter. Nixon is what America deserved and Nixon is what America got. (Photograph 5:5 April 78)

Boorstin, Daniel J. Our national politics has become a competition for images or between images, rather than between ideals. (Time 113:84 April 9, 79)

Brown, Edmund Gerald, Jr. The nation is not governable without new ideas. (Time 114:21 Nov 12, 79)

Caddell, Patrick. I don't know any politicians in America who could run against himself and win. (Time 115:18 April 7, 80)

Califano, Joseph A., Jr. No just society can deny the right of its citizens to the health care they need. We are the only industrial society that does. (New York Times 136:2 Jan 13, 87)

Carter, James Earl. In war, we offer our very lives as a matter of routine. We must be no less daring, no less steadfast, in the pursuit of peace. (Time 113:12 Mar 26, 79)

Carter, James Earl. The American people and our government will continue our firm commitment to promote respect for human rights not only in our own country but also abroad (to Andrei Sakharov). (Newsweek 89:17 Feb 28, 77)

Carter, James Earl. We must face a time of national austerity (1978). (US News & World Report 85:17 Nov 6, 78)

Church, Frank. Somehow, some day, this country has got to learn to live with revolution in the Third World. (Time 124:46 Dec 31, 84)

Clay, William. Whenever I see certain elements in the press show favoritism to a Black man running for a position of power, I know there's a nigger in the woodpile somewhere. (Sepia 26:10 May 76)

Colby, William Egan. I'm convinced it's possible to run a secret agency as part of a constitutional society. (Time 107:17 Jan 19, 76)

Dennis, Richard. Someone must support unpopular truths and unconventional points of view. (Town & Country 143:164 Dec 89)

Dorfman, Dan. To lie to the press on a public matter is, in effect, to lie to the people. (New York 10:9 May 9, 77)

Dudney, Bob. The country would have recovered from the death of John Kennedy, but it hasn't recovered yet from the death of Lee Harvey Oswald and probably never will. (Esquire 85:62 Feb 76)

Ehrlichman, John D. Narcotics suppression is a very sexy political issue. (Playboy 23:174 Nov 76)

Eisenhower, Dwight David. The path to America's future lies down the middle of the road. (Time 116:32 July 28, 80)

Foley, Thomas S. There is a mood in this country that government action is not necessarily always the perfect solution to social problems. (US News & World Report 84:24 Jan 23, 78)

Goldwater, Barry Morris. Extremism in the defense of liberty is no vice. Moderation in the pursuit of justice is no virtue. (Family Weekly 4 Dec 30, 84)

Gotlieb, Allan E. It's never over till it's over, and in the U.S. system of government it's never over. (New York Times 138:10 Jan 12, 89)

Greenfield, Jeff. You will get what you want if you vote for the candidate who says exactly the opposite of what you most deeply believe. (Penthouse 10:123 Nov 78)

Greider, William. When the Federal Reserve was created, the realm of acceptable political discourse shrank. (Harvard Business Review 66:23 May/June 88)

Harlow, Bryce N. Our only protection against the presidency is the character of the president. (Washingtonian 11:103 June 76)

Harris, Fred. Our current economic problems are not a failure of the system, they are a failure of economic leadership. (Village Voice 20:28 July 7, 75)

Heller, Joseph. No one governs. Everyone performs. Politics has become a social world. (New York Times 128:15 Section 6 Mar 4, 79)

Henderson, Vivian Wilson. We have programs for combatting racial discrimination, but not for combatting economic class distinctions. (Time 107:71 Feb 9, 76)

Hollow, Norman. In the olden days the Indian peoples defended themselves with bows and arrows. Now, politics is the only way our rights can be developed. (New York Times 125:1 Section 1 Dec 21, 75)

Holtzman, Elizabeth. Government follows Newton's law of physics. Objects stay at rest until they're pushed. (Newsweek 96:27 Sept 8, 80)

Jackson, Jesse. Whether I win or lose, American politics will never be the same. (Time 124:26 Dec 31, 84)

Lasch, Christopher. Radicalism in the United States has no great triumphs to record. (Time 110:67 Aug 15, 77)

Lisagor, Peter. Washington is a place where the truth is not necessarily the best defense. It surely runs a poor second to the statute of limitations. (Time 108:71 Dec 20, 76)

Marchetti, Victor. Ours is not yet a totalitarian government, but it is an elitist democracy—and becoming more so every year. (Inquiry 1:24 Feb 6, 78)

Marx, Leo. The establishment has taken over the art of anti-disestablishmentarianism. (M 6:84 Feb 89)

Mathias, Charles McCurdy. People tend to want to follow the beaten path. The difficulty is that the beaten path doesn't seem to be leading anywhere. (Time 106:12 Dec 8, 75)

Mondale, Walter Frederick. If you are sure you understand everything that is going on, you are hopelessly confused. (Book Digest 6:28 Dec 79)

Mondale, Walter Frederick. What we have today is government of the rich, by the rich and for the rich. (Newsweek 104:33 Aug 27, 83)

Morgan, Charles, Jr. If Moses had gone to Harvard Law School and spent three years working on the Hill, he would have written the Ten Commandments with three exceptions and a savings clause. (Rolling Stone 205:30 Jan 15, 76)

Nader, Ralph. The speed of exit of a civil servant is directly proportional to the quality of his service. (Town & Country 133:141 May 79)

Nessen, Ron. Press conferences force more policy decisions than anything else. (Time 106:32 May 5, 75)

Nixon, Richard Milhous. I'd like to see people, instead of spending so much time on the ethical problem, get after the problems that really affect the people of this country. (Newsweek 114:15 July 10, 89)

Nixon, Richard Milhous. There is one thing solid and fundamental in politics—the law of change. What's up today is down tomorrow. (Time 104:40 Aug 19, 74)

Nixon, Richard Milhous. We are a compromised country at the moment (1975). (Ladies' Home Journal 92:40 Nov 30, 75)

Nofziger, Lyn. Elections in this country are won in the center. (Newsweek 102:26 Oct 31, 83)

O'Neill, Thomas P. (Tip). If this were France, the Democratic Party would be five parties. (Time 112:42 Nov 20, 78)

Peters, Charles. In Washington, bureaucrats confer, the President proclaims and the

Congress legislates, but the impact on reality is negligible, if evident at all. (Time 115:14 June 30, 80)

Reagan, Ronald. America is back, standing tall. (Time 124:25 Dec 31, 84)

Reagan, Ronald. I believe that government is the problem, not the answer. (Washington Post 137:A5 April 20, 76)

Reston, James. Washington has no memory. (The Observer 9811:9 Sept 9, 79)

Rickover, Hyman G. Politics is to government like sex is to conception. (University Daily Kansan 94:1 Sept 30, 83)

Ridgeway, Matthew B. Candidates are no better or worse than those who choose and elect them, and therein lies the answer to what we are to become. (American Legion Magazine 101:21 Aug 76)

Robeson, Paul. American democracy is Hitler fascism. (Newsweek 86:58 Oct 6, 75)

Roosevelt, Franklin Delano. Government has the definite duty to use all its power and resources to meet new social problems with new social controls. (Newsweek 92:27 Nov 27, 78)

Roth, William V., Jr. Public confidence and trust in the federal government are low not only because of Watergate or our experience in Vietnam, but also because too many politicians have promised more than the government can deliver. (Chicago Tribune 311:1 Section 1 Nov 7, 75)

Sanders, Ed. Just because you're paranoid doesn't mean they're not trying to get you. (The Reader (Chicago's Free Weekly) 7:4 Section 1 April 7, 78)

Schroeder, Patricia. America is man enough to elect a woman President. (Time 130:20 Aug 3, 87)

Simon, William E. In the United States today, we already have more government than we need, more government than most people want, and certainly more government than we are willing to pay for. (Vital Speeches 42:72 Nov 15, 75)

Starr, Kevin O. Perhaps if we find a way to save our Presidents, we can find a way to save ourselves. (Newsweek 86:34 Oct 6, 75)

Steinfels, Peter. Rather than getting the government they want, the people should want the government they get; they should be retutored to fit its current capacities. (Newsweek 94:74 July 2, 79)

Stevenson, Adlai, II. It is better to light one candle than to curse the darkness. (New York Times Magazine 45 July 4, 76)

Stevenson, Adlai, III. I don't think ideas are incompatible with political reality. (Time 113:18 Feb 26, 79)

Stone, Isidor Feinstein. The biggest menace to American freedom is the intelligence community. (Wilson Library Bulletin 51:25 Sept 76)

Strauss, Robert S. Everybody in government is like a bunch of ants on a log floating down a river. Each one thinks he is guiding the log, but it's really just going with the flow. (Time 111:47 April 17, 78)

Strout, Richard. (American Democracy is) the only governmental vehicle on earth that has two steering wheels: one for the President, one for the Congress. You never can tell who's driving. (Time 111:83 Mar 27, 78)

Terkel, Studs. Dissent is not merely the right to dissent—it is the duty. (National Catholic Reporter 12:7 July 2, 76)

Vidal, Gore. The genius of the American ruling class, and this goes back to the beginning of the Republic, has been its ability to get people to vote against their own interests. (San Diego Magazine 34:156 Feb 82)

Wheaton, James R. Given what's happening today in Eastern Europe, in South America, even what the students have been trying to do in China, the state of democracy in America is shameful. (Los Angeles Times 109:A24 Mar 31, 90)

White, Kevin Hagen. Charismatic leadership is hungered for, but at the same time we fear it. (Time 107:10 Feb 9, 76)

White, Theodore. Politics in America is the binding secular religion. (Firing Line 5 July 26, 75)

Will, George F. When affirmative action came to Ann Arbor and Morningside Heights, dawn came up like thunder. (Newsweek 90:44 Nov 7, 77)

Woodson, Robert. A kinder, gentler nation doesn't have to be a more expensive one. (Chicago Tribune 4:15 Section 1 Jan 4, 89)

Wright, Jim. When people are drowning, there is no time to build a better ship. (Chicago Sun-Times 30:2 Feb 2, 77)

UNITED STATES—POSTAL SERVICE see POSTAL SERVICE—UNITED STATES

UNITED STATES—RACE QUESTION

Hooks, Benjamin Lawson. If we don't solve this race problem, this country isn't going to ever rest in peace. (Newsweek 88:46 Nov 22, 76)

Lowery, Joseph. Twenty years later, everything has changed and nothing has changed (on the 20th anniversary of the

assassination of Martin Luther King Jr.).
(Chicago Tribune 103:17 Section 1 April
12, 1988)

Mitterand, Francois. The day when racial
segragation ceases to be identified with
social segregation hasn't come yet. And
so long as racial protest is joined to social
protest, watch out. Even if there are
periods of calm, the awakening will be
rude (about the United States). (Village
Voice 31:32 June 3, 86)

Moynihan, Daniel Patrick. The time may
have come when the issue of race could
benefit from a period of 'benign neglect'
(to Richard Nixon in 1970). (Newsweek
94:90 Nov 19, 79)

UNITED STATES—SOCIAL CONDITIONS

Galbraith, John Kenneth. The (tax) revolt of
the affluent, which now has politicans so
frightened, is not a violent thing. The
response in the ghettoes if life there is
allowed further to deteriorate might be
different. (New York Times 128:A23 Jan
12, 79)

Iacocca, Lee A. A little righteous anger really
brings out the best in the American
personality. (Cleveland Magazine 12:149
Nov 83)

Vonnegut, Kurt. Life in our country has
become one big TV serial. (Lawrence
(Kansas) Journal-World 128:1 Oct 23, 86)

UNITED STATES. AIR FORCE

Matlovich, Leonard P. They gave me a medal
for killing two men and discharged me for
loving one. (Chicago Sun-Times 28:36
Aug 18, 75)

UNITED STATES. BUREAU OF INDIAN AFFAIRS

Tayac, Turkey (Chief of the Piscataway
Indians). They don't know about Indians
any more than a buzzard knows about ice
cream (about the Bureau of Indian
Affairs). (Washingtonian 10:103 May 75)

UNITED STATES. CENTRAL INTELLIGENCE AGENCY

Agee, Philip. The CIA claims that secrecy is
necessary to hide what it's doing from the
enemies of the United States. I claim that
the real reason for secrecy is to hide what
the CIA is doing from the American
people. (Playboy 22:49 Aug 75)

Agee, Philip. The CIA is nothing more than
the secret police of American capitalism,
plugging up leaks in the political dam
night and day so that shareholders of U.S.
companies operating in poor countries
can continue enjoying their rip-off. (Time
106:62 Aug 4, 75)

Angleton, James. Our generation believed
that you go in naked and you leave naked
(about working for the CIA). (Time 113:95

April 30, 79)

Codevilla, Angelo. I am aware that active
duty agents of the Central Intelligence
Agency worked for the George Bush
primary election campaign (in 1980).
(Village Voice 33:20 Oct 25, 1988)

Colby, William Egan. By the way, did you
ever work for the CIA? (to Bob Woodward
upon agreeing to issue an official denial
that Woodward had ever worked for the
CIA). (New York 8:50 July 28, 75)

Colby, William Egan. I'm convinced it's
possible to run a secret agency as part of
a constitutional society. (Time 107:17 Jan
19, 76)

Edwards, Don. The CIA is a real basket of
snakes compared to the FBI. (Chicago
Tribune 79:19 Mar 20, 87)

Ford, Gerald Rudolph. We cannot improve
this agency by destroying it (commenting
on the CIA at the installation ceremony for
George Bush as director). (New York
Times 125:1 Jan 31, 76)

Harriman, Averell. The Russians are not
nuts, they are not crazy people, they're
not Hitler. But they are trying to dominate
the world by their ideology and we are
killing the one instrument which we have
to fight that ideology, the CIA. (W 4:16
Nov 16, 75)

Harris, Fred. We've got to dismantle the
monster (about the CIA). (Time 106:24
Sept 29, 75)

Helms, Richard McGarrah. I think he was
yielding to that human impulse of the
greater good (explaining why the CIA
scientist in charge of the Chemical
Weapons Division did not destroy shellfish
toxin as ordered by President Nixon).
(Rolling Stone 199:34 Nov 6, 75)

Helms, Richard McGarrah. If I ever do
decide to talk, there are going to be some
very embarrassed people in this town,
you can bet on that (commenting after
testifying to the Watergate Committee on
CIA involvement in domestic intelligence
operations). (Newsweek 85:21 Feb 24,
75)

Helms, Richard McGarrah. We're not in the
Boy Scouts (about the Central Intelligence
Agency). (The Atlantic 244:36 Aug 79)

Mondale, Walter Frederick. It shows above
all that Americans are no good at all at
killing, lying and covering up and I'm glad
that's the case (on CIA assassination
attempts on foreign leaders). (Washington
Post 351:1 Nov 21, 75)

Mondale, Walter Frederick. There must be
some fundamental changes in America's
intelligence activities or they will
fundamentally change America. (Foreign

Policy 23:58 Summer 76)

Osborn, Kenneth Barton. There are
icebergs, and we are the Titanic (about
the Central Intelligence Agency). (Playboy
22:58 Aug 75)

Terkel, Studs. I would like to see the end of
institutional brutalities and stupidities. I
would like to see the abolition of the CIA,
which symbolizes those things, and I
would like people to look at the FBI as the
secret police system it is, rather than
something sacred. (Chicago Tribune
343:4 Section 1 Dec 8, 75)

Wills, Garry. The CIA is an unconstitutional
body. (Washington Post Magazine 32
June 28, 87)

**UNITED STATES. CENTRAL
INTELLIGENCE AGENCY** see also BUSH,
GEORGE; COLBY, WILLIAM EGAN

**UNITED STATES. CIVIL AERONAUTICS
BOARD** see also KAHN, ALFRED

UNITED STATES. CONGRESS

Abourezk, James. The bigger the
appropriations bill, the shorter the debate.
(Playboy 26:106 Mar 79)

Cohen, William. Congress is designed to be
slow and inefficient because it represents
the total diversity of this country. (Time
105:22 June 9, 75)

Connally, John Bowden. The power of this
country, in spite of all the misconceptions
that exist, is in the Congress of the United
States and not in the White House. (US
News & World Report 86:30 July 2, 79)

Ford, Gerald Rudolph. My motto towards
the Congress is communication,
conciliation, compromise and
cooperation. (Time 104:27 Dec 2, 74)

Rockefeller, Nelson Aldrich. Congressional
actions in the past few years, however
well intentioned, have hamstrung the
presidency and usurped the presidential
prerogative in the conduct of foreign
affairs. (Christian Science Monitor 68:2
May 11, 76)

Wright, Jim. Members (of Congress) are
now more concerned about image and
less about substance. (Time 119:13 April
26, 82)

Wright, Jim. The Wright broad rule is that
broads ought to be able to type
(commenting when asked to state a broad
rule for avoiding Congressional sex
scandals). (Wall Street Journal 57:1 Dec
31, 76)

UNITED STATES. CONGRESS. HOUSE

Bauman, Robert E. Anytime the House is in
session the American people are probably
in danger. (New York Times 125:31 April
6, 76)

UNITED STATES. CONGRESS. SENATE

Aiken, George David. I have never seen so
many incompetent persons in high office.
Politics and legislation have become more
mixed and smellier than ever
(commenting on the U.S. Senate in his
book Aiken: Senate Diary). (New York
Times 125:23 June 29, 76)

Byrd, Robert. The Senate is very much like a
violin. The sound will change with the
weather, the dampness, the humidity. The
Senate is a place of great moods. (Time
110:14 Oct 10, 77)

Goldwater, Barry Morris. I think the Senate is
beginning to look like a bunch of
jackasses. (Life 8:102 Jan 84)

Humphrey, Hubert Horatio. The Senate is a
place filled with goodwill and good
intentions, and if the road to hell is paved
with them, then it's a pretty good detour.
(Newsweek 91:23 Jan 23, 78)

Pryor, David. While this (the Senate) is said
to be the most exclusive club in the world,
no one ever said it's the most productive.
(Newsweek 111:17 Jan 4, 88)

Roosevelt, Franklin Delano. The only way to
do anything in the American government
is to bypass the Senate (returning from
Yalta). (Chicago Tribune 147:2 Section 2
May 29, 77)

**UNITED STATES. DEPARTMENT OF
DEFENSE**

McCarthy, Eugene Joseph. The selling of
arms is now one of the principal
occupations of the Defense Department.
(Center Report 8:11 Dec 75)

**UNITED STATES. DEPARTMENT OF
ENERGY**

Orben, Robert. I feel that if God had really
wanted us to have enough oil, He never
would have given us the Department of
Energy. (Time 113:71 Feb 26, 79)

**UNITED STATES. FEDERAL BUREAU OF
INVESTIGATION**

Edwards, Don. The CIA is a real basket of
snakes compared to the FBI. (Chicago
Tribune 79:19 Mar 20, 87)

Moore, George C. No, we never gave it a
thought (in response to whether the FBI
had ever discussed the constitutional or
legal authority for its Cointelpro Program).
(New York Times 125:1 Section 4 May 2,
76)

Terkel, Studs. I would like to see the end of
institutional brutalities and stupidities. I
would like to see the abolition of the CIA,
which symbolizes those things, and I
would like people to look at the FBI as the
secret police system it is, rather than
something sacred. (Chicago Tribune
343:4 Section 1 Dec 8, 75)

UNITED STATES. FEDERAL BUREAU OF

INVESTIGATION—RELATIONS—ORAL SEX

Hoover, John Edgar. I regret to say that we of the FBI are powerless to act in cases of oral-genital intimacy, unless it has in some way obstructed interstate commerce. (New York 13:14 Oct 6, 80)

UNITED STATES. LIBRARY OF CONGRESS

MacLeish, Archibald. What we know to be man is in these stacks (about the Library of Congress). (New York Times 129:B14 Oct 4, 79)

UNITED STATES. MARINE CORPS

Carroll, Larry. It's like that old saying that your're not a Marine until you've been shot. (Kansas City Times 120:D-3 Oct 22, 87)

UNITED STATES. SUPREME COURT

Brennan, William. It is my hope that the Court during my years of service has built a legacy of interpreting the Constitution and Federal laws to make them responsive to the needs of the people whom they were intended to benefit and protect. (Time 136:17 July 30, 90)

Dick, A. E. For thirty years, minorities, especially blacks, have been special wards of the [Supreme] Court. That no longer appears true (1989). (Newsweek 113:16-17 June 26, 89)

Jones, Bob. We're in a bad fix in America when eight evil old men and one vain and foolish woman can speak a verdict on American liberties. (The American Lawyer 5:93 Sept 83)

Neas, Ralph. There was more damage done to civil rights statutes in the last 2 1/2 weeks than in the last 2 1/2 decades (1989). (Chicago Tribune 181:3 Section 3 July 1, 89)

Nixon, Richard Milhous. Presidents come and go, but the Supreme Court, through its decisions, goes on forever. (Playboy 26:111 April 79)

Reagan, Ronald. If I have to appoint another one, I'll try to find one they'll object to just as much as this one (about Robert Bork). (Chicago Tribune 287:1 Oct 14, 87)

UNITED STATES. SUPREME COURT see also STEVENS, JOHN PAUL

UNIVERSAL DECLARATION OF HUMAN RIGHTS

Scranton, William W. The only universality that one can honestly associate with the Universal Declaration of Human Rights is universal lip service. (New York Times 126:10 Nov 25, 76)

UNIVERSE

Eddington, Arthur. The stuff of the universe is mind stuff. (Human Behavior 7:32 May 78)

Hoyle, Fred. There is a coherent plan in the universe, though I don't know what it's a plan for. (Omni 2:40 April 80)

Will, George F. The universe is not only stranger than we suppose, it is stranger than we suppose. (Kansas City Times 115:A-19 Nov 11, 82)

UNRUH, JESSE

Unruh, Jesse. If I had slain all my political enemies, I wouldn't have any friends today. (New West 1:8 Sept 13, 76)

UPPER CLASSES

Baltzell, Edward Digby, Jr. The masses who have no roots are far less dangerous to a society than an elite with no roots. (Town & Country 132:97 July 78)

Baltzell, Edward Digby, Jr. When class authority declines, money talks. (Town & Country 132:97 July 78)

VACCINES AND VACCINATION

Plotkin, Stanley. It is shameful that a country as rich as this does so poor a job immunizing its infants. (New York Times 139:A14 May 22, 90)

VAGUENESS

Brown, Edmund Gerald, Jr. In this business (politics) a little vagueness goes a long way. (New Times 6:18 May 28, 76)

VALIUM

Janov, Arthur. The world is having a nervous breakdown. Valium is the only glue that holds it together. (Rolling Stone 219:19 Aug 12, 76)

VALUES

Haskins, Caryl. It's funny that we often value what is rare and specialized. What is truly precious is what is common and unspecialized. (Washington Post 70:H7 Feb 13, 77)

Ringer, Robert J. Everything worthwhile has a price. (Playboy 28:97 Sept 81)

Wriston, Walter. I believe there are no institutional values, only personal values. (Guardian Weekly 124:16 Jan 25, 81)

VALUES see also SOCIAL VALUES; WORTH

VATICAN—FOREIGN RELATIONS— POLAND

John Paul II, Pope. Our times demand not to enclose ourselves in inflexible borders, especially when human good is concerned. (New York Times 128:1 June 11, 79)

VEECK, BILL

Veeck, Bill. I'd like to be devious, but I can't find it in myself. (Chicago 27:99 July 78)

VEGETARIANISM

Brenner, David. A vegetarian is a person who won't eat anything that can have children. (Cosmopolitan 197:184 Sept 84)

Singer, Isaac Bashevis. I did not become a vegetarian for my health. I did it for the health of the chickens. (Time 123:79 Jan 2, 84)

VENGEANCE

Menninger, Karl. The worst disease in the world is the plague of vengeance. (New York Times 133:24 Oct 30, 83)

VICE-PRESIDENTS—UNITED STATES

Bush, George. Everyone says they are going to reinvent the wheel, that their Vice President is going to be in on developing North-South strategy and other great projects. But it never happens. Two years later, you wake up and find he's still going to funerals. (Time 116:12 July 28, 80)

Cockburn, Alexander. A vice president traditionally has the same relationship to power as that of a circus cleaner to an elephant. (Spin 4:77 Nov 88)

Mondale, Walter Frederick. There is no way on earth people can take the Vice-president of the United States seriously (originally quoted by columnist Jim Klobuchar in the Minneapolis Tribune in 1974). (Rolling Stone 221:16 Sept 9, 76)

VICTIMS OF CRIME—RELATIONS— LIBERALISM—NEW YORK (CITY)

Wilson, James Q. There aren't any liberals left in New York. They've all been mugged by now. (American Spectator 18:18 April 85)

VIDAL, GORE

Vidal, Gore. Early on I wanted to be Franklin Roosevelt. (Vanity Fair 50:87 June 87)

Vidal, Gore. I write to make art and change society. (San Diego Magazine 34:156 Feb 82)

VIETNAM—POLITICS AND GOVERNMENT

Ho Chi Minh. It is better to sniff French dung for a while than to eat China's all our lives. (New York Times 128:1 Section 4 Feb 25, 79)

Nguyen Van Thieu, (former President of South Vietnam). A coalition (government) is like a sugar-coated poison pill. When the sugar melts, the poison kills you. (Time 105:12 April 14, 75)

VIETNAMESE

Ky, Nguyen Cao. Never believe what any Vietnamese tells you, including me (commenting in 1966). (Newsweek 85:17 May 19, 75)

VIETNAMESE WAR, 1957-1975

Aiken, George. The way to get out of Vietnam is to declare victory and leave (1966). (Time 124:46 Dec 31, 84)

Brown, Harold. A lesson we learned from Vietnam is that we should be very cautious about intervening in any place where there's a poor political base for our presence. (Time 109:24 May 23, 77)

Grass, Gunter. If you don't face it, it means two things: you lost the war and you've also lost the ability to make clear why it happened (about Vietnam). (Time 112:77 Nov 13, 78)

Humphrey, Hubert Horatio. We made judgements about that part of the world (Southeast Asia) based on our experience in Europe. We were a world power with a half-world knowledge. (Time 105:20 May 12, 75)

Johnson, Lyndon Baines. Boys, it is just like the Alamo. Somebody should have by God helped those Texans. I'm going to Viet Nam. (Time 105:28 May 12, 75)

Johnson, Lyndon Baines. I'm not going to be the first President to lose a war. (Time 105:28 May 12, 75)

Kissinger, Henry Alfred. We should have bombed the hell out of them the minute we got into office (a week after the 1973 Vietnam peace agreement). (Rolling Stone 188:35 June 5, 75)

Kohler, Jerry. I'd just as soon die in Vietnam as in the library. (Salina (Kansas) Journal 10 May 27, 76)

McCarthy, Eugene Joseph. Kissinger won a Nobel Peace Prize for watching a war end that he was for. (New York Times Magazine 100 Oct 24, 76)

Reagan, Ronald. We could pave the whole country and put parking stripes on it and still be home by Christmas (about winning the Vietnamese War). (New York 13:28 April 28, 80)

Westmoreland, William Childs. Despite the final failure of the South Vietnamese, the record of the American military services of never having lost a war is still intact. (Los Angeles Times 94:25 Part 1 Oct 30, 75)

Westmoreland, William Childs. We met the enemy, and he was us. (Rolling Stone 263:41 April 20, 78)

VIETNAMESE WAR, 1957-1975— AMERICAN PARTICIPATION

Westmoreland, William Childs. Despite the final failure of the South Vietnamese, the record of the American military services of never having lost a war is still intact. (Los Angeles Times 94:25 Part 1 Oct 30, 75)

VIETNAMESE WAR, 1957-1975— PROTESTS, DEMONSTRATIONS, ETC., AGAINST—KENT, OHIO

Capp, Al. The martyrs at Kent State were the kids in National Guard uniforms. (Newsweek 90:50 Oct 17, 77)

VINCENT, JAN-MICHAEL

Vincent, Jan-Michael. My father said if I was

too nervous to steal and too dumb to lie, than I'd better be an actor. (Kansas City Times 117:B-5 Aug 20, 85)

VIOLENCE

Billington, James. Violence is not only "as American as cherry pie," it is likely to remain a la mode for some time to come. (Newsweek 86:13 Oct 6, 75)

Colby, William Egan. I have definitional problems with the word violence. I don't know what the word violence means. (Rolling Stone 196:32 Sept 25, 75)

John Paul II, Pope. Violence always delays the day of justice (to the IRA). (The Observer 9814:1 Sept 30, 79)

VIOLENCE IN MOVING PICTURES

Marvin, Lee. There's too much damned violence on the screen. I don't go for it. Some of those producers and directors need some sense bashed into their heads. (The Star 4:2 Aug 30, 77)

VIOLENCE IN TELEVISION

Miller, Arthur. Violence is the last refuge of scoundrels (commenting on TV violence). (Christian Science Monitor 69:30 Aug 8, 77)

VIOLIN

Stern, Isaac. You don't realize how close it is to you, how much it is a part of your body, until it is gone (about the violin). (New York Times Magazine 15 Aug 12, 79)

VISSER, JERI LEE see TINKERBELLE

VOCATIONAL EDUCATION

Bell, Terrence H. We need to liberalize vocational education—and vocationalize liberal education. (Money 5:48 April 76)

VOLUNTEER SERVICE

Myrdal, Gunnar. It is natural for the ordinary American when he sees something wrong to feel not only that there should be a law against it but also that an organization should be formed to combat it. (Time 112:34 Aug 7, 78)

VORONEL, NINA

Voronel, Nina. Soviet life is so absurd that when I write realistically, it becomes the theatre of the absurd. (New York Times 125:28 Nov 7, 75)

WAGES see also MOVING PICTURE INDUSTRY— WAGES

WALDHEIM, KURT

Waldheim, Kurt. A head of state must not retreat in the face of slanders, hateful demonstrations and wholesale condemnations. (Chicago Tribune 55:17 Section 1 Feb 24, 88)

Waldheim, Kurt. The whole war generation would have to be incriminated if knowledge of atrocities was a crime. (Chicago Tribune 45:3 Section 4 Feb 15, 88)

WALES

Hepburn, Katharine. First God made England, Ireland and Scotland. That's when He corrected His mistakes and made Wales. (Time 112:69 Aug 7, 78)

WALESA, LECH

Walesa, Lech. I was always the leader of the class. (Time 119:16 Jan 4, 82)

WALKING

Stengel, Charles Dillon (Casey). If you walk backward you'll find out that you can go forward and people won't know if you're coming or going. (Newsweek 86:47 Aug 11, 75)

WALL STREET

Baruch, Bernard Mannes (attributed by William Flanagan). I buy low and sell high (when asked how he had made a fortune in the stock market). (New York 10:56 May 2, 77)

Galbraith, John Kenneth. There's just a growing feeling that Wall Street is a sort of irresponsible beehive of young people who don't know what they're doing. (Kansas City Star 108:6A Oct 27, 87)

Graham, Benjamin. (The stock market is) a Falstaffian joke that frequently degenerates into a madhouse. (Money 5:36 July 76)

LeFevre, William M. There are only two emotions in Wall Street: fear and greed. (Time 111:42 May 1, 78)

Perot, H. Ross. T There's only two places a 28-year-old can make a half million dollars—Wall Street and dealing dope. (Newsweek 112:143 July 11, 88)

Reagan, Ronald. I never found that Wall Street is a source of good economic advice. (Life 5:33 Jan 81)

Rogers, Jimmy. Nobody in government understands Wall Street. And very few people on Wall Street understands Wall Street. (Kansas City Star 108:6A Oct 27, 87)

Smith, Adam. If you don't know who you are, the stock market is an expensive place to find out. (Kansas City Star 109:2F Dec 25, 88)

WALL STREET JOURNAL

Nakagama, Sam. I would say that you can discount almost anything you read in the Wall Street Journal. (Manhattan, Inc. 5:56 Nov 88)

WALLACE, GEORGE CORLEY

Wallace, George Corley. Let 'em call me a racist in the press. It don't make any difference. Hell, I want 'em to. 'Cause if you want to know the truth, race is what's gonna win this thing for us. (Sepia 26:10 Feb 76)

Wallace, George Corley. Segregation is a moot question, and integration is the law of the land. It is a moot question, and therefore we don't want to go back, nor make any attempt to change what is now a fact accomplished. (Meet the Press 20:5 Mar 28, 76)

WALTERS, VERNON A.

Walters, Vernon A. I describe myself as a pragmatist tinged with idealism. (New York Times 134:6 May 31, 85)

WAR

Caputo, Philip J. The impetus or the impulse that makes people heroic in wars is the very thing that can make them monsters. (Chicago Tribune Magazine 23 Mar 19, 78)

Curtis, Carl Thomas. In the whole history of the world, whenever a meateating race has gone to war against a non-meateating race, the meat eaters won. It produces superior people. (Washingtonian 11:22-23 Dec 75)

Evtushenko, Evgenii Aleksandrovich. Distrust is the mother of war and political racism. (Atlas World Press Review 23:10 Nov 76)

Haig, Alexander M. The next war could be a come-as-you-are party. (Esquire 90:31 Sept 26, 78)

Hua, Kuo-Feng. Peace cannot be got by begging. War cannot be averted by yielding. (The Observer 9819:9 Nov 4, 79)

Kissinger, Henry Alfred. The likelihood of war is extremely low due to the nature of modern weapons. (M 1:48 July 84)

Mountbatten, Louis. If the Third World War is fought with nuclear weapons, the fourth will be fought with bows and arrows. (Maclean's 88:73 Nov 17, 75)

Patton, George S. In war, just as in loving, you've got to keep on shoving. (Playboy 26:26 Oct 79)

Patton, George S. Now I want you to remember that no bastard ever won a war by dying for his country. You won it by making the other poor dumb bastard die for his country. (American West 22:22 Nov 85)

West, Mae. I'm for peace. I have yet to wake up in the morning and hear a man say, I've just had a good war. (Viva 4:26 Aug 77)

WARHOL, ANDY

Capote, Truman. He's a sphinx without a secret (commenting on Andy Warhol). (People Weekly 5:15 May 10, 76)

Ultra Violet. He (Andy Warhol) was a shy, near-blind, bald, gay albino from an ethnic Pittsburgh ghetto. (Manchester Guardian Weekly 140:29 May 21, 89)

Warhol, Andy. I never fall apart because I never fall together. (Newsweek 86:69 Sept 15, 75)

Warhol, Andy. If I go into a hospital, I won't come out. (New York 20:40 Mar 9, 87)

Warhol, Andy. The best dates are when you take the office with you. (Manchester Guardian Weekly 140:29 May 21, 89)

WASHINGTON POST

Graham, Katharine. This company (The Washington Post) is not now and never has been antiunion. (Newsweek 86:44 Dec 22, 75)

WASHINGTON, BOOKER T.

Washington, Booker T., III. Being the sensitive man he was about his race, I think the present day Harlem scene would bring tears to my grandfather's eyes. (Sepia 26:10 Feb 77)

WASHINGTON, D.C.

Dean, John Wesley, III. Washington is a much better place if you are asking questions rather than answering them. (Washingtonian 14:153 Nov 78)

Dutton, Fred. Washington is like a woman who is always waiting to be seduced. (Time 109:26 Feb 7, 77)

Simon, John. The culture of the nation's capital would seem to be a capital joke. (New York 8:76 May 12, 75)

White, Kevin Hagen. Everybody knows that Washington, D.C. has no culture—they have to buy it. (Time 113:71 April 23, 79)

WASHINGTON, D.C.—DESCRIPTION

Connally, John Bowden (attributed by Henry Alfred Kissinger). You will be measured in (Washington D.C.) by the enemies you destroy. The bigger they are, the bigger you are. (Time 114:45 Oct 8, 79)

McCree, Wade. Washington is the only town in the world where sound travels faster than light. (Chicago Sun-Times 31:6 June 20, 78)

Simon, William E. Washington is the only city where sound travels faster than light. (Atlanta 16:130 Aug 76)

WASHINGTON, D.C.—SOCIAL LIFE AND CUSTOMS

Quinn, Sally. Washington society is ruled with unwavering severity by a handful of aging widows, dowagers and old maids who subsist on fortunes inherited from robber-baron husbands or corrupt political daddies. (Atlanta 16:124 Jan 76)

WATER POLLUTION

Babbitt, Bruce E. It's time we told every polluter: if you poison our water you will go to jail and your money will be spent to clean up the mess. (Chicago Tribune 70:4 Mar 11, 87)

WATERGATE CASE

Butz, Earl Lauer. It was stupid—like General Motors breaking into Ford to steal Edsel plans (commenting on Watergate, in the long term). (People Weekly 5:84 April 19, 76)

Colson, Charles Wendell. The only good guys to emerge from Watergate are those self-justified, upright fellows writing their own accounts. Since everyone has written a book, the sum of all the books is that no one was guilty, just everyone else.... (National Review 30:474 April 14, 78)

Dole, Robert J. Thank goodness whenever I was in the Oval Office I only nodded (commenting on the Watergate tapes). (Christian Science Monitor 68:17 Sept 10, 76)

Hellman, Lillian. I think (Watergate and the McCarthy Era) are deeply connected, with Mr. Nixon being the connection, the rope that carries it all through. (New York Times 125:28 Nov 7, 75)

Magruder, Jeb Stuart. I lost my moral compass. (Newsweek 85:49 May 5, 75)

Nixon, Richard Milhous. (Watergate) was worse than a crime, it was a blunder. (The Observer 9771:14 Dec 3, 78)

Nixon, Richard Milhous. All I want is a prosecution, not a persecution (upon firing Archibald Cox). (Washington Post National Weekly Edition 4:24 Mar 16, 87)

Nixon, Richard Milhous. History will justifiably record that my handling of the Watergate crisis was an unmitigated disaster. (Chicago Sun-Times 32:35 Sept 17, 79)

Nixon, Richard Milhous. If it hadn't been for Martha (Mitchell), there'd have been no Watergate. (Washingtonian 13:11 Nov 77)

Nixon, Richard Milhous. Just destroy all the tapes (on the greatest lesson of Watergate). (Newsweek 107:17 May 5, 86)

Trudeau, Pierre Elliott. The atmosphere of Watergate has polluted the atmosphere of other democratic countries. Nobody trusts anybody anymore. (American Legion Magazine 98:32 May 75)

WATERGATE CASE see also **HUNT, EVERETTE HOWARD**

WATERGATE TAPES

Dole, Robert J. Thank goodness whenever I was in the Oval Office I only nodded (commenting on the Watergate tapes). (Christian Science Monitor 68:17 Sept 10, 76)

Nixon, Patricia Ryan. If they had been my tapes, I would have burned or destroyed them because they were like a private diary, not public property. (Village Voice 23:62 Aug 7, 78)

WATERS, ETHEL

Graham, Billy. In her own way she (Ethel Waters) did as much for race relations as any American in the 20th Century. (Chicago Tribune 245:5 Sept 2, 77)

WATERS, JOHN

Waters, John. I always wanted to sell out, but nobody would buy me. (University Daily Kansan 98:3 Nov 17, 87)

WATTS TOWERS, LOS ANGELES

Rodia, Simon. I had in mind to do something big and I did (about the Watts Towers). (Travel & Leisure 8:67 Oct 78)

WATTS, ANDRE

Watts, Andre. Here lies a man who never played Petrouchka (on his epitaph). (Horizon 20:13 Dec 77)

WAUGH, EVELYN

Waugh, Evelyn. You have no idea how much nastier I would be if I was not a Catholic. Without supernatural aid I would hardly be a human being. (Newsweek 86:119 Nov 24, 75)

WAUGH, EVELYN—CHILDREN

Waugh, Evelyn. My children weary me. I can only see them as defective adults; feckless, destructive, frivolous, sensual, humourless. (Time 110:102 Oct 17, 77)

WAYNE, JOHN

Simon, John. Every era gets the leader it deserves; John Wayne is ours. (Newsweek 93:77 June 25, 79)

Wayne, John. I stay away from nuances. (Time 113:50 June 25, 79)

Wayne, John. Nobody likes my acting but the public. (The Tennessean 74:2 June 12, 79)

WEALTH

Baltzell, Edward Digby, Jr. I believe in inherited wealth. Society needs to have some people who are above it all. (Town & Country 132:97 July 78)

Baltzell, Edward Digby, Jr. When class authority declines, money talks. (Town & Country 132:97 July 78)

Boesky, Ivan F. It's OK to make money. It's a good thing. You go to heaven if you do it. (Kansas Cith Star 107:8A Nov 18, 86)

Bronfman, Edgar. To turn $100 into $110 is work. To turn $100 million into $110 million is inevitable. (Newsweek 106:62 Dec 2, 85)

Getty, Jean Paul. I suffer no guilt complexes or conscience pangs about my wealth. The Lord may have been disproportionate, but that is how He—or nature, if you like—operates. (Time 107:41 May 24, 76)

Getty, Jean Paul. If you can count your money, you don't have a billion dollars. (Newsweek 87:55 June 14, 76)

Getty, Jean Paul. Remember, a billion dollars isn't worth what it used to be. (Newsweek 94:166 Nov 19, 79)

Graham, Benjamin. Never having to balance your checkbook (a definition of financial success). (Money 5:37 July 76)

Hunt, Nelson Bunker. A billion dolalrs isn't what it used to be. (Life 7:39 Jan 83)

MacArthur, John D. Anybody who knows what he's worth, isn't worth very much (upon being asked how much he was worth). (Chicago Tribune 340:2 Section 1 Dec 5, 76)

Mellon, Paul. One of the main things money provides is privacy. (Time 111:79 May 8, 78)

Milligan, Spike. Money can't buy friends, but you can get a better class of enemy. (Washingtonian 21:120 Jan 85)

Poirot, Paul L. Multiplying wealth is by far the fastest way to help the poor. Dividing the wealth and subsidizing poverty is the fastest way to starve everyone. (American Opinion 18:29 Nov 75)

Tucker, Sophie. I've been rich and I've been poor, and rich is better. (Philadelphia 78:59 Aug 87)

Vanderbilt, William K. Inherited wealth is a real handicap to happiness. It is as certain a death to ambition as cocaine is to morality. (Times Literary Supplement 3960:198 Feb 17, 78)

WELLES, ORSON

Mankiewicz, Herman. There but for the grace of God goes God (about Orson Welles). (American Film 4:70 Feb 79)

WERTMUELLER, LINA

Wertmueller, Lina. I'm the last ballbuster left. (Time 107:59 Feb 16, 76)

WEST, MAE

West, Mae. I never needed Panavision and stereophonic sound to woo the world. I did it in black and white on a screen the size of a postage stamp. Honey, that's talent. (Rolling Stone 245:27 Aug 11, 77)

West, Mae. I'm for peace. I have yet to wake up in the morning and hear a man say, I've just had a good war. (Viva 4:26 Aug 77)

West, Mae. When I'm good, I'm very good; but when I'm bad, I'm better. (Oui 8:82 Jan 78)

WESTERN FILMS

Autry, Gene. We had no violence when I did the westerns, just fist fights and comedy. (Newsweek 85:9 Mar 3, 75)

WHITE, E. B.

White, E. B. Before I start to write, I always treat myself to a nice dry martini. (Writer's Digest 58:25 Oct 78)

WHITTLE, CHRISTOPHER

Whittle, Christopher. People call me a great salesman when they want to damn me with faint praise. (Vanity Fair 53:229 Mar 90)

WIDOWS

Hemingway, Mary. Books are helpful in bed. But they are not responsive (commenting on widowhood). (People Weekly 6:49 Dec 13, 76)

WILDER, BILLY

Wilder, Billy. If there's one thing I hate more than not being taken seriously, it's being taken too seriously. (New York 8:43 Nov 24, 75)

WILDER, GENE

Wilder, Gene. Everything I write is a love story and emotionally autobiographical. (Time 107:70 May 30, 77)

WILLIAMS, EDWARD BENNETT

Veeck, Bill. Baseball is the only orderly thing in a very unorderly world. If you get three strikes, even Edward Bennett Williams can't get you off. (Sports Illustrated 43:14 June 2, 75)

WILLIAMS, TENNESSEE

Brando, Marlon. If there are men who have a clean soul, he's (Tennessee Williams) one of them. (Playboy 26:140 Jan 77)

Williams, Tennessee. I was brought up puritanically. I try to outrage their puritanism. (Time 122:88 Mar 7, 83)

Williams, Tennessee. Men are rather inscrutable to me. (W 8:14 April 13, 79)

Williams, Tennessee. They teach it (The Glass Menagerie) in college now, and everybody approaches it as though it were a place of worship. Frankly, I fall asleep at times. (Time 106:31 Dec 29, 75)

WINNING

Allen, George. Only winners are truly alive. Winning is living. Every time you win, you're reborn. When you lose, you die a little. (Chicago Tribune 76:1 Section 2 Mar 17, 78)

Lombardi, Vince. Winning isn't everything. It is the only thing. (Newsweek 94:166 Nov 19, 79)

Rockne, Knute. You show me a good and gracious loser, and I'll show you a failure! (Argosy 384:15 Nov 76)

WINPISINGER, WILLIAM

Winpisinger, William (union leader). I don't mind being called a lefty. We're being centered to death. (Time 110:52 July 11, 77)

WISDOM

Hayakawa, Samuel Ichiye. There is only one thing age can give you, and that is wisdom. (New West 1:17 July 5, 76)

Levi-Strauss, Claude. Age removes the confusion, only possible in youth, between physical and moral characteristics. (Time 111:99 April 24, 78)

WISEMAN, FREDERICK

Wiseman, Frederick. The final film is a theory about the event, about the subject in the film. (Film Quarterly 31:15 Spring 78)

WIT AND HUMOR

Bond, Edward. Laughter that's not also an idea is cruel. (Washingtonian 21:42 Jan 85)

WIVES

Ronstadt, Linda. I'm so disorganized, what I really need is a good wife. (People Weekly 4:54 Nov 17, 75)

WIVES see also POLITICIANS—WIVES; PRESIDENTS—UNITED STATES—WIVES

WOLFE, THOMAS

Mailer, Norman. (Thomas Wolfe was) the greatest five-year-old who ever lived. (New York Times Book Review 3 Dec 2, 79)

O'Connor, Flannery. Anybody that admires Thomas Wolfe can be expected to like good fiction only by accident. (New York Times Book Review 3 Dec 2, 79)

WOMEN

Addams, Jane. I do not believe that women are better than men. We have not wrecked railroads, nor corrupted legislatures, nor done many unholy things that men have done; but then we must remember that we have not had the chance. (Working Woman 1:8 Nov 76)

Atwood, Margaret. Anybody who says they like all women just because they are women is an idiot—or lying. (Chicago Tribune 78:6 Section 6 Mar 19, 89)

Barrow, Willie. It's easier being black than being a woman. (Sepia 26:12 Sept 75)

Beauvoir, Simone De. One is not born a woman, one becomes one. (Ms 6:16 July 77)

Buckley, Pat. Women were born to be taken care of by men—I do think that's the law of the universe. (W 6:1 Oct 14, 77)

Carr, Jesse. Being powerful is like being a lady. If you have to tell people you are, you ain't. (Newsweek 88:77 Sept 27, 76)

Cleaver, Eldridge. If it came down to the choice between a woman and a radio, I'd choose a radio. It brings the outside world in. (Sepia 24:12 June 75)

Durant, Will. We are living in a time when woman thinks she has been emancipated, but I'm afraid that's a complimentary way of saying she's been industrialized. (Chicago Sun-Times 28:30 Nov 6, 75)

Fields, W. C. Women are like elephants. They're nice to look at but I wouldn't want to own one. (Viva 5:26 Dec 77)

Fontaine, Joan. The physical side of being a woman is detestable. (The Observer 9767:13 Nov 5, 78)

Foreman, Percy. Man's inhumanity to man is only exceeded by woman's inhumanity to woman. (Newsweek 88:93 Nov 8, 76)

Gonick, Jean. For women, life is a series of leaking tampons. (GQ 57:99 May 87)

Hearst, Austine. After 40, a woman needs a lover and a good facelift. And after 50, cash. (W 7:2 Oct 27, 78)

Johnston, Jill. All women are lesbians except those who don't know it yet. (Ms 4:80 Nov 75)

Jong, Erica. It seems to me that sooner or later all intelligent women become feminists. (New York Times 125:32 Nov 8, 75)

Koon, Larry. Women are best suited for secretarial work, decorating cakes and counter sales, like selling lingerie. (New Woman 10:12 May 80)

Lamarr, Hedy. Any girl can be glamorous. All you have to do is stand still and look stupid. (Chicago Sun-Times 30:21 Jan 28, 78)

Luce, Clare Boothe. There aren't many women now I'd like to see as President— but there are fewer men. (Newsweek 94:95 Oct 22, 79)

MacLaine, Shirley. I want women to be liberated and still be able to have a nice ass and shake it. (People Weekly 5:27 May 10, 76)

Masters, William Howell. Males have made asses of themselves writing about female sexual experience. (Newsweek 85:74 May 5, 75)

Mitford, Nancy. Sisters stand between one and life's cruel circumstances. (Ms 6:65 Sept 77)

Mohammed Reza Pahlevi, Shah of Iran. In a man's life, women count only if they're beautiful and graceful and know how to stay feminine. (Washingtonian 10:21 July 75)

Moore, Roger. My real attitude toward women is this, and it hasn't changed because of any movement or anything: basically, women like to be treated as sex objects. (Playboy 25:102 May 78)

Needham, Richard J. Men are foolish, they think money should be taken from the rich and given to the poor. Women are sensible, they think money should be taken from the rich and given to them. (Toronto Globe and Mail 134:6 July 13, 77)

Peterson, Esther. If a man fights his adversaries, he's called determined. If a woman does it, she's frustrated. (National Observer 16:18 June 13, 77)

Picasso, Pablo. For me there are only two kinds of women—goddesses and doormats. (People Weekly 13:37 May 26, 80)

Polykoff, Shirley. If I've only one life, let me live it as a blonde! (advertising slogan). (New York 9:37 Aug 23, 76)

Reagan, Nancy. A woman is like a teabag— only in hot water do you realize how strong she is. (The Observer 9931:13 Jan 3, 82)

Reagan, Ronald. I happen to be one who believes that it it wasn't for women, us men would still be walking around in skin suits carrying clubs. (Life 7:172 Jan 84)

Schreiner, Olive. We are men or women in the second place, human beings in the first. (Ms 6:94 Aug 77)

Skinner, Cornelia Otis. A woman's virtue is man's greatest invention. (Time 114:76 July 23, 79)

Smith, Alexis. Women who are only involved with how they look are always dull. (Chicago Tribune 123:16 Section 1 May 3, 77)

Steinem, Gloria. If the secretaries and wives told each other what we know, we could take over the world. (Chicago Sun-Times 34:41 April 27, 81)

Steinem, Gloria. Some of us are becoming the men we wanted to marry. (Chicago Sun-Times 34:41 April 27, 81)

Thatcher, Margaret Hilda. If you want anything said, ask a man; if you want anything done, ask a woman. (New York Times Magazine 52 April 29, 79)

Tucker, Sophie. From birth to age 18, a girl needs good parents. From 18 to 35, she needs good looks. From 35 to 55, she needs a good personality. From 55 on, she needs good cash. (Chicago Sun-Times 30:21 Jan 28, 78)

Vanderbilt, Gloria. A woman can never be too thin or too rich. (Chicago Sun-Times 32:3 Dec 18, 80)

Vizinczey, Stephen. No girl, however intelligent and warmhearted, can possibly know or feel half as much at 20 as she will at 35. (Time 111:99 April 24, 78)

Vreeland, Diana. Show me a fashionable woman, and I will show you a woman who accomplished something. (Newsweek 91:3 Jan 2, 78)

Wilson, Sloan. It is impossible to treat a woman too well. (New York 9:46 May 24, 76)

WOMEN see also MUSIC, JAZZ—WOMEN

WOMEN AND MEN

Algren, Nelson. Never eat at a place called Mom's. Never play cards with a man named Doc. And never lie down with a woman who's got more troubles than you. (Washingtonian 14:152 Nov 78)

Bardot, Brigitte. Men are beasts and even beasts don't behave as they do. (Viva 4:26 Feb 77)

Bergman, Ingmar. Possessiveness is neurotic, but this is how I am. (New West 2:24 April 25, 77)

Bocuse, Paul. The only place for them (women) is in bed. Anyone who doesn't change his woman every week or so lacks imagination. (Newsweek 86:53 Aug 11, 75)

Brown, Phyllis George. A smart woman will suggest things to a man and let him take the credit. (New Woman 10:12 May 80)

Buckley, Pat. Women were born to be taken care of by men—I do think that's the law of the universe. (W 6:1 Oct 14, 77)

Burgess, Anthony. Women cannot help moving, and men cannot help being moved. (Playboy 24:346 Dec 77)

Carmichael, Stokely. The only position for women in the movement is prone. (New York Times Magazine 91 April 10, 77)

Carrera, Barbara. Straight men make life very difficult. (M 1:87 Mar 84)

Cleaver, Eldridge. If it came down to the choice between a woman and a radio, I'd choose a radio. It brings the outside world in. (Sepia 24:12 June 75)

Curtis, Tony. There's simply no other way for a man to feel his manliness, his kingliness if you will, than to be loved by a beautiful woman. (The Observer 9778:10 Jan 21, 79)

DeCrow, Karen Lipshultz. I like the companionship of men. I don't want to cut myself off from half the human race. (New York Times 125:15 Oct 28, 75)

DeVore, Irven. Males are a vast breeding experiment run by females. (Time 110:63 Aug 1, 77)

Dietrich, Marlene. Once a woman has forgiven her man, she must not reheat his sins for breakfast. (Cosmopolitan 188:268 Feb 80)

Duffy, Sean. The chance of a meaningful relationship with a member of the opposite sex is inversely proportional to their amount of beauty. (Omni 1:132 May 79)

Gabor, Zsa Zsa. A man in love is incomplete until he has married. Then he's finished. (Village Voice 22:20 Dec 26, 77)

Gilder, George. This is what sexual liberation chiefly accomplishes—it liberates young women to pursue married men. (Newsweek 108:31 Dec 8, 86)

Hepburn, Katharine. Sometimes I wonder if men and women really suit each other. Perhaps they should live next door and just visit now and then. (Cosmopolitan 188:268 Feb 80)

James, Clive. Eloquence might get you started with a woman but it is often taciturnity that seals the bargain. (Chicago Tribune 19:3 Section 5 Jan 19, 87)

Jones, Franklin P. One thing in which the sexes are equal is in thinking that they're not. (Reader's Digest 108:261 May 76)

Jong, Erica. You don't have to beat a woman if you can make her feel guilty. (Viva 4:28 April 77)

King, Larry L. One receives an inverse ratio of romantic opportunities to that which one needs. (Viva 4:72 Dec 76)

Lartigue, Jacques-Henri. When you fall in love with a woman, it's because she's ready, she has chosen you. (Vanity Fair 47:82 April 84)

Leone, Mama. No one ever filed for divorce on a full stomach. (Viva 4:26 May 77)

Little Richard. Real women don't want to climb telephone poles. (New Woman 10:12 May 80)

Lodge, John Davis. Man is born into the world as a pig and is civilized by women. (W 6:2 Feb 18, 77)

Loos, Anita. Gentlemen don't prefer blondes. If I were writing that book today, I'd call it 'Gentlemen Prefer Gentlemen'. (Newsweek 85:72 May 12, 75)

Luce, Clare Boothe. It is ridiculous to think you can spend your entire life with just one person. Three is about the right number. Yes, I imagine three husbands would do it. (The Observer 9931:13 Jan 3, 82)

Mabley, Moms. A woman is a woman until the day she dies, but a man's a man only as long as he can. (Sepia 24:10 Jan 75)

Mailer, Norman. You don't know anything about a woman until you meet her in court. (Penthouse 16:152 Nov 84)

Marsh, Jean. We're not sent into this life to be alone, but two-by-two, like in the ark. (W 7:41 Oct 13, 78)

Mature, Victor. Apparently, the way to a girl's heart is to saw her in half. (Playboy 26:26 Oct 79)

Miller, Ann. No matter what you've achieved, if you're not loved (by a man), Honey, you ain't nothin' but a hound dog. (New Woman 10:12 May 80)

Morgan, Marabel. It is only when a woman surrenders her life to her husband, reveres and worships him, and is willing to serve him, that she becomes really beautiful to him. (Ms 7:64 June 79)

Nash, Ogden. Marriage is the alliance of two people, one of whom never remembers birthdays and the other never forgets them. (Cosmopolitan 188:268 Feb 80)

Novick, Julius. It is a well-known and infuriating fact of life that in any relationship, if one party really and truly does not give a damn, that party will inevitably have the upper hand. Indifference is power (ask any cat). (Village Voice 21:81 Feb 14, 77)

Pritchett, V. S. There are rules for old men who are in love with young girls, all the stricter when the young girls are in love with them. It has to be played as a game. (Time 114:127 Nov 12, 79)

Runyon, Damon. Man's only weapon against a woman is his hat. He should grab it and run. (Viva 4:28 April 77)

Schroeder, Patricia. When men talk about defense, they always claim to be protecting women and children, but they never ask the women and children what they think. (New York Times Book Review 35 Feb 17, 80)

Smith, Patti. As far as I'm concerned, being any gender is a drag. (Playboy 26:26 Oct 79)

Steinem, Gloria. The first problem for all of us, men and women, is not to learn, but to unlearn. (Human Behavior 7:17 May 78)

Steinem, Gloria. Today a woman without a man is like a fish without a bicycle. (New York 9:26 Aug 9, 76)

Summers, Andy. One night stands don't have to be tacky. (Playboy 31:90 April 84)

Toscanini, Arturo. I kissed my first girl and smoked my first cigarette on the same day. I haven't had time for tobacco since. (Playboy 32:16 Feb 85)

Ullmann, Liv. You must put more in your life than a man. (Time 113:65 Jan 29, 79)

Wertmueller, Lina. I'm the last ballbuster left. (Time 107:59 Feb 16, 76)

West, Mae. I've said it before and I'll say it again—I like a man that takes his time. (Coronet 13:37 Sept 75)

West, Rebecca. The main difference between men and women is that men are lunatics and women are idiots. (Chicago Tribune 303:1 Section 5 Oct 30, 87)

Wilson, Sloan. It is impossible to treat a woman too well. (New York 9:46 May 24, 76)

Woolf, Virginia. The history of men's opposition to women's emancipation is more interesting perhaps than the story of that emancipation itself. (Los Angeles Times 97:6 Part 4 Feb 3, 78)

WOMEN ARTISTS

Hofmann, Hans. They are so good you would not know they were done by a woman (about Lee Krasner's art). (Newsweek 104:23 July 2, 84)

WOMEN ASTRONAUTS

Lovell, James, Jr. We will fly women into space and use them the same way we use them on Earth—and for the same purpose. (Ms 6:49 July 77)

WOMEN ATHLETES

King, Billie Jean. You put a pink blanket on a little girl and a blue blanket on a little boy, and right there the difference starts. (The Sporting News 205:50 May 2, 88)

WOMEN AUTOMOBILE RACING DRIVERS

Guthrie, Janet. I am a racing driver who happens to be a woman. (New York Times 125:6 Section 5 April 18, 76)

WOMEN BASEBALL UMPIRES

Knepper, Bob. You can be a woman umpire if you want, but that doesn't mean it's right. (The Sporting News 205:36 Mar 28, 88)

WOMEN CRIMINALS

Ianni, Francis (American sociologist). As in business, politics and education, there will be equal opportunities in crime. You can't have Bella Abzugs without Bonnie Parkers. (Time 106:8 Dec 1, 75)

WOMEN POETS

Jong, Erica. I want to set an example of a woman poet who doesn't kill herself. (Kansas City Star 117:6B Dec 3, 84)

Lowell, Robert. Almost all good women poets are either divorced or lesbian. (San Francisco Chronicle 111:May 25, 77 (155))

WOMEN POLITICIANS

Byrne, Jane. Diamonds are a girl's best friend, and Federal grants are second. (Newsweek 96:24 Sept 29, 80)

WOMEN SOLDIERS

Goldwater, Barry Morris. I don't object to a woman doing anything in combat as long as she gets home in time to cook dinner. (Viva 5:29 Oct 77)

WOMEN'S LIBERATION MOVEMENT

Chapman, Marshall. As far as I'm concerned, feminists have done to women what the Baptists did to religion. (Stereo Review 41:90 Dec 78)

Charles, Prince of Wales. Women's liberationists rather annoy me because they tend to argue all the time and start calling you a male chauvinist pig and, frankly, it becomes rather uncivilized. (Los Angeles Times 94:2 Part 1 Nov 18, 75)

Ephron, Nora. For a lot of women, the women's movement has just given them a political rationalization for their fear of success. (Christian Science Monitor 69:2 Dec 10, 76)

Gilder, George. This is what sexual liberation chiefly accomplishes—it liberates young women to pursue married men. (Newsweek 108:31 Dec 8, 86)

Greer, Germaine. It's sheer myth that feminists are anti-child—we're the only people who're going to give children a better deal. (People Weekly 5:72 Jan 26, 76)

Harris, Marvin. Women's liberation did not create the working woman; rather the working woman—especially the working housewife—created women's liberation. (Time 119:89 Jan 11, 82)

Hefner, Hugh Marston. If I told you, for example that Playboy, in its 22 years, was one of the major things that contributed to the women's movement, you might find it a mindboggler, but it happens to be true. (Chicago Tribune 124:1 Section 1 May 3, 76)

Jong, Erica. It seems to me that sooner or later all intelligent women become feminists. (New York Times 125:32 Nov 8, 75)

Meyner, Helen. Let the best man win, whomever she may be. (Life 2:140 Dec 79)

Ringer, Robert J. The women behind the (women's liberation) movement want the same thing all group leaders want and have wanted through history: ego assuagement. (Playboy 25:110 May 78)

Ruckelshaus, Jill. It occurred to me when I was 13 and wearing white gloves and Mary Janes and going to dancing school, that no one should have to dance backwards all their lives. (Chicago Sun-Times 30:21 Jan 28, 78)

Schlafly, Phyllis. Ask yourself: When you are rescued from the third floor of a burning building, do you want to be carried down the ladder by a man or a woman? (National NOW Times 11:6 Aug 78)

WOMEN'S LIBERATION MOVEMENT— HISTORY

Anthony, Susan B. Failure is impossible. (Chicago Tribune 176:2 Section 2 June 25, 78)

Woolf, Virginia. The history of men's opposition to women's emancipation is more interesting perhaps than the story of that emancipation itself. (Los Angeles Times 97:6 Part 4 Feb 3, 78)

WOMEN—EMPLOYMENT

Hefferan, Colien. The woman who once saw marriage as a form of security now finds that she can provide her own security. (US News & World Report 85:83 Nov 27, 78)

Steinem, Gloria. The average secretary in the U.S. is better educated than the average boss. (Time 112:61 Sept 11, 78)

WOMEN—EQUAL RIGHTS

Bartholomew, Summer (Miss U.S.A.—1975). I believe in equal pay for equal jobs, but not communal toilets or anything like that. (Washingtonian 10:21 July 75)

Gillespie, Marcia Ann. I did not stand up for my rights as a black person in America to be told that I have to sit down because I'm a woman. (Time 114:99 Oct 29, 79)

Gray, Francine du Plessix. Women are the only exploited group in history who have been idealized into powerlessness. (Time 111:76 Jan 30, 78)

Hellman, Lillian. Nobody can argue any longer about the rights of women. It's like arguing about earthquakes. (Rolling Stone 233:56 Feb 24, 77)

Seaman, Barbara. (A feminist is) a woman who is for women, which does not mean being against men. (New York Times 125:32 Nov 8, 75)

Thomas, Marlo. A man has to be Joe McCarthy to be called ruthless. All a woman has to do is put you on hold. (New York Times Book Review 35 Feb 17, 80)

White, Theodore. It's about time women had their say in the laws governing them— laws that for 5,000 years have been made by old men, mostly with shriveled-up groins, who have long since forgotten what it was like to be young and never knew what it was like to be a woman. (W 7:41 Sept 15, 78)

WOMEN—OCCUPATIONAL MOBILITY

Peter, Laurence J. Most hierarchies were established by men who now occupy the upper levels, thus depriving women of an equal opportunity to achieve their levels of incompetence. (San Francisco Chronicle This World 1978:40 Jan 29, 78)

WOMEN—PSYCHOLOGY

Asimov, Isaac. Women tend to be dirtier but less clever than men. I don't know why, but they can be surprisingly vulgar (about women and limericks). (Time 111:74 April 24, 78)

Ephron, Nora. For a lot of women, the women's movement has just given them a political rationalization for their fear of success. (Christian Science Monitor 69:2 Dec 10, 76)

Gabor, Zsa Zsa. You're never too young to be younger. (Oui 8:82 Jan 78)

Greer, Germaine. Security is when everything is settled, when nothing can happen to you; security is a denial of life. (Redbook 148:57 Mar 77)

Jong, Erica. You don't have to beat a woman if you can make her feel guilty. (Viva 4:28 April 77)

Mature, Victor. Apparently, the way to a girl's heart is to saw her in half. (Playboy 26:26 Oct 79)

Steinem, Gloria. A pedestal is as much a prison as any small space. (Playboy 26:26 Oct 79)

WOODWARD, BOB

Colby, William Egan. By the way, did you ever work for the CIA? (to Bob Woodward upon agreeing to issue an official denial that Woodward had ever worked for the CIA). (New York 8:50 July 28, 75)

WOODWARD, BOB AND BERNSTEIN, CARL. THE FINAL DAYS

Bernstein, Carl. Let me say no one has successfully challenged the accuracy of this book (The Final Days) or any single assertion in it. (Meet the Press 20:9 April 18, 76)

WORD PROCESSING

Will, George F. People who use word processors should not be surprised if what they write is to prose as process cheese is to real cheese. (Lawrence (Kansas) Journal-World 125:4 Dec 18, 83)

WORDS

Compton-Burnett, Ivy. We must use words as they are used or stand aside from life. (Time 111:36 Jan 2, 78)

Schlesinger, Arthur, Jr. 'Gay' used to be one of the most agreeable words in the language. Its appropriation by a notably morose group is an act of piracy. (Time 111:36 Jan 2, 78)

WORK

Anonymous (Corollary to Murphy's Law). Everything will take longer than you think it will. (The Reader (Chicago's Free Weekly) 5:2 May 28, 76)

Anonymous (Corollary to Murphy's Law). Nothing is as easy as it looks. (The Reader (Chicago's Free Weekly) 5:2 May 28, 76)

Boyle, Charles. If not controlled, work will flow to the competent man until he submerges. (Time 113:25 Feb 26, 79)

Crow, Trammel. Work is so much more fun than fun, it is improperly called work. (New York Times 133:13 Aug 14, 84)

Drucker, Peter F. So much of what we call management consists in making it difficult for people to work. (New York Times 125:15 Section 3 May 16, 76)

Galbraith, John Kenneth. No ethic is as ethical as the work ethic. (Cosmopolitan 188:264 June 80)

Gossage, Howard. The only fit work for an adult is to save the world. (California 13:13 May 88)

Jerome, Jerome K. It is impossible to enjoy idling thoroughly unless one has plenty of work to do. (Rocky Mountain News 79:86 July 10, 80)

Kirkland, Lane. If hard work were such a wonderful thing, surely the rich would have kept it all to themselves. (Life 7:39 Jan 84)

McCarthy, Eugene Joseph. Work is the only kind of property many people have in America. (Center Report 8:12 Dec 75)

Parkinson, C. Northcote. Work expands to fill the time allotted to it, or, conversely, the amount of work completed is in inverse proportion to the number of people employed. (The Reader (Chicago's Free Weekly) 5:2 May 28, 76)

Weiler, A. H. Nothing is impossible for the man who doesn't have to do it himself. (Washingtonian 14:155 Nov 78)

Wilson, Sloan. A man who wants time to read and write must let the grass grow long. (New York 9:46 May 24, 76)

WORK ETHIC see **WORK**

WORK—PSYCHOLOGICAL ASPECTS

Liebow, Elliot. Most people would be ashamed for their children to see them at work. (Washingtonian 16:82 Mar 81)

WORK—RUSSIA

Anonymous. As long as the bosses pretend they are paying us a decent wage, we will pretend that we are working (Soviet worker's saying). (New York Times 126:25 Section 12 Jan 30, 77)

WORLD POLITICS

Evtushenko, Evgenii Aleksandrovich. Distrust is the mother of war and political racism. (Atlas World Press Review 23:10 Nov 76)

Ford, Gerald Rudolph. Most of the important things that happen in the world happen in the middle of the night. (San Francisco Chronicle This World 1978:2 Feb 26, 78)

Gasich, Welko (Vice President of Northrop Aircraft Corporation). Until we have a bona fide world police force, it's still Dodge City and everyone wants a rifle over his door. (Time 105:44 Mar 3, 75)

Goldberg, Arthur Joseph. We need a world in which it is safe to be human. (Kansas City Times 109:28 Jan 4, 77)

Jaruzelski, Wojceich. Thank goodness we don't live in medieval times when people fight wars over ideas. (Time 119:43 Jan 4, 82)

Khomeini, Ayatollah Ruhollah. All western governments are just thieves. Nothing but evil comes from them. (Time 115:22 Jan 7, 80)

Lord, Winston. The Trilateral Commission doesn't secretly run the world. The

Council on Foreign Relations does that. (W 7:9 Aug 4, 78)

Moynihan, Daniel Patrick. As the lights go out in the rest of the world, they shine all the brighter here. (Time 107:28 Jan 26, 76)

Singer, Isaac Bashevis. I'm afraid the whole world is going to become a second Lebanon. (New York 19:56 Nov 22, 86)

Solzhenitsyn, Aleksandr Isaevich. The entire period from 1945 to 1975 can be viewed as another world war that was lost by the West without a battle. (Time 115:48 Feb 18, 80)

Thomas, Lewis. We do not, in any real way, run the (world). It runs itself, and we are part of the running. (Time 111:85 May 29, 78)

Truman, Harry S. The C students run the world. (Time 108:32 Nov 8, 76)

WORLD WAR, 1939-1945

Will, George F. World War II was the last government program that really worked (to the Association of American Publishers). (Washingtonian 10:22 July 75)

WORRY

Allen, Woody. The lion and the calf shall lie down together, but the calf won't get much sleep. (Time 113:25 Feb 26, 79)

Moore, Mary Tyler. Worrying is a necessary part of life. (Chicago Tribune 32:16 Feb 1, 78)

WORTH

Arden, Elizabeth. Nothing that costs only a dollar is worth having. (Chicago Tribune 176:2 Section II June 25, 78)

Haskins, Caryl. It's funny that we often value what is rare and specialized. What is truly precious is what is common and unspecialized. (Washington Post 70:H7 Feb 13, 77)

Hunt, Nelson Bunker. People who know how much they're worth aren't usually worth that much. (Time 115:56 May 12, 80)

WRIGHT, FRANK LLOYD—FURNITURE

Wright, Frank Lloyd. I have been black and blue in some spot, somewhere, almost all my life from too intimate contact with my own early furniture. (Chicago Tribune 24:1 Section 2 Jan 24, 78)

WRIGHT, JIM

Oreskes, Michael. He (Jim Wright) is a man abundantly endowed with a quality in dangerously short supply in politics today: guts. (New York Times 138:12 May 22, 89)

WRITING

Califano, Joseph A., Jr. Writing things clearly does not necessarily mean writing them short. (Washingtonian 13:11 Nov 77)

Cowley, Malcolm. No complete son-of-a-bitch ever wrote a good sentence. (Inquiry 1:28 July 24, 78)

Doctorow, E. L. There is no longer any such thing as fiction or nonfiction; there's only narrative. (New York Times Book Review 3 Jan 27, 80)

Hall, Donald. Less is more, in prose as in architecture. (Writer's Digest 58:8 Nov 78)

McLuhan, Marshall. Most clear writing is a sign that there is no exploration going on. Clear prose indicates an absence of thought. (Time 106:36 Aug 25, 75)

Nixon, Richard Milhous. Writing is the toughest thing I've ever done. (Rolling Stone 227:43 Dec 2, 76)

Perkins, Maxwell. You have to throw yourself away when you write (to Elizabeth Lemmon). (Esquire 89:65 July 18, 78)

Roth, Philip. The road to hell is paved with works-in-progress. (New York Times Book Review 1 July 15, 79)

Steinbeck, John. The profession of book writing makes horse racing seem like a solid, stable business. (Time 112:68 Aug 28, 78)

Waugh, Evelyn. I regard writing not as investigation of character, but as an exercise in the use of language. (Time 113:96 Feb 12, 79)

WRITING—EQUIPMENT AND SUPPLIES

Will, George F. People who use word processors should not be surprised if what they write is to prose as process cheese is to real cheese. (Lawrence (Kansas) Journal-World 125:4 Dec 18, 83)

WRONG see **RIGHT AND WRONG**

WYNETTE, TAMMY

Wynette, Tammy. My life has been a soap opera. (US 3:64 June 30, 86)

YACHT RACING see also **TURNER, R.E. (TED)**

YOUNG, ANDREW

Young, Andrew. I was taught to fight when people called me nigger. That's when I learned that negotiation is better than fighting. (Time 108:13 Dec 27, 76)

YOUTH

Cartland, Barbara. Being 18 is like visiting Russia. You're glad you've had the experience, but you'd never want to repeat it. (The Observer 9764:14 Oct 15, 78)

Chanel, Coco. Youth is something very new: twenty years ago no one mentioned it. (Chicago Tribune 176:2 Section 2 June 25, 78)

Drabble, Margaret. I think when you are young, you are oblidged to be excessively interested in yourself. (Toronto Life Fashion Magazine 34 Fall 87)

Longworth, Alice Roosevelt. The secret of eternal youth is arrested development. (Washington Post 103:1 Section C Feb 24, 80)

White, William Allen. In education we are striving not to teach youth to make a living, but to make a life. (Kansas City Times 109:11B Feb 4, 77)

ZADORA, PIA

Zadora, Pia. I can buy and sell any of these people who are always criticizing me. (US 3:64 July 15, 85)

ZIEGLER, RONALD LOUIS

Ziegler, Ronald Louis. I never knowingly lied, but certainly history shows that many things I said were incorrect. (Newsweek 91:22 April 17, 78)

ZIMBABWE see also **CIVIL RIGHTS—ZIMBABWE; NKOMO, JOSHUA**

ZORINSKY, EDWARD

Dole, Robert J. Rural America never had a better friend (about Edward Zorinsky). (Chicago Tribune 67:7 Section 2 Mar 8, 87)

Dictionary of Contemporary Quotations Information Service

To locate new quotations in the *Dictionary of Contemporary Quotations Information Service*, our User's Diskette must be employed to gain access to our electronic information services. This diskette is furnished to all standing order *Dictionary of Contemporary Quotations* subscribers, and requires that it be used in an IBM™ (PC, XT, AT) or compatible personal computer equipped with a Hayes™ compatible modem.[1] There is no charge for the use of the *Dictionary of Contemporary Quotations Information Service* for standing order subscribers to the *Dictionary of Contemporary Quotations*. For institutions that wish only to subscribe to the *Dictionary of Contemporary Quotations Information Service*, a license arrangement is available from the publisher with annual subject updates. Please contact the publisher for details. The User's Diskette contains software which allows subscribers, upon the completion and return of our licensing agreement, to gain access to our data base. It is expected subscribers will have a telephone line dedicated to electronic searching which is not affected by local private branch exchange (PBX) systems. Note: There is a small handling charge for producing and/or replacing a User's Diskette; Further, prices and conditions of sale of this product are subject to change without notice.

Instructions for the use of the User Diskette are to be found on a Read.me file on the diskette as well as in an accompanying brochure sent with the diskette to subscribers. A complete subject authority list for the *Dictionary of Contemporary Quotations Information Service* as of October 1990 follows on page 288. This list is subject to regular change, but notice of significant revisions to this list is made on the Publication Schedule module of our electronic information services when they occur.

The current format of the *Dictionary of Contemporary Quotations Information Service* is identical to the format of Volume 6 of the *Dictionary of Contemporary Quotations*. Accordingly, no citations for source are provided in the subject section. There are also no see and see also references. Revisions are currently underway to the format of the *Dictionary of Contemporary Quotations Information Service* and it will become identical to this book. Steps are also being taken to make the data base available independent of our User's Diskette for subscribers who do not have access to the computer equipment presently required to use our information services.

---

[1] IBM and PC, XT and AT are registered trademarks of the International Business Machines Corporation and Hayes is a registered trademark of the Hayes Microcomputer Products, Inc.

This is a list of subjects under which quotations appear in the Dictionary of Contemporary Quotations Information Service effective 10/1/90. Please note that new subjects may appear in the data base monthly.

AARON, HENRY
ABBEY, EDWARD
ABILITY
ABORTION
ABORTION—LAWS AND LEGISLATION
ABORTION—POLITICAL ASPECTS
ABRAMS, ELLIOTT
ABZUG, BELLA
ACADEMIC FREEDOM
ACHIEVEMENT
ACTING
ACTORS AND ACTRESSES
ACUPUNCTURE
ADAMS, ANSEL
ADULTERY
ADVENTURE
ADVERTISING
ADVERTISING INDUSTRY
ADVICE
AESTHETICS
AFGHANISTAN
AFGHANISTAN—POLITICS AND
  GOVERNMENT
AFRICA
AFRICA, SOUTHERN—POLITICS AND
  GOVERNMENT
AFRICA—POLITICS AND GOVERNMENT
AFRICA—RACE QUESTION
AFRICANS
AGE
AGED
AGED—PSYCHOLOGY
AGED—RELATIONS—RUNNING
AGING
AGNEW, SPIRO THEODORE
AIDS
AIDS—CHILDREN
AIDS—NEW YORK(CITY)
AIDS—PREVENTION—STUDY AND
  TEACHING—PUBLIC SCHOOLS
AIKEN, CONRAD
AIKEN, GEORGE DAVID
AIR CONDITIONING
AIR POLLUTION
AIR POLLUTION—TEXAS
AIR SHIPS
AIR TRAVEL
AIRLINES—SAFETY
AIRPLANES, SUPERSONIC
ALAIA, AZZEDINE
ALASKA
ALASKA—POLITICS AND GOVERNMENT
ALBORNOZ, CLAUDIO SANCHEZ
ALCOHOL
ALCOHOLIC BEVERAGES

ALCOHOLISM
ALCOHOLISM AND AUTHORSHIP
ALDA, ALAN
ALGREN, NELSON
ALI, MUHAMMAD
ALICE COOPER
ALL THE PRESIDENT'S MEN (MOVING
  PICTURE)
ALLEN, GEORGE
ALLEN, WOODY
ALLENDE GOSSENS, SALVADOR
ALLMAN, GREGG
ALTMAN, ROBERT
AMBITION
AMERICA
AMERICAN FEDERATION OF LABOR AND
  CONGRESS OF INDUSTRIAL
  ORGANIZATIONS
AMERICAN MUSEUM OF NATURAL
  HISTORY, NEW YORK
AMERICAN PETROLEUM INSTITUTE
AMERICAN TELEPHONE AND TELEGRAPH
  COMPANY
AMERICANS
AMIN DADA, IDI
AMUSEMENT PARKS
ANDERSON, JOHN B.
ANDERSON, MIKE
ANDERSON, PAUL
ANDERSON, WENDELL
ANDRETTI, MARIO
ANGER
ANGER, KENNETH
ANGOLA
ANNE, PRINCESS OF GREAT BRITAIN
ANTI-CATHOLICISM
APARTHEID
ARAB STATES—POLITICS AND
  GOVERNMENT
ARABS
ARAFAT, YASIR
ARBUS, DIANE
ARCHITECTS
ARCHITECTURE
ARCHITECTURE—HOUSTON
ARGENTINA—DESCRIPTION
ARGENTINA—POLITICS AND
  GOVERNMENT
ARGUMENTS
ARMAMENTS
ARMSTRONG, LOUIS
ARMSTRONG, NEIL
ARNEZ, DESI
ARNOLD, BENEDICT
ARRAU, CLAUDIO
ART
ART AND POLITICS
ART CRITICISM
ART SALES
ART, MODERN
ART—MODERNISM

ARTERIOSCLEROSIS
ARTIFICIAL INTELLIGENCE
ARTISTS
ARTISTS—SELF PERCEPTION
ARTS
ARTS AND SOCIETY
ARTS—AFRICA
ARTS—CHICAGO
ARTS—CRITICISM
ARTS—NEW YORK (CITY)
ARTS—RUSSIA
ARTS—UNITED STATES
ASHBERY, JOHN
ASHE, ARTHUR
ASIMOV, ISAAC
ASPEN, COLORADO
ASSASSINATION
ASSASSINATION—UNITED STATES
ASSAULT AND BATTERY
ASTAIRE, FRED
ASTOR, NANCY
ASTROLOGY
ASTROTURF
ATGET, EUGENE
ATHEISM
ATHLETES
ATHLETES—UNITED STATES
ATLANTIS
ATOMIC BOMB
ATOMIC BOMB—PAKISTAN
ATOMIC POWER
ATOMIC POWER INDUSTRY
ATOMIC POWER PLANTS
ATOMIC POWER PLANTS—KOREA
  (REPUBLIC)
ATOMIC POWER—FRANCE
ATOMIC WARFARE
ATOMIC WEAPONS
ATTICA PRISON
AUCHINCLOSS, LOUIS
AUDEN, WYSTAN HUGH
AUDIENCES
AUSCHWITZ CONCENTRATION CAMP
AUTH, TONY
AUTHORS
AUTHORS RIGHTS
AUTHORS, AMERICAN
AUTHORS, AMERICAN—TEXAS
AUTHORS, AMERICAN—WOMEN
AUTHORS, RUSSIAN
AUTHORS—FAME
AUTHORS—RELATIONS—MOVING
  PICTURE INDUSTRY
AUTHORSHIP
AUTHORSHIP—HISTORY
AUTHORSHIP—POETRY
AUTHORSHIP—PSYCHOLOGICAL
  ASPECTS
AUTOBIOGRAPHY
AUTOMOBILE DRIVING
AUTOMOBILE RACING

AUTOMOBILES
AUTOMOBILES—POLLUTION
AUTOMOBILES—PURCHASING
AUTOMOBILES—USED
AUTRY, GENE
AVARICE
AVIATION
BABBITT, BRUCE E.
BACON, FRANCIS
BAEZ, JOAN
BAGNOLD, ENID
BAILEY, F. LEE
BAILEY, PEARL
BAKER, HOWARD HENRY
BAKER, JOSEPHINE
BAKER, JOY
BAKER, RUSSELL
BAKKER, JIM
BAKKER, TAMMY
BALANCHINE, GEORGE
BALDNESS
BALDWIN, ROGER
BALTIMORE. BASEBALL CLUB (AMERICAN
  LEAGUE)
BANKHEAD, TALLULAH
BANKS AND BANKING
BANKS AND BANKING—LAWS AND
  REGULATIONS
BANKS AND BANKING—UNITED STATES
BAPTISTS
BARDOT, BRIGITTE
BARRINGER, JOHN W.
BARS AND BARROOMS
BARS AND BARROOMS—CHICAGO
BARTH, JOHN
BARUCH, BERNARD MANNES
BARYSHNIKOV, MIKHAIL
BASEBALL
BASEBALL FANS—CHICAGO
BASEBALL PLAYERS—HITTING
BASEBALL—FAILURE
BASEBALL—HITTING—RECORDS
BASEBALL—MANAGERS
BASEBALL—SALARIES, PENSIONS, ETC.
BASEBALL—STUDY AND TEACHING
BASEBALL—UMPIRING
BASIE, WILLIAM (COUNT)
BASKETBALL
BASKETBALL, COLLEGE
BASKETBALL, COLLEGE—COACHES
BASKETBALL, PROFESSIONAL
BASKETBALL, PROFESSIONAL—BLACKS
BATTLE, BILL
BEAME, ABRAHAM DAVID
BEATLES (MUSICAL GROUP)
BEATNIKS
BEATON, SIR CECIL
BEATTY, WARREN
BEAUTY CONTESTS
BEAUTY, PERSONAL
BEAUTY, PERSONAL—MEN

BEAUVOIR, SIMONE DE
BECKETT, SAMUEL
BEER
BEGIN, MENACHEM
BEHAVIOR (PSYCHOLOGY)
BELGIUM—FOREIGN POLICY—AFRICA
BELIEF
BELIEF AND DOUBT
BELL, GRIFFIN
BELLOW, SAUL
BELOFF, NORA
BENCHLEY, ROBERT
BENNETT, WILLIAM
BENNY, JACK
BENTON, THOMAS HART
BERGMAN, INGMAR
BERGMAN, INGRID
BERKOWITZ, DAVID
BERNHARDT, SARAH
BERNSTEIN, LEONARD
BERRY, CHUCK
BEVERLY HILLS, CALIFORNIA
BHUTTO, ZULFIKAR ALI
BIKO, STEVE
BILLY JACK (MOVING PICTURE
   CHARACTER)
BIOGRAPHY
BIRD STUDY
BIRTH CONTROL
BISEXUALITY
BISMARCK, OTTO FUERST VON
BLACK MUSICIANS
BLACK MUSLIMS
BLACK POLITICIANS
BLACK, SHIRLEY TEMPLE
BLACKBURN, BEN B.
BLACKS
BLACKS AND POLITICS
BLACKS—CIVIL RIGHTS
BLACKS—CIVIL RIGHTS—HISTORY
BLACKS—ECONOMIC CONDITIONS
BLACKS—EDUCATION
BLACKS—EMPLOYMENT
BLACKS—PSYCHOLOGY
BLACKS—SEGREGATION—CHICAGO
BLACKS—SEGREGATION—PLAINS,
   GEORGIA
BLACKS—SOCIAL CONDITIONS
BLACKS—UNITED STATES
BLAKE, EUBIE
BLASS, BILL
BLOCH, ROBERT
BLOOMINGDALE'S (DEPARTMENT STORE)
BLOOMINGDALE, BETSY
BOCUSE, PAUL
BOESKY, IVAN F
BOGART, HUMPHREY
BOHR, NIELS
BOLKAN, FLORINDA
BONO, SONNY
BOOK REVIEWERS AND REVIEWING

BOOKS
BOOKS AND READING
BOOKS—COLLECTORS AND COLLECTING
BOOKSELLERS AND BOOKSELLING
BOONE, PAT
BOREDOM
BORGE, VICTOR
BORGES, JORGE LUIS
BORK, ROBERT
BOSS RULE
BOSTON—DESCRIPTION
BOSTON. BASKETBALL CLUB (NATIONAL
   ASSOCIATION)
BOTHA, PIETER WILLEM
BOULANGER, NADIA
BOUTON, JIM
BOWEN, ELIZABETH
BOWIE, DAVID
BOWLING
BOXING
BOY GEORGE
BRADLEY, THOMAS
BRADSHAW, TERRY
BRAGA, SONIA
BRAIN
BRAIN-WASHING
BRAINE, JOHN
BRAND, STEWART
BRANDO, MARLON
BRANDT, WILLY
BRAZIL
BREAKFASTS
BRECHT, BERTOLT
BRESLIN, JIMMY
BREZHNEV, LEONID I.
BRIBERY
BROCK, LOU
BRONSON, CHARLES
BROOKS, LOUISE
BROOKS, MEL
BROWN, EDMUND GERALD, JR.
BROWN, GEORGE S.
BROWN, JAMES
BROWN, WILLIE
BRUCE, LENNY
BRYANT, ANITA
BUCHWALD, ART
BUCKLEY, WILLIAM FRANK, JR.
BUDDHA AND BUDDHISM
BUDGET
BUDGET, PERSONAL
BUDGET—UNITED STATES
BUDGETING
BUJOLD, GENEVIEVE
BUKOVSKY, VLADIMIR
BULGAKOV, MIKHAIL AFANAS'EVICH. THE
   MASTER AND MARGARITA
BUNDY, THEODORE
BUNEUL, LUIS
BURDEN, CHRIS
BUREAUCRACY

BURGER KING, INC.
BURGER, WARREN EARL
BURNS, ARTHUR FRANK
BURNS, GEORGE
BURTON, RICHARD
BUSBY, STEVE
BUSH, BARBARA
BUSH, GEORGE
BUSH, GEORGE—PRESIDENTIAL
  CAMPAIGN—1988
BUSINESS
BUSINESS ETHICS
BUSINESS MANAGEMENT AND
  ORGANIZATION
BUSINESS—INTERNATIONAL ASPECTS
BUSINESS—PUBLIC RELATIONS
BUSINESS—RELATIONS—FOOTBALL
BUSINESS—STUDY AND TEACHING
BUSINESS—UNITED STATES
BUSINESSMEN
BUSINESSMEN—GREAT BRITAIN
BUSINESSMEN—PUBLIC RELATIONS
BUSINESSMEN—TAX DEDUCTIONS
BUSINESSMEN—UNITED STATES
BUTZ, EARL LAUER
BYRD, ROBERT
BYRNE, JANE
CAAN, JAMES
CADDELL, PATRICK
CAESAR, SID
CAGNEY, JAMES
CALDER, ALEXANDER
CALDWELL, SARAH
CALDWELL, TAYLOR
CALIFANO, JOSEPH A., JR.
CALIFORNIA
CALIFORNIA—DESCRIPTION
CALIFORNIA—POLITICS AND
  GOVERNMENT
CALLAS, MARIA
CALLEY, WILLIAM LAWS, JR.
CALLOWAY, CAB
CAMBODIA
CAMBODIA—POLITICS AND
  GOVERNMENT
CANADA
CANADA—DESCRIPTION
CANADA—POLITICS AND GOVERNMENT
CANADA—RELATIONS—UNITED STATES
CANADIANS
CANCER
CANCER—CAUSES
CANCER—THERAPY
CANETTI, ELIAS
CANNES INTERNATIONAL FILM FESTIVAL
CAPITAL
CAPITAL INVESTMENTS
CAPITAL PUNISHMENT
CAPITALISM
CAPITALISM AND SOCIETY
CAPONE, ALPHONSE

CAPOTE, TRUMAN
CAPP, AL
CARAMANLIS, CONSTANTINE
CARDIN, PIERRE
CARDS
CAREW, RODNEY
CAREY, HUGH
CAROLINE, PRINCESS OF MONACO
CARSWELL, HAROLD G.
CARTER, AMY
CARTER, BILLY
CARTER, JAMES EARL
CARTER, JAMES EARL—ENERGY
  PROGRAM
CARTER, JAMES EARL—FAMILY
CARTER, JAMES
  EARL—FAMILY—FINANCE, PERSONAL
CARTER, JAMES EARL—RELATION WITH
  THE PRESS
CARTER, JAMES
  EARL—RELATIONS—RELIGION
CARTER, JAMES EARL—STAFF
CARTER, LILLIAN
CARTER, ROSALYNN
CARTER, RUBIN (HURRICANE)
CARTIER-BRESSON, HENRI
CARTLAND, BARBARA
CASH, JOHNNY
CASH, KEVIN
CASSIDY, SHAUN
CASTRO, FIDEL
CATHOLIC CHURCH
CATHOLIC CHURCH IN THE UNITED
  STATES
CATHOLIC CHURCH—FINANCE
CATHOLIC COLLEGES AND UNIVERSITIES
CATHOLICISM
CAUCASIAN RACE
CAUSATION
CELEBRITIES
CELEBRITIES—CONDUCT OF LIFE
CELEBRITIES—SEXUAL BEHAVIOR
CENSORSHIP
CENSORSHIP—SOUTH AFRICA
CENTRAL AMERICA—POLITICS AND
  GOVERNMENT
CERF, BENNETT
CEZANNE, PAUL
CHABROL, CLAUDE
CHAGALL, MARC
CHAMBERS, MARILYN
CHAMPAGNE
CHANCE
CHANDLER, RAYMOND
CHANGE
CHAPLIN, CHARLES SPENCER
CHARACTER
CHARACTERS AND CHARACTERISTICS
CHARACTERS AND
  CHARACTERISTICS—ENGLAND
CHARACTERS AND

CHARACTERISTICS—FRANCE
CHARACTERS AND
  CHARACTERISTICS—GREAT BRITAIN
CHARACTERS AND
  CHARACTERISTICS—IRELAND
CHARACTERS AND
  CHARACTERISTICS—ITALY
CHARACTERS AND
  CHARACTERISTICS—MEN
CHARACTERS AND
  CHARACTERISTICS—NEW YORK (CITY)
CHARACTERS AND
  CHARACTERISTICS—SOUTH
CHARACTERS AND
  CHARACTERISTICS—UNITED STATES
CHARLES, PRINCE OF WALES
CHARO
CHAVEZ, CESAR
CHEEVER, JOHN
CHER
CHICAGO
CHICAGO SYMPHONY ORCHESTRA
CHICAGO—DESCRIPTION
CHICAGO—POLICE
CHICAGO—POLITICS AND GOVERNMENT
CHICAGO—SOCIAL LIFE AND
  CUSTOMS—PROHIBITION
CHICAGO. BASEBALL CLUB (AMERICAN
  LEAGUE)
CHICAGO. BASEBALL CLUB (NATIONAL
  LEAGUE)
CHILDBIRTH
CHILDREN
CHILDREN—CLOTHING AND DRESS
CHILDREN—GROWTH AND
  DEVELOPMENT
CHILDREN—MANAGEMENT AND
  TRAINING
CHILDREN—SEXUAL BEHAVIOR
CHILE—POLITICS AND GOVERNMENT
CHINA (PEOPLE'S REPUBLIC)
CHINA (PEOPLE'S
  REPUBLIC)—DESCRIPTION
CHINA (PEOPLE'S REPUBLIC)—MILITARY
  POLICY
CHINA (PEOPLE'S REPUBLIC)—POLITICS
  AND GOVERNMENT
CHINA (PEOPLE'S
  REPUBLIC)—RELATIONS—COCA-COLA
  COMPANY
CHOREOGRAPHY
CHRISTIANITY
CHRISTIANS
CHRISTIE, AGATHA
CHRYSLER CORPORATION
CHUNG, CONNIE
CHURCH AND BELIEF
CHURCH AND RACE PROBLEMS
CHURCH AND STATE
CHURCH ATTENDANCE—SEGREGATION
CHURCH, FRANK

CHURCHES
CHURCHES—DESEGREGATION
CIGARS
CITIES AND TOWNS
CITY AND TOWN LIFE
CIVIL DISOBEDIENCE
CIVIL RIGHTS
CIVIL RIGHTS—PARAGUAY
CIVIL RIGHTS—RUSSIA
CIVILIZATION
CIVILIZATION AND LEISURE
CLARK, JOE
CLEAVER, ELDRIDGE
CLEAVER, KATHLEEN
CLEMENTS, BILL
CLERGY
CLEVELAND, GROVER
CLEVELAND—POLITICS AND
  GOVERNMENT
CLOTHING AND DRESS
CLOTHING AND DRESS—MEN
CLOTHING AND DRESS—WOMEN
CLOTHING INDUSTRY
CLUBS
COACHES (ATHLETICS)
COCA, IMOGENE
COCA-COLA COMPANY
COCAINE
COCHRANE, ELIZABETH
COFFEE
COHEN, MICKEY
COHN, ROY
COLBERT, CLAUDETTE
COLBY, WILLIAM EGAN
COLD (DISEASE)
COLICOS, JOHN
COLLECTORS AND COLLECTING
COLLEGE EDUCATION
COLLEGE EDUCATION, VALUE OF
COLLEGE GRADUATES
COLLEGE PROFESSORS AND
  INSTRUCTORS
COLLEGES AND UNIVERSITIES
COLLEGES AND
  UNIVERSITIES—CHEATING
  (EDUCATION)
COLORADO—POWER RESOURCES
COLSON, CHARLES WENDELL
COLUMBIA BROADCASTING SYSTEM, INC.
COMEDIANS
COMEDY
COMICS (BOOKS, STRIPS, ETC.)
COMMERCIAL PRODUCTS
COMMITTEES
COMMON SENSE
COMMUNES
COMMUNICATION
COMMUNISM
COMMUNISM—AFRICA
COMMUNISM—CHINA (PEOPLE'S
  REPUBLIC)

COMMUNISM—EUROPE
COMMUNISM—RELATIONS—
  JOURNALISTS
COMMUNISM—RUSSIA
COMPASSION
COMPETENCE
COMPETITION
COMPETITIONS
COMPOSERS
COMPROMISE
COMPUTER INDUSTRY
COMPUTERS
COMPUTERS—SOCIAL ASPECTS
CONABLE, BARBER
CONCEIT
CONCERTS
CONCORD, MASSACHUSETTS—POLITICS
  AND GOVERNMENT
CONDON, RICHARD
CONDUCT OF LIFE
CONDUCTORS (MUSIC)
CONFLICT OF GENERATIONS
CONFORMITY
CONGRESSMEN
CONGRESSMEN—SEXUAL BEHAVIOR
CONNALLY, JOHN BOWDEN
CONNALLY, MARK
CONNOLLY, CYRIL
CONRAD, JOSEPH
CONSERVATION
CONSERVATION ASSOCIATIONS
CONSERVATION OF RESOURCES
CONSERVATISM
CONSUMER PROTECTION
CONSUMERS
CONSUMPTION (ECONOMICS)
CONTRACTS
CONVERSATION
COOKE, ALISTAIR
COOKERY
COOKERY, CAJUN
COOKERY—MIDWEST
COOKERY—UNITED STATES
COOKS
COOLIDGE, CALVIN
COOPER, GARY
COPYRIGHT—UNITED STATES
CORPORAL PUNISHMENT
CORPORATIONS
CORPORATIONS, INTERNATIONAL
CORSARO, FRANK
COSELL, HOWARD
COSMOLOGY
COST OF LIVING
COSTA RICA—FOREIGN
  POLICY—NICARAGUA
COUNCIL ON FOREIGN RELATIONS
COUNTRY LIFE
COURAGE
COUSINS, NORMAN
COWARD, NOEL

COWBOYS
CREATION
CREATION (LITERARY, ARTISTIC, ETC.)
CREATION—STUDY AND TEACHING
CREDIT
CREDIT UNIONS
CRICHTON, MICHAEL
CRIME AND CRIMINALS
CRIME AND CRIMINALS—NEW YORK
  (CITY)
CRIME AND CRIMINALS—PHILADELPHIA
CRIME AND
  CRIMINALS—RELATIONS—MENTAL
  HYGIENE
CRIME AND CRIMINALS—UNITED STATES
CRIME PREVENTION
CRIMINAL JUSTICE, ADMINISTRATION OF
CRIMINAL JUSTICE, ADMINISTRATION
  OF—IRAN
CRISWELL, W. A.
CRITICISM
CRITICS
CRONKITE, WALTER
CROSBY, BING
CROSBY, HARRY
CUBA
CUBA—DESCRIPTION
CUBA—FOREIGN RELATIONS—UNITED
  STATES
CUBAN MISSILE CRISIS, 1962
CULTS
CULTURE
CURIOSITY
CYNICISM
CYPRUS—POLITICS AND GOVERNMENT
D'AUBUISSON, ROBERTO
DALEY, RICHARD J.
DALI, SALVADOR
DALLAS COUNTY, TEXAS
DALLAS. FOOTBALL CLUB (NATIONAL
  LEAGUE)
DALTREY, ROGER
DANCE
DANCE THEATER OF HARLEM
DANCING
DANCING, FOLK
DAVIS, BETTE
DAVIS, CULLEN
DAVIS, STUART
DAY, DOROTHY
DAY, MORRIS—RELATIONS—WOMEN
DAYAN, MOSHE
DE CHIRICO, GIORGIO
DE GAULLE, CHARLES
DE MILLE, AGNES
DEAN, JOHN WESLEY, III
DEATH
DEBT, PUBLIC—UNITED STATES
DECENTRALIZATION IN GOVERNMENT
DECISION MAKING (POLITICAL SCIENCE)
DECROW, KAREN LIPSHULTZ

DEDERICH, CHARLES
DELEGATION OF AUTHORITY
DELLA FEMINA, JERRY
DEMOCRACY
DEMOCRATIC PARTY
DEMOCRATIC PARTY—CHICAGO
DEMOCRATIC PARTY—PRESIDENTIAL
  CANDIDATES
DEMOCRATIC PARTY. NATIONAL
  CONVENTION, CHICAGO, 1968
DENIRO, ROBERT
DENVER, JOHN
DEPRESSION, MENTAL
DEPRESSIONS
DESIGN
DETECTIVE AND MYSTERY STORIES
DETENTE (POLITICAL SCIENCE)
DEVIL
DEVRIES, PETER
DIARIES
DICKINSON, ANGIE
DICTATORSHIP
DIET
DIETRICH, MARLENE
DIMAGGIO, JOE
DIPLOMACY
DIPLOMATS
DISARMAMENT
DISCOVERY
DISCRIMINATION IN EMPLOYMENT
DISNEY, WALT
DISSENTERS
DISSENTERS—CHINA (PEOPLE'S
  REPUBLIC)
DISSENTERS—RUSSIA
DISSENTERS—UNITED STATES
DISTRUST
DIVORCE
DIXON, PAUL RAND
DNA
DOBLER, CONRAD
DOGS
DOLE, ELIZABETH
DOLE, ROBERT J.
DOLLAR (MONEY)
DONAHUE, MARK
DONALD DUCK
DONLEAVY, J. P.
DONOVAN, THOMAS
DOUGLAS, WILLIAM ORVILLE
DRAMA
DRAMATIC CRITICISM
DRAMATISTS
DRAWING
DROUGHTS—WEST
DRUG INDUSTRY
DRUGS
DRUGS AND THE AGED
DRUNKENNESS
DUBUFFET, JEAN
DUCHAMP, MARCEL

DUKAKIS, MICHAEL S.
DUKE, DAVID
DULLES, JOHN FOSTER
DULLNESS
DUNAWAY, FAYE
DUNCAN, ISADORA
DURANT, WILL
DURANTE, JIMMY
DURKIN, JOHN
DUTY
DYLAN, BOB
E.T. (MOVING PICTURE CHARACTER)
EASTWOOD, CLINT
EATING
ECHEVERRIA ALVAREZ, LUIS
ECOLOGY
ECONOMIC ASSISTANCE, AMERICAN
ECONOMIC CONDITIONS
ECONOMIC FORECASTING
ECONOMIC POLICY
ECONOMIC STATISTICS
ECONOMICS
ECONOMICS—STUDY AND TEACHING
ECONOMISTS
EDER, RICHARD
EDISON, THOMAS ALVA
EDITORS AND EDITING
EDUCATION
EDUCATION, HIGHER
EDUCATION—AIMS AND OBJECTIVES
EDUCATION—JAPAN
EDUCATION—PHILADELPHIA
EDUCATION—UNITED STATES
EDUCATORS
EFFICIENCY, ADMINISTRATIVE
EGALITARIANISM
EGGLESTON, JUSTINE JUDD
EGYPT—FOREIGN RELATIONS—ISRAEL
EGYPT—FOREIGN RELATIONS—RUSSIA
EGYPT—FOREIGN RELATIONS—UNITED
  STATES
EHRLICHMAN, JOHN D.
EIKERENKOETER, FREDERICK J.
EINSTEIN, ALBERT
EISENHOWER, DWIGHT DAVID
EISENHOWER, MAMIE GENEVA (DOUD)
EIZENSTAT, STUART
EKLAND, BRITT
EL SALVADOR
EL SALVADOR—POLITICS AND
  GOVERNMENT
ELKINS, WEST VIRGINIA—DESCRIPTION
EMIGRATION AND IMMIGRATION LAW
EMOTIONS
EMPLOYEES
EMPLOYEES, DISMISSAL OF
EMPLOYEES, PUBLIC
EMPLOYMENT
ENEMIES
ENERGY CONSERVATION
ENGLISH LANGUAGE

ENGLISH LANGUAGE—COMPOSITION
ENGLISH LANGUAGE—GRAMMAR
ENGLISH LANGUAGE—STUDY AND
   TEACHING
ENGLISH LANGUAGE—USAGE
ENTERTAINERS
ENTERTAINING
ENTERTAINMENT INDUSTRY
ENTREPRENEURS
ENTREPRENEURS—UNITED STATES
ENVIRONMENT
ENVIRONMENTAL ACTION
   (ORGANIZATION)
ENVIRONMENTAL MOVEMENT
ENVIRONMENTAL POLICY
EQUALITY
ERHARD SEMINARS TRAINING
ERHARD, LUDWIG
ERHARD, WERNER
ERRORS
ERVIN, SAMUEL JAMES
ESPOSITO, MEADE H.
ESTES, BILLIE SOL
ETHICS
ETIQUETTE
ETIQUETTE—IOWA
EUROPE
EUROPE—POLITICS AND GOVERNMENT
EUROPEANS
EVANGELICALISM
EVANS, CHICK
EVOLUTION—STUDY AND TEACHING
EXCESS
EXERCISE
EXNER, JUDITH CAMPBELL
EXPENDITURES, PUBLIC
EXPERTS
EXPLANATION
FACTS
FAILURE
FAIRCHILD, MORGAN
FAITH
FALLACI, ORIANA
FALWELL, JERRY
FAME
FAMILY
FAMILY LIFE
FANATICISM
FARM LABOR—CALIFORNIA
FARMING
FASCISM
FASHION
FASHION DESIGN
FASHION DESIGNERS
FASHION—NEW YORK (CITY)
FATE
FATHERS
FAULK, JOHN HENRY
FAULKNER, WILLIAM
FAWCETT-MAJORS, FARRAH
FEAR

FEDERAL GOVERNMENT
FEDERAL-STATE CONTROVERSIES
FELA
FELDMAN, MARTY
FELLINI, FEDERICO
FERRARO, GERALDINE
FICTION
FIELD, MARSHALL, V.—FAMILY
FIELDS, W. C.
FINANCE, PERSONAL
FINCH, PETER
FINKS, JIM
FINLEY, CHARLES OSCAR
FINLEY, CHARLES
   OSCAR—RELATIONS—BASEBALL
   PLAYERS
FIREARMS—LAWS AND REGULATIONS
FISHER, EDDIE
FISHER, M. F. K.
FISHERMEN
FISHING
FITZGERALD, F. SCOTT
FITZGERALD, ZELDA
FITZSIMMONS, FRANK E.
FLAGS—MUTILATION, DEFACEMENT, ETC.
FLANNER, JANET
FLATTERY
FLIGHT
FLOOD, CURT
FLOREZ, ELISA (MISSY)
FLY FISHING
FLYNT, LARRY
FONDA, HENRY
FONDA, PETER
FOOD
FOOD HABITS
FOOD INDUSTRY—COMPETITION
FOOD LAW AND LEGISLATION
FOOD, HEALTH
FOOD, ORGANIC
FOOTBALL
FOOTBALL, COLLEGE
FOOTBALL, COLLEGE—COACHES
FOOTBALL, COLLEGE—RECRUITMENT
FOOTBALL, COLLEGE—TRAINING
FOOTBALL, PROFESSIONAL
FOOTBALL,
   PROFESSIONAL—QUARTERBACKS
FOOTBALL, PROFESSIONAL—SALARIES,
   PENSIONS, ETC.
FOOTBALL—GAMBLING
FOOTBALL—TEXAS
FORBES, MALCOLM
FORD MOTOR COMPANY
FORD, CHARLOTTE
FORD, EDSEL, II
FORD, GERALD RUDOLPH
FORD, GERALD RUDOLPH—STAFF
FORD, GERALD RUDOLPH—THOUGHT
   AND THINKING
FORD, HENRY, II

FORD, JACK
FORECASTING
FOREMAN, GEORGE
FOREST CONSERVATION
FORGERY
FORM
FORSTER, E. M.
FOSTER, JODIE
FRAMPTON, PETER
FRANCE
FRANCE—FOREIGN POLICY
FRANCE—FOREIGN POLICY—AFRICA
FRANCE—POLITICS AND GOVERNMENT
FRANCO, FRANCISCO
FRANKEL'S LAW (QUOTATION)
FRANKLIN, BENJAMIN
FRANKLIN, BONNIE
FRAZIER, JOE
FREE ENTERPRISE
FREE SPEECH
FREE TRADE AND PROTECTION
FREEDOM
FREEDOM (THEOLOGY)
FREEDOM OF THE PRESS
FRENCH
FREUD, SIGMUND
FRIEDMAN, MILTON
FRIENDSHIP
FROMME, LYNETTE (SQUEAKY)
FUEL INDUSTRY
FUEL INDUSTRY—WESTERN STATES
FULBRIGHT, JAMES WILLIAM
FUND RAISING
FUNERALS
FUR BEARING ANIMALS
FUR COATS, WRAPS, ETC.
FURNESS, BETTY
FUTURE
GABLE, CLARK
GABO, NAUM
GABOR, ZSA ZSA
GALLICO, PAUL
GAMBLING
GAMES
GANDHI, INDIRA (NEHRU)
GARDENING
GARLAND, JUDY
GARN, JAKE
GASTRONOMY
GEMS
GENERAL MOTORS CORPORATION
GENERALIZATIONS
GENEROSITY
GENETIC ENGINEERING
GEORGIA—POLITICS AND GOVERNMENT
GERMAN REUNIFICATION QUESTION
GERMANY (FEDERAL
  REPUBLIC)—FOREIGN RELATIONS
GERMANY—HISTORY
GETTY, GORDON PETER
GETTY, JEAN PAUL

GIFTS
GILLESPIE, DIZZY
GILMORE, GARY MARK
GINGRICH, NEWT
GINSBERG, ALLEN
GIONO, JEAN
GISCARD D'ESTAING, VALERY
GISH, LILLIAN
GIULINI, CARLO MARIA
GIVENCHY, HUBERT DE
THE GLASS MENAGERIE (THEATRICAL
  PRODUCTION)
GLEASON, JACKIE
GOD
GOEBBELS, JOSEPH
GOELET, ROBERT G.
GOETZ, BERNHARD
GOLD
GOLDWATER, BARRY MORRIS
GOLDWIN, ROBERT
GOLDWYN, SAMUEL
GOLF
GOODMAN, BENNY
GOODWIN, RICHARD N.
GORBACHEV, MIKHAIL
GOSSIP
GOVERNMENT
GOVERNMENT AND THE PRESS
GOVERNMENT AND THE PRESS—GREAT
  BRITAIN
GOVERNMENT EMPLOYEES
GOVERNMENT SPENDING POLICY
GOVERNMENTAL INVESTIGATIONS
GOVERNORS
GRABLE, BETTY
GRAHAM, BILLY
GRAHAM, MARTHA
GRAND JURY
GRANDMOTHERS
GRANT, CARY
GRASSO, ELLA
GRATITUDE
GRAVES, ROBERT
GRAZIANO, ROCKY
GREAT BRITAIN—DESCRIPTION
GREAT BRITAIN—ECONOMIC
  CONDITIONS
GREAT BRITAIN—ECONOMIC POLICY
GREAT BRITAIN—FOREIGN POLICY
GREAT BRITAIN—FOREIGN
  POLICY—RHODESIA
GREAT BRITAIN—FOREIGN RELATIONS
GREAT BRITAIN—POLITICS AND
  GOVERNMENT
GREAT BRITAIN—POWER RESOURCES
GREAT BRITAIN—SOCIAL LIFE AND
  CUSTOMS
GREECE—POLITICS AND GOVERNMENT
GREENE, GAEL
GREENE, GRAHAM
GREENMAIL

GREENSPAN, ALAN
GREER, GERMAINE
GRETZKY, WAYNE
GROPPI, JAMES E.
GUCCI (DEPARTMENT STORE)
GUGGENHEIM, PEGGY
GUILT
GUINNESS, SIR ALEC
GUMBEL, BRYANT
GURNEY, EDWARD JOHN
GUTHRIE, ARLO
HABIT
HACKMAN, GENE
HAGGARD, MERLE
HAHN, JESSICA
HAIG, ALEXANDER M.
HAIR—CARE
HAITI
HAITI—ECONOMIC CONDITIONS
HAITI—POLITICS AND GOVERNMENT
HALDEMAN, HARRY ROBBINS
HALEY, JACK
HALL, JERRY
HAMBURGERS
HAMMER, ARMAND
HAMMER, MIKE (LITERARY CHARACTER)
HAPPINESS
HARDING, WARREN GAMALIEL
HARRIMAN, AVERELL
HARRIS, FRED
HARRIS, PATRICIA ROBERTS
HARRISON, REX
HART, GARY
HARVARD UNIVERSITY. SCHOOL OF LAW
HATE
HAUPTMANN, BRUNO RICHARD
HAWKINS, PAULA
HAYAKAWA, SAMUEL ICHIYE
HAYDEN, THOMAS
HAZARDOUS SUBSTANCES—DISPOSAL
HEARST, PATRICIA CAMPBELL
HEATH, EDWARD
HEFNER, HUGH MARSTON
HEIDE, WILMA SCOTT
HEIDEGGER, MARTIN
HELION, JEAN
HELL
HELLER, JOSEPH
HELLMAN, LILLIAN
HELM, LEVON
HELMS, JESSE
HELMS, RICHARD MCGARRAH
HEMINGWAY, ERNEST
HEMINGWAY, MARGAUX
HEMINGWAY, MARY
HEROES
HEROIN
HESTON, CHARLTON
HIGH SCHOOLS
HINCKLE, WARREN
HINDSIGHT

HIPPIES
HISTORIANS
HISTORY
HITCHCOCK, ALFRED JOSEPH
HITCHENS, IVON
HITLER, ADOLF
HOCHMAN, SANDRA
HOCKEY
HOCKEY—VIOLENCE
HOCKNEY, DAVID
HOFFA, JAMES RIDDLE
HOFFER, ERIC
HOFFMAN, ABBIE
HOFFMAN, DUSTIN
HOLIDAYS
HOLLYWOOD, CALIFORNIA
HOLLYWOOD,
    CALIFORNIA—DESCRIPTION
HOLOCAUSTS
HOLTZ, LOU
HOLY SPIRIT ASSOCIATION FOR THE
    UNIFICATION OF WORLD CHRISTIANITY
HOME
HOMOSEXUALITY
HOMOSEXUALS—CIVIL RIGHTS
HOMOSEXUALS—CIVIL
    RIGHTS—CALIFORNIA
HOMOSEXUALS—CIVIL RIGHTS—MIAMI
HONEGGER, BARBARA
HONESTY
HOOVER, JOHN EDGAR
HOPE
HOPE, BOB
HOROWITZ, VLADIMIR
HORSES
HOSPITALITY
HOSPITALS
HOUSE DECORATION
HOUSTON
HOWAR, BARBARA
HOWE, TINA
HUBBARD, L. RON
HUDSON, ROCK
HUGHES, HOWARD ROBARD
HULL, MA
HUMOR
HUMPHREY, HUBERT HORATIO
HUNGER—UNITED STATES
HUNT FAMILY
HUNT, EVERETTE HOWARD
HUNT, HAROLDSON LAFAYETTE
HUNTER, ALBERTA
HUSBANDS
HUSTLER (PERIODICAL)
HUTTON, BARBARA
IDEA (PHILOSOPHY)
IDEAS
IDEAS IN ART
IDEAS, HISTORY OF
IDENTITY (PSYCHOLOGY)
IGNORANCE

IMAGINATION
IMMIGRANTS IN THE UNITED STATES
IMMORTALITY
INCOME
INCOME TAX
INDIA—POLITICS AND GOVERNMENT
INDIANA. UNIVERSITY (BASKETBALL)
INDIANS OF NORTH AMERICA
INDIANS OF NORTH
  AMERICA—GOVERNMENT RELATIONS
INDIVIDUAL AND SOCIETY
INDIVIDUALISM
INFANTS
INFANTS—PURCHASE AND SALE
INFINITY
INFLATION (FINANCE)
INFLUENCE
INFORMATION
INFORMATION THEORY
INNOCENCE
INSANITY
INSTITUTIONS
INSURANCE COMPANIES
INTEGRATION
INTELLECT
INTELLECTUALS
INTELLECTUALS—MOSCOW
INTELLECTUALS—RELATIONS—WOMEN
INTELLIGENCE
INTELLIGENCE LEVELS
INTELLIGENCE LEVELS—UNITED STATES
INTELLIGENCE SERVICE—UNITED
  STATES
INTERIOR DECORATION
INTERNAL SECURITY
INTERNATIONAL BROTHERHOOD OF
  TEAMSTERS, CHAUFFEURS,
  WAREHOUSEMEN AND HELPERS OF
  AMERICA
INTERNATIONAL RELATIONS
INTERPERSONAL RELATIONS
INTERVIEWING
INVESTMENT ADVISERS
INVESTMENTS
IONESCO, EUGENE
IRAN—FOREIGN RELATIONS—UNITED
  STATES
IRAN—POLITICS AND GOVERNMENT
IRAN-CONTRA AFFAIR
IRANIAN-IRAQI WAR, 1980-1988
IRISH
IRISH REPUBLICAN ARMY
IRVING, JOHN
IRWIN, ROBERT
ISOLATIONISM (UNITED STATES)
ISRAEL
ISRAEL—ECONOMIC CONDITIONS
ISRAEL—FOREIGN POLICY
ISRAEL—FOREIGN RELATIONS—ARAB
  STATES
ISRAEL—FOREIGN RELATIONS—EGYPT

ISRAEL—FOREIGN RELATIONS—UNITED
  STATES
ISRAEL—MILITARY POLICY
ISRAEL—POLITICS AND GOVERNMENT
ISRAEL—PUBLIC RELATIONS
ITALIANS
ITALY
ITALY—DESCRIPTION
ITALY—POLITICS AND GOVERNMENT
JACKSON, GLENDA
JACKSON, HENRY MARTIN
JACKSON, REGGIE
JACOBS, ANDY
JAGGER, BIANCA
JAGGER, MICK
JAMES, HENRY
JAMISON, JUDITH
JAPAN
JAPAN—COMMERCE—UNITED STATES
JAPAN—POLITICS AND GOVERNMENT
JARVIS, HOWARD
JAVITS, JACOB KOPPEL
JAVITS, MARION
JEANS
JEFFERSON, THOMAS
JENNER, BRUCE
JERUSALEM
JESSYE, EVA
JESUITS
JESUS CHRIST
JEWELRY—MEN
JEWISH-ARAB RELATIONS
JEWS
JEWS—IRAN
JEWS—UNITED STATES
JOBS
JOHN F. KENNEDY CENTER FOR THE
  PERFORMING ARTS, WASHINGTON,
  D.C.
JOHN PAUL I, POPE
JOHN PAUL II, POPE
JOHN PAUL II,
  POPE—RELATIONS—WOMEN
JOHNS, GLYNNIS
JOHNSON, LYNDON BAINES
JOHNSON, NICHOLAS
JOHNSON, PHILIP
JONES, JAMES
JONES, JAMES THURMAN
JONES, JOHN
JONES, PRESTON
JORDAN
JORDAN, BARBARA
JORDAN, HAMILTON
JOURNALISM
JOURNALISM—NEW YORK (CITY)
JOURNALISM—WASHINGTON, D. C.
JOURNALISTIC ETHICS
JOURNALISTS
JUAN CARLOS I, KING OF SPAIN
JUDGES

JUDGES—CHICAGO
JURY
JUSTICE
JUSTICE, ADMINISTRATION OF
JUSTICE, ADMINISTRATION OF—RUSSIA
JUSTICE, ADMINISTRATION OF—UNITED
    STATES
KAFKA, FRANZ
KAHN, ALFRED
KAIDA, IVAN IVANOVICH
KANSAS CITY, MISSOURI—POLITICS AND
    GOVERNMENT
KARRAS, ALEX
KARSH, YOUSUF
KEATON, DIANE
KELLY, EDWARD J.
KELLY, GENE
KEMP, JACK
KENNEDY FAMILY
KENNEDY, EDWARD MOORE
KENNEDY, JOAN
KENNEDY, JOHN FITZGERALD
KENNEDY, JOHN
    FITZGERALD—ASSASSINATION
KENNEDY, JOSEPH P., III
KENNEDY, ROBERT FRANCIS
KENNEDY, ROSE
KEROUAC, JACK
KEYNES, JOHN MAYNARD
KHOMEINI, AYATOLLAH RUHOLLAH
KIDD, BRUCE
KINDNESS
KING'S LAW (QUOTATION)
KING, DONALD
KING, MARTIN LUTHER, JR.
KING, MARTIN LUTHER,
    JR.—ASSASSINATION
KINGMAN, DAVID ARTHUR
KIRBO, CHARLES
KIRKLAND, GELSEY
KIRKPATRICK, JEANE
KISSING
KISSINGER, HENRY ALFRED
KISSINGER, HENRY ALFRED—RELATIONS
    WITH THE PRESS
KISSLING, FRANCES
KLORES, STANLEY
KLUGE, ALEXANDER
KNIEVEL, EVEL
KNOPF, ALFRED A.
KNOWLEDGE
KNOWLEDGE, SOCIOLOGY OF
KNOWLEDGE, THEORY OF
KOCH, EDWARD I.
KOJAK, THEO (TELEVISION CHARACTER)
KOOP, C. EVERETT
KORDA, MICHAEL
KOREA (REPUBLIC)
KOREA (REPUBLIC)—FOREIGN
    RELATIONS—UNITED STATES
KORFF, BARUCH
KOSINSKI, JERZY
KOVIC, RON
KREMENTZ, JILL
KU KLUX KLAN
KUBRICK, STANLEY
KY, NGUYEN CAO
LA COSTA, CALIFORNIA
LABOR AND LABORING CLASSES
LABOR AND LABORING
    CLASSES—RUSSIA
LAETRILE
LANCE, THOMAS BERTRAM
LAND, EDWIN
LANE, MARK
LANGE, JESSICA
LANGLOIS, HENRI
LANGUAGE AND LANGUAGES
LAROUCHE, LYNDON
LASORDA, TOM
LASSER, LOUISE
LATIN AMERICA
LAUDER, ESTEE
LAUGHTER
LAUREN, RALPH
LAW
LAW—PRACTICE—UNITED STATES
LAWYERS
LAYNE, BOBBY
LE BRIS, MICHEL
LE CARRE, JOHN
LEADERSHIP
LEAR, AMANDA
LEARNING AND SCHOLARSHIP
LEARY, TIMOTHY
LEBANON
LEBOWITZ, FRAN
LEBRON, LOLITA
LEDBETTER, HUDDIE
LEFEBVRE, MARCEL
LEFT WING POLITICS
LEGISLATION
LEISURE
LEMMON, JACK
LEMON, BOB
LENNON, JOHN
LESBIANISM
LETTERS
LEVANT, OSCAR
LEVI, EDWARD
LEWIS, JOHN L.
LIBEL AND SLANDER
LIBERACE
LIBERALISM
LIBERATION THEOLOGY
LIBERTY
LIBRARIANS
LIBRARIES
LIBRARIES AND PUBLISHERS
LIBYA—FOREIGN RELATIONS—UNITED
    STATES
LIDDY, G. GORDON

LIEBLING, A. J.
LIFE
LIFE (PERIODICAL)
LIFE ON OTHER PLANETS
LILLY, DENNIS
LINDBERGH, CHARLES AUGUSTUS
LINDBERGH, CHARLES
  AUGUSTUS—KIDNAPPING CASE
LINDGREN, LYNN
LINDSAY, JOHN VLIET
LIPPMANN, WALTER
LIQUOR
  TRAFFIC—CHICAGO—PROHIBITION
LITERATURE
LITERATURE—AWARDS, PRIZES, ETC.
LITERATURE—CRITICISM
LITERATURE—LATIN AMERICA
LITTLE RICHARD
LITTLE, JOAN
LOBBYING
LOCAL GOVERNMENT—FEDERAL AID
LOGIC
LOMBARDO, GUY
LONE RANGER (RADIO PERSONALITY)
LONELINESS
LONG, RUSSELL
LONGEVITY
LONGWORTH, ALICE ROOSEVELT
LOPES, DAVE
LOREN, SOPHIA
LOS ANGELES
LOS ANGELES—DESCRIPTION
LOS ANGELES—POLICE
LOSING
LOUISIANA
LOVE
LOVELL, JAMES, JR.
LOWER CLASSES—GREAT BRITAIN
LUBBOCK, TEXAS
LUCAS, GEORGE
LUCE, CLARE BOOTHE
LUCE, HENRY
LUCK
LUDLAM, CHARLES
LUNG CANCER
LYING
LYSERGIC ACID DIETHYLAMIDE
MACARTHUR, DOUGLAS
MACARTHUR, JOHN D.
MACHISMO
MACK, JOHN
MACLAINE, SHIRLEY
MACNELLY, JEFF
MADDOX, LESTER GARFIELD
MADONNA (ROCK MUSICIAN)
MAFIA
MAFIA—LAS VEGAS
MAFIA—NEW YORK (CITY)
MAHFOUZ, NAGUIB
MAILER, NORMAN
MAKARIOS III, ARCHBISHOP

MAKAROVA, NATALIA
MALAMUD, BERNARD
MALCOLM X
MALLE, LOUIS
MALRAUX, ANDRE
MAMET, DAVID
MAN
MAN—INFLUENCE OF ENVIRONMENT
MAN—INFLUENCE ON NATURE
MAN—RESPONSIBILITY
MANAGEMENT
MANDELA, NELSON
MANNERS AND CUSTOMS
MANSFIELD, KATHERINE
MANSFIELD, MIKE
MAO, TSE-TUNG
MARCEAU, MARCEL
MARCOS, FERDINAND
MARCOVICCI, ANDREA
MARIJUANA
MARINE POLLUTION
MARKETING
MARRIAGE
MARS (PLANET)
MARTIN, BILLY
MARTIN, MARY
MARTINIS
MARTYRDOM
MARX, GROUCHO
MARX, KARL
MARXISM
MARY HARTMAN, MARY HARTMAN
  (TELEVISION PROGRAM)
MARZULLO, VITO
MASON, JAMES
MASS
MASS MEDIA
MASS MEDIA—UNITED STATES
MASS SOCIETY
MASTURBATION
MATERIALISM
MATTER
MAUGHAM, WILLIAM SOMERSET
MAXWELL, ELSA
MAYS, WILLIE
MCCARTHY, EUGENE JOSEPH
MCCARTHY, JOSEPH RAYMOND
MCCARTNEY, LINDA
MCCARTNEY, PAUL
MCCULLERS, CARSON
MCGOFF, JOHN
MCGOVERN, GEORGE STANLEY
MCHUGH, VICKI
MCINTYRE, BRUCE
MCINTYRE, JAMES
MCKUEN, ROD
MCLUHAN, MARSHALL
MEAD, MARGARET
MEANS, JACQUELINE
MEANY, GEORGE
MEDIA

MEDICAL LAWS AND LEGISLATION
MEDICAL SERVICE
MEDICAL SERVICE, COST OF
MEDICAL SERVICE—UNITED STATES
MEDICARE
MEDICINE
MEDICINE—PRACTICE—UNITED STATES
MEDIOCRITY
MEDITATION
MEEKNESS
MEIR, GOLDA
MEKAS, JONAS
MEMORY
MEN
MEN—BEHAVIOR
MEN—FRANCE
MEN—POWER (SOCIAL SCIENCES)
MEN—PSYCHOLOGY
MENOTTI, GIAN CARLO
MENTAL HYGIENE
MERCOURI, MELINA
MERCURY POISONING
MERMAN, ETHEL
METTERNICH, KLEMENS WENZEL
  NEPOMUK LOTHAR, VON, PRINCE
MEXICO
MEXICO—DESCRIPTION
MEXICO—FOREIGN RELATIONS—UNITED
  STATES
MEXICO—POLITICS AND GOVERNMENT
MEYER, RUSS
MEYERS, VICTOR ALOYSIUS
MIAMI
MIAMI—DESCRIPTION
MIDDLE AGE
MIDDLE CLASSES—UNITED STATES
MIDDLE EAST
MIDDLE EAST—FOREIGN RELATIONS
MIDDLE EAST—PEACE AND MEDIATION
MIDDLE EAST—POLITICS AND
  GIVERNMENT
MIDDLE EAST—POLITICS AND
  GOVERNMENT
MIDLER, BETTE
MIGRATION, INTERNAL—CALIFORNIA
MIKULSKI, BARBARA A.
MILITARY ASSISTANCE
MILITARY ASSISTANCE,
  AMERICAN—NICARAGUA
MILITARY HISTORY
MILITARY INTELLIGENCE
MILITARY SERVICE AS A PROFESSION
MILITARY-INDUSTRIAL COMPLEX
MILLER, ANN
MILLER, ARNOLD
MILLER, ARTHUR
MILLER, GEORGE WILLIAM
MILLER, HENRY
MILLIONAIRES
MILLS, CHUCK
MILLS, WILBUR DAIGH

MILNES, RICHARD MONCKTON
MIND
MINELLI, LIZA
MINERAL RIGHTS
MINGUS, CHARLES
MINIMUM WAGE
MINNESOTA. FOOTBALL CLUB (NATIONAL
  LEAGUE)
MINNESOTA. UNIVERSITY (FOOTBALL)
MINORITIES—EQUAL RIGHTS
MIRACLES
MISERY
MISFORTUNE
MISTAKES
MITCHELL, JOHN
MITCHELL, MARTHA
MITCHUM, ROBERT
MOBS—PSYCHOLOGY
MODERATION
MODESTY
MOHAMMED REZA PAHLEVI, SHAH OF
  IRAN
MONDALE, JOAN
MONDALE, WALTER FREDERICK
MONDAY, RICK
MONEY
MONEY—INTERNATIONAL ASPECTS
MONK, THELONIOUS
MONNIER, VALENTINE
MONROE, MARILYN
MOON, KEITH
MOON, SUN MYUNG
MOON—EXPLORATION
MOORE, HENRY
MOORE, MARIANNE
MOORE, ROGER
MOORE, SARA JANE
MORAL ATTITUDES
MORMONS AND MORMONISM
MORO, ALDO
MOROCCO—FOREIGN
  RELATIONS—SPAIN
MOROCCO—POLITICS AND
  GOVERNMENT
MOSCOW—DESCRIPTION
MOSES
MOSES, ROBERT
MOTHER TERESA
MOTHERS
MOTHERS AND SONS
MOTHERWELL, ROBERT
MOTORCYCLE RACING
MOTORCYCLING
MOUNT EVEREST
MOUNTAINEERING
MOUNTBATTEN OF BURMA, LOUIS
  MOUNTBATTEN, EARL, 1900-1979
MOVING PICTURE ACTORS AND
  ACTRESSES
MOVING PICTURE AUDIENCES
MOVING PICTURE AUTHORSHIP

MOVING PICTURE INDUSTRY
MOVING PICTURE INDUSTRY—GREAT
    BRITAIN
MOVING PICTURE INDUSTRY—WAGES
MOVING PICTURES
MOVING PICTURES, EXPERIMENTAL
MOVING PICTURES—DIRECTORS
MOVING PICTURES—FINANCE
MOVING PICTURES—PORNOGRAPHY
MOVING
    PICTURES—PORNOGRAPHY—FRANCE
MOVING PICTURES—PRODUCTION AND
    DIRECTION
MOWAT, FARLEY
MOYERS, BILL D.
MOYNIHAN, DANIEL PATRICK
MOZAMBIQUE—POLITICS AND
    GOVERNMENT
MUHAMMAD, WALLACE D.
MUNICIPAL FINANCE
MUNITIONS
MURDER
MURDOCH, IRIS
MURDOCH, RUPERT
MURPHY'S LAW (QUOTATION)
MUSGRAVE, THEA
MUSIC
MUSIC, BLUEGRASS
MUSIC, BLUES
MUSIC, CALYPSO
MUSIC, CLASSICAL
MUSIC, DISCO
MUSIC, FOLK
MUSIC, JAZZ
MUSIC, JAZZ—WOMEN
MUSIC, POPULAR
MUSIC, ROCK
MUSIC, ROCK—FESTIVALS
MUSIC, ROCK—JOURNALISM
MUSIC—APPRECIATION
MUSIC—APPRECIATION—YOUTH
MUSIC—CRITICISM
MUSIC—UNITED STATES
MUSICAL COMEDIES, REVUES, ETC.
MUSICIANS
MUSICIANS, ROCK
MUSICIANS—CONDUCT OF LIFE
MYERS, MICHAEL (OZZIE)
MYTHOLOGY
NABOKOV, VLADIMIR
NADER, RALPH
NAIVETE
NAMATH, JOE
NAMIBIA—DESCRIPTION
NARCOTICS
NARCOTICS AND BLACKS
NASSER, GAMAL ABDEL
NATIONAL ASSOCIATION FOR THE
    ADVANCEMENT OF COLORED PEOPLE
NATIONAL BROADCASTING COMPANY
NATIONAL BROADCASTING COMPANY.

NEWS
NATIONAL COLLEGIATE ATHLETIC
    ASSOCIATION
NATIONAL ENQUIRER (NEWSPAPER)
NATIONALISM
NATURE IN ART
NAVRATILOVA, MARTINA
NEBRASKA. UNIVERSITY (FOOTBALL)
NECESSITY
NEED (PSYCHOLOGY)
NEIGHBORHOODS
NEIGHBORS
NELSON, WILLIE
NESSEN, RON
NEUROSES
NEUTRON BOMB
NEW JERSEY—DESCRIPTION
NEW ORLEANS—DESCRIPTION
NEW YORK (CITY)
NEW YORK (CITY)—DEBT
NEW YORK (CITY)—DESCRIPTION
NEW YORK (CITY)—ELLIS ISLAND
NEW YORK
    (CITY)—HARLEM—DESCRIPTION
NEW YORK (CITY)—HISTORY
NEW YORK (CITY)—POLITICS AND
    GOVERNMENT
NEW YORK (CITY). BASEBALL CLUB
    (AMERICAN LEAGUE)
NEW YORK (STATE)—POLITICS AND
    GOVERNMENT
NEW YORK TIMES
NEW YORKER (PERIODICAL)
NEW YORKERS
NEWMAN, PAUL
NEWSPAPER EDITORS AND EDITING
NEWSPAPER PUBLISHERS AND
    PUBLISHING
NEWSPAPERS
NEWSPAPERS AND TELEVISION
NEWSPAPERS—PHILADELPHIA
NEWSPAPERS—RELATIONS—TRADE
    UNIONS
NEWSPAPERS—SECTIONS, COLUMNS,
    ETC.
NEWSPAPERS—SOUTH AFRICA
NEWTON, C. M.
NGUYEN VAN THIEU
NICARAGUA—POLITICS AND
    GOVERNMENT
NIGERIA—POLITICS AND GOVERNMENT
NIGHT LIFE
NIKOLAIS, ALWIN
NIN, ANAIS
1960'S
1970'S
1975
1978
1980'S
NIVEN, DAVID
NIXON, PATRICIA RYAN

NIXON, RICHARD MILHOUS
NIXON, RICHARD MILHOUS—CONDUCT
  OF LIFE
NIXON, RICHARD MILHOUS—STAFF
NKOMO, JOSHUA
NOBEL PRIZES
NOGUCHI, ISAMU
NONVIOLENCE
NORODOM SIHANOUK, KING OF
  CAMBODIA (ABDICATED 1955)
NORTH AMERICA
NORTH, OLIVER L., JR.
NORTHERN IRELAND
NORTHERN IRELAND—DESCRIPTION
NORTHERN IRELAND—POLITICS AND
  GOVERNMENT
NORTHERN IRELAND—RELIGION
NORTHERN IRISH AID COMMITTEE
NOTHING (PHILOSOPHY)
NUDISM
NUNN, SAM
NUREEV, RUDOLF
NURSEMAIDS
NYE, BLAINE
NYIREGYHAZI, ERVIN
O'KEEFFE, GEORGIA
O'NEILL, EUGENE
O'NEILL, THOMAS P. (TIP)
O'ROURKE, P. J.
OAKLAND. BASEBALL CLUB (AMERICAN
  LEAGUE)—ORGANIZATION AND
  ADMINISTRATION
OATES, JOYCE CAROL
OBESITY
OBEY, DAVID R.
OBSCENITY (LAW)
OCCUPATIONS
OFFICES—ETIQUETTE
OFFICIAL SECRETS
OHIO. KENT STATE UNIVERSITY, KENT
OKLAHOMA—POLITICS AND
  GOVERNMENT
OKLAHOMA. UNIVERSITY—FOOTBALL
OLDENBURG, CLAES
OLIVIER, LAURENCE
OLYMPIC GAMES
OLYMPIC GAMES, 1980
OMNISCIENCE
ONASSIS, JACQUELINE LEE (BOUVIER)
  KENNEDY
ONO, YOKO
OPERA
OPERA SINGERS
OPPORTUNITY
OPPRESSION
OPTIMISM
ORCHESTRAS
ORGANIZATION OF PETROLEUM
  EXPORTING COUNTRIES
ORGANIZATIONS
ORWELL, GEORGE

OSWALD, LEE HARVEY
OUTDOOR LIFE—NEW YORK (CITY)
PACIFISM
PAGE, GERALDINE
PAINTERS
PAINTING
PAINTING—REALISM
PAKISTAN—POLITICS AND GOVERNMENT
PALESTINE
PALESTINE LIBERATION ORGANIZATION
PALESTINIAN ARABS
PALEY, WILLIAM S.
PANAMA CANAL
PANAMA—FOREIGN RELATIONS—UNITED
  STATES
PARAGUAY—POLITICS AND
  GOVERNMENT
PARANOIA
PARENT-CHILD RELATIONSHIP
PARENTS
PARIS
PARIS—DESCRIPTION
PARK, TONGSUN
PARKINSON'S LAW (QUOTATION)
PARKINSON'S LAW
  (QUOTATION)—COROLLARY
PARKS
PARSONS, BETTY
PARTON, DOLLY
PARTRIDGE, ERIC
PAST (TIME)
PASTORE, JOHN O.
PATERSON, NEW JERSEY
PATRIOTISM
PAUL VI, POPE
PAUL, SAINT
PAYTON, WALTER
PEACE
PEACE—MIDDLE EAST
PECKINPAH, SAM
PELE
PENN, IRVING
PENTHOUSE (PERIODICAL)
PEOPLE'S BICENTENNIAL COMMISSION
PEREZ, MANUEL BENITEZ
PERFECTION
PERIODICALS
PERIODICALS—COVERS
PERKINS, FRANCES
PERKINS, MAXWELL
PERON, MARIA ESTELA MARTINEZ ISABEL
PEROT, H. ROSS
PERSISTENCE
PERSONALITY
PERSONALITY AND CULTURE
PERSUASION (PSYCHOLOGY)
PERSUASION (RHETORIC)
PESSIMISM
PETER PRINCIPLE (QUOTATION)
PETROLEUM INDUSTRY
PETROLEUM SUPPLY

PETROLEUM SUPPLY—TEXAS
PETROLEUM—GREAT BRITAIN
PETROLEUM—PIPE LINES—ALASKA
PETROLEUM—PRICES
PHILADELPHIA ORCHESTRA
PHILADELPHIA—DESCRIPTION
PHILADELPHIA—POLITICS AND
    GOVERNMENT
PHILADELPHIA. HOCKEY CLUB (NATIONAL
    LEAGUE)
PHILIPPINES
PHILIPPINES—FOREIGN
    RELATIONS—UNITED STATES
PHILIPPINES—POLITICS AND
    GOVERNMENT
PHILLIPS, MICHELLE
PHILOSOPHY
PHILOSOPHY—FRANCE
PHOBIAS
PHONOGRAPH RECORD INDUSTRY
PHOTOGRAPHERS
PHOTOGRAPHY
PHYSICAL FITNESS
PHYSICIAN AND PATIENT
PHYSICIANS
PHYSICIANS—CHICAGO
PHYSICIANS—PSYCHOLOGY
PHYSICS
PIANISTS
PICASSO, PABLO
PIERCE, WEBB
PINERO, MIGUEL
PINIELLA, LOU
PIPPIN, HORACE
PITCHING (BASEBALL)
PITTSBURGH. FOOTBALL CLUB
    (NATIONAL LEAGUE)
PITY
PLAGIARISM
PLAINS, GEORGIA—DESCRIPTION
PLANNING
PLAYBOY (PERIODICAL)
PLAYBOY ENTERPRISES, INC.
PLEASURE
POETRY
POETRY—RUSSIA
POETS
POINDEXTER, JOHN M.
POLAND—POLITICS AND GOVERNMENT
POLICE
POLITICAL CAMPAIGNS
POLITICAL CAMPAIGNS—TEXAS
POLITICAL CANDIDATES
POLITICAL PATRONAGE
POLITICAL PRISONERS
POLITICAL SCIENCE
POLITICIANS
POLITICIANS—CONDUCT OF LIFE
POLITICIANS—FUND RAISING
POLITICIANS—RELATION WITH THE
    PRESS
POLITICIANS—SEXUAL BEHAVIOR
POLITICIANS—UNITED STATES
POLITICIANS—WIVES
POLITICS
POLITICS, CORRUPTION IN
POLITICS, CORRUPTION IN—ILLINOIS
POLITICS, CORRUPTION IN—NEW YORK
    (CITY)
POLITICS—SOUTH
POLLOCK, JACKSON
POLLUTION
POOR
POOR—UNITED STATES
POPES
POPULAR CULTURE
PORNOGRAPHY
PORTER, COLE
PORTUGAL—POLITICS AND
    GOVERNMENT
POSTAL SERVICE—UNITED STATES
POSTEMA, PAM
POTENTIAL
POUND, EZRA
POVERTY
POWELL, JODY
POWELL, PAUL
POWER (SOCIAL SCIENCES)
POWER RESOURCES
PRAISE
PRAYER
PREJUDICE
PRESENT (TIME)
PRESIDENTIAL CAMPAIGNS
PRESIDENTIAL CAMPAIGNS—1976
PRESIDENTIAL CAMPAIGNS—1980
PRESIDENTIAL CAMPAIGNS—1984
PRESIDENTIAL CAMPAIGNS—1988
PRESIDENTIAL CANDIDATES
PRESIDENTIAL CANDIDATES—CONDUCT
    OF LIFE
PRESIDENTIAL CANDIDATES—SEXUAL
    BEHAVIOR
PRESIDENTS—INAUGURAL
    ADDRESSES—1893
PRESIDENTS—INAUGURAL
    ADDRESSES—1921
PRESIDENTS—INAUGURAL
    ADDRESSES—1933
PRESIDENTS—INAUGURAL
    ADDRESSES—1961
PRESIDENTS—INAUGURAL
    ADDRESSES—1973
PRESIDENTS—UNITED STATES
PRESIDENTS—UNITED
    STATES—ELECTION—1984
PRESIDENTS—UNITED
    STATES—POWERS AND DUTIES
PRESIDENTS—UNITED STATES—PRESS
    SECRETARY
PRESIDENTS—UNITED
    STATES—PROTECTION

PRESIDENTS—UNITED STATES—PUBLIC
 RELATIONS
PRESIDENTS—UNITED STATES—STAFF
PRESIDENTS—UNITED STATES—WIVES
PRESLEY, ELVIS
PRESS
PRETTY BABY (MOVING PICTURE)
PRICES
PRIESTS
PRINCE (MUSICIAN)
PRINCETON, NEW JERSEY
PRINCIPLE (PHILOSOPHY)
PRISONS
PRISONS—BRAZIL
PRIVACY, RIGHT OF
PROBLEM SOLVING
PRODUCTION
PRODUCTION STANDARDS
PROFESSIONALISM
PROFIT
PROGRESS
PRONUNCIATION
PROPAGANDA
PROPERTY
PROPHETS
PROSTITUTION
PROTESTANT EPISCOPAL CHURCH
PRYOR, RICHARD
PSYCHIATRISTS
PSYCHIATRY
PSYCHOLOGY
PSYCHOTHERAPY
PUBLIC OFFICE
PUBLIC OFFICERS
PUBLIC OFFICERS—SALARIES,
 PENSIONS, ETC.
PUBLIC OPINION
PUBLIC SCHOOLS AND RELIGION
PUBLIC SCHOOLS—DESEGREGATION
PUBLIC SCHOOLS—PHILADELPHIA
PUBLIC SERVICE
PUBLIC WELFARE
PUBLIC WELFARE—FEDERAL AID
PUBLISHERS AND PUBLISHING
PUERTO RICO—POLITICS AND
 GOVERNMENT
PULITZER PRIZES
PUNCTUALITY
PURCHASING
QADDAFI, MUAMMAR
QUALITY
QUALITY (PHILOSOPHY)
QUARRY, JERRY
QUAYLE, DAN
QUAYLE, MARILYN
QUINLAN, KAREN ANNE
QUOTATIONS
RABIN, YITZHAK
RACE DISCRIMINATION
RACE RELATIONS
RACIAL DIFFERENCES

RADICALISM
RADIO ADVERTISING
RADIO BROADCASTING
RADNER, GILDA
RADZIWILL, LEE
RAFKO, KAYE LANI RAE
RAM DASS
RAND, AYN
RAND, SALLY
RAPE
RARE ANIMALS
RATHER, DAN
RATTIGAN, TERRENCE
RAUSCHENBERG, ROBERT
RAY, MAN
REACTIONARIES
READING
REAGAN, NANCY
REAGAN, RONALD
REAGAN, RONALD—ECONOMIC POLICY
REAGAN, RONALD—RELATIONS—LEFT
 WING POLITICS
REAGAN, RONALD—STAFF
REAL ESTATE DEVELOPMENT
REAL ESTATE INVESTMENT
REALITY
REASON
REASONER, HARRY
REBOZO, CHARLES GREGORY
REDDY, HELEN
REDFORD, ROBERT
REDNECKS
REED, LOU
REEVE, CHRISTOPHER
REFORM
REFUGEES, VIETNAMESE
REGAN, DON
REGULATION
RELATIVITY THEORY
RELIGION
RELIGION—UNITED STATES
REPORTERS AND REPORTING
REPUBLICAN PARTY
REPUBLICAN PARTY—CALIFORNIA
REPUBLICAN
 PARTY—RELATIONS—WOMEN
REPUBLICAN PARTY. NATIONAL
 CONVENTION, DETROIT, 1980
REPUBLICAN PARTY. NATIONAL
 CONVENTION, KANSAS CITY, 1976
RESEARCH
RESPECTABILITY
RESTAURANTS
RESTAURANTS—CHINA (PEOPLE'S
 REPUBLIC)
RESTAURANTS—FRANCHISE SYSTEM
RESTAURANTS—UNITED STATES
RETIREMENT
REUBEN, DON
REVENGE
REVOLUTIONISTS

REVOLUTIONISTS, CAMBODIAN
REVOLUTIONS
REVOLUTIONS—AFGHANISTAN
REVOLUTIONS—NICARAGUA
REVSON, CHARLES
REWARDS, PRIZES, ETC.
REXROTH, KENNETH
REYNOLDS, BURT
RHODES, JAMES
RHODESIA—DESCRIPTION
RHODESIA—POLITICS AND
  GOVERNMENT
RHODESIA—RACE QUESTION
RHYS, JEAN
RICE, DONNA
RICH
RICH, FRANK
RICH—POLITICAL ACTIVITY
RICH—SEXUAL BEHAVIOR
RICH—SOCIAL LIFE AND CUSTOMS
RICHARD, KEITH
RICHARDS, PAUL
RICHARDSON, ELLIOT LEE
RICKOVER, HYMAN GEORGE
RIGGS, BOBBY
RIGHT AND WRONG
RIGHT TO LIFE (MOVEMENT)
RIMBAUD, ARTHUR
RIOTS
RITTER, JOHN
RIVERA, DIEGO
RIZZO, FRANK LAZZARO
ROADS
ROBBERY
ROBBINS, HAROLD
ROBERTSON, PAT
ROBESON, PAUL
ROBINSON, FRANK
ROBINSON, JACKIE
ROBINSON, JOAN
ROCKEFELLER FAMILY
ROCKEFELLER, DAVID
ROCKEFELLER, JOHN DAVISON, III
ROCKEFELLER, NELSON ALDRICH
ROCKNE, KNUTE
RODGERS, RICHARD
RODRIGUEZ, ARMANDO
RODRIGUEZ, CHI CHI
ROLLING STONES (MUSICAL GROUP)
ROLLINS, SONNY
ROMANCE
ROME
RONALD REAGAN
RONSTADT, LINDA
ROONEY, MICKEY
ROOSEVELT, ELEANOR
ROOSEVELT, FRANKLIN DELANO
ROOTS (TELEVISION PROGRAM)
ROREM, NED
ROSE, BILLY
ROSE, PETE

ROSENBLOOM, CARROLL
ROSSINI, GIOACCHINO
ROSSNER, JUDITH
ROSTROPOVICH, MSTISLAV
ROTHSCHILD, MARIE-HELEN DE
ROWEN, PHYLLIS
ROWSE, A. L.
ROYALTY—ENGLAND
RUBIN, JERRY
RUBINSTEIN, ARTUR
RUCKLESHAUS, JILL
RULES
RUMANIA—FOREIGN POLICY
RUNNING
RUSHDIE, SALMAN
RUSHDIE, SALMAN. THE SATANIC VERSES
RUSSELL, ROSALIND
RUSSIA
RUSSIA—DESCRIPTION
RUSSIA—ECONOMIC CONDITIONS
RUSSIA—ECONOMIC POLICY
RUSSIA—FOREIGN POLICY
RUSSIA—FOREIGN POLICY—UNITED
  STATES
RUSSIA—FOREIGN RELATIONS
RUSSIA—FOREIGN RELATIONS—AFRICA
RUSSIA—FOREIGN RELATIONS—EGYPT
RUSSIA—FOREIGN
  RELATIONS—EUROPE, EASTERN
RUSSIA—FOREIGN RELATIONS—MIDDLE
  EAST
RUSSIA—FOREIGN RELATIONS—UNITED
  STATES
RUSSIA—HISTORY
RUSSIA—MILITARY POLICY
RUSSIA—POLITICS AND GOVERNMENT
RUSSIA—RACE QUESTION
RUSSIANS
RUSSIANS IN ISRAEL
RUTHERFORD, MARGARET
RYAN, NOLAN
RYUN, JIM
SADAT, ANWAR
SADAT, ANWAR—VISIT TO JERUSALEM,
  1977
SAFETY
SAFIRE, WILLIAM
SAHL, MORT
SAILING
SAINTS
SAKHAROV, ANDREI DMITRIEVICH
SALINGER, J. D.
SALVATION
SAN ANTONIO, TEXAS
SAN FRANCISCO
SANS SOUCI (RESTAURANT),
  WASHINGTON, D.C.
SAROYAN, WILLIAM
SASSOON, VIDAL
SATIRE
SAUDI ARABIA—POLITICS AND

GOVERNMENT
SAVALAS, TELLY
SAVING AND SAVINGS
SAVORY, ALLEN
SCANDAL
SCHEER, ROBERT
SCHIZOPHRENIA
SCHLAFLY, PHYLLIS
SCHLESINGER, ARTHUR, JR.
SCHLESINGER, JAMES RODNEY
SCHMIDT, HELMUT
SCHNEIDERMAN, DAVID
SCHOOL CHILDREN—TRANSPORTATION
FOR INTEGRATION
SCHOOL CHILDREN—TRANSPORTATION
FOR INTEGRATION—BOSTON
SCHOOLS
SCHORR, DANIEL
SCHRADER, PAUL
SCHROEDER, PATRICIA
SCHUMACHER, ERNST F.
SCHUMAN, WILLIAM
SCHWEIKER, RICHARD S.
SCIENCE
SCIENCE FICTION
SCIENCE—RESEARCH
SCIENTISTS
SCOTT, HUGH
SCOTT, WILLIAM
SCREW (PERIODICAL)
SCULPTURE
SECRET SERVICE—UNITED STATES
SECRETS
SECURITY (PSYCHOLOGY)
SEGREGATION
SEGREGATION IN EDUCATION
SELF EVALUATION
SELF INTEREST
SELF PERCEPTION
SELLECK, TOM
SELLERS, PETER
SENATORS
SENATORS—WIVES
SENGHOR, LEOPOLD SEDAR
SERVANTS
SETON, ELIZABETH, SAINT
SEVAREID, ERIC
SEX
SEX (PSYCHOLOGY)
SEX—CUBA
SEXUAL BEHAVIOR
SEXUAL ETHICS
SHAKESPEARE, WILLIAM
SHANKER, ALBERT
SHANLEY, JOHN PATRICK
SHAW, GEORGE BERNARD
SHCHARANSKY, ANATOLY
SHEEN, MARTIN
SHEPARD, SAM
SHEPHERD, CYBILL
SHOFNER, JIM

SICILY
SICK
SICKNESS
SILENCE
SILLS, BEVERLY
SILVERMAN, FRED
SIMON, JOHN
SIMON, PAUL
SIMON, WILLIAM E.
SIN
SINATRA, FRANK
SINCLAIR, UPTON
SINGER, ISAAC BASHEVIS
SINGERS
SINGLE PEOPLE
SINS
SKELTON, RED
SKEPTICISM
SKIN—CARE AND HYGIENE
SKIS AND SKIING
SKYLAB
SLANG
SLEEP
SLICK, GRACE
SLUMS
SMALL TOWN LIFE—TEXAS
SMITH, IAN DOUGLAS
SMITH, JACLYN
SMITH, MAGGIE
SMITH, MARGARET CHASE
SMITH, PATTI
SMITH, W. EUGENE
SMITH, WALTER (RED)
SMOKING
SNYDER, TOM
SOCCER
SOCIAL CHANGE
SOCIAL CLASSES
SOCIAL CLASSES—UNITED STATES
SOCIAL INTERACTION
SOCIAL POLICY
SOCIAL PROBLEMS
SOCIAL VALUES
SOCIALISM
SOCIALISM—GREAT BRITAIN
SOCIALISM—SWEDEN
SOCIALISM—UNITED STATES
SOCIETY
SOLAR ENERGY
SOLDIER OF FORTUNE (PERIODICAL)
SOLDIERS
SOLITUDE
SOLTI, SIR GEORG
SOLZHENITSYN, ALEKSANDR ISAEVICH
SOMOZA DEBAYLE, ANASTASIO
SONGS
SONTAG, SUSAN
SOREL, EDWARD
SORENSEN, THEODORE CHAIKIN
SOUTH
SOUTH AFRICA

SOUTH AFRICA—DESCRIPTION
SOUTH AFRICA—POLITICS AND
   GOVERNMENT
SOUTH AFRICA—RACE QUESTION
SOUTHERN METHODIST UNIVERSITY
   (FOOTBALL)
SOUTHERNERS
SPACE
SPACE, OUTER—EXPLORATION
SPAIN—HISTORY—CIVIL WAR, 1936-1939
SPAIN—POLITICS AND GOVERNMENT
SPANISH SAHARA
SPEECH
SPIELBERG, STEVEN
SPILLANE, MICKEY
SPIRITUAL LEADERSHIP
SPITZ, MARK
SPORTS
SPORTS JOURNALISM
SPORTS—FAILURE
SPORTS—SUCCESS
STAFFORD, JEAN
STALIN, JOSEF V.
STALLONE, SLY
STALLONE, SYLVESTER
STALLONE, SYLVESTER—THOUGHT AND
   THINKING
STAPLETON, RUTH CARTER
STARGELL, WILLIE
STATE GOVERNMENTS
STATESMEN
STATISTICS
STEEL INDUSTRY
STEINBECK, JOHN
STEINBERG, SAUL
STEINBRENNER, GEORGE
STEINEM, GLORIA
STENGEL, CHARLES DILLON (CASEY)
STERNBACH, LEO HENRYK
STEVENS, CAT
STEVENS, JOHN PAUL
STEVENSON, ADLAI, II
STEVENSON, ADLAI, III
STEWART, ROD
STOCK EXCHANGES—NEW YORK
   EXCHANGE
STOCKBROKERS
STOCKS
STOKOWSKI, LEOPOLD
STONE, EDWARD DURRELL
STONE, ISIDOR FEINSTEIN
STONEHENGE
STOPPARD, TOM
STOWE, HARRIET BEECHER
STRATEGIC ARMS LIMITATION TALKS
STRATEGIC DEFENSE INITIATIVE
STRAUSS, ROBERT S.
STRAVINSKY, VERA
STRESS
STRIKES—ITALY
STRIKES—NEWSPAPERS

STROUT, RICHARD
STUDENT MILITANTS
STUDENTS
STUDIO 54 (DISCOTHEQUE), NEW YORK
   (CITY)
STUPIDITY
STYLE
SUBURBS
SUCCESS
SUCCESS—IRELAND
SUCCESS—NEW YORK (CITY)
SUCCESS—PSYCHOLOGICAL ASPECTS
SUICIDE
SULLIVAN, ED
SUNUNU, JOHN H.
SUPPLY SIDE ECONOMICS
SUSANN, JACQUELINE
SUTTON, WILLIE
SWAGGART, JIMMY LEE
SWAN LAKE (BALLET)
SWEARINGEN, BONNIE
SWITZERLAND
SYMBIONESE LIBERATION ARMY
SYMPATHY
SYNANON (ORGANIZATION)
TAIWAN
TALENT
TALMADGE, HERMAN
TASTE (AESTHETICS)
TAX RETURNS
TAXATION
TAXATION—CALIFORNIA
TAXATION—UNITED STATES
TAYLOR, ELIZABETH
TEACHERS
TEACHING
TECHNOLOGICAL CHANGE
TECHNOLOGY AND CIVILIZATION
TECHNOLOGY TRANSFER
TELEPHONE COMPANIES
TELEVISION
TELEVISION ADVERTISING
TELEVISION ADVERTISING AND POLITICS
TELEVISION AUDIENCES
TELEVISION AUTHORSHIP
TELEVISION BROADCASTING
TELEVISION BROADCASTING,
   NONCOMMERCIAL
TELEVISION BROADCASTING—NEWS
TELEVISION
   BROADCASTING—PROGRAMMING
TELEVISION
   BROADCASTING—RELIGIOUS
   PROGRAMS
TELEVISION CHARACTERS
TELEVISION PERFORMERS
TELEVISION PROGRAMS
TELLER, EDWARD
TEMPTATION
TENNIS
TERROR

TERRORISM
TERRORISM—GREAT BRITAIN
TERRORISM—ITALY
TERRORISM—NETHERLANDS
TEXANS
TEXAS
TEXAS IN LITERATURE
TEXAS—POLITICS AND GOVERNMENT
TEXTBOOKS
THARP, TWYLA
THATCHER, MARGARET HILDA
THEATER
THEATRICAL DIRECTORS
THEATRICAL PRODUCTION AND
   DIRECTION
THEOLOGY
THICKE, ALAN
THOMAS, CAITLIN
THOMAS, DYLAN
THOMAS, LOWELL
THOMPSON, HUNTER S.
THOMPSON, JAMES
THOMPSON, LORD ROY HERBERT
THOMSON, VIRGIL
THOUGHT AND ACTION
THOUGHT AND THINKING
THURMOND, STROM
TIFFANY'S, INC.
TIME
TIME (PERIODICAL)
TIME, USE OF
TINKERBELLE
TOBACCO
TOMLIN, LILY
TORRIJOS, OMAR
TOSCANINI, ARTURO
TOTALITARIANISM
TOUREL, JENNIE
TOWER, JOHN
TOWNSHEND, PETE
TRACK ATHLETICS
TRADE UNIONS
TRADE UNIONS—ACTORS AND
   ACTRESSES
TRADE UNIONS—GREAT BRITAIN
TRADE UNIONS—ITALY
TRADE UNIONS—UNITED STATES
TRAN VAN HUONG
TRANSCENDENTAL MEDITATION
TRANSLATIONS AND TRANSLATING
TRAVEL
TRAVEL WITH CHILDREN
TREATIES
TRIBUNE COMPANY
TRILATERAL COMMISSION
TRILLIN, CALVIN
TROLLOPE, ANTHONY
TRUDEAU, GARRY
TRUDEAU, MARGARET
TRUFFAUT, FRANCOIS
TRUMAN, HARRY S.

TRUMP, DONALD
TRUST
TRUSTS AND TRUSTEES
TRUTH
TUCHMAN, BARBARA
TURBEVILLE, DEBORAH
TURNER, LANA
TURNER, R. E. (TED)
TWEED, WILLIAM MARCY (BOSS)
TWENTIETH CENTURY
UDALL, MORRIS KING
UGANDA—POLITICS AND GOVERNMENT
UNDERDEVELOPED AREAS
UNEMPLOYED
UNEMPLOYMENT
UNEMPLOYMENT—RELIEF MEASURES
UNITED FARM WORKERS UNION
UNITED MINE WORKERS
UNITED NATIONS
UNITED STATES
UNITED STATES MILITARY ACADEMY,
   WEST POINT
UNITED STATES—APPROPRIATION AND
   EXPENDITURES
UNITED STATES—ARMED FORCES
UNITED STATES—CENTENNIAL
   CELEBRATIONS, ETC.
UNITED STATES—CONGRESS—STAFF
UNITED STATES—CONSTITUTION
UNITED STATES—CONSTITUTION—
   AMENDMENTS
UNITED STATES—CONSTITUTION—
   AMENDMENTS—FIRST
   AMENDMENT
UNITED STATES—CONSTITUTION—BILL
   OF RIGHTS
UNITED STATES—DEFENSES
UNITED STATES—DESCRIPTION
UNITED STATES—ECONOMIC
   CONDITIONS
UNITED STATES—ECONOMIC POLICY
UNITED STATES—ECONOMIC
   RELATIONS—EUROPE
UNITED STATES—ECONOMIC
   RELATIONS—INDIANS OF NORTH
   AMERICA
UNITED STATES—ECONOMIC
   RELATIONS—VIETNAM
UNITED STATES—ELECTIONS—1984
UNITED STATES—ENERGY POLICY
UNITED STATES—FOREIGN OPINION
UNITED STATES—FOREIGN POLICY
UNITED STATES—FOREIGN
   POLICY—1960
UNITED STATES—FOREIGN
   POLICY—CENTRAL AMERICA
UNITED STATES—FOREIGN
   POLICY—CIVIL RIGHTS
UNITED STATES—FOREIGN
   POLICY—CUBA
UNITED STATES—FOREIGN POLICY—EL

SALVADOR
UNITED STATES—FOREIGN
POLICY—NICARAGUA
UNITED STATES—FOREIGN
POLICY—RELATIONS—UNITED STATES.
CONGRESS
UNITED STATES—FOREIGN
POLICY—RUSSIA
UNITED STATES—FOREIGN
POLICY—SOUTH AFRICA
UNITED STATES—FOREIGN
POLICY—VIETNAM
UNITED STATES—FOREIGN POPULATION
UNITED STATES—FOREIGN RELATIONS
UNITED STATES—FOREIGN
RELATIONS—ANGOLA
UNITED STATES—FOREIGN
RELATIONS—ARAB STATES
UNITED STATES—FOREIGN
RELATIONS—ASIA
UNITED STATES—FOREIGN
RELATIONS—BRAZIL
UNITED STATES—FOREIGN
RELATIONS—CENTRAL AMERICA
UNITED STATES—FOREIGN
RELATIONS—CHINA (PEOPLE'S
REPUBLIC)
UNITED STATES—FOREIGN
RELATIONS—CUBA
UNITED STATES—FOREIGN
RELATIONS—IRAN
UNITED STATES—FOREIGN
RELATIONS—ISRAEL
UNITED STATES—FOREIGN
RELATIONS—KOREA (REPUBLIC)
UNITED STATES—FOREIGN
RELATIONS—LATIN AMERICA
UNITED STATES—FOREIGN
RELATIONS—MEXICO
UNITED STATES—FOREIGN
RELATIONS—MIDDLE EAST
UNITED STATES—FOREIGN
RELATIONS—NICARAGUA
UNITED STATES—FOREIGN
RELATIONS—PANAMA
UNITED STATES—FOREIGN
RELATIONS—PHILIPPINES
UNITED STATES—FOREIGN
RELATIONS—RUSSIA
UNITED STATES—FOREIGN
RELATIONS—SOUTH AFRICA
UNITED STATES—HISTORY
UNITED STATES—HISTORY—CIVIL WAR
UNITED STATES—INTELLECTUAL LIFE
UNITED STATES—MILITARY POLICY
UNITED STATES—MILITARY POLICY—IRAN
UNITED STATES—POLITICS AND
GOVERNMENT
UNITED STATES—PRESIDENTS
UNITED STATES—RACE QUESTION
UNITED STATES—SOCIAL CONDITIONS

UNITED STATES—SOCIAL
CONDITIONS—FOREIGN OPINION
UNITED STATES—SOCIAL LIFE AND
CUSTOMS
UNITED STATES—SOCIAL POLICY
UNITED STATES. AIR FORCE
UNITED STATES. BUREAU OF INDIAN
AFFAIRS
UNITED STATES. CENTRAL INTELLIGENCE
AGENCY
UNITED STATES. COMMISSION ON CIA
ACTIVITIES WITHIN THE UNITED STATES
UNITED STATES. CONGRESS
UNITED STATES. CONGRESS. HOUSE
UNITED STATES. CONGRESS. HOUSE.
SELECT COMMITTEE ON INTELLIGENCE
UNITED STATES. CONGRESS. SENATE
UNITED STATES. DEPARTMENT OF
DEFENSE
UNITED STATES. DEPARTMENT OF
ENERGY
UNITED STATES. DEPARTMENT OF
HEALTH, EDUCATION, AND WELFARE.
OFFICE OF EDUCATION
UNITED STATES. DEPARTMENT OF LABOR
UNITED STATES. DEPARTMENT OF STATE
UNITED STATES. FEDERAL AVIATION
ADMINISTRATION
UNITED STATES. FEDERAL BUREAU OF
INVESTIGATION
UNITED STATES. FEDERAL BUREAU OF
INVESTIGATION—RELATIONS—ORAL
SEX
UNITED STATES. FEDERAL
COMMUNICATIONS COMMISSION
UNITED STATES. LIBRARY OF CONGRESS
UNITED STATES. MARINE CORPS
UNITED STATES. NATIONAL SECURITY
AGENCY
UNITED STATES. NAVY
UNITED STATES. SUPREME COURT
UNITED STATES. SUPREME
COURT—ABORTION DECISIONS
UNITED STEELWORKERS OF AMERICA
UNIVERSAL DECLARATION OF HUMAN
RIGHTS
UNIVERSE
UNIVERSITY PRESSES
UNRUH, JESSE
UPPER CLASSES
UPPER CLASSES—GREAT BRITAIN
UPSTAIRS, DOWNSTAIRS (TELEVISION
PROGRAM)
USERY, WILLIAM J.
USTINOV, PETER
UTAH. UNIVERSITY (FOOTBALL)
VAGUENESS
VALIUM
VALUES
VANCE, CYRUS
VATICAN—FOREIGN

RELATIONS—POLAND
VEECK, BILL
VEGETARIANISM
VELLECA, CARL
VENGEANCE
VICE-PRESIDENTIAL CANDIDATES
VICE-PRESIDENTS
VICE-PRESIDENTS—UNITED STATES
VICTIMS OF CRIME
VICTIMS OF CRIME—RELATIONS—
  LIBERALISM—NEW YORK
  (CITY)
VIDAL, GORE
VIDAL, GORE—POLITICAL
  CAMPAIGN—CALIFORNIA
VIETNAM—POLITICS AND GOVERNMENT
VIETNAMESE
VIETNAMESE IN THE UNITED STATES
VIETNAMESE WAR, 1957-1975
VIETNAMESE WAR,
  1957-1975—AMERICAN PARTICIPATION
VIETNAMESE WAR,
  1957-1975—ATROCITIES—MY LAI
VIETNAMESE WAR,
  1957-1975—PROTESTS,
  DEMONSTRATIONS, ETC., AGAINST
VIETNAMESE WAR,
  1957-1975—PROTESTS,
  DEMONSTRATIONS, ETC.,
  AGAINST—KENT, OHIO
VIGILANTES
VINCENT, JAN-MICHAEL
VIOLENCE
VIOLENCE IN MOVING PICTURES
VIOLENCE IN TELEVISION
VIOLIN
VIRGINIA. UNIVERSITY (FOOTBALL)
VIRGINITY
VIVA
VOCATIONAL EDUCATION
VOLLBRACHT, MICHAELE
VOLUNTEER SERVICE
VORONEL, NINA
VOTING
WAGES
WALDHEIM, KURT
WALES
WALESA, LECH
WALKING
WALL STREET
WALL STREET JOURNAL
WALLACE, CORNELIA
WALLACE, GEORGE CORLEY
WALTERS, BARBARA
WALTERS, VERNON A.
WAR
WAR—CASUALITIES
WARHOL, ANDY
WASHINGTON POST
WASHINGTON, BOOKER T.
WASHINGTON, D.C.

WASHINGTON, D.C.—DESCRIPTION
WASHINGTON, D.C.—SOCIAL LIFE AND
  CUSTOMS
WATER POLLUTION
WATER PURIFICATION
WATER TREATMENT PLANTS
WATERGATE CASE
WATERGATE SPECIAL PROSECUTION
  FORCE
WATERGATE TAPES
WATERS, ETHEL
WATERS, JOHN
WATT, JAMES
WATTS TOWERS, LOS ANGELES
WATTS, ANDRE
WAUGH, EVELYN
WAUGH, EVELYN—CHILDREN
WAYNE, JOHN
WEALTH
WELCH, RAQUEL
WELD, TUESDAY
WELK, LAWRENCE
WELLES, ORSON
WERTMUELLER, LINA
WEST, MAE
WESTERN FILMS
WEXLER, ANNE
WHISKEY
WHITE, DAN
WHITE, DWIGHT
WHITE, E. B.
WIDOWS
WILDE, OSCAR
WILDER, BILLY
WILDER, GENE
WILLIAMS, EDWARD BENNETT
WILLIAMS, TENNESSEE
WILSON, HAROLD
WINNING
WINPISINGER, WILLIAM
WIRE TAPPING
WISDOM
WISEMAN, FREDERICK
WIT AND HUMOR
WITCHCRAFT
WIVES
WOLFE, THOMAS
WOMEN
WOMEN AND FASHION
WOMEN AND MEN
WOMEN AND POLITICS
WOMEN ARTISTS
WOMEN ASTRONAUTS
WOMEN ATHLETES
WOMEN AUTOMOBILE RACING DRIVERS
WOMEN BASEBALL UMPIRES
WOMEN CRIMINALS
WOMEN JOURNALISTS
WOMEN POETS
WOMEN POLITICIANS
WOMEN PRIESTS

WOMEN SOLDIERS
WOMEN'S LIBERATION MOVEMENT
WOMEN'S LIBERATION
  MOVEMENT—HISTORY
WOMEN, AMERICAN
WOMEN, ENGLISH
WOMEN—CIVIL RIGHTS
WOMEN—EMPLOYMENT
WOMEN—EQUAL RIGHTS
WOMEN—HISTORY—GREAT BRITAIN
WOMEN—OCCUPATIONAL MOBILITY
WOMEN—POWER (SOCIAL SCIENCES)
WOMEN—PSYCHOLOGY
WOMEN—SUCCESS
WOMEN—WASHINGTON, D.C.
WOODWARD, BOB
WOODWARD, BOB AND BERNSTEIN,
  CARL. THE FINAL DAYS
WORD PROCESSING
WORDS
WORK
WORK—PSYCHOLOGICAL ASPECTS
WORK—RUSSIA

WORLD POLITICS
WORLD WAR, 1939-1945
WORRY
WORTH
WRIGHT, FRANK LLOYD—FURNITURE
WRIGHT, JIM
WRITING
WRITING—EQUIPMENT AND SUPPLIES
WYETH, ANDREW
WYNETTE, TAMMY
YANKEE STADIUM, NEW YORK
YOSHIMURA, WENDY
YOUNG, ANDREW
YOUTH
YOUTH—RELATIONS—WALL STREET
ZADORA, PIA
ZIEGLER, RONALD LOUIS
ZIMBABWE—CIVIL RIGHTS
ZIMBABWE—DESCRIPTION
ZIONISM
ZORINSKY, EDWARD
ZUKOR, ADOLPH